Teacher Edition

VISIONS

Language ◆ Literature ◆ Content

Mary Lou McCloskey

Lydia Stack

Australia ◆ Canada ◆ Mexico ◆ Singapore ◆ United Kingdom ◆ United States

TEXAS TEACHER EDITION BOOK B
Mary Lou McCloskey and Lydia Stack

Publisher: *Phyllis Dobbins*
Director of Development: *Anita Raducanu*
Developmental Editor: *Tania Maundrell-Brown*
Associate Developmental Editor: *Yeny Kim*
Associate Developmental Editor: *Kasia Zagorski*
Editorial Assistant: *Audra Longert*
Production Supervisor: *Mike Burggren*
Marketing Manager: *Jim McDonough*
Manufacturing Manager: *Marcia Locke*
Director, ELL Training and Development: *Evelyn Nelson*
Photography Manager: *Sheri Blaney*
Development: *Weston Editorial*
Design and Production: *Proof Positive/Farrowlyne Associates, Inc.*
Cover Designer: *Studio Montage*
Printer: *R.R. Donnelley and Sons Company, Willard*

Cover Image: © *Grant Heilman Photography*

Printed in the United States of America.
1 2 3 4 5 6 7 8 9 10   08 07 06 05 04 03

For more information, contact Heinle, 25 Thomson Place, Boston, Massachusetts 02210 USA, or you can visit our Internet site at http://www.heinle.com

For permission to use material from this text or product contact us:
Tel 1-800-730-2214
Fax 1-800-730-2215
Web www.thomsonrights.com

ISBN: 0-8837-7078-4

Contents

Program Introduction Tiv

Components-At-A-Glance Tvi

Scope and Sequence Tviii

Scientifically Based Research Txiv

Visions Assessment Program At-A-Glance Txvi

Unit 1: Challenges 1

Unit 2: Changes 78

Unit 3: Courage 152

Unit 4: Discoveries 222

Unit 5: Communication 284

Unit 6: Frontiers 348

Skills Index 412

Author and Reading Selection Index T421

Skills Index T421

Activity Book Contents T430

Student CD-ROM Contents T432

English-Spanish Cognates from the Reading Selections T434

VISIONS

Language Acquisition through Literature and Content

Visions is Heinle's newest four-level language development program that supports students from the newcomer level through transition into mainstream classrooms.

By incorporating literature with content, students are taught, and have ample practice with, the skills they need to meet grade-level TEKS while being introduced to the academic language needed for school success.

Visions is TEKS-Based to ensure that learners have the best materials to guide them in their language acquisition.

Features:

- **4 levels:** Newcomer (Basic)
  Beginning (A)
  Intermediate (B)
  Advanced/Transition (C)
- **Basic level for non-schooled and low-beginning students** provides systematic language development as well as literacy instruction.
- **Staff development handbook and video** is designed for easy program access.
- High-interest, low-level **literature and content-based readings** motivate students.
- **Scaffolding throughout all four books** uses a three-pronged approach to meeting the standards: Introduce, Practice, Assess.
- **Writing activities** reinforce and recycle strategic skills.
- **Quality assessment materials** and ExamView® test generating software are aligned with the TEKS.
- **Technology** reinforces listening/speaking, reading skills, and phonemic development.
- **Heinle Reading Library** gives students practice in independent reading with stories tied to Student Book themes.

Here's what teachers in Texas and beyond have to say:

"All chapters were very relative to the themes. The vocabulary building activities are excellent!"

Minerva Anzaldua
Martin Middle School, Corpus Christi, TX

"This is the type of literature and language series I've been looking for! I really like how each activity flows together and keeps the theme together."

Elia Corona
Liberty Middle School, Pharr, TX

"The readings were well-written. Students can relate and understand."

"The chapter goals and selections are clear and relevant to students' needs."

"The activities help students understand literary conventions."

James Harris
DeLeon Middle School, McAllen, TX

"The themes are well-developed. They provide conceptual frameworks within which students can understand the literature and learn language."

"The skills and information presented are important for students' academic success."

"The chapters are excellent because every activity has accessible vocabulary for ELL."

Donald Hoyt
Cooper Middle School, Fresno, CA

"Great ESL strategies for any level!"

"Clear directions for students!"

Gail Lulek
Safety Harbor Middle School, Safety Harbor, FL

Components-At-A-Glance

Visions: Texas Teacher Edition "Your guide to TEKS-based instruction"

For Students		Basic Level	Level A	Level B	Level C
Student Book	offers accessible, authentic literature with a balance of fiction and nonfiction, including excerpts from novels, short stories, plays, poetry, narratives, biographies, and informational and content-based readings.	●	●	●	●
Activity Book	provides step-by-step reinforcement of the TEKS and highlights state test-taking tips.	●	●	●	●
Student Handbook	provides students with helpful learning strategies.	●	●	●	●
The Heinle Reading Library	offers 18 classic stories that are tied to every theme of Visions and designed for student independent reading.		●	●	●
Student CD-ROM	provides an opportunity for practicing, reteaching, and reinforcing listening/speaking skills, reading skills, and phonemic awareness.	●	●	●	●
Audio CD*	features all reading selections recorded for building listening/speaking skills and auditory learning.	●	●	●	●
Newbury House Dictionary with CD-ROM	helps students develop essential dictionary and vocabulary building skills. Featuring a pronunciation CD-ROM.		●	●	●
More Grammar Practice, Texas Edition	helps students learn and review essential grammar skills.		●	●	●
Website (http://visions.heinle.com)	features additional skill-building activities for students.	●	●	●	●

***Also featured on Audio Tape.**

For Teachers		Basic Level	Level A	Level B	Level C
Teacher Edition	contains point-of-use lesson suggestions and multi-level activities developed specifically to meet TEKS requirements.		●	●	●
Teacher Resource Book	provides easy-to-use and implement lesson plans aligned with the TEKS. Additional support includes graphic organizers to support lesson activities, CNN® video transcripts and Video Worksheets for students, and summaries of each reading in English and translated into Cambodian, Haitian Creole, Hmong, Cantonese, Spanish, and Vietnamese. School-to-Home Newsletters, in English and the six languages, encourage family involvement. This component is also available on CD-ROM for teacher customization.	●	●	●	●
Assessment Program	features diagnostic tests and TEKS-based assessment items to ensure accountability, and tracking systems to monitor student progress. Assessment Program is available on CD-ROM with the ExamView® test-generating software, designed to create customizable tests in minutes from a test bank from each chapter of *Visions.*	●	●	●	●
Transparencies	offer graphic organizers, reading summaries, and grammar charts for interactive teaching.	●	●	●	●
TEKS Lesson Planning Correlation	provides point-of-use standards accountability at each lesson.	●	●	●	●
Staff Development Handbook and Video	provide step-by-step training for all teachers.	●	●	●	●
CNN® Video	features thematic news segments from today's headlines to help build content comprehension through meaningful viewing activities.		●	●	●
Website (http://visions.heinle.com)	features additional teaching resources and an opportunity for teachers to share classroom management techniques with an online community.	●	●	●	●

Scope and Sequence

Unit 1: Challenges

Chapter	Build Vocabulary	Text Structure	Reading Strategy	Spelling/ Punctuation/ Capitalization	Build Reading Fluency	Elements of Literature	Word Study	Grammar Focus	From Reading to Writing	Across Content Areas
1. "The Race," by Jennifer Trujillo, and "The Camel Dances," by Arnold Lobel p. 2	Find Synonyms Using a Reference	Poem and Fable	Make Inferences	Capitalization: Names Spelling: Plural nouns	Reading Key Phrases	Distinguish Sounds of Rhyming Words	Analyze the Suffix *-er*	Study Past Tense Verbs	Write a Poem	Science: Classify Animals
2. "Hatchet" by Gary Paulsen p. 14	Use Context	Realistic Adventure Fiction	Identify Cause and Effect	Spelling: *R*-controlled vowels Punctuation: Periods at the end of sentences Punctuation: Quotation marks for direct quotes	Reading Chunks	Use Figurative Language	Understand Compound Words	Use the Past Tense of the Verb *Be*	Write a Realistic Adventure Story	Science: Learn About Combustion
3. "Antarctic Adventure" by Meredith Hooper p. 28	Identify Words About Ships	Historical Narrative	Predict	Spelling: Abbreviations Capitalization: Days of the week and months of the year	Rapid Word Recognition	Identify Personification	Use Adverbs	Use *And* to Join Words and Sentences	Write a Historical Novel	Social Studies: Learn About Bodies of Land and Water
4. "Yang the Youngest" by Lensey Namioka p. 40	Identify Homonyms	First-Person Narrative	Compare a Reading with Your Experiences	Punctuation: Apostrophes in contractions Capitalization: Countries and languages Spelling: Use the sound /au/	Adjusting Reading Rate	Analyze Characters	Define Words with a Latin Root	Study Complex Sentences with Dependent Clauses	Write a First-Person Narrative	Social Studies: Learn the Meanings of *Culture*
5. "The Scholarship Jacket" by Marta Salinas p. 54	Learn Words About Emotions	Short Story	Find the Main Idea and Details	Punctuation: Commas in appositives Punctuation: Use of ellipses for omitted text Spelling: Words with the long *e* sound Spelling: Words ending with the sound /k/ Spelling: Words ending with *-l* or *-ll*	Reading Chunks of Words Silently	Analyze Character Motivation	Identify Root Words	Use *Could* and *Couldn't* for Past Ability	Write a Short Story	Science: Learn About Nutrition

Apply and Expand

Listening and Speaking Workshop p. 72	**Viewing Workshop** p. 73	**Writer's Workshop** p. 74	**Projects** p. 76
Make a Speech: News Report	Compare and Contrast Electronic Media with Written Stories	Write to Narrate: Tell How Someone Faced a Challenge	1. Create a Poster About Meeting Challenges 2. Write a Magazine Article or a Web Article

Unit 2: Changes

Chapter	Build Vocabulary	Text Structure	Reading Strategy	Spelling/ Punctuation/ Capitalization	Build Reading Fluency	Elements of Literature	Word Study	Grammar Focus	From Reading to Writing	Across Content Areas
1. "Why Do Leaves Change Color in the Fall?" from the World Wide Web p. 80	Use a Word Wheel	Scientific Informational Text	Make Inferences	Spelling: Use *ch* for /k/ sound Spelling: Use *c* for /s/ sound	Repeated Reading	Identify Processes	Use Pronunciation in Context: *ph*	Identify and Use the Simple Present Tense	Write a Scientific Informational Text	Science: Learn About Trees
2. "Elizabeth's Diary" by Patricia Hermes p. 92	Use Varied Word Choices	Historical Fiction Diary	Summarize	Punctuation: Hyphens in numbers	Rapid Word Recognition	Identify Flashbacks	Understand the Suffix *-ty*	Use the Future Tense with *Will*	Write a Diary Entry	Language Arts: Understand Genres of Literature
3. "And Now Miguel" by Joseph Krumgold p. 102	Use the LINK Strategy	Play	Determine the Sequence of Events	Spelling: Silent *b* Spelling: Silent *gh* Punctuation: Question marks Capitalization: Place names	Adjust Your Reading Rate	Understand Scenes in a Play	Contrast *Its* and *It's*	Identify and Use the Future Conditional	Write Dialogue for a Scene in a Play	Social Studies: Understand State Flags
4. "Tuck Triumphant" by Theodore Taylor p. 118	Identify Related Words	Realistic Fiction	Draw Conclusions	Spelling: Adverbs with the suffix *-ly* Punctuation: Apostrophes for possession Spelling: Use the prefix *dis-*	Choral Read Aloud	Recognize Style in a First-Person Narrative	Use the Suffix *-less*	Use Adjectives Before Nouns	Write a Realistic Story	Social Studies: Learn About Families
5. "The Journal of Jesse Smoke," by Joseph Bruchac, and "Ancient Ways," by Elvania Toledo p. 132	Find Root Words	Historical Fiction Journal	Understand the Sequence of Events	Spelling: Use *ie* or *ei* Spelling: Silent *l* Spelling: Words with sound /aw/	Read to Memorize	Understand Metaphors	Use the Suffix *-ness*	Use the Present Continuous Tense	Write a Poem	Math: Use Rank Order

Apply and Expand

Listening and Speaking Workshop p. 146	**Viewing Workshop** p. 147	**Writer's Workshop** p. 148	**Projects** p. 150
Interview and Report	Analyze Film or Video: Tell How a Scene Is Effective	Write to Persuade: Write a Letter to the Editor	1. Research Life in the United States Since the Colonial Period 2. Write a Magazine Article About a Historical Site

Unit 3: Courage

Chapter	Build Vocabulary	Text Structure	Reading Strategy	Spelling/ Punctuation/ Capitalization	Build Reading Fluency	Elements of Literature	Word Study	Grammar Focus	From Reading to Writing	Across Content Areas
1. "Life Doesn't Frighten Me" by Maya Angelou p. 154	Preview New Vocabulary	Poem	Use Images to Understand and Enjoy Poetry	Capitalization: Titles of poems Spelling: *It's* and *its*	Echo Read Aloud	Identify Rhyming Words	Identify Contractions	Use Prepositional Phrases	Write a Poem About a Feeling	Science: Learn About the Respiratory System
2. "Matthew A. Henson" by Wade Hudson p. 166	Learn Synonyms with Reference Aids	Biography	Find the Main Idea and Supporting Details	Punctuation: Commas in a series Capitalization: Places and abbreviations of names	Repeated Reading	Recognize Chronological Order and Transitions	Recognize Proper Nouns	Identify Two-Word Verbs	Write a Short Biography	Science: Learn About Temperature
3. "Anne Frank: The Diary of a Young Girl" by Anne Frank p. 178	Use Context	Diary	Use Chronology to Locate and Recall Information	Punctuation: Semicolons Capitalization: Opening and closing a letter or diary	Reading Chunks of Words Silently	Understand Tone	Use the Suffix *-ion*	Use Conjunctions to Form Compound Sentences	Write a Diary	Social Studies: Describe Social Groups
4. "Lance Armstrong: Champion Cyclist" by President George W. Bush p. 190	Use Multiple Reference Aids	Speech	Distinguish Fact from Opinion	Spelling: To/two/too Punctuation: Colons and dashes	Adjust Your Reading Rate	Identify Style, Tone, and Mood in a Speech	Interpret Figurative Language	Use Superlative Adjectives	Write a Speech	Social Studies: Read a Chart
5. "Earthquake" by Huynh Quang Nhuong p. 202	Use the Dictionary	Memoir	Draw Conclusions and Give Support	Spelling: Plurals Spelling: Adding *-ed* and doubling final consonants Spelling: Past tense of words ending in *-y*	Rapid Word Recognition	Recognize Foreshadowing	Form Compound Words	Identify Pronoun Referents	Write a Memoir	Social Studies: Read a Map

Apply and Expand

Listening and Speaking Workshop p. 216	**Viewing Workshop** p. 217	**Writer's Workshop** p. 218	**Projects** p. 220
Present a Biographical Narrative	Compare and Contrast Visual and Electronic Media with Written Stories: Compare Points of View	Response to Literature	1. Give a Speech 2. Design a Web Page or an Art Exhibit

Unit 4: Discoveries

Chapter	Build Vocabulary	Text Structure	Reading Strategy	Spelling/ Punctuation/ Capitalization	Build Reading Fluency	Elements of Literature	Word Study	Grammar Focus	From Reading to Writing	Across Content Areas
1. "The Library Card," by Jerry Spinelli, and "At the Library," by Nikki Grimes p. 224	Use Repetition to Find Meaning	Fiction	Compare and Contrast	Capitalization: Direct quotations Spelling: Long vowel sounds Punctuation: Italics for emphasis	Reading Chunks of Words Silently	Recognize a Writing Style	Understand Historical Influences on English Words	Identify Sentences with Relative Clauses	Write a Story	Language Arts: Use the Library
2. "Discovering the Inca Ice Maiden" by Johan Reinhard p. 238	Understand Key Words and Related Words	Nonfiction Narrative	Use Graphic Sources of Information	Capitalization: Proper adjectives Spelling: Forming words with double consonants Punctuation: Commas within large numbers	Read to Scan for Information	Understand First-Person Point of View	Spell *-ed* Forms of Verbs	Identify *Be* + Adjective + Infinitive	Write a First-Person Nonfiction Narrative	Social Studies: Understand the Atmosphere and Altitude
3. "The Art of Swordsmanship" by Rafe Martin p. 252	Identify Related Words	Folktale	Use Dialogue to Understand Character	Punctuation: Commas within quotes Spelling: Silent *k*	Repeated Reading	Examine Character Traits and Changes	Find Word Origins and Prefixes	Use Adverbs to Show Time	Write a Folktale	The Arts: Learn About Art in Everyday Objects
4. "Mae Jemison, Space Scientist" by Gail Sakurai p. 264	Adjust Reading Rate	Biography	Find the Main Idea and Supporting Details	Capitalization: Proper nouns Capitalization: Acronyms as proper nouns Punctuation: Parentheses for information	Reading Silently	Recognize Flashbacks	Identify Greek and Latin Word Origins	Use and Punctuate Dependent Clauses with *Although* and *When*	Write a Short Biography	Science: Understand Gravity

Apply and Expand

Listening and Speaking Workshop p. 278	**Viewing Workshop** p. 279	**Writer's Workshop** p. 280	**Projects** p. 282
Report a Biographical Sketch About a Person's Hobby	Interpret Important Ideas from Maps: View a Historical Atlas	Write to Inform: Write an E-mail	1. Make a Future-Discovery Poster 2. Make Discoveries About Your Community

Unit 5: Communication

Chapter	Build Vocabulary	Text Structure	Reading Strategy	Spelling/ Punctuation/ Capitalization	Build Reading Fluency	Elements of Literature	Word Study	Grammar Focus	From Reading to Writing	Across Content Areas
1. "How Tía Lola Came to Visit Stay" by Julia Alvarez p. 286	Use Context Clues	Narrative	Predict	Spelling: Words with two spellings Capitalization: Commas after introductory time clauses Spelling: Their, there, they're Punctuation: Italics for words in other languages	Reading Silently	Recognize Point of View	Use the Prefixes *un-* and *im-*	Recognize the Present Perfect Tense	Write a Narrative with Dialogue	Social Studies: Read a Weather Map
2. "Helen Keller," by George Sullivan, and "The Miracle Worker," by William Gibson p. 302	Find Synonyms for Action Verbs	Biography and Drama	Compare and Contrast	Punctuation: Hyphens Punctuation: Italics for stage directions Punctuation: Colons	Adjust Your Reading Rate	Analyze Stage Directions	Use the Suffix *-ly*	Recognize and Use Past Progressive Verbs	Write a Scene from a Play	Science: Learn About Some Causes of Diseases
3. "Hearing: The Ear" p. 316	Identify Science Vocabulary	Textbook	Represent Text Information in an Outline	Capitalization: Titles and headings Spelling: Words ending in *-ing*	Read to Scan for Information	Recognize Descriptive Language	Identify Words with Greek Origins	Recognize Subject and Verb Agreement in the Present Tense	Write to Inform	The Arts: Learn About the Voice
4. "The Art of Making Comic Books" by Michael Morgan Pellowski p. 328	Learn Words About Art	Illustrated "How-to" Book	Make Inferences Using Text Evidence	Punctuation: Hyphens Spelling: Silent *w* Capitalization: Exclamations	Repeated Reading	Recognize Writing Style	The Suffix *-ian*	Understand the Present Conditional	Write an Illustrated "How-to" Article	The Arts: Learn About Art Forms

Apply and Expand

Listening and Speaking Workshop p. 342	**Viewing Workshop** p. 343	**Writer's Workshop** p. 344	**Projects** p. 346
Present an Oral Summary of a Reading	View and Think: Evaluate Visual Media	Write a Persuasive Editorial	1. List Types of Foreign-Language Communication 2. Design Your Own Media

Unit 6: Frontiers

Chapter	Build Vocabulary	Text Structure	Reading Strategy	Spelling/ Punctuation/ Capitalization	Build Reading Fluency	Elements of Literature	Word Study	Grammar Focus	From Reading to Writing	Across Content Areas
1. "The Lewis and Clark Expedition" p. 350	Use a Word Wheel	Informational Text	Use Chronology to Locate and Recall Information	Punctuation: Commas after introductory phrases Spelling: *the* and *t*; *thr* and *tr*	Reading Silently	Analyze Characters	Use a Thesaurus and Synonym Finder to Find Synonyms	Use Appositives	Write an Informational Text	Social Studies: Use Headings as You Read
2. "A Wrinkle in Time" by Madeleine L'Engle p. 362	Use Context Clues	Science Fiction	Describe Mental Images	Spelling: The *f* sound using *f, ph, gh* Spelling: Ordinal numbers Capitalization: Titles Spelling: Silent *h* Punctuation: Italics for emphasis	Echo Reading Aloud	Understand Mood	Understand Prefixes *un-, in-*, and *im-*	Identify the Past Perfect Tense	Write a Science Fiction Narrative	Science: Learn About the Speed of Light
3. "I Have a Dream" by Martin Luther King Jr. p. 380	Distinguish Denotative and Connotative Meanings	Speech	Draw Conclusions with Text Evidence	Spelling: Irregular plurals Punctuation: Apostrophes for singular and plural possessives	Adjust Your Reading Rate	Identify Audience and Purpose	Recognize Figurative Language	Use Dependent Clauses with *That*	Write a Persuasive Speech	Social Studies: Learn About the United States Constitution
4. "Lyndon Baines Johnson: Our Thirty-Sixth President," by Melissa Maupin, and "Speech to the Nation: July 2, 1964," by Lyndon Baines Johnson p. 392	Identify Key Words About Government	Biography	Distinguish Fact from Opinion	Spelling: *qu* for the *kw* sound Punctuation: Commas in dates Capitalization: Proper names	Choral Read Aloud	Recognize Repetition in a Speech	Identify Adjectives	Use the Conjunction *Yet* to Show Contrast	Write a Biography	Social Studies: Learn About the Branches of Government

Apply and Expand

Listening and Speaking Workshop p. 406	**Viewing Workshop** p. 407	**Writer's Workshop** p. 408	**Projects** p. 410
Give a Persuasive Speech	View and Think: View Videos of Speeches	Write a Research Report	1. Make a Book About a New Place 2. Write a Letter to the President

Scientifically Based Research in the *Visions* Program

The *Visions* program was developed utilizing current, scientifically based research findings of the most effective methods to teach language mastery. The references for each section below identify specific areas within the *Visions* student materials where the research has been applied.

Vocabulary Development

Research shows students need to consistently work on vocabulary in three critical areas (Anderson, 1999) and to meet standards (California Dept. of Education, 1998).

Word Meaning: Students study vocabulary meanings and concepts, relate them to prior experience, and record them in their personal dictionary. See *Build Vocabulary* sections.

Word Identification Strategies: Students learn important skills such as context clues, roots, and affixes. See *Word Study* sections.

Vocabulary Across Content Areas: Students learn key words in science, math, and social studies in the *Content Connection* and *Across Content Areas* sections.

Reading Comprehension

Strategies: Reading strategies such as fact/opinion, cause/effect, prediction, summarization, and paraphrasing need to be directly taught before the reading, practiced during the reading, and then evaluated (Anderson, 1999). See *Reading Strategy* sections.

Types of Questions: Readings that are followed by literal, inferential, and evaluative comprehension questions develop higher order thinking skills (Fowler, 2003). See *Reading Comprehension* sections.

Reading Fluency

The ability to read rapidly, smoothly, and automatically while adjusting rate and reading with expression (Mather and Goldstein, 2001) defines reading fluency. English language learners and at-risk students need systematic scaffolding activities with repeated oral reading to become fluent readers (De la Colina, Parker, Hasbrouck, Lara-Alecia, 2001). See *Build Reading Fluency* sections.

Rapid Word Recognition: Practice of this skill can increase students' fluency (Cunningham and Stanovich, 1998; Torgesen et al., 2001).

Reading Chunks and Key Phrases: This helps ELL and at-risk students become more fluent and to understand what they read.

Adjusting Reading Rate: Students learn to vary reading rate according to the purpose and type of text.

Repeated Reading: Students reread words, phrases, and passages a specific number of times (Meyer and Felton, 1999) for consistent, positive support of effectiveness in increasing reading fluency (National Reading Panel, 2000). Six minutes a day of repeated oral reading practice (Mercer, et al., in press) was found to be highly effective in increasing fluency.

Reading Silently and Aloud: Practice and support using the teacher, a peer (Li and Nes, 2001), and the Audio CD (Blum, Koskinen, Tennant, and Parker, 1995) has been proven to increase reading fluency.

Sheltered Content Instruction

Using the strategies from Cognitive Academic Language Learning Approach (CALLA) and the Sheltered Instruction Observation Protocol (SIOP), students apply learning strategies to help them succeed academically in their content area classes. See *Use Prior Knowledge* and *Content Connection* sections.

Spelling Instruction

Students are taught orthographic patterns and frequently used words in conjunction with the readings. Students who receive direct instruction in word analysis and how to analyze speech sounds and spell words are more successful in reading and writing (Whittlesea, 1987). See *Visions Activity Book* and *Teacher Edition.*

Traits of Writing and Oral Presentations

Students can learn to write and give oral presentations with greater success when they are based on the model presented in their reading and when they are made cognitively aware of the traits that good writers and presenters use. In *Visions,* students write and present narrative, descriptive, technical, and persuasive writing, as well as research reports. Students analyze types of text structure used in various writing models. The writing process is used throughout. See *Text Structure, Writing Workshops,* and *Listening and Speaking Workshops.*

References

Anderson, Neil. *Exploring Second Language Reading.* Boston, MA: Heinle, 1999.

Becker, H. and Hayman, E. *Teaching ESL K-12: Views from the Classroom.* Boston, MA: Heinle, 2001.

Blum, I.H.; Koskinen, P.S.; Tennant, N.; and Parker, E.M. "Using Audio Taped Books to Extend Classroom Literacy Instruction into the Homes of Second-language Learners." *Journal of Reading Behavior* 27 (1995): 535–563.

California Department of Education. *English-Language Arts Content Standards for California Public Schools Kindergarten Through Grade Twelve.* Sacramento, CA: 2001.

California Department of Education. *Strategic Thinking and Learning.* Sacramento, CA: 2001.

Chamot, A. and O'Malley, J. *The CALLA Handbook Addison-Wesley.* Reading, MA: 1995.

Cognitive Academic Language Learning Approach (CALLA) <http://www.writing.berkely.edu/TESL-EJ/ej07/r5.html>.

Cunningham, A.E. and Stanovich, K.E. "What Reading Does for the Mind." *American Educator* 22 (1998): 1–2, 8–15.

De la Colina, M.G.; Parker, R.I.; Hasbrouck, J.E.; Lara-Alecia, R. "Intensive Intervention in Reading Fluency For At-Risk Beginning Spanish Readers." *Bilingual Research Journal* 25 (2001): 503–38.

Fowler, B. *Critical Thinking Across the Curriculum Home Page* "Blooms Taxonomy and Critical Thinking (Questions)." Longview Community College, 1996. 22 January 2003 <http://www.kcmetro.cc.mo.us/longview/ctac/blooms.htm>.

Li, D., and Nes, S. "Using Paired Reading to Help ESL Students Become Fluent and Accurate Readers." *Reading Improvement* 38 (2001): 50–61.

Mercer, C.; Campbell, K.; Miller, M.; Mercer, K.; and Lane, H. in press. "Effects of a Reading Fluency Intervention for Middle Schoolers with Specific Learning Disabilities." *Learning Disabilities Research and Practice.*

Meyer, M.S., and Felton, R.H. "Repeated Reading to Enhance Fluency: Old Approaches and New Directions." *Annals of Dyslexia* 49 (1999): 283–306.

National Reading Panel. *Teaching Children to Read: An Evidence-based Assessment of the Scientific Research Literature on Reading and Its Implications for Reading Instruction* (National Institute of Health Publ. No 00-4769) Washington, DC: 2002 National Institute of Child Health and Human Development.

Nixon, Susan. *Six Traits Writing Assessment Home Page.* 22 January 2003 <http://6traits.cyberspaces.net>.

Short, Deborah J., and Echevarria, Jana. *ERIC Clearinghouse on Languages and Linguistics.* "Sheltered Instruction Observation Protocol: A Tool for Teacher-Researcher Collaboration and Professional Development." 1999. 22 January 2003 <http:// www.cal.org/ericcll/digest/sheltered.html>.

Torgesen, J.K.; Alexander, A.W.; Wagner, R.K.; Rashotte, C.A.; Voeller, K; Conway, T.; and Rose, E. "Intensive Remedial Instruction for Children with Severe Reading Disabilities: Immediate and Long-term Outcomes from Two Instructional Approaches." *Journal of Learning Disabilities* 34 (2001): 33–58.

Visions Assessment Program At-A-Glance

The *Visions* Assessment Program was designed to ensure TEKS-based accountability for teachers and students alike. It begins with a Diagnostic Test to assess what students already know and to target students' needs in specific skill areas. The Assessment Program ensures on-going as well as summative evaluation with the Chapter Quizzes, Unit Tests, and Mid-Book and End-of-Book Exams. Portfolio Assessment is also taken into account to measure the students' overall progress.

VISIONS Assessment Program		
	Name	**Purpose of Assessment**
Entry Level	**Diagnostic Test**	To enable teachers to ascertain their students' proficiency skills in vocabulary, reading, grammar, spelling, and writing, and to do a Needs Analysis in order to target specific instructional needs.
Monitor Progress	**Chapter Quizzes**	To monitor students' on-going progress in vocabulary, grammar, reading, and writing. There are 27 Chapter Quizzes.
	Unit Tests	To monitor students' on-going progress toward meeting strategies and standards in vocabulary, grammar, reading, and writing at the end of each unit. There are 6 Unit Tests.
	Mid-Book Exam	To monitor students' on-going progress toward meeting strategies and standards in vocabulary, grammar, reading, and writing as taught throughout the first three units of the book.
	Student Resources Checklists	To promote student responsibility in meeting the standards. Students self-assess their strengths and weaknesses for purposes of reteaching if necessary.
Summative	**End-of-Book Exam**	To measure students' achievement and mastery in meeting the standards in vocabulary, reading, and writing as taught throughout the book.
Additional Tools to Monitor Progress	**Peer Editing Checklists**	To collaboratively involve classmates in giving and gaining feedback on their progress toward meeting the standards in writing.
	Active Listening Checklist	To collaboratively involve classmates in giving and gaining feedback on their progress in the area of listening and speaking during oral presentations.
	Teacher Resources Listening, Speaking, Reading, Writing, Viewing, and Content Area Checklists	To track on-going progress of students in all domains of the standards, and to serve as a vehicle in planning instruction.
	Reading Fluency	To check students' progress in learning to read silently and aloud with expression, and to adjust their reading rates according to the purpose of their reading.
	Rubrics	To evaluate students' overall performance using a fixed measurement scale and a list of criteria taken from formal and informal outcomes. These rubrics should be part of each student's permanent record.
	Portfolio Assessment	To involve students in self-reflection on their progress in meeting their learning goals. This on-going assessment is a collection of student work that exhibits the student's best efforts and progress.
	ExamView ® CD-ROM	To empower teachers to choose and customize test items to meet students' targeted needs; items chosen may be used to retest after intervention activities.

VISIONS

Language ✧ Literature ✧ Content

Mary Lou McCloskey
Lydia Stack

Australia ✧ Canada ✧ Mexico ✧ Singapore ✧ United Kingdom ✧ United States

VISIONS STUDENT BOOK B
Mary Lou McCloskey and Lydia Stack

Publisher: *Phyllis Dobbins*
Director of Development: *Anita Raducanu*
Developmental Editor: *Tania Maundrell-Brown*
Associate Developmental Editor: *Yeny Kim*
Associate Developmental Editor: *Kasia Zagorski*
Editorial Assistant: *Audra Longert*
Production Supervisor: *Mike Burggren*
Marketing Manager: *Jim McDonough*
Manufacturing Manager: *Marcia Locke*
Director, ELL Training and Development: *Evelyn Nelson*
Photography Manager: *Sheri Blaney*
Development: *Proof Positive/Farrowlyne Associates, Inc.; Quest Language Systems*
Design and Production: *Proof Positive/Farrowlyne Associates, Inc.*
Cover Designer: *Studio Montage*
Printer: *R.R. Donnelley and Sons Company, Willard*

Cover Image: *© Grant Heilman Photography*

Printed in the United States of America.
1 2 3 4 5 6 7 8 9 10 08 07 06 05 04 03

For more information, contact Heinle, 25 Thomson Place, Boston, Massachusetts 02210 USA, or you can visit our Internet site at http://www.heinle.com

For permission to use material from this text or product contact us:
Tel 1-800-730-2214
Fax 1-800-730-2215
Web www.thomsonrights.com

ISBN: 0-8384-5248-5

Reviewers and Consultants

We gratefully acknowledge the contribution of the following educators, consultants, and librarians who reviewed materials at various stages of development. Their input and insight provided us with valuable perspective and ensured the integrity of the entire program.

Program Advisor

Evelyn Nelson

Consultants

Deborah Barker
Nimitz High School
Houston, Texas

Sharon Bippus
Labay Middle School
Houston, Texas

Sheralee Connors
Portland, Oregon

Kathleen Fischer
Norwalk LaMirada Unified School District
Norwalk, California

Willa Jean Harner
Tiffin-Seneca Public Library
Tiffin, Ohio

Nancy King
Bleyl Middle School
Houston, Texas

Amy Hirasaki Moore
Houston, Texas

Julie Rines
The Thomas Crane Library
Quincy, MA

Lynn Silbernagel
The Catlin Gabel School
Portland, Oregon

Cherylyn Smith
Fresno Unified School District
Fresno, California

Jennifer Trujillo
Fort Lewis College
Teacher Education Department
Durango, Colorado

Teresa Walter
Chollas Elementary School
San Diego, California

Reviewers

Susan Alexandre
Trimble Technical High School
Fort Worth, Texas

Deborah Almonte
Franklin Middle School
Tampa, Florida

Donna Altes
Silverado Middle School
Napa, California

Ruben Alvarado
Webb Middle School
Austin, TX

Sheila Alvarez
Robinson Middle School
Plano, Texas

Cally Androtis-Williams
Newcomers High School
Long Island City, New York

Minerva Anzaldua
Martin Middle School
Corpus Christi, Texas

Alicia Arroyos
Eastwood Middle School
El Paso, Texas

Douglas Black
Montwood High School
El Paso, Texas

Jessica Briggeman
International Newcomer Academy
Fort Worth, Texas

Diane Buffett
East Side High School
Newark, New Jersey

Eva Chapman
San Jose Unified School District Office
San Jose, California

Elia Corona
Memorial Middle School
Pharr, Texas

Alicia Cron
Alamo Middle School
Alamo, Texas

Florence Decker
El Paso Independent School District (retired)
El Paso, Texas

Janeece Docal
Bell Multicultural Senior High School
Washington, DC

Addea Dontino
Miami-Dade County School District
Miami, FL

Kathy Dwyer
Tomlin Middle School
Plant City, Florida

Olga Figol
Barringer High School
Newark, New Jersey

James Harris
DeLeon Middle School
McAllen, Texas

Audrey Heining-Boynton
University of North Carolina-Chapel Hill
School of Education
Chapel Hill, North Carolina

Carolyn Ho
North Harris Community College
Houston, Texas

Donald Hoyt
Cooper Middle School
Fresno, California

Nancy A. Humbach
Miami University
Department of Teacher Education
Oxford, Ohio

Erik Johansen
Oxnard High School
Oxnard, California

Marguerite Joralemon
East Side High School
Newark, New Jersey

Karen Poling Kapeluck
Lacey Instructional Center
Annandale, Virginia

Lorraine Kleinschuster
Intermediate School 10 Q
Long Island City, New York

Fran Lacas
NYC Board of Education (retired)
New York, New York

Robert Lamont
Newcomer Center
Arlington, Texas

Mao-ju Catherine Lee
Alief Middle School
Houston, Texas

Gail Lulek
Safety Harbor Middle School
Safety Harbor, Florida

Natalie Mangini
Serrano International School
Lake Forest, California

Graciela Morales
Austin Independent School District
Austin, Texas

Karen Morante
School District of Philadelphia
Philadelphia, Pennsylvania

Lorraine Morgan
Hanshaw Middle School
Modesto, California

Dianne Mortensen
Pershing Intermediate School 220
Brooklyn, New York

Denis O'Leary
Rio del Valle Junior High School
Oxnard, California

Jeanette Page
School District of Philadelphia (retired)
Philadelphia, Pennsylvania

Claudia Peréz
Hosler Middle School
Lynwood, California

Yvonne Perez
Alief Middle School
Houston, Texas

Penny Phariss
Plano Independent School District
Plano, Texas

Bari Ramírez
L.V. Stockard Middle School
Dallas, Texas

Jacqueline Ray
Samuel High School
Dallas, Texas

Howard Riddles
Oak Grove Middle School
Clearwater, Florida

Randy Soderman
Community School District Six
New York, New York

Rita LaNell Stahl
Sinagua High School
Flagstaff, Arizona

Dean Stecker
School District of Palm Beach County
West Palm Beach, Florida

Mary Sterling-Cruz
Jackson Middle School
Friendswood, Texas

Rosemary Tejada
Carlsbad High School
Carlsbad, California

Camille Sloan Telthorster
Bleye Middle School
Houston, Texas

Vickie Thomas
Robinson Middle School
Plano, Texas

Claudio Toledo
Lynwood Middle School
Lynwood, CA

Christopher Tracy
Garnet-Patterson Middle School
Washington, DC

Stephanie Vreeland
T.A. Howard Middle School
Arlington, Texas

Jennifer Zelenitz
Long Island City High School
Long Island City, New York

We wish to thank the students at the following schools who helped us select high-interest readings at an appropriate language level. Their feedback was invaluable.

Student reviewers

Intermediate School 10 Q
Long Island City, New York

Jackson Middle School
Friendswood, Texas

L.V. Stockard Middle School
Dallas, Texas

Memorial Middle School
Pharr, Texas

Newcomer Center
Arlington, Texas

Nimitz High School
Houston, Texas

Oxnard High School
Oxnard, California

Pershing Intermediate School 220
Brooklyn, New York

Samuel High School
Dallas, Texas

Silverado Middle School
Napa, California

T.A. Howard Middle School
Arlington, Texas

Trimble Technical High School
Fort Worth, Texas

Contents

UNIT 1 Challenges 1

Chapter 1 2

Reading Strategy: Make Inferences 4

Jennifer Trujillo ■ **The Race** • poem 6

Arnold Lobel ■ **The Camel Dances** • fable 8

Across Content Areas: Science: Classify Animals 13

Chapter 2 14

Reading Strategy: Identify Cause and Effect 16

Gary Paulsen ■ **Hatchet** • excerpt from a novel 17

Across Content Areas: Science: Learn About Combustion 27

Chapter 3 28

Reading Strategy: Predict 30

Meredith Hooper ■ **Antarctic Adventure** • excerpt from a historical narrative 31

Across Content Areas: Social Studies: Learn About Bodies of Land and Water 39

Chapter 4 40

Reading Strategy: Compare a Reading with Your Experiences 42

Lensey Namioka ■ **Yang the Youngest** • excerpt from a novel 43

Across Content Areas: Social Studies: Learn the Meanings of *Culture* 53

Chapter 5 54

Reading Strategy: Find the Main Idea and Details 56

Marta Salinas ■ **The Scholarship Jacket** • short story 57

Across Content Areas: Science: Learn About Nutrition 71

Apply and Expand 72

Listening and Speaking Workshop: Make a Speech: News Report 72

Viewing Workshop: Compare and Contrast Electronic Media with Written Stories 73

Writer's Workshop: Write to Narrate: Tell How Someone Faced a Challenge 74

Projects 76

Further Reading 77

UNIT 2 Changes 78

Chapter 1 80

Reading Strategy: Make Inferences 82

World Wide Web ■ **Why Do Leaves Change Color in the Fall?** • excerpt from a science article from the World Wide Web 83

Across Content Areas: Science: Learn About Trees 91

Chapter 2 92

Reading Strategy: Summarize 94

Patricia Hermes ■ **Elizabeth's Diary** • excerpt from a historical fiction diary 95

Across Content Areas: Language Arts: Understand Genres of Literature 101

Chapter 3 102

Reading Strategy: Determine the Sequence of Events 104

Joseph Krumgold ■ **And Now Miguel** • play based on a novel 105

Across Content Areas: Social Studies: Understand State Flags 117

Chapter 4 118

Reading Strategy: Draw Conclusions 120

Theodore Taylor ■ **Tuck Triumphant** • excerpt from a novel 121

Across Content Areas: Social Studies: Learn About Families 131

Chapter 5 132

Reading Strategy: Understand the Sequence of Events 134

Joseph Bruchac ■ **The Journal of Jesse Smoke** • excerpt from a historical fiction journal 136

Elvania Toledo ■ **Ancient Ways** • poem 140

Across Content Areas: Math: Use Rank Order 145

Apply and Expand 146

Listening and Speaking Workshop: Interview and Report 146
Viewing Workshop: Analyze Film or Video 147
Writer's Workshop: Write to Persuade: Write a Letter to the Editor 148
Projects 150
Further Reading 151

UNIT 3 Courage 152

Chapter 1 154

Reading Strategy: Use Images to Understand and Enjoy Poetry 156

Maya Angelou ■ **Life Doesn't Frighten Me** • poem 157

Across Content Areas: Science: Learn About the Respiratory System 165

Chapter 2 166

Reading Strategy: Find the Main Idea and Supporting Details 168

Wade Hudson ■ **Matthew A. Henson** • excerpt from a biography 169

Across Content Areas: Science: Learn About Temperature 177

Chapter 3 178

Reading Strategy: Use Chronology to Locate and Recall Information 180

Anne Frank ■ **Anne Frank: The Diary of a Young Girl** • excerpt from a diary 181

Across Content Areas: Social Studies: Describe Social Groups 189

Chapter 4 190

Reading Strategy: Distinguish Fact from Opinion 192

President George W. Bush ■ **Lance Armstrong: Champion Cyclist** • speech 193

Across Content Areas: Social Studies: Read a Chart 201

Chapter 5 202

Reading Strategy: Draw Conclusions and Give Support 204

Huynh Quang Nhuong ■ **Earthquake** • excerpt from a memoir 205

Across Content Areas: Social Studies: Read a Map 215

Apply and Expand 216

Listening and Speaking Workshop: Present a Biographical Narrative 216
Viewing Workshop: Compare and Contrast Visual and Electronic Media with Written Stories 217
Writer's Workshop: Response to Literature 218
Projects 220
Further Reading 221

UNIT 4 Discoveries 222

Chapter 1 224

Reading Strategy: Compare and Contrast 226

Jerry Spinelli ■ **The Library Card** • excerpt from a novel 228

Nikki Grimes ■ **At the Library** • poem 232

Across Content Areas: Language Arts: Use the Library 237

Chapter 2 238

Reading Strategy: Use Graphic Sources 240

Johan Reinhard ■ **Discovering the Inca Ice Maiden** • nonfiction narrative 241

Across Content Areas: Social Studies: Understand the Atmosphere and Altitude 251

Chapter 3 252

Reading Strategy: Use Dialogue to Understand Character 254

Rafe Martin ■ **The Art of Swordsmanship** • folktale 255

Across Content Areas: The Arts: Learn About Art in Everyday Objects 263

Chapter 4 264

Reading Strategy: Find the Main Idea and Supporting Details 266

Gail Sakurai ■ **Mae Jemison, Space Scientist** • biography 267

Across Content Areas: Science: Understand Gravity 277

Apply and Expand 278

Listening and Speaking Workshop: Report a Biographical Sketch About a Person's Hobby 278

Viewing Workshop: Interpret Important Ideas from Maps 279

Writer's Workshop: Write to Inform: Write an E-mail 280

Projects 282

Further Reading 283

UNIT 5 Communication 284

Chapter 1 286

Reading Strategy: Predict 288

Julia Alvarez ■ **How Tía Lola Came to ~~Visit~~ Stay** • excerpt from a novel 289

Across Content Areas: Social Studies: Read a Weather Map 301

Chapter 2 302

Reading Strategy: Compare and Contrast 304

George Sullivan ■ **Helen Keller** • excerpt from a biography 306

William Gibson ■ **The Miracle Worker** • excerpt from a play 309

Across Content Areas: Science: Learn About Some Causes of Diseases 315

Chapter 3 316

Reading Strategy: Represent Text Information in an Outline 318

■ **Hearing: The Ear** • excerpt from a textbook 319

Across Content Areas: The Arts: Learn About the Voice 327

Chapter 4 328

Reading Strategy: Make Inferences Using Text Evidence 330

Michael Morgan Pellowski ■ **The Art of Making Comic Books** • illustrated "how-to" book 331

Across Content Areas: The Arts: Learn About Art Forms 341

Apply and Expand 342

Listening and Speaking Workshop: Present an Oral Summary of a Reading 342

Viewing Workshop: View and Think 343

Writer's Workshop: Write a Persuasive Editorial 344

Projects 346

Further Reading 347

UNIT 6 Frontiers 348

Chapter 1 350

Reading Strategy: Use Chronology to Locate and Recall Information 352

■ **The Lewis and Clark Expedition** • excerpt from a textbook 353

Across Content Areas: Language Arts: Use Headings as You Read 361

Chapter 2 362

Reading Strategy: Describe Mental Images 364

Madeleine L'Engle ■ **A Wrinkle in Time** • excerpt from a science fiction novel 365

Across Content Areas: Science: Learn About the Speed of Light 379

Chapter 3 380

Reading Strategy: Draw Conclusions with Text Evidence 382

Martin Luther King Jr. ■ **I Have a Dream** • excerpt from a speech 383

Across Content Areas: Social Studies: Learn About the United States Constitution 391

Chapter 4 392

Reading Strategy: Distinguish Fact from Opinion 394

Melissa Maupin ■ **Lyndon Baines Johnson: Our Thirty-Sixth President** • excerpt from a biography 396

Lyndon Baines Johnson ■ **Speech to the Nation: July 2, 1964** • excerpt from a speech 398

Across Content Areas: Social Studies: Learn About the Branches of Government 405

Apply and Expand 406

Listening and Speaking Workshop: Give a Persuasive Speech 406
Viewing Workshop: View and Think 407
Writer's Workshop: Write a Research Report 408
Projects 410
Further Reading 411

Skills Index 412

Credits 419

To the Student

We hope you like *Visions*
We wrote it for you
To learn speaking, reading, writing,
And listening, too.

You'll read all kinds of things —
Stories, poems, and plays,
And texts that will help you understand
What your content teacher says.

Use this book to "grow" your English,
To talk about what you write and read.
Use it to learn lots of new words
And new reading strategies you'll need.

Good authors, good activities,
And especially your good teachers,
Can also help you learn grammar and writing,
And lots of other language features.

So please open this book
And learn everything you can.
Then write and show us how far you've come
Since you first began.

M.L.M. and L.S.

Mary Lou McCloskey

Lydia Stack

www.visions@heinle.com

UNIT 1

Introduce the Unit

Unit Materials

Activity Book: *pp. 1–40*
Audio: *Unit 1*
Student Handbook
Student CD-ROM: *Unit 1*
CNN Video: *Unit 1*
Teacher Resource Book: *Lesson Plans, Teacher Resources, Reading Summaries, Home-School Connection, Video Script, Video Worksheet, Activity Book Answer Key*
Teacher Resource CD-ROM
Assessment Program: *Quizzes and Test, pp. 7–22; Teacher and Student Resources, pp. 115–144*
Assessment CD-ROM
Transparencies
The Heinle Newbury House Dictionary/CD-ROM
More Grammar Practice workbook
Heinle Reading Library
Web Site: www.heinle.visions.com

Heinle Staff Development Handbook

Refer to the Heinle Staff Development Handbook for more teacher support.

Unit Theme: Challenges

1. **Teacher think aloud** *Say: A challenge is something that is hard to do. Waking up early every morning is a challenge. Eating healthy food is a challenge, too. I face challenges every day.*
2. **Use personal experience** *Ask: What challenges do you face in school?*

Unit Preview: Table of Contents

1. **Use the table of contents to locate information** Ask questions about the titles and number of chapters in this unit. *Ask: How many chapters are in this unit?* Read the chapter titles and authors of the reading selections. *Ask: What page is Chapter 1 on? Who are the authors of the selections in Chapter 1?* Continue with the other examples.
2. **Identify genres** *Say: The first selection is a poem. What other kinds of readings are in this unit?* (fable, excerpts of novels and historical narrative, short story)
3. **Connect** *Ask: Which titles interest you?*

UNIT 1

Challenges

CHAPTER 1 *page 2* — **The Race**
a poem by Jennifer Trujillo

The Camel Dances
a fable by Arnold Lobel

CHAPTER 2 *page 14* — **Hatchet**
an excerpt from a novel by Gary Paulsen

CHAPTER 3 *page 28* — **Antarctic Adventure**
an excerpt from a historical narrative by Meredith Hooper

CHAPTER 4 *page 40* — **Yang the Youngest**
an excerpt from a novel by Lensey Namioka

CHAPTER 5 *page 54* — **The Scholarship Jacket**
a short story by Marta Salinas

UNIT OBJECTIVES

Reading

Make inferences as you read a poem and a fable • Identify cause and effect as you read a realistic adventure story • Predict events as you read a historical narrative • Compare a reading with your experiences as you read a first-person narrative • Find the main idea and details as you read a short story

Listening and Speaking

Describe something you like to do • Act out events in a story • Retell order of events • Identify and use colloquial speech • Debate issues

Runners, Robert Delaunay, 1926.

View the Picture

1. What challenge are the people in the picture facing?
2. Compare your ideas with those of a partner.

In this unit, you will read a poem, a fable, stories, and a historical narrative. In these readings, people face challenges in their lives, such as staying alive or learning to feel comfortable in a new place. You will learn about the features of these writing forms and how to write them yourself.

1

Grammar
Study past tense verbs • Use the past tense of the verb *be* • Use *and* to join words and sentences • Study complex sentences with dependent clauses • Use *could* and *couldn't* for past ability

Writing
Write a poem • Write a realistic adventure story • Write a historical narrative • Write a first-person narrative • Write a short story

Content
Science: Classify animals • Science: Learn about combustion • Social Studies: Learn about bodies of land and water • Social Studies: Learn the meanings of *culture* • Science: Learn about nutrition

UNIT 1
Introduce the Unit

View the Picture

1. **Art background** Robert Delaunay (1855–1941) was born in Paris, France. He loved art and began painting at a young age. Delaunay often changed artistic styles throughout his career. His first paintings were of an Impressionist style, but later in life he became known as a Cubist painter. A Cubist painting tries to show an object from many different points of view, all at the same time.
2. **Art interpretation** Have students discuss how the painting looks like it has been painted from multiple points of view.
   a. **Explore style** Have students discuss the color and texture of the painting. ***Ask:*** *Why does the painting look slightly blurry?* (the men are moving fast) *Why does the painting look like it has three frames?* (each frame is from a different perspective) *Why did the artist use such bright, vivid colors?* (to grab your attention)
   b. **Interpret the painting** Ask students to think about the people in the painting. ***Ask:*** *Why are they runnning? Where are they? How do the runners feel?*
   c. **Connect to the theme** ***Say:*** *The theme of this unit is challenges. What challenge do you see in this painting?* (Running is a challenge. Some people run to compete against other people. Some people run just to challenge themselves.)

ASSESS

Have students draw pictures of themselves meeting a challenge. ***Say:*** *Try to use a part of the art on this page in your drawing, such as a color or the look on a face.*

UNIT 1 • CHAPTER 1
Into the Reading

Chapter Materials

Activity Book: *pp. 1–8*
Audio: *Unit 1, Chapter 1*
Student Handbook
Student CD-ROM: *Unit 1, Chapter 1*
Teacher Resource Book: *Lesson Plan, Teacher Resources, Reading Summary, Activity Book Answer Key*
Teacher Resource CD-ROM
Assessment Program: *Quiz, pp. 7–8; Teacher and Student Resources, pp. 115–144*
Assessment CD-ROM
Transparencies
The Heinle Newbury House Dictionary/CD-ROM
Web Site: www.heinle.visions.com

Objectives

Preview *Say: These objectives are what we will learn in Chapter 1. Is there an objective you already know?*

Use Prior Knowledge

Discuss Competition

Teacher Resource Book: *Web, p. 37*

Teacher think aloud *Say: I know what a competition is. A soccer game is a competition. Winning, losing, trying, and teamwork are parts of a competition. I can use this information as I read the selections.*

Answers

1. *Examples:* auto races, baseball games, soccer matches, board games

CHAPTER 1

Into the Reading

The Race
a poem
by Jennifer Trujillo

The Camel Dances
a fable
by Arnold Lobel

Objectives

Reading Make inferences as you read a poem and a fable.

Listening and Speaking Describe something you like to do.

Grammar Study past tense verbs.

Writing Write a poem.

Content Science: Classify animals.

Use Prior Knowledge

Discuss Competition

Prior knowledge is something that you already know. Use your prior knowledge to help you understand what you do not know.

When you try to win against someone else, or against another team, this is called a competition.

1. With a partner, talk about competitions people take part in.
2. Copy the web on a piece of paper. Write your ideas in the web. Add more ovals if necessary.
3. Talk about an activity that you have each competed in. Use the following questions as a guide:
   a. What was the activity?
   b. Were you on a team or alone?
   c. How did you feel before you competed? After?
   d. Did you win?

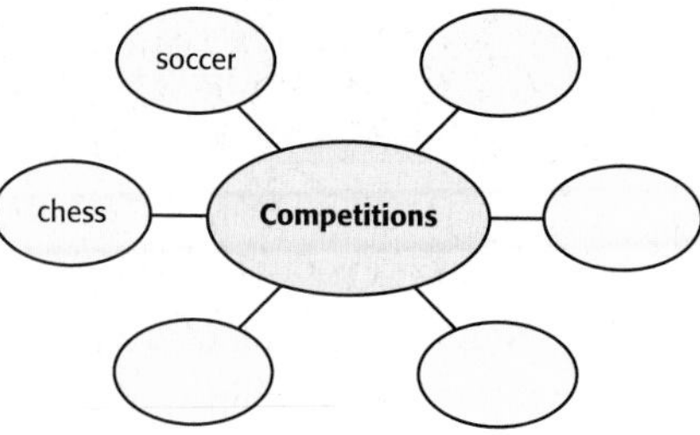

MULTI-LEVEL OPTIONS *Build Vocabulary*

Newcomer Write *happy* and *mad* on the board. Model a facial expression for each. Point to one word. ***Ask:*** *How do you look when you're happy or glad? How do you look when you're mad or angry?* Have students demonstrate an expression for each word and its synonym.

Beginning Ask students to work in pairs. Have them take turns acting out a word as the partner guesses the synonym pair.

Intermediate In pairs, have one student use a word from the chart in a sentence and the other student restate the sentence using a synonym. Have students alternate turns.

Advanced Divide students into pairs. Have one student make up a story that is as short as possible using all the words on the list. Then have the other student retell the story using synonyms.

Build Background

Ballet

Background is information that can help you understand what you hear or read.

You will read about ballet in one of the readings. Ballet is a kind of dance. Ballet steps and body positions take a lot of practice. Dancers learn special ways to stand. These are called the five basic positions.

Content Connection

In a *pirouette,* dancers spin around on the toes or ball of one foot.

First Steps in Ballet

Build Vocabulary

Find Synonyms Using a Reference Aid

When you learn new words, you **build your vocabulary.**

A **synonym** is a word that has a similar meaning to another word.

happy = glad   mad = angry

A dictionary is a **reference** book that gives the meanings of words. Dictionaries often use synonyms for meanings.

1. The word *gallop* is used in "The Race." Look at this dictionary entry.

> **gal•lop** /'gæləp/ *n.* the fastest run of four-legged animals, esp. horses: *The horse raced to the rescue at full gallop.* —*v.* (usu. of horses) to run at a gallop: *Race horses gallop around the race track.*

2. Notice that the word *run* is used in the definition of *gallop.* A synonym for *gallop* is *run.*
3. Copy this chart. Use a dictionary to look up the words. Find synonyms for them in the definitions. Write the words and their synonyms in your Personal Dictionary.

Word	Synonym
whoop	
shy	
chuckle	

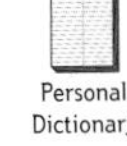
Personal Dictionary

The Heinle Newbury House Dictionary

Activity Book p. 1

Student CD-ROM

Home Connection

Build Vocabulary Have students copy a synonym chart to use at home. Give students these words: *sofa/couch* and *rug/carpet* and words with a blank space next to each: *automobile/______, job/______, house/______.* Tell them to ask people at home or friends to help them find a synonym for each word.

Learning Styles *Kinesthetic*

Build Background Have small groups demonstrate the basic ballet positions pictured. Ask them to show different ways of moving from one position to another. Then have groups demonstrate their work.

Build Background

Ballet

1. **Relate to personal experiences** Ask students to share information about dancing they like to do. Point to the ballet positions. *Ask: Do you think ballet steps are hard or easy? Who can show us the steps?*
2. **Content Connection** *Ask: Can you name some ways ballet dancers move?* (jump, spin, run, hop on one foot, slide) Have volunteers demonstrate one or two moves.

Build Vocabulary

Find Synonyms Using a Reference Aid

Teacher Resource Book: *Personal Dictionary, p. 63*

1. **Locate pronunciations** Have students use a dictionary to locate the pronunciations of unfamiliar words. Ask them to pronounce the words.
2. **Use a dictionary** Introduce students to The Heinle Newbury House Dictionary. Walk them through the Introduction on pp. xiii–xxii. These notes instruct students on how to use a dictionary to clarify meaning, pronunciation, and usage.
3. **Use other sources** Tell students that dictionaries are also available online and as CD-ROMs. Students will find meanings, pronunciations, derivations, and usage notes in these other sources. The CD-ROM version of The Heinle Newbury House Dictionary is found on the inside back cover.
4. **Reading selection vocabulary** You may want to introduce the glossed words in the reading selections before students begin reading. Key words: *twinkle, dawn, fling, recital, bow, applause, audience.* Instruct students to write the words with correct spelling and their definitions in their Personal Dictionaries. Have them pronounce each word and divide it into syllables.
5. **Multi-level options** See MULTI-LEVEL OPTIONS on p. 2.

Answers

3. *Possible synonyms:* whoop/shout, shy/bashful, chuckle/laugh

ASSESS

Have students write two sentences with a synonym pair.

UNIT 1 • CHAPTER 1
Into the Reading

Text Structure

Poem and Fable

Use graphic organizers to compare features In pairs, have students identify and describe the information in each graphic organizer. Ask students to compare and contrast the features of a poem and a fable.

Reading Strategy

Make Inferences

1. **Teacher think aloud** *Say: When I walk past the cafeteria and I smell food, I know what time it is. I know that the cafeteria has food ready at lunchtime. I can make an inference that it's time to eat lunch.*
2. **Locate derivation** Have students locate the derivation of *inference* in the glossary in the Student Handbook and record it in their Reading Logs.
3. **Multi-level options** See MULTI-LEVEL OPTIONS below.

Answers

1. *Example:* The girl rode a horse named Fina. Women didn't ride horses then. She was a brave girl. She was an unusual and a special girl.

ASSESS

Ask: What are three features of a poem? (rhyming words, images, stanzas) *What are three features of a fable?* (short beginning, middle, end; animals as main characters; moral)

Text Structure

Poem and Fable

The **text structure** of a reading is its main parts and how they fit together.

This chapter contains two reading selections, a poem and a fable.

1. "The Race" is a poem. Look for these things as you read or listen to it.

Poem	
Rhyming Words	words that sound the same at the end
Images	words that help you make pictures in your mind
Stanzas	groups of lines

2. "The Camel Dances" is a fable. Look for these things as you read or listen to it.

Fable	
Structure	short beginning, middle, and end
Characters	animals are often the main characters
A Moral	a lesson about life

3. As you read the poem and the fable, think about how they are the same and how they are different.

Student CD-ROM

Reading Strategy

Make Inferences

A **reading strategy** is a way to understand what you read. You can become a better reader if you learn good reading strategies.

To **make an inference** is to make a guess. You use what you know when you make the guess. For example, if your brother comes home sweating and wearing his running shoes and shorts, you can make an inference that he went running. When you read, you use information from the reading selection and your own life to make inferences.

1. Read the first two lines of "The Race" on page 6. What do you learn about the girl? What inference can you make?
2. As you read or listen to "The Race" and "The Camel Dances," look for information about the characters. Use this information to make inferences.

The Girl	The Camel
lets her hair down when she rides	likes to dance

Student CD-ROM

4 **Unit 1** Challenges

MULTI-LEVEL OPTIONS *Reading Strategy*

Newcomer Help students to make inferences about the picture on p. 5. ***Ask:*** *Are the horses moving?* (no) *Are the horses excited?* (yes) *Do you think the horses will race?* (yes)

Beginning Direct students to the picture on p. 5. ***Ask:*** *How do the horses feel?* (excited) *What are the riders doing?* (They are getting ready to race.) *Can you tell who is going to win?* (no) Explain that when they answer these questions, they are making inferences.

Intermediate Direct students to the picture on p. 5. In pairs, have students list three things that they can tell about the horses and their riders in the picture. Then ask each pair to compare their inferences with another pair.

Advanced Have students make up a story about the picture on p. 5. Tell them to make inferences in their story about who the horses and their riders are, why they are gathered together, and how they feel. Have them share their story with a partner.

The Race

a poem
by Jennifer Trujillo

The Camel Dances

a fable
by Arnold Lobel

5

UNIT 1 • CHAPTER 1
Reading Selection

Reading Selection Materials

Audio: *Unit 1, Chapter 1*
Teacher Resource Book: *Reading Summary, pp. 65–66*

Preview the Selections

1. **Interpret the image** ***Ask:*** *What kind of colors, shapes, and lines do you see in the picture? What do they tell us about the artist's message?* Tell students that the picture relates to both the poem and the fable in this chapter. ***Ask:*** *What is happening in this picture? What inference can you make about the selections from this picture?*
2. **Connect** Remind students that the unit theme is *challenges*. Ask them how the picture relates to challenges. Say that in some challenges, people compete and try to win. In other challenges, people do something for themselves. Tell students they will read about both types of challenges in this unit.

Community Connection

Ask students where they go to participate in competitions. (after-school programs, a special club) Ask them what kinds of challenges they like best. (playing an instrument, playing a sport, learning about computers)

Learning Styles ***Intrapersonal***

Ask: *How do you prepare yourself for a challenge like a race or competition? What can you do to help you do your best? Can you picture yourself finding your own special way to meet the challenge?* Have students write a list of steps they take or draw a picture of their visualization.

Reading Selection

Read the Selection

1. **Use text features** Direct students to the numbers for each stanza. Explain their purpose and use. Then direct students to glossed words. Explain that the information helps them understand the boldfaced words.
2. **Choral reading** Have students do a choral reading of the poem as they listen to the audio. In choral readings, everyone reads together aloud. A teacher or student may stand in front of the class as the "leader."
3. **Make inferences** *Ask: Why do you think the girl's great-grandma planned to stop her from riding?* (Girls didn't ride in those days.)

Sample Answer to Guide Question
She is shy. "Up there she wasn't shy!"

See Teacher Edition pp. 434–435 for a list of English-Spanish cognates in the reading selection.

The Race

a poem by Jennifer Trujillo

Audio

1 She rode a horse named Fina
when women didn't ride.
They galloped around the mountain,
her legs on Fina's side.

2 She let her hair down from its **bun**
and felt it whip and fly.
She laughed and sang and whooped out loud.
Up there she wasn't shy!

Make Inferences
What is the rider like when she is not on a horse? What words in the poem support your answer?

3 One day great-grandma found her out
and planned to stop it all.
But down in town they'd heard some news . . .
they told her of a call.

4 A call for the caballeros
from all **the highs and lows**
to race their fancy **caballos**
to try and win the rose.

bun hair wrapped in a round shape
the highs and lows land up high (mountains) and low (valleys)
caballos horses

MULTI-LEVEL OPTIONS *Read the Selection*

Newcomer Play the audio. Pause at the rhyming words (*ride/side, fly/shy,* and so on). Write them on the board. Read the poem again. Have students raise their hands when they hear a rhyming word. ***Ask:*** *Is the girl's name Fina?* (no) *Do many girls ride in this race?* (no) *Does the girl win the rose?* (yes)

Beginning Read the Reading Summary aloud. Then do a paired reading. Seat students side by side and have them take turns reading aloud. ***Ask:*** *What is the horse's name?* (Fina) *Does the girl ride fast or slow?* (She rides fast.) *Who is Abuela?* (the girl's great-grandma) *What is the prize in this race?* (a rose)

Intermediate Have students do a paired reading. ***Ask:*** *Why does the girl's great-grandma want to stop the girl?* (She doesn't think girls should ride or race horses.) *Why does Abuela change her mind?* (She likes a challenge.) *Who feels proud at the end of the poem?* (the girl, Abuela, and Fina)

Advanced Have students do a partner read aloud. Direct pairs to face each other and read alternate stanzas. ***Ask:*** *What is the girl like when she isn't riding Fina?* (shy, quiet, careful, neat) *What does the prize of a rose tell you about this race?* (It's a tradition. It's done for love of riding, not for money.)

5 Abuela looked at Fina,
a **twinkle** in her eye.
Abuela said, "Let's enter!
This race deserves a try."

6 At **dawn** she was the only girl,
but didn't even care.
She came to meet the challenge, and
her horse was waiting there.

Make Inferences

Did the girl think she would win? What information supports your answer?

7 They swept across the finish line
much faster than the rest.
She **flung** her hat without surprise;
she'd always done her best.

8 Fina shook her **mane** and stomped.
Abuela flashed a smile.
She sniffed the rose and trotted off
in **caballera** style!

---

twinkle a shine that goes on and off
dawn sunrise
flung threw or tossed
mane the hair on a horse's neck
caballera proud horse-riding style

About the Author

Jennifer Trujillo (born 1970)

Jennifer Trujillo was born in Denver, Colorado. Her family came from Caracas, Venezuela. She spent part of her childhood there and part of it in Colorado. Today Trujillo teaches at a Navajo Indian Reservation and at Fort Lewis College in Colorado. She says, "Writing is like swimming. Sometimes I dive in with a splash! Other times, I have to step in slowly—one toe at a time."

➤ What advice do you think Jennifer Trujillo would give a girl or a boy who wants to enter a competition?

Read the Selection

1. **Recognize a stanza** Have students identify the stanzas by number. Ask them to count the number of lines in each stanza.
2. **Understand terms** Tell students to find the meanings of the glossed words below the poem. Clarify meanings as needed.
3. **Choral reading** Play the audio or read the poem to students. Have small groups do choral readings of different stanzas.
4. **Role-play the order of events** Ask questions to help students summarize the events of the poem. Then have small groups role-play each event in the poem in order.
5. **Multi-level options** See MULTI-LEVEL OPTIONS on p. 6.

Sample Answer to Guide Question

Yes, the girl thought she would win. "She flung her hat without surprise;"

About the Author

Evaluate information about the author
Read the author biography to students. ***Ask:*** *Where does she teach?* (at a Navajo Indian Reservation, Fort Lewis College) Explain the difference between diving in and stepping in slowly. Ask students which one describes the way they write.

A Capitalization

Names

Tell students that the first letter in names of people and characters is always capitalized. ***Ask:*** *What letters in the author's name are capitalized?* (*J* and *T*) *Why does Jennifer Trujillo's name start with capital letters?* (It's the name of a person.) *Why does Fina's name start with a capital letter?* (It's the name of a character.) *Can you find another name that is capitalized in the poem?* (Abuela)

Apply Write these sentences on the board. Have students correct the capitalization errors.

maria gomez wants to race her horse.

Mr. gomez is afraid she will be hurt.

Mrs. gomez knows maria can do it.

Read the Selection

1. **Teacher read aloud** Read paragraphs 1 and 2 aloud to students while they listen silently. ***Ask:*** *Why does the Camel want to become a ballet dancer?* (to move with grace and beauty) *What does the Camel do to reach her goal?* (She practices.)
2. **Identify the main character** Remind students that this reading selection is a fable. ***Ask:*** *What kind of main characters does a fable have?* (animals) Have students identify the main character in this fable. Ask if anyone has seen a camel. Share facts about camels. (have one or two humps; can go for days without drinking water; used for transportation; and so on)

Sample Answer to Guide Question
She is a hard worker. She is determined.

See Teacher Edition pp. 434–435 for a list of English-Spanish cognates in the reading selection.

The Camel Dances
a fable by Arnold Lobel

Audio

Make Inferences
What does the Camel's practicing tell you about her character?

1 The Camel had her heart set on becoming a ballet dancer. "To make every movement a thing of grace and beauty," said the Camel. "That is my one and only desire."

2 Again and again she practiced her pirouettes, her **relevés,** and her **arabesques.** She repeated the five basic positions a hundred times each day. She worked for long months under the hot desert sun. Her feet were **blistered,** and her body ached with fatigue, but not once did she think of stopping.

relevés ballet steps in which the dancer rises on tiptoe on one or both legs

arabesques movements in ballet in which the dancer stands on one leg with the other leg extended straight back

blistered covered with pockets of skin filled with fluid

8 **Unit 1** Challenges

MULTI-LEVEL OPTIONS *Read the Selection*

Newcomer Play the audio. Have students point to the paragraph numbers as they listen. ***Ask:*** *Does the Camel practice again and again?* (yes) *Does the Camel give up?* (no) *Do her friends like her dancing?* (no) *Is the Camel happy?* (yes)

Beginning Prepare a cloze exercise of the Reading Summary. Have students complete it as you read the summary aloud. ***Ask:*** *What does the Camel want to be?* (a ballet dancer) *What does the audience think of the Camel's dancing?* (They don't like it.) *Who does she dance for now?* (herself)

Intermediate Have three groups write and present a summary of one part of the reading: the beginning, middle, or end. ***Ask:*** *How does the Camel feel about dancing?* (She loves it.) *What do the other camels think about her dancing?* (They don't think she is a good dancer.) *Will she give up her dancing?* (No)

Advanced Have students work in small groups to write summaries of the whole fable. Have each group share summaries with the other groups. ***Ask:*** *Do you think the Camel would act the same way if she wanted to do something else? Explain.* (Yes. She is very determined and has high expectations of herself.)

3 At last the Camel said, "Now I am a dancer." She announced a **recital** and danced before an invited group of camel friends and **critics.** When her dance was over, she made a deep **bow.**

4 There was no **applause.**

5 "I must tell you **frankly,**" said a member of the audience, "as a critic and a **spokesman** for this group, that you are lumpy and humpy. You are baggy and bumpy. You are, like the rest of us, simply a camel. You are *not* and never will be a ballet dancer!"

6 Chuckling and laughing, the **audience** moved away across the sand.

7 "How very wrong they are!" said the Camel. "I have worked hard. There can be no doubt that I am a splendid dancer. I will dance and dance just for myself."

8 That is what she did. It gave her many years of pleasure.

9 *Satisfaction will come to those who please themselves.*

Make Inferences

Do you think the audience liked the recital? What information supports your answer?

---

recital a show of dancing or music for people to watch
critics people who give opinions about the arts
bow bend at the waist
applause clapping that shows approval
frankly truthfully
spokesman one who speaks for a larger group
audience the people who come to watch an event

About the Author — Arnold Lobel (1933–1987)

Arnold Lobel grew up in Schenectady, New York. He studied art at the Pratt Institute in Brooklyn, New York. There he became interested in book illustration. Most of Lobel's books include characters who are animals. His most famous book, *Frog and Toad Are Friends,* contains humorous stories about friendship.

➤ Why do you think Arnold Lobel chose to tell this story using animals instead of people?

UNIT 1 • CHAPTER 1
Reading Selection

Read the Selection

1. **Shared text reading** Play the audio of the story once. Then have students read aloud together from a shared text, such as a Big Book, an overhead transparency, or a chart. *Ask: Did the Camel stop dancing?* (no) *Why not?* (She enjoys dancing.)
2. **Recognize text structure** *Ask: What did you learn about the structure of a fable?* (short beginning, middle, and end) Have students identify what happens in the beginning, middle, and end of this fable.
3. **Multi-level options** See MULTI-LEVEL OPTIONS on p. 8.

Sample Answer to Guide Question
No, the audience didn't like the recital. "There was no applause."

About the Author

1. **Explain author challenges** Arnold Lobel had many serious childhood illnesses. He spent a lot of time in the hospital. He felt lonely there, but he got many of his ideas for his books from his childhood and from watching his own children.
2. **Interpret the facts** *Ask: How do you think the challenges in Arnold Lobel's life helped him write this fable? What kind of challenges in your life might make an interesting story?*

Across Selections

Use a Venn diagram Discuss the ways the two readings in this chapter are alike and different. For example, both of the selections tell about a challenge, but one is a poem and the other is a fable. Have students record their ideas on a Venn diagram.

Spelling

Plural nouns

Make a two-column chart labeled *Singular* and *Plural.* Write in the correct columns: *1 position, 5 positions; 1 friend, 2 friends. Say: Plural means more than one. Most plurals are made by adding -s to a noun.*

Apply Write these words on the board for students to copy: *heart, dancer, month, recital, critic, year. Say: Find these words in the fable. Which words are plural?* (months, critics, years)

Evaluate Your Reading Strategy

Make Inferences *Say: You have practiced an important reading strategy. Now you can decide how well you have done. Does this statement describe how you read?*

I use details to make inferences about how characters act or feel. This helps me understand characters.

Reading Comprehension

Question-Answer Relationships

Sample Answers

1. She likes to ride her horse very fast.
2. The girl wins the race.
3. She likes to dance.
4. They are proud and pleased.
5. They don't like it.
6. She learns ballet positions and practices them. She works hard for months.
7. She feels excited. She is not shy.
8. She does not think that girls should ride horses.
9. The Camel feels happy and satisfied.
10. Work at things for your own pleasure, not to please others.
11. Many students may say that they also feel happy in doing things that are important to them.

Build Reading Fluency

Reading Key Phrases

Assessment Program: *Reading Fluency Chart, p. 116*

When students have completed the reading fluency activity, record their progress in the Reading Fluency Chart.

Beyond the Reading

Reading Comprehension

Question-Answer Relationships (QAR)

You can understand a reading better if you answer different kinds of questions.

"Right There" Questions

1. **Recall Facts** In "The Race," what does the main character like to do?
2. **Recall Facts** How does the race end?
3. **Recall Facts** In "The Camel Dances," what does the Camel like to do?

"Think and Search" Questions

4. **Understand Characters** How do Abuela and her granddaughter feel at the end of the race?
5. **Understand Characters** What steps does the Camel take to become a ballet dancer?
6. **Understand Main Ideas** What does the Camel's audience think of her dancing?

"Author and You" Questions

7. **Recognize Character Traits** How do you think the girl from "The Race" feels when she is riding horses?
8. **Make Inferences** In the beginning of "The Race," why do you think Abuela wants to stop her granddaughter from riding horses?
9. **Recognize Character Traits** How do you think the Camel feels when she is dancing?
10. **Explain Main Ideas** What is the moral, or lesson, of "The Camel Dances"?

"On Your Own" Question

11. **Compare** How do you feel when you are doing something that is special to you?

Activity Book p. 2

Student CD-ROM

Build Reading Fluency

Reading Key Phrases

When you build reading fluency, you learn to read faster and to understand better.

Reading key phrases will help you learn to read faster. Read these phrases aloud and raise your hand each time you read the key phrase: "rode a horse."

rode a horse	ride a horse	race horses
ride ponies	ride horses	rode a horse
raced a horse	rode a horse	raced horses
rode a horse	raced horses	rode horses

MULTI-LEVEL OPTIONS *Elements of Literature*

Newcomer Replay the audio of "The Race." Tell students to raise their hands when they hear rhyming words. Have pairs practice reading the poem aloud. Suggest ways they can emphasize the rhyming words (standing up, clapping, and so on).

Beginning Write *ride* and *side* on the board. Read the words aloud and have students repeat. Then read aloud stanza 1 from "The Race." Direct students to say the rhymes aloud as they read each one. Then write *fly* and *shy*. Read the second stanza with students responding chorally. Repeat the process for the rest of the poem.

Intermediate Tell students to work independently to list the rhyming words in each stanza. Have them write a third word that rhymes with each pair. Ask them to share their lists with a small group.

Advanced Point out that rhyming words are used in commercials and songs. Have small groups of students sing or say examples from their favorite songs. Have other students record the rhyming words they hear.

Listen, Speak, Interact 

Describe Something You Like to Do

When people listen and talk to each other, they **interact.**

In both the poem and the fable, the characters like to do something.

1. Reread the poem and fable with a partner. Identify the activity each main character likes to do.
2. Tell your partner about an activity that you like to do. What do you like about it? How does it make you feel? Are you good at it?
3. How is your activity similar to or different from the activities the main characters like to do?

Elements of Literature

Distinguish Sounds of Rhyming Words

Literature is something that you read. Writers use many different ways to express themselves. These ways are the **elements of literature.**

Poetry often contains words that **rhyme.** Words that rhyme have the same ending sound. In stanza 1 of "The Race," *side* and *ride* are rhyming words. Often, the words that rhyme appear at the end of a line of poetry.

1. Read "The Race" with a partner. Take turns reading it out loud.
2. Be sure you make the correct sounds as you read. This will help you distinguish rhyming words. Ask your teacher to help you pronounce words you do not know.
3. Listen for the rhyming words as your partner reads. What similar sounds do the words have? How do the words sound different?
4. As you listen, think about the effects of the rhyming words. What mood, or feeling, do the rhyming words give the poem? Why do you think the author uses this style of writing?
5. List the rhyming words for each stanza in the poem in a chart.

Stanza (Group of Lines)	Rhyming Words
1	ride, side
2	fly, ___

Activity Book p. 3

Student CD-ROM

Content Connection *The Arts*

Use a stanza from "The Race" to model word substitutions of verbs, nouns, and end rhymes. For example, *We flew a plane named Fina/when women didn't fly. /It soared around the mountain, /green and sharp and high.* Have students identify the changed words (flew, plane, soared, green and sharp) and new end rhymes (fly, high). Then tell them to write a group poem. Monitor their progress and help with end rhymes.

Learning Styles *Visual*

Have students draw the main character from either "The Race" or "The Camel Dances." Direct them to show the character doing her favorite activity.

Listen, Speak, Interact

Describe Something You Like to Do

1. **Reread in pairs** Pair beginning and advanced students. Have them read alternate stanzas and paragraphs.
2. **Newcomers** Reread with this group. Have them identify activities they like to do. Write these activities on the board. Add key words to identify why they like them. Have students record details about their activities in their Reading Logs.

Answers

1. horse riding, ballet dancing
2. *Example:* playing the piano. I can make and listen to music at the same time. It makes me feel happy.
3. *Example:* It is similar to ballet dancing because of the music. It is different from horse riding because I use an instrument instead of an animal.

Elements of Literature

Distinguish Sounds of Rhyming Words

1. Review the rhyming words in the text. Provide additional examples (*rest/best, smile/style).* Ask students to tell you other rhyming words by prompting them with the first word and a clue. ***Ask:*** *What word rhymes with* hook *and is something that you read?* (book)
2. **Use personal experience** Point out that rhyming words are used in commercials and songs. Share a song or advertising slogan with students.
3. **Multi-level options** See MULTI-LEVEL OPTIONS on p. 10.

Answers

4. *Example:* A light, fun, musical mood. To avoid making it too serious. To make it interesting.
5. Stanza 1: ride, side; stanza 2: fly, shy; stanza 3: all, call; stanza 4: lows, rose; stanza 5: eye, try; stanza 6: care, there; stanza 7: rest, best; stanza 8: smile, style.

Recite the poem, "Roses Are Red," or another simple rhyme. Have students identify the rhyming word pairs.

Beyond the Reading

Word Study

Analyze the Suffix *-er*

Make a word map Write the word *ride* on the board and say it. Then write the suffix *-er* and pronounce it. Then put the word parts together and pronounce the new word. Write the new word.

Answers

1. singer, painter, speaker
2. dancer
3. dance, *-er*

Grammar Focus

Study Past Tense Verbs

Apply Ask students to write a sentence in the present tense. Have them exchange sentences with a classmate and rewrite the sentences in the past tense. ***Ask:*** *Is the verb regular or irregular?*

ASSESS

On the board, write: *The man who bakes sells bread.* Underline *man who bakes* and *sells.* Have students rewrite the sentence twice. First use the *-er* suffix. Next use the past tense.

Word Study

Analyze the Suffix *-er*

Words can have several parts. In this section, you will learn what the different parts mean.

A **suffix** is a group of letters added to the end of a word. A suffix changes the meaning of a word.

The suffix *-er* often means that something or someone does something. For example, a teach**er** is someone who teaches.

Note that most base words ending in *-e* drop the final *-e* before adding the suffix *-er*. For example: *ride* ⟶ *rider.*

1. Here are some action words. On a piece of paper, add *-er* to the words to make a word meaning someone who does the action.
   a. sing **b.** paint **c.** speak
2. Find a word with the suffix *-er* in "The Camel Dances." Write the word on a piece of paper.
3. Divide the word into the base word and the suffix *-er*.

Activity Book
p. 4

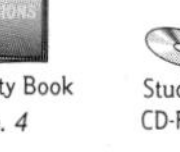

Student CD-ROM

Grammar Focus

Study Past Tense Verbs

Grammar is the way that a language is put together. Grammar helps us understand each other.

To tell about actions in the past, use the past tense of verbs. Regular verbs form the past tense like this:

Simple Form	Ending	Past Tense
gallop	**-ed**	gallop**ed**

Most verbs are regular verbs. Irregular verbs form the past tense in different ways.

Simple Form	Past Tense
feel	**felt**
find	**found**
hear	**heard**
ride	**rode**
sweep	**swept**

Activity Book
pp. 4–5

Student Handbook

Student CD-ROM

MULTI-LEVEL OPTIONS *From Reading to Writing*

Newcomer Have students draw a picture of a challenge they have faced. Tell them to explain their drawing to a partner. Have them list five words that describe each picture. Work with students to find rhymes for their word lists.

Beginning Have students draw a picture to illustrate their challenge. Help them list key words to use in their poems. Have them explain their challenges in small groups. Tell group members to help each other identify rhyming words for their key words.

Intermediate Have students write the first line of their poems. Ask pairs to brainstorm and list words that rhyme with the last word. Tell them to use the list to write the second line of their poems. Have them repeat the process as they work through the poem.

Advanced Have students exchange poems with a partner. Tell them to check for capitalization, plurals, *-er* suffixes, and past tense verbs. They may also suggest additional rhyming words. Remind students to be tactful. Point out that final changes are up to the author.

From Reading to Writing 

Write a Poem

In school, after you read some literature, you often have to write about it. This section shows you how to do this.

Write a short poem that tells about a challenge.

1. Choose an event that was a challenge for you or someone you know.
2. Give your poem a title.
3. Group your lines into sets of two lines. Use rhyme at the end of your lines. Look at the example.

What Went Wrong
She didn't want to be friends anymore.
She said this as she went out the door.

4. Use past tense verbs.
5. Produce a visual such as a picture to go with your poem.
6. Present your poem to the class. Speak clearly and with expression.

Activity Book
p. 7

Across Content Areas 

Classify Animals

Content areas are the subjects you study in school. Math, science, social studies, language arts, and other arts such as music and drawing are content areas.

Scientists who study animals **classify** them, or put them in groups. We can classify animals by what they eat.

Herbivores eat mostly plants.
Carnivores eat mostly other animals (meat).

1. Look at this list of animals.

	Animals	
camels	tigers	boa constrictors
wolves	cows	chimpanzees
elephants		

2. Work with a partner. Decide whether the animals in the list are herbivores or carnivores. If you do not know, use a reference resource such as an encyclopedia.
3. Copy this chart on a piece of paper. Write the name of each animal in the correct column.

Herbivores	*Carnivores*
horses	

Activity Book
p. 8

Student
CD-ROM

From Reading to Writing

Write a Poem

1. **Brainstorm** Have students brainstorm a list of topics for their poems. Remind them to write down all their ideas first. Then they can choose the best idea.
2. **Think-Quickwrite-Pair-Share** Ask students to think about their chosen idea and write as much as they can about it. Have them group their lines into sets of two. As students share with a partner, they can help find rhyming words to end their lines.
3. **Multi-level options** See MULTI-LEVEL OPTIONS on p. 12.

Across Content Areas: Science

Classify Animals

Define and clarify Explain the meanings of *classify, herbivores,* and *carnivores.* ***Say:*** *Name an animal that eats nuts or fruit.* (squirrel, monkey) ***Ask:*** *How do you classify it?* (herbivore) Then give examples for fish or meat eaters. (eagle, bear) Have students name and classify animals that they are familiar with. Ask them to explain what those animals eat.

Answers

2. Camels, elephants, cows, and chimpanzees are herbivores.
3. Tigers, wolves, and boa constrictors are carnivores.

ASSESS

Have students write two sentences that describe two different animals. Tell them to find rhyming words for the last words in each sentence.

Assessment Program: *Unit 1, Chapter 1 Quiz, pp. 7–8*

Reteach and Reassess

Text Structure Draw two trees with three branches each on the board. Label the "roots" of one tree "poem" and the other tree "fable." Have students name and describe text features. (Poem: rhyming words, images, stanzas. Fable: structure, characters, moral.) Call on students to label each branch with appropriate features.

Reading Strategy Have small groups write three facts about a school event. Have groups exchange lists and make inferences about the event.

Elements of Literature Write ten words from the readings on index cards. Distribute cards to small groups. Have them name as many rhyming words as they can.

Reassess Create a two-column chart labeled *"The Race"* and *"The Camel Dances."* Label three rows *Features, Challenge,* and *Inferences*. Have students complete the chart.

Chapter Materials

Activity Book: *pp. 9–16*
Audio: *Unit 1, Chapter 2*
Student Handbook
Student CD-ROM: *Unit 1, Chapter 2*
Teacher Resource Book: *Lesson Plan, Teacher Resources, Reading Summary, Activity Book Answer Key*
Teacher Resource CD-ROM
Assessment Program: *Quiz, pp. 9–10; Teacher and Student Resources, pp. 115–144*
Assessment CD-ROM
Transparencies
The Heinle Newbury House Dictionary/CD-ROM
Web Site: www.heinle.visions.com

Objectives

Teacher think aloud Read the objectives. ***Say:*** *The word* cause *reminds me of* because. *That answers the question* why. *As I read this story, I can look for why different things happen.*

Use Prior Knowledge

Share Knowledge About Forests

Make a semantic web Assign groups these topics: *Things that live in the forest. Things to do in the forest. Things people take to the forest.* After groups list items for their topics, use them to create a semantic web for students' ideas and for more vocabulary building during the reading of the selection.

Answers
1. **a.** T **b.** T **c.** T **d.** T **e.** F **f.** T

CHAPTER 2

Into the Reading

Hatchet

an excerpt from a novel
by Gary Paulsen

Objectives

Reading Identify cause and effect as you read a realistic adventure story.

Listening and Speaking Act out events in a story.

Grammar Use the past tense of the verb *be.*

Writing Write a realistic adventure story.

Content Science: Learn about combustion.

Use Prior Knowledge

Share Knowledge About Forests

A forest is a large area with many trees. What do you already know about forests?

1. Read these statements. Decide if each one is true or false. Write your answers on a piece of paper.
   - **a.** A forest has things in it that can be used to make a campfire.
   - **b.** Dry leaves can catch fire—they are flammable.
   - **c.** There is food that people can eat in a forest.
   - **d.** Some forests have lakes and rivers.
   - **e.** A dry, empty bird's nest is not flammable.
   - **f.** A forest can have rocks in it.
2. Compare your answers with a partner's.
3. Check your answers with other students or your teacher.

MULTI-LEVEL OPTIONS *Build Vocabulary*

Newcomer Show a picture of a face without a nose. ***Ask:*** *What's missing?* Explain that students can guess the answer because they already know the context. Show a tree branch with several twigs. ***Say:*** *A twig is the smallest part of a tree.* Point to a twig. ***Say:*** *You can figure out new words from the context and what you already know.*

Beginning Show a tree branch with several twigs. ***Say:*** *A twig is the smallest branch of a tree.* Point to a twig. ***Say:*** *You can figure out new words from the context and information you already know.* On the board, write: *A salad is a combination of lettuce, tomatoes, and onions.* ***Ask:*** *Is a combination more or less than one thing?* (more)

Intermediate Read the sentence that begins "He tried small twigs . . ." ***Say:*** *Twigs come from trees. Draw a picture of a twig.* Show twig drawings. ***Say:*** *You figured out what* twig *means because you know about trees. You have a context.* Read the next sentence. ***Ask:*** *How many things do you need to make a combination?* (more than one)

Advanced Have small groups of students discuss the examples on p. 15. ***Ask:*** *What information in the sentences helps you figure out what* twig *or* combination *mean?* (little pieces, worse than grass, of the two). Have students write sentences for the vocabulary words giving additional context clues. Have them share their sentences in groups.

Build Background

Fire

People who camp in forests often make a campfire. Campfires are used for cooking and staying warm.

It is easy to start a campfire with matches. If you do not have matches, you can start a fire with sparks (bits of light and heat). You make sparks by scraping two hard surfaces such as stone together.

Fire can be very dangerous. You should always have sand or water close by when you make a campfire.

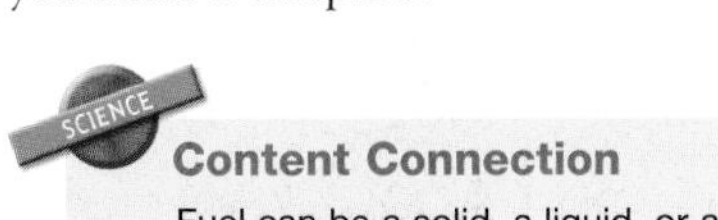

Content Connection

Fuel can be a solid, a liquid, or a gas.

Build Vocabulary

Use Context

Sometimes you can guess the meanings of new words by using the **context,** or nearby words and sentences.

1. In "Hatchet," the sparks made by the boy in the story "just *sputtered* and died." You can use the word *died* to guess what *sputtered* means.
2. Look at the underlined words in the following sentences. Use the context to help you understand the meaning of each word.

He tried small <u>twigs</u>, breaking them into little pieces, but that was worse than the grass.

Then he tried a <u>combination</u> of the two, grass and twigs.

3. Write the underlined words and your definitions in your Personal Dictionary. Then check your definitions in a dictionary.

Personal Dictionary

The Heinle Newbury House Dictionary

Activity Book *p. 9*

Student CD-ROM

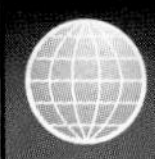

Content Connection *Social Studies*

Build Background Explain to students that forest fires are a big problem in areas of the U.S. Assign groups to find information about forest fires in national parks. They can do an Internet search with the key words *forest fires, national parks.* Or they can use the school or public library. Have students write a paragraph or draw a picture about problems that forest fires cause to wildlife or to people who live nearby.

Learning Styles *Natural*

Prior Knowledge Have small groups brainstorm a list of items they would expect to find in a forest. Then have them make a chart with categories to classify the items on their list. Assist groups by suggesting categories such as animals, plants, living or nonliving things, and so on. Display the charts.

UNIT 1 • CHAPTER 2
Into the Reading

Build Background

Fire

1. **Activate prior knowledge** Show a picture of a campfire. Have students identify parts and colors of the fire: flames, sparks, smoke, red, yellow.
2. **Content Connection** Show a lighted candle with wax melting. Point out the three states as the candle burns. (The candlestick is a solid; when it melts it's a liquid; the heat it gives off is a gas.) ***Ask:*** *What other fuels do you know?* (wood, oil, gas) *Are they solids, liquids, or gases?*

Build Vocabulary

Use Context

Teacher Resource Book: *Personal Dictionary, p. 63*

1. **Teacher think aloud** Write on the board: *The sparks fell on the wet leaf and <u>sputtered</u> and died.* ***Say:*** *I know that the sparks died or they went out. So I guess the word* sputtered *means they started to go out. I can use other words in the sentence to guess the meanings of new words.*
2. **Reading selection vocabulary** You may want to introduce the glossed words in the reading selection before students begin reading. Key words: *sparks, exasperation, pitiful, painstaking, position, inhale.* Instruct students to write the words with correct spelling and their definitions in their Personal Dictionaries. Have them pronounce each word and divide it into syllables.
3. **Multi-level options** See MULTI-LEVEL OPTIONS on p. 14.

Answers

2. *Possible answers:* Twigs are very small branches or pieces of wood from trees. A combination is several things together.

Have students write sentences using the new vocabulary words.

Text Structure

Realistic Adventure Fiction

Define and explain Use question words that will identify the genre's features. ***Say:*** *To learn about the setting, ask, "Where?" To learn about the characters, ask, "Who?"* Continue with the remaining features.

Reading Strategy

Identify Cause and Effect

Teacher Resource Book: *Two-Column Chart, p. 44*

1. **Use a graphic organizer** *Say: I sharpened my pencil. Why? Because the point broke.* Help students identify the cause and effect. Model filling in this example on the chart.
2. **Multi-level options** See MULTI-LEVEL OPTIONS below.

ASSESS

On the board, write the features of realistic adventure fiction. ***Ask:*** *Who is in the story?* (characters) *What happens?* (events) *Where does the story happen?* (setting) *Why is it difficult for the characters?* (problem)

Text Structure

Realistic Adventure Fiction

Fiction is a **genre** (kind) of literature. In fiction, the writer makes up people and events. A novel is a kind of fiction. Novels are long. They are published as entire books.

You are going to read an excerpt (a short part) from a novel. This novel is **realistic adventure fiction.** The features of realistic adventure fiction are listed in the chart.

As you read, look for these features of realistic adventure fiction.

Realistic Adventure Fiction	
Setting	where the story takes place
Characters	people in the story
Events	things that could happen in real life
Problem	difficulty that the characters face

Reading Strategy

Identify Cause and Effect

A **cause** is an action or event that produces an effect or makes something happen. An **effect** is the result that happens. For example:

Cause: You study hard.

Effect: You get better grades.

Understanding the connection between a cause and an effect can help you better understand your reading.

1. As you read "Hatchet," ask yourself: What happens? What causes it to happen?
2. List your answers in a chart like the one on the right.

Cause	*Effect*

MULTI-LEVEL OPTIONS *Reading Strategy*

Newcomer Copy the book's chart. Turn the classroom light off. ***Say:*** *I turned the switch. I caused the lights to go off.* Under *cause* write: *turned the switch off.* Under *effect* write: *lights went out.* Other examples: a flat tire and a nail; exercising and strong muscles.

Beginning Copy the book's chart. Under *cause* write: *light a match/feel hungry/feel thirsty.* Ask students to speculate about what might happen as a result of each cause. Record their answers. Have the class decide which effect is most likely.

Intermediate Copy the book's chart. Under *effect* write: *paper starts burning/you eat wild berries/you drink water from a lake.* Have small groups brainstorm and record possible causes of each effect. Have groups share their lists.

Advanced On the board, write: *What happens when you water a plant? What happens when you don't water a plant?* ***Say:*** *These questions are causes. You have to write three sentences to describe their effects.* Have students share their paragraphs with a partner.

HATCHET

an excerpt from a novel
by Gary Paulsen

17

Reading Selection Materials

Audio: *Unit 1, Chapter 2*
Teacher Resource Book: *Reading Summary, pp. 67–68*

Preview the Selection

1. **Brainstorm** Bring in a picture of a hatchet. Ask students how a hatchet might be used in a forest. List students' ideas. Then have students think of other items they would want to take with them on a camping trip in a forest. Tell them to explain why they would take the items.
2. **Interpret the image** *Ask: Where is this place? What do you see there? What do you need to live there?*
3. **Connect** Remind students that the unit theme is *challenges.* Ask what challenges might be found in the setting. Tell students they will read about the challenges that a boy faces trying to survive in a similar setting.

Cultural Connection

Tell students that many families in the U.S. go on camping trips during their vacations. ***Ask:*** *What kind of vacations does your family take? Where do you stay on vacation? What places do you visit? Do you know what families from other cultures do on vacations?* Compare the similarities and differences. Plan a vacation trip with a small group.

Learning Styles *Visual*

Tell students to close their eyes. They should imagine they are in the place where this picture was taken. Have them describe to a partner what they see, hear, or smell. Have them describe how they feel. Tell them to describe something they need but don't have with them.

UNIT 1 • CHAPTER 2
Reading Selection

Read the Selection

1. **Use text features** Point out the prologue and explain its purpose. Direct students to the numbers, which indicate the paragraphs in the reading selection. Call attention to the glossed words. Remind students to use the illustration to help them understand.
2. **Teacher read aloud** Read the selection aloud. Pause to check understanding and to identify features: setting, character, events, problem.
3. **Identify cause and effect** *Ask: Why do you think Brian wants a fire?* (He needs to keep warm or cook food.)

Sample Answer to Guide Question
He can't start the fire. He can't find anything easy to burn.

See Teacher Edition pp. 434–435 for a list of English-Spanish cognates in the reading selection.

Audio

Prologue

In this story, the main character is a teenager named Brian Robeson. He is on a plane to visit his father in the oil fields in Canada. The only other person on the plane is the pilot. When the pilot has a heart attack, Brian must guide the plane to land. After he lands on a lake, he finds himself alone and scared. The only belongings he has are his clothing and a small ax called a hatchet. Brian must find a way to survive alone in the wilderness.

1 Brian found it was a long way from sparks to fire.

2 Clearly there had to be something for the sparks to ignite, some kind of tinder or kindling—but what? He brought some dried grass in, tapped sparks into it and watched them die. He tried small twigs, breaking them into little pieces, but that was worse than the grass. Then he tried a combination of the two, grass and twigs.

3 Nothing. He had no trouble getting **sparks,** but the tiny bits of hot stone or metal—he couldn't tell which they were—just sputtered and died.

4 He settled back **on his haunches** in **exasperation,** looking at the **pitiful** clump of grass and twigs.

5 He needed something finer, something soft and fine and fluffy to catch the bits of fire.

6 Shredded paper would be nice, but he had no paper.

7 "So close," he said aloud, "so close . . ."

Identify Cause and Effect
Why is Brian exasperated (frustrated)?

sparks small bits of light caused by hard surfaces scraping together
on his haunches sitting in a crouching position close to the ground
exasperation extreme frustration
pitiful sad, worth feeling sorry for

MULTI-LEVEL OPTIONS *Read the Selection*

Newcomer Play the audio. Encourage students to read aloud as they listen. *Ask: Does Brian land the plane?* (yes) *Does he try to start a fire with grass and twigs?* (yes) *Does his 20-dollar bill burn?* (no) *Does the bark look like paper?* (yes)

Beginning Read the prologue. *Ask: Why is Brian in the wilderness?* (The pilot of his plane had a heart attack.) *What does Brian have with him?* (clothing and a hatchet) *What is the first thing he tries to do?* (start a fire) *Does he succeed?* (no)

Intermediate Have students do a reciprocal reading. Have each student take a turn reading a short passage and asking questions about it to the class. *Ask: Why is Brian alone?* (The pilot had a heart attack and died.) *Why is he limping?* (He hurt his leg.) *What does Brian find in his pocket?* (a 20-dollar bill) *Is it useful to him?* (no)

Advanced Have students read silently. Then ***ask:*** *How does Brian make sparks?* (with the hatchet and a rock) *Where does he look for things to burn?* (on the ground, from the birch trees) *How does he feel when his experiments don't work?* (He gets exasperated.)

8 He put the hatchet back in his belt and went out of the shelter, limping on his sore leg. There had to be something, had to be. Man had made fire. There had been fire for thousands, millions of years. There had to be a way. He dug in his pockets and found the twenty-dollar bill in his wallet. Paper. Worthless paper out here. But if he could get a fire going . . .

Identify Cause and Effect

What happens when Brian tries to light his twenty-dollar bill? Why?

9 He ripped the twenty into tiny pieces, made a pile of pieces, and hit sparks into them. Nothing happened. They just wouldn't take the sparks. But there had to be a way—some way to do it.

10 Not twenty feet to his right, leaning out over the water were birches and he stood looking at them for a full half-minute before they **registered** on his mind. They were a beautiful white with bark like clean, slightly speckled paper.

11 Paper.

12 He moved to the trees. Where the bark was peeling from the trunks it lifted in tiny **tendrils,** almost fluffs. Brian plucked some of them loose, rolled them in his fingers. They seemed flammable, dry and nearly powdery. He pulled and twisted bits off the trees, packing them in one hand while he picked them with the other, picking and gathering until he had a **wad** close to the size of a baseball.

---

registered made an impression on, came to the attention of

tendrils thin pieces, like hairs

wad a ball made by pressing something soft together

Read the Selection

1. **Use the illustration** Ask students to describe the trees in the illustration. Introduce the name of the tree. (birch) Point out features of the tree. (leaves, trunk, branches, bark)
2. **Understand terms** Have students find the meanings of the glossed words below the selection. Clarify meanings as needed.
3. **Paired reading** Play the audio or read the selection aloud. Have students reread it in pairs.
4. **Identify cause and effect** *Ask: Why did Brian rip up the 20-dollar bill?* (to try to burn it) *Why is Brian peeling the bark from the tree?* (It may burn easily.)
5. **Multi-level options** See MULTI-LEVEL OPTIONS on p. 18.

Sample Answer to Guide Question

The paper money doesn't burn. It may be wet or the pieces may be too big.

th Spelling

R-controlled vowels

Write *bark* on the board. Pronounce the word slowly while you point to each sound. *Ask: Which two letters make only one sound?* (*ar*) Repeat this process with *person* (*er*) and *bird* (*ir*). Explain that when vowels are followed by the letter *-r*, they sound different. Have student pairs practice pronouncing the following words from "Hatchet": *spark, dollar, paper, shelter, thirteen, birch.*

Apply Have pairs find and pronounce *r*-controlled vowels in paragraph 12 (powdery), paragraph 17 (thirty), and paragraph 24 (starving).

UNIT 1 • CHAPTER 2

Reading Selection

Read the Selection

1. **Analyze character** *Ask: Is Brian brave?* (yes) *Why do you think so?* (He doesn't seem scared. He tries to do something.) *Is he patient?* (yes) *Why?* (He keeps trying different ideas.)
2. **Paired reading** Read paragraphs 13–16 aloud to students. ***Ask:*** *Why does Brian rip the bark?* (to make it smaller and finer) *How long did he work on it?* (two hours) Have students reread the selection in pairs.
3. **Identify cause and effect** *Ask: Why didn't the spark start a fire?* (The bark was not dry or small enough.) *Why does Brian work so long to build a fire?* (Because it's important for him to keep warm.)

Sample Answer to Guide Question
The sparks might start a fire. It will be easier for the sparks to stay together and heat up the bark.

13 Then he went back into the shelter and arranged the ball of birchbark peelings at the base of the black rock. As an afterthought he threw in the remains of the twenty-dollar bill. He struck and a stream of sparks fell into the bark and quickly died. But this time one spark fell on one small hair of dry bark—almost a thread of bark—and seemed to glow a bit brighter before it died.

14 The material had to be finer. There had to be a soft and incredibly fine nest for the sparks.

15 I must make a home for the sparks, he thought. A perfect home or they won't stay, they won't make fire.

16 He started ripping the bark, using his fingernails at first, and when that didn't work he used the sharp edge of the hatchet, cutting the bark in thin slivers, hairs so fine they were almost not there. It was **painstaking** work, slow work, and he stayed with it for over two hours. Twice he stopped for a handful of berries and once to go to the lake for a drink. Then back to work, the sun on his back, until at last he had a ball of fluff as big as a grapefruit—dry birchbark fluff.

Identify Cause and Effect

What do you think will happen if Brian makes a home for the sparks? Why?

painstaking needing great care and effort

MULTI-LEVEL OPTIONS *Read the Selection*

Newcomer *Ask: Does Brian use the birch bark?* (yes) *Does he make a nest out of pieces of the bark?* (yes) *Does the nest of bark catch fire?* (no) *Does Brian eat candy?* (no) *Does Brian hit the rock with a hatchet?* (yes)

Beginning *Ask: Does Brian use bigger pieces or smaller pieces of bark?* (smaller) *Is it easy work or hard work?* (hard) *Do the sparks start a fire or do they go out?* (go out) *How does Brian hit the rocks?* (fast, with a hatchet)

Intermediate *Ask: How does Brian cut the bark into slivers?* (with the hatchet) *Why does he stop working?* (to get berries and a drink of water) *What happens to the sparks when he hits the rock fast?* (They seem to take, but then they die.)

Advanced *Ask: How does Brian feel as he tries one thing after another?* (exasperated, frustrated) *What does he think is the difference between Cro-Magnon man and himself?* (A Cro-Magnon would have a fire by now.) *Will he give up? Why or why not?* (No. He knows how important a fire is to him.)

Identify Cause and Effect

Why does Brian hit his hatchet against the rock?

17 He **positioned** his spark nest—as he thought of it—at the base of the rock, used his thumb to make a small **depression** in the middle, and slammed the back of the hatchet down across the black rock. A cloud of sparks rained down, most of them missing the nest, but some, perhaps thirty or so, hit in the depression and of those six or seven found fuel and grew, smoldered and caused the bark to take on the red glow.

18 Then they went out.

19 Close—he was close. He repositioned the nest, made a new and smaller dent with his thumb, and struck again.

20 More sparks, a slight glow, then nothing.

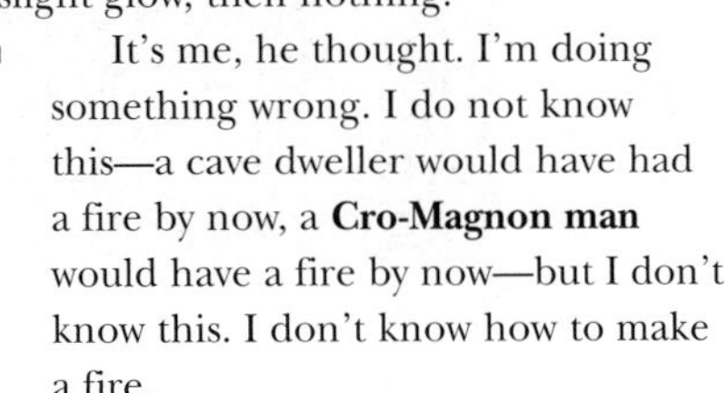

21 It's me, he thought. I'm doing something wrong. I do not know this—a cave dweller would have had a fire by now, a **Cro-Magnon man** would have a fire by now—but I don't know this. I don't know how to make a fire.

22 Maybe not enough sparks. He settled the nest in place once more and hit the rock with a series of blows, as fast as he could. The sparks poured like a golden waterfall. At first they seemed to take, there were several, many sparks that found life and took briefly, but they all died.

23 Starved.

24 He leaned back. They are like me. They are starving. It wasn't quantity, there were plenty of sparks, but they needed more.

positioned put into the right place
depression an area that is lower than what is nearby
Cro-Magnon man a prehistoric human

Punctuation

Periods at the end of sentences

Direct students to the last word on the page, *died*. ***Ask:** What do you see after* died? (a period) ***Say:** Look at line 18. What do you see at the end of that sentence?* (a period) *What does a period do in a sentence?* (It ends it.) *What does a period tell the reader to do?* (Stop.)

Apply Reproduce paragraph 21 on p. 21 without periods. Direct students to take turns reading the paragraph aloud. Then discuss and analyze the problems of reading a paragraph without periods. Have pairs put periods into the paragraph. Do another partner read aloud. Compare the two readings.

Read the Selection

1. **Use the illustration** Ask students to identify the items in the illustration: bark, twigs, smoke, sparks.
2. **Understand terms** Point out the glossed words below the selection. Clarify meanings as needed.
3. **Shared reading** Play the audio as students follow along silently with the reading. Model how to join in at the end of sentences. Play the audio again. Tell students to join in by reading aloud when they can.
4. **Multi-level options** See MULTI-LEVEL OPTIONS on p. 20.

Sample Answer to Guide Question
He hits the hatchet to make the sparks.

Read the Selection

1. **Shared reading** Read the story aloud as students follow along silently. Ask volunteers to join in by reading sections aloud. Refer to the illustration to clarify actions as needed.
2. **Dramatize** Have students work in pairs to examine the actions and emotions described in paragraphs 24, 27, 29, and 30. Have one partner read the sentence as the other acts it out.

Sample Answer to Guide Question
He blows to give the fire more air, or oxygen.

25 I would kill, he thought suddenly, for a book of matches. Just one book. Just one match. I would kill.

26 What makes fire? He thought back to school. To all those science classes. Had he ever learned what made a fire? Did a teacher ever stand up there and say, "This is what makes a fire . . ."

27 He shook his head, tried to focus his thoughts. What did it take? You have to have fuel, he thought—and he had that. The bark was fuel. Oxygen—there had to be air.

28 He needed to add air. He had to fan on it, blow on it.

29 He made the nest ready again, held the hatchet backward, **tensed,** and struck four quick blows. Sparks came down and he leaned forward as fast as he could and blew.

30 Too hard. There was a bright, almost intense glow, then it was gone. He had blown it out.

Identify Cause and Effect

Why does Brian blow on his nest of shredded bark?

---

tensed held the muscles tightly just before using them

MULTI-LEVEL OPTIONS *Read the Selection*

Newcomer ***Ask:*** *Does Brian have any matches?* (no) *Do you need air for a fire?* (yes) *Does Brian make more sparks?* (yes) *Does the glowing bark look like red butterflies?* (no) *Does the bark finally catch fire?* (yes)

Beginning ***Ask:*** *What does Brian wish for?* (matches) *What extra thing does he need to make fire?* (air) *Is it better to blow hard or gently?* (gently) *What does the glowing bark look like?* (red worms) *What happens at the end?* (The bark catches fire.)

Intermediate ***Ask:*** *Why does Brian want matches so much?* (He could make a fire fast and easily.) *What does Brian try to remember?* (what makes a fire) *What mistake does he make when the bark begins to glow?* (He blows too hard.) *What does he do differently next time?* (He blows gently.)

Advanced ***Ask:*** *How are Brian and the sparks alike?* (Both are starved.) *What does Brian forget when he tries to make a fire?* (A fire needs air.) *What does Brian realize after he blows out the sparks?* (He needs to blow gently.) *How do you think he will use the fire?* (to keep warm, to cook, to signal rescuers)

31 Another set of strikes, more sparks. He leaned and blew, but gently this time, holding back and aiming the stream of air from his mouth to hit the brightest spot. Five or six sparks had fallen in a tight mass of bark hair and Brian centered his efforts there.

32 The sparks grew with his gentle breath. The red glow moved from the sparks themselves into the bark, moved and grew and became worms, glowing red worms that crawled up the bark hairs and caught other threads of bark and grew until there was a pocket of red as big as a quarter, a glowing red coal of heat.

33 And when he ran out of breath and paused to **inhale,** the red ball suddenly burst into flame.

34 "Fire!" He yelled. "I've got fire! I've got it, I've got it, I've got it . . ."

---

inhale breathe in to take in air

About the Author — Gary Paulsen (born 1939)

Gary Paulsen has written many novels for young readers. Several involve young characters facing challenges. Paulsen also faced some difficult problems as a child. His father was in the army, and Paulsen had to change schools often. Paulsen was a shy boy and changing schools was very hard for him. One day, a librarian gave him a library card and books, and he found a new world. Paulsen said, "I write because it's all I can do . . . [Because I want my] years on this ball of earth to mean something. Writing furnishes a way for that to happen."

➤ If you could ask Gary Paulsen a question about this story, what would it be?

UNIT 1 • CHAPTER 2
Reading Selection

Read the Selection

1. **Paired reading** After you read aloud the selection, have pairs of students read it again.
2. **Identify cause and effect** Write on the board: *The sparks started a fire. Brian blew on the sparks.* Ask students to decide which sentence states the cause and which states the effect. Ask students to justify their answers.
3. **Multi-level options** See MULTI-LEVEL OPTIONS on p. 22.

About the Author

1. **Explain author challenges** Gary Paulsen has led a life filled with adventure and challenges. He had many different jobs until he settled in northern Minnesota. He began racing dogs and competed twice in the Alaskan Iditarod. He uses his past experiences in his stories.
2. **Interpret the facts** *Ask: What problems and challenges do you think he had living in the woods?* (keeping warm, living in very cold weather, being alone)

Across Selections

Make comparisons Use a two-column chart to compare Brian's challenge to the Camel's on pp. 8–9. ***Ask:*** *How are the characters similar and different?* (They both work hard. The Camel worked for her own pleasure. Brian worked to stay alive. The Camel had an audience. Brian was alone.)

Punctuation

Quotation marks for direct quotes

Write on the board: *"I've got fire!"* Circle the quotation marks. Explain that quotation marks show the words a character says aloud. Direct students to read paragraph 34 silently as you ***say,*** *"Fire! I've got fire! I've got it! I've got it! I've got it . . ."* ***Ask:*** *Why did I leave out* He yelled? (It's not in quotation marks.) Have student pairs find quotations in paragraphs 7 and 26.

Evaluate Your Reading Strategy

Identify Cause and Effect *Say: You have practiced an important reading strategy. Now you can decide how well you have done. Does this statement describe how you read?*

> To identify causes and effects, I ask, "Why did this event happen?" This helps me understand what I am reading.

Reading Comprehension

Question-Answer Relationships

Sample Answers

1. He's a 13-year old boy.
2. He's in the wilderness by himself and needs to survive. He was in a small plane when the pilot died, and Brian had to land the plane.
3. He tries to burn twigs and grass.
4. A teenager is alone in the wilderness. He tries to start a fire by using his hatchet, a stone, twigs, and grass, but it doesn't work. He thinks about what he knows about fires. He uses his knowledge to try other ways. In the end, he is able to start a fire.
5. It's easier to start a fire with very small pieces of bark.
6. Brian thinks about why things don't work. Then he tries again. He's patient and works hard to solve the problem.
7. Brian is happy at the end because he was finally able to start the fire.
8. Brian will try to make the fire bigger so that others will see it and save him. He may also look for some food to cook.
9. Many students may ask what strategies the author uses or what is the most important strategy. The author might say using details or showing how characters feel.

Build Reading Fluency

Reading Chunks

Explain that reading chunks of underlined words helps improve reading fluency. Ask students to listen as you model reading chunks before they practice silently with a partner.

Beyond the Reading

Reading Comprehension

Question-Answer Relationships (QAR)

"Right There" Questions

1. **Recall Facts** Who is Brian?
2. **Recall Facts** What problem does Brian have? Why does Brian have this problem?
3. **Recall Facts** What is the first thing Brian tries to burn?

"Think and Search" Questions

4. **Paraphrase Text** Tell someone what the story is about in your own words. What details do you recall when you paraphrase the story?
5. **Identify Cause and Effect** Why does Brian chop the peeled bark into smaller pieces?

"Author and You" Question

6. **Analyze Characters** What do you learn about Brian from his efforts to start the fire?

"On Your Own" Questions

7. **Analyze Characters** How does Brian feel at the end of the story? Why do you think he feels this way?
8. **Predict** What do you think Brian will do now that he has a fire going?
9. **Identify Author's Strategy** What would you ask the author about strategies he uses to make the story seem real? How do you think he would answer?

Activity Book p. 10

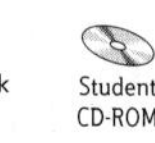
Student CD-ROM

Build Reading Fluency

Reading Chunks

Reading chunks, or groups, of words is better than reading word by word. With a partner, practice reading the underlined chunks of words aloud two times.

Clearly there had to be something for the sparks to ignite, some kind of tinder or kindling—but what? He brought some dried grass in, tapped sparks into it and watched them die. He tried small twigs, breaking them into little pieces, but that was worse than the grass. Then he tried a combination of the two, grass and twigs. Nothing. He had no trouble getting sparks, but the tiny bits of hot stone or metal—he couldn't tell which they were—just sputtered and died.

MULTI-LEVEL OPTIONS *Elements of Literature*

Newcomer Divide students into small groups. Assign each group a simile based on the reading. Have the groups draw or act out their similes for another group. Ask the audience to identify the simile.

Beginning Have students illustrate one simile from the reading. For example, *The ball of fluff was as big as a grapefruit.* Then students trade drawings with a partner. Each partner finds the simile in the reading and writes it as a caption under the drawing.

Intermediate Prepare slips of paper with similes based on the reading. Examples include: *The bark was like clean, slightly speckled paper. The ball of fluff was as big as a grapefruit.* Cut the strips in half to divide the figurative language. Give out the slips randomly. Direct students to find a person to complete the simile.

Advanced Give students the first half of each simile based on the reading. Examples include: *The bark was like _____. The ball of fluff was as _____. The sparks poured like _____.* Have students work in pairs to create new similes. Share them with the class.

Listen, Speak, Interact 

Act Out Events in a Story

Brian is lost in the woods with only a hatchet for a tool. He faces difficult challenges, but does not give up. He keeps trying.

1. With a partner, reread the story. List the challenges that Brian faces.
2. Find and discuss the different things Brian does to meet these challenges.
3. Find clues that show how Brian feels about his situation. When does he show frustration or excitement?
4. Choose one of the challenges in the story to act out for the class.
5. When you present the event, speak slowly and clearly. Show how Brian feels through his words and his actions.

Elements of Literature

Use Figurative Language

To make their stories more interesting, writers often describe one thing by comparing it to another thing. This is called **figurative language. Similes** are one kind of figurative language. Similes use the words *like* or *as* to show comparison: *Brian ran like the wind.*

1. Read paragraphs 10, 16, 22, and 32 aloud with a small group. Find the simile in each paragraph.
2. Make a section called "Similes" in your Reading Log. Copy the sentences from the selection with similes.
3. Record other similes that you find as you read other pieces of literature.

   The chair is like a throne.

   She is as tall as the sky.

Reading Log

Activity Book *p. 11*

Student CD-ROM

Community Connection

Invite a speaker from a local camping or outdoors organization. Ask the speaker to explain how to prepare for a safe outdoor adventure. Have students write questions before the visit. Categorize and consolidate the questions in small groups. Remind students about asking questions with appropriate rate, volume, and eye contact.

Learning Styles *Mathematical*

Show students how to make a 4-column chart. Label the columns *Steps, Failed, Worked Partly, Worked.* ***Say:*** *It took Brian many steps to start a fire. In column 1, list the steps he took. Then check the column that best describes the result.* Write this example: *Brian tried to light dry grass.* ***Ask:*** *What happened to that experiment?* (It failed.) Demonstrate which column to check. Have students work in pairs to complete their own charts.

UNIT 1 • CHAPTER 2

Beyond the Reading

Listen, Speak, Interact

Act Out Events in a Story

1. **Reread in pairs** Pair beginning and advanced students. Have them read alternate paragraphs.
2. **Newcomers** Reread with this group. Help them identify challenges that Brian faced. Write these on the board. Add key words to identify how he felt. Have students record the key words in their Reading Logs.

Answers

1. making a fire without matches; finding materials for the fire; figuring out what will burn
2. looks for a substitute for matches (hatchet, stone, twigs, grass, etc.); uses material he has and finds in the wilderness (20-dollar bill, bark, etc.); tries different materials and methods until he gets closer and closer to starting a fire
3. settled back on his haunches in frustration; yelled, "Fire! I've got fire!" frustration: when grass and twigs didn't burn; excitement: when the fire started

Elements of Literature

Use Figurative Language

Teacher Resource Book: *Reading Log, p. 64*

1. **Model creating a simile** Review examples of similes in the text. ***Say:*** *Brian is brave. What animal is brave?* (a lion; Brian is as brave as a lion.)
2. **Personal experience** Share examples of common similes, such as: as fast as lightning; as quiet as a mouse.
3. **Multi-level options** See MULTI-LEVEL OPTIONS on p. 24.

Answers

1. . . . bark like clean, slightly speckled paper; . . . a ball of fluff as big as a grapefruit; . . . sparks poured like a golden waterfall; . . . pocket of red as big as a quarter

ASSESS

Have students complete these two similes: *The lake was as cold as _____. The smoke was like a _____.*

Word Study

Understand Compound Words

Teacher Resource Book: *Personal Dictionary, p. 63*

Make a vocabulary game Write on the board: *classroom, lunchbox, homework.* Identify the individual words that make up each compound word. Create a matching game with separated parts of compound words. Have students match and pronounce the words.

Answers
1. **a.** afterthought **b.** fingernails **c.** waterfall
2. **a.** after, thought **b.** finger, nails **c.** water, fall

Grammar Focus

Use the Past Tense of the Verb *Be*

Apply Ask students to write a sentence with *am, is,* or *are.* Have them exchange sentences and rewrite them in the past tense.

Answers
1. . . . it was a long way; . . . that was worse . . .; over the water were birches . . . They were a beautiful white . . .

ASSESS

On the board, write: *Brian _____ in the forest. The trees _____ dark and tall.* Have students complete the sentences using *was* or *were.*

Word Study

Understand Compound Words

Some words are made up of two other words. These are called **compound words.** You can usually guess the meaning of a compound word if you look at each part separately. Look at this example from "Hatchet."

> Then he went back into the shelter and arranged the ball of birchbark peelings at the base of the black rock.

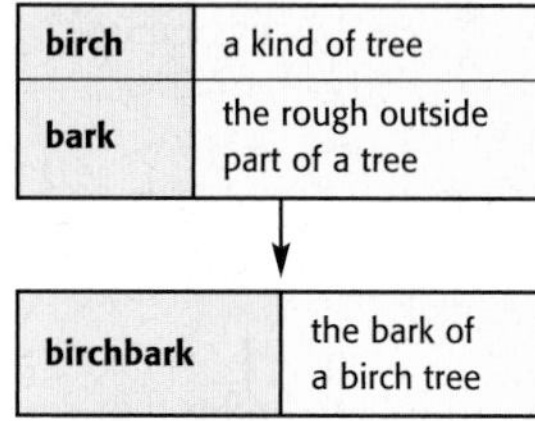

1. Copy the following sentences on a piece of paper. Find the compound words and underline them.
   a. As an afterthought, he threw in the remains of the paper.
   b. He started ripping the bark, using his fingernails at first . . .
   c. The sparks poured like a golden waterfall.
2. Divide each compound word into two words.
3. Write these compound words and their meanings in your Personal Dictionary. If you need help with the meanings, look them up in a dictionary or ask your teacher.

Personal Dictionary

The Heinle Newbury House Dictionary

Activity Book *p. 12*

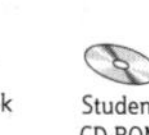
Student CD-ROM

Grammar Focus

Use the Past Tense of the Verb *Be*

The verb **be** is an irregular verb. The past tense of **be** has two forms, **was** and **were.**

1. Find examples of the past tense of *be* in paragraphs 1, 2, and 10.
2. Write a sentence using each subject in the chart. Include a past tense of *be* in each sentence.

Subjects	Past Tense of *Be*
I He/She/It/Brian	**was** in the forest.
You We They/The students	**were** in the forest.

Activity Book *pp. 13–14*

Student Handbook

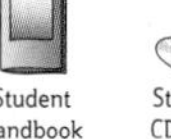
Student CD-ROM

MULTI-LEVEL OPTIONS *From Reading to Writing*

Newcomer Pair a beginning and an advanced student to create a story together. Have them brainstorm and list characters, setting, events, and problems. Have advanced students write the stories as beginning students illustrate them.

Beginning Write a group story. Have small groups work cooperatively to tell their story with storyboards. Assist them in writing captions for their stories. Have students read their stories chorally to another group.

Intermediate Have pairs of students develop and write a story together. Remind them to focus attention on step 3 so they use similes in their stories. Have students share their stories in small groups.

Advanced Pair an advanced student and a beginner to create a story together. See the Newcomer section for more information.

From Reading to Writing 

Write a Realistic Adventure Story

You have analyzed "Hatchet" and looked at its text structure. Use the selection as a model for writing your own adventure story.

1. Organize your story using the chart. Decide where the story takes place. Who are the characters? What is the problem?
2. Use the past tense of *be* correctly.
3. Include similes to help readers picture the people, places, and things you are describing.
4. Be sure your story has a beginning, a middle, and an end.
5. Indent each paragraph.

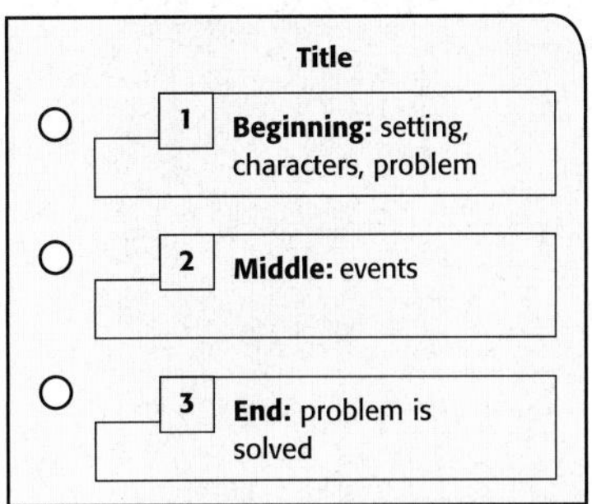

6. Be sure to capitalize the title of your story, the names of the characters, and other proper nouns.

Activity Book p. 15

Across Content Areas 

Learn About Combustion

When scientists talk about fire, they use the word **combustion.** Combustion requires three things:

fuel	something that will burn, such as paper or wood
oxygen	a colorless, odorless gas in the air (you must breathe oxygen in order to live)
heat	to start, or **ignite,** the combustion

Which of these does Brian use in each of the following situations?

1. Brian blew on the fire.
2. He gathered birchbark.
3. He made sparks with his hatchet and a rock.

a. fuel **b.** oxygen **c.** heat

Remember: Always observe fire safety rules. Always have something that can **extinguish** (put out) the fire. In the science lab, always follow instructions.

Activity Book p. 16

Reteach and Reassess

Text Structure Give student pairs one blank of the realistic adventure fiction chart on p. 16. Ask them to complete the chart with details from "Hatchet." Then have students compare their charts with another pair.

Reading Strategy Copy the cause-and-effect chart from p. 16. Have pairs of students chart four examples from the reading.

Elements of Literature Have students write similes to complete these sentences: *Brian is as _____. Starting a fire without matches is like _____.*

Reassess Have students write an "I Am" poem. Have them reflect on Brian and his challenge. Have them write a poem from Brian's point of view.

From Reading to Writing

Write a Realistic Adventure Story

1. **Draw pictures** Have students brainstorm a list of problems for an adventure story. Have students choose one and draw pictures to show how they would solve the problem.
2. **Think-Pair-Share** In pairs, have students explain their pictures or events in the story. Then, have students write their story. Remind them to identify the setting and character(s) in it.
3. **Multi-level options** See MULTI-LEVEL OPTIONS on p. 26.

Across Content Areas: Science

Learn About Combustion

Connect Explain the meanings of *combustion, fuel, oxygen, heat,* and *ignite, extinguish.* ***Ask:*** *What fuel did Brian use in his fire?* (birch bark) Have students identify other fuels. Ask them to explain what is used to ignite fires and to extinguish fires.

Answers
1. oxygen 2. fuel 3. heat

ASSESS

Have students write three sentences about how they can start a fire—one mentioning the fuel, another about air or oxygen, and a third about the source of heat.

Assessment Program: *Unit 1, Chapter 2, Quiz, pp. 9–10*

UNIT 1 • CHAPTER 3

Into the Reading

Chapter Materials

Activity Book: *pp. 17–24*
Audio: *Unit 1, Chapter 3*
Student Handbook
Student CD-ROM: *Unit 1, Chapter 3*
Teacher Resource Book: *Lesson Plan, Teacher Resources, Reading Summary, Activity Book Answer Key*
Teacher Resource CD-ROM
Assessment Program: *Quiz, pp. 11–12; Teacher and Student Resources, pp. 115–144*
Assessment CD-ROM
Transparencies
The Heinle Newbury House Dictionary/CD-ROM
Web Site: www.heinle.visions.com

Objectives

Pair reading Have students work in pairs and take turns reading the objectives section. Explain the objectives. Point out key words.

Use Prior Knowledge

Discuss Directions

1. **Use a map** Show a map of your state, the U.S., or the world. Ask students to identify the directions: north, south, east, west.
2. **Relate to personal experience** Have students locate places they have visited or lived in. Ask if the places are north, south, east, or west of where they live now.

Answers
1. **a.** Oklahoma **b.** New Mexico **c.** Mexico **d.** east

CHAPTER 3

Antarctic Adventure

an excerpt from
a historical narrative
by Meredith Hooper

Objectives

Reading Predict events as you read a historical narrative.

Listening and Speaking Retell order of events.

Grammar Use *and* to join words and sentences.

Writing Write a historical narrative.

Content Social Studies: Learn about bodies of land and water.

Use Prior Knowledge

Discuss Directions

What do you know about directions?

1. Look at the map and answer these questions.
   a. Which state is to the north of Texas?
   b. Which state is to the west?
   c. What country is to the south?
   d. Which direction is Louisiana from Texas?
2. Choose a city, state, or country where you have lived. Draw a map and label the directions. Tell your partner what is to the north, south, east, and west of it.

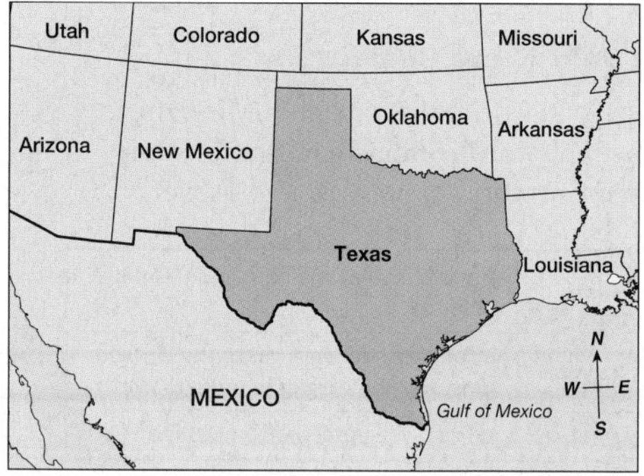

MULTI-LEVEL OPTIONS *Build Vocabulary*

Newcomer Point out that a ship is a large boat. Preteach key words from the sentences. Examples: front, back, standing, specific, direction, wind, blows, move.

Beginning Teach students how to pronounce the new words. Have small groups work together to discuss and complete the sentences.

Intermediate Have students work in pairs to complete the sentences. Tell them to write one original sentence using two new words. Have them share their sentences with another pair.

Advanced Have students complete the sentences independently. Tell them to write a short paragraph using the new vocabulary words. Have them share their paragraphs with a partner.

Build Background

Antarctica

Antarctica is a continent located at the South Pole, the most southern point on Earth. The temperature in Antarctica is rarely above 32°F (0°C). Antarctica is almost completely covered by ice. Today, scientists live in and study Antarctica from underground buildings. No other people live in this very cold place.

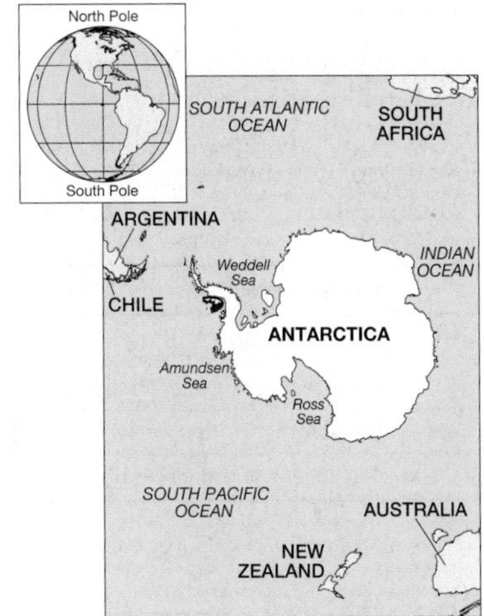

Content Connection

Explorers began trying to reach the South Pole in the early 1900s.

Build Vocabulary

Identify Words About Ships

You are going to read a story about a ship that sinks. To understand the action, learn some words about ships.

Write these sentences in your Personal Dictionary. Complete the sentences with words from the picture.

1. The front of a ship is the ____.
2. The back of the ship is the ____.
3. The man is standing on the ____.
4. The ____ makes the ship move in a specific direction.
5. The wind blows into the ____ and makes the ship move.

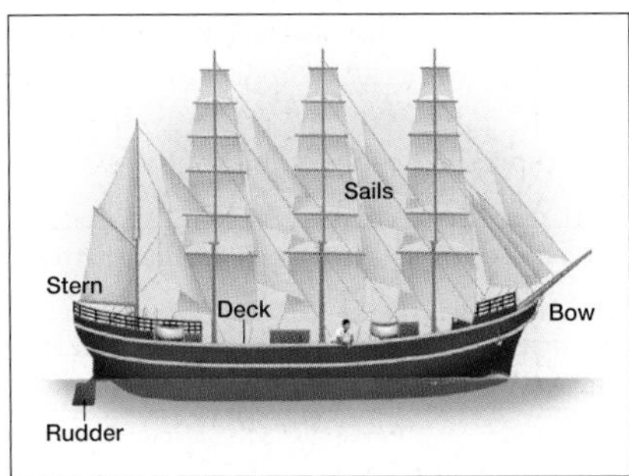

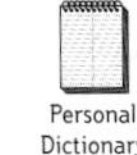
Personal Dictionary

Activity Book p. 17

Student CD-ROM

Content Connection
Social Studies

Build Background Display an atlas. Explain that an atlas contains many different maps. Tell students they can find information about cities, states, countries, bodies of water, and continents. Show them how to look up information. Have students compare the map of Antarctica on p. 29 with the map in the atlas. Ask them to find the other six continents in the atlas. (Africa, Asia, Australia, Europe, North America, and South America)

Learning Styles
Kinesthetic

Build Vocabulary Have students dramatize a day of the life of a sailor on board a ship to Antarctica. Ask them to act out the work they do and how they might entertain themselves.

Build Background

Antarctica

1. **Use a map** Have students locate Antarctica on a map or globe. Ask them to share any information they know about this continent. *Ask: Do you think it is easy or difficult to stay in Antarctica? Why?*
2. **Content Connection** *Ask: How do you think early explorers traveled to Antarctica?* (by boat) *How did they travel within Antarctica?* (by foot, sleds, skis) *What do you think they took with them?* (food, warm clothes)

Build Vocabulary

Identify Words About Ships

Teacher Resource Book: *Personal Dictionary, p. 63*

1. **Use experiences** Ask students to share any experiences they have had with boats. Write key words on the board. Direct students to the illustration. Have them compare similarities and differences to boats they know.
2. **Use graphic features to locate information** Ask students to locate the vocabulary labels in the illustration to explain the parts of the ship. Have students look in the dictionary as needed.
3. **Reading selection vocabulary** You may want to introduce the glossed words in the reading selection before students begin reading. Key words: *fatal, sickening, abandon, uninhabited, exhausted.* Instruct students to write the words with correct spelling and their definitions in their Personal Dictionaries. Have them pronounce each word and divide it into syllables.
4. **Multi-level option** See MULTI-LEVEL OPTIONS on p. 28.

Answers
1. The front of the ship is the bow.
2. The back of the ship is the stern.
3. The man is standing on the deck.
4. The rudder makes the ship move in a specific direction.
5. The wind blows into the sails and makes the ship move.

ASSESS

Have students draw a ship and label the bow, stern, deck, rudder, and sails.

Into the Reading

Text Structure

Historical Narrative

Clarify features Have students suggest examples for each of the features mentioned in the graphic organizer for the first day of this school year or someone's last birthday.

Reading Strategy

Predict

1. **Share experiences** *Say: I see dark clouds in the sky. The wind is starting to blow. I* predict *it is going to rain.* Write on the board: *predict.* Explain its meaning. Have students make their own predictions based on situations you describe. For example: *It's 2:30. The bell rings. What are students going to do?* (leave school, get on the bus, go home)
2. **Multi-level options** See MULTI-LEVEL OPTIONS below.

Answers

1. *Example:* I think the ship will break apart.
2. *Example:* Yes.

ASSESS

Ask: What are four features of a historical narrative? (dates, characters, setting, events)

Text Structure

Historical Narrative

"Antarctic Adventure" is a **historical narrative.** It tells a story about the experiences of real people from history. As you read, look for these features of a historical narrative:

Historical Narrative	
Events	what happened
Dates	when events happened in history
Characters	real people
Setting	descriptions of real places

As you read "Antarctic Adventure," identify the real people in the narrative. Think about what their experiences were like.

Student CD-ROM

Reading Strategy

Predict

As you read "Antarctic Adventure," try to **predict,** or guess, what you think will happen next in the narrative. When you predict as you read, you are a more active reader.

To predict what will happen:

Use clues.	Clues are hints from what you read.
Change predictions.	New clues may change what you think.

1. Read paragraphs 3 and 4 on page 32. What do you think will happen next? Why?
2. Now read paragraph 5. Was your prediction correct?
3. Did you use clues from the story (the cracking sound) and your prior knowledge (boats with holes can sink) to make your prediction?
4. Continue predicting as you read the selection.

Student CD-ROM

MULTI-LEVEL OPTIONS *Reading Strategy*

Newcomer Draw or show students a pair of boots and an umbrella. *Ask: What can you predict about the weather?* (rain) Have students draw items for another weather prediction. Share them with a partner. Then direct students to look at the picture. *Ask: Can you predict what the water feels like?* (cold, icy)

Beginning Draw or show students a pair of mittens, a scarf, and a cap. *Say: Look at these clothes. What kind of weather can you predict?* Then direct students to look at the picture. *Ask: Can you predict what people wear in this story?* (parkas, gloves, hats) *Is the antarctic adventure going to be fun?* (No, it will be hard.)

Intermediate Tell students to think about the ship on p. 29. *Say: You know this reading is a historical narrative. Make a prediction about when the "Antarctic Adventure" takes place.* (long ago, in the last century)

Advanced Have students write predictions about the clothes, food, and supplies the men in "Antarctic Adventure" take with them. As they read, have them check if their predictions were correct.

Antarctic Adventure

an excerpt from a historical narrative
by Meredith Hooper

31

Reading Selection Materials

Audio: *Unit 1, Chapter 3*
Teacher Resource Book: *Reading Summary, pp. 69–70*

Preview the Selection

1. **Use a graphic organizer** Have students examine the photo and create a KWL chart. Use guiding questions: *Where is this? What is the weather like? How can people travel here? What animals live here? Is it safe or dangerous on the ice?*
2. **Connect** Ask students if they have ever been to a very cold place. Have them share their experiences. Tell students they will read about the challenges that a group of men faced in this cold environment.

Content Connection *Technology*

Have students search the Internet for information about Antarctic scientific and weather research stations. (key words: Antarctica, weather stations, scientific studies, environment) Ask pairs of students to record three facts they learn. Have them share their facts with another pair.

Learning Styles *Linguistic*

The Inuit language is supposed to have many more words for snow than English does. Have one group of students search the Internet to find as many Inuit words related to snow as possible (key words: words for snow, Inuit language). Have another group of students use a dictionary or thesaurus to find snow-related words in English. Compare the lists.

UNIT 1 • CHAPTER 3
Reading Selection

Read the Selection

1. **Use section headings** Direct students to the prologue. Remind them of its purpose and use. Have students guess the meaning of the section heading, *The* Endurance *Sinks*. Call attention to the illustration below and have students make guesses. Then direct students to glossed words and have them find their meanings at the bottom of the page.
2. **Shared reading** Play the audio or read the selection to students. Have volunteers join in by reading different paragraphs aloud.
3. **Make predictions** *Ask: Are the men going to be able to fix the ship?* (no)

Sample Answer to Guide Question
It's going to break into pieces and sink.

See Teacher Edition pp. 434–435 for a list of English-Spanish cognates in the reading selection.

Prologue

Ernest Shackleton was an explorer who wanted to cross Antarctica on foot. He formed a crew and was the leader of a brave expedition that set sail for this continent in 1914. The name of his ship was *Endurance.* After six weeks of pushing through ice, the ship became locked in ice.

The *Endurance* Sinks

1 The beginning of the end came on Sunday, October 24, 1915, just after dinner. The *Endurance* lost the fight.

2 For 278 days the wooden ship had been stuck fast in the dangerous **pack ice** of the Weddell Sea.

Audio

3 Now three huge ice **floes** were pressing **relentlessly** around the ship. The *Endurance* groaned and quivered. Suddenly, there was a terrible crash! Twisted and **fatally** bent, the *Endurance* began to let in water.

4 The men pumped water out until they were exhausted. But still the ice floes pressed in, twisting and grinding with a dreadful roaring noise. The ship's **timbers** cracked and splintered under the pressure.

Predict
What do you think will happen to the *Endurance?*

The *Endurance.*

pack ice a large area of sea ice with a mixture of floating ice pieces packed together
floes sheets of floating ice
relentlessly without stopping
fatally in a way that causes death
timbers large pieces of wood

MULTI-LEVEL OPTIONS *Read the Selection*

Newcomer Play the audio. Then have students do a paired reading. ***Ask:*** *Is Ernest Shackleton an explorer?* (yes) *Does he want to explore Africa?* (no) *Does his ship get stuck in the ice?* (yes) *Is his ship crushed by the ice?* (yes) *Do Shackleton and his crew stay on the ship?* (no)

Beginning Read the Reading Summary aloud. Then have students write questions about what they heard. ***Ask:*** *What is the name of Ernest Shackleton's ship?* (the *Endurance*) *What crushes his ship?* (the ice) *Where does the crew go after the ship is crushed?* (onto the ice)

Intermediate Have students do a paired reading. ***Ask:*** *Why does Ernest Shackleton go to Antarctica?* (to explore it) *Why does his ship the* Endurance *stop moving?* (It is stuck in the ice.) *Why is the ice able to crush the ship?* (It is made of wood.) *How else can you say "Abandon ship"?* (Leave now! Save yourselves!)

Advanced Assign students into small groups for a jigsaw reading. Divide the reading selection into different sections. Have one or two students in each group read each section. Then have students teach their sections of the reading to the rest of the group. ***Ask:*** *What happens when the ice crushes the ship?* (Wood snaps. Seawater pours in. Engines move out of place.)

Photographer Frank Hurley and Ernest Shackleton.

5 The end came on Wednesday. The *Endurance* was being crushed. It was **sickening** to feel the decks breaking up and the ship's great wooden beams bending, then snapping with a noise like gunfire.

6 The ship's stern lifted 20 feet into the air, the rudder tore off, and water rushed forward and froze, weighing down the bow. The icy black sea poured in.

Predict

Will Shackleton tell his men to leave the ship?

7 Ernest Shackleton looked down into the engine room and saw the engines dropping sideways. He gave the order: **abandon** ship!

8 The men tumbled out onto the ice, shocked and exhausted. They were standing on a shaking ice floe, just 2 feet thick, floating on the surface of the deep, dark ocean.

9 That night they camped on the ice. All around them the ice floes groaned and crashed. Three times the ice started splitting and smashing underneath them, and they had to move their tents.

sickening making you feel sick

abandon leave without planning to return

UNIT 1 • CHAPTER 3
Reading Selection

Read the Selection

1. **Understand terms** Direct students to the glossed words below the selection. Clarify meanings as needed.
2. **Retell the order of events** Assist students to retell the order of events. If necessary, list the events and model using time order words in the retelling: *first, then, after that, finally.*
3. **Paired reading** Have students reread the selection in pairs. ***Ask:*** *How did the crew feel when they abandoned ship?* (shocked and exhausted)
4. **Multi-level options** See MULTI-LEVEL OPTIONS on p. 32.

Sample Answer to Guide Question

Yes. Shackleton will tell his men to leave the ship.

 **Spelling**

Abbreviations

Make a two-column chart on the board labeled *Abbreviation* and *Word.* Tell students that they will see many abbreviations in English. Write *lb.* and *pound* under the correct headings. Explain that an abbreviation is a short version of a word. It ends in a period. Explain that it is useful to know the common abbreviations for weights, measures, and time. Write *ft.*, *mi.*, and *mos.* under *Abbreviation.*

Apply Direct students to paragraph 6. Ask them to find the word the first abbreviation in the chart stands for. (feet) Tell students they will complete the chart as they continue the reading selection.

Read the Selection

1. **Teacher read aloud** Read paragraphs 10–16 aloud to students. ***Ask:*** *Why does Shackleton want to walk across the ice?* (to find land) *How did the men get food and water?* (from the ice and the animals)
2. **Share feelings** Ask questions to help students explain how the people in the story felt during these events. For example, ***ask:*** *How did the crew feel when the ship sank?*

Sample Answer to Guide Question
No. It's very far and the weather is so cold.

10 Shackleton decided that they had to walk across the pack ice to reach land. But the land he was aiming for was 312 miles away.

11 They set out on Saturday, dragging food, equipment, and the lifeboats from the *Endurance* over the ice. But in three days, they traveled less than 2 miles.

12 Shackleton decided they had to stop and camp on the ice. The ice would drift north, taking them nearer to land and safety.

> **Predict**
> Do you think the men will reach the land 312 miles away?

In a way, the ice was friendly. It was solid underfoot. It gave them water to drink. Seals and penguins used the ice, so there would be food to catch. 13

They chose a large, thick floe for "Ocean Camp." They could still see the *Endurance* in the distance. Parties of men **salvaged** what they could from the crushed wreck. 14

One evening, Shackleton saw the *Endurance* begin to sink. "She's going, boys!" he shouted sadly. The men ran to watch. Their ship **upended,** bow first, and sank slowly under the ice. 15

The *Endurance* had been their home for so long. She was their last link with the outside world. They felt very lonely now. 16

salvaged rescued objects sure to be lost in the ship

upended turned so that one end points upward and the other downward

MULTI-LEVEL OPTIONS *Read the Selection*

Newcomer ***Ask:*** *Does the ship finally sink?* (yes) *Is the walk to the nearest land a short one?* (no) *Is there a lot of room on the lifeboats?* (no) *Do Shackleton and five of his men finally find help at a whaling station?* (yes)

Beginning ***Ask:*** *What finally happens to the ship?* (It sinks.) *Why doesn't the crew walk to find help?* (It is too far away.) *What does the crew use to get off the ice?* (lifeboats) *Where do Shackleton and the five other men finally find help?* (at a whaling station)

Intermediate ***Ask:*** *What does the crew do with the ship before it sinks?* (They take off everything they can.) *Why is the crew finally able to use the lifeboats?* (The ice breaks up.) *What do Shackleton and the five other men do next?* (They sail 800 miles to a whaling station.)

Advanced ***Ask:*** *Do you think the crew expects to be rescued? Why or why not? How do they survive?* (They use what they can from the ship. They have food and fresh water.) *What kind of man is Shackleton?* (He's very brave. He never gives up. He meets challenges.)

17 Five months later they were still camping. They had drifted slowly north, and now the floes were starting to break up. Their floe heaved and suddenly split. The men crammed into their three lifeboats.

18 After seven days they managed to reach **uninhabited** Elephant Island and set up camp on the coast. There, Shackleton left 22 of his men in a small hut.

19 With five men, he planned to make a dangerous and daring journey. The island of South Georgia lay 800 miles away, across the wild ocean. They would sail there and get help at one of the whaling stations.

20 In the little ***James Caird,*** they made one of the greatest sea journeys ever. After 17 days, they stumbled **exhausted** onto the shore of South Georgia. But they were on the wrong side of the island.

21 No one had ever crossed the glaciers and mountains of South Georgia on foot, but Shackleton and two of his men did it to reach help.

22 It took three months before Shackleton was able to rescue the men on Elephant Island. But everyone who had sailed on the *Endurance* had been saved.

---

uninhabited without any people living there
James Caird the name of a ship
exhausted very tired

About the Author — Meredith Hooper (born 1939)

Meredith Hooper has written more than 20 nonfiction books for young readers. She researches each book carefully to make sure that it contains correct information. She explains this challenge, "I bring . . . research skills to bear on each subject, believing that each audience deserves the best." Many of Hooper's books are about science or history.

➤ Why do you think that Meredith Hooper wrote about Shackleton's trip to Antarctica? To inform the reader? To entertain the reader? To influence the reader?

A Capitalization

Days of the week and months of the year

Ask students to name the seven days of the week as you write them on the board. Exaggerate the size of each first letter. Tell students that the days of the week and the months of the year always start with a capital letter. Have them name the months. Ask volunteers to write them on the board.

Evaluate Your Reading Strategy

Predict *Say: You have practiced an important reading strategy. Now you can decide how well you have done. Does this statement describe how you read?*

> I use clues from the story and my own experience to make predictions. Making predictions prepares me to understand what will happen later.

Read the Selection

1. **Shared reading** Play the audio or read aloud to complete the reading of the story as students follow along. Ask volunteers to join in by reading parts aloud. ***Ask:*** *How did the men get to Elephant Island?* (in the lifeboats) *Why did Shackleton want to go to South Georgia?* (There were whaling stations where they could get help.)
2. **Multi-level options** See MULTI-LEVEL OPTIONS on p. 34.

About the Author

1. **Explain author's background** Meredith Hooper is Australian but she loves Antarctica. She has been to the South Pole several times. She received a medal from the American government for her work at the South Pole. Many of her books are about the natural history of Antarctica, the importance of the natural world, and man's place in the world.
2. **Interpret the facts** ***Ask:*** *What challenges do you think Meredith Hooper experienced during her trips to Antarctica and the South Pole?*

Answer
Example: She wanted to tell a story about Antarctica and use her experiences.

Across Selections

Compare and contrast Compare and contrast Brian's challenges in the forest with Shackleton's challenges in Antarctica. What characteristics and qualities did both Brian and Shackleton have? How were they different? Have students record their ideas on a Venn diagram.

UNIT 1 • CHAPTER 3
Beyond the Reading

Reading Comprehension

Question-Answer Relationships

Sample Answers

1. The events happened in 1915–1916.
2. Ernest Shackleton is the leader of an exploring expedition to Antarctica.
3. The problem was the ship was stuck in the ice for about nine months.
4. The ice was pressing against the ship and started breaking the ship.
5. The ice made holes in the ship and water started coming in.
6. He saw there was no way to save the ship.
7. The walk across the ice was very slow and difficult. It would take too long to walk to safety.
8. Shackleton was brave, strong, intelligent, determined, and hopeful.
9. It was cold, scary, and lonely on the ice.
10. The photos showed some of the scenery from Antarctica and how cold and lonely it is there.
11. Many students may say that they don't want to take such a long, cold trip like this.

Build Reading Fluency

Rapid Word Recognition

Rapid word recognition is an excellent activity for students who struggle with irregular spelling patterns. Time students for 1 minute as they read the words in the squares aloud.

Beyond the Reading

Reading Comprehension

Question-Answer Relationships (QAR)

"Right There" Questions

1. **Recall Facts** When do the events in this narrative happen?
2. **Recall Facts** What is Ernest Shackleton's role?
3. **Recall Facts** What problems do Shackleton and his men face?
4. **Recall Facts** What is the first thing that goes wrong for the *Endurance?*

"Think and Search" Questions

5. **Find Cause and Effect** Why does the *Endurance* begin to sink after 278 days stuck in the ice?
6. **Identify the Main Idea** Why does Ernest Shackleton give the order to abandon ship?
7. **Analyze Characters** Why does Shackleton decide to stop crossing the ice and camp out instead?

"Author and You" Questions

8. **Understand Character Traits** What words would you use to describe Ernest Shackleton as a leader?
9. **Understand Plot** What do you think it was like to be stranded on the ice of Antarctica?
10. **Use Visual Elements** How did looking at the photographs on the pages of the selection help you to understand the narrative?

"On Your Own" Question

11. **Express Your Opinion** Would you like to take a challenging trip like the one in this story? Why or why not?

Activity Book p. 18

Student CD-ROM

Build Reading Fluency

Rapid Word Recognition

Rapidly recognizing words helps increase your reading speed.

1. With a partner, review the words in the box.
2. Next, read the words aloud for one minute. Your teacher or partner can time you. How many words did you read in one minute?

fight	deck	ice	pack	ice	fight
stuck	pack	deck	ice	pack	stuck
pack	huge	stuck	fight	huge	pack
ice	ice	each	stuck	fight	ice
huge	stuck	deck	huge	deck	deck

36 Unit 1 Challenges

MULTI-LEVEL OPTIONS *Elements of Literature*

Newcomer Reread the first sentence in paragraph 13. ***Say:*** *The ice isn't really friendly. It's not a person. But you get the idea that the men felt safe on it.* Write on the board: *The wind howled in anger. The sun smiled down.* Have pairs discuss what they can tell about the wind and the sun from the personification.

Beginning Have students reread the first sentence in paragraph 13. ***Ask:*** *Was the ice really friendly?* (no) ***Say:*** *When a* thing *is described like a person, it is called personification.* Have students work in pairs to discover the way the crew personifies the *Endurance* in paragraphs 15 and 16. (as a woman)

Intermediate On the board, write: *The* Endurance *lost the fight. The ice floes groaned.* ***Ask:*** *Was the ship really in a fight? Can ice really groan? Why might a writer describe an animal or a thing as if it were a person?* Assign groups to find examples of personification in paragraphs 3, 4, 13, and 16. Have them report to the class.

Advanced Have students work in pairs. Ask them to complete these examples of personification: *The ship was _____. The wind seemed _____. The ocean looked _____. The glaciers on South Georgia Island were _____.* Then have students pick one sentence to illustrate.

UNIT 1 • CHAPTER 3
Beyond the Reading

Listen, Speak, Interact 

Retell Order of Events

The events in "Antarctic Adventure" cover nearly two years. The writer tells the events in the order they happened. Time words help you keep track of events.

Examples of Time Words
Dates (June 15, 2003)
Days of the week (Monday, Tuesday . . .)
Months of the year (January, February . . .)

1. Read the selection aloud as a partner listens. Stop each time you come to a time word. On a piece of paper, list the words and the events in time order.
2. Then make a timeline that shows the events you recorded.
3. Using the timeline as a guide, retell the events to your partner.
4. Tell your partner about an adventure you had. Keep all events in the correct time order. Use time words to make the order of events clear.

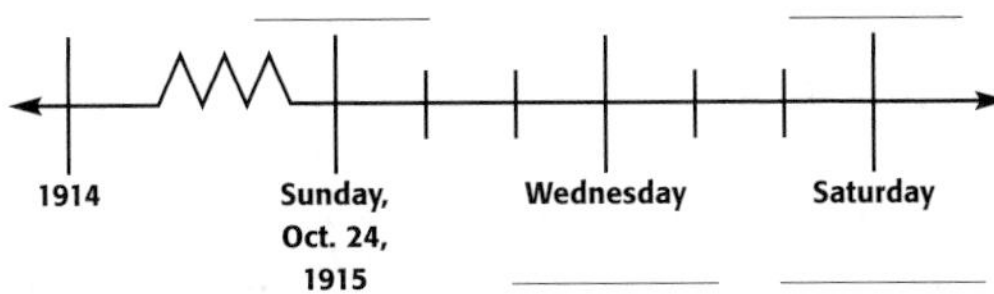

Elements of Literature

Identify Personification

Writers use **personification** to make nonfiction writing more interesting. Personification gives human thoughts, feelings, and actions to an object or animal.

In "Antarctic Adventure," the author describes the ship as if it were a person. For example: "The *Endurance* groaned."

Groaned is a word usually used for people and animals. The use of the word makes the ship seem alive.

Look through the rest of the selection and find other examples of personification. Record them in your Reading Log.

Reading Log

Activity Book p. 19

Student CD-ROM

Home Connection

Have students create timelines of their personal histories, starting with the date they were born. Have them ask parents or relatives about important events, such as moving to another place, interesting trips, or new schools. Tell them to include the month, date, and year when possible. Remind them to put the events in order before they put the dates on their timeline. Allow time for students to share their histories in small groups.

Learning Styles *Visual*

Have students illustrate their own image of life in Antarctica. Point out they can include people, transportation, clothing, or animals in their pictures. Have students write a caption about the picture using personification.

Listen, Speak, Interact

Retell Order of Events

1. **Reread in pairs** Pair beginning and advanced students. Have them read alternate paragraphs.
2. **Newcomers** Reread with this group. Have them identify dates, time words, and events.
3. **Relate events in a sequence** In their Reading Logs, have students record a timeline and details about an adventure they have had or read about.

Elements of Literature

Identify Personification

Teacher Resource Book: *Reading Log, p. 64*

1. Point out and clarify the examples of personification in the text. Give other examples. (The wind whispered through the trees. The flowers in the garden put on their prettiest colors.) Ask students to create other examples of personification.
2. **Locate derivation** Have students locate the derivation of *personification* in the glossary in the Student Handbook or other sources, such as online or CD-ROM dictionaries. Ask students to record the meaning and derivation in their Reading Logs.
3. **Use personal experience** Point out that personification is used in commercials where objects such as computers or cars act like people. Ask students to give examples from commercials they have seen.
4. **Multi-level options** See MULTI-LEVEL OPTIONS on p. 36.

ASSESS

Have students write about three things that they have already done this week. Ask them to use time expressions to show the order of the events.

Word Study

Use Adverbs

Teacher Resource Book: *Personal Dictionary, p. 63*

Roundtable Write on the board: *The men walked _____ on the ice.* Divide students into small groups. Have them say adverbs to complete the sentence. List students' words on the board.

Answers

1. relentlessly, sadly, slowly

Grammar Focus

Use *And* to Join Words and Sentences

Modeling *Say: The leaves are green. The grass is green. The leaves and grass are green.* Point out that the sentence with *and* is shorter and less repetitive than the two separate sentences. Have students suggest other same-color items and combine the nouns using *and.*

Answers

1. Paragraph 4: twisting and grinding; paragraph 6: cracked and splintered; the rudder tore off and water rushed forward and froze; paragraph 7: looked down into the engine room and saw the engines dropping sideways.
2. The ship made a terrible noise and sank.

ASSESS

Write: *The ship is old. The ship is small.* Have students rewrite the sentence combining words and groups of words with *and.*

Word Study

Use Adverbs

Adverbs can describe verbs. Many adverbs end in *-ly.*

The ship sailed slow**ly.**

Writers use adverbs to make their writing more precise or vivid.

1. In "Antarctic Adventure," find examples of adverbs that end in *-ly.* Look in paragraphs 3 and 15.
2. Write the adverbs in your Personal Dictionary. Underline the *-ly.*
3. Write an example sentence of your own using one of the adverbs.

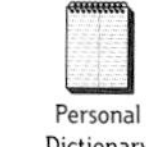
Personal Dictionary

Activity Book *p. 20*

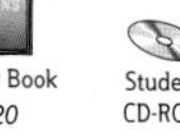
Student CD-ROM

Grammar Focus

Use *And* to Join Words and Sentences

The word *and* means "also." *And* can join words and sentences.

And joining nouns:	They set out on Saturday, dragging food, equipment, **and** the lifeboats.
And joining verbs:	The ice floes groaned **and** crashed.
And joining adjectives:	The men tumbled out onto the ice, shocked **and** exhausted.
And joining adverbs:	Slowly **and** sadly, the people left the ship.
And joining sentences:	The ice started splitting, **and** they had to move their tents.

1. Find the uses of *and* in paragraphs 4, 6, and 7 of "Antarctic Adventure." What words or groups of words are joined?
2. Combine these two sentences into one. Use *and.*

   The ship made a terrible noise.
   It sank.

Activity Book *pp. 21–22*

Student Handbook

Student CD-ROM

MULTI-LEVEL OPTIONS *From Reading to Writing*

Newcomer Have students draw a series of pictures that shows the important events in their narratives. Have them write important names and dates. Ask them to tell their stories to partners.

Beginning Give students sentence starters to help organize their stories: *This story is about _____. It happened in _____. The people in this story are _____. First, _____. Next, _____. Then, _____. Finally, _____.* Have them read their stories to partners.

Intermediate Have students prepare a timeline of events and a list of people for their narratives. Then have them draft a sentence about each event on the timeline. Revise the drafts in pairs. Tell pairs to think of ways to include personification in each narrative.

Advanced Have students work independently to prepare an outline of events. Ask them to use their outlines to write a three-paragraph narrative with a clear beginning, middle, and end. Have them read their narratives in small groups. Direct the groups to make suggestions about ways to include personification.

From Reading to Writing 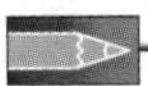

Write a Historical Narrative

Write a historical narrative about someone who faced danger. You may write about a person you know or someone you have learned about.

1. Use time words to tell when the events took place.
2. Make sure that your narrative has a beginning, a middle, and an end.
3. Use personification to bring things to life.
4. Use *and* to join words and sentences.
5. Be sure to indent each paragraph.
6. Add a timeline that shows the order in which important events occur.
7. Be sure to capitalize days of the week and months of the year.

Activity Book
p. 23

Across Content Areas 

Learn About Bodies of Land and Water

The surface of Earth is made up of land and water. The main bodies of land are called **continents.** The main bodies of water are called **oceans.**

Continents	**Oceans**
Asia	The Atlantic Ocean
Africa	The Pacific Ocean
North America	The Indian Ocean
South America	The Arctic Ocean
Australia	
Europe	
Antarctica	

Smaller bodies of salt water are called **seas.** Some examples are the Mediterranean Sea (between Europe, Asia, and Africa) and the Caribbean Sea (along the coasts of Venezuela, Colombia, and Central America). Seas are often parts of oceans.

Islands are smaller bodies of land completely surrounded by water. Puerto Rico is an island in the Caribbean Sea.

1. Look at a map of the world and find the continents and oceans.
2. Look at the map of Antarctica on page 29. List the oceans, seas, continents, and islands that you see on the map.

Activity Book
p. 24

From Reading to Writing

Write a Historical Narrative

Teacher Resource Book: *Chronological Order, p. 50; Timelines, p. 39*

1. **Review historical narrative** Remind students that a historical narrative tells about something that actually happened. Tell them that even though they should use personification to bring things to life, their narratives must be about real-life, not made-up, events.
2. **Multi-level options** See MULTI-LEVEL OPTIONS on p. 38.

Across Content Areas: Social Studies

Learn About Bodies of Land and Water

Use a map Have students locate and identify the continents and oceans on a world map or a globe. Ask students to point out countries they have lived in or visited and identify the continent where they are located.

Answers

2. Oceans: South Atlantic, South Pacific, Indian; Seas: Ross, Amundsen, Weddell; Continents: Africa, South America, Australia, Antarctica; Islands: New Zealand.

ASSESS

Ask: Is the Atlantic an ocean or a sea? (an ocean) *Which is larger—an ocean or a sea?* (an ocean) *Is Puerto Rico a continent or an island?* (an island) *Name a continent.* (Some answers might be: North America or Antarctica.)

Assessment Program: *Unit 1, Chapter 3 Quiz, pp. 11–12*

Reteach and Reassess

Text Structure Have students list the features of a historical narrative. Then ask them to find examples of each feature in the reading selection.

Reading Strategy Tell students to review the predictions they made on pages 33 and 34. Have small groups discuss how accurate they were.

Elements of Literature Have each student use personification to write a sentence about an object or animal in "Antarctic Adventure." Ask them to trade papers with a partner and have the partners underline the personification.

Reassess Have students write a one-paragraph prediction about what the crew did after they were rescued.

Chapter Materials

Activity Book: *pp. 25–32*
Audio: *Unit 1, Chapter 4*
Student Handbook
Student CD-ROM: *Unit 1, Chapter 4*
Teacher Resource Book: *Lesson Plan, Teacher Resources, Reading Summary, Activity Book Answer Key*
Teacher Resource CD-ROM
Assessment Program: *Quiz, pp. 13–14; Teacher and Student Resources, pp. 115–144*
Assessment CD-ROM
Transparencies
The Heinle Newbury House Dictionary/CD-ROM
Web Site: www.heinle.visions.com

Objectives

Make connections Read the objectives aloud. *Ask: What narrative did we already read?* ("Antarctic Adventure," a historical narrative) Have students identify words they know.

Use Prior Knowledge

Discuss the First Day of School

Teacher Resource Book: *Web, p. 37*

Visualize *Say: Imagine that you are in a new school. What is happening? Who do you meet?* Have students close their eyes and visualize the scene. Ask students to describe their ideas.

CHAPTER 4

Into the Reading

Yang the Youngest

an excerpt from a novel by Lensey Namioka

Objectives

Reading Compare a reading with your experiences as you read a first-person narrative.

Listening and Speaking Identify and use colloquial speech.

Grammar Study complex sentences with dependent clauses.

Writing Write a first-person narrative.

Content Social Studies: Learn the meanings of *culture*.

Use Prior Knowledge

Discuss the First Day of School

The main character in "Yang the Youngest" is attending a new school. In most cultures, the first day of school is a big day. You introduce yourself, meet new people, and learn school rules.

1. Copy the web on a piece of paper.
2. With a partner, brainstorm things that might happen on the first day of school. Write your ideas on the web.
3. Share your information with the class.

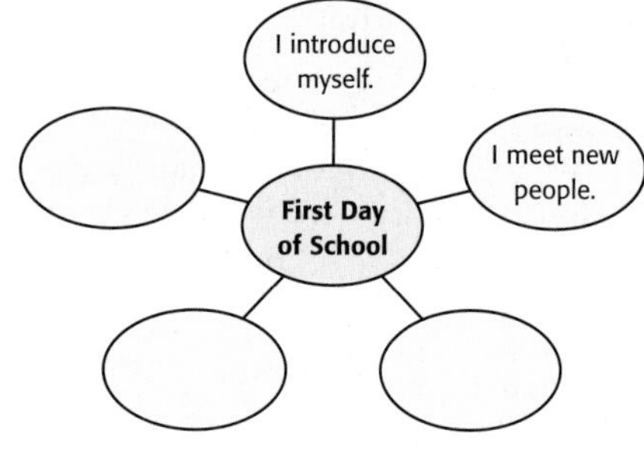

MULTI-LEVEL OPTIONS *Build Vocabulary*

Newcomer Write on the board: *1a. I swim in a pool. 1b. I play pool. 2a. I rose from my chair. 2b. A rose is a flower.* Mime swimming as you point to 1a and read the sentence. Mime or demonstrate the meanings of the other sentences. Then point to a sentence and have students act out the meaning.

Beginning Write on the board: *pool, rose, pen.* Mime swimming as you point to *pool.* ***Say:*** *I swim in a pool. Pool is also a game.* (Mime playing.) Then stand up. ***Say:*** *I stood up. I rose. A rose is also a flower.* (Mime smelling.) Then have students write sentences with the homonyms. Let them share their sentences with a partner.

Intermediate Have students answer the homonym questions and check their answers in pairs. Then have each pair write a sentence using the homonyms *pool, rose,* and *pen.* Have them share their sentences with another pair.

Advanced Have students write a sentence using both meanings of the homonyms *pool, rose,* and *pen.* For example, ***say:*** *There's a pool table next to the swimming pool.*

Build Background

China

China is a very large country in eastern Asia. It has a long history and has had a great influence on other countries. Paper and silk were first developed there. Family life, politeness, and respect for authority are very important in China.

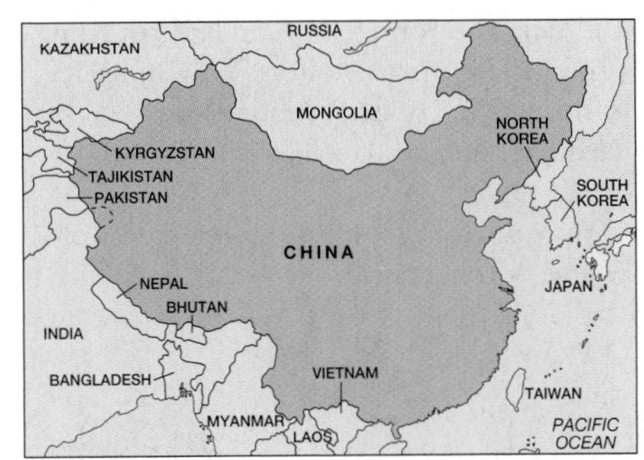

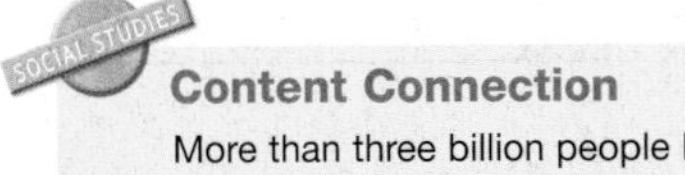

Content Connection

More than three billion people live in Asia. Over one billion live in China.

Build Vocabulary

Identify Homonyms

Homonyms are words that are pronounced and usually spelled the same but have different meanings.

Read these sentences. Choose the definitions that make sense.

1. "It was really hot, so I went to the pool to swim." In this sentence, *pool* means:
   a. a small body of water
   b. a game played on a special table
2. "When the teacher called my name, I rose." In this sentence, *rose* means:
   a. got up from my seat
   b. a flower with a beautiful smell
3. "May I borrow your pen?" In this sentence, *pen* means:
   a. a place to put animals in
   b. something to write with

Write these homonyms in your Personal Dictionary.

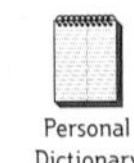
Personal Dictionary

Activity Book *p. 25*

Student CD-ROM

Content Connection
The Arts

Build Background Have students create a travel poster inviting people to visit China. Tell students to use pictures of famous historical or cultural sites in China. Have them create a title and theme for each poster.

Learning Styles
Mathematical

Build Background Use an almanac to have students research the sizes and populations of China and the United States. Have pairs of students create charts that compare their data.

Build Background

China

1. **Use a map** Have students locate China on a globe or world map. Have them identify surrounding countries and bodies of water. ***Ask:*** *What country is north of China?* (Mongolia) *Where is the Yellow Sea?* (to the east)
2. **Content Connection** ***Say:*** *There are more than 6 billion people in the world.* Help students determine the percentage of people in the world who are Asian (50%) and the percentage of people in the world who are Chinese (16.7%).

Build Vocabulary

Identify Homonyms

Teacher Resource Book: *Personal Dictionary, p. 63*

1. **Identify homonyms** Use pictures to show both meanings of *pool, rose, pen.* Explain their meanings. Say sentences using the homonyms and have students identify the correct picture/meaning.
2. **Reading selection vocabulary** You may want to introduce the glossed words in the reading selection before students begin reading. Key words: *wink, stomp, chat, respect, cranky, in spite of, puzzled.* Instruct students to write the words with correct spelling and their definitions in their Personal Dictionaries. Have them pronounce each word and divide it into syllbales.
3. **Multi-level options** See MULTI-LEVEL OPTIONS on p. 40.

Answers

1. a **2.** a **3.** b

ASSESS

Have students write a sentence for each meaning of *pool, rose,* and *pen.*

Into the Reading

Text Structure

First-Person Narrative

1. **Recognize features** Direct students to the feature chart. Discuss and explain the features of a first-person narrative.
2. **Multi-level options** See MULTI-LEVEL OPTIONS below.

Reading Strategy

Compare a Reading with Your Experiences

Teacher think aloud *Say: When I read about a student's first day of school, I think about my first day of school. He didn't have any friends, and I didn't have any friends. I think I know how he felt.* Ask students to think about their own experiences and use them to understand Yang.

ASSESS

Ask: What pronouns are in a first-person narrative? (I, me, we, us)

Text Structure

First-Person Narrative

"Yang the Youngest" is an excerpt from a novel. The story is told by Yang himself. In this type of writing, **first-person narrative,** the speaker tells you about his or her life.

As you read, look for these features of first-person narrative.

First-Person Narrative	
Story	beginning, middle, end
Personal Pronouns	*I, me, we, us*
Problem	The speaker faces a problem.
Problem Resolution	The speaker tells how he or she resolves the problem.

Student CD-ROM

Reading Strategy

Compare a Reading with Your Experiences

As you read, think about how the experiences of the main character, Yang, might be like yours. Yang feels he does not know enough English to make friends. He also surprises his parents with his "American" behavior.

1. Read paragraph 1 on page 44. Compare your experiences with what happens in the paragraph by answering questions such as these:
   a. Have I ever had trouble because I did not know anyone?
   b. Have my parents ever been surprised by changes in my behavior?
2. As you read the selection, continue making comparisons between your experiences and the story. For example, have you ever felt afraid to meet new people?

Student CD-ROM

MULTI-LEVEL OPTIONS *Text Structure*

Newcomer On the board, write: *I, me, we, us.* Ask which pronouns describe one person (I, me) and which describe more than one (we, us). Have students work in groups to write a sentence using each pronoun. Ask them to share their sentences with another group. Monitor their work during the group sharing.

Beginning Write this story on the board: *I just moved to town. I want to look good at my new school. I asked my cousin to help me find a new jacket. He took me to a big store. We found a jacket there. Now I'm ready for my new school.* Have students identify the pronouns that make this a first-person narrative. (I, me, my)

Intermediate Have students write a short first-person narrative. A topic might be picking out clothes for school. Remind them to use the text features for their narrative: a beginning, a middle, and an end; personal pronouns; a problem and a solution.

Advanced Provide students with a short article written in the third person. Have them rewrite it as a first-person narrative.

YANG THE YOUNGEST

an excerpt from a novel
by Lensey Namioka

43

Reading Selection Materials

Audio: *Unit 1, Chapter 4*
Teacher Resource Book: *Reading Summary, pp. 71–72*

Preview the Selection

1. **Relate to personal experience** Have students describe the school in the photo. *Ask: Is it in China or in the U.S.? Why do you think so? Does this school look like our school? How is it similar or different? Would you like to go to this school? Why or why not? What was your first day at our school like?*
2. **Connect** Remind students that the unit theme is *challenges*. Ask students what kind of challenges the main character might face. *Ask: What can you tell about Yang's family from the title?* (He is the youngest, so he must have older siblings.)

Community Connection

Invite a former student or an adult from the neighborhood to speak to the class. Ask the guest to talk about his or her experiences in school. Have students prepare for the visit by discussing how school might have been different 5, 10, or 20 years earlier. Then have them write questions to ask the speaker.

Learning Styles *Musical*

Tell students to find out if the school has a school song. If it does, learn it and perform it as a class. If it doesn't, have groups write a song or poem about what it is like to be a new student in school.

UNIT 1 • CHAPTER 4
Reading Selection

Read the Selection

1. **Use the illustration** Have students look at the illustration. ***Ask:*** *Which student is the main character?* Encourage them to explain their choice. Point out the expressions on students' faces and what the students are doing. Have students speculate about how different students are feeling.
2. **Choral reading** Have pairs of students prepare different paragraphs for a choral reading. Give them time to practice. Then have the class "put the pieces together" by reading aloud in sequence.
3. **Compare the selection with your experiences** ***Ask:*** *How did you feel your first day in a new school or in a new class? Was it easy or difficult for you? Why?*

Sample Answer to Guide Question
Yes. I wasn't sure if the other people would like me. I wasn't sure what to do or say.

See Teacher Edition pp. 434–435 for a list of English-Spanish cognates in the reading selection.

Audio

Compare a Reading with Your Experiences

Have you ever been afraid to join a new situation? What made you feel afraid?

1 Our family arrived in America in the winter, and the school year was almost half over. So when I started school, the other students in my class already knew each other. To make things worse, I didn't even know enough English to try to make friends.

2 But language was only one of my problems. American kids scared me at first. They yelled terribly loud and ran fast in the hallways.

3 For the first few weeks, I found myself hugging the walls. It was like the time in China when I learned to swim. I was afraid to let go of the side of the pool because in the middle were other swimmers splashing around like sharks.

4 Once when I was walking in the hallway at school, I turned a corner and bumped into a boy. He was running so fast that he knocked me off my feet.

5 He pulled me **upright** and shook me a little. Maybe he wanted to see if any parts were **rattling** loose. When he saw that I wasn't hurt, he **winked** at me, laughed, and said, "Hey, no sweat!"

---

upright standing up
rattling making short, sharp noises by banging around
winked closed only one eye in order to make a friendly face

MULTI-LEVEL OPTIONS *Read the Selection*

Newcomer Play the audio. Then replay it and have students do a paired reading as they listen. ***Ask:*** *Does the main character like school at first?* (no) *Are his parents happy with the way he acts?* (no) *Does he jump up when his teacher enters the classroom?* (yes) *Do some kids laugh at him?* (yes)

Beginning Read the Reading Summary aloud. Then have students do a paired reading. ***Ask:*** *How does the main character feel about school at first?* (He doesn't like it.) *How do his parents feel about the way he acts?* (He's too rough.) *What does he do when his teacher comes into the classroom?* (He jumps up.)

Intermediate Have small groups do a reciprocal reading. ***Ask:*** *How does the main character think he can make new friends?* (by learning more English) *What do his parents complain about?* (He's too rough and he stomps his feet too hard.) *Why does he jump up when his teacher enters the room?* (It's a sign of respect.)

Advanced Have students read silently. ***Ask:*** *Why doesn't the main character like school at first?* (He doesn't know enough English to make friends. Other students scare him.) *What does he learn after a few weeks?* (He learns to walk as fast and shove as hard as the other kids. He stops jumping up when the teacher comes in.)

6 He looked so cheerful that I laughed, too. "No sweat" sounded like a good phrase, and I told Third Sister about it. She added it to her list.

7 In a few weeks I learned to walk just as fast and shove my way just as hard as the other kids.

8 My parents even complained about it. "You're becoming too rough, Yingtao. Why do you have to **stomp** your feet so hard?"

Compare a Reading with Your Experiences

Have you ever been embarrassed by behaving differently from others?

9 Before I got used to the American school, the other kids laughed at some of the things I did. Each morning, as soon as the teacher came into the room, I jumped to my feet and stood **stiffly** at attention. That was how we showed our **respect** to the teacher in China.

10 The first time I did it here, the teacher asked me whether I needed something. I looked around and saw that nobody else was standing up. Feeling foolish, I shook my head and sat down.

11 When I did it again the next day, a couple of kids behind me started to **snigger.** After that, I remembered not to jump up, but I half rose a few times. One boy used to watch me, and if he saw my bottom leave my seat, he would whisper, "Down, **Fido!**"

12 Third Sister was a great help during those early days. While the other kids were busy talking or playing games at **recess,** she and I stood in a corner and kept each other company.

---

stomp walk heavily or loudly
stiffly in a formal manner, not bending the body
respect honor, admiration
snigger snicker, laugh meanly
Fido a traditional name for a dog
recess a break from work or school to relax

UNIT 1 • CHAPTER 4
Reading Selection

Read the Selection

1. **Use the illustration** *Ask: Who are the people?* (students, a teacher) *Who is entering the room?* (the teacher) *Why do you think the boy is standing?* (Maybe he wants to ask a question. Maybe he doesn't have a seat.)
2. **Understand terms** Have students find the meanings of the glossed words at the bottom of the page. Clarify meanings as needed.
3. **Guided reading** After students listen to the audio or to you read the selection, have them reread each paragraph, pausing as you ask comprehension questions and clarify meanings.
4. **Compare the selection with your experiences** Ask questions to help students discuss their actions when the teacher enters a room. Students can act out their reactions.
5. **Multi-level options** See MULTI-LEVEL OPTIONS on p. 44.

Sample Answer to Guide Question

Yes. I was embarrassed when other students used forks to eat lunch but I used chopsticks.

9 Punctuation

Apostrophes in contractions

Write *did not* = *didn't* on the board. Tell students that there are many contractions in English. ***Say:*** *Contractions are short ways to say and spell words. To make contractions, you join words together and leave out one or two letters. When you leave out letters, you must put an apostrophe in place of the missing letters.* Point to the example on the board. ***Ask:*** *What letter was left out?* (*o*) *What is in its place?* (an apostrophe)

Apply Have students find the contractions in paragraphs 5 (wasn't) and 8 (You're). Have them tell a partner the uncontracted form of each and what letters were left out. Tell them to write the contractions they find as they read in their Reading Logs.

UNIT 1 • CHAPTER 4
Reading Selection

Read the Selection

1. **Guided reading** Read or ask volunteers to read the paragraphs aloud. *Ask: Why was Second Sister lonely? When do you feel lonely or sad? How do you act when you are lonely and sad? Why did Third Sister have lots of friends?*
2. **Identify text structure** Have students reread the paragraphs with partners and find personal pronouns that show this is a first-person narrative.

Sample Answer to Guide Question
Yes. I tried to do things to make them happy or to make them smile.

13 Every day we walked together to our **elementary school,** which was not far from our house. Eldest Brother and Second Sister took a big yellow bus to a school that was farther away.

14 If Eldest Brother had trouble making friends, it didn't seem to bother him. Music was the only thing he really cared about.

15 I think Second Sister felt the loneliest. In China, people always said she would turn out to be a real beauty. She had been popular at school there, always surrounded by friends. But in America not many people told her she was beautiful. These days she was often **cranky** and sad. Mother told the rest of us that we just had to be patient with Second Sister.

16 Third Sister had no trouble at all making friends. Even before she could speak much English, she began **chatting** with other kids. She could always fill in the gaps with laughter.

Compare a Reading with Your Experiences

Have you ever had a friend or family member who was often sad? How did you treat the person?

---

elementary school a school for grades 1–6 and students about the ages of 6–12

cranky acting annoyed, in a bad mood

chatting talking in a friendly and informal way

MULTI-LEVEL OPTIONS *Read the Selection*

Newcomer *Ask: Does Second Sister feel lonely?* (yes) *Does Third Sister have trouble making friends?* (no) *Does the main character sit with Asian-Americans?* (yes) *Does the girl in his class speak Chinese?* (no) *Was she born in America?* (yes)

Beginning *Ask: How does Second Sister feel?* (lonely) *What is Third Sister good at?* (making friends) *Who sits with the main character at lunchtime?* (Asian-Americans) *What language does the girl in his class speak?* (English) *Where was she born?* (America)

Intermediate *Ask: Why is Second Sister so lonely?* (She was more popular in China.) *Why is Third Sister so cheerful?* (She has no trouble making friends.) *Why does Yang's teacher seat him next to an Asian-American?* (She thinks it will be easier for him to make friends if they are both Asian-American.)

Advanced *Ask: How do the main character's brothers and sisters feel?* (Eldest Brother only cares about music. Second Sister is lonely. Third Sister is happy.) *Why does the term* Asian-Americans *confuse the main character?* (He thinks they are Chinese like him, but they are Americans and Koreans, too.)

17 During lunch she and I sat at a table with mostly **Asian-Americans.** At first we didn't understand what Asian-Americans were. When we were filling out **registration forms** at school, we put down "Chinese" in the space marked "race."

18 The secretary at the school told us to change it to "Asian-American." With a big smile, she said, "We have a number of Asian-Americans at this school, so you'll be able to make friends easily."

Compare a Reading with Your Experiences

Has anyone ever tried to make you feel comfortable in a new situation? Did it help?

19 My teacher must have felt the same because on my first day in class, she seated me next to a girl who was also Asian-American.

20 I greeted her in Chinese, but she just shook her head. "I'm afraid I don't understand Japanese," she said in English.

21 "I wasn't speaking Japanese," I told her. "I was speaking Chinese."

22 "Sorry. I don't understand that, either. My family is from Korea."

23 I didn't know much about Korea, except that my country had once **invaded** her country. I hoped she didn't hold it against me.

24 "You speak good English," I said. "When did you arrive?"

25 "I was born in America," she said. "So were my parents."

26 **In spite of** this bad start, she tried to be helpful to me. But we never became close friends.

27 So I was lonely. After Third Sister made friends in her class, she began to spend less and less time with me.

Asian-Americans Americans whose parents or ancestors came from Asia

registration forms papers showing lists of students who are signed up for school

invaded sent armies to take over and control

in spite of *in spite of* introduces an idea that may seem surprising

Read the Selection

1. **Guided reading** Read or ask volunteers to read the paragraphs as students follow along in their books. ***Ask:** Do all Asian-Americans speak the same language?* (no) *Do you think the girl can speak Korean? Why?* (No. She was born in the U.S.)
2. **Role-play** Have pairs of students choose different roles (the secretary, the Korean girl, the main character) and perform the dialogues in the story.
3. **Multi-level options** See MULTI-LEVEL OPTIONS on p. 46.

Sample Answer to Guide Question

Yes. It helps a lot.

A Capitalization

Countries and languages

Make a two-column chart labeled *Countries* and *Languages.* Write in column 1: *China, the United States.* ***Say:** The names of countries and languages always start with a capital letter. Sometimes the names are the same or very similar. Sometimes they are very different.* Then ask students to identify the two languages for the chart (Chinese, English).

Apply Have students find another language and country in paragraphs 20–23. (Japanese, Korea). Tell them to record the information on their charts. Then have them volunteer other languages or countries they know.

Read the Selection

1. **Quaker reading** Play the audio of paragraphs 28–35. Tell students to note which paragraph they liked the best. Then have students read their paragraphs aloud. Point out that they can repeat sections other students have read aloud.
2. **Role-play** Have students reread the selection in pairs. Ask volunteers to act out the incident with the pen.
3. **Compare the selection with your experiences** *Ask: How do you feel when you don't know an English word that you want to use?* (frustrated, embarrassed)

Sample Answer to Guide Question
Yes. I was angry. I was embarrassed.

---

28 Then I met Matthew. During recess one day, Third Sister was busy talking to some new friends, and I was looking **wistfully** at some boys playing catch and wondering if I could find the nerve to join them.

Compare a Reading with Your Experiences

Has anyone ever teased you? How did you feel?

29 Suddenly I felt someone **pluck** my pen from my pocket. This was a ballpoint pen I had brought with me from China, with a picture of a panda on the side of it. Whenever I thought about China and missed the friends I had left behind, I would take out the pen and look at the picture.

30 The boy who had taken the pen was running away, laughing. I ran after him, shouting. The teacher came up and asked me what the trouble was.

31 "He took my . . . my . . ." I stopped, because I didn't know the English word for pen. In Chinese we have the same word, *bi,* for pen, pencil, and brush. "He took my writing stick," I finished **lamely.**

32 The boy **who'd** taken the pen stood there and grinned, while the teacher looked **puzzled.**

33 "Jake took his ballpoint pen," said a tall, **freckled** boy with curly brown hair. "I saw the whole thing."

34 The teacher turned and frowned at Jake. "Is this true?"

35 "Aw, I was just teasing him a little," said Jake, quickly handing the pen back to me. "He's always playing with it, so I got curious."

36 I thanked the boy with the curly hair. "Don't mind Jake," he said. "He didn't mean anything."

---

wistfully in a manner that is sadly wishful
pluck pull or grab
lamely in a manner that is weak or not convincing
who'd who had
puzzled confused
freckled having small spots of darker skin on the skin

MULTI-LEVEL OPTIONS *Read the Selection*

Newcomer *Ask: Does a boy take a wallet from the main character's pocket?* (no) *Does anyone help get the pen back?* (yes) *Is the boy with the curly hair named Jake?* (no) *Does Yang still feel lonely after he meets Matthew?* (no)

Beginning *Ask: What does Jake take from the main character's pocket?* (a pen) *What picture is on it?* (a panda) *Who helps Yang get the pen back?* (Matthew) *How does Yang feel then?* (a little less lonely)

Intermediate *Ask: What does the pen remind the main character of?* (friends back in China) *What does he call the pen when he can't remember its name in English?* (a writing stick) *How does Yang explain his name to Matthew?* (Yang Yingtao in China and Yingtao Yang in America)

Advanced *Ask: Why does the main character have trouble telling the teacher what happened?* (He couldn't remember the word for *pen.*) *Why does Jake take the pen away?* (He's curious. He is teasing.) *Why is Yang a little less lonely at the end of the story?* (He's meeting people and feeling more comfortable.)

37 "My name is Yang Yingtao," I introduced myself. Then I remembered that in America people said their **family name** last and their **given name** first.

38 "Yingtao is my last name," I told him. "Except that in America my last name is really my first name and my first name is my last name. So I'm Yang Yingtao in China and Yingtao Yang in America."

39 The boy looked confused. Just then the bell rang. "I'm Matthew Conner," he said quickly. "See you around."

40 I began to feel a little less lonely.

Compare a Reading with Your Experiences

Have you ever confused anyone? What happened? How did you feel?

---

family name the name you share with your parents and brothers or sisters

given name the name given to you by your parents when you were born

About the Author

Lensey Namioka (born 1929)

Like her character Yang, Lensey Namioka was born in China and later came to the United States. Her father worked for the Chinese government, and the family moved around a lot. Because of this, Namioka understands some of the problems young people face when they come to a new place or feel that they do not fit into the group. She says that she writes books "because it's fun. There's nothing else I enjoy more."

➤ Why do you think Lensey Namioka wrote "Yang the Youngest"? To entertain? To inform? To persuade?

Spelling

Use the sound /au/

Explain that the letters *ou* and *ow* often make the same sound. Write *house* and *brown* on the board. Then point to each word and pronounce it clearly. Have students repeat them. Have students find other words with the sounds in paragraphs 30 (shouting), 34 (frowned), and 39 (around).

Apply Have small groups create lists of rhyming words for each *ou* and *ow* word they find.

Evaluate Your Reading Strategy

Compare the Selection with Your Experiences *Say: You have practiced an important reading strategy. Now you can decide how well you have done. Does this statement describe how you read?*

> I read what the characters say and do, and I compare these things with my own experiences. My own experiences help me understand the characters in literature.

UNIT 1 • CHAPTER 4

Reading Selection

Read the Selection

1. **Paired reading** Have pairs of students read the selection and practice the last dialogue between Jake and Yang. ***Ask:*** *What is different about Chinese names and American names?* (the order of the first and last names)
2. **Multi-level options** See MULTI-LEVEL OPTIONS on p. 48.

Sample Answer to Guide Question

Yes. I couldn't explain what I wanted in a store. I had to point to things. I felt embarrassed. I wanted to leave quickly.

About the Author

1. **Explain author challenges** Lensey Namioka moved many times as a child. She knows the challenges children face in unfamiliar places.
2. **Interpret the facts** ***Ask:*** *How do you think Lensey Namioka used her experiences in this story? Are her experiences similar to yours?*

Answer

Example: Lensey Namioka wrote "Yang the Youngest" to entertain.

Across Selections

1. **Compare point of view** Discuss the differences between the realistic narrative story about Brian (pp. 18–23) and the first-person narrative story about Yang. Remind students to examine the point of view of the narrator. ***Ask:*** *What is different about who is telling the stories? Do you feel closer to Brian or to Yang when you read the stories? Which character do you think you know better?*

Reading Comprehension

Question-Answer Relationships

Sample Answers

1. The setting is Yang's new school.
2. One of Yang's sisters, Third Sister, walks to school with him.
3. Yang's new school was a busy school with many active students.
4. Yang doesn't know enough English.
5. Yang's problem is making new friends.
6. Yang begins to act more like American students and learns to do what they do.
7. Another student stops to help Yang and introduces himself.
8. She is having a hard time making new friends. She misses people saying that she is beautiful. She misses her old friends.
9. In Chinese culture, being quiet is good; families are close; and teachers are respected.
10. I think Yang and Matthew will become friends.
11. Yang should say hi to everyone. He should not worry about his English.

Build Reading Fluency

Adjusting Reading Rate

Demonstrate to the students how you change your rate of reading depending on the purpose and type of reading material.

Beyond the Reading

Reading Comprehension

Question-Answer Relationships (QAR)

"Right There" Questions

1. **Recall Facts** What is the setting of the story?
2. **Recall Facts** Who walks to school with Yang?

"Think and Search" Questions

3. **Analyze Setting** How would you describe the place where the story happens?
4. **Recognize Character Traits** Why does Yang have trouble sharing his thoughts and feelings at school?
5. **Understand Characters** What is the main problem Yang faces?
6. **Analyze Characters** How does Yang change as he gets used to his new school?
7. **Draw a Conclusion** What happens to change Yang's feelings?

"Author and You" Questions

8. **Analyze Characters** Why do you think Second Sister is crankier in the United States than she had been in China?
9. **Compare and Contrast** What did you learn about Chinese culture from the selection? What things are similar to your culture? What things are different?

"On Your Own" Questions

10. **Predict** What do you think will happen between Yang and Matthew?
11. **Express Your Opinion** What do you think Yang should do to be more comfortable in his new school?

Activity Book p. 26

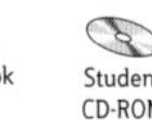
Student CD-ROM

Build Reading Fluency

Adjusting Reading Rate

You read many quotations in "Yang the Youngest." Reading quotations aloud helps you learn to adjust your reading rate. Pause and read as if you are speaking to a person.

1. With a partner, practice rereading paragraphs 18–25 on page 47.
2. Read the quotations with expression.
3. Pause after each quotation.
4. Choose the quotation you like the best and read it aloud in front of the class.

MULTI-LEVEL OPTIONS *Elements of Literature*

Newcomer Direct students to examples on p. 51. Ask students to brainstorm a list of words or phrases that describe Yang. (shy, polite, nervous, wants to make friends) Help students copy the web from p. 51 into their Reading Logs. Have them transfer the four phrases they think best describe Yang onto their webs.

Beginning Have students work in small groups to find two sentences that describe *how Yang feels.* Then have them find two sentences that describe *what Yang does.* Have them copy the web from p. 51 into their Reading Logs. Have them write their sentences on their webs.

Intermediate Have each student find two sentences that describe *how Yang feels* and two sentences that describe *what Yang does.* Have small groups discuss whether their sentences are examples of direct or indirect characterization. Monitor the groups as they work.

Advanced Have students work in pairs. Ask each pair to find one direct and one indirect characterization of Yang. Have them share their examples with another pair.

Listen, Speak, Interact 

Identify and Use Colloquial Speech

When the boy runs into Yang in the hallway, he says, "Hey, no sweat." This kind of language is called **colloquial speech.** Colloquial speech is the way you speak with friends in everyday conversation. Using colloquial speech helps authors create characters that sound like real people.

1. Read aloud or listen to paragraphs 1–7 with a partner.
   a. Act out the scene when Yang bumps into another student.
   b. Discuss what you think the phrase "Hey, no sweat" means.
2. Together, find three other examples of colloquial speech in paragraphs 11, 35, and 39. What do they mean?
3. Colloquial speech can reflect a region or culture. What examples of colloquial speech do you know? How do they reflect a region or culture?

Elements of Literature

Analyze Characters

Characters are the people in a story. Writers tell about characters in two ways:

Direct Characterization	The author tells you how the character feels. Example: "The character is happy."
Indirect Characterization	The author *suggests* how a character feels or what a character is like. Example: "The character is laughing."

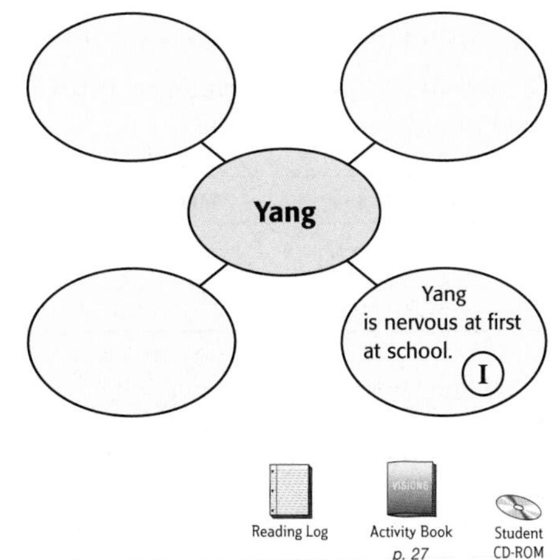

1. Copy the character web in your Reading Log.
2. Complete the web with details about Yang. Next to each detail write *D* if it shows *direct characterization* and *I* if it shows *indirect characterization.*

Reading Log | Activity Book *p. 27* | Student CD-ROM

Content Connection
The Arts

Have students copy the lyrics from a favorite song. Tell them to underline sentences in which colloquial language is used. Then have them rewrite the underlined sentences into standard English. Have them share their analysis in small groups.

Learning Styles
Kinesthetic

Ask students to present a role-play about a challenging or funny event in school. Remind them to include gestures, expressions, and colloquial language. Have the class discuss what they were able to learn about the characters from the role-play.

Listen, Speak, Interact

Identify and Use Colloquial Speech

1. **Reread in pairs** Model the dialogues, exaggerating the inflection slightly. Have pairs of students read alternate paragraphs.
2. **Newcomers** Have students locate the colloquial expressions in the selection. Write these phrases on the board. Have students guess their meanings. Students can copy the expressions into their Reading Logs.

Answers

2. Paragraph 11: Down, Fido. (Sit down.); paragraph 35: Aw, I was just teasing him a little. (I was playing a little. I'm not trying to hurt him.); paragraph 39: See you around (Good-bye. See you later.).
3. *Example:* Y'all. Southern U.S.

Elements of Literature

Analyze Characters

Teacher Resource Book: *Reading Log, p. 64*

1. **Interpret characters' feelings** Brainstorm and record a list of words to describe Yang. Explain direct and indirect characterization. *Say: Yang ran after Jake shouting.* (indirect) *Yang was very upset.* (direct) Have students look back through the story and decide if the author used direct or indirect characterization for each of the feelings on the list.
2. **Multi-level options** See MULTI-LEVEL OPTIONS on p. 50.

Answers

2. *Example:* Yang felt: nervous (I), scared (D), embarrassed (I), lonely (D)

ASSESS

Have students explain these examples of indirect characterization with direct words. On the board write: *I'm crying.* (sad) *They are singing and dancing.* (happy)

Word Study

Define Words with a Latin Root

Teacher Resource Book: *Personal Dictionary, p. 63*

Make a word map Write on the board and say the root *spect.* Then write the prefix *re-* and pronounce it. Then put the parts together and pronounce the new word. Point to the new word in the chart. Ask students to use the word in a sentence. Repeat with the prefix *in-* and the suffix *-ator.*

Grammar Focus

Study Complex Sentences with Dependent Clauses

Demonstrate knowledge of clauses Write on the board: *When I got home, I did my homework.* Point out the dependent clause. (When I got home) Ask students to substitute other dependent clauses. Have small groups find sentences with dependent clauses in paragraphs 4 and 5.

Answers

1. Examples can be found in paragraphs 1, 4, 9, 11, and 12.

ASSESS

Have students combine these sentences by using a dependent clause: *Yang met Matthew. They became good friends.* (When Yang met Matthew, they became good friends.)

Word Study

Define Words with a Latin Root

Many English words and spellings come from other languages and cultures. For example, the word *respect* has the word part *spect. Spect* comes from the Latin word *spectare* that means "to look." (People who lived in Rome long ago spoke Latin.) The word *respect* means "to look at with honor."

Word	Meaning
re**spect**	to look at with honor
in**spect**	to look at closely
spectator	someone who watches something

Personal Dictionary

Activity Book *p. 28*

Student CD-ROM

1. Copy the words and definitions in the chart in your Personal Dictionary.
2. Work with a partner to write three sentences. Include one *spect* word in each sentence.

Grammar Focus

Study Complex Sentences with Dependent Clauses

A **clause** is a part of a sentence. It has a subject (S) and a verb (V).

Dependent Clause	Main Clause
When I study hard, ↑ (S) ↑ (V) ↑ (comma)	I get good grades.

Main clauses can be sentences by themselves. **Dependent clauses** must be used with main clauses. They cannot stand alone.

Dependent clauses can start with time words like *when, after, before, as soon as,* and *while.*

Before I got used to the American school, the other kids laughed at some of the things I did.

When the dependent clause comes first, a comma is used.

As soon as I finish**,** I will call you.

I will call you as soon as I finish.

1. Find other examples of sentences from the reading with clauses. Look in paragraphs 1, 4, 9, 11, 12.
2. Write three sentences with dependent clauses and main clauses. Use correct punctuation.

Activity Book *pp. 29–30*

Student Handbook

Student CD-ROM

52 Unit 1 Challenges

MULTI-LEVEL OPTIONS *From Reading to Writing*

Newcomer Have students draw a sequence of events about their first-person narratives. Help them write a caption for each picture. Remind them to use the pronouns *I, me, we,* and *us* and to put their drawings in order. Then have them share their narratives in small groups.

Beginning Have students fill in the chart on p. 53 with key words or short sentences for their first-person narratives. Help them create a story map to clarify the structure. Let them read their narratives in small groups. Have groups suggest ideas for additional colloquial speech.

Intermediate Have students prepare an outline of their first-person narratives from their completed charts. Discuss outlines individually. Monitor use of the features of a narrative: beginning, middle, end; pronouns; and a problem that is faced. Have students share narratives in small groups.

Advanced Have students prepare an outline of their first-person narratives from their completed charts. Tell them to write a draft to share in small groups. Direct groups to make suggestions for improving structure, using personal pronouns, and adding colloquial speech and dependent clauses.

From Reading to Writing 

Write a First-Person Narrative

Write a first-person narrative about a challenge you are facing. A challenge usually involves a problem. Tell how you will resolve the problem.

1. Use the first-person pronouns *I*, *me*, *we*, and *us*.
2. Use direct and indirect characterization.
3. Write sentences with dependent and independent clauses. Use correct punctuation.
4. Be sure your narrative has a beginning, a middle, and an end.

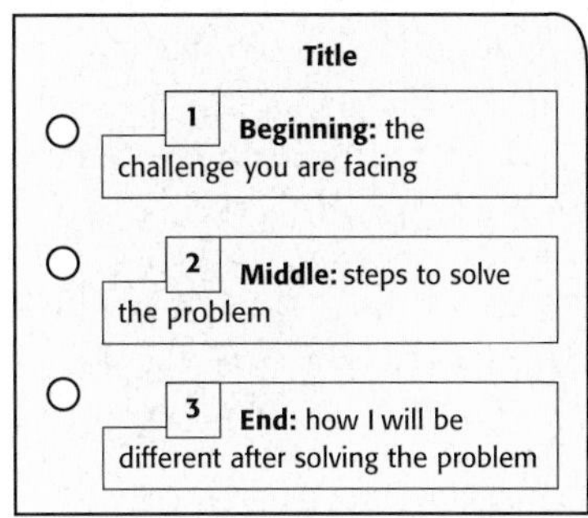

Activity Book
p. 31

Across Content Areas 

Learn the Meanings of *Culture*

The word **culture** has two main meanings when it applies to people. Read this dictionary entry:

> **cul•ture** /'kʌl+ʃər/ *n.* **1** the ideas, activities (art, foods, businesses), and ways of behaving that are special to a country, people, or region: *In North American culture, men do not kiss men when meeting each other. They shake hands.* **2** the achievements of a people or nation in art, music, literature, etc.: *The Chinese have had a high culture for thousands of years.||She is a person of culture and refinement.*

Read these sentences. Decide which definition—**1** or **2**—matches each sentence.

1. My sister goes to museums a lot because she loves art.
2. In many East Asian countries, most people eat with chopsticks.
3. Jazz music originated in the United States.
4. In Mexico, taking a siesta (a short nap) after lunch used to be common.

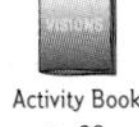

Activity Book
p. 32

Reteach and Reassess

Text Structure Have students compare and contrast the features of the historical narrative on p. 30 with a first-person narrative. Use a Venn diagram to compare the features.

Reading Strategy Have students select an event from "Yang the Youngest" to compare to a personal experience of their own.

Elements of Literature Have students read paragraphs from "Yang the Youngest" in groups. Tell them to identify examples of direct and indirect characterization.

Reassess Have students write a paragraph that is a first-person narrative. Tell them to write about an event in "Yang the Youngest" from a different character's point of view (for example: Third Sister or Jake).

From Reading to Writing

Write a First-Person Narrative

1. **Brainstorm** Have students brainstorm a list of topics for their first-person narratives. Remind them to write down all their ideas. Have them pick the idea they like best.
2. **Think-Quickwrite-Pair-Share** Ask students to think about their topics and write as much as they can on the chart. In pairs, have students share their stories. Direct students to try to include examples of direct and indirect language to describe their feelings.
3. **Multi-level options** See MULTI-LEVEL OPTIONS on p. 52.

Across Content Areas: Social Studies

Learn the Meanings of *Culture*

Define and connect Explain the two meanings of *culture. Ask: How do people greet each other in the American culture?* (shake hands, wave) *Do you know how people greet each other in other cultures?* (bow, kiss) Discuss other differences between cultures in behavior at school, with relatives, in public places, and so on.

Answers
1. 2 2. 1 3. 2 4. 1

ASSESS

Have students write two sentences or draw pictures indicating the different meanings of culture.

Assessment Program: *Unit 1, Chapter 4 Quiz, pp. 13–14*

UNIT 1 • CHAPTER 5
Into the Reading

Chapter Materials

Activity Book: *pp. 33–40*
Audio: *Unit 1, Chapter 5*
Student Handbook
Student CD-ROM: *Unit 1, Chapter 5*
Teacher Resource Book: *Lesson Plan, Teacher Resources, Reading Summary, Activity Book Answer Key*
Teacher Resource CD-ROM
Assessment Program: *Quiz, pp. 15–16; Teacher and Student Resources, pp. 115–144*
Assessment CD-ROM
Transparencies
The Heinle Newbury House Dictionary/CD-ROM
Web Site: www.heinle.visions.com

Objectives

Teacher think aloud Read the first objective. *Say: I know that* main *means something very important, so the main idea must be an important idea in the story.*

Use Prior Knowledge

Discuss Awards

Gather and organize Explain that students will gather and organize information about events and awards. Have students share experiences about awards they have won.

Answers

2. *Examples:* medal, blue ribbon, trophy, certificate, money, gift certificate.

CHAPTER 5

The Scholarship Jacket

a short story
by Marta Salinas

Into the Reading

Objectives

Reading Find the main idea and details as you read a short story.

Listening and Speaking Debate issues.

Grammar Use *could* and *couldn't* for past ability.

Writing Write a short story.

Content Science: Learn about nutrition.

Use Prior Knowledge

Discuss Awards

An award is a prize or a special honor. The main character in this selection believes that she will win an award. Have you ever worked hard to win a prize or special honor?

1. Work in a small group.
2. On a piece of paper, list as many awards as you can.
3. Identify what a person needs to do in order to win the award. For example, in a footrace, a person needs to cross the finish line first.
4. Copy the chart. Complete it with information about how the awards are won.

Event	Prize	How You Win It
Essay Contest	1st place ribbon	Write the best essay
Soccer	1st place trophy	
Spelling Contest	1st place trophy	

5. Many people all over the world work hard to win awards. Discuss with a partner why this is a common theme in many cultures.

MULTI-LEVEL OPTIONS *Build Vocabulary*

Newcomer As you read sentence 1 aloud, mime *fidgeted.* Then read the answer choices *a* and *b* and mime the answers. Have the group decide which answer is correct. Repeat the process for the remaining sentences. Have students practice the new words in pairs.

Beginning As you read sentence 1 aloud, mime *fidgeted.* Then read the answer choices *a* and *b.* Ask volunteers to mime the choices. Have the group decide which answer is correct. Repeat the process for the remaining sentences. Have students say sentences with the new words as others mime the meaning.

Intermediate After students complete the exercises, have them rewrite the underlined text using an alternate phrase. For example*: I played nervously with the papers. . . .*

Advanced Have students complete the activity and check it with a partner. Then tell each student to write sentences to describe a time when they fidgeted, despaired, and were in shock.

Build Background

School Traditions

Schools around the world have special traditions or customs. Some schools give awards to the best student. Others put pictures of the best athletes up on a wall. One tradition in schools in the United States is to give a jacket that has the initial, or first letter, of the school's name on it. For example, if your school is called Martinez School, the initial would be *M.*

Discuss school traditions with a partner. Describe traditions you know about from your school or schools in other cultures.

Content Connection

The valedictorian is the student in the graduating class who has the best grades. The valedictorian sometimes gives a speech on graduation day.

Build Vocabulary

Learn Words About Emotions

In "The Scholarship Jacket," the characters show their emotions. With a partner, read these sentences and choose the best explanation for the underlined words in each one. Check your answers in a dictionary.

1. I fidgeted with the papers on my desk because I didn't know what to say.
   a. I was happy.
   b. I was nervous.
2. I despaired every time I thought about the race. I knew I couldn't win.
   a. I had no hope.
   b. I felt excited.
3. When I won the contest, I was in shock.
   a. I was very surprised.
   b. I was very tired.

Write the words *fidget, despair,* and *in shock* in your Personal Dictionary, along with their meanings.

Personal Dictionary

The Heinle Newbury House Dictionary

Activity Book *p. 33*

Student CD-ROM

Home Connection

Build Background Discuss holidays in the United States, such as Thanksgiving or Independence Day. Give examples of traditional meals and events. Ask students if they know of holidays in other countries. Have them share about ways they celebrate holidays at home. Direct students to draw pictures of how they celebrate holidays.

Learning Styles ***Musical***

Build Background Tell students to find the lyrics to the school song or write one of their own. Have them perform for themselves or for another class.

Build Background

School Traditions

1. **Relate to personal experiences** Have students give examples of special traditions in your school. Point out any colors, songs, or mascots, that are part of the school tradition.
2. **Content Connection** The word *valedictorian* comes from Latin. It means "the one who says good-bye," or gives the final speech at graduation. ***Ask:*** *What would you say at a graduation speech?*

Build Vocabulary

Learn Words About Emotions

Teacher Resource Book: *Personal Dictionary, p. 63*

1. **Use experiences** Act out the vocabulary words as you explain situations that cause these feelings. ***Say:*** *I didn't have my homework. I didn't want the teacher to know, so I looked through my papers and moved my pencil around. I fidgeted.* Ask students to share times when they fidget.
2. **Clarify meaning and usage** Have students use a print, online, and CD-ROM dictionary and thesaurus to clarify the meaning and usage of the new words.
3. **Reading selection vocabulary** You may want to introduce the glossed words in the reading selection before students begin reading. Key words: *scholarship, agile, coincidence, appreciate, expectation, eager, adrenaline.* Instruct students to write the words with correct spelling and their definitions in their Personal Dictionaries. Have them pronounce each word and divide it into syllables.
4. **Multi-level options** See MULTI-LEVEL OPTIONS on p. 54.

Answers
1. b **2.** a **3.** a

ASSESS

Have students write a sentence for each of the vocabulary words.

Into the Reading

Text Structure

Short Story

1. **Define and explain** Ask information questions to identify the features. For example, ***ask:*** *What comes at the beginning of the story?* (main problem)
2. **Multi-level options** See MULTI-LEVEL OPTIONS below.

Reading Strategy

Find the Main Idea and Details

Teacher Resource Book: *Two-Column Chart, p. 44*

Use a graphic organizer Use a two-column chart and label the columns *Main Idea* and *Details.* Then fill in an example. ***Say:*** *I love music.* (main idea) *I listen to the radio; I sing with my sister; I play the guitar.* (details)

Answers

1. *Sample answer:* Main idea: The main character wants to win the scholarship jacket. Details: Her sister won it. She is a good student. She can't get a sports school jacket.
2. *Sample answer:* The details are all about the girl wanting the scholarship jacket.

ASSESS

Ask: *What are four features of a short story?* (characters, main problem, dialogue, narration)

Text Structure

Short Story

"The Scholarship Jacket" is a **short story.** Short stories develop the characters and action very quickly. Look at the chart. It shows some features of a short story.

Short Story	
Characters	a few are presented in the story
Main Problem	comes at the beginning of the story
Narration	the author's words that describe the action and the characters
Dialogue	the words that the characters speak; the words are in quotation marks (" . . . ")

1. As you read "The Scholarship Jacket," notice how the writer carefully develops the characters and the story.
2. Stop at the end of each page and ask yourself, "What do I know about Martha? What is happening now?"

Student CD-ROM

Reading Strategy

Find the Main Idea and Details

The **main idea** of a paragraph is the most important idea in the paragraph. The **details** include all the information that helps you understand the main idea.

Sometimes the author does not directly state the main idea. When this happens, you have to find it by paying attention to the details. Ask yourself, "What topic do the details share?"

1. Read paragraph 2 of "The Scholarship Jacket," on page 58. What is the paragraph's main idea? What are the details that you find?
2. Think about what the details tell you. How do they support the main idea?

Student CD-ROM

MULTI-LEVEL OPTIONS *Reading Strategy*

Newcomer Bring in a picture with a clear central focus, such as a sporting event or a rescue. ***Ask:*** *What is the most important thing in this picture? That's the main idea.* Then point to a specific item such as the type of clothing or equipment being used. ***Say:*** *This is a detail. Can you find other details?*

Beginning Bring in a picture with a clear central focus, such as a sporting event or a rescue. Write these sentence starters: *This is a picture of* ______. *I also see* ______ *and* ______. Have students complete the sentences and share them with a partner.

Intermediate/Advanced Have an intermediate and an advanced student work together in pairs to do a reciprocal reading. Tell them to identify the main idea and at least two details.

THE SCHOLARSHIP JACKET

a short story by Marta Salinas

57

Reading Selection

Reading Selection Materials

Audio: *Unit 1, Chapter 5*
Teacher Resource Book: *Reading Summary, pp. 73–74*

Preview the Selection

1. **Use the illustration** Have students describe the picture. ***Ask:*** *Who is the girl? Where is she? What is she doing? Do you think she is a good student? Why? Why do you think she is studying so hard?*
2. **Relate to personal experiences** ***Ask:*** *Is this the way you study? What is the same? What is different? Why is it important to study?*
3. **Connect** Have students suggest what kind of challenges might be in a story about a scholarship jacket. ***Ask:*** *What do you think a scholarship jacket is? What will be the problem in the story? Why do you think so?*

Cultural Connection

Tell students that sports fans in the U.S. like to display their support for teams. Some fans dress up as the team mascot; they have special cheers; or they wear caps with their team logos. Ask students if they know the ways fans display their support for teams in other countries. Have them draw a comparison chart.

Learning Styles ***Linguistic***

Have students work in pairs to create a role-play between a student award winner and the school principal. The award can be for sports, for music, or for an essay contest. Ask students to think about how a principal might announce the award, discuss what the award means to the school, or praise the student. Each role-play must have at least three exchanges. Have pairs present their role-plays to small groups.

Reading Selection

Read the Selection

1. **Use the illustration** Help students describe the girl in the picture. Have them guess what she is thinking about. Ask them to compare how the girl is feeling in the picture and in her dreams.
2. **Teacher read aloud** Read paragraphs 1 and 2 aloud.
3. **Find the main idea and details** In pairs, have students reread the paragraphs. ***Ask:*** *Is the first paragraph about the girl or about a jacket?* (a jacket) *What do you know about the jacket?* (It's green and gold. It's for the student with the highest grades. It has a large gold *S* and the student's name.) Use a cluster map to record the main idea and details.

Sample Answer to Guide Question
The main idea is that the girl wants to win the scholarship jacket.

See Teacher Edition pp. 434–435 for a list of English-Spanish cognates in the reading selection.

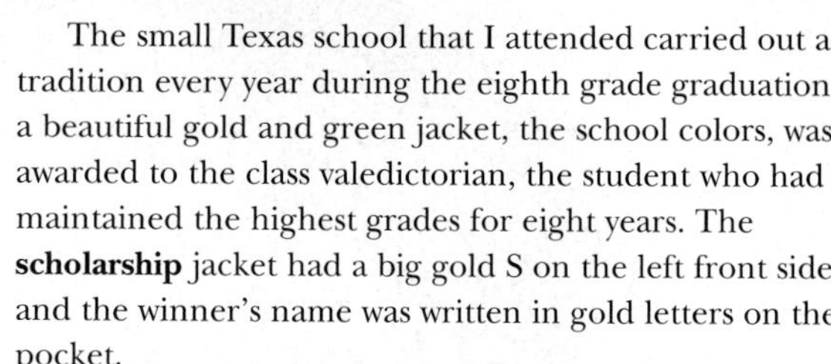

Audio

1 The small Texas school that I attended carried out a tradition every year during the eighth grade graduation; a beautiful gold and green jacket, the school colors, was awarded to the class valedictorian, the student who had maintained the highest grades for eight years. The **scholarship** jacket had a big gold S on the left front side and the winner's name was written in gold letters on the pocket.

Find the Main Idea and Details

What is the main idea of this paragraph?

2 My oldest sister Rosie had won the jacket a few years back and I fully expected to win also. I was fourteen and in the eighth grade. I had been a straight A student since the first grade, and the last year I had looked forward to owning that jacket. My father was a farm laborer who couldn't earn enough money to feed eight children, so when I was six I was given to my grandparents to raise. We couldn't participate in sports at school because there were registration fees, uniform costs, and trips out of town; so even though we were quite **agile** and athletic, there would never be a sports school jacket for us. This one, the scholarship jacket, was our only chance.

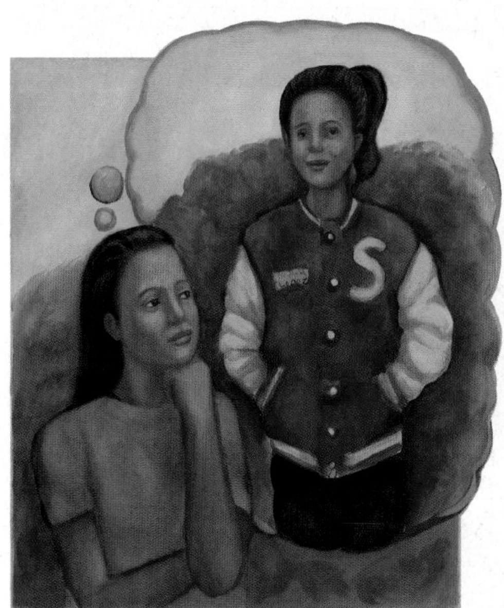

3 In May, close to graduation, **spring fever** struck, and no one paid any attention in class; instead we stared out the windows and at each other, wanting to speed up the last few weeks of school.

scholarship study, schoolwork
agile quick, able to move well
spring fever a feeling of great energy due to the warm weather of spring

MULTI-LEVEL OPTIONS *Read the Selection*

Newcomer Play the audio. Encourage students to whisper-read as they listen. ***Ask:*** *Does Martha think she will win the scholarship jacket?* (yes) *Is her father poor?* (yes) *Can she win a jacket for sports?* (no) *Does she think she's good-looking?* (no) *Does she hear her teachers arguing?* (yes)

Beginning Play the audio. Then have students do a paired reading. ***Ask:*** *What does the girl want to win?* (the scholarship jacket) *Who is raising her?* (her grandparents) *What do other kids call her?* (beanpole, string bean) *What does she overhear?* (teachers arguing about her)

Intermediate Do a paired reading. ***Ask:*** *Why does the girl think she'll win the jacket?* (She got straight A's for eight years.) *Who won it two years ago?* (her sister) *Why does everyone have trouble concentrating in class?* (It's close to graduation.) *What are her teachers arguing about?* (Martha)

Advanced Have students do a think-quickwrite-pair-share to explore the reading selection. ***Ask:*** *Why is it so important for the girl to win the jacket?* (It's the only jacket she can win.) *Why can't she win a jacket for sports?* (She can't afford to pay for fees, uniforms, or trips out of town, so she can't join a team.)

I despaired every time I looked in the mirror. Pencil thin, not a curve anywhere, I was called "Beanpole" and "String Bean" and I knew that's what I looked like. A flat chest, no hips, and a brain, that's what I had. That really isn't much for a fourteen-year-old to work with, I thought, as I **absentmindedly** wandered from my history class to the gym. Another hour of sweating in basketball and displaying my toothpick legs was coming up. Then I remembered my P.E. shorts were still in a bag under my desk where I'd forgotten them. I had to walk all the way back and get them. Coach Thompson was a real bear if anyone wasn't dressed for **P.E.** She had said I was a good forward and once she even tried to talk Grandma into letting me join the team. Grandma, of course, said no.

Find the Main Idea and Details

How does the style (look and feeling) of the illustration help express the main idea of this paragraph?

4 I was almost back at my classroom's door when I heard angry voices and arguing. I stopped. I didn't mean to **eavesdrop;** I just hesitated, not knowing what to do. I needed those shorts and I was going to be late, but I didn't want to interrupt an argument between my teachers. I recognized the voices: Mr. Schmidt, my history teacher, and Mr. Boone, my math teacher. They seemed to be arguing about me. I couldn't believe it. I still remember the shock that rooted me flat against the wall as if I were trying to blend in with the graffiti written there.

absentmindedly without one's mind on the task, thinking about other things

P.E. physical education or gym class

eavesdrop listen in on another person's conversation

Read the Selection

1. **Understand terms** Have students find the meanings of the glossed words at the bottom of the page. Clarify meanings as needed.
2. **Reciprocal reading** Play the audio of paragraphs 3 and 4. Arrange students in groups for reciprocal reading. Assign each student a different portion of the selection. Students should read aloud the portion, answer questions of others in the group, and summarize.
3. **Find the main idea and details** Ask questions to help students identify the main idea and the details that support it.
4. **Multi-level options** See MULTI-LEVEL OPTIONS on p. 58.

Sample Answer to Guide Question

The illustration shows two scenes. This shows that two events are happening at the same time. Two of Martha's teachers are arguing and Martha is watching them. The picture of the teachers is smaller than the one of Martha. This shows that the teachers' argument is a detail and how Martha feels about it is the main idea.

Punctuation

Commas in appositives

Tell students that appositives give extra information about a person, place, or thing. Instruct students to put a comma before and after appositives. On the board, write: *Mr. Schmidt, my history teacher, is in the hall.* ***Ask:*** *What part of the sentence is an appositive?* (my history teacher) *Who does it give extra information about?* (Mr. Schmidt) *What punctuation is before and after it?* (commas) Direct students to the last sentence in paragraph 2. ***Ask:*** *What is the appositive?* (the scholarship jacket) *What does it give extra information about?* (this one) *What punctuation is before and after it?* (commas). Ask students to pay attention to sentences with appositives as they read the selection.

UNIT 1 • CHAPTER 5
Reading Selection

Read the Selection

Paired reading Have students read the selection in pairs. Monitor their comprehension. *Ask: What does Mr. Boone want Mr. Schmidt to do?* (He wants him to lie or change some records.) *Why?* (Joann's father is on the School Board and owns a store.)

Sample Answer to Guide Question

The details are important because they explain the reason Mr. Boone wants to change the records. Mr. Boone is telling Mr. Schmidt that Joann's father is important to the school and the town. He thinks the school should give special treatment to Joann.

5 "I refuse to do it! I don't care who her father is, her grades don't even begin to compare to Martha's. I won't lie or **falsify** records. Martha has a straight A plus average and you know it." That was Mr. Schmidt and he sounded very angry. Mr. Boone's voice sounded calm and quiet.

6 "Look, Joann's father is not only on the Board, he owns the only store in town; we could say it was a close tie and—"

7 The pounding in my ears drowned out the rest of the words, only a word here and there filtered through. ". . . Martha is Mexican. . . . **resign**. . . . won't do it. . . ." Mr. Schmidt came rushing out, and luckily for me went down the opposite way toward the **auditorium,** so he didn't see me. Shaking, I waited a few minutes and then went in and grabbed my bag and fled from the room. Mr. Boone looked up when I came in but didn't say anything. To this day I don't remember if I got in trouble in P.E. for being late or how I made it through the rest of the afternoon. I went home very sad and cried into my pillow that night so grandmother wouldn't hear me. It seemed a cruel **coincidence** that I had overheard that conversation.

Find the Main Idea and Details

How are the details about Joann's father important to the main idea of Mr. Boone's message? What is the main idea or meaning of his words to Mr. Schmidt?

---

falsify make false, change to say something untrue
resign choose to leave one's job
auditorium a large room with seats as in a theater
coincidence a combination of events that happens by chance but seems arranged or planned

MULTI-LEVEL OPTIONS *Read the Selection*

Newcomer *Ask: Does Mr. Schmidt want Martha to get the jacket?* (yes) *Does Mr. Boone want her to get the jacket?* (no) *Does Mr. Schmidt say he won't lie?* (yes) *Is Joann's father on the Board?* (yes) *Is Martha a Mexican girl?* (yes) *Did the jacket always cost $15?* (no)

Beginning *Ask: Which teacher wants Martha to get the jacket?* (Mr. Schmidt) *Which teacher doesn't want her to get it?* (Mr. Boone) *What does Mr. Schmidt say he won't do?* (lie) *What does Mr. Boone say about Joann's father?* (He's on the School Board. He owns the only store in town.) *How much does the jacket cost this year?* ($15)

Intermediate *Ask: Why is Mr. Schmidt angry?* (He's been asked to lie about who has the best grades.) *Why does Mr. Boone want to give the jacket to Joann?* (He wants to please Joann's father.) *Why won't the principal look Martha in the eye?* (He knows that what he is doing is wrong.)

Advanced *Ask: What does Mr. Boone want Mr. Schmidt to do so Joann gets the jacket?* (He wants Mr. Boone to say Joann's grades are better than Martha's.) *What reasons does he give?* (Joann's father is important. Martha is a Mexican.) *Why is the price of the jacket raised to $15?* (so Martha can't buy it, but Joann can)

Find the Main Idea and Details

The speaker tells us that the principal fidgeted with his papers. How does this detail help you identify the main idea in this paragraph?

8 The next day when the principal called me into his office, I knew what it would be about. He looked uncomfortable and unhappy. I decided I wasn't going to make it any easier for him so I looked him straight in the eye. He looked away and fidgeted with the papers on his desk.

9 "Martha," he said, "there's been a change in policy this year regarding the scholarship jacket. As you know, it has always been free." He cleared his throat and continued. "This year the Board decided to charge fifteen dollars—which still won't cover the complete cost of the jacket."

10 I stared at him in shock and a small sound of **dismay** escaped my throat. I hadn't expected this. He still avoided looking in my eyes.

11 "So if you are unable to pay the fifteen dollars for the jacket, it will be given to the next one in line."

dismay unhappiness, shock

Read the Selection

1. **Shared reading** Continue reading the story by reading aloud as students follow along. Ask pairs to join in by reading different parts. *Ask: What did the principal tell Martha about the scholarship jacket?* (The School Board had changed the policy. They wanted to charge $15 for it.) *How did Martha feel about that?* (She was shocked.)
2. **Role-play** Have pairs of students read the selection, practicing the dialogue in the story. Ask students to predict what they think Martha will do.
3. **Multi-level options** See MULTI-LEVEL OPTIONS on p. 60.

Sample Answer to Guide Question

The principal fidgets because he is nervous and does not feel right about the School Board's decision.

Punctuation

Use ellipses for omitted text

Tell students that sometimes they will see three periods together in a sentence. This is called an ellipsis. They tell the reader that some words have been left out. Direct them to paragraph 7 and play the audio. Ask them to guess some of the missing words.

Apply Have students work in pairs. Work with each pair to select a conversation. Remind them that direct speech always begins and ends with quotation marks. Have them rewrite the sentences, replacing a few phrases with ellipses. Direct them to trade papers with another pair. Have the other pair try to remember or guess the missing text.

Reading Selection

Read the Selection

1. **Reciprocal reading** Read the Reading Summary aloud. Arrange students in groups for reciprocal reading. Assign each student a different portion of the selection. Students should read aloud the portion, answer questions of others in the group, and help summarize the selection.
2. **Identify main problem** Have students work in pairs to identify the main problem of this short story. *Ask: How do you think this problem will be solved? Why?*

Sample Answer to Guide Question

The jacket is a symbol of her hard work and achievement. Martha has been working for the jacket ever since she started school.

12 Standing with all the **dignity** I could **muster,** I said, "I'll speak to my grandfather about it, sir, and let you know tomorrow." I cried on the walk home from the bus stop. The dirt road was a quarter of a mile from the highway, so by the time I got home, my eyes were red and puffy.

13 "Where's Grandpa?" I asked Grandma, looking down at the floor so she wouldn't ask me why I'd been crying. She was sewing on a quilt and didn't look up.

14 "I think he's out back working in the bean field."

15 I went outside and looked out at the fields. There he was. I could see him walking between the rows, his body bent over the little plants, hoe in hand. I walked slowly out to him, trying to think how I could best ask him for the money. There was a cool breeze blowing and a sweet smell of mesquite in the air, but I didn't **appreciate** it. I kicked at a dirt clod. I wanted that jacket so much. It was more than just being a valedictorian and giving a little thank you speech for the jacket on graduation night. It represented eight years of hard work and **expectation.** I knew I had to be honest with Grandpa; it was my only chance. He saw me and looked up.

Find the Main Idea and Details

Why is the jacket so important to Martha? How do the details "eight years of hard work and expectation" help you understand the main idea?

dignity pride
muster collect, find
appreciate enjoy
expectation hope, desire

MULTI-LEVEL OPTIONS *Read the Selection*

Newcomer *Ask: Does Martha cry on the way home?* (yes) *Does she talk to her grandfather?* (yes) *Does he ask her what happened?* (yes) *Does he give her the $15?* (no)

Beginning *Ask: What does Martha do on the way home?* (cries) *Who does she go to talk to?* (her grandfather) *What does she tell him?* (that the jacket now costs $15) *What does he tell Martha?* (to say to her principal that he will not pay the $15)

Intermediate *Ask: Why is Martha so upset?* (She knows she deserves the jacket after eight years of hard work.) *Why does she speak to her grandfather in Spanish?* (It is the only language he speaks.) *How does she feel when she tells her grandfather what happened?* (nervous, desperate, hopeful)

Advanced *Ask: Why does Martha feel that being honest with her grandpa is her only hope?* (He will give her the money if she has a good reason.) *What does he ask her?* (to explain what the jacket means to her) *What does Martha realize?* (Getting the jacket is meaningful only if it is earned; paying money for it would make it worthless.)

Find the Main Idea and Details

Do you think Grandpa will give her the money for the jacket? What details make you think this?

16 He waited for me to speak. I cleared my throat nervously and clasped my hands behind my back so he wouldn't see them shaking. "Grandpa, I have a big favor to ask you," I said in Spanish, the only language he knew. He still waited silently. I tried again. "Grandpa, this year the principal said the scholarship jacket is not going to be free. It's going to cost fifteen dollars and I have to take the money in tomorrow, otherwise it'll be given to someone else." The last words came out in an **eager** rush. Grandpa straightened up tiredly and leaned his chin on the hoe handle. He looked out over the field that was filled with the tiny green bean plants. I waited, desperately hoping he'd say I could have the money.

17 He turned to me and asked quietly, "What does a scholarship jacket mean?"

18 I answered quickly; maybe there was a chance. "It means you've earned it by having the highest grades for eight years and that's why they're giving it to you." Too late I realized the **significance** of my words. Grandpa knew that I understood it was not a matter of money. It wasn't that. He went back to hoeing the weeds that sprang up between the **delicate** little bean plants. It was a **time consuming** job; sometimes the small shoots were right next to each other. Finally he spoke again.

19 "Then if you pay for it, Marta, it's not a scholarship jacket, is it? Tell your principal I will not pay the fifteen dollars."

eager hurried, fast, excited
significance importance
delicate fragile, easily broken
time consuming taking a lot of time

Read the Selection

1. **Shared reading** Read or ask a volunteer to read aloud paragraphs 16–19 as students follow along in their books. Tell students to join in at the end of sentences. ***Ask:*** *How does Martha feel when she asks her grandfather?* (nervous) *Did he answer her?* (no) *What question did he ask Martha?* (What does a scholarship jacket mean?) *How did Martha explain the scholarship jacket?* (It's something you earn, not buy.)
2. **Role-play** Have pairs of students read the selection. Tell them to select a dialogue in the story to present to the class. Ask students to predict how Martha is going to react to her grandfather's answer.
3. **Multi-level options** See MULTI-LEVEL OPTIONS on p. 62.

Sample Answer to Guide Question

I don't think he will give her the money. He doesn't answer Martha right away.

Spelling

Words with the long *e* sounds

Write on the board and ***Say:*** *speak* and *sweet.* Ask students what vowel sound they hear. (long *e*) Explain that the letters *ea* or *ee* are long vowels that are both pronounced /ee/.

Apply Create a two-column chart labeled *ea/ee.* Direct students to complete the chart with words from paragraphs 12–18 of the selection. (12: speak; 14: bean; 15: breeze, speech; 16: free, fifteen, eager, leaned, green; 17: mean; 18: weeds, each) Have students write five sentences using the words from their charts. Ask them to read their sentences in small groups.

UNIT 1 • CHAPTER 5
Reading Selection

Read the Selection

1. **Reciprocal reading** Play the audio. Then arrange students in groups for reciprocal reading. After assigning each student a different portion of the selection, students should read aloud the portion. Have others ask questions for the "leader" to answer.
2. **Find the main idea and details** Help students to identify the main idea in each paragraph.

Sample Answer to Guide Question
"very sad and withdrawn" and "who dragged into the principal's office . . ."

20 I walked back to the house and locked myself in the bathroom for a long time. I was angry with grandfather even though I knew he was right, and I was angry with the Board, whoever they were. Why did they have to change the rules just when it was my turn to win the jacket?

Find the Main Idea and Details

What words help you understand how Martha is feeling in this paragraph?

21 It was a very sad and **withdrawn** girl who dragged into the principal's office the next day. This time he did look me in the eyes.

22 "What did your grandfather say?"

23 I sat very straight in my chair.

24 "He said to tell you he won't pay the fifteen dollars."

25 The principal **muttered** something I couldn't understand under his breath, and walked over to the window. He stood looking out at something outside. He looked bigger than usual when he stood up; he was a tall **gaunt** man with gray hair, and I watched the back of his head while I waited for him to speak.

---

withdrawn silent, not wanting to talk to anyone, unhappy

muttered complained, spoken unclearly or quietly

gaunt very thin

MULTI-LEVEL OPTIONS *Read the Selection*

Newcomer *Ask: Was Martha happy with her grandfather and the Board?* (no) *Did she tell the principal she had the money?* (no) *Did she tell him what her grandfather had said to her?* (yes) *Did the principal tell her that she would get the jacket anyway?* (yes)

Beginning *Ask: How did Martha feel toward her grandfather and the Board?* (angry) *What did she tell the principal?* (Her grandfather wouldn't pay for the jacket.) *What did the principal finally say?* (She could have it anyway.)

Intermediate *Ask: Why was Martha angry on the way to school?* (She wanted the jacket, but her grandfather and the Board were standing in her way.) *What did she tell the principal that her grandpa said about the jacket?* (that it wasn't a scholarship jacket if Martha had to pay for it)

Advanced *Ask: Why was the principal disappointed when Martha didn't bring the money?* (He believed Martha deserved the jacket but was ordered to charge her money.) *Why did the principal stop her before she left?* (because he knew that she had earned the jacket)

26 "Why?" he finally asked. "Your grandfather has the money. Doesn't he own a small bean farm?"

27 I looked at him, forcing my eyes to stay dry. "He said if I had to pay for it, then it wouldn't be a scholarship jacket," I said and stood up to leave. "I guess you'll just have to give it to Joann." I hadn't meant to say that; it had just slipped out. I was almost to the door when he stopped me.

28 "Martha—wait."

29 I turned and looked at him, waiting. What did he want now? I could feel my heart pounding. Something bitter and **vile** tasting was coming up in my mouth; I was afraid I was going to be sick. I didn't need any sympathy speeches. He sighed loudly and went back to his big desk. He looked at me, biting his lip, as if thinking.

30 "Okay. We'll make an exception in your case. I'll tell the Board, you'll get your jacket."

Find the Main Idea and Details

What is the main emotion of this paragraph? How do Martha and the principal feel? Use details from the paragraph to support your ideas.

---

vile terrible

UNIT 1 • CHAPTER 5
Reading Selection

Read the Selection

1. **Student read aloud** Ask volunteers to read aloud paragraphs 26–30 as students follow along in their books. ***Ask:*** *What did Martha expect the principal to say?* (She expected him to say he was sorry.) *What did he say?* (that Martha would get the jacket)
2. **Role-play** Have pairs of students read the selection, practicing the dialogue in the story. Ask students how Martha will react to the principal's statement.
3. **Multi-level options** See MULTI-LEVEL OPTIONS on p. 64.

Sample Answer to Guide Question
The main emotion is sadness and despair. Martha and the principal are very upset about the situation. Martha's heart was pounding. She felt that she was going to be sick. The principal sighed and was biting his lip.

Spelling

Words ending with the sound /k/

Write *back* and *speak* on the board. Explain these rules: To decide if a word should end in *-ck* or *-k*, examine the letters before the final /k/ sound. When a one-syllable word has *one* vowel before the final /k/ sound, the word ends in *-ck* (lock, back). When a one-syllable word has *two* vowels before the final /k/ sound, the word ends in *-k* (speak, book). When the letter before the final /k/ sound in a one-syllable word is a consonant, the word ends in *-k* (walk, desk).

Apply Draw a three-column chart with the headings *1 vowel + /k/, 2 vowels + /k/,* and *1 consonant + /k/.* Write the samples *lock, speak,* and *walk* in the correct columns. Then ask students to find additional examples from the reading selection and from previous selections.

Read the Selection

1. **Reciprocal reading** Listen to the audio of paragraphs 20–25. Then arrange students in groups for reciprocal reading. Assign each student a different portion to read and to lead in group discussions.
2. **Identify characters** Direct small groups of students to make a list of all the characters in the reading. Tell them to identify where they appear in the story (beginning, middle, end). ***Ask:*** *Who do you think is the most important character? Why?*

Sample Answer to Guide Question
Everyone is happy that Martha is going to get what she deserves. She has a hard time speaking. She wanted to run and jump. She was full of energy.

Find the Main Idea and Details

What do you think the main idea of this paragraph is? What details support the main idea?

31 I could hardly believe it. I spoke in a trembling rush. "Oh, thank you sir!" Suddenly I felt great. I didn't know about **adrenaline** in those days, but I knew something was pumping through me, making me feel as tall as the sky. I wanted to yell, jump, run the mile, do something. I ran out so I could cry in the hall where there was no one to see me. At the end of the day, Mr. Schmidt winked at me and said, "I hear you're getting a scholarship jacket this year."

32 His face looked as happy and innocent as a baby's, but I knew better. Without answering I gave him a quick hug and ran to the bus. I cried on the walk home again, but this time because I was so happy. I couldn't wait to tell Grandpa and ran straight to the field. I joined him in the row where he was working and without saying anything I crouched down and started pulling up the weeds with my hands. Grandpa worked alongside me for a few minutes, but he didn't ask what had happened. After I had a little pile of weeds between the rows, I stood up and faced him.

adrenaline a chemical that the body makes when a person is very excited; it gives a boost of energy

MULTI-LEVEL OPTIONS *Read the Selection*

Newcomer ***Ask:*** *Was Martha unhappy after she heard she was getting the jacket?* (no) *Did Martha give Mr. Schmidt a hug?* (yes) *Did she run to the field to see grandfather?* (yes) *Did her grandfather give her a pat on the shoulder and a smile?* (yes)

Beginning ***Ask:*** *How did Martha feel after she learned she was getting the jacket?* (excited) *What did she do when she saw Mr. Schmidt?* (She hugged him.) *Where did she go next?* (to her grandfather's field) *What did her grandfather do when she told him the news?* (He patted her and smiled.)

Intermediate ***Ask:*** *Why did Mr. Schmidt wink at Martha at the end of the day?* (He was happy for her.) *Why did she run straight to the field?* (to tell her grandfather) *Why did she tell her grandfather that she told the principal what he said?* (to let him know that she understood he was right not to pay for the jacket)

Advanced ***Ask:*** *Why did she hug Mr. Schmidt?* (because he always believed she should get the jacket) *Why wasn't she fooled by her grandfather's silence?* (She could tell by his smile and his pat on her shoulder how happy he was for her.)

33 "The principal said he's making an exception for me, Grandpa, and I'm getting the jacket after all. That's after I told him what you said."

34 Grandpa didn't say anything, he just gave me a pat on the shoulder and a smile. He pulled out the crumpled red handkerchief that he always carried in his back pocket and wiped the sweat off his forehead.

35 "Better go see if your grandmother needs any help with supper."

36 I gave him a big grin. He didn't fool me. I skipped and ran back to the house whistling some silly tune.

Find the Main Idea and Details

How would you describe Martha and Grandpa at this point in the story? What details or words tell you how they feel about each other at the end?

About the Author

Marta Salinas (born 1949)

Marta Salinas was born in California. She studied writing and received her degree from the University of California at Irvine. Her short story "The Scholarship Jacket" was first published in *Nosotras: Latina Literature Today,* a collection of works by Hispanic women writers.

➤ Based on this story, how do you think Marta Salinas feels about fighting for fairness?

Spelling

Words ending with *-l* or *-ll*

On the board, write: *still, cool,* and *principal.* Explain these rules: When a one-syllable word ends with a single vowel and the sound /l/, it is spelled *-ll* (still). When a one-syllable word ends with two vowels and the sound /l/, it is spelled *-l* (cool). Words with more than one syllable usually end with a single *-l* (principal). Have students find and explain examples in paragraphs 3 (pencil), 33 (all), and 36 (fool).

Evaluate Your Reading Strategy

Find the Main Idea and Details *Say: You have practiced an important reading strategy. Now you can decide how well you have done. Does this statement describe how you read?*

When I reread a paragraph, I ask myself, "What is this paragraph mostly about?" Finding the main idea helps me remember important information.

Read the Selection

1. **Shared reading** Read or ask volunteers to read paragraphs 33–36 as students follow along in their books. Have groups of students join in for the end of sentences. *Ask: Do you think the grandfather is happy?* (Yes, he patted Martha on the shoulder.)
2. **Role-play** Have pairs of students read the selection. Invite pairs to act out the scene between Martha and her grandfather.
3. **Multi-level options** See MULTI-LEVEL OPTIONS on p. 64.

Sample Answer to Guide Question

Martha and Grandpa are very happy that Martha received the jacket after all. ". . . big grin," ". . . skipped and ran . . . ," ". . . whistling some silly tune."

About the Author

1. **Explain author's background** Marta Salinas has been a strong activist for environmental concerns and social issues. Her story illustrates her concern and belief that people should fight for what is right and that they should expect to be treated fairly.
2. **Interpret the facts** *Ask: What qualities do people need to fight for fairness?*

Answer

Sample answer: Marta Salinas thinks fighting for fairness is very important.

Across Selections

Use a Venn diagram Discuss how Martha's challenge and fight were different from the other challenges faced by people in this unit. *Ask: Was her challenge easier or more difficult than the others? Why do you think so?* Have students record their ideas on a Venn diagram or chart.

Reading Comprehension

Question-Answer Relationships

Sample Answers

1. Martha is the main character.
2. The scholarship jacket.
3. She hears her teachers arguing about who should receive the jacket.
4. Mr. Boone wants to give the jacket to Joann because her father is thought to be more important in the town.
5. Because the school board changed its policy this year.
6. He believes that everyone should be treated fairly. He believes an award should be earned, not bought.
7. This non-verbal language shows that the principal is thinking about something very serious and is burdened by it.
8. Because she wants the jacket and knows he could give her the money.
9. The people who want to give the jacket to Joann are not fair or have been persuaded to do something unjust.
10. I might try to borrow the money from someone else and pay it back later.
11. Yes, he made the right choice. He did what was fair and just and it worked out well in the end.

Build Reading Fluency

Reading Chunks of Words Silently

Assessment Program: *Reading Fluency Chart, p. 116*

When students have completed the reading fluency activity, record their progress in the Reading Fluency Chart.

Beyond the Reading

Reading Comprehension

Question-Answer Relationships (QAR)

"Right There" Questions

1. **Recall Facts** Who is the story's main character?
2. **Explain the Main Idea** What does Martha hope to win?
3. **Recall Facts** What happens when Martha returns to her classroom to get her P.E. clothes?
4. **Recall Facts** To whom does Mr. Boone want to give the scholarship jacket? Why?

"Think and Search" Questions

5. **Summarize** Why does the principal tell Martha that she must pay fifteen dollars for the scholarship jacket?
6. **Analyze Characters** What do you learn about Grandpa when he refuses to pay the fifteen dollars?
7. **Analyze Characters** In paragraph 29, the principal uses nonverbal language: "he sighed loudly . . . biting his lip . . ." What does this nonverbal language tell you about what he is thinking and feeling?

"Author and You" Question

8. **Make an Inference** Why is Martha angry at her grandfather, even though she knows he is right?

"On Your Own" Questions

9. **Draw a Conclusion** What do you think about the people who want to give the jacket to Joann?
10. **Put Yourself in a Character's Place** What would you do in Martha's position?
11. **Express Your Opinion** Did Grandpa make the right choice?

Activity Book p. 34

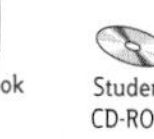
Student CD-ROM

Build Reading Fluency

Reading Chunks of Words Silently

Reading silently is good practice. It helps you learn to read faster.

1. Listen to paragraph 1 of "The Scholarship Jacket" on the Audio CD.
2. Listen to the chunks of words.
3. Reread paragraph 1 silently two times.
4. Your teacher will time your second reading.

MULTI-LEVEL OPTIONS *Elements of Literature*

Newcomer Play the audio of paragraph 4 as students listen. On the board, write: *What made Martha stop? **Say:** Martha didn't go into the classroom. Something made her stop.* Point to the question and ask it again. (She hears her teachers arguing.) Use this format to ask about Martha's motivation in paragraphs 16 and 27.

Beginning Read paragraph 16 aloud. Write on the board: *Why does Martha want to talk to her grandfather?* Have students work in small groups. Ask them to identify two sentences in paragraph 16 that answer the question. ("I wanted that jacket so much. It was more than just being valedictorian. . . .")

Intermediate Explain that finding motivation helps the reader understand the *reason* a character takes an action. Read paragraphs 5–6 aloud. ***Ask:** Why does Mr. Boone want to give the jacket to Joann?* (Her father is on the school board and he is an important person in town.)

Advanced Have students read paragraphs 17–19. ***Say:** Grandfather decides not to pay for the jacket.* Discuss how those paragraphs explain his decision. Assign other characters from the story (Martha, Mr. Boone, Mr. Schmidt) to small groups. Have them find an example of their character's motivation.

Listen, Speak, Interact 

Debate Issues

Should Martha and her grandfather have paid the money for the jacket? Debate this issue with your classmates.

In a debate, some people support one side of an issue. Other people support the other side. Good debaters make the best arguments possible, even if they disagree with the side that they are arguing.

Position	Argument	Facts and Opinions to Support the Position
1	Martha and her grandfather should pay for the jacket.	
2	Martha and her grandfather should not pay for the jacket.	

1. Fill out a chart like this. Be prepared to argue both sides.
2. Present one position in the debate. Be sure to support your position with facts and opinions.
3. Listen to your classmates' arguments. What evidence do your classmates use to support their opinions?
4. How do their opinions compare to yours? Do their arguments cause you to change your opinions? Why or why not?

Elements of Literature

Analyze Character Motivation

Motivation is the reason why a character acts in a certain way. To understand a character's motivation, ask: Why does the character say or do this? For example:

Why does Martha want the scholarship jacket?

She wants to be like her sister.
She wants to make her family proud.

1. Analyze the motivations of the following characters. Write your answers in your Reading Log.
   a. Mr. Boone: Why does he want to give the jacket to Joann?
   b. Grandpa: Why doesn't he want to pay for the jacket?
2. Work with a partner to explain other character motivations in the story. Be sure to look for nonverbal messages such as gestures, facial expressions, and body language (how the person moves his or her body).

Reading Log

Activity Book p. 35

Student CD-ROM

Listen, Speak, Interact

Debate Issues

Teacher Resource Book: *Persuasive—Debate and Writing, p. 51*

1. **Reread in pairs** Pair beginning and advanced students. Have them read alternate paragraphs.
2. **Newcomers** Reread with this group. Point out details to support the different sides in the debate. Write the ideas on the board. Add key words and expressions that students can use to try to persuade others.

Elements of Literature

Analyze Character Motivation

Teacher Resource Book: *Open Mind Diagram, p. 47; Reading Log, p. 64*

1. **Teacher think aloud** *Say: Last night, I went to bed at eight o'clock! What made me go to bed so early? I got up early yesterday and worked all day. I was tired. That was the motivation, or reason, why I went to bed so early.* Provide other examples (went to the nurse, stayed home from school) and have students suggest what might motivate a person to do that.
2. **Use personal experience** Ask students what motivates them to study or play their best in a sport or game.
3. **Multi-level options** See MULTI-LEVEL OPTIONS on p. 68.

Answers

1. a. *Sample answer:* Mr. Boone wants to give the jacket to Joann because her father is on the school board, owns the only store in town, and is a powerful person in their town.
   b. *Sample answer:* Grandpa doesn't want to pay for the jacket because paying for a jacket means it will lose its meaning as an award for the highest grades.

ASSESS

Ask: What motivated Martha to work hard in school for eight years? (the jacket) *What motivated Mr. Boone to try to give the jacket to Joann?* (He wanted to make Joann's father happy.)

Content Connection *Technology*

Have students interview school leaders (principal, coaches, advisors, etc.) to find out what prizes or awards the school gives. Have groups write the names of each prize or award and summarize the requirements for winning. Have them publish the summaries on the school or class web site.

Learning Styles *Interpersonal*

Point out that sometimes a character's motivation isn't *stated* in a text. Assign groups to explore the following questions about motivation: *Why did Mr. Schmidt defend Martha? Why did the principal decide to cancel the $15 fee after all? Why did Mr. Boone think Joann should get the jacket?* Have students share their analysis with another group.

UNIT 1 • CHAPTER 5

Beyond the Reading

Word Study

Identify Root Words

Teacher Resource Book: *Personal Dictionary, p. 63*

Make a word map Write on the board and say *except.* Add the suffix *-ion* and say it. Add *-al* to the map and pronounce it. Add the prefix *un-.* Put the word parts together and pronounce the new words.

Answers
a. expect b. labor c. false d. comfort, happy

Grammar Focus

Use *Could* and *Couldn't* for Past Ability

Use a graphic organizer Make a two-column chart labeled *Now* and *Yesterday.* Ask students about things they can and cannot do. Write them under *Now.* Model the sentences in the past using *could* and *couldn't.* Have students use *could* and *couldn't* to talk about *Now* items. Write the new sentences under *Yesterday.*

ASSESS

On the board, write: *We can play soccer. We can't watch a movie.* Have students rewrite the sentences by adding *Yesterday* and changing the underlined words.

Word Study

Identify Root Words

Root words are the words from which other words are made. You can see the root word inside the larger words.

Root Word	Words Using the Root Word
except	exception, exceptional, unexceptional

Recognizing root words can help you understand and spell the larger words that include them.

1. Look at the underlined words in the following sentences. What root word do you see in them? Write the root words and the larger words in your Personal Dictionary.
   a. The jacket stood for eight years of hard work and expectation.
   b. My father was a farm laborer.
   c. I won't lie or falsify records.
   d. He looked uncomfortable and unhappy.
2. Each time you find a root word inside a larger word, write both words in your Personal Dictionary. This will increase your vocabulary.

Personal Dictionary

Activity Book p. 36

Student CD-ROM

Grammar Focus

Use *Could* and *Couldn't* for Past Ability

Use **could** to describe past abilities. If you were able to do something yesterday, then you *could* do it. If you were not able to do something yesterday, then you *could not* do it.

Sometimes writers combine *could* and *not* into the contraction **couldn't.** For example, "We *couldn't* participate in sports at school."

1. Find other examples of *could* and *couldn't* in the story. See paragraphs 2, 4, 15, and 29.
2. Write one sentence using *could* to describe something you were able to do sometime in the past. Write another sentence using *couldn't* to describe something you were not able to do in the past.

Activity Book pp. 37–38

Student Handbook

Student CD-ROM

MULTI-LEVEL OPTIONS *From Reading to Writing*

Newcomer Brainstorm and write a list of story ideas. Have small groups choose an idea and create a storyboard. Tell them to illustrate the characters, the problem, the actions, and the ending of their stories. Provide key words for each frame. Have them share their stories with another group.

Beginning Brainstorm and write a list of story ideas. Have students work in pairs to choose an idea. Assist pairs in creating a story map. Have students write sentences describing characters, the problem, and the events that happen. Then have students explain the story ending to another pair.

Intermediate Have students use their outlines to expand their ideas into sentences. Remind them to identify characters, the problem, the events that happen, and the ending. Have them meet in groups to respond to one another's work. Tell reviewers to discuss character motivation.

Advanced Direct students to write a first draft from their outlines. Have them share their drafts in pairs. Ask partners to suggest revisions and ways of adding dialogue. Have students complete a final draft to read to a group.

From Reading to Writing 

Write a Short Story

Write a short story about working for something that you want. Use the model to plan the important parts of your story.

1. Be sure your story has a beginning, a middle, and an end.
2. Introduce the characters right away.
3. Introduce the goal quickly.
4. Include only a few events.

Title

1 Beginning
Who are the characters? What are they like? Remember: You are the main character.

2 Middle
What is your goal? What is your motivation? What events take place?

3 End
How do you meet your goal? How does the story end?

Activity Book
p. 39

Across Content Areas 

Learn About Nutrition

Nutrition is the study of how the body needs and uses food. Look at these words related to nutrition.

nutritionist	someone who gives advice about nutrition
nutrient	something in food that feeds the body
nutritious	good for the health of your body

1. Copy these sentences on a piece of paper.
2. Complete each one with the correct word: *nutritionist, nutrient,* or *nutritious.*
   - **a.** Are beans good for you? Many ____ say "Yes!"
   - **b.** Beans are ____ because they contain protein, a ____ that builds muscles and other body tissues.

Reteach and Reassess

Text Structure Have small groups discuss a movie they all know. Have them discuss its characters, its main problem, events that happen, and its ending.

Reading Strategy Have small groups create a "class award." Tell them to explain the purpose of the award and details such as how to win it, when it is given, etc.

Elements of Literature Direct students to write a short description of one character in "The Scholarship Jacket." Remind them to include information about motivation.

Reassess Reread paragraphs 33–35. ***Say:*** *Grandpa doesn't say anything, but Martha knows what he's thinking.* Write a paragraph that describes what Grandpa is thinking.

From Reading to Writing

Write a Short Story

1. **Model an outline** Give students copies of the chart on p. 71. Model planning an outline for a short story as you fill in a sample chart. Talk about students' ideas for the characters, the problem, what happens, and the ending of their stories. Allow students to plan their own outlines.
2. **Think-Quickwrite-Pair-Share** Ask students to use their outlines to quickly write as much as they can. Have students work in pairs to add details and explain what motivates their characters to do certain things.
3. **Multi-level options** See MULTI-LEVEL OPTIONS on p. 70.

Across Content Areas: Science

Learn About Nutrition

1. **Define and clarify** Explain the meanings of *nutrition, nutritionist, nutrient,* and *nutritious.* ***Ask:*** *Which is more nutritious—candy or soup?* (soup) ***Ask:*** *Who knows about good nutrition?* (a nutritionist) Have students check the sides of food packages for examples of nutrients.
2. **Create a record** Have students work in pairs to record their diet for a week. Instruct pairs to choose 5 nutrients they will record. Then have them collaborate to compose and organize a record for these nutrients. After recording information for a week, have pairs revise their records.

Answers
2. **a.** nutritious **b.** nutritious **c.** nutrient

ASSESS

Have students write sentences using *nutritionist, nutrient,* and *nutritious.*

Assessment Program: *Unit 1, Chapter 5 Quiz, pp. 15–16*

UNIT 1
Apply and Expand

Materials

Student Handbook
CNN Video: *Unit 1*
Teacher Resource Book: *Lesson Plan, p. 6; Teacher Resources, pp. 35–64; Video Script, pp. 161–162; Video Worksheet, p. 173; School-Home Connection, pp. 119–125*
Teacher Resource CD-ROM
Assessment Program: *Unit 1 Test, pp. 17–22; Teacher and Student Resources, pp. 115–144*
Assessment CD-ROM Transparencies
The Heinle Newbury House Dictionary/CD-ROM
Heinle Reading Library
Web Site: www.heinle.visions.com

Listening and Speaking Workshop

Make a Speech: News Report

Teacher Resource Book: *Web, p. 37*

Use past tense in writing *Say: News stories report what happened in the past.* Remind students to add *-d* or *-ed* to regular verbs to form the past tense.

Step 1: Use a graphic feature such as a sunshine organizer to organize your news report.
Have students write the names of main characters from reading selections they enjoyed. Connect the characters to the challenges they faced. Then add details to show how the characters solved their problems and met their challenges.

UNIT 1 Apply and Expand

Listening and Speaking Workshop

Make a Speech: News Report

> **Topic**
> Choose one of the chapter stories you read and present it as a news report. Focus on the challenge or problem the characters faced.

Step 1: Use a graphic feature such as a Sunshine Organizer to organize your news report.

Step 2: Be specific.

Answer the following questions:

1. *Who* faces the challenge or problem?
2. *What* is the challenge or problem? Describe it in detail.
3. *When* do the main events take place? In the present or in the past?
4. *Where* do the main events take place (the setting)?
5. *Why* do the characters face the problem? (Describe how the problem came up.)

Step 3: Use an attention-grabbing opening.

Use one of these hints for openings:

1. Ask a question.
2. Say something funny.
3. Make a dramatic statement.
4. Refer to an authority and use quotes.

Step 4: Stay on the topic and use visuals.

1. The topic is about "A challenge." Don't wander.
2. Notecards will help you stay on track.
3. Use visuals with your speech to make it more interesting.
   a. Use pictures from a magazine or the Internet, or use a drawing.
   b. Consider using a video or a technology presentation.

Step 5: Practice your speech.

After you have at least one idea for an opening:

1. Put each group of ideas on a notecard.
2. Practice with a partner.
3. Answer the questions on the Checklists.
4. Revise your report based on feedback.
5. Practice with visuals.

MULTI-LEVEL OPTIONS *Listening and Speaking Workshop*

Newcomer Make a two-column chart labeled *Who?* and *What happened?* Help students identify and complete these elements from their chosen work. Tell them they may illustrate characters or important objects, such as a ship, a horse, or a jacket. Then have them practice retelling the stories to a partner.

Beginning Make a four-column chart labeled *Who?, Where?, When?,* and *What happened?* Provide students with a short news article. Read the article aloud. Have them discuss answers to the *wh*-questions. Then help them complete the chart about their chosen reading. Have them restate the information in groups.

Intermediate Have students work in pairs to collaborate as they compose their news reports. Remind them to use a sunshine graphic organizer as they work together to organize their news reports. After practicing their news reports, have them work with their partner to revise their reports based on feedback.

Advanced Have students practice their reports in pairs. Direct reviewers to note if reports have the following: an attention-grabbing opening, a clear statement of the problem, important details, and an explanation of how the problem was solved.

Active Listening Checklist

1. I liked ____ because ____ .
2. I want to know more about ____ .
3. I thought the opening was interesting / not interesting.
4. You stayed on the topic. Yes / No

Speaking Checklist

1. Did I speak too slowly, too quickly, or just right?
2. Did I speak loudly enough for the audience to hear me?
3. Was my voice too high, too low, or just right?
4. Did I use visuals to make the speech interesting?
5. Did I look at the audience?

Viewing Workshop

Compare and Contrast Electronic Media with Written Stories

Analyze Information

In Unit 1, you read about Ernest Shackleton and the ship the *Endurance*.

1. Get a video from the school or public library about Ernest Shackleton.
2. Compare and contrast the video to the reading selection "Antarctic Adventure." What new information do you learn from the video? What information is the same? What information do you learn only in the reading selection?

Further Viewing

Watch the *Visions* CNN video for Unit 1. Do the Video Worksheet.

CNN Video

Content Connection *Social Studies*

Bring in a video of a suitable news program or ask a school librarian for a video of a school event. View the tape. Have students work in pairs to write four *wh*-questions about the video. Direct students to do a practice interview of another pair. Videotape or audiotape the students if possible.

Learning Styles *Visual*

Have students create a "news set" as a background for their broadcasts. In a corner of the classroom, have students assemble an "anchor desk" where each presenter sits to give his or her news report.

Step 2: Be specific.

Remind students that every main idea needs details to support it. Tell them to include as many details as they can when answering the *wh*-questions.

Step 3: Use an attention-grabbing opening.

Brainstorm a list of suggestions for each of the four possible openings.

Step 4: Stay on the topic and use visuals.

Tell students to share the topics of their stories in small groups. Then have students brainstorm ideas for visuals that would help illustrate important points in the storyline.

Step 5: Practice your speech.

Go over the procedure and the checklists before students practice in pairs.

ASSESS

Have students write two sentences. Sentence 1 tells what they liked the best about their own speech. Sentence 2 tells what they would like to do better next time.

Portfolio

Students may choose to record or videotape their speeches to place in their portfolios.

Viewing Workshop

Compare and Contrast Electronic Media with Written Stories

Teacher Resource Book: *Venn Diagram, p. 35*

1. **Make observations** As you view the video, pause occasionally and allow students to comment on the events and people. Keep a list on the board for later use.
2. **Use graphic organizers** Use a Venn diagram to help students as they compare and contrast the video and the reading selection. Students can refer to the list of events and ideas on the board and to their textbooks as they complete their Venn diagrams.
3. **Evaluate information** Have students use the diagrams to discuss the content of the video and the reading selection.

UNIT 1
Apply and Expand

Writer's Workshop

Write to Narrate: Tell How Someone Faced a Challenge

Teacher Resource Book: *Chronological Order, p. 50*

Create a story chart Have students analyze the organization of the story chart as a model for their own writing.

Step 1: Make lists.
Remind students to label the lists. After the lists are completed, have students review and circle the most important items.

Step 2: Write your first draft.
Explain and clarify the meanings of the boldfaced words. Model some examples as needed. Remind students of examples from reading selections in this unit.

Writer's Workshop

Write to Narrate: Tell How Someone Faced a Challenge

Writing Prompt

Choose someone you admire who has faced a challenge. Write his or her story. It could be someone in your family or community, a friend, or someone you know about from history or the news. You are writing because you think that the story is inspiring and you want to share it with other people.

Story Chart

Title of Your Story

I. Beginning
   A. Strong opening
   B. State the topic
   C. Identify the characters and the setting
II. Middle
   A. Sequence of events
   B. Details
   C. Dialogue in quotation marks
III. End
   A. Connect the details of the story
   B. Tell why you admire the person and why

Step 1: Make lists.

1. List important events, background information, and other details that are important to the challenge.
2. List other people who are important to the challenge.
3. Make a list of events. Put them in correct time order.

Step 2: Write your first draft.

1. Begin with a strong opening that makes the reader want to know what is coming next.
2. Write a sentence to introduce the topic.
3. Use details to describe the characters and their actions.
4. Use *and* to connect words.
5. Follow correct time order. Use time words like dates and *first, then, next* in dependent clauses.
6. In your ending, show that the story is over. Use a word like *finally.*

MULTI-LEVEL OPTIONS *Writer's Workshop*

Newcomer Have students tell their stories aloud while you record them. Have pairs listen to their tapes and write down key words and phrases. Monitor and assist as needed. Then have students work in pairs to dramatize one scene from their narrative using their key words. Have pairs perform their dramatizations.

Beginning Make copies of a simplified story chart. Have students write two sentences under *Beginning, Middle,* and *End.* Tell them to read their sentences to a partner. Ask them to add details as they read.

Intermediate Have students write a first draft. Remind them to add dialogue to each section. Provide useful phrases such as *The boy said, . . .* or *Her mother answered, . . .* Remind students that dialogue is written between quotation marks. Have pairs of students dramatize their dialogues.

Advanced Have students organize a class "archive." As students publish their narratives, have groups be responsible for displaying and compiling the class's work.

Step 3: Revise.

Collaborate with a partner to revise and organize your work. Listen as your partner reads your story aloud to you. Check for these things:

1. Did you use correct pronouns when talking about each character (*he, she, him, her*)?
2. Did you pay attention to the audience and your purpose for writing?
3. Did you use details to make the story interesting and exciting?
4. Did you describe actions?
5. Did you use correct time order?
6. Did you rearrange the text to give your story a clear beginning, middle, and end?

Step 4: Edit and proofread.

Read your story carefully and check for these things. If you have written your story on a computer, use the checks for spelling, punctuation, and grammar.

1. Did you write clearly by combining important parts of text? Did you delete parts that were not important to your story?
2. Did you use different sentence types to keep your writing interesting?
3. Did you use a dictionary or glossary to make sure your spelling is correct?
4. Did you use punctuation correctly to clarify and enhance your ideas?
5. Did you indent paragraphs?
6. Use the Editor's Checklist in your Student Handbook.

Step 5: Publish.

Prepare your story for presentation to your audience:

1. If you wrote your story on a computer, choose a font (style of type) that is easy to read. If you wrote it by hand, use your best handwriting.
2. Write a title page with the title of your story and "by (your name)."
3. Create a class collection of the stories. Make a Table of Contents to organize everyone's work.
4. As you read the stories, review them for their strengths and weaknesses.
5. Set your goals as a writer based on your writing and the writing of your classmates.
6. Meet with a small group to talk about each other's stories. Talk about challenges you and your classmates faced in writing the stories. Then talk about strategies you used to express your ideas.

The Heinle Newbury House Dictionary

Student Handbook

UNIT 1
Apply and Expand

Step 3: Revise.
Review the questions for students to use as they listen to one another's stories. Then, in pairs, have students share their stories and provide feedback on drafts.

Step 4: Edit and proofread.
Review the different editing and proofreading points. Give clarification and explanation as needed.

Step 5: Publish.
Encourage students to make their stories attractive and interesting so others will want to read them. Allow time for students to read one another's stories or for students to read their stories to younger students.

Have students identify the beginning, the middle, and the end of their narratives.

Portfolio
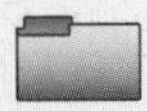

Students may choose to include their writing in their portfolios.

Home Connection

Say: Think about a time you had a problem. Did you go to a friend or family member for help? Direct students to draft a paragraph about the event and the kind of help or advice they received. Help students revise and edit their paragraphs, and publish them in a class book. Have students invite friends and family to a choral reading of their work.

Learning Styles *Musical*

Explain to students that a ballad is a song or poem that tells a story. A ballad usually tells about a challenge that the main character faces. Read some examples such as "Casey at the Bat" by Ernest Lawrence Thayer or "Greensleeves." Have students work in pairs to write a sentence identifying the problem faced and the way it was met.

UNIT 1
Apply and Expand

Projects

Project 1: Create a Poster About Meeting Challenges

Teacher Resource Book: *Note-Taking, p. 58*

1. **Gather and organize** Model the process of polling individuals, recording the information on a chart, and analyzing the results. Then have students conduct their polls.
2. **Create posters and visual displays** Help students identify the three most popular qualities. Brainstorm ways to illustrate them.

Project 2: Write a Magazine Article or a Web Article

Teacher Resource Book: *Research Report, p. 60*

1. **Generate research questions** Brainstorm questions about challenging places to live. Then have students select questions to include on their charts.
2. **Take notes** Have students record information and notes on the chart next to the corresponding questions.

Portfolio 

Students may choose to include their projects in their portfolios.

Projects

Project 1: Create a Poster About Meeting Challenges

Do you know people who have successfully met challenges? In your opinion, what qualities do these people share?

1. Take a poll of ten people of different ages and/or cultures. Ask, "What are the three most important qualities to help people meet challenges?"
2. List each person's name and response in a chart.

My Mother
1. intelligence
2. courage
3. keeps trying

3. Look at your list. Are the qualities mentioned the same or different for all ages? For all cultures?
4. Find the three qualities named most often. Make a poster with illustrations that show these qualities.
5. Present your poster to the class and to your family.

Project 2: Write a Magazine Article or a Web Article

Research a place where it is difficult to live. It can be a place from the unit or a place that you have read or know about.

1. Make a list of five questions you want to answer about the challenge of living in the place. Include any questions you formed as you read the unit selections.
2. Use reference books and the Internet to answer your questions.
3. Your questions may change as you research. Revise your questions if you need to. Then continue to research answers.
4. Complete a chart with your questions and answers. Use these to write your article.

What I Want to Know	What I Learned
How does cold weather affect life there?	It is dangerous to go out without the right clothing and equipment.

5. Find photographs or make illustrations that show your place. Write short captions that tell about each image.
6. Compare and contrast your magazine or Web article with a reading selection that mentions a difficult place to live. How is your information similar? How is it different?

76 **Unit 1** Challenges

MULTI-LEVEL OPTIONS *Projects*

Newcomer Work with students to create a series of illustrations or a photo essay of a challenging place to live. They can draw images or download them from the Internet. Help them write short captions to explain the images.

Beginning Help students select and write descriptions of challenging places to live. Ask questions such as: *How hot does the temperature get? How long is the winter?* Then have them find Internet images to illustrate their descriptions.

Intermediate Provide students with magazine articles or web sites as models for their own articles. Help them use reference books and web sites to research information on challenging places to live.

Advanced Encourage students to add quotations to their articles. Tell them to record interviews or to find quotations from people in their Internet research. Review the use of quotation marks.

Further Reading

Here is some information about books that tell how people have faced challenges. Choose one or more of them. Record the ones you read in your Reading Log. Write your thoughts and feelings about what you read. Take notes about your answers to these questions:

1. What challenge did this book describe?
2. How did the people meet their challenges?

Hatchet
by Gary Paulsen, Pocket Books, 1996. After a plane crash, Brian must learn how to survive alone in the Canadian wilderness. With only a hatchet that his mother gave him, Brian must make it on his own.

Yang the Youngest and His Terrible Ear
by Lensey Namioka, Yearling Books, 1994. Yingtao recently moved with his family of musicians from China to Seattle, Washington. He is tone-deaf and is afraid of ruining the family recital.

That Was Then, This Is Now
by S. E. Hinton, Puffin, 1998. This book by the award-winning author of *The Outsiders* is about two 16-year-old friends, Byron and Mark, who have been close friends since childhood. However, their friendship suddenly changes when Byron discovers that Mark has committed a crime. Byron turns Mark over to the police. Now he must learn to face the guilt of betrayal and the loss of his best friend.

Quilted Landscape: Conversations with Young Immigrants
by Yale Strom, Simon & Schuster Children's, 1996. This book tells the stories of 26 immigrant children ages 11 through 17. They describe how they feel about living in the United States and discuss the challenges of adjusting to a new country.

The Cay
by Theodore Taylor, Yearling Books, 2002. In this award-winning book, a boy named Phillip travels on a freight boat that is torpedoed during World War II. Blinded by a blow to the head, he finds himself on a deserted Caribbean island.

Raptor
by Paul Zindel, Hyperion Press, 1999. Zack and his American Indian friend, Ute, are trapped in a cave with a living dinosaur, the deadly Utah raptor. In this thriller, the two boys struggle to outwit the dinosaur and escape from the cave.

Selkirk's Island: The True and Strange Adventures of the Real Robinson Crusoe
by Diana Souhami, Harvest Books, 2002. This book tells the true story of Alexander Selkirk, who spent four years on a deserted island in the eighteenth century.

Reading Log

Heinle Reading Library

UNIT 1
Apply and Expand

Further Reading

Teacher Resource Book: *Reading Log, p. 64*

1. **Locate Resources** Arrange for students to tour the school or a local library to familiarize themselves with the different items available to them. Discuss proper behavior in the library.
2. Explain procedures for getting a library card and checking out books. Point out the usual amount of time that books can be borrowed. Encourage students to ask questions.
3. Point out sections with books for their age group. Have students find sections for fiction and nonfiction books.

Assessment Program: *Unit 1 Test, pp. 17–22*

Introduce the Unit

Unit Materials

Activity Book: *pp. 41–80*
Audio: *Unit 2*
Student Handbook
Student CD-ROM: *Unit 2*
CNN Video: *Unit 2*
Teacher Resource Book: *Lesson Plans, Teacher Resources, Reading Summaries, Home-School Connection, Video Script, Video Worksheet, Activity Book Answer Key*
Teacher Resource CD-ROM
Assessment Program: *Quizzes and Test, pp. 23–38; Teacher and Student Resources, pp. 115–144*
Assessment CD-ROM
Transparencies
The Heinle Newbury House Dictionary/CD-ROM
More Grammar Practice workbook
Heinle Reading Library
Web Site: www.heinle.visions.com

Heinle Staff Development Handbook

Refer to the Heinle Staff Development Handbook for more teacher support.

Unit Theme: Changes

1. **Share knowledge** *Say: I see changes around me. The weather changes all the time. People change, too. Last year I didn't like to eat salads. Now I like them.*
2. **Use personal experience** *Ask: How have you changed in the past five years? What changes are happening around you?*

Unit Preview: Table of Contents

1. **Use the table of contents to make predictions** Read the table of contents. *Ask: Which titles do you think are about people? What names of people do you see? What page is Chapter 1 on? Is there an author of the selection in Chapter 1?* Continue with other examples.
2. **Identify genres** *Say: The first selection is from a science article. What other kinds of readings are in this unit?* (a play, an excerpt from a novel, a historical fiction journal, a historical fiction diary, a poem)
3. **Connect** *Ask: Which type of reading in this unit do you think you will enjoy most?*

Changes

CHAPTER 1 *page 80* — **Why Do Leaves Change Color in the Fall?** an excerpt from a science article from the World Wide Web

CHAPTER 2 *page 92* — **Elizabeth's Diary** an excerpt from a historical fiction diary by Patricia Hermes

CHAPTER 3 *page 102* — **And Now Miguel** a play based on a novel by Joseph Krumgold

CHAPTER 4 *page 118* — **Tuck Triumphant** an excerpt from a novel by Theodore Taylor

CHAPTER 5 *page 132* — **The Journal of Jesse Smoke** an excerpt from a historical fiction journal by Joseph Bruchac

Ancient Ways a poem by Elvania Toledo

78

UNIT OBJECTIVES

Reading

Make inferences about a scientific informational text • Summarize a historical fiction diary • Determine the sequence of events in a play • Draw conclusions as you read realistic fiction • Understand the sequence of events as you read a historical fiction journal

Listening and Speaking

Role-play a scientific interview • Talk about the sequence of events • Perform a scene • Interview a newcomer • Identify how language reflects culture and regions

Day and Night, M. C. Escher, woodcut, 1938.

View the Picture

1. Describe the changes that take place in the picture.
2. With a partner, discuss a change in your life.

In this unit, you will read a science article, a diary, a play, a story, a journal, and a poem about changes. You will learn some of the reasons for change, and some of the challenges that changes bring. You will learn about the features of these writing forms and how to write them yourself.

79

Grammar

Identify and use the simple present tense • Use the future tense with *will* • Identify and use the future conditional • Use adjectives before nouns • Use the present continuous tense

Writing

Write a scientific informational text • Write a diary entry • Write dialogue for a scene in a play • Write a realistic story • Write a poem

Content

Science: Learn about trees • Language Arts: Understand genres of literature • Social Studies: Understand state flags • Social Studies: Learn about families • Math: Use rank order

UNIT 1

Introduce the Unit

View the Picture

1. **Art background** The Dutch artist M.C. Escher (1898–1972) was fascinated by graphic techniques his whole life. Using these techniques on woodcuts and lithographs, Escher created surprising, but very precise, distortions in perspectives and apparent shifts in reality. To make a woodcut, he had to carve a picture in reverse on a wooden block, roll ink over its surface, press paper against the inked surface, and finally peel off the imprinted paper.
2. **Art interpretation** Have students discuss what the artist can emphasize using the medium of a woodcut.
   a. **Interpret the image** Have students discuss the title of the picture. Point out that each side of the woodcut reflects the opposite side. ***Ask:*** *How do the simple colors show a message?* (black birds point toward day and the white birds point toward night) *What shapes change and flow into other shapes in the woodcut?* (the fields transform into the shapes of the birds; the rivers seem to flow into each other beyond the horizon) *What shapes are fixed and don't change form?* (the man-made structures of windmills, bridges, city, and roads)
   b. **Connect to theme** *Say: The theme of this unit is* changes. *What changes does Escher examine in this woodcut?*

ASSESS

Have students draw all the geometric shapes they can find in Escher's woodcut.

Chapter Materials

Activity Book: *pp. 41–48*
Audio: *Unit 2, Chapter 1*
Student Handbook
Student CD-ROM: *Unit 2, Chapter 1*
Teacher Resource Book: *Lesson Plan, Teacher Resources, Reading Summary, Activity Book Answer Key*
Teacher Resource CD-ROM
Assessment Program: *Quiz, pp. 23–24; Teacher and Student Resources, pp. 115–144*
Assessment CD-ROM
Transparencies
The Heinle Newbury House Dictionary/CD-ROM
Web Site: www.heinle.visions.com

Objectives

Preview Read aloud the objectives. *Say: We will learn these objectives in Chapter 1. Is there an objective you already know?*

Use Prior Knowledge

Discuss the Changing of Seasons

1. **Share knowledge** *Say: My favorite season is spring. I like warm weather and playing baseball. What is your favorite season? Why?*
2. **Gather and organize** Model ways to fill in the chart.

CHAPTER 1

Into the Reading

Why Do Leaves Change Color in the Fall?

an excerpt from a science article from the World Wide Web

Objectives

Reading Make inferences about a scientific informational text.

Listening and Speaking Role-play a scientific interview.

Grammar Identify and use the simple present tense.

Writing Write a scientific informational text.

Content Science: Learn about trees.

Use Prior Knowledge

Discuss the Change of Seasons

A season is several months that have a certain kind of weather. The northern part of North America has four seasons—summer, autumn (fall), winter, and spring. In some parts of the world, there are only two seasons—the dry season and the rainy season.

1. On a piece of paper, make a chart like the one here.
2. Choose a place where you have lived. On the chart, fill in the name of the place and the seasons.
3. Fill in the chart with information about each of the seasons.
4. Share your information with a partner.

Change of Seasons in ______				
Season				
Temperature is (hot, warm, cool, cold)				
Weather (rainy, sunny, snowy, windy)				
Clothes People Wear				
Things People Do				

MULTI-LEVEL OPTIONS *Build Vocabulary*

Newcomer Have students draw pictures of green plants. Help them label parts, such as stem, leaf, petal, flower, and roots.

Beginning Write on the board and *say: photosynthesis.* Have students work in pairs. Show them how to use the letters in the word to list smaller words they know, such as *photo, top, they,* etc. Have pairs share their list.

Intermediate *Ask: Why are plants important to people?* (for food, clean air, shade) Tell students that plants help people because of photosynthesis. Write and say the word. Have students pronounce it. Brainstorm a list of words about plants. Direct small groups to make sentences using words from the list.

Advanced Have students work in pairs. Direct them to write sentences using all the words from their word wheels. Have them share their sentences with another pair.

Build Background

North America and Climate

Climate is the kind of weather that an area has. The United States has many different climates. The southwestern United States has a desert climate—it is hot and dry. The Northeast and Midwest have a temperate climate—it is not extremely hot, and it is not extremely cold.

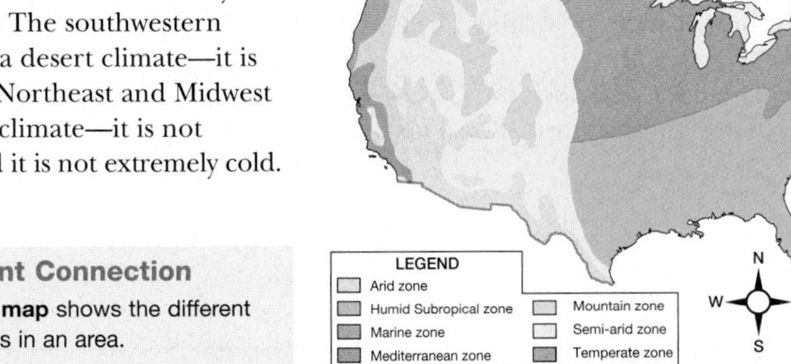

SOCIAL STUDIES

Content Connection

A **climate map** shows the different weather patterns in an area.

Build Vocabulary

Use a Word Wheel

Making a **Word Wheel** will help you remember new words.

1. In your Personal Dictionary, draw a large circle. Divide it into four parts.
2. Write *photosynthesis* in one part of the circle.
3. Look up the word *photosynthesis* in the dictionary. What is the meaning of this word?
4. Write three words that are related to *photosynthesis*. Write the words in the other three parts of the circle.

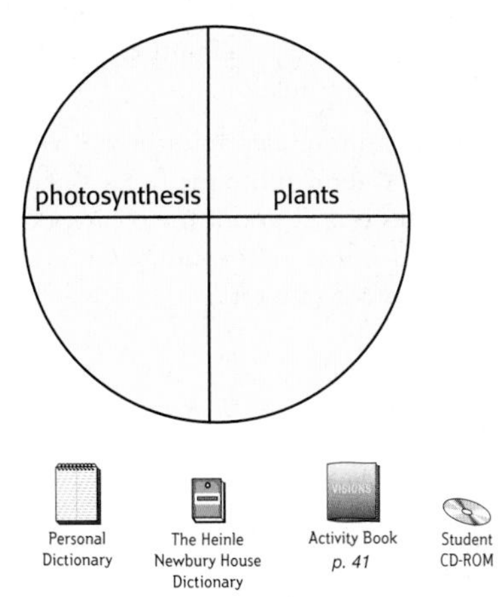

Personal Dictionary | The Heinle Newbury House Dictionary | Activity Book *p. 41* | Student CD-ROM

Build Background

North America and Climate

1. **Use a map** Refer students to the climate map in their books. Point out different places on the map and ask them to identify the climates. ***Ask:*** *Is there a desert climate in the Northeast or in the Southwest? Is it hot and dry or cold and wet in a desert climate?*
2. **Content Connection** *Ask: What type of climate do we have?* Have students talk about the climates of places where they have visited or lived.

Build Vocabulary

Use a Word Wheel

Teacher Resource Book: *Personal Dictionary, p. 63*

1. **Use a dictionary** Write: *photosynthesis.* Help students to pronounce it. Ask them to find the definition in a dictionary. ***Ask:*** *What is photosynthesis? Does photosynthesis happen in animals or plants?* Help students make a list of words related to photosynthesis for their word wheels.
2. **Reading selection vocabulary** You may want to introduce the glossed words in the reading selection before students begin reading. Key words: *factory, excess, deciduous trees, renew, disintegrate.* Instruct students to write the words with correct spelling and their definitions in their Personal Dictionaries. Have them pronounce each word and divide it into syllables.
3. **Multi-level options** See MULTI-LEVEL OPTIONS on p. 80.

Answers

4. *Possible answers:* sunlight, green color, food, process, leaves.

Have students write sentences using the words from their word wheels.

Community Connection

Build Vocabulary Invite a local florist or member of a horticultural club to talk about the importance of plants to community and the environment. Prepare the class by having students write questions to ask the guest.

Learning Styles
Visual

Build Background Make a class climate map. Have students work in groups. Assign each group a climate: desert, temperate, tropical, or subarctic. ***Say:*** *Find plants that grow in each climate.* Students can use the library or the Internet. Suggest that they draw or find images of the plants. Have groups write their plant lists and attach the art to appropriate places on the climate map.

Text Structure

Scientific Informational Text

Understand terms Copy the chart on the board. Point out key words in the chart. Give examples to clarify meaning (why there is day and night, what happens when you plant a seed).

Reading Strategy

Make Inferences

1. **Teacher think aloud** Model making inferences. *Say: I hear buses in front of the school. I know that buses come to pick up students when school is finished. I can make an inference that it's almost time to go home.* Give other events or clues and have students make their own inferences.
2. **Multi-level options** See MULTI-LEVEL OPTIONS below.

ASSESS

Ask: What are three features of a scientific informational text? (event, explanation, cause and effect)

Text Structure

Scientific Informational Text

"Why Do Leaves Change Color in the Fall?" is a **scientific informational text.** It describes how changes in weather affect the color of leaves.

As you read the text, look for these features of a scientific informational text.

Scientific Informational Text	
Event	description of a natural event
Explanation	scientific explanation of how and why the event takes place
Cause and Effect	statements that describe a scientific process

Student CD-ROM

Reading Strategy

Make Inferences

When you use what you already know to understand a reading, you **make inferences.** As you read "Why Do Leaves Change Color in the Fall?" make inferences about the text. This will help you understand the new ideas and information.

1. Read the selection title on page 83, and look at the pictures. Make inferences about the topic of the selection. Write your inferences on a piece of paper.
2. Read paragraphs 1 and 2. Were your inferences correct? Write down some facts from the selection that support your inferences.
3. As you read the rest of the selection, continue to make inferences.

Student CD-ROM

82 **Unit 2** Changes

MULTI-LEVEL OPTIONS *Reading Strategy*

Newcomer Direct students to the picture on p. 83. Tell them to make guesses about the picture. *Ask: Is this a picture of summer?* (no) *Is the temperature warm or cool?* (cool) *What's making the leaves fall down?* (the wind)

Beginning Direct students to the picture on p. 83. *Ask: Is this a photograph of spring or fall?* (fall) *What's making the leaves fall down?* (the wind) *Were the leaves always brown, red, and orange?* (no) Explain that when they make a guess to answer the question using information they know, they are making an inference.

Intermediate Direct students to the picture on p. 83. *Ask: What happens to trees in the fall?* (Leaves turn colors and fall down.) *What's the temperature like?* (cool) *What kinds of clothes do people wear?* (jackets, gloves, caps) Explain that each time they guess an answer using information they know, they are making an inference.

Advanced Direct students to the picture on p. 83. Tell them to write a question about the weather, climate, season, or kinds of clothing people might wear in this picture. Have them ask the question to a partner. Explain that when they guess those answers using information they know, they are making inferences.

Why Do Leaves Change Color in the Fall?

an excerpt from a science article from the World Wide Web from *Science Made Simple*

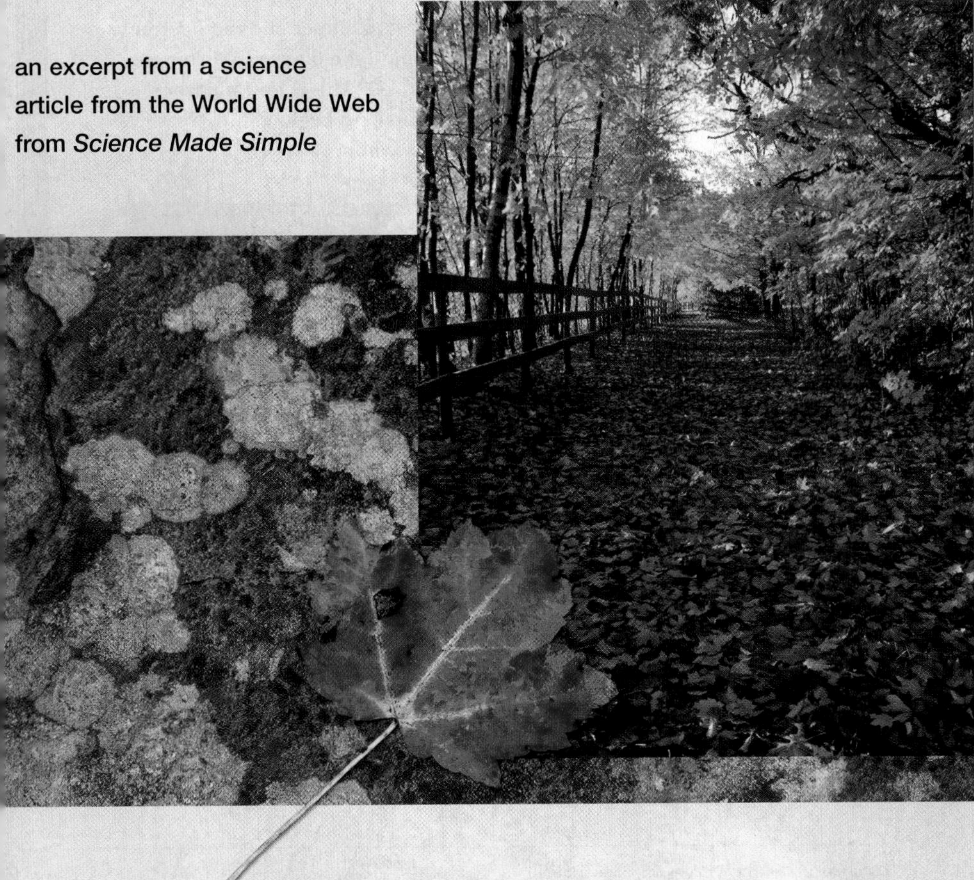

83

UNIT 2 • CHAPTER 1
Reading Selection

Reading Selection Materials

Audio: *Unit 2, Chapter 1*
Teacher Resource Book: *Reading Summary, pp. 75–76*

Preview the Selection

1. **Interpret the image** Explore and describe how color, shape, and line influence the message. ***Ask:*** *What is happening in this picture? What season is it? How do you know it is fall? What inference can you make about the weather from this picture?*
2. **Connect** Ask students how the picture relates to *changes*, the unit theme. Point out that changes in nature can take a long time and involve many little steps. Change can be gradual or sudden. Tell students they will read about changes in nature and changes in people's lives in this unit.

Cultural Connection

Discuss fall harvest holidays with students. Point out that people traditionally celebrate them in the fall at the end of the growing season. In the U.S., Thanksgiving Day is celebrated with a traditional meal of turkey, sweet potatoes, and pumpkin pie. Ask students to describe activities or foods of harvest holidays from other countries that they know about. Make a comparison chart with dates, foods, and activities.

Learning Styles *Mathematical*

Have students research the dates of this year's winter and summer solstices, and the spring and fall equinoxes. Then have them estimate the number of days between each (about 90 days or three months).

Reading Selection

Read the Selection

1. **Use illustrations and labels** Direct students to the illustration and labels. Point out the placement of the labels and their meanings. Explain that the information in the illustration and labels helps them understand the content of the reading.
2. **Shared reading** Play the audio or read paragraphs 1–3 to students. Direct them to the illustration to clarify the process of photosynthesis that is described in paragraph 2. Have students read the selection again with partners.
3. **Make inferences** *Ask: How are plants like factories?* (They both use materials to make something new and useful.)

Sample Answer to Guide Question

In winter the weather is usually much colder and not as sunny, so the trees need to be ready for the cold, dark time.

See Teacher Edition pp. 434–435 for a list of English-Spanish cognates in the reading selection.

Back Forward Reload Home Address: Search

Audio

1 We all enjoy the beautiful show of colors as leaves change each autumn. Did you ever wonder how and why this happens? To answer that question, we first have to understand what leaves are and what they do.

2 Leaves are nature's food **factories.** Plants take water from the ground through their roots. They take a gas called carbon dioxide from the air. Plants use sunlight to turn water and carbon dioxide into glucose. Glucose is a kind of sugar. Plants use glucose as food for energy and as a building block for growing. The way plants turn water and carbon dioxide into sugar is called photosynthesis. That means "putting together with light." A chemical called chlorophyll helps make photosynthesis happen. Chlorophyll is what gives plants their green color.

3 As summer ends and autumn comes, the days get shorter and shorter. This is how the trees "know" to begin getting ready for winter.

Make Inferences

Why do trees have to "get ready" for winter?

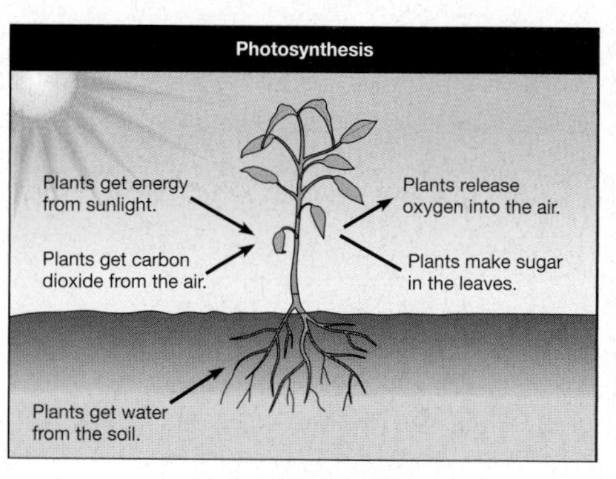

factories places where things are manufactured, or made

MULTI-LEVEL OPTIONS *Read the Selection*

Newcomer Play the audio. Do a guided reading of the Reading Summary. Match beginning and advanced students to do a paired reading of the Summary. ***Ask:*** *Are leaves nature's food factories?* (yes) *Do plants make glucose for energy?* (yes) *Do plants keep making sugar in cool weather?* (no)

Beginning Do a guided reading of the Reading Summary. Match beginning and intermediate students to do a paired reading of the Summary. ***Ask:*** *What parts of plants are nature's food factories?* (leaves) *What is glucose?* (a kind of sugar) *When do plants stop making sugar?* (in cool weather)

Intermediate Do a reciprocal reading with small groups. Then have each group summarize and present a different part of the article. ***Ask:*** *What three things do plants need to make sugar?* (sunlight, water, and carbon dioxide) *What do plants do when the weather gets cool?* (They stop making sugar.)

Advanced Do a jigsaw reading of the article. Assign small groups to present a different section of the reading. ***Ask:*** *What do plants use sugar for?* (food for energy) *What gives plants their green color?* (chlorophyll) *What happens when the chlorophyll disappears from leaves?* (They turn colors.)

4 During winter, there is not enough light or water for photosynthesis. The trees will rest, and live off the food they stored during the summer. They begin to shut down their food-making factories. The green chlorophyll disappears from the leaves. As the bright green fades away, we begin to see yellow and orange colors. Small amounts of these colors have been in the leaves all along. We just can't see them in the summer, because they are covered up by the green chlorophyll.

5 The bright reds and purples we see in leaves are made mostly in the fall. In some trees, like maples, glucose is trapped in leaves after photosynthesis stops. Sunlight and the cool nights of autumn turn this glucose into a red color. The brown color of trees like oaks is made from wastes left in the leaves.

An oak tree in autumn.

Make Inferences

Do oak trees have glucose trapped in their leaves after photosynthesis stops?

6 It is the combination of all these things that make the beautiful colors we enjoy in the fall.

7 During summer days, leaves make more glucose than the plant needs for energy and growth. The **excess** is turned into **starch** and stored until needed. As the daylight gets shorter in the autumn, plants begin to shut down their food production.

---

excess extra, more than is needed

starch food for the plant

Read the Selection

1. **Interpret the photo** Have students read the caption under the photo and describe the leaves in the photo.
2. **Understand terms** Have students find the meanings of the glossed words at the bottom of the page. Clarify meanings as needed.
3. **Paired reading** Play the audio. Then have students read the selection in pairs.
4. **Identify cause and effect** Ask questions to help students recognize the scientific processes—the causes and effects.
5. **Multi-level options** See MULTI-LEVEL OPTIONS on p. 84.

Sample Answer to Guide Question

No. Glucose in the oak leaves would make them turn red. The oak leaves turn brown, so there isn't much glucose trapped in them.

Spelling

Use *ch* for /k/ sound

Tell students that several science words have the sound /k/ but are spelled with *ch*. Have students find two science words in paragraph 2 that start with *ch* but sound like /k/. (chemical, chlorophyll)

Read the Selection

1. **Teacher read aloud** Read paragraphs 8–9 aloud to students. Use the illustration to clarify the process of leaf separation. ***Ask:*** *What happens to the leaf when the separation layer is complete?* (It forms a tear-line and falls off the tree.) *What other foods have carotene and xanthophyll?* (carrots, bananas, squashes)
2. **Reread text** Have students reread the selection with partners. ***Ask:*** *How do water and sugar travel through the leaves and the plants?* (in small tubes in the leaves and in the plants)

Sample Answer to Guide Question
When the chlorophyll disappears, the leaves change color.

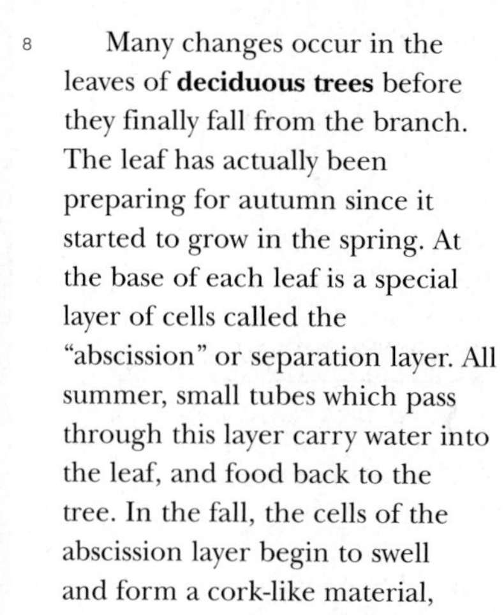

8 Many changes occur in the leaves of **deciduous trees** before they finally fall from the branch. The leaf has actually been preparing for autumn since it started to grow in the spring. At the base of each leaf is a special layer of cells called the "abscission" or separation layer. All summer, small tubes which pass through this layer carry water into the leaf, and food back to the tree. In the fall, the cells of the abscission layer begin to swell and form a cork-like material, reducing and finally cutting off flow between leaf and tree.

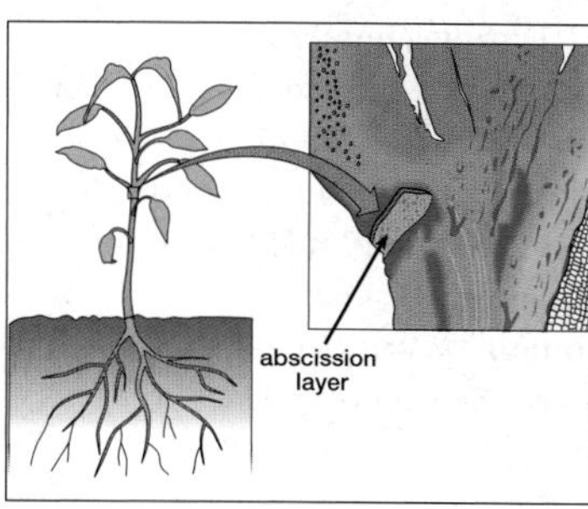

Glucose and waste products are trapped in the leaf. Without fresh water to **renew** it, chlorophyll begins to disappear.

Make Inferences
What do you think will happen to the leaf when chlorophyll begins to disappear?

9 Other colors, which have been there all along then become visible. The orange colors come from carotene ('kar-uh-teen) and the yellows from xanthophyll ('zan-thuh-fil). They are common pigments, also found in flowers, and foods like carrots, bananas and egg yolks. We do not know their exact role in leaves, but scientists think they may be involved somehow in photosynthesis.

10 The bright red and purple colors come from anthocyanin (an-thuh-'si-uh-nuhn) **pigments.**

deciduous trees trees that lose their leaves
renew make new or better
pigments colors in plants

86 Unit 2 Changes

MULTI-LEVEL OPTIONS *Read the Selection*

Newcomer ***Ask:*** *Is* pigment *another name for* color? (yes) *Do carrots, flowers, and bananas have green pigments?* (no) *Are there red and purple pigments in beets, apples, and violets?* (yes) *After the leaves change color, do they fall off the trees?* (yes)

Beginning ***Ask:*** *When the weather turns cool, what happens to the leaves on trees?* (They change color.) *What is another word for color?* (pigment) *What happens after the leaves turn different colors?* (They fall off the trees.)

Intermediate ***Ask:*** *What happens when chlorophyll begins to disappear?* (Leaves turn different colors.) *What happens to the green color of leaves without water?* (The color disappears.) *What can you see in the leaves when the green color disappears?* (other colors)

Advanced ***Ask:*** *What does chlorophyll need to keep leaves green?* (water) *What happens to the chlorophyll when water doesn't get to the leaves?* (It disappears.) *Why can't we see the bright colors any other time?* (They are hidden by the chlorophyll's green color.)

These are also common in plants; for example, beets, red apples, and purple grapes, and flowers like violets and hyacinths. In the leaves, these pigments are formed in the autumn from trapped glucose. Brown colors come from tannin, a bitter waste product. Different combinations of these pigments give us a wide range of colors each fall.

As the bottom cells in the 11
separation layer form a seal between leaf and tree, the cells in the top of the separation layer begin to **disintegrate.** They form a tear-line, and eventually the leaf is blown away or simply falls from the tree.

Make Inferences

Are pigments present in leaves?

disintegrate dissolve or break into pieces

Spelling

Use *c* for /s/ sound

Tell students that when *c* is followed by the letters *e, i,* or *y,* it sounds like /s/ (excess, cells). Have them work in pairs to find words in paragraphs 8–10 that follow the rule. (8: deciduous, abscission; 9: scientists; 10: anthocyanin, hyacinths)

Evaluate Your Reading Strategy

Make Inferences *Say: You have practiced an important reading strategy. Now you can decide how well you have done. Does this statement describe how you read?*

> I use details to make inferences about how characters act or feel. This helps me understand characters.

Read the Selection

1. **Teacher read aloud** Read paragraphs 10–11 as students follow along in their books. ***Ask:*** *What happens when the top separation layer breaks into pieces?* (The leaves fall off the trees.) *What are pigments?* (colors in plants)
2. **Multi-level options** See MULTI-LEVEL OPTIONS on p. 84.

Sample Answer to Guide Question

Yes. They appear after the chlorophyll disappears and when there is glucose trapped in the leaves.

Across Selections

Teacher Resource Book: *Venn Diagram, p. 35*

Use a Venn diagram Compare and contrast a scientific informational text with the "Antarctic Adventure" in Unit 1. For example, they both use facts about science, but the purpose of the historical narrative is to tell a story. The purpose of the scientific text is to explain a process or describe a scientific event. Have students record their ideas on a Venn diagram.

Reading Comprehension

Question-Answer Relationships

Sample Answers

1. Plants take water through their roots.
2. Glucose is sugar. It's the plant's food and building material.
3. Plants use sunlight to turn the water and carbon dioxide into glucose. Chlorophyll helps make the process of photosynthesis happen.
4. First the plants begin to shut down their food production. Then the green chlorophyll disappears from the leaves. Finally the red color can be seen.
5. In summer, the trees have green leaves. In winter, there are no leaves. In summer, they are making food. In winter, they are using the stored food.
6. Eventually the leaves are blown away or fall from the leaves.
7. In spring, the trees get ready to make glucose again. They grow new leaves and start sending water up to the leaves.
8. Some trees have sharp pointed needles instead of leaves. The needles are green, so they probably use photosynthesis to make food.
9. The fall season is the time when the leaves fall to the ground.
10. Because the illustrations can show things that photos can't, like the roots of a plant in soil.

Build Reading Fluency

Repeated Reading

Assessment Program: *Reading Fluency Chart, p. 116*

As students read aloud, time the reading and count the number of incorrectly pronounced words. Record their results in the Reading Fluency Chart.

Beyond the Reading

Reading Comprehension

Question-Answer Relationships (QAR)

"Right There" Questions

1. **Recall Facts** How do plants take water from the ground?
2. **Recall Facts** What is glucose? Why is glucose important for plants?

"Think and Search" Questions

3. **Recall Steps in a Process** How do plants turn water and carbon dioxide into sugar?
4. **Recall Steps in a Process** What are the steps that make maple leaves red?
5. **Compare and Contrast** How are trees different in the winter and the summer?

"Author and You" Questions

6. **Determine Causes and Effects** What eventually happens to the leaves?
7. **Make Inferences** What do you think happens to the trees in the spring?

"On Your Own" Questions

8. **Make Inferences** Some kinds of trees do not change color in the autumn. Do you think that these trees also use photosynthesis to make food?
9. **Think About Language** English has two words for one of the seasons—*autumn* and *fall*. Why do you think the word *fall* is used for this season?
10. **Interpret Visual Images** Why do you think illustrations are used instead of photos on pages 84 and 86? How do different parts of the illustrations help you understand the text?

Activity Book *p. 42*

Student CD-ROM

Build Reading Fluency

Repeated Reading

Rereading one paragraph at a time can help increase your reading rate and build confidence.

1. With a partner read aloud paragraph 1 in "Why Do Leaves Change Color in the Fall?" three times.
2. Did your reading rate increase each time?
3. Next, read paragraph 2 three times.
4. Continue rereading each paragraph.
5. Stop after ten minutes.

MULTI-LEVEL OPTIONS *Elements of Literature*

Newcomer Have students illustrate the life cycle of a chicken. Help them label each phase with key words: *egg, chick, adult, egg-laying hen.*

Beginning Have students illustrate the life cycle of a chicken: egg, chick, adult, egg-laying hen. Help them write captions that describe each phase of the cycle.

Intermediate Direct students to paragraph 2 on p. 84. Have them work in pairs to write the steps in photosynthesis. Point out that the last step is the first step of the next cycle.

Advanced Direct students to paragraph 8 on p. 86. Have groups discuss the cycle of change in leaves in autumn. Point out that the last step is the first step of the next cycle. Have each group write a summary of their discussion. Ask them to compare their summary with another group.

Listen, Speak, Interact 

Role-Play a Scientific Interview

Scientists who understand processes such as photosynthesis must be able to answer questions about the subject.

1. With a partner, reread the selection.
2. Ask each other questions about the text. Be sure you both understand the steps of photosynthesis.
3. Role-play an interview. One of you will be a scientist and one of you will be an interviewer. Write five questions about photosynthesis that the interviewer will ask the scientist.
   a. Use several different question words, such as *why, where, how, when,* and *what.*
   b. Use a question mark at the end of each question.
4. Prepare answers to all five questions.

> **Interviewer:** Dr. Perez, what does the word *photosynthesis* mean?

> **Scientist:** It means "made with light." It is also the way that plants make sugar.

5. Perform your interview for the class.

Elements of Literature

Identify Processes

Scientific writing describes **processes,** or the order in which things happen. One kind of process is a cycle. A cycle is a process that begins and ends with the same thing. For example, the life cycle of a chicken is from an egg to a baby chick to an adult chicken. The adult chicken then lays eggs.

1. Find the paragraph in the reading that gives the cycle of a plant making food.
2. Find the paragraph that gives the cycle of what happens to leaves in the autumn.

Activity Book p. 43

Student CD-ROM

Home Connection

Brainstorm and write the steps in the life cycle of human beings—infant, child, teenager, adult, senior. Invite students to bring in pictures of themselves as infants, toddlers, and children. Use these photos to illustrate their life cycles until the present. Ask them to predict their later ages with drawings of what they want or hope to be later in life.

Learning Styles *Natural*

Have students find out about how cities are cleaning the air and saving energy by planting gardens on the roofs of tall buildings. Students can do an Internet search with key words: *roof gardens.* Have groups choose the kinds of plants they would put in their roof garden. They can also design a garden plan.

Listen, Speak, Interact

Role-Play a Scientific Interview

Teacher Resource Book: *Interview, p. 54; Reading Log, p. 64*

1. **Reread in pairs** Pair beginning and advanced students. Have them read alternate paragraphs. The student that is listening should ask questions for the reader to answer.
2. **Newcomers** Reread with this group. Have them identify the steps in the process of photosynthesis. Write these steps on the board. Add key words to explain and describe them. Have students record these steps in their Reading Logs.
3. **Prepare questions** Write question words on the board. Have pairs write and practice their questions and answers for their role-play. After pairs have practiced, have them perform their interviews.

Elements of Literature

Identify Processes

1. As you review the process in the text, include a circle with the different stages of the life cycle of a chicken. Point out that cycles are continuous processes.
2. **Use a graphic organizer** After students find the two cycles in the text, have them write them in a circle to show the continuous process.
3. **Multi-level options** See MULTI-LEVEL OPTIONS on p. 88.

Answers
1. paragraph 2
2. paragraph 8

ASSESS

In random order, write the steps of the plant-making-food cycle on the board. Have students arrange the steps in the proper order to complete the cycle.

Word Study

Use Pronunciation in Context: *ph*

Use a glossary or other sources Have students skim the glossary of their science textbook and locate words with *ph,* such as *photon,* whose pronunciation is given. Ask them to use the pronunciation symbols to pronounce the word.

Answers

3. photo (light); graph (to write); physi (science of nature); phone (sound); alpha (first); phony (sound).

Grammar Focus

Identify and Use the Simple Present Tense

Roundtable Arrange the class into small groups. Have one student start by saying what he/she usually does after school. The next student repeats the information and adds his/her own. *Marco goes to the library. I play basketball.* Continue around the group.

Answers

Sample answers: Plants take water . . . Plants use sunlight . . . Plants use glucose . . . That means "putting together . . ." A chemical called chlorophyll helps make . . .

ASSESS

Have students write three sentences using the simple present tense.

Word Study

Use Pronunciation in Context: *ph*

Some English words and spellings come from the Greek language. Some Greek words use the letters *ph* together. They are pronounced like an *f.*

photosynthesis	telephone
graph	alphabet
physical	symphony

1. The box lists six words that have the letters *ph.*
2. Say the words aloud. Pronounce the *ph* like an *f* as in *fact.* Say the word *fact* so you can feel and hear the correct sound. Use the pronunciation in the dictionary to help you say the word.
3. Find the meaning of the Greek roots underlined in each word. Use a dictionary or glossary.
4. Write original sentences using the words in the box.

The Heinle Newbury House Dictionary

Activity Book *p. 44*

Student CD-ROM

Grammar Focus

Identify and Use the Simple Present Tense

The **simple present tense** is used to describe things that happen regularly or are generally true.

The green chlorophyll **disappears.**

The simple present tense is the **simple form** of the verb or the simple form plus *-s* or, sometimes, *-es.* The simple form of a verb is the verb with no endings or other changes.

1. Find the uses of the simple present tense in paragraph 2.
2. Write three sentences about things you do every day. Use the simple present tense.

Simple Present Tense	
Subject	**Verb**
I You We They The leaves	disappear.
He She It The color	disappear**s.**

Activity Book *pp. 45–46*

Student Handbook

Student CD-ROM

MULTI-LEVEL OPTIONS *From Reading to Writing*

Newcomer Have students draw a pair of pictures to illustrate what happens when it rains and when the rain stops. Have them label the pictures: *precipitation* and *evaporation.*

Beginning Direct students to the illustration on p. 91. Show them a picture of snow as an example of precipitation. Ask them to say other words they know related to precipitation. (rain, storm, showers) Have them record the words in their Reading Logs.

Intermediate Have students work in pairs to look up the meanings of *precipitation* and *evaporation* in the dictionary. Tell students to complete these sentence starters: _____ *happens when it rains.* _____ *happens when the water dries.*

Advanced Have students check the meanings of *precipitation, evaporation,* and *condensation* in the dictionary. Then ask them to write a short summary of the cycle of water in nature. Remind them to use the simple present tense.

From Reading to Writing 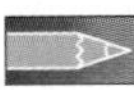

Write a Scientific Informational Text

Write an informational text that explains a scientific process—the water cycle. Use the terms *evaporation, condensation,* and *precipitation.* Look at the Water Cycle diagram to plan your informational text.

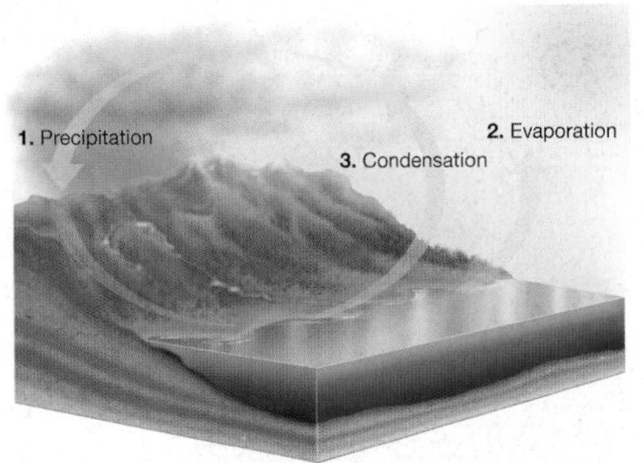

1. Use the simple present tense.
2. Be sure to add *-s* to a verb if its subject is *he, she, it,* or a singular noun.
3. List events in order.
4. Collaborate with a partner to revise your writing. Add or delete text to make your writing clearer.

Activity Book *p. 47*

Across Content Areas 

Learn About Trees

You read about **deciduous trees**—trees whose leaves change color and drop off in the fall. Not all trees are deciduous. Some stay green all year. These trees have **needles** instead of leaves. They also have **cones** (rounded, woody structures). They are called **coniferous** trees. The needles of coniferous trees do die and drop off, but they do this at different times. Therefore, the tree is always green.

Complete the diagram to show the similarities and differences between deciduous and coniferous trees.

Deciduous Trees	Both	Coniferous Trees
leaves change color	grow in northeast of U.S.	have needles

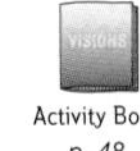
Activity Book *p. 48*

From Reading to Writing

Write a Scientific Informational Text

Teacher Resource Book: *Chronological Order, p. 50*

1. **Use the illustration** Direct students to the illustration and labels. Explain the terms for students unfamiliar with the water cycle. Help students describe the process illustrated. Remind them to use the simple present tense for facts. Write additional words that students suggest on the board.
2. **Think-Quickwrite-Pair-Share** Ask students to think about the process and write as much as they can about it. As students share with a partner, remind them to check the use of the simple present tense verb forms.
3. **Multi-level options** See MULTI-LEVEL OPTIONS on p. 90.

Across Content Areas: Science

Learn About Trees

Teacher Resource Book: *Venn Diagram, p. 35*

Define and clarify Explain the meanings of *deciduous, coniferous, needles,* and *cones.* Bring in pictures of the different types of trees and have students describe them. Point to different trees and have students identify them as deciduous or coniferous. Ask students to identify similarities and differences between the two groups of trees. Have them record their responses on a Venn diagram.

Have students write one sentence about a coniferous tree and one sentence about a deciduous tree.

Assessment Program: *Unit 2, Chapter 1 Quiz, pp. 23–24*

Reteach and Reassess

Text Structure Ask pairs of students to give examples of the features of a scientific informational text from the reading.

Reading Strategy Tell students to describe the clothes that people wear in one kind of weather. Have a partner make an inference about the season.

Elements of Literature Prepare sets of five cards. On each card write one word: *infant, child, teenager, adult,* or *senior.* Distribute the cards randomly to students. Direct them to form groups so that each group has all five words. Have each member tell one change that happens during its stage in the human life cycle.

Reassess Have students write about one change that happens to trees in the fall. Ask students to use the simple present tense.

Chapter Materials

Activity Book: *pp. 49–56*
Audio: *Unit 2, Chapter 2*
Student Handbook
Student CD-ROM: *Unit 2, Chapter 2*
Teacher Resource Book: *Lesson Plan, Teacher Resources, Reading Summary, Activity Book Answer Key*
Teacher Resource CD-ROM
Assessment Program: *Quiz, pp. 25–26; Teacher and Student Resources, pp. 115–144*
Assessment CD-ROM
Transparencies
The Heinle Newbury House Dictionary/CD-ROM
Web Site: www.heinle.visions.com

Objectives

Teacher think aloud Read the objectives. ***Say:*** *I know* the sequence of events *is about the order of events. Maybe* flashback *is about the past. As I read this story, I can watch out for changes that happened in the past.*

Use Prior Knowledge

Discuss Moving to a New Place

Think-Pair-Share Arrange students in pairs. Have them think about moving to a new place. Students can list the changes they wrote on the chart and tell their partners about their experiences.

Elizabeth's Diary

an excerpt from a historical fiction diary by Patricia Hermes

Into the Reading

Objectives

Reading Summarize a historical fiction diary.

Listening and Speaking Talk about the sequence of events.

Grammar Use the future tense with *will*.

Writing Write a diary entry.

Content Language Arts: Understand genres of literature.

Use Prior Knowledge

Discuss Moving to a New Place

Have you, or has someone you know, ever moved to a new place? What was it like to move?

1. With a partner, discuss what you know about moving to a new place. What changes were hard? What changes were easy? What changes were surprising? Complete a chart like the one here.
2. Find a map in your classroom or in a textbook. With your finger, mark the path of the move—from country to country or city to city.

Hard Changes	Easy Changes	Surprising Changes

MULTI-LEVEL OPTIONS *Build Vocabulary*

Newcomer Write the numbers 1–10 on the board. Then erase number 5. ***Say:*** *The number 5 is* gone. *The number 5 is* missing. Write: *gone = missing.* Demonstrate *cried* and *swatted* with gestures and expressions. Write: *cried = could not hold back my tears* and *swatted = hit.* Have students practice acting out and saying the words in pairs.

Beginning On the board, write: *Five of our ships were gone.* Read the sentence aloud. Have students repeat it. Write *missing* underneath *gone.* Reread the sentence, substituting *missing* for the underlined word. Point to the words as you read. Then have students repeat the sentence as you point to either word. Continue the process with the remaining sentences.

Intermediate Have students write sentences with the words *gone, cried,* and *swatted.* Then direct them to trade papers with a partner and rewrite the sentences using different word choices. Tell pairs to read their new sentences together. Have them check the meanings in a dictionary.

Advanced Have students write two sentences using both word choices for each pair of words: *gone/missing, swatted/hit,* and *blacker than night/dark.* Tell them to share their sentences with a partner.

UNIT 2 • CHAPTER 2
Into the Reading

Build Background

Jamestown

In 1607, a group of English people traveled by ship to make new homes on the east coast of North America. They settled in what is now Virginia, in a place called Jamestown. It was the first permanent English colony in North America.

You are going to read about a girl and her family who moved to this new land.

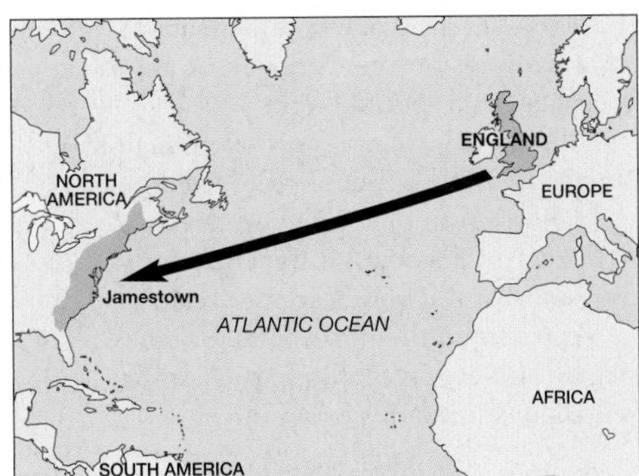

Content Connection

A **colony** is a new place where a group of people have moved but are still governed by their home country.

Build Vocabulary

Use Varied Word Choices

Writers often find different ways to say similar things. This makes their writing more vivid and precise. Sometimes you can understand a word or a phrase by finding another one nearby with a similar meaning. Here is an example from "Elizabeth's Diary":

> Five of our ships were gone. One missing ship is the *Sea Venture.*

In these sentences, *gone* and *missing* mean almost the same thing.

Work with a partner. Read these sentences and look at the **bold** words or phrases. Then find a word in the right-hand column that has a similar meaning.

1. I **could not hold back my tears.**
2. I **swatted** three mosquitoes.
3. The sky was **blacker than night.**

a. hit
b. cried
c. dark

The Heinle Newbury House Dictionary

Activity Book p. 49

Student CD-ROM

Build Background

Jamestown

1. **Use a map** Show a map of Europe and North America. Have students identify England and the United States. ***Ask:*** *What direction is North America from England: east, west, north, or south?*
2. **Content Connection** Give background information on the American colonies. ***Say:*** *The United States was originally a group of English colonies. The colonies became an independent country. America's independence is celebrated every year on July 4th.* ***Ask:*** *What other countries were colonies before they became independent? When do they celebrate their independence?*

Build Vocabulary

Use Varied Word Choices

1. **Teacher think aloud** Write on the board: *Five of our ships were* gone. *One* missing *ship is the* Sea Venture. ***Say:*** *I know that* missing *means "not there." So I guess the word* gone *also means "not there." I can use other words in the sentence to guess the meanings of new words.*
2. **Reading selection vocabulary** You may want to introduce the glossed words in the reading selection before students begin reading. Key words: *slam, twin, mosquito, expedition.* Instruct students to write the words with correct spelling and their definitions in their Personal Dictionaries. Have them pronounce each word and divide it into syllables.
3. **Multi-level options** See MULTI-LEVEL OPTIONS on p. 92.

Answers

1. b 2. a 3. c

ASSESS

Have students write sentences using the new vocabulary words.

Content Connection
The Arts

Build Vocabulary Have students imagine traveling across an ocean in a ship. Help them create a role-play in pairs. Remind them to make careful word choices so their audience can understand new words. Have them perform for another pair.

Learning Styles
Visual

Build Background Remind students that Jamestown was a settlement in Virginia. Find out where two other colonies, Plymouth and New Amsterdam, were settled. (Massachusetts and New York) Do an Internet search with key words: *early American colonies*. Have students find the states on a map and compare their information in small groups.

Text Structure

Historical Fiction Diary

Compare and contrast genres Discuss the features of historical fiction. Remind students of the features of a historical narrative. Point out that both use real dates and places. In historical narratives, the events are real. In historical fiction, some events are made up.

Reading Strategy

Summarize

1. **Teacher think aloud** *Say: When I summarize, I only give important information. Yesterday afternoon I left school at 4:00. I got on the bus. I went to the supermarket. I went inside. I looked around. I bought . . . Wait a minute! This is getting too long. Let me summarize! Yesterday, I went shopping at the supermarket after school.* Help students pick out only important information when they summarize.
2. **Multi-level options** See MULTI-LEVEL OPTIONS below.

ASSESS

Ask: Are the places and dates of historical fiction real? (yes) *Are the events real?* (probably not)

Text Structure

Historical Fiction Diary

If you keep a **diary,** you write about what happens to you every day, or almost every day, in a special book.

"Elizabeth's Diary" is historical fiction. It tells the story of people who lived in early North America. The author bases the story on history, but the characters and some of the events are not real.

As you read the diary, look for dates, places, and events that help the author tell about Elizabeth's experiences.

Historical Fiction	
Dates	The months, days, and years are real dates.
Setting	The cities and countries are real places.
Events	Some events really happened. Other events are made up.
Characters	Some characters are real. Some are made up.

Student CD-ROM

Reading Strategy

Summarize

When you **summarize** a reading you say or write down the most important information or events.

As you read "Elizabeth's Diary," summarize the information in each paragraph. Summarizing will help you understand and remember what you read.

1. Read the first and the last sentence in each paragraph. The most important information is often found there.
2. Read the entire paragraph quickly. The other sentences provide details.
3. Ask yourself, "What is the most important idea in the paragraph?"

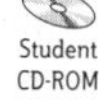

Student CD-ROM

MULTI-LEVEL OPTIONS *Reading Strategy*

Newcomer Make a large class calendar for the week or month. Record special dates and events such as holidays, birthdays, and field trips. Say that you will be keeping a diary of class work. At the end of each day, write words to describe class activities. For example: *Listened to the audio of "Elizabeth's Diary"* or *Located places on a map.*

Beginning Provide each student with a blank calendar page for the current month. Help them record special dates and events such as holidays, birthdays, and field trips. At the end of each day, tell students to summarize the classroom activities. Have them record a summary statement on their calendars.

Intermediate Provide each student with a blank calendar page for the current month. Have students work in groups to fill in special dates and events such as holidays, birthdays, and field trips. At the end of each class, direct pairs of students to summarize and record on their calendars the work they did that day.

Advanced Provide each student with a blank calendar page for the current month. Have students fill in special dates and events such as holidays, birthdays, and field trips. At the end of each day, direct students to summarize and record on their calendars the work they did in class that day.

Elizabeth's Diary

an excerpt from a historical fiction diary by Patricia Hermes

95

Reading Selection

Reading Selection Materials

Audio: *Unit 2, Chapter 2*
Teacher Resource Book: *Reading Summary, pp. 77–78*

Preview the Selection

1. **Interpret the image** *Ask: What do you see? Where is the ship? What is happening to it? Is this an easy trip or a dangerous trip? How do you think the people on the ship feel? Where do you think they are going? Why are they on this ship? Do people use these ships today? When did people use them?*
2. **Connect** Remind students that the unit theme is *changes*. Ask what changes the people might find in the colonies compared with their lives back in England.

Content Connection
Science

In groups, have students brainstorm and list changes that happen to the water, the air, and the sky when the ocean goes from calm to stormy. Then tell each group to write a summary statement of their ideas. Have groups share their statements.

Learning Styles
Kinesthetic

Assign groups of students roles as passengers and crewmembers of a ship at sea. Tell them their ship is in a storm like the one in the illustration. Have them mime the actions that each crewmember takes during the storm as they create a role-play. Then tell groups to perform their role-plays for one another.

Reading Selection

Read the Selection

1. **Use text features** Point out the date at the top of the page. Remind students that this is a girl's diary. Explain that she lived in a different time. Direct students to the illustration. Ask them to suggest some ways that Elizabeth is different from them. Remind students to use the illustration to help them understand the reading selection.
2. **Teacher read aloud** Read the selection aloud. Pause to check understanding and to identify features: date, place, events, and characters.
3. **Summarize** Ask students to reread the first paragraph and pick out the most important events to summarize.

Sample Answer to Guide Question
There was a bad hurricane. Five ships and many people were lost.

See Teacher Edition pp. 434–435 for a list of English-Spanish cognates in the reading selection.

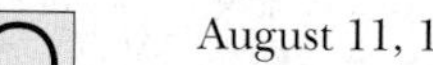

Audio

Summarize

What happened during the trip?

August 11, 1609

1 Today, we came to land at last! It seems there are no bones in my legs. I hugged my friend Jessie. We held each other up. Still, the land seemed to bob around beneath us. Seventy-one days. That is how long we were on the ocean.

2 Nine ships sailed from Plymouth, England. But at sea, a hurricane struck. Oh, how it struck! It became blacker than night. The waves brought us up into the dark sky, and then **slammed** us down. Men were washed off deck and into the sea. Some men tied themselves to the **mast.** But then—the mast broke off. Our ship rolled and rats came out. I tried to hold back tears, but could not. Jessie cried, too. Mama said we should not show fear or **dismay.** But soon, she cried, too. Prayers flew up to heaven like little birds. After the storm, when it became quiet, we looked about. Then, even Papa had tears in his eyes. For five of our ships were gone. One missing ship is the *Sea Venture.* It held our food! Were the ships blown off course? Or are they at the bottom of the ocean? We do not know.

3 Still, we are safely in Jamestown. I am here with my mama and papa. Soon, our new baby will be born. But it will be a home without Caleb, my **twin.** He stayed behind with Mama's cousin because his lungs are weak. He will join us come spring. I pray that spring comes soon, because without Caleb it will be a sad home.

slammed struck or hit with great force
mast a very tall pole on a ship that holds up the sails
dismay upset or worry
twin one of two children born to the same mother at the same time

96 **Unit 2** Changes

MULTI-LEVEL OPTIONS *Read the Selection*

Newcomer Play the audio. Then stand in front of the class and lead a choral reading **Ask:** *Was there a hurricane during the trip?* (yes) *Are all the ships safe?* (no) *Does Elizabeth land in Jamestown?* (yes) *Is it cold inside the fort?* (no) *Does Elizabeth like Gabriel Archer?* (no)

Beginning Do a teacher read aloud. Then have a volunteer stand in front of the class and lead a choral reading. **Ask:** *What broke off the ship during the hurricane?* (the mast) *Where does the ship land?* (in Jamestown) *Who stayed in England with a cousin?* (Elizabeth's twin brother, Caleb) *Is it hot or cold inside the fort?* (hot)

Intermediate Do a paired reading. Then **ask:** *What happened to some men during the storm?* (They were washed into the sea.) *What is the name of the ship with all the food?* (the *Sea Venture*) *What bothers Elizabeth the most inside the fort?* (mosquitoes) *How does she feel about Captain Archer?* (She doesn't like him.)

Advanced Have students read silently. **Ask:** *What terrible things happen during the trip?* (a hurricane, men washed into the sea, ships are lost) *Do you think Elizabeth was happy or unhappy or both when she reached Jamestown? Explain your answer.*

Summarize

What problem does Elizabeth have?

August 11, later

4 It is *hot* inside this fort where we shall live for a while. Nothing stirs but nasty **mosquitoes.** They bite and sting. They get in my ears. Jessie and I **compete** for who can swat the most. I have killed twenty-seven. Jessie is winning, for she has **slain** thirty. Mama rubs **fennel** into the bites. Already, though, my neck is as fat as a **melon.**

5 Papa says that tomorrow we shall begin to build our house. He says there will be no bugs inside our house. Captain Gabriel Archer was one of those in charge of our **expedition.** He has lived here before. He says, "You wait and see. There are always bugs."

6 Gabriel Archer is a **dreadful,** unpleasant man.

---

mosquitoes small insects that bite and suck blood
compete work hard to beat others at a contest or race
slain killed
fennel a tall herb or plant used as a medicine or to flavor food
melon a kind of juicy, large fruit
expedition a long journey with a goal such as exploring a new land
dreadful awful, terrible

About the Author

Patricia Hermes (born 1936)

Patricia Hermes was born in Brooklyn, New York. She writes fiction and nonfiction. One of her novels, *Fly Away Home* (1996), was made into a movie. She enjoys writing because it allows her to be any character that she wants to be. Hermes says, "It gives me the opportunity to live other lives . . . I can write about things that scare me. . . . I can be silly. I can be brave. I can make everything work out." *Our Strange New Land: Elizabeth's Diary* is the first part of two books. The second book is *The Starving Time: Elizabeth's Diary.*

➤ Describe how Patricia Hermes' point of view affects "Elizabeth's Diary." Do you think she enjoyed writing the book?

Read the Selection

1. **Understand terms** Have students find the meanings of the glossed words below the selection. Clarify meanings as needed.
2. **Paired reading** Play the audio. Then have students reread the selection in pairs.
3. **Summarize** *Ask: What do the mosquitoes do?* (They bite and sting and get in Elizabeth's ears.) Have students summarize paragraph 5.
4. **Multi-level options** See MULTI-LEVEL OPTIONS on p. 96.

Sample Answer to Guide Question
The mosquitoes. There are a lot of them, and they bite and sting her.

About the Author

1. **Explain author background** In her books, Patricia Hermes has her characters face many different types of serious problems, but she often includes humor in the stories.
2. **Interpret the facts** *Ask: When do you think Elizabeth is being a little silly?* (when she writes about the mosquitoes and not liking Gabriel Archer)

Across Selections

Teacher Resource Book: *Reading Log, p. 64*

Discuss personal preferences Compare and contrast the scientific informational text in Chapter 1 and the example of historical fiction in this chapter. Ask students to discuss which of the two selections they enjoyed more. *Ask: Which reading did you like better? Why?* (The diary. It was easier to read. It has more adventure in it.) Have students record their responses in their Reading Logs.

Punctuation

Hyphens in numbers

Write on the board: *21 = twenty-one.* Tell students that some numbers over twenty are made up of two numbers. Some examples are 21 through 29 or 71 through 79. ***Say:*** *When you write those numbers in words, you must put a hyphen between the two words.* Ask students to find two spelled-out numbers with hyphens in paragraphs 1 (seventy-one) and 4 (twenty-seven).

Evaluate Your Reading Strategy

Summarize ***Say:*** *You have practiced an important reading strategy. Now you can decide how well you have done. Does this statement describe how you read?*

If I do not understand something I read, I go back and reread to summarize. Summarizing helps me understand and remember important information.

UNIT 2 • CHAPTER 2
Beyond the Reading

Reading Comprehension

Question-Answer Relationships

Sample Answers

1. August 11, 1609
2. Jessie is Elizabeth's friend.
3. It sailed from Plymouth, England.
4. They traveled to Jamestown, Virginia.
5. Caleb is Elizabeth's twin brother.
6. When the hurricane struck, the mast, some men, and five ships were lost.
7. Elizabeth's mother and father traveled with her. Her brother, Caleb, stayed behind.
8. Elizabeth is living in the fort. Her family does not have a house yet.
9. I think Elizabeth is happy to be in North America. She is glad they are safely in Jamestown.
10. I think the fort is made of wood and is rough. There are no windows to keep bugs out. Forts are usually safe.
11. Students may mention that they feel sorry for her because her life will be very difficult. There are very few places built. She will probably have to work very hard.

Build Reading Fluency

Rapid Word Recognition

Rapid word recognition is an excellent activity for students who struggle with irregular spelling patterns. Time students for 1 minute as they read the words in the squares aloud.

Beyond the Reading

Reading Comprehension

Question-Answer Relationships (QAR)

"Right There" Questions

1. **Determine Chronological Order** What is the date of the first diary entry?
2. **Identify** Who is Jessie?
3. **Recall Facts** Where did Elizabeth's ship sail from?

"Think and Search" Questions

4. **Identify** Where did Elizabeth and her family travel to?
5. **Identify** Who is Caleb?
6. **Explain** What happened when the hurricane struck?

"Author and You" Questions

7. **Draw Conclusions** What members of Elizabeth's family traveled with her? Who stayed behind?
8. **Analyze Setting** Where is Elizabeth living? Why?
9. **Understand Characterization** Is Elizabeth happy to be in North America? How do you know?
10. **Visualize** What is the fort like? Do you think it is a safe place to live? Why or why not?

"On Your Own" Question

11. **Compare with Your Experiences** How would you feel if you were in Elizabeth's situation?

Activity Book p. 50

Student CD-ROM

Build Reading Fluency

Rapid Word Recognition

Rapidly recognizing words helps increase your reading speed.

1. With a partner, review the words in the box.
2. Next, read the words aloud for one minute. Your teacher or partner will time you.
3. How many words did you read in one minute? Was it more than on page 36?

there	tied	struck	each	night
each	night	there	sea	tied
struck	each	sea	night	stuck
night	sea	each	there	sea
sea	there	tied	tied	each

MULTI-LEVEL OPTIONS *Elements of Literature*

Newcomer Review the calendars students have been keeping in class. Have them illustrate some of the events or activities that they recorded.

Beginning *Say: A diary is usually private. People don't want others to read their diaries.* Then review the calendars that students have been keeping in class. Ask them how their calendars are like Elizabeth's diary. (The calendars have dates. They tell what happened in class.)

Intermediate Have students review the calendars they have been keeping in class. Ask them to write a paragraph for a private diary about an event or activity they recorded on the calendar. Tell them they may share their paragraphs with a partner if they wish.

Advanced Have students review the calendars they have been keeping in class. Then ask them to write a paragraph for a public journal about an event or activity they recorded. Have them share their paragraphs with a partner.

Listen, Speak, Interact 

Talk About the Sequence of Events

"Elizabeth's Diary" tells Elizabeth's thoughts. She writes about her present, past, and future.

1. With a partner, reread the story. Find one event that happens in the past, one event that happens in the present, and one event that will happen in the future. How do you think Elizabeth feels about each of these events?
2. Tell your partner about three events:
   a. an important event in your past
   b. an important event in your present
   c. an important event that you want for your future
3. Draw a timeline that shows the sequence of these events. Include small pictures in your timeline.
4. Present a short speech about your life using the illustrated timeline.
5. When your classmates present their speeches, listen to be sure you understand. If you do not, ask your classmate to repeat or to use different words.

Elements of Literature

Identify Flashbacks

Writers use **flashbacks** to tell about something that happened to a character before the time that the story is set. A character remembers something that happened in the past. In "Elizabeth's Diary," there is a flashback.

1. Copy the following sentences in your Reading Log. The sentences are listed in the order that they appear in the diary.
   a. Today, we came to land at last!
   b. But at sea, a hurricane struck.
   c. Still, we are safely in Jamestown.
   d. It is *hot* inside this fort.
   e. Papa says that tomorrow we shall begin to build our house.
2. Now rewrite the sentences in the order they really happened.

Reading Log

Activity Book p. 51

Student CD-ROM

Home Connection

Ask students to interview a parent or family member who has moved to a new country, city, or state. Tell students to ask the person to name one change that was easy to deal with and one change that was hard. Then have small groups complete a two-column chart of hard and easy changes. Direct them to compare and contrast their charts with another group.

Teacher Resource Book: *Interview, p. 54*

Learning Styles *Musical*

Tell small groups to find songs about changes. Have them ask a librarian to help find recordings or do an Internet search using key words: *songs of change.* Work with students to find or write the lyrics. Have students perform the songs for the class.

Listen, Speak, Interact

Talk About the Sequence of Events

Teacher Resource Book: *Timelines, p.39; Reading Log, p. 64*

1. **Reread in pairs** Arrange pairs of beginning and advanced students. Have them reread the selection with their partners and identify past, present, and future events.
2. **Newcomers** Reread with this group. Pause to have students identify events and indicate the time: past, present, or future. Help students explain how Elizabeth might have felt. Have them record past, present, and future events from their own lives in their Reading Logs.

Answer

1. *Examples:* Past: The ship rolled and rats came out. Present: Jessie and Elizabeth compete for who can swat the most. Future: Caleb will join them in the spring.

Elements of Literature

Identify Flashbacks

Teacher Resource Book: *Reading Log, p. 64*

1. **Teacher think aloud** *Say: Now we are reading about a ship that traveled to Jamestown. I remember we studied about another ship that traveled to Antarctica . . .*
2. **Personal experience** Ask students to share examples of flashbacks in stories from books, television programs, or movies.
3. **Multi-level options** See MULTI-LEVEL OPTIONS on p. 98.

Answer

2. b, a, c, d, e

ASSESS

Have students identify past, present, or future in these sentences. *Say: I will meet you tomorrow.* (future) *We visited some relatives last weekend.* (past) *He's sitting in class now.* (present)

Word Study

Understand the Suffix *-ty*

Teacher Resource Book: *Personal Dictionary, p. 63*

Make a vocabulary game Write number words on one set of cards and the digits on another set to create a concentration game. Have students match words and numbers and say the number words aloud.

Answers
2. seven + -ty = seventy
eight + -ty = eighty
nine + -ty = ninety
3. seventy-one, twenty-seven, thirty

Grammar Focus

Use the Future Tense with *Will*

Apply Ask students to write a sentence in the present tense. Have them trade papers with a classmate and rewrite the sentences in the future tense.

Answer
Examples: Soon, our new baby will be born. He will join us come spring.

ASSESS

On the board, write: *Elizabeth hugged Jessie. She missed her brother, Caleb.* Have students rewrite the sentences changing the verbs to the future using *will.*

Word Study

Understand the Suffix *-ty*

A **suffix** is a word part added to the end of a word. A suffix changes the word's meaning. The suffix *-ty* added to a number word means *tens* or *times ten.*

six + *-ty* = six**ty**

Note that the spelling of the numbers two through five changes when the suffix *-ty* is added.

1. Copy the chart in your Personal Dictionary.
2. Complete the chart. Follow the example.
3. Find three number words ending with the suffix *-ty* in paragraphs 1 and 4.

Suffix + ty (times ten)		
2	two + ty ⇒ twenty	20
3	three + ty ⇒ thirty	30
4	four + ty ⇒ forty	40
5	five + ty ⇒ fifty	50
6	*six + ty ⇒ sixty*	60
7		70
8		80
9		90

Personal Dictionary

The Heinle Newbury House Dictionary

Activity Book *p. 52*

Student CD-ROM

Grammar Focus

Use the Future Tense with *Will*

"Elizabeth's Diary" tells about some events that take place in the future. One way to form the **future tense** is:

will + base form of verb

Look at this example:

Without Caleb it <u>will be</u> a sad home.

Find other examples of the future tense with *will* in paragraphs 3 and 5 of "Elizabeth's Diary." Write them on a piece of paper.

Activity Book *pp. 53–54*

Student Handbook

Student CD-ROM

MULTI-LEVEL OPTIONS *From Reading to Writing*

Newcomer Have each student create a storyboard of a change in his/her life. Help students write captions to explain if the change was easy or hard. Then have students present their stories to a small group.

Beginning Work with students to complete sentence starters for their diary: *I was born in _____. Now I live in _____. An easy change for me was _____. A hard change for me was _____. Now I feel _____.*

Intermediate Have students write a diary entry about an important change in their lives. Remind them to check their use of past, present, and future tenses.

Advanced Tell students to write a diary entry about an important change they want to make in their lives. Remind them to check their use of past, present, and future tense.

From Reading to Writing 

Write a Diary Entry

Write a diary entry about your past and your future.

1. Brainstorm ideas for a diary entry. Use a chart to organize your ideas.

Past	Future
I lived in ___.	I will live in ___.

2. In your chart, write answers to these questions.
   a. What important things happened to you last year? How did you feel?
   b. Think about your future. How will your life change?
3. Write a diary entry using the information in your chart. Be sure to use the appropriate diary form shown in the reading.
4. Check your work for the following:
   a. Did you indent each paragraph?
   b. Did you write the date?
   c. Did you use *I* or *we*?
   d. Did you use a question mark (?) when you asked a question?
   e. Did you use an exclamation point (!) when you wanted to show excitement?

Activity Book
p. 55

Across Content Areas 

Understand Genres of Literature

In literature, people write about their experiences in several **genres**, or forms, of literature.

A **diary** is a book with blank pages in which you record your experiences every day. Diaries are usually very private.

A **journal** is like a diary, but it is often a record of special events. Journals are often written for other people to read.

A **memoir** is a record of the writer's experiences in the distant past.

In this book, there are selections from two diaries, one journal, and one memoir. Find these selections in the table of contents at the beginning of this book.

Activity Book
p. 56

UNIT 2 • CHAPTER 2

Beyond the Reading

From Reading to Writing

Write a Diary Entry

Teacher Resource Book: *Two-Column Chart, p. 44*

1. **Brainstorm** Ask students to suggest events to include in their past and future diary entries. List them on the board.
2. **Think-Quickwrite-Pair-Share** Allow several minutes of thinking time. Then tell students to write as much as they can about their past events. Then have them write about their future events. Tell students to share their diary entries in pairs. Later, have students rewrite their entries making sure to follow proper writing conventions.
3. **Multi-level options** See MULTI-LEVEL OPTIONS on p. 100.

Across Content Areas: Language Arts

Understand Genres of Literature

1. **Connect** Explain the meanings of *genre, diary, journal,* and *memoir. Ask: Are Elizabeth's entries in a diary or a journal?* (diary) Have students talk about journals or diaries that they or their friends keep.
2. **Locate derivation** Have students locate the derivation of *genre* in the glossary in the Student Handbook or other sources, such as online or CD-ROM dictionaries. Ask students to record the meaning and derivation in their Reading Logs.
3. **Use a table of contents** Direct students to the unit table of contents on page 78. Ask them to identify the journal entry. ("The Journal of Jesse Smoke")

Answer
Two diaries ("Elizabeth's Diary" and "Anne Frank: The Diary of a Young Girl"); journal ("The Journal of Jesse Smoke"); memoir ("Earthquake")

Have students write three sentences for a diary entry about today.

Assessment Program: *Unit 2, Chapter 2 Quiz, pp. 25–26*

Reteach and Reassess

Text Structure Have students work in pairs. Tell them to write the dates and places that are recorded in "Elizabeth's Diary."

Reading Strategy Assign small groups to summarize one of the first five paragraphs. Then have groups read their summaries in order.

Elements of Literature Tell students to identify the flashback that Elizabeth writes about in paragraph 2.

Reassess Have students summarize Elizabeth's second diary entry on August 11 (p. 97). Remind them to pay attention to the tenses they use.

Chapter Materials

Activity Book: *pp. 57–64*
Audio: *Unit 2, Chapter 3*
Student Handbook
Student CD-ROM: *Unit 2, Chapter 3*
Teacher Resource Book: *Lesson Plan, Teacher Resources, Reading Summary, Activity Book Answer Key*
Teacher Resource CD-ROM
Assessment Program: *Quiz, pp. 27–28; Teacher and Student Resources, pp. 115–144*
Assessment CD-ROM
Transparencies
The Heinle Newbury House Dictionary/CD-ROM
Web Site: www.heinle.visions.com

Objectives

Read in pairs In pairs, have students take turns reading the objectives section aloud. Tell them to list the words they don't know. Then have pairs ask other pairs if they know any words on their lists. Clarify meanings of key words.

Use Prior Knowledge

Talk About Farming

1. **Relate to personal experience** Ask students to describe farms they have visited or lived on.
2. **Use a graphic organizer** Students can complete their own chart of farm tasks. Have them compare and contrast in small groups.

CHAPTER 3

And Now Miguel

a play based on a novel
by Joseph Krumgold

Objectives

Reading Determine the sequence of events in a play.

Listening and Speaking Perform a scene.

Grammar Identify and use the future conditional.

Writing Write dialogue for a scene in a play.

Content Social Studies: Understand state flags.

Use Prior Knowledge

Talk About Farming

In the selection you are going to read, Miguel and his family make their living by farming. What do you know about farming?

1. Make a chart like the one here.
2. With a partner, brainstorm a list of daily tasks (jobs) on a farm.
3. Guess the time it would take to do each job.
4. Add up the time for all the jobs.
5. Share your chart with the rest of the class. Discuss how many people it might take to run a farm.

Daily Tasks on a Farm	Time
care for animals	3–4 hrs. a day
fix equipment	2 hrs. a day

MULTI-LEVEL OPTIONS *Build Vocabulary*

Newcomer Ask students to think about their goals for school or an extracurricular activity. Have them illustrate one of their goals. Help them write a label for their illustration.

Beginning Ask students to think about their goals for school or an extracurricular activity. Instruct students to share their goals in pairs.

Intermediate Ask students to think about their goals. Have them list three goals for school or an extracurricular activity. Have them share their goals in small groups.

Advanced Have students write a paragraph stating their goals for school or an extracurricular activity. Have them read their paragraphs to a partner.

Build Background

The Sangre de Cristo Mountains

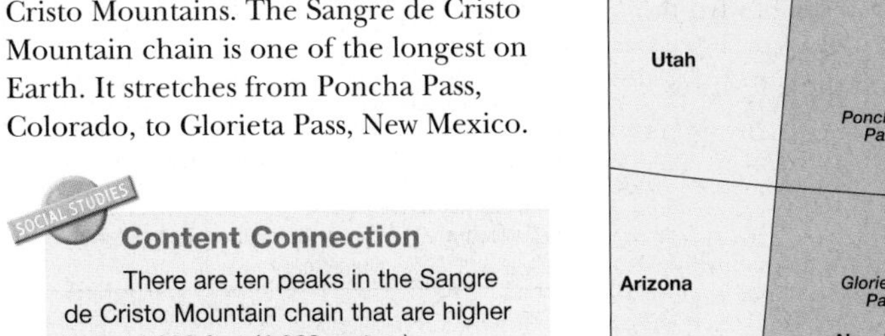

Miguel, the main character of the selection, hopes to go to the Sangre de Cristo Mountains. The Sangre de Cristo Mountain chain is one of the longest on Earth. It stretches from Poncha Pass, Colorado, to Glorieta Pass, New Mexico.

Content Connection

There are ten peaks in the Sangre de Cristo Mountain chain that are higher than 14,000 feet (4,268 meters).

Build Vocabulary

Use the LINK Strategy

The LINK strategy is one way for you to build your vocabulary. LINK stands for **L**ist, **I**nquire, **N**ote, and **K**now.

Use the word *goal* as an example. A *goal* is something that you want to achieve. Complete a LINK chart for your goals in your Personal Dictionary.

L	**L**ist words related to a topic.
I	**I**nquire, or ask about the meanings of words.
N	**N**ote ideas using the words from your list.
K	**K**now more about a topic.

1. **List:** List all the words you can think of that relate to your goals in life.
2. **Inquire:** Share your list of words with a partner. If your partner wrote any words you do not know, ask what they mean.
3. **Note:** Write sentences about your goals. Use as many words as you can from your lists.
4. **Know:** Think about what you know about goals.

Personal Dictionary

Activity Book *p. 57*

Student CD-ROM

Content Connection ***The Arts***

Build Vocabulary Have students work in pairs to create a role-play. ***Say:*** *You want to get a job after school. Your family wants you to study. You and your partner are going to create a role-play about a conflict between your goals and your family's goals for you.* Have pairs practice and perform the role-plays for the class.

Learning Styles ***Natural***

Build Background Have students plan a weekend "field trip" to the Sangre de Cristo Mountains. Tell them to decide what kind of food, clothing, and supplies they will need to take. Have them find out what animals or plant life they can expect to see.

Build Background

The Sangre de Cristo Mountains

1. **Use a map** Instruct students to locate the Sangre de Cristo Mountains on a map of the United States. Have them trace its chain from New Mexico to Colorado. ***Ask:*** *Are the names in this area from Spanish or English?* (Spanish) *Why?* (Many Spanish explorers came to this area.)
2. **Content Connection** Explain to students that the height of mountains is measured from sea level. ***Ask:*** *What is the highest mountain peak in the U.S.?* (Mt. McKinley in Alaska) *How high is it?* (20,000 ft.) *What is the highest mountain peak in the world?* (Mt. Everest in the Himalayas, on the border of Nepal and Tibet) *How high is it?* (29,000 ft.)

Build Vocabulary

Use the LINK Strategy

Teacher Resource Book: *Personal Dictionary, p. 63*

1. **Teacher think aloud** ***Say:*** *I know a goal in soccer is when someone kicks the ball into the net. The team gets a point. So I think a goal is something good or something you work hard to get.*
2. **Relate to personal experience** Ask students to suggest goals they have in life. Write key words on the board. Then have students create their own list of words.
3. **Reading selection vocabulary** You may want to introduce the glossed words in the reading selection before students begin reading. Key words: *dozen, search, lamb, flock, snap.* Instruct students to write the words with correct spelling and their definitions in their Personal Dictionaries. Have them pronounce each word and divide it into syllables.
4. **Multi-level options** See MULTI-LEVEL OPTIONS on p. 102.

ASSESS

Have students write one sentence about one of their goals.

Text Structure

Play

Clarify features Introduce and explain the features of a play. Ask students to describe plays they have seen or read.

Reading Strategy

Determine the Sequence of Events

1. **Draw on experiences** Ask a volunteer to explain how to do a simple task, such as sharpening a pencil. List the steps as the student explains them. Point out any time words.
2. **Multi-level options** See MULTI-LEVEL OPTIONS below.

Answer

1. 1st: b; 2nd: a; 3rd: d; 4th: c

ASSESS

On the board, write: *The _____ describes the scenes.* (narrator) *The _____ is the conversations between characters.* (dialogue) *The _____ are the parts of the story in the play.* (scenes) Tell students to fill in the blanks with the features of a play.

Text Structure

Play

"And Now Miguel" is a **play.** In a play, actors pretend to be the characters. They memorize and perform a script of what the characters say.

In a play, you will find these features.

Play	
Scenes	parts of the story in the play
Narrator	the person who describes the scene and gives background information
Characters	their names appear before each line of dialogue to tell who is speaking
Dialogue	conversations between different characters

Student CD-ROM

Reading Strategy

Determine the Sequence of Events

The **plot,** or main events, of a play follows a certain order. This is called the **sequence of events.**

1. Below you will find a group of sentences from the play. They are not in the right order. On a piece of paper write the sentences in the order in which they happen in the play. To help you decide the sequence of events, look for words that serve as clues such as *before, after,* and *next.*
   - **a.** The next morning, more than a dozen sheep are gone.
   - **b.** One night, there is a storm.
   - **c.** "It's all right Miguel. We'll find them. This is not a job for you."
   - **d.** Miguel says, "I can find them! I can help!"
2. As you read the play, check to see if you put the events in the correct sequence.

Student CD-ROM

MULTI-LEVEL OPTIONS *Reading Strategy*

Newcomer Prepare seven index cards with one day of the week written on each card. Mix the cards up and distribute them randomly. ***Say:*** *Stand in the front of the room. Put yourselves in correct sequence. Hold up your cards.* After students arrange themselves, have their classmates check the sequence by reciting the days.

Beginning Prepare 12 index cards with one month written on each card. Mix the cards up and distribute them randomly. ***Say:*** *Stand in the front of the room. Put yourselves in correct sequence. Hold up your cards.* After students arrange themselves, have their classmates check the sequence by reciting the months.

Intermediate Have students work in pairs. Instruct them to copy sentences 1. a–d in a logical order. Tell them to check their work with another pair.

Advanced Instruct students to copy sentences 1. a–d in a logical order. Then have them write a sixth sentence. ***Say:*** *Write another sentence to follow the last sentence in the book. Write a sentence about what Miguel says to his father.* Have students share their sentences with a partner.

And Now Miguel

a play based on a novel
by Joseph Krumgold

105

UNIT 2 • CHAPTER 3
Reading Selection

Reading Selection Materials

Audio: *Unit 2, Chapter 3*
Teacher Resource Book: *Reading Summary, pp. 79–80*

Preview the Selection

Teacher Resource Book: *Know / Want to Know / Learned Chart, p. 42*

1. **Use a graphic organizer** Ask students to think about the title and the photo. Help them create a KWL chart. Use guiding questions: *Where is this? Who do you think Miguel is? What does he do? What other farming tasks do you think he has to do? Do you think he likes this work? Why or why not?* Instruct them to complete the *learned* column in the chart after reading the selection.
2. **Connect** Ask what changes Miguel might observe or experience. Tell students they will read about Miguel's goal and the changes that allow him to reach his goal.

Cultural Connection

Say: *In many cultures, children do the same work as their parents. We call that "following in their parents' footsteps." Do your parents want you to "follow in their footsteps"? Do you want to do the same work as your parents?* Have students discuss the subject in small groups and report back to the class.

Learning Styles
Intrapersonal

Direct your students to think about their dreams and goals. Ask if they know what they are good at and what their strengths are. Have them write about how their goals and their strengths are connected in their Reading Logs.

Read the Selection

1. **Use text features** Direct students to the features of a play on the page: scene number, names of characters, and dialogue. Tell students to identify the names of the characters who are speaking. Direct students to the illustration to make guesses about where Gabriel and Miguel are.
2. **Shared reading** Play the audio. Ask volunteers to read the parts of different characters in scene 1.
3. **Analyze character** *Ask: What does Miguel want to be and do?* (He wants to be a man so he can take the sheep into the mountains.)

Sample Answer to Guide Question
Gabriel is older, so he was born first.

See Teacher Edition pp. 434–435 for a list of English-Spanish cognates in the reading selection.

Audio

Scene 1

1 **Miguel:** *I am Miguel Chavez. To my family, I am just a boy. But I want to be a man. The men in my family raise sheep in the mountains of New Mexico. It has been our work for hundreds of years. I, too, will be a shepherd someday. I hope and I wait. But "someday" never comes.*

2 **Narrator:** Miguel and his brother Gabriel are driving out to the new **pasture.** Miguel is quiet.

3 **Gabriel:** What's up, Miguel?

4 **Miguel:** I've been thinking how easy it is for you—to be Gabriel.

Determine the Sequence of Events

Who was born first, Miguel or Gabriel?

5 **Gabriel** *(laughing):* I guess so, little brother. After all, that's who I am!

6 **Miguel:** But it's not easy for me—to be Miguel.

7 **Gabriel:** Maybe not. It takes a little time. Wait a year or two, and it'll be easier.

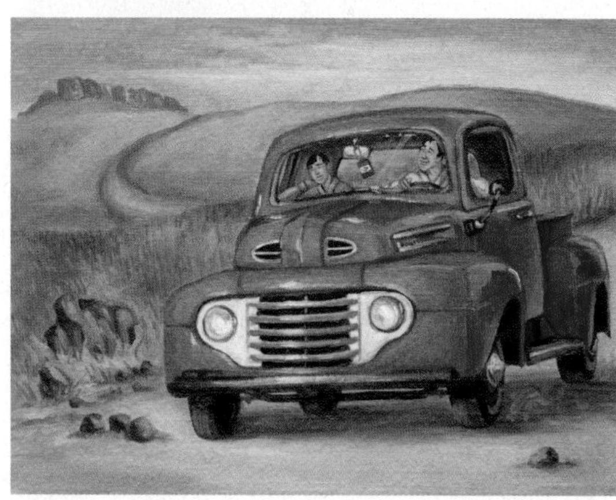

8 **Miguel:** Isn't there something I can do *now?* Like practice?

9 **Gabriel** *(shaking his head):* Being Miguel—it's not like playing basketball. As I say, it takes time.

---

pasture land with grass where animals can eat

MULTI-LEVEL OPTIONS *Read the Selection*

Newcomer Play the audio. Then stand in front of the class and do a choral reading. ***Ask:*** *Does Miguel want to be a shepherd?* (yes) *Is Miguel the older brother?* (no) *Does Miguel want to take the sheep into the mountains?* (yes) *Does Grandfather say yes?* (no)

Beginning Play the audio. Then assign groups of students to different roles. Play it again as students read their roles along with the audio. ***Ask:*** *What does Miguel want to be?* (a shepherd) *Who is Miguel's brother?* (Gabriel) *Where does Miguel want to take the sheep?* (into the mountains) *Who says no?* (Grandfather)

Intermediate Play the audio. Then have volunteers play different roles. ***Ask:*** *What do the men in Miguel's family do?* (raise sheep) *What does Miguel want to do before he's a shepherd?* (practice) *What is Miguel's wish?* (to take the sheep into the mountains) *What job does Miguel get?* (painting numbers on the sheep)

Advanced Ask groups of students to prepare and present different scenes of the play. ***Ask:*** *What advice does Gabriel give Miguel about learning to be himself?* (wait a year or two) *Why does Grandfather say that sheep are like people?* (When people don't stick together, they get lost too.)

Scene 2

10 **Miguel:** *I had a wish, to take the sheep into the Sangre de Cristo Mountains along with the other men.*

If they know you are ready, you will go. But if they don't, you must wait again for another year.

I must try to make them see that I am ready.

11 **Narrator:** The first **lamb** of the year is born. Before long, there are many new lambs. Miguel gets the job of painting numbers on the sheep. That way, it is easy to tell which lamb belongs to which mother in case they get separated. During a break in the work, Miguel's grandfather speaks to him.

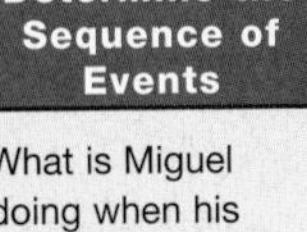

Determine the Sequence of Events

What is Miguel doing when his grandfather speaks to him?

12 **Grandfather:** That's the real work of a *pastor,* of a shepherd. To see that no sheep **strays** away from the **flock.** All must stay together.

13 **Miguel:** Why do they go off by themselves? Why are sheep so dumb?

14 **Grandfather** *(laughing):* That's a good question! Sheep are like people.

15 **Miguel** *(confused):* What do you mean?

16 **Grandfather:** When people don't stick together, they get lost. Now let's get back to work!

lamb a baby sheep
strays leaves a group, gets lost
flock a group of animals

Read the Selection

1. **Understand terms** Have students find the meanings of the glossed words below the selection. Point out the illustration of a pasture on p. 105.
2. **Teacher read aloud** Do a teacher read aloud of scene 2. Then have students read it again in small groups.
3. **Identify events** Ask students to retell the events in order. List the events and model using time-order words in the retelling: *first, then, after that, next, finally.*
4. **Interpret feelings** Ask questions to help students explain how Miguel feels during this scene.
5. **Multi-level options** See MULTI-LEVEL OPTIONS on p. 106.

Sample Answer to Guide Question
Miguel is painting numbers on the mother sheep and the lambs.

Spelling

Silent *b*

Tell students that the letter *b* is silent when it comes after *m.* Point out an example in paragraph 11 (lamb). Ask students to find the other example in paragraph 13 (dumb).

Apply On the board, write: *crab, thumb, beam, comb, plumber, brother.* **Say:** *Circle the three words with a silent* b. (thumb, comb, plumber) Then ask volunteers to pronounce the words.

Read the Selection

1. **Teacher read aloud** Read scene 3 aloud to students. *Ask: Why doesn't Miguel want to go to school?* (He wants to help find the missing sheep.) *Who saw the sheep?* (Miguel's friend Juby)
2. **Discuss scenes** Ask students which scene begins on this page (scene 3). *Ask: Why do you think the author started a new scene here?* (a different place/time, different characters, a different event)

Sample Answer to Guide Question

1. There was a storm.
2. Miguel went to school.
3. Juby said he saw the sheep.

Scene 3

17 **Miguel:** *Some boys dream of becoming policemen or airplane pilots. But for me, there is only one kind of work. At night, I look at the mountains and I dream of becoming a shepherd.*

18 **Narrator:** One night, there is a storm. The next morning, more than a **dozen** sheep are gone. At breakfast, Miguel and his father talk.

19 **Miguel** *(excited):* I can find them! I can help!

20 **Father:** It's time for school, isn't it?

21 **Miguel:** All I want to say—

22 **Father** *(shaking his head):* It's all right, Miguel. We'll find them. This is not a job for you.

23 **Narrator:** Miguel runs out of the house. At school, a boy tells Miguel he saw the sheep.

24 **Miguel:** Where did you see them? Where?

25 **Juby:** What's the matter, Miguel? Is something wrong?

26 **Miguel** *(impatiently):* Just tell me, where are the sheep?

27 **Juby:** Give me a chance, OK?

28 **Narrator:** The bell rings as Juby explains where he saw the sheep. It's in the opposite direction from where the others plan to look.

29 **Miguel:** *I stood there thinking. But not for long. I knew if I came home with the missing sheep, they would have to say I'm ready.*

I didn't look back as I ran down the hill, away from the school.

30 **Narrator:** Miguel **searches** for hours, but he can't find the sheep. He is tired, and his feet hurt. He is about to give up when he spots the sheep coming up the hill toward him.

Determine the Sequence of Events

Put these events in order:
Miguel went to school.
There was a storm.
Juby said he saw the sheep.

dozen twelve

searches looks for someone or something

MULTI-LEVEL OPTIONS *Read the Selection*

Newcomer *Ask: Are some sheep gone in the morning?* (yes) *Does Miguel want Gabriel to find them?* (no) *Does Miguel return home with the missing sheep?* (yes) *Does Father say Miguel can go to the mountains soon?* (no)

Beginning *Ask: What's missing in the morning?* (sheep) *What does Miguel say he can do?* (find them) *What does Miguel return home with?* (the missing sheep) *Who says Miguel can't go to the mountains this summer?* (Father)

Intermediate *Ask: How does Miguel feel when the sheep are missing?* (excited) *What does Juby tell Miguel at school?* (He saw the sheep.) *What does Father say is more important than sheep?* (school) *Why does Father tell Miguel that he will grow up to be a burro if he misses school?* (Miguel will be uneducated. Burros are not very smart.)

Advanced *Ask: What happens each night when Miguel goes to sleep?* (He dreams of being a shepherd.) *Where are the missing sheep?* (in the opposite direction of where the men plan to look) *Why is Miguel disappointed?* (His father says Miguel can't go to the mountains.)

Scene 4

Determine the Sequence of Events

What happens after the men shout "Bravo!"?

31 **Narrator:** A little while later, Miguel arrives home with the sheep. *"Bravo!"* the men shout. But Miguel's father has something to say.

32 **Father:** I am glad that the sheep are back. Sheep are important. But school is even more important. If you stayed away from school every time something had to be done, you'd grow up to be a ***burro.***

33 **Miguel:** I understand, Papá.

34 **Father** *(smiling):* I want to thank you for what you did, though.

35 **Narrator:** Later, Miguel tries to ask his father about going up to the mountains when school is over.

36 **Miguel:** I can go to the mountains? Yes?

37 **Father** *(firmly):* No! It cannot be arranged. Not this year. *(He nods toward Gabriel.)* Gabriel will go. That is part of his work. It's not yet time for you to go.

38 **Miguel** *(disappointed):* Yes, Papá.

39 **Narrator:** That night, Miguel prays to San Ysidro.

40 **Miguel** *(praying):* If you think it is a good idea, please arrange it so I may go up into the Sangre de Cristo Mountains.

---

burro Spanish word for "donkey," a person who is not very smart

Read the Selection

1. **Choral reading** Do a choral reading of scene 4. Divide students into three groups. Assign each group one of the three characters. ***Ask:*** *Who found the sheep?* (Miguel) *Why can't Miguel go to the mountains?* (His father said that it's not time yet.)
2. **Understand the narrator** Have students reread the part of the narrator in scene 4. ***Ask:*** *What information does the narrator give?* (how much time has passed, events that have happened, events happening now) Explain that the narrator helps readers understand the sequence of events.
3. **Multi-level options** See MULTI-LEVEL OPTIONS on p. 108.

Sample Answer to Guide Question

After the men shout, Miguel's father talks to Miguel. He says school is more important for Miguel.

th Spelling

Silent *gh*

Tell students that the letters *gh* are silent in some words. On the board, write: *night.* Underline the letter *i.* Say *night,* exaggerating the long *i* sound. ***Say:*** *In* night, *the letter* i *makes a long sound, so it is a long vowel. When the vowel before* gh *is long,* gh *is silent. The letter* i *in* night *is long, so the* gh *is silent. Can you find words in paragraphs 22 and 34 with a silent* gh? (right, though)

Read the Selection

1. **Teacher read aloud** Read scene 5 aloud to students. *Ask: Why does Miguel want to do a good job sweeping?* (so his father will think he is a man and let him go to the mountains)
2. **Recognize features** *Ask: In scene 5, who is the narrator speaking to?* (audience) *Who is Father speaking to?* (Miguel) *Who is Miguel speaking to?* (audience) *Does Miguel always speak to the audience?* (No, sometimes he speaks to the other characters in the play.) Point out that when Miguel's speech is in italics, it shows he's speaking to the audience.

Sample Answer to Guide Question
Miguel falling into a fleece bag and the other men laughing at him made Father unhappy with Miguel's behavior.

Scene 5

41 **Narrator:** It's June. After the sheep are **sheared,** the flock will leave for the mountains. During the shearing, Miguel sweeps the floor.

42 **Miguel:** *It's a big job, to be the one with the broom. When the fleeces come off the sheep, they fall on the floor. And if they get dirty, the buyer is disappointed. So the floor has to be swept in the best and most careful way.*

My father trusts me to do a good job. Maybe he believes I'm becoming a man.

43 **Narrator:** Miguel is a hard worker. The men praise him because he sweeps up so much dust. Miguel feels proud. But suddenly one day, Miguel slips. He falls into the bottom of a big sack of fleeces.

44 **Eli:** Did anyone see Miguel?

45 **Gabriel** *(looking down in the sack):* Here! He's in the sack!

46 **Narrator:** All the men yell and laugh, except for Miguel's father.

47 **Father** ***(snapping)****:* Is this any time to start playing games, like you were a little boy? Now come on! Up!

48 **Miguel:** *I was ashamed. I no longer felt like a man. If I could have stayed at the bottom of the sack, I would have stayed there.*

Determine the Sequence of Events

What events made Father unhappy with Miguel's behavior?

sheared cut (the wool of the sheep)

snapping speaking in an annoyed or angry voice

MULTI-LEVEL OPTIONS *Read the Selection*

Newcomer *Ask: Does Miguel paint the floor?* (no) *Does Miguel fall into a sack of fleece?* (yes) *Does Miguel's father say he can go to the mountains?* (yes) *Is Gabriel going to college?* (no)

Beginning *Ask: What is Miguel's job?* (He sweeps the floor.) *What does Miguel fall into?* (a sack of fleece) *Where will Miguel go?* (to the mountains) *Where will Gabriel go?* (to the army)

Intermediate *Ask: Why are the men happy with Miguel?* (because he sweeps up a lot of dust) *How does Miguel feel when he falls into the sack?* (embarrassed, ashamed) *How does his father feel?* (angry) *What will Gabriel do in the army?* (train to be a soldier)

Advanced *Ask: What happens if Miguel does a poor job sweeping?* (The fleece gets dirty.) *Why is Miguel ashamed when he falls into the sack?* (He feels like a little boy.) *How does Miguel feel about Gabriel leaving?* (confused, upset; He doesn't want his brother to leave, but he wants to go to the mountains.)

Scene 6

49 **Narrator:** Two days later, Miguel's father has news for Miguel.

50 **Father** *(seriously):* You will go with us to the mountains, Miguel.

51 **Miguel** ***(puzzled):*** Me? Go to the Sangre de Cristo Mountains for the whole summer?

52 **Father:** Yes.

53 **Miguel:** I'm glad, Papá.

54 **Father:** I'm glad, too.

55 **Miguel:** How did this happen?

56 **Father:** Gabriel can't go. He has to go into the army to train to be a soldier. There was a letter this morning.

57 **Miguel:** *I stood there quietly. I did not know what to think. There was too much good mixed up with the bad.*

Determine the Sequence of Events

What happened earlier that Miguel did not know about?

puzzled not understanding

Read the Selection

1. **Shared reading** Continue reading scene 6 as students join in. Divide students into two groups. Have one group join in for Father's parts and the other for Miguel's parts. ***Ask:*** *What news does Miguel's father have?* (Miguel is going to the mountains.) *Who isn't going to the mountains?* (Gabriel)
2. **Identify character feelings** Have students reread scene 6 in pairs. Ask questions to help students analyze the feelings of Father and Miguel at the news about Gabriel. Direct students to character feelings in parentheses next to character names.
3. **Multi-level options** See MULTI-LEVEL OPTIONS on p. 110.

Sample Answer to Guide Question
Gabriel had received a letter from the army.

Punctuation

Question marks

Draw a question mark on the board. Tell students to use it at the end of every question, even if the question is not a complete sentence. Direct students to paragraphs 51 and 55. ***Ask:*** ***Which question is an incomplete sentence?*** (Me?) Have students identify additional questions in paragraphs 44 and 47.

Apply Write on the board: *Gabriel can't go. There was a letter this morning.* Have students work in pairs to rewrite the sentences as questions. Remind them to end their questions with a question mark.

Read the Selection

1. **Teacher read aloud** Read scene 7 aloud to students. *Ask: Why does Miguel feel bad?* (He thinks his prayers caused Gabriel to go away.) *What did Gabriel wish for?* (to see other places)
2. **Role-play** Have students reread the dialogue between Miguel and Gabriel in pairs. *Ask: What does Gabriel want Miguel to do?* (He wants Miguel to learn everything about sheep.) *Why?* (so they can work together and be the best *pastores,* or shepherds, in New Mexico)

Sample Answer to Guide Question

1. Miguel prayed to St. Ysidro.
2. Gabriel has to go away.

Determine the Sequence of Events

Put these events in order: Miguel prayed to St. Ysidro. Gabriel has to go away.

Scene 7

58 **Narrator:** Miguel feels terrible. He thinks it's because of his prayers that Gabriel has to go away. Finally, he and Gabriel talk together.

59 **Gabriel:** It's dangerous to wish so hard, Miguel. Sometimes wishes come true in ways that surprise you.

60 **Miguel:** I'm sorry.

61 **Gabriel:** I made a wish, too. For a long time, I have wished to see other places—like an ocean. Now I have my wish.

62 **Miguel:** I think I understand.

63 **Gabriel:** While I'm gone, Miguel, you learn everything about sheep. When I come back, you and I will be the best two ***pastores*** in all New Mexico.

64 **Miguel** *(smiling):* I promise.

pastores Spanish word for "shepherds"

MULTI-LEVEL OPTIONS *From Reading to Writing*

Newcomer *Ask: Does Miguel feel bad?* (yes) *Does Gabriel tell Miguel to learn about goats?* (no) *Does Gabriel go to the army?* (yes) *Does Miguel go to the mountains?* (yes)

Beginning *Ask: How does Miguel feel?* (bad, terrible) *What should Miguel learn more about?* (sheep) *Where does Gabriel go?* (to the army) *Where does Miguel go?* (to the mountains)

Intermediate *Ask: What does Gabriel tell Miguel about wishing for things?* (It can be dangerous to wish too hard.) *What does Gabriel wish for?* (to see other places) *Who goes with Miguel to the mountains?* (the men) *How long does it take to reach the camp?* (five days) *Do you think the trip is hard or easy? Why?*

Advanced *Ask: Why does Miguel feel terrible?* (He thinks his wishes caused Gabriel to leave.) *What makes Miguel feel better?* (Gabriel says that he wants to see new places.) *How does Miguel feel when he gets to the camp in the mountains?* (proud, like a man) *Explain why.*

Scene 8

65 **Miguel:** *The next morning, I left with the men for the mountains. And Gabriel left for the army.*

Five days later, we reached our camp, high up in the Sangre de Cristo Mountains. Many men named Chavez had come to this place. And now, watching the country below I, Miguel, stood there at last.

Determine the Sequence of Events

What two events happened at the same time?

About the Author — Joseph Krumgold (1908–1980)

Joseph Krumgold was born in New Jersey. He wrote novels, children's books, and screenplays for movies. Krumgold's books tell stories about growing up and how we learn to accept and respect one another. In 1966, his book *About Miguel Chavez* was made into a movie called *And Now Miguel.*

➤ Krumgold wrote this story as a narrative. It was adapted into a play. How are the two genres the same? How are they different? Which one do you like better? Why?

A Capitalization

Place names

Tell students that the first letter in names of places such as cities, states, or provinces is always capitalized. On the board, write: *New Jersey.* ***Ask:*** *Why are the letters* N *and* J *capitalized?* (New Jersey is the name of a state.) *Can you find the name of another state in paragraph 63?* (New Mexico)

Apply Have students write the names of cities, towns, states, or provinces they have lived in or visited. Monitor for correct capitalization.

Evaluate Your Reading Strategy

Determine the Sequence of Events *Say: You have practiced an important reading strategy. Now you can decide how well you have done. Does this statement describe how you read?*

When I read a play, I notice the order of events. Knowing the order of events helps me remember important things in a play.

Read the Selection

1. **Teacher read aloud** Read scene 8. ***Ask:*** *Where does Miguel go?* (to the mountains) *Where does Gabriel go?* (to the army) *How do you think Miguel felt in the Sangre de Cristo Mountains?* (proud, but a little sad because he missed his brother) *Did Miguel change? How?*
2. **Multi-level options** See MULTI-LEVEL OPTIONS on p. 108.

Sample Answer to Guide Question
Miguel went to the mountains and Gabriel went to the army.

About the Author

Express ideas and opinions ***Ask:*** *Is it important to accept and respect others? What do you think is the difference between a man and a boy? Is there something special that adults know?*

Across Selections

Teacher Resource Book: *Two-Column Chart, p. 44*

Make comparisons and contrasts Compare and contrast the changes that happened in Elizabeth's life traveling to a new land with those in Miguel's life, which made him grow up and accept a man's work. Ask students how both Elizabeth and Miguel change and grow up. ***Ask:*** *In what ways were they different?* Have students record their ideas on a two-column chart.

Reading Comprehension

Question-Answer Relationships

Sample Answers

1. The men in Miguel's family take care of sheep.
2. Some sheep are missing.
3. Miguel paints numbers on the sheep and lambs and sweeps the floor.
4. Both jobs are important: One helps keep the flock together and the other helps keep the fleece clean.
5. He thinks he will be able to go to the mountains with the men.
6. His brother knows that Miguel wants to grow up fast, but it's not easy to be patient and wait for the right time.
7. The father wants Miguel to understand how important school is.
8. Miguel feels happy because he finally goes to the mountains, but he feels bad because his brother has to go away.
9. I think Miguel will spend the rest of his life taking care of sheep.
10. Most students will say that they want to get a car and a driver's license, stay out late with their friends, or get a job instead of going to school.

Build Reading Fluency

Adjust Your Reading Rate

Demonstrate to the students how you change your rate of reading depending on the purpose and type of reading material.

Beyond the Reading

Reading Comprehension

Question-Answer Relationships (QAR)

"Right There" Questions

1. **Recall Facts** What job do the men in Miguel's family do for a living?
2. **Understand Chronological Order** What happens after the storm?

"Think and Search" Questions

3. **Identify** What two jobs does Miguel get to do?
4. **Analyze** How important are these two jobs?
5. **Explain** What does Miguel think will happen if he comes home with the missing sheep?

"Author and You" Questions

6. **Draw Conclusions** Why do you think Miguel tells his brother that "it is not easy to be Miguel"?
7. **Analyze Characters** Why do you think Father tells Miguel he will be a *burro* if he does not go to school?
8. **Analyze Characters** In paragraph 57, what does Miguel mean when he says, "There was too much good mixed up with the bad"?
9. **Make Inferences** How do you think Miguel will spend the rest of his life?

"On Your Own" Question

10. **Relate the Story to Your Life** What is something that you would like to do, but your parents think you are too young to do?

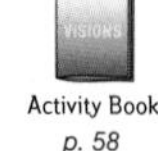
Activity Book
p. 58

Build Reading Fluency

Adjust Your Reading Rate

When you read a play you must adjust your reading rate to read with expression.

1. Listen to the Audio CD for "And Now Miguel."
2. Read along with the Audio CD.
3. Read with expression.

MULTI-LEVEL OPTIONS *Elements of Literature*

Newcomer Have students work in four groups with advanced students. Assign one of scenes 1–4 to each group. Instruct groups to complete the chart on p. 115 for their scene. If possible, have them collect props and make costumes. Tell them to practice with other groups.

Invite families or another class to see the play.

Beginning Have students work in four groups with intermediate students. Assign one of scenes 5–8 to each group. Instruct groups to complete the chart on p. 115 for their scene. If possible, have them collect props and make costumes. Have them practice with other groups.

Invite families or another class to see the play.

Intermediate See MULTI-LEVEL OPTIONS for Beginning students.

Advanced See MULTI-LEVEL OPTIONS for Newcomers.

Listen, Speak, Interact 

Perform a Scene

Good actors read their lines as if they are feeling the characters' emotions. Choose one scene from "And Now Miguel" and perform it with a small group.

1. Decide how the events in the story would affect the characters' emotions.
2. Perform the scene for the class, acting out the emotions you discussed. Use your own experiences to help you in your presentation.
3. If possible, record the presentation on video.
4. Listen to the other groups in the class. What emotions do you hear and see in their presentations?

Elements of Literature

Understand Scenes in a Play

Playwrights (people who write plays) usually divide a play into different parts, or **scenes.** In "And Now Miguel," each scene happens in a different place, or setting. Sometimes the narrator describes the setting. Other times you have to guess where the scene takes place by getting clues from the dialogue.

1. Choose one scene in "And Now Miguel" and describe how to show the setting in a theater. What is the scenery behind the actors? List props (things on the stage such as chairs and tables), and costumes (what the actors are wearing), lighting, and sounds you would use.
2. Copy this chart in your Reading Log. Complete it with your ideas.
3. Draw your scene.

Scene	Setting	Props	Costumes	Lighting
1	in a truck	wheel	work clothes	bright

Reading Log | Activity Book p. 59 | Student CD-ROM

Home Connection

Have students prepare a choral reading of scenes from the play. Assign roles to volunteers or small groups. Assign "directors" to lead the readings. Ask students to invite family and friends to attend the performance.

Learning Styles *Visual*

Instruct students to work in groups to design a "set" for the play. Have them prepare props, make costumes, and paint backgrounds for scenes that are being performed.

Beyond the Reading

Listen, Speak, Interact

Perform a Scene

Teacher Resource Book: *Open Mind Diagram, p. 47*

1. **Reread in small groups** Assign groups different scenes to perform. Have them read the scene together and decide on roles. Tell them to look for clues to character feelings.
2. **Newcomers** Reread with this group. Have them consider the events that change Miguel's life and how Miguel felt. Help students with inflection and pauses as they read the dialogues.
3. **Draw conclusions about the characters** Tell students to write about the feelings and emotions of the character they portrayed. Have them explain why their character was experiencing those emotions.

Elements of Literature

Understand Scenes in a Play

Teacher Resource Book: *Reading Log, p. 64*

1. Point out and clarify examples of setting, props, costumes, and lighting for scene 1. Have students choose another scene and imagine the setting. Students can draw their pictures of the setting, label them first, and then fill in the details on the chart.
2. **Use personal experience** Point out that settings are used in television, movies, and plays. Have students describe the setting of a favorite program. Ask other students to guess the show.
3. **Multi-level options** See MULTI-LEVEL OPTIONS on p. 114.

ASSESS

Tell students to identify the different components that are a scene and give an example of each. (setting: on the mountain; props: shepherd's staff; costumes: boots, jeans; lighting: bright)

Word Study

Contrast *Its* and *It's*

Teacher Resource Book: *Personal Dictionary, p. 63*

Use flash cards Instruct students to make their own pair of flash cards for *its* and *it's.* Say different sentences and have students decide which word is correct by holding up the flash card.

Answers

Examples: But it's not easy for me. But it is not easy for me.
It's not like playing basketball. It is not like playing basketball.

Grammar Focus

Identify and Use the Future Conditional

Model a sentence Model a sentence with the future conditional. *Say: If it rains this afternoon, I will watch a movie.* Then have students complete the same *if*-clauses with their own result clauses. Remind them to use *will* with the future conditional. Point out that the simple present tense is used in the *if*-clause.

ASSESS

Write on the board: *If we don't have homework, I _____. If I _____, the teacher will be pleased.* Instruct students to complete the sentences using the future conditional.

Word Study

Contrast *Its* and *It's*

The words **its** and **it's** look alike but have different meanings.

Its is used to show possession. *It's* is a **contraction** (short form) of *it* and *is.* The apostrophe (') shows that a letter has been left out.

Possessive Form: *Its*
The sheep's ears are soft.
Its ears are soft.
Contraction Form: *It's*
It is rainy on the mountains.
It's rainy on the mountains.

1. Skim the reading to find examples of *its* and *it's.* Write the sentences with these words in your Personal Dictionary.
2. Rewrite the sentences to include the nouns and verbs.
3. Note that most possessive forms include apostrophes. For example, *Anna's book* means "the book that belongs to Anna."

Personal Dictionary

Activity Book *p. 60*

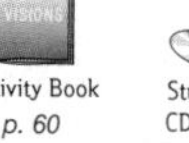
Student CD-ROM

Grammar Focus

Identify and Use the Future Conditional

The **future conditional** is used to describe what might happen in the future. The condition is what must happen first. It begins with the word *if.* The result happens later. It has a verb referring to the future, often with *will.*

If Joe needs help, he will ask the teacher.

Write three sentences like these using the future conditional:

If Miguel finds the sheep, he will be happy.

If I save some money, I might buy some CDs.

Activity Book *pp. 61–62*

Student Handbook

Student CD-ROM

MULTI-LEVEL OPTIONS *From Reading to Writing*

Newcomer Have students draw a picture of something they want to do but cannot do yet, such as drive a car or get a job. Give them this sentence starter: *I want to _____, but I can't do it right now.* Help students to complete the sentence to describe their picture.

Beginning Brainstorm a list of conflicts between a student and a parent. Have students work in pairs. Have them discuss one conflict and complete this dialogue: (Student): *I think I should _____. I can _____.* (Parent): *You can't because _____.* Help students complete the sentences. Tell them to perform for another pair.

Intermediate Brainstorm and write a list of conflicts between a student and a parent. Instruct students to work in pairs to write a dialogue about one of the conflicts. Remind them that both the parent and child must give reasons for their positions. Have students perform their dialogues for the class.

Advanced Tell students to work in pairs. Direct them to write about a conflict between a student and a parent. Remind them to include reasons for each position. Have students perform their dialogues for the class.

From Reading to Writing 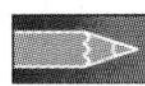

Write Dialogue for a Scene in a Play

Write dialogue for a scene in a play with two characters. One character wants to do something, but the other character does not.

1. Write your characters' names.
2. Decide the reason for the conflict.
   a. Write the first character's reasons for wanting to do the activity.
   b. Write the second character's reasons for why the first character cannot do the activity.
   c. Use the future conditional.
   d. Be sure to use apostrophes correctly when writing contractions and possessives.
3. Write the dialogue between the two characters.
4. Perform a dramatic interpretation of the scene. Speak with expression. Use gestures and body language.

Activity Book p. 63

Across Content Areas 

Understand State Flags

Each state in the United States has its own flag. The colors and symbols on a state flag usually tell something about the state's people and history.

For example, the New Mexico flag shows a Native American symbol for the sun. The red and yellow colors come from the Spanish flag because Spanish explorers came to New Mexico in the 1500s.

1. Draw the flag for your state or another state.
2. Research what the design and colors stand for. Use the library or the Internet.
3. Explain the colors and symbols in your flag.

Activity Book p. 64

Reteach and Reassess

Text Structure Have students identify the features of a play. (scenes, narrator, characters, dialogue)

Reading Strategy Write on the board: *Juby tells Miguel where the missing sheep are.* Direct students to write one sentence about an event that happens *before* Miguel and Juby talk and one sentence about an event that happens *after* they talk.

Elements of Literature Have students pick one scene. Ask them to describe the setting and lighting. Then have them list the props and costumes the characters need.

Reassess Have students write a paragraph describing what Miguel and Gabriel do together in the play. Ask students to include details such as setting and props for each scene. Remind students to check that the events are in correct order.

Beyond the Reading

From Reading to Writing

Write Dialogue for a Scene in a Play

Teacher Resource Book: *Two-Column Chart, p. 44*

1. **Use a graphic organizer** Use the information about Miguel and his father's dialogue to model the process for preparing a dialogue. Make a two-column chart on the board. Write the characters' names at the top of the chart. Then identify the conflict or disagreement. Ask students to suggest ways for the characters to talk about it as you complete the chart.
2. **Organize information** Ask students to suggest topics for conflicts. List them on the board. Add helpful words and phrases. Then instruct students to work in pairs to create a dialogue about a conflict between two characters.
3. **Language experience dialogue** Have them dictate their dialogues as you write them. Then tell students to practice reading their lines with their partners.
4. **Multi-level options** See MULTI-LEVEL OPTIONS on p. 116.

Across Content Areas: Social Studies

Understand State Flags

1. **Connect** Tell students to describe flags of countries they have lived in or visited. Ask them to describe the colors, symbols, or other items on the flag. If possible, have them explain the historical significance of the flag and its symbols.
2. **Draw a picture** Instruct students to create a new flag for your school. Have the class brainstorm and list possible symbols to use. Ask students to explain their completed flags.

ASSESS

Have students write two or three sentences describing their state or country flag. Have them explain what they think the symbols mean.

Assessment Program: *Unit 2, Chapter 3 Quiz, pp. 27–28*

Chapter Materials

Activity Book: *pp. 65–72*
Audio: *Unit 2, Chapter 4*
Student Handbook
Student CD-ROM: *Unit 2, Chapter 4*
Teacher Resource Book: *Lesson Plan, Teacher Resources, Reading Summary, Activity Book Answer Key*
Teacher Resource CD-ROM
Assessment Program: *Quiz, pp. 29–30; Teacher and Student Resources, pp. 115–144*
Assessment CD-ROM
Transparencies
The Heinle Newbury House Dictionary/CD-ROM
Web Site: www.heinle.visions.com

Objectives

Teacher think aloud *Say: I know that* real *means that something is true. But* fiction *means a story is not true. I think* realistic *might be something that is similar to something real but is not real. So* realistic fiction *must be a story that is made-up but could be a true story.*

Use Prior Knowledge

Discuss Surprises

Teacher Resource Book: *Sunshine Organizer, p. 40*

Share knowledge Make a Sunshine Organizer on the board as you explain surprising news you heard recently.

CHAPTER 4

Tuck Triumphant

an excerpt from a novel by Theodore Taylor

Into the Reading

Objectives

Reading Draw conclusions as you read realistic fiction.

Listening and Speaking Interview a newcomer.

Grammar Use adjectives before nouns.

Writing Write a realistic story.

Content Social Studies: Learn about families.

Use Prior Knowledge

Discuss Surprises

Think about a time when you heard surprising news.

1. Copy the Sunshine Organizer on a piece of paper.
2. Name the surprise in the center of the circle.
3. Write answers to these questions around the circle.
   a. Who told you the surprising news?
   b. What was the surprise?
   c. When did you learn about the surprise?
   d. Where did the surprise happen?
   e. Why was it a surprise?
   f. How did you react to the surprise?

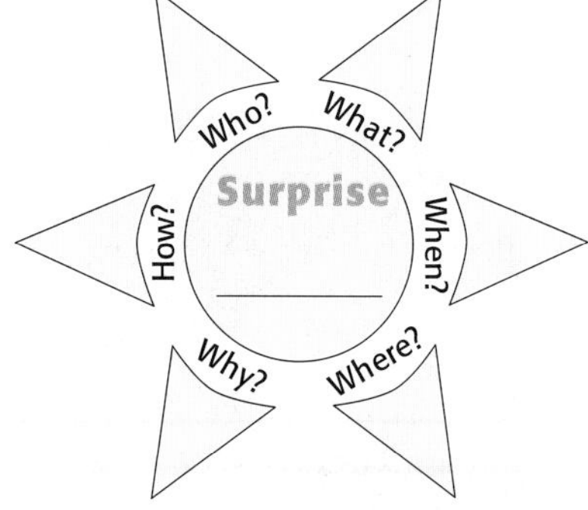

4. Share your outline information with a partner.

118 **Unit 2** Changes

MULTI-LEVEL OPTIONS *Build Vocabulary*

Newcomer Have students create a collage of pictures relating to travel and airports. Help students label the pictures.

Beginning Brainstorm a list of travel words with students. Instruct small groups to categorize items in the list. Help students name their categories. Then have groups compare their categories.

Intermediate Tell students to brainstorm a list of travel words. Instruct small groups to categorize items in the list and name each category. Have groups compare and expand their lists.

Advanced Ask students to brainstorm a list of travel words. Tell each student to find at least three categories for the items on the list. Have them compare their categories with other students.

Build Background

Korea

Korea is a part of Asia south of China. Approximately 70 million people live there. A few years after World War II, Korea was divided into North Korea and South Korea.

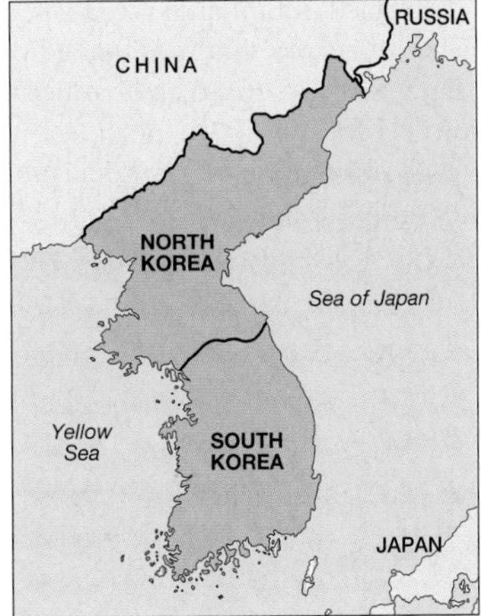

Content Connection

Korea is a **peninsula**. A peninsula is a body of land that has water on three sides.

Build Vocabulary

Identify Related Words

"Tuck Triumphant" takes place in an airport in Los Angeles, California. There are several words about travel in the story.

1. On a piece of paper, draw a web like the one here.
2. Read the sentences below and find five words that relate to travel. Write these words in the web.
   a. Passengers began to come and go out of Customs and Immigration.
   b. We saw a pretty Korean stewardess.
   c. Handing over his Korean passport, she said, "I admire your courage."

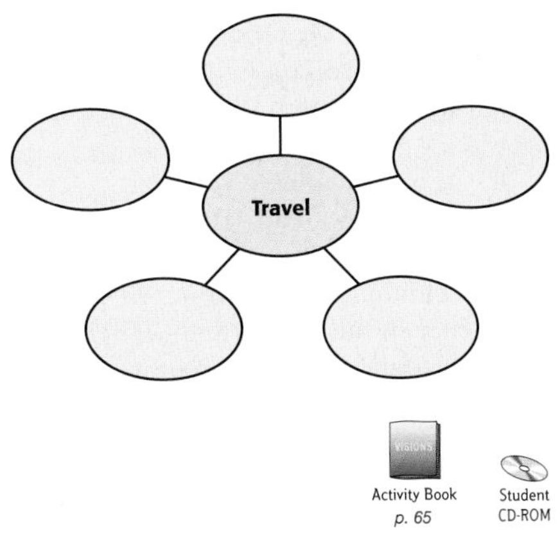

Activity Book *p. 65* Student CD-ROM

Cultural Connection

Build Vocabulary Have students plan a trip to Korea. Ask them to find special sights to see and places to visit. Then have small groups create a "To Do" list for their trip. Instruct them to write everything they will need to do or to take with them on their trip.

Learning Styles *Mathematical*

Build Background Ask students to find out the name of Korean currency (won) and its present exchange rate with the dollar. Tell them to look in the travel section of a newspaper or do an Internet search. Then have students calculate the exchange of $100 into Korean currency.

Build Background

Korea

1. **Use a map** Have students locate Korea on a map or globe. Tell them to identify surrounding countries and bodies of water. *Ask: What country is north of Korea?* (China) *What country is east of Korea?* (Japan) *What seas are to the east and west of Korea?* (Sea of Japan, Yellow Sea)
2. **Content Connection** Have students find and identify other peninsulas on a world map or a map of the United States.

Build Vocabulary

Identify Related Words

Teacher Resource Book: *Web, p. 37*

1. **Use a semantic word map** Have students brainstorm phrases associated with airplanes, air travel, and airports. Create a word map. Add the related words from the textbook to the word map. Use the map for vocabulary reference throughout this chapter.
2. **Reading selection vocabulary** You may want to introduce the glossed words in the reading selection before students begin reading. Key words: *adoption, embarrassed, orphan, bewildered, disbelief, breathless.* Instruct students to write each word with correct spelling and their definitions in their Personal Dictionaries. Have them pronounce each word and divide it into syllables.
3. **Multi-level options** See MULTI-LEVEL OPTIONS on p. 118.

Answers

1. a. passengers, Customs, Immigration
   b. stewardess
   c. passport

ASSESS

Have students write sentences using three of the related vocabulary words.

UNIT 2 • CHAPTER 4
Into the Reading

Text Structure

Realistic Fiction

Teacher Resource Book: *Reading Log, p. 64; Two-Column Chart, p. 44*

Recognize features Direct students to the feature chart. Have students think of other examples of realistic fiction they have read, such as "Hatchet" from Unit 1. Create a two-column chart for students to record the setting, characters, and plot for this reading selection.

Reading Strategy

Draw Conclusions

1. **Teacher think aloud** *Say: I know that insects have six legs. This new bug has eight legs. I can use facts to draw the conclusion that this new bug is not an insect.*
2. **Locate derivation** Have students locate the derivation of *conclusion* in the glossary in the Student Handbook and record it in their Reading Logs.
3. **Multi-level options** See MULTI-LEVEL OPTIONS below.

ASSESS

Have students match the features of realistic fiction with the definitions:

1. setting	a. events that could happen
2. plot	b. the people
3. characters	c. a real place

Text Structure

Realistic Fiction

"Tuck Triumphant" is **realistic fiction**—a story that uses made-up characters and events that could happen in real life.

As you read, look for details such as the setting and events that could be real. Write two examples of each in your Reading Log.

Realistic Fiction	
Setting	a real place
Plot	events that could happen in real life
Characters	people who take part in the events; they talk and act like real people

Reading Log

Student CD-ROM

Reading Strategy

Draw Conclusions

You **draw a conclusion** when you decide that something is true, or not true, after thinking carefully about all of the facts. For example, if you see that your friend never chooses broccoli in the cafeteria (a fact), and if she makes a face when she sees broccoli (a fact), you can draw a conclusion that she does not like broccoli.

Use the chart to help you draw conclusions as you read "Tuck Triumphant." List facts from the reading in one column. List facts from your experience in the next column. Then write the conclusion you can draw.

Facts from Reading	Facts from Experience	Conclusions
Helen calls the other person "Mother."	Children call only their mothers "Mother."	The other person is Helen's mother.

Student CD-ROM

MULTI-LEVEL OPTIONS *Reading Strategy*

Newcomer Give students simple facts and have them draw conclusions. For example, ***say:*** *The weather is cold. The days are short. Can you draw a conclusion about the season of the year?* (It's winter.)

Beginning Give students simple facts and have them draw conclusions. For example, write on the board: *Today is Thursday. Tomorrow I have band practice. I can draw the conclusion that band practice is on _____.* (Friday)

Intermediate Model drawing a conclusion. ***Say:*** *Today is Thursday. Tomorrow I have band practice. I can draw the conclusion that band practice is on Friday.* Then have groups of students write two or three facts. Have another group draw a conclusion based on those facts.

Advanced Model drawing a conclusion. ***Say:*** *Today is Thursday. Tomorrow I have band practice. I can draw the conclusion that band practice is on Friday.* Then have students write their own facts and ask a partner to draw a conclusion about them.

TUCK Triumphant

an excerpt from a novel
by Theodore Taylor

121

Reading Selection Materials

Audio: *Unit 2, Chapter 4*
Teacher Resource Book: *Reading Summary, pp. 81–82*

Preview the Selection

1. **Use the illustration** Have students describe the illustration. ***Ask:*** *Where is this place? Who is in the picture? What are they doing? What are they wearing? Do you think this story is happening now or did it happen a long time ago? Why do you think so?*
2. **Connect** Remind students that the unit theme is *changes*. ***Ask:*** *What kind of changes do you think these people might face?*

Content Connection *The Arts*

Instruct students to work in pairs to create a role-play about picking someone up at the airport. Tell them that they don't know the person they are meeting. Have them decide who the person is, how they will identify the person, and how they feel about the meeting. Then have students perform for another pair.

Learning Styles *Linguistic*

On the board, write: *I'm packing my bag for a trip to Korea. I'm packing _____.* Arrange students in a circle. ***Say:*** *We are pretending to pack for a trip to Korea. Each person will pack one thing. But first you must name everything else already in the bag.* Model this game by pointing to the words and saying them: *I'm packing my bag for a trip to Korea. I'm packing a passport.* Continue modeling a few additional items until students understand the steps.

Reading Selection

Read the Selection

Teacher Resource Book: *Two-Column Chart, p. 44*

1. **Understanding terms** Have students find the boldfaced words in the reading selection. Students can try to figure out the meaning from the text or from the glosses at the bottom of the page. Ask students which words are related to travel and airplanes.
2. **Teacher read aloud** Read paragraphs 1–7 to the students. Then have pairs of students do a reciprocal reading, asking questions as they read.
3. **Identify setting, characters, plot** Use questions to help students identify these features. Have students begin filling them in on a story feature chart.

Sample Answer to Guide Question
Stan is probably the narrator's brother.

See Teacher Edition pp. 434–435 for a list of English-Spanish cognates in the reading selection.

Audio

1 "Will that **adoption** lady be here?" I asked again, wishing I were somewhere else. At the very best, I'd gone along with this whole thing **halfheartedly,** hiding my true feelings, since learning we weren't getting a baby.

2 *Here* was the old, **tottering** Los Angeles airport of my childhood, mostly wood and **corrugated** iron. A new one was being built.

3 Mother shook her head. "She called yesterday. She had to go to Salt Lake City. We're on our own, Helen."

4 We'd survive, I thought. As usual.

5 There was a family poem that we all recited on appropriate occasions. Birthdays and such.

We are the Ogdens
Tougher than leather
We are the Ogdens
We stick together

Draw Conclusions

Who do you think Stan is?

6 Stan had written it when he was about ten and now thought it was silly. He was **embarrassed** by it.

7 After a while passengers from Pan Am Flight 12, a three-tailed, four-motored **Constellation,** began to come out of **Customs and Immigration,** relatives running to meet them, hugging and kissing, **jabbering,** laughing. Most of the passengers were carrying packages wrapped in straw. The greeters had bouquets of flowers.

adoption the act of choosing to take legal responsibility for a child
halfheartedly without interest or energy
tottering moving unsteadily, almost falling down
corrugated having a wavy surface
embarrassed feeling ashamed
Constellation a type of airplane
Customs and Immigration the part of government that keeps track of the goods and people entering a country
jabbering talking quickly without making much sense

MULTI-LEVEL OPTIONS *Read the Selection*

Newcomer Play the audio. Have students do a paired reading of the Reading Summary. ***Ask:*** *Is the family getting a baby?* (no) *Did Stan write a poem?* (yes) *Does a little girl come off the plane?* (no) *Is the boy from Korea?* (yes) *Does he have a round face?* (yes)

Beginning Read the Reading Summary aloud. Then have students do a paired reading of it. ***Ask:*** *What does Helen want for the family?* (a baby) *What did Stan write?* (a poem) *Who comes off the plane?* (a little boy) *Where does he come from?* (Korea) *What shape is his face?* (round)

Intermediate Do a paired reading. ***Ask:*** *Where is the family?* (at the airport) *How does Stan feel about his poem?* (embarrassed) *What is on the boy's chest?* (a sign with his name on it) *What does Helen think when she sees him?* (that he's beautiful)

Advanced Have students read the story silently. ***Ask:*** *Why is the narrator unhappy at the beginning of the story?* (She wanted the family to adopt a baby.) *In Stan's poem, what do the Ogdens always do?* (stick together) *Why did the boy come to America?* (He's being adopted.) *What did Helen do when she first saw him?* (She melted.)

8 I'd left Tuck and Daisy* at home, telling them this was the day their new brother was arriving.

Draw Conclusions

Who is the family waiting for?

9 The rest of us Ogdens—father, mother, Luke and myself—stood silently watching for *our* passenger. Finally, we saw a pretty Korean stewardess holding the hand of a little boy who looked even younger than six. On his chest was a big sign: Chok-Do Choi. In his right hand was a small straw bag. In her free hand the stewardess held a little gray stuffed **koala.**

10 Chok-Do was a war **orphan** and war orphans usually had few possessions. The fighting between North Korea and South Korea hadn't been over too long.

11 *He's beautiful,* I thought, flat admitted it. I melted at the sight of him, unlike the new me.

* Tuck and Daisy are the Ogden family's dogs.

koala a small, furry animal from Australia that lives in trees

orphan a child whose parents have died

UNIT 2 • CHAPTER 4
Reading Selection

Read the Selection

1. **Use the illustration** *Ask: Who are these people?* (a stewardess and a small child) *Where are they?* (at the airport) *Why do you think the child is holding a sign?* (Maybe it's a name.) *Do you think the child speaks English? Why or why not?* (No. The name doesn't look like an English name.)
2. **Understand terms** Have students find the meanings of the glossed words at the bottom of the page. Clarify meanings as needed.
3. **Guided reading** Play the audio. Then have students reread each paragraph, pausing as you clarify and ask questions.
4. **Analyze characters** Ask questions to help students draw conclusions about the narrator. *Ask: How does Helen describe Chok-Do? Do you think she expected to like her new brother? Why or why not?*
5. **Multi-level options** See MULTI-LEVEL OPTIONS on p. 122.

Sample Answer to Guide Question

They were waiting for the Korean orphan boy they are adopting.

Spelling

Adverbs with the suffix *-ly*

Tell students that adverbs are words that answer questions about where, when, how, how much, or how often. Tell them many adverbs end in *-ly.* Ask them to identify an adverb in paragraph 9. (silently) *Say:* Silently *tells* how *the family waited for the little boy.* Have pairs of students identify additional *-ly* adverbs in paragraphs 1 (half-heartedly), 9 (finally), 10 (usually), and 12 (truly).

Read the Selection

Paired reading Arrange students in pairs and have them reread the selection. ***Ask:*** *Who is crying?* (the whole family) *Why?* (They were very happy to see Chok-Do, the boy they are adopting.) *Who is Tony Ogden?* (the father) *Who learned a little Korean?* (everyone in the family) *Why did they learn it?* (so they could speak a little to Chok-Do) *How do you feel when you meet someone new? How do you think Chok-Do is feeling right now?*

Sample Answer to Guide Question
Yes, they all were full of emotion.

Draw Conclusions

Did each member of the family have a similar reaction when they saw Chok-Do?

12 He was wearing a white shirt and his dark shorts were held up by **suspenders.** Beneath sturdy legs, shiny black shoes were on his small feet. His black-black hair was **crew-cut** and his face was as round as a lemon pie and about the same color. Truly beautiful.

13 I glanced at my mother and saw tears. I saw that my father was **dabbing** at his eyes. Luke was swallowing. Why were we all so sad? Then I suddenly realized my own eyes were wet. I couldn't believe myself.

14 We moved to meet him.

15 Smiling widely, the stewardess said, "You are Chok-Do's new family?"

16 My father said, "Yes, I'm Tony Ogden."

suspenders straps worn over the shoulders to hold up a pair of pants, used instead of a belt

crew-cut a haircut with the hair cut very short

dabbing touching quickly

MULTI-LEVEL OPTIONS *Read the Selection*

Newcomer ***Ask:*** *Does the family cry?* (yes) *Does the family know a little Korean?* (yes) *Does the boy speak to the family?* (no) *Are his eyes big and brown?* (yes)

Beginning *What does the family do?* (cry) *What language does the family try to learn a little of?* (Korean) *What does the boy say?* (nothing) *What are his eyes like?* (big and brown)

Intermediate *What is the boy's name?* (Chok-Do) *How does Helen's mother greet him?* (She hugs and kisses him.) *What does she ask him in Korean?* ("How are you?") *How does Chok-Do feel?* (bewildered)

Advanced *What does the stewardess ask the family?* ("Are you Chok-Do's new family?") *Why does the family learn a little Korean?* (so they can communicate with Chok-Do) *How does Chok-Do look at them?* (as if they were Martians)

17 Mother was already kneeling down, hugging her new son, kissing him, saying "*An-nyŏng-ha-shim-ni-kka.*"

18 "How are you?"

19 We'd all learned a little Korean.

20 Then she stood up, wiping her eyes, introducing the family. "This is your father and this is Helen, your sister, and this is Luke, your brother."

21 **Bewildered,** he looked at us as if we were Martians, saying nothing. His eyes were huge and brown and I was wishing they were mine.

22 "Do you have identification?" asked the stewardess.

23 My father quickly displayed the adoption papers and his driver's license.

24 She glanced at them and then seemed to be sizing up Chok-Do's new family, going to each of our faces, an **inquisitive** look on hers.

---

bewildered very confused

inquisitive curious, asking a lot of questions

Punctuation

Apostrophes for possession

Write on the board: *Chok-Do's new family*
Ask: *Whose new family is it?* (Chok-Do's)
Point to the apostrophe and the *-s.* ***Say:*** *When you add an apostrophe and an -s to a noun, you are showing ownership or possession.*

Apply Ask students to find another example of an apostrophe for possession in paragraph 23 (father's drivers license) and tell what it means.

UNIT 2 • CHAPTER 4
Reading Selection

Read the Selection

1. **Shared reading** Play the audio or read the paragraphs aloud. Instruct students to follow along in their books and join in for paragraphs 21 and 23. ***Ask:*** *Do you think Chok-Do understands what the mother says?* (no) *What papers does the father show the stewardess?* (adoption papers and his driver's license) *Why?* (The stewardess wants to make sure that Chok-Do is going to the right family.)
2. **Draw conclusions** ***Say:*** *Families often change when there is a new member. Can you draw a conclusion about how the Ogden family may change now that they have adopted Chok-Do?*
3. **Multi-level options** See MULTI-LEVEL OPTIONS on p. 124.

Read the Selection

1. **Shared reading** Play the audio or read the paragraphs aloud. Instruct students to follow along in their books and join in for quotations. ***Ask:*** *What papers did the stewardess give the Ogdens?* (Chok-Do's passport and visa) *Why does she think the Ogdens have courage?* (It is not easy to raise a deaf child.) *How did the Ogdens react when they heard Chok-Do was deaf?* (very surprised and shocked)
2. **Analyze characters** Have students think about the stewardess. ***Ask:*** *Why does she just walk away? Do you think she should help the Ogdens a little more? What does the family think of her? How would you feel if you were part of the Ogden family?* Have students discuss their ideas in groups.

Sample Answer to Guide Question
No. They were all very surprised when the stewardess told them.

25 Finally handing over his Korean passport and a visa, she said, in almost **flawless** English, "Well, I have delivered him as I promised. I must say I admire your courage to adopt a little deaf boy."

26 She glanced down at Chok-Do and smiled.

27 I heard my mother gasp and then my father said, in a squeezed voice, "What? What did you say?"

28 "Deaf boy?" Mother said. "There's some mistake." On her face was shock, **disbelief.**

29 "Weren't you told?" asked the stewardess. "He does not hear, does not speak."

30 Staring at her and then at Chok-Do, my parents answered together a **breathless:** "No!"

31 "I'm sorry," said the stewardess. "I wish you good luck."

32 Then she knelt down by the boy, kissed his cheek, smiled briefly, handed him the koala and disappeared back into Customs and Immigration.

Draw Conclusions
Did the Ogdens know that Chok-Do was deaf? How can you tell?

flawless perfect
disbelief unable or unwilling to believe
breathless out of breath

MULTI-LEVEL OPTIONS *Read the Selection*

Newcomer ***Ask:*** *Can Chok-Do hear?* (no) *Is the family shocked?* (yes) *Is Chok-Do also blind?* (no) *Does the mother take Chok-Do's hand?* (yes) *Does the father want to ask the stewardess more questions?* (yes) *Does he ask them?* (no)

Beginning ***Ask:*** *What does the family learn from the stewardess?* (Chok-Do cannot hear or speak.) *How does the family feel?* (shocked) *What does the mother do?* (She takes Chok-Do's hand.) *What does the father do?* (He sits down next to the mother.)

Intermediate ***Ask:*** *What does the stewardess think the family has a lot of?* (courage) *What does she say when she leaves?* ("I wish you good luck.") *What does the mother say she has to do?* (sit down) *Why?* (She's in shock.)

Advanced ***Ask:*** *Why is the family surprised by the stewardess?* (No one told them that Chok-Do can't hear or speak.) *Why does the mother say, "There must be some mistake"?* (She can't believe no one told them that Chok-Do is deaf.) *Why does Helen say at the end, "So much for the tough Ogdens"?* (They aren't really tough.)

33 Daddy called after her, "Wait a minute!"

34 Mother said she had to sit down and went over to a low **concrete-block** wall, taking Chok-Do by the hand. My father went over and sat down beside her. They were in a state of **shock.** So were Luke and myself. So much for the tough Ogdens.

Draw Conclusions

How do the Ogdens feel about the news that Chok-Do is deaf?

concrete-block large bricks made of concrete

shock upsetting surprise

About the Author — Theodore Taylor (born 1921)

Theodore Taylor grew up during the Great Depression, a time when many people in the United States didn't have jobs or money. Taylor helped his family by delivering newspapers and selling candy. His parents worked very hard, and Taylor learned to take care of himself. He started writing when he was 13 years old. He wrote about sports for a local newspaper. In his books, Taylor's characters face problems alone, the same way he did as a child. He said, "I like that kind of kid. I think kids like that kind too, and if it helps them aim for self-reliance, then I've done a good job."

➤ Based on what you know about Taylor's writing, how do you think the Ogden family will react to this change in their lives?

Spelling

Use the prefix *dis-*

Write on the board and say the word *appears.* Write the prefix *dis-* and pronounce it. Then write the complete word and pronounce it. ***Say:*** *The prefix* dis- *means "not" or "the opposite of." When something appears, you see it. When it* dis*appears, you don't see it.* Repeat to form other words: *disagree, disobey,* and *disapprove.* Have students find another word with the prefix *dis-* in paragraph 28. (disbelief)

Evaluate Your Reading Strategy

Draw Conclusions ***Say:*** *You have practiced an important reading strategy. Now you can decide how well you have done. Does this statement describe how you read?*

When I draw conclusions, I look for facts in the text to help me. Drawing conclusions helps me get the most out of a reading.

Read the Selection

1. **Shared reading** Read paragraphs 33–34 as students follow along in their books and join in for alternating sentences. ***Ask:*** *How does everyone feel?* (shocked and helpless) *Why?* (They didn't know Chok-Do was deaf.)
2. **Make predictions** Have students think about what the family might do next. ***Ask:*** *Will they take Chok-Do home with them? Will they try to call the adoption lady? How will they communicate with Chok-Do?* Lead a discussion of students' ideas.
3. **Multi-level options** See MULTI-LEVEL OPTIONS on p. 126.

Sample Answer to Guide Question

The family is very surprised and shocked.

About the Author

1. **Explain author background** Theodore Taylor was a naval officer during World War II. He also served in the Korean War. He has won many awards for his books, including the Lewis Carroll Shelf Award for *The Cay.*
2. **Interpret the facts** ***Ask:*** *In what ways do you think Taylor's experience helped him describe the characters in this story?*

Across Selections

Teacher Resource Book: *Two-Column Chart, p. 44; Venn Diagram, p. 35*

Compare content Have students suggest changes that Chok-Do and his new family may be experiencing. Instruct them to compare them with changes that Elizabeth faced when she came to North America in "Elizabeth's Diary." Have students record their ideas on a chart or Venn diagram.

Reading Comprehension

Question-Answer Relationships

Sample Answers

1. Helen Ogden is the daughter. She is the narrator.
2. The Odgen family is at the airport to meet a Korean war orphan that they are adopting.
3. Chok-Do is deaf and cannot speak.
4. Because he wrote it when he was ten years old. Now it sounds silly to him.
5. Chok-Do probably became an orphan because of the war. Maybe his parents died in the war.
6. The family was happy, but then they were shocked. They were prepared to adopt a child, but they didn't know he was deaf.
7. Chok-Do is probably confused and scared. He doesn't know anybody. Everything is very different.
8. I think the Ogdens will work together and help Chok-Do. They will learn to communicate with him.
9. Students will probably say they were nervous or scared at first until they got to know the people.

Build Reading Fluency

Choral Read Aloud

Ask students to read aloud with you for 5–10 minutes daily. Remind them to keep their eyes on the words. This will help students with phrasing, intonation, and pronunciation.

Beyond the Reading

Reading Comprehension

Question-Answer Relationships (QAR)

"Right There" Questions

1. **Recall Facts** Who is Helen?
2. **Recall Facts** Why is Helen at the airport with her parents?
3. **Recall Facts** What surprise do the Ogdens learn about Chok-Do?

"Think and Search" Questions

4. **Make Inferences** Why do you think Stan is embarrassed by the Ogden family poem?
5. **Make Inferences** How did Chok-Do become an orphan?
6. **Compare and Contrast** How do the family's feelings change after they learn that Chok-Do is deaf?

"Author and You" Question

7. **Draw Conclusions** How do you think Chok-Do feels about traveling to another country and having a new family?

"On Your Own" Questions

8. **Predict** What do you think will happen between the Ogdens and Chok-Do? Explain.
9. **Relate the Reading to Your Personal Experiences** Have you ever had to stay with strangers? How did you feel, or how do you think you would feel?

Activity Book p. 66

Student CD-ROM

Build Reading Fluency

Choral Read Aloud

A choral read aloud means the teacher reads aloud together with the class. This helps you connect spoken language with the text.

1. Read "Tuck Triumphant" aloud with your teacher.
2. Try to keep up with the class.
3. You may point to the text as you read.

MULTI-LEVEL OPTIONS *Elements of Literature*

Newcomer On the board, write: *Chok-Do is deaf.* and *Can't hear.* ***Ask:*** *Which sentence is a complete sentence?* (the first one) ***Say:*** *Some writers use incomplete sentences to show what a character is thinking.* Have students work in pairs. Direct them to paragraph 4. ***Ask:*** *Can you find the incomplete sentence?* (As usual.)

Beginning On the board, write: *Chok-Do is deaf.* and *Can't hear.* ***Ask:*** *Which one is a complete sentence?* (the first one) ***Say:*** *Some writers use incomplete sentences to show what a character is thinking.* Have students work in pairs. Direct them to paragraphs 4 and 12. Ask students to identify the incomplete sentences. (4: As usual. 12: Truly beautiful.)

Intermediate Direct students to paragraph 4. ***Ask:*** *Which sentence is incomplete?* (the second one) *What's missing?* (a subject and verb) Tell students that writers sometimes use incomplete sentences to show what a character is thinking. Direct them to paragraph 12. Ask them to identify the incomplete sentence. (Truly beautiful.)

Advanced Tell students that writers sometimes use incomplete sentences to show what a character is thinking. Direct them to paragraphs 4 and 12. Have them find the sentences that are incomplete and decide what is missing from each. (4: As usual. 12: Truly beautiful. They're missing subjects and verbs.) Have them rewrite the sentences into complete sentences.

Listen, Speak, Interact 

Interview a Newcomer

One of your cousins is coming to your city for a visit. However, you have never met this cousin. You are meeting at the airport. You want to find out about your cousin, and your cousin wants to find out about you.

1. With a partner, decide who lives in the city and who is the visitor. What would you like to learn about each other? Use the list of questions in the box. Add your own questions.
2. Practice your interview. Be sure to use intonation to show you are asking a question.
3. Record your interview or present it to the class.

Questions
1. How old are you? 2. What do you like to do? 3. What classes do you like at school? 4. What sports do you like? 5. What is your favorite (food, movie, band, television program)?

Elements of Literature

Recognize Style in a First-Person Narrative

In a **first-person narrative,** a character in the story tells the story. This character is the **narrator.**

In "Tuck Triumphant," Helen Ogden is the narrator.

We'd survive, I thought. As usual.

The first sentence is a complete sentence. The second sentence is an incomplete sentence. It does not have a subject or a verb.

Sometimes writers use incomplete sentences as part of their **style.** Style is the way that writers use language to express themselves.

In "Tuck Triumphant," the author uses incomplete sentences as part of his style. Helen's incomplete sentences make her thinking seem real to us, because we often use incomplete sentences when we think.

1. Find two examples of incomplete sentences in Helen's thoughts. Look in paragraphs 5 and 12.
2. Listen to the Audio CD for these paragraphs. How does this language make the reader feel?

Activity Book p. 67

Student CD-ROM

Content Connection
The Arts

Brainstorm and write a list of appropriate and inappropriate phrases students can use to introduce themselves to new people. Then have pairs of students create a useful "greetings" dialogue. Have them perform their dialogues for another pair.

Learning Styles
Interpersonal

Ask students to think about how Chok-Do feels when he arrives in Los Angeles. Have them work in pairs to write a first-person narrative from Chok-Do's point of view. On the board, write these questions to help them get started: *Where does Chok-Do think he is? What does he see? Who does Chok-Do think the Ogdens are? What does he think when the stewardess leaves? How does he feel when Mrs. Ogden takes his hand?*

Listen, Speak, Interact

Interview a Newcomer

Teacher Resource Book: *Interview, p. 54; Reading Log, p. 64*

1. **Inside-outside circle** Model the situation and role-play with a volunteer. Then have students form two circles, one inside the other. Tell them to practice the questions and answers. Instruct students in the outer circle to move one space to the right before practicing the next question.
2. **Newcomers** Assist students in writing their answers in their Reading Logs.

Elements of Literature

Recognize Style in a First-Person Narrative

Teacher Resource Book: *Two-Column Chart, p. 44*

1. **Recognize complete sentences** Review the difference between complete and incomplete sentences. Write examples on the board and have students identify which ones are incomplete. Tell students to look back through the story for examples of incomplete sentences.
2. **Summarize** Ask students to think about times when they need to use complete sentences and when they can use incomplete sentences. Make a two-column chart to record their ideas. Help summarize the findings on the chart. Point out the difference in style and its appropriateness for certain situations.
3. **Multi-level options** See MULTI-LEVEL OPTIONS on p. 128.

Answers

1. paragraph 5: Birthdays and such. paragraph 12: Truly beautiful.
2. It makes the reader feel like Helen is speaking directly to him/her because it is like listening to her thoughts.

ASSESS

Have students write one complete and one incomplete answer to the question: *How are you today?* (Great. I feel great.)

Word Study

Use the Suffix *-less*

Teacher Resource Book: *Personal Dictionary, p. 63*

Make a word map Write on the board and *Say: help.* Then write the suffix *-less* and pronounce it. Next, write the parts together and pronounce the new word. Tell students to use the adjective in a sentence. Repeat to form: *careless, colorless, painless, tasteless.*

Answers
3. a. endless b. homeless

Grammar Focus

Use Adjectives Before Nouns

Demonstrate knowledge of adjectives and nouns Write on the board: *It's a(n) _____ book.* Hold up a book. *Ask: What is it?* Then ask students to add an adjective. Have students suggest other adjectives. Repeat with other objects.

Answers
1. and 2. *Sample answers:* (white) shirt, (dark) shorts, (sturdy) legs
3. *Sample Answers:* I have a blue book. adjective: blue; noun: book

Have students write three sentences describing their best friend. Tell them to use at least three adjectives.

Word Study

Use the Suffix *-less*

A **suffix** is a group of letters added to the end of a word. It changes the word's meaning. The words *flawless* and *breathless* have the suffix *-less*.

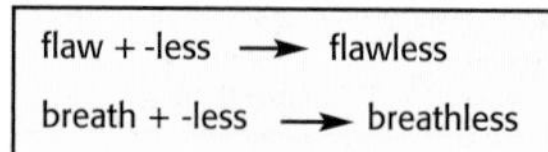

The suffix *-less* means "without." When *-less* is added to the end of the nouns *flaw* and *breath*, the meanings of the words change.

She spoke in almost flaw**less** English.

My parents answered together, a breath**less**: "No!"

1. Look up the definitions of *flaw* and *breath* in a dictionary.
2. Use your knowledge of these words and the suffix *-less* to guess the meanings of *flawless* and *breathless*. Look these words up in a dictionary to check your answers.
3. Copy the sentences below in your Personal Dictionary. Complete each sentence with a word that ends in the suffix *-less*.
   a. The long road ahead seemed without end. The road seemed _____ .
   b. During the storm, the family lost its home. The family was _____ .

Personal Dictionary

The Heinle Newbury House Dictionary

Activity Book *p. 68*

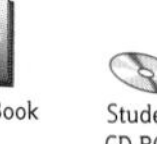
Student CD-ROM

Grammar Focus

Use Adjectives Before Nouns

An **adjective** describes a **noun** (a person, place, or thing). Adjectives go before the nouns they describe.

a big sign: The adjective *big* tells you about the noun *sign*.

a little boy: The adjective *little* tells you about the noun *boy*.

1. Find three examples of adjectives in paragraph 12.
2. Name the nouns that the adjectives describe.
3. Write a sentence containing an adjective on a piece of paper. Identify the adjective and the noun.

Activity Book *pp. 69–70*

Student Handbook

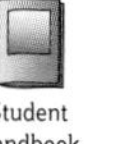
Student CD-ROM

MULTI-LEVEL OPTIONS *From Reading to Writing*

Newcomer Discuss, demonstrate, and write typical gestures people make when they first meet a new person. (shake hands, make eye-contact, smile) Have students illustrate a meeting between themselves and a stranger. Tell them to write word bubbles with useful greetings such as: *Hi. My name's _____. Hello, I'm _____.*

Beginning Have students think about a time they met someone new. Then instruct them to write a sentence describing one thing they knew about the person before they met and one thing they learned later. Tell them to read their sentences in pairs.

Intermediate Have students think about a time they met someone new to help them complete the chart on p. 131. Instruct them to write a short paragraph about the meeting. Remind them to write in the first-person voice. Tell them to share their paragraphs in small groups.

Advanced Tell students to think about a time they met someone new to help them complete the chart on p. 131. Have them write a paragraph in the first-person voice about the meeting. Remind them to use adjectives to make their writing more detailed. Ask them to share their paragraphs in groups.

From Reading to Writing 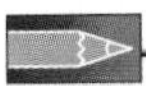

Write a Realistic Story

Write a story about meeting someone new. You can write about someone you really met, or you can make up a realistic character.

Use the chart below to plan the main parts of your story. List what you knew about the person before the meeting. Then list what you learned from the meeting.

What I Knew Before We Met	What I Learned When We Met

1. Write in the first-person voice, using the pronouns *I, me, we,* and *us.*
2. Use incomplete sentences to express some of your thoughts.
3. Use adjectives before some of your nouns to make your writing more interesting and precise.
4. Include realistic details about the characters, events, and setting so that readers can picture the story.
5. Produce a visual such as a drawing that shows something about the setting and characters of your story.

Activity Book *p. 71*

Across Content Areas 

Learn About Families

In "Tuck Triumphant," we meet the mother, the father, and the two children of the Ogden family. This is called a **nuclear family.**

However, the Ogden family is more than just four people. There are probably grandparents, aunts, uncles, and cousins. This larger family is called an **extended family.**

In some parts of the world, it is traditional for many members of an extended family to live together. In the United States, members of a nuclear family usually live together, but sometimes other family members live with them, too.

How are families in your culture the same as the Ogden family? How are they different?

What do you think are the advantages and disadvantages of each kind of family?

Activity Book *p. 72*

Student CD-ROM

From Reading to Writing

Write a Realistic Story

1. **Share experiences** Tell students about a time you met someone new. Include information you knew about the person before you met and things you learned after meeting. Model filling out the chart on p. 131 as you talk. Have students talk about a new person they met. ***Ask:*** *Who did you meet? Did you know anything about the person before the meeting? When did you meet? Where did you meet? What did you learn about the person?*
2. **Think-Pair-Share** Ask students to think about the person for their stories and write as much as they can on the chart. Have students share their stories in pairs. Direct students to add adjectives to describe their subject.
3. **Multi-level options** See MULTI-LEVEL OPTIONS on p. 130.

Across Content Areas: Social Studies

Learn About Families

Define and connect Explain *nuclear* and *extended families.* ***Ask:*** *Do you know any countries where extended families are more common than nuclear families? Which describes your family?*

ASSESS

Have students write two sentences: one about the members of their nuclear family and one about their extended family.

Assessment Program: *Unit 2, Chapter 4 Quiz, pp. 29–30*

Reteach and Reassess

Text Structure Have students describe the setting of "Tuck Triumphant," list the characters, and write three sentences describing the events in the story.

Reading Strategy ***Ask:*** *Can you draw a conclusion about how well the poem in paragraph 5 describes the Ogden family?*

Elements of Literature Ask students to pretend that they are Chok-Do. Tell them to write his thoughts as he gets hugs and kisses from Mrs. Ogden. Remind students that the sentences can be incomplete.

Reassess Instruct students to select a character from the story and write an "I Am" poem from the character's point of view.

UNIT 2 • CHAPTER 5
Into the Reading

Chapter Materials

Activity Book: *pp. 73–80*
Audio: *Unit 2, Chapter 5*
Student Handbook
Student CD-ROM: *Unit 2, Chapter 5*
Teacher Resource Book: *Lesson Plan, Teacher Resources, Reading Summary, Activity Book Answer Key*
Teacher Resource CD-ROM
Assessment Program: *Quiz and Test, pp. 31–39; Teacher and Student Resources, pp. 115–144*
Assessment CD-ROM
Transparencies
The Heinle Newbury House Dictionary/CD-ROM
Web Site: www.heinle.visions.com

Objectives

Read aloud Read the objectives aloud. ***Ask:*** *What will you be able to do at the end of this chapter?*

Use Prior Knowledge

Plan for a Trip

Gather and organize Have students suggest destinations and complete the chart. Tell them to share their trip preparations in pairs.

Answers

Sample answer: Destination: Hawaii; Clothes: T-shirts; Food: snacks; Other needs: toothbrush

The Journal of Jesse Smoke

an excerpt from a historical fiction journal by Joesph Bruchac

Ancient Ways

a poem by Elvania Toledo

Into the Reading

Objectives

Reading Understand the sequence of events as you read a historical fiction journal.

Listening and Speaking Identify how language reflects culture and regions.

Grammar Use the present continuous tense.

Writing Write a poem.

Content Math: Use rank order.

Use Prior Knowledge

Plan for a Trip

How do you get ready for a trip?

1. On a piece of paper, draw a chart like the one here.
2. Decide where you are going. Write the name of your destination (the place where you are going) on the chart.
3. Complete the chart. Under each heading, list the things that you will take on a trip. Add more headings if you wish.
4. Using your chart, share your ideas with the class. Ask for suggestions to add to your list.

Destination: ______		
Clothes	Food	Other Needs
jacket		
hiking boots		

132 **Unit 2** Changes

MULTI-LEVEL OPTIONS *Build Vocabulary*

Newcomer Prepare index cards with a root word that students know, such as *sleep*, and affixes, such as *a-*, *-y*, *-ing*, and *-s*. Show how to combine the root and affix to make a new word. ***Say:*** *When you know the meaning of a root, you can often guess the meaning of a new word that has the root in it.*

Beginning On the board, write: *unhappy.* Ask students to identify its root (happy). Then list other words students know with the root *happy* (happiness, unhappier, happiest). ***Say:*** *When you know the meaning of a word's root, you can often guess the meaning of a new word that has the root in it.*

Intermediate ***Ask:*** *What shorter word do you see in* possession? (possess) ***Say:*** Possess *is called a root. Roots are the main parts of words.* Tell students that knowing the meanings of roots can help them guess the meanings of new words. Have them work in pairs to complete the chart.

Advanced Instruct students to complete the chart and share their information with a partner. Have them check the dictionary for any words they are uncertain about.

Build Background

The Trail of Tears

"The Journal of Jesse Smoke" describes a time when Cherokee Native Americans were forced to leave their homes. Other people wanted their land. In 1838, General Winfield Scott forced thousands of Cherokee to march to a new home in what is now the state of Oklahoma. They called the route they took "The Trail of Tears" because many of them died.

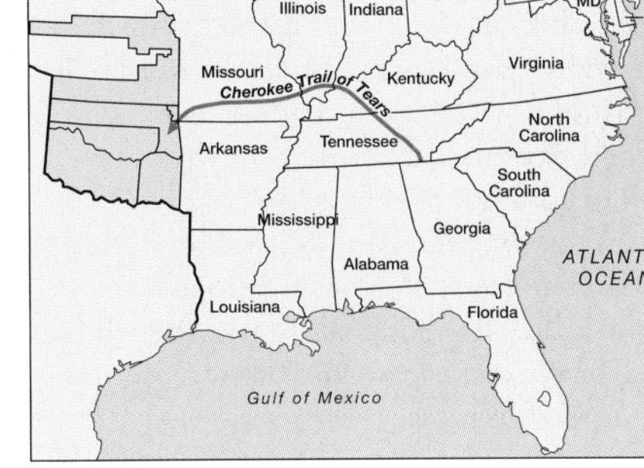

SOCIAL STUDIES

Content Connection

Other Native American tribes include the Cheyenne, Seminole, Apache, Comanche, Sioux, and Navajo.

Build Vocabulary

Find Root Words

You can sometimes understand the meaning of a word by looking at the word's **root,** or base.

1. Copy the chart in your Personal Dictionary.
2. Find the root of each word. Write it in the chart.
3. Write the meaning of the root word. Use a dictionary if you need to.
4. What is the meaning of the original word? If you are still uncertain, look it up in the dictionary.

Word	Root	Meaning of Root
possession	possess	own
approaching		
traditional		
existence		
plantation		

Personal Dictionary

The Heinle Newbury House Dictionary

Activity Book p. 73

Student CD-ROM

Cultural Connection

Build Vocabulary Ask students to share cognates from other languages they know for the root words in the chart.

Learning Styles *Mathematical*

Build Background Direct students to a map of the United States. Have them use the map's scale to calculate the distance from the beginning to the end of the Trail of Tears.

Build Background

The Trail of Tears

1. **Use a map** Tell students to locate the Cherokee's homelands on the map. Have them trace the Trail of Tears and name the states that it goes through.
2. **Content Connection** Bring in resource materials for students to use to find the location of these and other Native American tribes. Compare their original range to the current Native American reservations.

Build Vocabulary

Find Root Words

Teacher Resource Book: *Personal Dictionary, p. 63*

1. **Offer observations** Write *historical* on the board. ***Say:*** *I can see the word* history *in this word. I know* history *means "a record of the past." So, I guess that* historical *means "something about history or the past."* Have students check the meaning in a dictionary.
2. **Use a dictionary** Have students use a dictionary to find the root words and check their meanings.
3. **Reading selection vocabulary** You may want to introduce the glossed words in the reading selections before students begin reading. Key words: *emigration, address, plantation, used to.* Instruct students to write the words with correct spelling and their definitions in their Personal Dictionaries. Have them pronounce each word and divide it into syllables.
4. **Multi-level options** See MULTI-LEVEL OPTIONS on p. 132.

Answers

approach (to go toward something); tradition (a custom or behavior); exist (to be present); plant (a living thing that grows in the earth)

ASSESS

Have students write a sentence for each of the vocabulary words.

Into the Reading

Text Structure

Historical Fiction Journal

Understand terms Review the elements of historical fiction: plot, characters, dialogue. Explain *chronological.*

Reading Strategy

Teacher Resource Book: *Timelines, p. 39*

Understand the Sequence of Events

1. **Use a graphic organizer** Make a timeline on the board. Use it to plot some school events. Explain that a timeline can help students remember the order of events in the past.
2. **Multi-level options** See MULTI-LEVEL OPTIONS below.

ASSESS

Say: *Name two types of writing that record daily experiences.* (a journal and a diary) ***Ask:*** *Which is private?* (diary) *Which is more public?* (journal)

Text Structure

Historical Fiction Journal

A journal is similar to a diary. They are both books in which you record your daily experiences. A journal is usually public. It is written for others to read. A diary is usually private. It is written only for the author to read.

In this chapter, you will read an excerpt from "The Journal of Jesse Smoke," a **historical fiction** journal. It tells the story of a Native American youth whose people are forced to move.

As you read "The Journal of Jesse Smoke," look for these features:

Historical Fiction	
Dates	chronological sequence of events
Characters	people in the story; they can be real or made-up
Dialogue	speech between characters; what real people might have said

Student CD-ROM

Reading Strategy

Understand the Sequence of Events

The **sequence of events** in a story is the order in which events happen.

Remembering the most important events in a story can help you recall details that go with the events.

1. Draw a timeline like this on a piece of paper.
2. Read paragraphs 1–5 of "The Journal of Jesse Smoke."
3. Write the important events and dates on your timeline.
4. Continue reading the journal, writing the important events on your timeline.

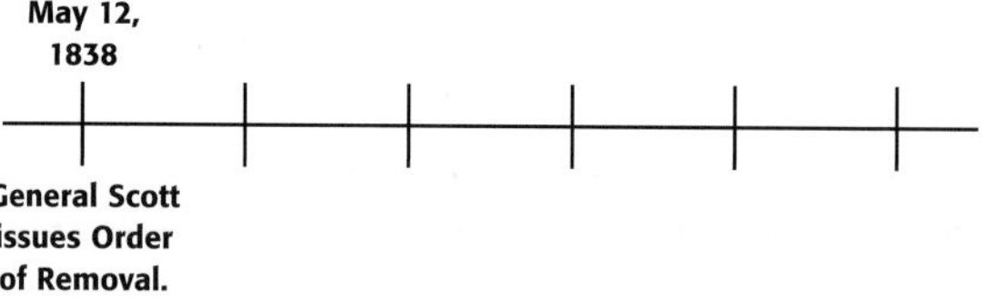

Student CD-ROM

MULTI-LEVEL OPTIONS *Reading Strategy*

Newcomer Have students prepare a timeline that they will fill in as they read through "The Journal of Jesse Smoke." The timeline can be taped along the wall so students can add words and pictures.

Beginning Help small groups prepare timelines that they will fill in as they read through "The Journal of Jesse Smoke." Remind students that dates go above the timeline and events go below. Tell them they may write key words or illustrate information on their timelines.

Intermediate Help pairs of students prepare timelines of "The Journal of Jesse Smoke." Guide students as they edit sentences to explain the dates and events they chose to record.

Advanced Have students create a timeline. Instruct them to practice filling in events from the story in paragraphs 1–5. Tell them they will continue to fill in their timelines as they read through the story.

The Journal of Jesse Smoke

an excerpt from a historical fiction journal
by Joseph Bruchac

Ancient Ways

a poem by Elvania Toledo

135

Reading Selection

Reading Selection Materials

Audio: *Unit 2, Chapter 5*
Teacher Resource Book: *Reading Summary, pp. 83–84*

Preview the Selections

1. **Evaluate the meanings of the titles** Direct students to the titles of the reading selections. ***Ask:*** *What is the title of the first selection? What do you think Jesse will write about in his journal? It's historical fiction, so what will be true in the journal? What is the title of the second reading? What do you think the title means? What is* ancient? *Do you think Native Americans follow ancient ways or do you think they have changed some?*
2. **Connect** Have students suggest what changes Jesse might include in his journal. ***Ask:*** *Do you think Jesse and the Cherokee people want the changes? Are all changes good?*

Content Connection
Social Studies

Instruct students to find out where the Cherokee people live today. They can ask a librarian for help or do an Internet search with the key word *Cherokee.*

Learning Styles
Natural

Tell students that it was important for Native Americans to live in harmony with nature. Have students find out about the ways Native Americans lived before the Indian Removal Act forced them off their lands. Some areas students can research include the kinds of homes they lived in, what foods they grew, which animals they hunted or raised, and what tools they made and used.

UNIT 2 • CHAPTER 5
Reading Selection

Read the Selection

1. **Use graphic elements** Ask students to find clues that this is a journal. (dates) Point out the words with an asterisk. Direct students to the explanations at the bottom of the page. Have students describe the boy in the illustration and tell what he is doing.
2. **Teacher read aloud** Read paragraph 1 aloud. *Ask: What event is Jesse describing?* Then continue with paragraphs 2–5.
3. **Understand the sequence of events** Have students reread the paragraphs in pairs. Tell them to record important events on their timelines.

Sample Answer to Guide Question
The important event: a few people are following the order for the Cherokees to move; some important details: they are taking possessions they can, there are three collection points by rivers, they will be taken west on flatboats.

See Teacher Edition pp. 434–435 for a list of English-Spanish cognates in the reading selection.

Audio

The Journal of Jesse Smoke
an excerpt from a historical fiction journal by Joseph Bruchac

May 12, 1838

1 The worst has happened. Scott has issued an order for our immediate Removal*. All must hasten to prepare for **emigration** and come forward so that we may be transported. His **address,** dated May 10, has been posted widely throughout the Cherokee Nation.

May 15, 1838

2 A few of our people are following the orders of General Scott. Carrying what possessions they can, they are making their way to one of the three collection points. They are along the rivers at Gunter's Landing, Ross's Landing, and Cherokee Agency. Although the waters are low in the Tennessee, they plan to take us west on flatboats.

Understand the Sequence of Events
What important event happens in this paragraph? Which details should you remember?

3 Many of my people, like my mother, have made no preparations for leaving.

4 "We shall trust in Kooweeskoowee*," my mother says. "John Ross has a plan."

5 Our second chief, George Lowrey, has remained here in our Cherokee Nation while John Ross fights for us in Washington. Whenever he speaks, he echoes my mother's words. He also reminded us of the words spoken in council by the old warrior Woman Killer, who died not long after speaking these words that many of us know by heart.

*Removal was the government's policy of ordering American Indians to leave their land and go to reservations.

*Kooweeskoowee, or John Ross, was a leader of the Cherokee Nation.

emigration leaving one's country to live in another

address a speech

MULTI-LEVEL OPTIONS *Read the Selection*

Newcomer Play the audio. Then do a guided reading. Point out important dates and have students record and illustrate them on the class timeline. ***Ask:*** *Do the Cherokees have to leave their land?* (yes) *Do they want to leave?* (no) *Do most Cherokees speak English?* (no) *Is their land good land?* (yes)

Beginning Read the Reading Summary. Then do a guided reading of the journal. Have students identify and record dates on their timelines. ***Ask:*** *What does General Scott's order say?* (The Cherokees must leave their land.) *What do the Cherokees want to do?* (stay on their land) *Do most Cherokees follow old ways or new ways?* (old ways)

Intermediate Play the audio. Have students do a paired reading of the journal. ***Ask:*** *Where are the Cherokees supposed to go?* (to a reservation) *Who is John Ross?* (a Cherokee chief) *How do the Cherokees feel about their land?* (They love it.) *How do the Cherokees feel about their leaders?* (They trust them.)

Advanced Have students do a paired reading. ***Ask:*** *Why does the government want the Cherokees to leave?* (so white men can take their land) *What is John Ross doing in Washington?* (fighting for his people) *What did the secretary of war promise?* (Cherokees won't have to leave before the fall.)

6 "My companions," Woman Killer said, "men of renown, in council, who now sleep in the dust, spoke the same language and I now stand on the verge of the grave to bear witness to their love of country. My sun of existence is fast approaching to its setting, and my aged bones will soon be laid in the bosom of this earth we have received from our fathers, who had it from the Great Being above. When I sleep in forgetfulness, I hope my bones will not be deserted by you."

Understand the Sequence of Events

What important event is reported in this paragraph? Which details should you remember?

7 Chief Lowrey has assured us that John Ross is still **negotiating** and having some success. The secretary of war himself has promised that there will be no forcible roundup of our people before the fall, when it is more practical to travel.

8 The great majority of our people speak no English, have no great **plantations,** and live closer to our old ways. They have little or no knowledge of all that is happening. All they have is their deep love for this land and their trust that our leaders, especially Tsan Usdi, will abide by the will of our people.

---

negotiating talking in order to reach an agreement **plantations** large farms

Read the Selection

1. **Understand terms** Have students find the meanings of the glossed words at the bottom of the page. Clarify meanings as needed.
2. **Reciprocal reading** After you read paragraphs 6–9 aloud, arrange students in small groups for reciprocal reading. Assign each student a different portion of the selection. Students should read aloud the portion, answer questions of others in the group, and help summarize the portion.
3. **Understand sequence of events** Ask questions to help students identify the main event and the details.
4. **Analyze characters** Read aloud again the speech made by Woman Killer in paragraph 6. Explain that he talks about many things in nature. Have students identify the different references to nature.
5. **Multi-level options** See MULTI-LEVEL OPTIONS on p. 136.

Sample Answer to Guide Question

The important event: talks between John Ross and the government; some important details: the promise made by the secretary of war, the move will not be before fall.

 Spelling

Use *ie* or *ei*

Tell students that *ie* is more common than *ei.* Have them learn the rhyme:

Use *i* before *e*
except after *c,*
or when sounded like *ay,*
as in *neighbor* or *weigh.*

Direct students to examples of each spelling in paragraph 2 (their) and in paragraph 6 (received).

Apply Have students work in pairs. Write on the board: *eight, chief, deceive.* Have pairs say the words and explain why the *ie* or *ei* spelling in each word is correct. (The *ei* in *eight* is pronounced *ay. Chief* follows the rule that *ie* is most common. The *ei* in *deceive* follows the letter *c.*)

Read the Selection

Shared reading Ask students to join in as you read aloud. *Ask: Who is Standing Turkey?* (Jesse's friend) *Where do you think the soldiers are going?* (to the village) *Is Standing Turkey worried about the soldiers?* (no) *Why does Standing Turkey think Jesse's journal is a good thing?* (Maybe he wants a record of the soldiers and their activities.)

Sample Answer to Guide Question
The important event: Standing Turkey asks about Jesse's journal; some important details: motions with his chin, journal under Jesse's arm.

9 I observed this today when I spoke to a friend of mine. His name is Standing Turkey. His family numbers ten and they farm land along the Hiwassee River. He and three others in the family are readers of Cherokee. He and his brother are mechanics, and the four women in their family are weavers. Though their place is small, it has fine soil, good water, a small herd of cattle. It is much **coveted** by the white men who have been surveying it with hungry eyes.

10 Standing Turkey was on his way to the blacksmith to have a tool mended. He greeted me as we passed on the road. I turned and followed him. Neither of us spoke for half a mile or so as we walked together.

11 "You are still filling your book with words?" he said to me at last, motioning with his chin at the journal under my arm.

Understand the Sequence of Events

What important event happens in this paragraph? Which details should you remember?

coveted wanted with great desire and envy

MULTI-LEVEL OPTIONS *Read the Selection*

Newcomer *Ask: Do Jesse Smoke and Standing Turkey walk together?* (yes) *Do white soldiers ride by?* (yes) *Do the soldiers look happy?* (no) *Do they have guns and bayonets?* (yes) *Does Standing Turkey think the soldiers will win?* (no)

Beginning *Ask: Who does Jesse Smoke walk with?* (his friend Standing Turkey) *Who rides by?* (white soldiers) *How do they look?* (grim) *What do they have with them?* (guns and bayonets) *Who does Standing Turkey think will defeat the soldiers?* (the Cherokee chief)

Intermediate *Ask: What does Standing Turkey ask Jesse Smoke about?* (his journal) *What do Standing Turkey and Jesse Smoke do when the soldiers ride by?* (climb over a fence) *What do the soldiers leave behind?* (clouds of dust) *What does Standing Turkey think of the soldiers?* (They won't win.)

Advanced *Ask: How do people feel about Jesse's journal?* (They approve of it.) *What would happen if Jesse and Standing Turkey didn't jump over the fence?* (They would have been run over.) *How does Standing Turkey describe the soldiers?* (determined) *How do you think he sees his own people?* (determined, winners)

12 I nodded. It seems that everyone knows of my journal now. I have been teased about it often. Such gentle teasing, though, means that people approve of what I am doing.

Understand the Sequence of Events

What important event is reported in this paragraph? Which details should you remember?

13 The sound of galloping hooves approaching came from around the bend. We stepped to the side, climbing over a rail fence just in time to avoid being run over by a **company** of white soldiers on horseback. Their faces were grim, and the sun glinted off their guns and bayonets. They seemed to take no notice of us and they soon disappeared, leaving nothing behind but the choking clouds of swirling dust.

14 Standing Turkey and I returned to the road, clouds of red dust rising from us as well as we brush ourselves off.

15 "They seem determined," Standing Turkey said. "But Kooweeskoowee will defeat them."

---

company a military unit of soldiers

About the Author — Joseph Bruchac (born 1942)

Joseph Bruchac is of Abenaki Indian descent. He says: "I think I always knew I would be a writer someday, but it wasn't until I was grown and had children of my own that I turned to telling Native American stories. My Indian grandfather never told those stories to me. Instead, I began to seek them out from other Native elders as soon as I left home for college. I wanted to share those stories with my sons."

Bruchac still lives in the house he grew up in, near the foothills of the Adirondack Mountains in New York.

➤When authors write, they often have a perspective (opinions and attitudes) about what they describe. What do you think Joseph Bruchac's perspective is on the removal of the Cherokee people?

UNIT 2 • CHAPTER 5

Reading Selection

Read the Selection

1. **Shared reading** Complete the reading of the journal as students follow along. Have students join in for alternating sentences. ***Ask:*** *Who does Standing Turkey think will defeat the soldiers?* (Kooweeskoowee) *Do you think he will?*
2. **Make predictions** Have pairs of students reread the selection. Ask them to predict what will happen to Jesse, Standing Turkey, and their families. Ask them to explain why they think so.
3. **Multi-level options** See MULTI-LEVEL OPTIONS on p. 138.

Sample Answer to Guide Question

The important event: a group of white soldiers riding to the town; some important details: soldiers have guns and bayonets, their determined looks, they don't notice anyone on the road.

About the Author

1. **Explain author's background** Joseph Bruchac won many awards for his books based on Native American stories. His series, *Keepers of the Earth,* illustrates how the Native Americans feel about the earth, nature, and other people.
2. **Point of view** Storytelling is an important way of teaching lessons. ***Ask:*** *What lessons do you think Joseph Bruchac is showing with his stories?*

Spelling

Silent *l*

Tell students that the letter *l* is silent when it comes before *f, d,* or *k.* Point out examples in paragraph 10 (half, walked) and in *would.*

Apply On the board, write: *cloud, talk, journal, could, calf, mile.* ***Ask:*** *Which three words have a silent* l? (talk, could, calf) Then ask volunteers to pronounce the words.

Read the Selection

1. **Use text features** Direct students to the numbers for each stanza. Have students notice the number of lines in the different stanzas. Then direct students to glossed words and their meanings below.
2. **Choral reading** Play the audio. Have different groups do a choral reading of different stanzas.
3. **Compare and contrast** *Ask: Which are the ancient ways?* (the hogan, the village, the sheep herd for food, exercise) *Which are the new ways?* (the trailer, the neighborhood, the grocery store, using vehicles, i.e., cars and trucks) *How are they similar?* (They are just different forms that provide the same things.) *How are they different?* (The old ways were natural and closer to the earth. The new ways are unnatural or man-made.)

See Teacher Edition pp. 434–435 for a list of English-Spanish cognates in the reading selection.

Audio

Ancient Ways
a poem by Elvania Toledo

1 They're traditional.

2 They **used to** live in a **hogan**
but now they live in a trailer.

3 They used to live in a village
but now they live in a neighborhood.

4 They used to herd sheep
but now they go to the grocery store.

5 They used to exercise
but now they drive vehicles.

6 The father tells his daughter
"Things are changing."

---

used to *used to* means that something happened in the past, but it does not happen in the present

hogan a traditional American Indian house

MULTI-LEVEL OPTIONS *Read the Selection*

Newcomer Have students illustrate different stanzas. Play the audio as students hold up their drawings to relate to each stanza. ***Ask:*** *Did they used to live in a hogan?* (yes) *Do they now live in a trailer?* (yes) *Did they used to live in a village?* (yes) *Do they live in a city now?* (no) *Did they used to herd sheep?* (yes)

Beginning Play the audio. Then do a shared reading. Have students join in when they can. ***Ask:*** *What were their first houses called?* (hogans) *Where did they live after they lived in a village?* (a neighborhood) *How do they get around now?* (in vehicles)

Intermediate Have students work in pairs. Direct them to read alternate stanzas. ***Ask:*** *Where did they used to live?* (in a hogan, in a village) *Where do they now live?* (in a trailer, in a neighborhood) *Why don't they exercise anymore?* (They drive vehicles.)

Advanced Do a choral reading. ***Ask:*** *What old ways of life are named?* (a hogan, a village, herding sheep, exercise) *What are the new ways of life?* (a trailer, a neighborhood, a grocery store, driving vehicles) *Do you think the father likes the changes? Why or why not?*

About the Author — Elvania Toledo

Elvania Toledo is a Native American and a resident of a Navajo community in New Mexico. Toledo wrote "Ancient Ways" when she was a student at Atza Biyaazh Community School in Shiprock, New Mexico.

➤ What do you think Elvania Toledo's perspective is on the changes that she describes in this poem? Compare and contrast changes in your culture to those in the Navajo community.

When you listen to the poem, how does the use of "but now they . . ." make you feel?

Spelling

Words with sound /aw/

Tell students that the sound /aw/ has two spellings. It can be spelled as *aw* in words such as *paw* and *awful.* It can also be spelled as *au* as in *daughter* and *caught.* Ask students to list other words with *aw* and *au.*

Evaluate Your Reading Strategy

Understand the Sequence of Events *Say: You have practiced an important reading strategy. Now you can decide how well you have done. Does this statement describe how you read?*

> When I read a story with a complex plot, I write down the important events. Understanding the sequence of events helps me remember details later.

Read the Selection

1. **Choral reading** Read the poem aloud. Have students do a choral rereading of the poem.
2. **Analyze poetic forms** Have students reread stanzas 2–5. ***Ask:*** *How does each line of those stanzas begin?* (They used to . . .) *How does the second line of the stanzas begin?* (but now they . . .) *What do you notice about each stanza?* (It gives the old way and contrasts it with the new way.) *How does this help show the changes that are happening in the father's and daughter's lives?* (It links the old and new, but it also makes the old ways look better than the new.)
3. **Multi-level options** See MULTI-LEVEL OPTIONS on p. 140.

About the Author

Explain author's background Read the biographical information about Elvania Toledo. Discuss the types of changes she may have experienced between her life in the Navajo community and student life in Shiprock, New Mexico.

Across Selections

Teacher Resource Book: *Two-Column Chart, p. 44*

Points of view Discuss the authors' points of view in "The Journal of Jesse Smoke" and "Ancient Ways." ***Ask:*** *How did the authors feel about the changes that were happening to the Native Americans?* Have students record their ideas on a two-column chart.

Reading Comprehension

Question-Answer Relationships

Sample Answers

1. He begins on May 12, 1838.
2. General Scott gave the orders.
3. Jesse's mother will not make plans to leave. She thinks John Ross will help them.
4. where they live, how they get their food, and how they travel
5. I don't think the people of the Cherokee Nation want to move. The Nation lived there a long time. Their houses and land are there.
6. The Cherokee people are being forced to move to a different place. They don't have a choice.
7. Students may say that they think Jesse keeps a journal as a record for John Ross.
8. The Cherokee people believe that Kooweeskoowee will save them because they believe that is right and fair. The Native Americans respected fairness and honesty. They believe the soldiers and people in Washington will respect their request.
9. Standing Turkey and Jesse Smoke were not afraid of the white soldiers. They returned to the road as soon as the soldiers were gone. They were sure Kooweeskoowee would defeat them.
10. Once my family had to move because a big company wanted to build an office building where my apartment was. I was angry about it.
11. One good change was I got a new little sister. One bad change was I got braces.

Build Reading Fluency

Read to Memorize

Demonstrate to students that reading to memorize means adjusting your reading to be slow with stops to review your progress.

Beyond the Reading

Reading Comprehension

Question-Answer Relationships (QAR)

"Right There" Questions

1. **Recall Facts** On what day does Jesse Smoke begin his journal?
2. **Recall Facts** Who gave the orders to the people to make their way to the collection points?
3. **Recall Facts** Will Jesse Smoke's mother make preparations to leave her land?
4. **Recall Facts** List three things that changed for the people in "Ancient Ways."

"Think and Search" Questions

5. **Evaluate Evidence** Do you think the people of the Cherokee Nation want to move away from their land? Why or why not?
6. **Summarize** What is happening to the Cherokee people?

"Author and You" Questions

7. **Analyze Characters** Why do you think Jesse is keeping a journal about what is happening?
8. **Draw Conclusions** Why do you think the Cherokee people believe that Kooweeskoowee will save them from the Removal?

"On Your Own" Questions

9. **Analyze Characters** Do you think Standing Turkey and Jesse Smoke were afraid when the white soldiers with guns and bayonets came behind them on the road? Why or why not?
10. **Relate to Your Experience** Have you or any people you know had a similar experience to the Cherokee's? Describe it.
11. **Relate to Your Experience** In "Ancient Ways," people's lives changed. How has your life changed over the years? Have the changes been good, bad, or both?

Activity Book p. 74

Student CD-ROM

Build Reading Fluency

Read to Memorize

You must adjust your reading rate to read slowly when you memorize.

1. Use the Audio CD to listen to "Ancient Ways."
2. Read each line slowly.
3. Practice memorizing the poem.
4. In small groups, present the poem without looking at the words.

142 **Unit 2** Changes

MULTI-LEVEL OPTIONS *Elements of Literature*

Newcomer Have students illustrate one of these metaphors: *a heart of stone* or *the sun of my existence.* Help them write the metaphors as captions for their pictures.

Beginning On the board, write: *He is a mountain of a man. The child is a bundle of energy.* Ask students to discuss what these metaphors say about the two people. Point out that metaphors are kinds of comparisons. Have students illustrate one metaphor.

Intermediate Write on the board: *The road was a swirling storm of dust.* Tell students that a metaphor makes a comparison. *Ask: What does this metaphor compare the dusty road to?* (a storm) Ask students to work in pairs. Have them decide if there are any metaphors in "Ancient Ways." (no)

Advanced Have students work in small groups to discuss the metaphors in "The Journal of Jesse Smoke." Ask them to rewrite the metaphors as sentences that explain each metaphor's meaning. Have them share their sentences with another group.

Listen, Speak, Interact 

Identify How Language Reflects Culture and Regions

Speakers' choices of words can tell listeners about their culture and their country or region.

1. With a partner, listen to the audio recording of page 137 as you read. Find words that tell you about Cherokee culture and the region where they live. What do these words tell you?
2. With a partner, find a sentence in paragraph 6 that means "When I die, I hope that you will not forget me." Discuss how the two ways of expressing this idea are different. What does the speaker's choice of expression tell you about his role in Cherokee culture and society?
3. Think of a story that was passed down to you in your family. Tell your partner the story. Use words that say something about your culture or region.
4. Tell your story to the class. Listen to your partner's story. What do the words he or she uses tell you about the culture or region? Talk about your ideas with your partner.

Elements of Literature

Understand Metaphors

A **metaphor** is a way of describing something by comparing it to something else. For example, if you say that someone has "a heart of stone," you do not really mean that the person's heart is made of stone. You are using a metaphor to compare this person's heart to a stone. Both are cold and hard.

1. Look at these metaphors. Explain what they mean to a partner.
   a. My sun of existence is fast approaching to its setting.
   b. When I sleep in forgetfulness, I hope my bones will not be deserted by you.
2. On a piece of paper, write two or three metaphors to describe someone or something you know.

Activity Book p. 75

Student CD-ROM

Home Connection

Ask students to compare and contrast the home they live in now with another place they have lived. Have them create a two-column chart entitled *Home before* and *Home now.* Brainstorm a list of features they can compare, such as city or country; number of rooms; rural, suburban, or urban. Instruct them to ask their families to help them complete the chart. Let them present their charts in small groups.

Learning Styles *Linguistic*

Have students write a Language Experience Poem. Tell them the topic can be about the language and words they used to use and the language and words they can use now. Instruct them to use the structure of "Ancient Ways," starting with a statement such as *We're bilingual.* Then tell them to write several stanzas with *We used to ____, but now we can ____.* and ending with an observation about the changes. Have students write their poems in their Reading Logs.

Listen, Speak, Interact

Identify How Language Reflects Culture and Regions

1. **Reread in pairs** Read paragraph 6. Then pair beginning and advanced students. Have them read the speech together.
2. **Newcomers** Reread with this group. Instruct students to pick out words that refer to nature and write these on the board. Have students record the words in their Reading Logs.

Answers

1. *Sample answers:* in the dust; my sun of existence is approaching to its setting; my bones will soon be laid in the bosom of this earth.
2. "When I sleep in forgetfulness, I hope my bones will not be deserted by you." This version is more poetic. Death is like sleeping. It is important to remember the customs and traditions.

Elements of Literature

Understand Metaphors

1. **Teacher think aloud** On the board, write: *You are the sunshine of my life.* ***Say:*** *I know that a person does not give off light like the sun, but the sunshine is nice. It makes me feel happy. So, I think this person makes me happy.* Then in pairs, have students discuss the metaphors used in the journal.
2. **Locate derivation** Have students locate the derivation of *metaphor* in the glossary in the Student Handbook or other sources, such as online or CD-ROM dictionaries. Ask students to record the meaning and derivation in their Reading Logs.
3. **Multi-level options** See MULTI-LEVEL OPTIONS on p. 142.

Answers

1. *Sample answers:*
   a. My life will end soon.
   b. When I die . . .

ASSESS

On the board, write: *He's a mouse. She's a lion.* Have students explain what the metaphors mean.

Word Study

Use the Suffix *-ness*

Teacher Resource Book: *Personal Dictionary, p. 63*

Make a word map Write *sad* on the board and pronounce it. Then write the suffix *-ness* and pronounce it. Point out that the suffix changes the adjective to a noun. Have students create other nouns by adding the suffix *-ness* to *good, cold, complete.* (goodness, coldness, completeness)

Answer

2. happiness (*y* changes to an *i*)

Grammar Focus

Use the Present Continuous Tense

Play charades Have volunteers choose an action verb. Direct one student to mime an action. Others in the class try to guess the action verb by saying a sentence in the present continuous using the verb.

Answers

2. paragraph 2: are following, are making their way; paragraph 6: is fast approaching. . . .

ASSESS

Have students write a sentence in the present continuous tense to describe what they are doing right now.

Word Study

Use the Suffix *-ness*

When the suffix *-ness* is added to some adjectives, it forms a noun. This noun describes the condition that the adjective describes. Look at this example:

When I sleep in forgetfulness, I hope my bones will not be deserted by you.

The adjective *forgetful* is the base, or root, of the noun *forgetfulness.*

I am a very forgetful person.

My forgetfulness sometimes gets me into trouble.

1. Copy this chart in your Personal Dictionary.

2. The last letters of some adjectives change when you add the suffix *-ness.* Find an example in the chart.

The Suffix *-ness*	
Adjective	**Noun**
forgetful	forgetfulness
kind	kindness
happy	happiness
loud	loudness

Personal Dictionary

Activity Book *p. 76*

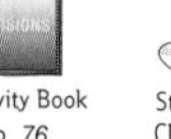
Student CD-ROM

Grammar Focus

Use the Present Continuous Tense

The **present continuous tense** describes an action that is happening *right now.* Look at this example:

John Ross is still negotiating.

Look at the chart to see how this tense is formed.

1. Find three examples of the present continuous tense. Look in paragraphs 2 and 6.
2. Write two sentences of your own that use the present continuous.

The Present Continuous Tense		
Subject	***am/are/is***	**Verb + *ing***
I	am	working.
You We They	are	working.
He She It	is	working.

Activity Book *pp. 77–78*

Student Handbook

Student CD-ROM

MULTI-LEVEL OPTIONS *From Reading to Writing*

Newcomer Tell students to think about changes they have gone through from childhood to the present. Have students draw a series of pictures of their ideas. Help them write dates or ages for each picture.

Beginning Have students draw a series of pictures. Direct them to illustrate changes they have gone through from childhood to the present. Help them write dates and key words to explain each picture.

Intermediate Have students do a Think-Pair-Share. First tell students to write a list of ideas from their poems. Then have them work in pairs to share their ideas and refine their poems. Tell students to make drawings to illustrate some of the ideas of their poems.

Advanced Instruct students to write their poems and then read them to a partner. Have partners help refine the poems by checking for patterns and rhythm and making suggestions to the authors. Remind students that authors make the final decisions about their poems.

From Reading to Writing 

Write a Poem

Write a poem with six to ten lines that describes how you have changed since you were younger. Brainstorm a list of ways you have changed. Use the list to help you plan your poem.

1. Use the structure of "Ancient Ways":

   I used to eat mangoes
   but now I eat apples.

2. Make sure your poem has a pattern or rhythm.
3. Separate your lines into stanzas.
4. Read your poem to the class. Read it dramatically. Use gestures and body language to show meaning.

Activity Book p. 79

Across Content Areas 

Use Rank Order

Rank order places things according to quantity or importance.

1. On a piece of paper, write a list of the numbers 1–10.
2. Put the states in the chart in rank order of Native American population.
3. The first state should have the largest population. The last state should have the smallest population.
4. Include the population numbers in your list.

State	Native American Population
Arizona	265,367
California	345,011
Florida	49,190
Michigan	59,945
New Mexico	173,773
New York	76,046
North Carolina	98,235
Oklahoma	273,348
Texas	127,950
Washington	95,808

Activity Book p. 80

Student CD-ROM

Reteach and Reassess

Text Structure Have students write three *wh*-questions to help them remember the three elements of historical fiction.

Reading Strategy Have students list five events from "The Journal of Jesse Smoke." Then ask them to number the events in chronological order.

Elements of Literature Have students write a metaphor that compares themselves to an animal or a bird.

Reassess Have students use their timelines to write a paragraph about the events in Jesse Smoke's journal.

From Reading to Writing

Write a Poem

1. **Brainstorm and list** Have students suggest ways they have changed. List the ideas on the board. Model planning a poem using some of the ideas on the board. Remind students of the structures: *I used to . . . , but now I . . . .* Then have students write their poems individually and share them in small groups.
2. **Multi-level options** See MULTI-LEVEL OPTIONS on p. 144.

Across Content Areas: Math

Use Rank Order

1. **Use graphic organizers** Direct students to the titles and column headings on the chart. Point out that the chart on this page is arranged in alphabetical order. Have students locate information using the chart. *Ask: Which state has 76,046 Native Americans?* (New York) *Which state has the smallest number of Native Americans?* (Florida)

Answers

From largest to smallest populations: CA, OK, AZ, NM, TX, NC, WA, NY, MI, FL.

Have students arrange themselves in rank order by age or height.

Assessment Program: *Unit 2, Chapter 5 Quiz, pp. 31–32*

UNIT 2
Apply and Expand

Materials

Student Handbook
CNN Video: *Unit 2*
Teacher Resource Book: *Lesson Plan, p. 12; Teacher Resources, pp. 35–64; Video Script, pp. 163–164; Video Worksheet, p. 174; Home-School Connection, pp. 126–132*
Teacher Resource CD-ROM
Assessment Program: *Unit 2 Test, pp. 33–38; Teacher and Student Resources, pp. 115–144*
Assessment CD-ROM
Transparencies
The Heinle Newbury House Dictionary/CD-ROM
Heinle Reading Library
Web Site: www.heinle.visions.com

Listening and Speaking Workshop

Interview and Report

Teacher Resource Book: *Interview, p. 54; Note-Taking, p. 58*

Use questions in interviews Questions are important for interviews. Review *wh-* question words and question formation as needed.

Step 1: Write interview questions. Have students prepare questions based on the issues and concerns. Write the question words on the board for reference.

UNIT 2 **Apply and Expand**

Listening and Speaking Workshop

Interview and Report

> **Topic**
> In small groups, prepare an interview about changes that should take place in your school.

Before you begin, assign roles:
The interviewer: asks questions to gain information
The interviewees: answer the questions
The reporter: reports the interview results to the class

Step 1: Write interview questions.

Use your own experience to list issues and concerns about your school. Then form questions for your interview.

Issues / Concerns	*Questions*
The school day starts too early.	*What time do you think school should start?*

Step 2: Ask and answer the questions.

1. The interviewer should show respect when asking questions.
   a. Ask if the interviewee wants to be interviewed.

   "Excuse me. Could I ask you a few questions about our school?"

   b. The interviewer should pay attention to the interviewee. Look the interviewee in the eyes when he or she is speaking. Accept the answers. Do not argue.

   "I see. My next question is, . . ."

   "That is an interesting answer."

   c. At the end of the interview, thank the interviewee.

   "Thank you for your time."

2. The reporter should take notes.

Step 3: Summarize and report the responses to the class.

1. All group members should go over the reporter's notes and choose the most interesting answers.

> ***Wei-Mon:***
> *school should start at 9:00*
> *has to help her mother in the morning*
> ***Rosa:***
> *wants school to start at 7:00*
> *works in the afternoon*

2. Organize the answers that you chose into a report.
3. The reporter reports to the class.

MULTI-LEVEL OPTIONS *Listening and Speaking Workshop*

Newcomer Work with students to write several information questions. Have them role-play asking and answering the questions in pairs. Remind students to look at the other person when asking a question.

Beginning Work with students to write information questions. Create a "script" to use when they approach and ask other students their questions. Have them role-play asking and answering the questions in small groups. Direct groups to comment on eye contact and respectfulness.

Intermediate Direct students to work in pairs to develop a list of interview questions. Instruct them to role-play both parts and practice taking notes. Have them discuss the easy and hard parts of interviewing another person.

Advanced Instruct students to develop individual lists of interview questions. Then have them ask questions in pairs as they practice taking notes. Remind students to ask questions to clarify meaning when they don't understand their partners. Have them discuss the easy and hard parts of interviewing another person.

Step 4: Ask classmates to evaluate your report.

Ask your classmates to evaluate the report by using the Active Listening Checklist. Then have a discussion in your group about how you could improve your performance.

Active Listening Checklist

1. I liked ____ because ____.
2. I didn't like ____ because ____.
3. I want to know more about ____.
4. I don't understand ____.

Viewing Workshop

Analyze Film or Video

Tell How a Scene Is Effective

In this unit, you read a selection about the Cherokee Native Americans in the 1830s and a selection about the English colonists in Virginia. Select one of these two topics. Then compare and contrast the written account with a video story.

1. Rent a video about the Native Americans or the colonists, or borrow a video from your school library.
2. Watch the video. What is the purpose of the video? To inform, entertain, persuade? How does the video show this purpose?
3. Identify a scene that was powerful for you. Maybe it made you think, or maybe it gave you strong emotional reactions.
4. Think about how the video created this effect. Consider the following elements: the acting, the dialogue, the music, the images themselves.
5. Compare and contrast the video to the selections. How are they similar? How are they different?
6. Take notes on your thoughts. How does the maker of the video use these things to show important ideas? What are the strengths and weaknesses of these elements? Describe the scene to your class and explain how it was effective.

Further Viewing

Watch the *Visions* CNN Video for Unit 2. Do the Video Worksheet.

CNN Video

Home Connection

Direct students to use their questions to interview a person at home. Have them bring in their notes. ***Ask:*** *Are the responses from home similar to or different than responses from other students?* Have them discuss their answers in small groups and report back to the class.

Learning Styles *Interpersonal*

Have pairs brainstorm a list of appropriate and inappropriate actions students should be aware of when they interview others. Tell them to include verbal cues, such as how to persuade someone to be interviewed, and nonverbal cues, such as eye contact or body language.

Apply and Expand

Step 2: Ask and answer the questions.

Model interviewing a person. Point out appropriate behavior and politeness markers. Then have students practice asking each other their questions before conducting the real interviews.

Step 3: Summarize and report the responses to the class.

Have students work in groups to read and discuss their response notes. Monitor students as they change the notes into complete sentences.

Step 4: Ask classmates to evaluate your report.

Provide checklists for students to complete as they listen to the reports. After groups review the checklists, have students discuss ideas on how they can perform better for the next oral presentation.

ASSESS

Have students write a sentence telling what they might do differently the next time.

Portfolio

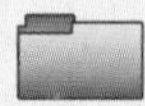

Students may choose to record or videotape their reports to place in their portfolios.

Viewing Workshop

Analyze Film or Video

Teacher Resource Book: *Venn Diagram, p. 35; Cluster Map, p. 38*

1. **Interpret a visual image** After students choose a scene, view it again. On the board, list items to consider: acting, dialogue, music, images. Arrange students in groups to share thoughts about what made it memorable.
2. **Evaluate the impact of a scene** Have students record their thoughts and notes on a cluster map.
3. **Share information** Have students use the diagrams to share their evaluations of their chosen video scenes.

Writer's Workshop

Write to Persuade: Write a Letter to the Editor

Write a persuasive letter Read and discuss the prompt. Point out that strong opinions and facts are needed to convince someone to do something.

Step 1: Research.
Have students work in group roundtables to list advantages of staying in school and disadvantages of dropping out. Have groups read their ideas and use them to plan further research in the library or on the Internet.

Step 2: Write your first draft.
Explain conventions for writing a letter to the editor. Point out the importance of clear, strong opinions and arguments to persuade. Have students identify the strongest arguments on their charts to include in their letters.

Writer's Workshop

Write to Persuade: Write a Letter to the Editor

> **Writing Prompt**
>
> Suppose you know someone who is no longer interested in school and wants to quit and get a job. Write a persuasive letter to the editor of a newspaper. You want to persuade readers that it is better to stay in school than to drop out.

Step 1: Research.

1. Make a list of all the reasons why people should stay in school. Fill out a Comparison Chart like this one.

Advantages of Staying in School	Disadvantages of Dropping Out
gain knowledge and skills	low pay

2. Use your own experience and the library or the Internet to find facts and statistics about why people should stay in school. Look for information in the following subject areas or search topics: employment, level of education, U.S. Department of Labor, and jobs.
3. Use tables of contents and headings in books to find these topics. Use key words to find them on the Internet.
4. Organize and summarize the facts you find. Write them in the chart to help you create your persuasive letter.

Step 2: Write your first draft.

1. Write the letter opening.
2. In the first paragraph, write an introduction. Explain why you are writing, and give an idea of what your letter will be about.
3. Write a paragraph that summarizes your ideas. Use full sentences. A good way to write persuasive letters is to ask and answer questions. For example:
   "Do students who work always earn more than those who stay in school? The evidence says no."
4. Write a conclusion sentence to summarize your ideas and finish your letter.
5. End your letter with the closing.

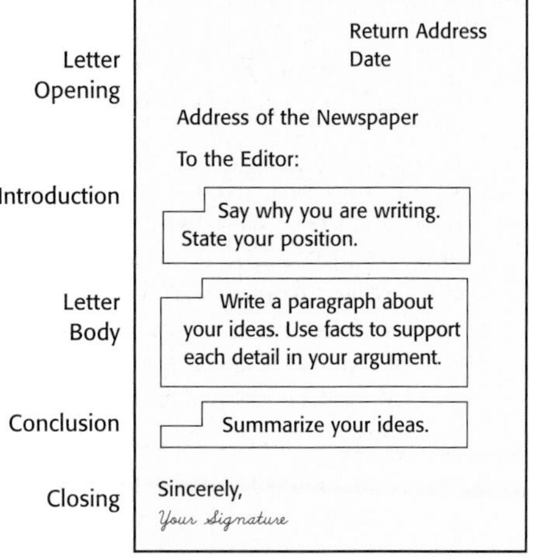

MULTI-LEVEL OPTIONS *Writer's Workshop*

Newcomer Instruct students to write a Language Experience Activity letter. Have students write a friendly letter of persuasion for the class bulletin board in small groups. Tell them to brainstorm and record the group's ideas on the topic. Then, have groups rewrite them as complete sentences. Show students how to write the date, the salutation, the body, and the closing of a friendly letter.

Beginning Instruct students to write a Language Experience Activity letter to the school newspaper in small groups. Tell them to brainstorm and record the group's ideas on the topic. Then have groups expand the ideas into complete sentences. Work with the groups to understand and apply the opening, body, and closing of a letter to the editor.

Intermediate Have students work in groups to research the topic and write a group letter to the editor of a local newspaper. Instruct students to collaborate with their groups to compose, organize, and revise their letters.

Advanced Instruct students to work in pairs to write a persuasive letter to the editor. Have them share their letters with another pair. Direct the reviewers to check that the conventions of a letter to the editor have been followed. Have them send their letters to a local newspaper.

Step 3: Revise.

1. Reread your draft and ask yourself these questions:
   a. Is my introduction clear?
   b. Did I present my ideas in a logical order?
   c. Did I use persuasive language?
   d. Did I support my opinions with facts and details?

   Revise your work using the points above. Combine and rearrange text to make your ideas clear.
2. Be sure you have all the facts and details you need to write your letter. Use the Internet or school library if you need to find more information. Use the information to revise your letter.
3. Collaborate with a partner. Ask each other the following questions to help revise and organize your work:
   a. Would the letter persuade me to stay in school?
   b. If not, how could the letter be more persuasive?
   c. How can I add or delete text to make it more persuasive?
4. Use your partner's responses to the questions above to make any final changes to your letter.

Step 4: Edit and proofread.

1. Proofread your work. Check your spelling. Use a dictionary to check the spelling of difficult words. Make sure you have ended all sentences with a punctuation mark.
2. Be sure you used apostrophes correctly when writing possessives and contractions.
3. Use the Editor's Checklist in your Student Handbook.

Step 5: Publish.

Write the final version of your letter. Follow these steps:

1. If possible, use a computer to make your final version. If not, copy the letter onto writing paper. Use your best handwriting so that others can read your work.
2. Put the letter in an envelope. Address the envelope to "Editor." Add the name and address of the newspaper. Ask your teacher to help you send the letter to a local newspaper.
3. Read a copy of your letter to the class. Ask your classmates for feedback.
4. Listen to your classmates read their letters. Would their letters persuade someone to stay in school? What facts and details helped you to believe your classmates' opinions?

The Heinle Newbury House Dictionary

Student Handbook

UNIT 2
Apply and Expand

Step 3: Revise.
Clarify and explain the questions as needed. Give examples of persuasive language for students to incorporate into their letters. Have pairs read and give feedback on the letters.

Step 4: Edit and proofread.
Review punctuation. You may want to have students focus on specific editing and proofreading points.

Step 5: Publish.
For the final copy, have students complete envelopes for their letters. Display the letters for others to read and discuss.

Have students choose the letter they thought was the most persuasive and write why they liked it.

Portfolio 

Students may choose to include their writing in their portfolios.

Community Connection

Bring in or have students bring in local and community newspapers. Examine and discuss the formats of the letters to the editor. ***Ask:*** *What are some of the topics of these letters? What topics are interesting to you?*

Learning Styles *Linguistic*

Ask students to write a persuasive speech to a group of students who want to drop out of school. Tell them to use their research for their letters to the editor. Have them practice their speeches with a small group. Then have them revise and deliver them to the class.

UNIT 2
Apply and Expand

Projects

Project 1: Research Life in the United States Since the Colonial Period

Teacher Resource Book: *Note-Taking, p. 58; Two-Column Chart, p. 44*

1. **Gather and organize** After students choose topics, have them locate resources in the library or on the Internet. Instruct students to take notes and organize the information on a chart.
2. **Create posters** Remind students to plan their posters. Have them identify the main point of the poster and create a title and content to support the main idea.

Project 2: Write a Magazine Article About a Historical Site

Teacher Resource Book: *Know/Want to Know/Learned Chart, p. 42*

1. **Gather information** Have students use a KWL chart to guide their search for information.
2. **Write a research paper** Instruct students to use their notes to make an outline for their final reports.

Portfolio

Students may choose to include their projects in their portfolios.

Projects

In this unit, you learned about changes. In these projects, consider what changes are taking place.

Project 1: Research Life in the United States Since the Colonial Period

Present a compare and contrast poster between life in the United States now and in the colonial period (1607 to 1776). Use the library or the Internet to gather information and images to present to classmates. Examples include:

Population: Were there more people or fewer people living in the United States than there are today?
City Life Versus Country Life: Did more people or fewer people live in cities than they do now?
Transportation and Travel: How has the way people move from place to place changed?
Employment: What jobs from today were more common in the colonial period than today? What jobs did not exist in the colonial period?
Entertainment: How has the way people spend their free time changed?

Project 2: Write a Magazine Article About a Historical Site

In the United States, there are several places where buildings have been returned to their original condition. In some of these places, people dress as the early settlers did. They also show you how the original people lived and worked.

Choose one of the sites below or another site that you know about. Research using the Internet or the library, and write an article for a travel magazine about it. Answer these questions:

Where is the site?
Who lived in this area originally?
When did they live there?
How did they live?
What can you see and do there?
Why do people like to go there to visit?

1. As you research, form new questions you want to find answers to.
2. List your sources with your article. (Sources are places where you gathered information.)

Some Historical Restorations in the United States:

Colonial Williamsburg, in Williamsburg, Virginia (Search: Colonial Williamsburg)
Plimoth Plantation, in Plymouth, Massachusetts (Search: Plimoth Plantation)
Old City Park, in Dallas, Texas (Search: Old City Park)
Calico Ghost Town in Barstow, California (Search: Calico Ghost Town)
St. Augustine Lighthouse, in St. Augustine, Florida (Search: St. Augustine Lighthouse)

MULTI-LEVEL OPTIONS *Projects*

Newcomer Assign students to work in groups. Have each group create a poster for one of the historical sites in project 2. Have them visit the Web site for ideas. Ask students to draw or download photographs or other art. Help them write a title for the poster.

Beginning Assign students to work in groups. Have each group create a brochure for one of the historical sites in project 2. Have them visit the Web site for ideas. Ask students to draw or download maps, photographs, or other art. Help them write interesting captions for each visual.

Intermediate Assign students to work in pairs. Have them visit the Web site for one of the historical sites in project 2. Tell students to decide on two or three of the most interesting aspects of the site to create an advertisement for the site. Encourage them to include maps and art in the design.

Advanced Have students do research in the library or on the Internet about one of the historical sites in project 2. Ask students to decide on two or three of the most interesting aspects of the site to write about. Tell them to write a paragraph on each aspect. Instruct them to include maps and art to highlight their ideas.

Further Reading

These books tell how people have dealt with changes in their lives. Choose one or more of them to read. Write your thoughts and feelings about what you read in your Reading Log. Take notes about your answers to these questions:

1. Did any of the changes you read about remind you of an experience that you have had?
2. In the books you read, how did the characters adjust to the changes?

Our Strange New Land: Elizabeth's Jamestown Colony Diary
by Patricia Hermes, Scholastic, Inc., 2002. Elizabeth is a member of the first English colony in Jamestown, Virginia. She keeps a diary of her experiences.

And Now Miguel
by Joseph Krumgold, HarperTrophy, 1984. Miguel Chavez spends the entire year trying to convince the Chavez men that he is ready to help herd the sheep to the mountains.

Tuck Triumphant
by Theodore Taylor, Camelot, 1996. Helen tries to convince her family to keep the deaf Korean boy they adopted. Helen's blind Labrador, Friar Tuck, helps her accomplish her goal.

Eagle Song
by Joseph Bruchac, Puffin, 1999. Danny's family moves from a Mohawk reservation to Brooklyn, New York. Danny must learn how to deal with not fitting in and being teased at school. He learns the value of courage and how to adjust to his new home.

Dream Soul
by Laurence Yep, HarperTrophy, 2002. Joanie's parents are immigrants from China. Joanie faces the conflict of living in two cultures, American and Chinese, when she moves to West Virginia.

Taking Sides
by Gary Soto, Harcourt, 1992. Fourteen-year-old Lincoln Mendoza moves from a Hispanic inner-city neighborhood to a suburb. An aspiring basketball player, Lincoln must learn how to handle a difficult new coach and his new team.

The Giver
by Lois Lowry, Laurel Leaf, 1994. This Newbery Award–winning book is set in a future society governed by a Committee of Elders. At the annual Ceremony of Twelve, the elders assign each 12-year-old person a life assignment. They select Jonas to be a "receiver of memories." In his new assignment, Jonas begins to uncover the truth about his society.

Reading Log

Heinle Reading Library

UNIT 2
Apply and Expand

Further Reading

Respond to literature Have students select a book about people facing changes and write a review of it. Instruct students to organize their review into three paragraphs. In the first paragraph, have them write about the title and main idea with a brief summary of the important events. In the second paragraph, tell them to explain their reaction to the story by telling how they feel and why they feel that way. In the last paragraph, direct students to tell what they learned from the story and from the characters' responses to the changes.

Assessment Program: *Unit 2 Test, pp. 33–38*

Introduce the Unit

Unit Materials

Activity Book: *pp. 1–120*
Audio: *Unit 3*
Student Handbook
Student CD-ROM: *Unit 3*
CNN Video: *Unit 3*
Teacher Resource Book: *Lesson Plans, Teacher Resources, Reading Summaries, School-Home Connection, Video Script, Video Worksheet, Activity Book Answer Key*
Teacher Resource CD-ROM
Assessment Program: *Quizzes, Test, and Mid-Book Exam, pp. 39–60; Teacher and Student Resources, pp. 115–144*
Assessment CD-ROM
Transparencies
The Heinle Newbury House Dictionary/CD-ROM
More Grammar Practice workbook
Heinle Reading Library
Web Site: www.heinle.visions.com

Heinle Staff Development Handbook

Refer to the Heinle Staff Development Handbook for more teacher support.

Unit Theme: Courage

1. **Teacher think aloud** *Say: What is courage? I think courage is something that helps people do difficult or dangerous things. I think a firefighter has courage to go into a house that is burning. An astronaut needs courage to fly into space in a rocket ship.*
2. **Use personal knowledge** *Ask: Do you know someone who has a lot of courage?* Have students talk about the courageous people they know. Point out that the adjective form of *courage* is *courageous.*

Unit Preview: Table of Contents

1. **Identify genres** *Say: The first selection is a poem. What other readings are in this unit?* (biography, diary, speech, memoir) Have students decide if these readings are about real or made-up (fictional) people and events.
2. **Connect** *Ask: What dangerous or difficult situations do you need courage for?*

UNIT 3

Courage

CHAPTER 1 **Life Doesn't Frighten Me**
page 154 a poem by Maya Angelou

CHAPTER 2 **Matthew A. Henson**
page 166 an excerpt from a biography by Wade Hudson

CHAPTER 3 **Anne Frank: The Diary of a Young Girl**
page 178 an excerpt from a diary by Anne Frank

CHAPTER 4 **Lance Armstrong: Champion Cyclist**
page 190 a speech by President George W. Bush

CHAPTER 5 **Earthquake**
page 202 an excerpt from a memoir by Huynh Quang Nhuong

UNIT OBJECTIVES

Reading

Use images to understand and enjoy poetry • Find the main idea and supporting details as you read a biography • Use chronology to locate and recall information as you read a diary • Distinguish fact from opinion as you read a speech • Draw conclusions and give support as you read a memoir

Listening and Speaking

Discuss personal experiences • Role-play an interview with a character • Act out a dialogue • Listen to and discuss a speech • Discuss emergencies

The Glacier de Tacconay, from *Scenes from the Snowfields,* Vincent Brooks, engraving, 1859.

View the Picture

1. How do you think this picture shows courage?
2. With a partner, discuss times when you needed courage.

In this unit, you will read a poem, a biography, a diary, a speech, and a memoir about courage. You will learn about situations in which people needed courage to survive or to face a challenge in their lives. You will also learn about the features of these writing forms and how to write them yourself.

153

Grammar
Use prepositional phrases • Identify two-word verbs • Use conjunctions to form compound sentences • Use superlative adjectives • Identify pronoun referents

Writing
Write a poem about a feeling • Write a short biography • Write a diary • Write a speech • Write a memoir

Content
Science: Learn about the respiratory system • Science: Learn about temperature • Social Studies: Describe social groups • Social Studies: Read a chart • Social Studies: Read a map

UNIT 3
Introduce the Unit

View the Picture

1. **Art background** Glaciers are massive formations of ice and rock. They begin to form when snow and ice accumulate in a larger amount than can melt in the summer. This accumulation continues over centuries. These great rivers of ice have had a major effect on Earth's surface, sculpting mountains and carving valleys as they expand and contract.
2. **Art interpretation** Ask students to describe the landscape and what people are doing in this engraving.
   a. **Explore contrasts** Have students contrast the glaciers and the people. Ask them to look at color (cool and warm), size (monumental and tiny), and shapes (rounded and vertical). Ask them what message these contrasts carry.
   b. **Connect to theme** *Say: The theme of this unit is* courage. *Think about the people in the picture. What kinds of courage do you think they needed to get here and will need to survive here?*

ASSESS

Have students draw a picture of a person showing courage in a dangerous place.

UNIT 3 • CHAPTER 1
Into the Reading

Chapter Materials

Activity Book: *pp. 81–88*
Audio: *Unit 3, Chapter 1*
Student Handbook
Student CD-ROM: *Unit 3, Chapter 1*
Teacher Resource Book: *Lesson Plan, Teacher Resources, Reading Summary, Activity Book Answer Key*
Teacher Resource CD-ROM
Assessment Program: *Quiz, pp. 39–40; Teacher and Student Resources, pp. 115–144*
Assessment CD-ROM
Transparencies
The Heinle Newbury House Dictionary/CD-ROM
Web Site: www.heinle.visions.com

Objectives

Preview Have students work in pairs to read and discuss the objectives. *Ask: Is there an objective you already know?*

Use Prior Knowledge

Discuss What Frightens You

1. **Share knowledge** Brainstorm and record a list of things that frighten students.
2. **Use a graphic organizer** Demonstrate how to complete the chart. Have students work in pairs to complete the chart.

Into the Reading

Objectives

Reading Use images to understand and enjoy poetry.

Listening and Speaking Discuss personal experiences.

Grammar Use prepositional phrases.

Writing Write a poem about a feeling.

Content Science: Learn about the respiratory system.

Use Prior Knowledge

Discuss What Frightens You

Everyone has fears. What frightens you (makes you afraid)?

1. With a partner, make a list of things that frighten you. Think about places, animals, noises, and events.
2. Copy the chart on a piece of paper. Write the words from your list where you think they should go.
3. Draw a picture for one or two of the frightening things.
4. Share your chart and pictures with the class.

Very, Very Frightening	Very Frightening	Frightening	A Little Frightening

MULTI-LEVEL OPTIONS *Build Vocabulary*

Newcomer Have students line up in alphabetical order by their last names. Then tell them to write their names alphabetically on the board.

Beginning Demonstrate a shadow with your hand. Write *shadow* on the board. Show or draw a picture and label on the board: *ghost, frog,* and *snake.* Then point to a word and have a volunteer imitate each one.

Intermediate Have students work in pairs. Tell each student to make up a short story using all the words in the box. Then have the students read their stories to their partners.

Advanced Ask students to write the words on p. 155 in alphabetical order. For each word, have students locate and write the dictionary word entries that come directly before and after it.

Build Background

Nursery Rhymes

Poems for very young children are called nursery rhymes. One famous collection of nursery rhymes is "Mother Goose." Some pictures show the character as a frightening woman.

Tell the class about nursery rhymes you have heard. Compare and contrast nursery rhymes from parts of the United States and other cultures.

LANGUAGE ARTS

Content Connection

Nursery rhymes are one kind of **oral tradition.** They are told out loud by grandparents to parents to children for hundreds of years.

Build Vocabulary

Preview New Vocabulary

The poem in this chapter includes words that name frightening things.

1. Work with a partner to guess the meanings of these words.

shadow	ghost	frog	snake

2. Read the dictionary entry for the first word.

shad•ow /ˈʃædoʊ/ *n.* **1** the dark shape formed when someone or something blocks the sun or other light: *The houses made long shadows in the late afternoon.*|| *At night, scary things hide in the shadows on city streets.*

3. Look up the other words in the dictionary. Read the definition. Use the pronunciation key to help you say each word.
4. Write the words in your Personal Dictionary and look for them as you read the poem.

Personal Dictionary

The Heinle Newbury House Dictionary

Activity Book *p. 81*

Student CD-ROM

Content Connection
Technology

Build Vocabulary Ask students to think of five things that can be frightening or scary. Instruct them to use an electronic dictionary to locate and write a definition for each word. Then have them write a sentence for each word.

Learning Styles
Interpersonal

Build Background Have small groups work together to plan a short skit based on a nursery rhyme. Ask groups to act out their nursery rhyme skits for the class.

Into the Reading

Build Background

Nursery Rhymes

1. **Recite songs and poems** Bring in a book of nursery rhymes and share some with the class. Ask students to share songs and poems that their parents or grandparents shared with them.
2. **Content Connection** *Ask: What nursery rhymes did you learn when you were young? Who taught them to you?*

Build Vocabulary

Preview New Vocabulary

Teacher Resource Book: *Personal Dictionary, p. 63*

1. **Use a dictionary** Review alphabetical order and how to find words in a dictionary. Have students find the first word and locate the word's meaning and pronunciation. Then arrange students in pairs to look up the other words in a dictionary.
2. **Reading selection vocabulary** You may want to introduce the glossed words in the reading selection before students begin reading. Key words: *on the loose, boo, shoo, way, strangers.* Instruct students to write the words with correct spelling and their definitions in their Personal Dictionaries. Have them pronounce each word and divide it into syllables.
3. **Multi-level options** See MULTI-LEVEL OPTIONS on p. 154.

ASSESS

On the board, write: *shadow, ghost, frog, snake.* Ask students to put them in alphabetical order.

Text Structure

Poem

1. **Recognize features** Explain terms in the feature chart for poems. Ask students to identify the features of a poem in poems or nursery rhymes they know.
2. **Multi-level options** See MULTI-LEVEL OPTIONS below.

Reading Strategy

Use Images to Understand and Enjoy Poetry

Visualize *Say: Think of the color red. Does it feel warm or cold? Think of blue. Think about a small kitten. Does it make you feel happy or scared?* Explain that sometimes poems have images that help us understand the thoughts of the poet.

ASSESS

Ask students to name the features of a poem (rhyming words, repetition, images, stanzas).

Text Structure

Poem

"Life Doesn't Frighten Me" is a **poem.** Poems let writers share what is important to them. They express their feelings.

As you read "Life Doesn't Frighten Me," look for the distinguishing features of a poem. Notice the speaker's thoughts and feelings.

Poem	
Stanzas	groups of lines
Rhyming Words	words that have the same or similar sounds; they are often used at the ends of lines
Repetition	a repeated idea or theme
Images	words that help you make a picture in your mind

Reading Strategy

Use Images to Understand and Enjoy Poetry

Poems include words that help readers make pictures in their minds. These images (pictures) allow readers to understand and enjoy a poem better.

1. Read or listen to the audio recording of "Life Doesn't Frighten Me." What images do you see in your mind? Read each line slowly and carefully to help you understand each image.
2. How do these images help you understand and enjoy the poem? Which words help you to make the best images in your mind?
3. Draw a picture of a line from the poem. Make your picture show what the poet is saying in the poem.

MULTI-LEVEL OPTIONS *Text Structure*

Newcomer Write on the board: *sad/mad; dog/frog; pen/ten.* Say each word pair. Then have students repeat them aloud. Write on the board: *day, fun, big, pet.* ***Ask:*** *Which word rhymes with* say*?* (day) Repeat for other words. (run/fun; pig/big; get/pet)

Beginning On the board, write: *floor, same, fright, hair, blue, there, store, game, two, kite.* Say each word. Then have students repeat them aloud. ***Ask:*** *Which word on the board rhymes with* floor*?* (store) Point out that rhyming words can have very similar *(same/game)* or very different *(two/blue)* spellings.

Intermediate Have students read or recite a familiar nursery rhyme. Ask them to think about the images created by the words. Instruct students to close their eyes and visualize the words. Then have them take turns describing the pictures in their minds.

Advanced Have students work in groups. Direct them to use words from their "frightening ideas" charts on p. 154. Tell them to find as many rhyming words as possible for each idea.

Life Doesn't Frighten Me

a poem by Maya Angelou

157

Reading Selection Materials

Audio: *Unit 3, Chapter 1*
Teacher Resource Book: *Reading Summary, pp. 85–86*

Preview the Selection

1. **Interpret the image** Explore and describe how color, shape, and line influence the message. ***Ask:*** *Are the lines straight or curved?* (curved) *Why do you think the artist used curved lines?* (to show quick movement or action) Ask students how the picture is connected to the title of the poem. ***Ask:*** *What is frightening about the picture? What do you think is scary in life?*
2. **Connect** Remind students that the unit theme is *courage.* Ask them how courage might help a person deal with a frightening animal. Have students think of other times in life when people need courage. Point out there may be situations that are emergencies and very dangerous and other times when something is new. Tell students to look for these different types of situations where courage is needed as they read the poem.

Content Connection *Social Studies*

Ask students to name historical figures who they think are courageous. (Martin Luther King Jr.; astronauts; heroes from other cultures) Ask them how each person showed courage. Then have students describe a time they were courageous. (trying out for a play; singing a solo in front of a large audience; standing up to a bully)

Learning Styles *Intrapersonal*

Direct students to the picture on p. 157. ***Ask:*** *What do you think of when you look at this picture? How does this picture make you feel? What would you do if you were faced with a creature like that?* Have students write their answers in their Reading Logs.

Teacher Resource Book: *Reading Log, p. 64*

Read the Selection

1. **Use text features** Have students find the number of lines in the first stanza. Refer students to the illustration. ***Ask:*** *Where are the lions? Do lions really walk around on the street? How do they make you feel?*
2. **Choral reading** Play the audio. Assign small groups to do a choral reading of different stanzas.
3. **Use images to understand and enjoy poetry** *Ask: What are some things that can frighten people?* (shadows, noises, bad dogs, ghosts)

Sample Answer to Guide Question
I see large gray clouds that look like ghosts. The clouds are growing and getting bigger and scarier.

See Teacher Edition pp. 434–435 for a list of English-Spanish cognates in the reading selection.

Use Images to Understand and Enjoy Poetry

What images do you make in your mind when you read the words *Big ghosts in a cloud?*

1 Shadows on the wall
Noises down the hall
Life doesn't frighten me at all
Bad dogs barking loud
Big ghosts in a cloud
Life doesn't frighten me at all

MULTI-LEVEL OPTIONS *Read the Selection*

Newcomer Read the poem aloud. Pause at the rhyming words (*wall, hall, fun, run,* etc.). Write them on the board. Read the poem again. Have students raise their hands when they hear a rhyming word. Then ***ask:*** *Are the ghosts big?* (yes) *Is the author afraid of the lions?* (no)

Beginning Play the audio. ***Ask:*** *Where are the ghosts?* (in a cloud) *Who is mean?* (Mother Goose) *What is breathing flame?* (dragons)

Intermediate Have students do a paired reading. Then ***ask:*** *How do the dogs bark?* ("dogs barking loud") *What are some ways the author makes scary things go away?* (says "boo," makes fun of them, smiles at them)

Advanced Have students read the poem silently to themselves. Then ***ask:*** *Are dogs and lions always scary?* (No, pet dogs and lions at the zoo aren't scary.) *How do the scary things change as the poem goes on?* (They get scarier; shadows and noises aren't as scary as lions and dragons.)

Use Images to Understand and Enjoy Poetry

Describe what images you see in your mind after reading this stanza.

2 Mean old Mother Goose
Lions **on the loose**
They don't frighten me at all
Dragons breathing flame
on my **counterpane**
That doesn't frighten me at all.

3 I go **boo**
Make them **shoo**
I make fun
Way they run
I won't cry
So they fly
I just smile
They go wild
Life doesn't frighten me at all.

---

on the loose set free
counterpane a bedspread or quilt
boo a sound made to frighten or surprise
shoo tell someone or something to go away by using motions
way = away

A Capitalization

Titles of poems

Tell students that the first letter of each main word in a poem's title is always capitalized. Then tell students that the titles of poems are written with quotation marks around them. ***Ask:*** *What letters in the poem's title are capitalized?* (L, D, F, and M) *Why does "Life Doesn't Frighten Me" have quotation marks around it?* (It's the title of the poem.)

Apply Have students correct the capitalization and punctuation errors in the following sentences. On the board, write: *My favorite nursery rhyme is "little miss muffet."* ("Little Miss Muffet") *We read Humpty Dumpty in class today.* ("Humpty Dumpty")

Read the Selection

1. **Use text features** Call attention to the numbers for each stanza. Have students find the meanings below for the glossed words.
2. **Choral reading** Play the audio. Have different groups do choral readings of different stanzas.
3. **Use images to understand and enjoy poetry** ***Ask:*** *What animals are mentioned in the poem?* (Mother Goose, lions, dragons)
4. **Identify features of a poem** Have students point out examples of rhyming words and lines that are repeated.
5. **Multi-level options** See MULTI-LEVEL OPTIONS on p. 158.

Sample Answer to Guide Question

In stanza 2, I see mean lions walking around, dragons breathing fire, and smoke at the foot of my bed.

Read the Selection

1. **Use text features** Ask students to count how many stanzas there are on p. 160. (three) Remind them to check the meanings of the boldfaced words at the bottom of the page. Have students describe the illustration and explain what is frightening about it.
2. **Choral reading** Play the audio or read the poem to students. Have different groups do choral readings of different stanzas.
3. **Use images to understand and enjoy poetry** *Ask: Which image is the most frightening to you? Why?*

Sample Answer to Guide Question
A new girl is in class and the boys are mean. They pull her hair and it hurts.

4 Tough guys in a fight
All alone at night
life doesn't frighten me at all.
Panthers in the park
Strangers in the dark
No, they don't frighten me at all

Use Images to Understand and Enjoy Poetry

What images do you see in your mind when you read "That new classroom where Boys all pull my hair"?

5 That new classroom where
Boys all pull my hair
(Kissy little girls
with their hair in curls)
They don't frighten me at all

6 Don't show me frogs and snakes
And listen for my scream
If I'm afraid at all
It's only in my dreams

panthers large, wild cats, usually all black

strangers people that you do not know

MULTI-LEVEL OPTIONS *Read the Selection*

Newcomer *Ask: Are the strangers in the park?* (no) *Are the boys and girls in the classroom?* (yes) *Does the poet have a magic charm?* (yes)

Beginning *Ask: What are in the park?* (panthers) *What do the boys do to the girl?* (They pull her hair.) *Where does the poet keep her magic charm?* (up her sleeve)

Intermediate *Ask: What are some places the poet writes about?* (the park, the dark, school, the ocean) *When is the only time she is afraid?* (in her dreams) *What does the magic charm do?* (It keeps her safe; it allows her to breathe underwater.)

Advanced *Ask: What do you think the author would say about monsters under a bed?* ("They don't frighten me! I'm not afraid of them!") *What do you think the author meant by "That new classroom"? Why might that be scary? Explain.*

7 I've got a magic **charm**
That I keep up my sleeve,
I can walk the ocean floor
And never have to breathe.

8 Life doesn't frighten me at all
Not at all
Not at all
Life doesn't frighten me at all.

Use Images to Understand and Enjoy Poetry

What images stay in your mind after reading this poem?

charm an object that is believed to bring luck

About the Author

Maya Angelou (born 1928)

Maya Angelou faced frightening situations during her childhood. Her family was poor and her parents were divorced. She had to move many times and sometimes lived in places where African-Americans were treated badly. However, people such as Angelou's grandmother taught her how to have courage. Angelou has worked as an actress, a writer, and a teacher. She has also worked for equal treatment of African-Americans.

➤ Why did Maya Angelou write this poem? Was it to entertain us or to express herself?

What challenges do you think Maya Angelou faced in becoming an author?

Read the Selection

1. **Make predictions** Ask students to make predictions about the poem's ending. ***Ask:*** *Will there be more scary things? Will the poet tell why she has courage?*
2. **Choral reading** Play the audio. Then have students reread the poem chorally.
3. **Multi-level options** See MULTI-LEVEL OPTIONS on p. 160.

Sample Answer to Guide Question
Images of shadows, lions, dragons, boys pulling hair, etc.

About the Author

1. **Explain author's background** Read the author biography aloud. Explain that Maya Angelou has written five collections of poetry. She uses imagery so that readers can experience her feelings. Tell students that in 1993 she read her poem "On the Pulse of Morning" at the presidential inauguration of Bill Clinton.
2. **Analyze point of view** ***Ask:*** *What experiences helped Maya Angelou learn about courage?* (her difficult childhood) *How does the first-person point of view of the poem make you feel about her experiences?* (I feel like she wrote about her personal experiences in the poem. I feel like I know her better.)

Across Selections

Analyze text features Have students reread "Ancient Ways" on p. 140. Instruct students to analyze the text features of that poem and "Life Doesn't Frighten Me." ***Ask:*** *Which text features do the two poems have in common?* (stanzas, repetition, images)

Spelling

It's* and *its

Write *it's* and *its* on the board. Explain that the word *it's* means "it is." Explain that the word *its* is a possessive pronoun and means "of it" or "belonging to it." On the board, write: *It's good to have friends.* ***Say:*** *It's good to have friends. It is good to have friends.* Then write: *We climbed the tree and hung from its branches.* ***Say:*** *We hung from its branches. We hung from the branches of the tree.*

Evaluate Your Reading Strategy

Use Images to Understand and Enjoy Poetry ***Say:*** *You have practiced an important reading strategy. Now you can decide how well you have done. Does this statement describe how you read?*

When I read poetry, I try to "see" the images in my mind. When I "see" the images in a poem, I understand it better and enjoy it more.

Reading Comprehension

Question-Answer Relationships

Sample Answers

1. She is not frightened by being in a new classroom.
2. She is frightened in her dreams, but not in real life.
3. She has a magic charm that protects her. She knows many of the things are not real.
4. Shadows can be from car lights going by. Noises can be people walking or buildings creaking in the wind.
5. I would be frightened of tough guys fighting and being alone at night.
6. I think the illustrations show different images and help you realize that the frightening things in the poem are not real, but imaginary. Photos would show real things. The illustrations show me that things that seem frightening are not real although they are scary.
7. The illustrations have a dark, mysterious style and show important elements in the poem, such as lions and dragons. These help me understand the poem by helping me create more complete mental images than I could from the poem alone.
8. I think a person should be afraid of strangers in the dark and tough guys in a fight.

Build Reading Fluency

Echo Read Aloud

Model reading aloud with expression. Read one line at a time. Ask the class to read (echo) the same line you just read before going on to the next line or sentence.

Beyond the Reading

Reading Comprehension

Question-Answer Relationships (QAR)

"Right There" Questions

1. **Recall Facts** Name something that does not frighten the author.
2. **Recall Facts** What is one thing that does frighten the author?

"Think and Search" Questions

3. **Give Reasons** What makes the author not afraid of the frightening things in this poem?
4. **Make Inferences** What might really cause shadows on the wall or noises down the hall?

"Author and You" Questions

5. **Evaluate Ideas** Which of the things in the poem would frighten you the most?
6. **Analyze Illustrations** Why do you think illustrations are placed with the poem instead of photos? How does this help you understand the text?
7. **Analyze Illustrations** How do the style (look and feeling) and elements (parts) of the illustrations help you understand the poem?

"On Your Own" Question

8. **Make Judgments** Are there any things in the poem that you think a person *should* be frightened of?

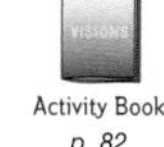

Activity Book
p. 82

Build Reading Fluency

Echo Read Aloud

Echo reading helps you learn to read with expression. Your teacher reads a line of "Life Doesn't Frighten Me." Then the class reads the same line aloud.

1. Listen to your teacher read the poem.
2. Next, read the same line aloud with expression.
3. Continue listening then reading.

MULTI-LEVEL OPTIONS *Elements of Literature*

Newcomer Play the audio of "Life Doesn't Frighten Me." Ask students to raise their hands for all rhyming words. Have pairs practice reading the poem aloud, clapping to emphasize syllables and each rhyming word.

Beginning Write on the board and ***say:*** *wall* and *hall.* Have students repeat. Then read aloud the first stanza of "Life Doesn't Frighten Me." Direct students to say the rhymes aloud as you reach each one. Continue the process throughout the poem.

Intermediate Tell students to work independently to list the rhymes in each stanza. Then have them write a third word that rhymes with each pair. Tell them to share their lists in small groups.

Advanced Remind students that some of the rhymes in the poem are exact rhymes and some are similar. Have students work independently to list the pairs of similar rhymes in the poem. Then ask students to write as many additional similar rhymes for each pair as they can.

Listen, Speak, Interact 

Discuss Personal Experiences

"Life Doesn't Frighten Me" includes real-life situations that you may have experienced.

1. Read the poem aloud with a partner. List frightening things in the poem, such as "Shadows on the wall."
2. Discuss experiences that have frightened you. For example, "There was a hurricane." Compare and contrast your experiences.
3. Present a dramatic interpretation of one of your experiences. Act out the situation that frightened you.

Elements of Literature

Identify Rhyming Words

"Life Doesn't Frighten Me" uses **rhyming words** at the ends of some lines. The ends of rhyming words can sound exactly the same, such as *wall* and *hall.* Sometimes the word endings sound similar, such as *sleeve* and *breathe.*

1. With a partner, find an example in the poem of rhyming words that sound exactly the same at the end. Say the words aloud.
2. Find an example of rhyming words that sound similar at the end. Say the words aloud.
3. Use the pronunciation guide in a dictionary to help you say words you do not know.
4. In your Reading Log, make a chart like the one here. Find examples of each kind of rhyming words and write them in the chart.

Exact Rhyme	Similar Rhyme
wall / hall	sleeve / breathe

Reading Log

Activity Book p. 83

Student CD-ROM

Content Connection *The Arts*

Tell students that some poems, songs, and nursery rhymes are about things that can be frightening. ***Ask:*** *What are some animals that can be scary?* Elicit responses such as tigers, sharks, and bears. Ask small groups of students to find a song, poem, or nursery rhyme that is about a frightening animal. Allow groups to rehearse their selections and perform them for the class.

Learning Styles *Kinesthetic*

Ask pairs of students to select one frightening image from the poem. Have pairs mime the image using no verbal cues. Allow students to guess which image each pair is acting out.

Listen, Speak, Interact

Discuss Personal Experiences

1. **Reread in pairs** Pair beginning and advanced students. Have them read alternate stanzas of the poem.
2. **Newcomers** Reread with this group. Ask them to name things that frighten them. Write these on the board. Have them write the words in their Reading Logs.

Answers

1. Shadows; noises down the hall; dogs barking; ghosts in a cloud; Mother Goose; lions; dragons; tough guys in a fight; being alone at night; panthers; strangers; a new classroom; frogs; snakes.

Elements of Literature

Identify Rhyming Words

Teacher Resource Book: *Reading Log, p. 64*

1. Point out exact rhymes (*hall/wall*) and similar rhymes (*flame/counterpane*) in the poem. Prompt students to find other rhyming words. ***Ask:*** *What word rhymes with* loud *and is something that you see in the sky?* (cloud) *Do these words sound the same or similar?* (same)
2. **Multi-level options** See MULTI-LEVEL OPTIONS on p. 162.

Answers

1. wall/hall/all; loud/cloud; Goose/loose; boo/shoo; fun/run; cry/fly; fight/night; park/dark; where/hair; girls/curls
2. flame/counterpane; smile/wild; scream/dreams; sleeve/breathe

ASSESS

Recite "Little Miss Muffet" or another simple rhyme. Have students identify the rhyming pairs.

Beyond the Reading

Word Study

Identify Contractions

Make a word map Write on the board and *say: does not.* Then write the contraction *doesn't* and pronounce it. Ask students to identify the missing letter in the contraction. Tell them that an apostrophe takes the place of missing letters.

Answers

1. a. do not; b. I am; c. It is; d. I have
2. don't/do not; I'm/I am; it's/it is; I've/I have

Grammar Focus

Use Prepositional Phrases

Apply Ask questions about the location of people and objects. Have students respond with prepositional phrases. Ask students to write a sentence using a prepositional phrase. Have them exchange sentences and underline their partner's prepositional phrase.

Answers

1. a. down/the hall; b. in/a cloud; c. on/my counterpane; d. in/the park

ASSESS

On the board, write: *That does not* scare me. It *is not* real. Have students write contractions for the underlined words.

Word Study

Identify Contractions

Contractions are shortened forms of words.

Life doesn't frighten me at all.

The word *doesn't* is a contraction for the words *does not.* The **apostrophe** (') shows where the word *not* has been shortened. It replaces the letter *o.* Notice that the two words become one word.

1. Read the following sentences. Which of these words make up each contraction?

   I am   I have   it is   do not

   a. They don't frighten me at all.
   b. If I'm afraid at all.
   c. It's only in my dreams.
   d. I've got a magic charm.
2. Write the contractions and the two words that make up the contractions in a chart like the one here.

Contraction	Two Words
doesn't	does not

Activity Book p. 84

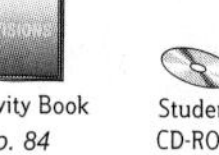
Student CD-ROM

Grammar Focus

Use Prepositional Phrases

A **prepositional phrase** often answers the question *when, where,* or *how.*

Shadows on the wall

A prepositional phrase is made up of a preposition and an object. Some prepositions are: *about, at, down, for, in, on, over, under, up, with.*

Preposition	Object
in	the closet
on	the wall

1. Read the following lines from the poem. Write the prepositions and the objects in a chart.
   a. Noises down the hall
   b. Big ghosts in a cloud
   c. Dragons breathing flame on my counterpane
   d. Panthers in the park
2. Write your own sentence using a prepositional phrase.

Activity Book pp. 85–86

Student Handbook

Student CD-ROM

164 **Unit 3** Courage

MULTI-LEVEL OPTIONS *From Reading to Writing*

Newcomer Write *afraid* on the board. Model a facial expression for *afraid. Say: This is how I look when I'm afraid.* Write *angry, sad, happy,* and *surprised* on the board. Ask students to model facial expressions for each. Have students draw and label faces with each expression.

Beginning Tell students to list key words that they might use in their poems. Have them read their lists aloud in small groups. Ask groups to assist members by suggesting rhymes for the words on one another's lists.

Intermediate Have students write the first line of their poems. Instruct students to work in pairs to brainstorm words that rhyme with the last word. Tell them to use their ideas to write the second line. Have them repeat the process as they work through the poem.

Advanced Tell students to exchange poems with a partner. Reviewers should check for prepositional phrases, imagery, and rhyming. Remind students to be tactful. Also point out that final changes are up to the author.

From Reading to Writing 

Write a Poem About a Feeling

Brainstorm ideas about a feeling you sometimes have. Use these ideas to write a poem. Some feelings are: afraid, happy, sad, angry, surprised, confused.

1. Write your ideas in a web.
2. Use at least two prepositional phrases to tell when and where you feel this. Use the web to write your poem.
3. Use images to help the reader "see" what you are saying.
4. Use rhyming words at the end of the lines.
5. Read your poem aloud to the class. Use expression and gestures to help your classmates understand.

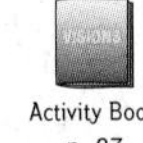
Activity Book p. 87

Across Content Areas 

Learn About the Respiratory System

Your **respiratory system** consists of the **lungs** and the body's air passages. When you breathe in, you **inhale.** When you breathe out, you **exhale.** You breathe in **oxygen,** a gas in the air. In the lungs, the oxygen enters the blood. **Blood** is the red liquid that flows through your body. Blood carries the oxygen to all parts of your body. Oxygen is exhaled as **carbon dioxide,** a compound of carbon and oxygen.

Inhale
Exhale
Lungs

Copy these sentences. Fill in the blanks with the correct words.

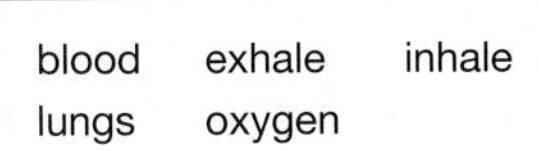

1. When you ____ , air fills your ____ .
2. You breathe in a gas called ____ .
3. Your ____ takes the oxygen to parts of your body.
4. When you ____ , carbon dioxide leaves the body.

Activity Book p. 88

Reteach and Reassess

Text Structure Divide students into four groups. Assign one text feature to each group (stanzas, repetition, images, rhyming words). Instruct each group to write a definition of their assigned text feature. Have volunteers write their group's definition on the board.

Reading Strategy Tell students to select one stanza from the poem. Ask them to draw a picture that represents the image or images in that stanza. Allow students to share their drawings.

Elements of Literature Select ten easily rhymed words. Write the words on the board. For each word, ask students to name as many rhyming words as they can.

Reassess Write *Rhyming Words, Repetition, Images* on index cards. Display one card at a time. For each card, ask students to provide examples from "Life Doesn't Frighten Me."

Beyond the Reading

From Reading to Writing

Write a Poem About a Feeling

Teacher Resource Book: *Web, p. 37*

1. **Gather and organize** Brainstorm and record a list of feelings on the board. Have students use a web to record details and ideas that illustrate the chosen feeling. Tell them to number the ideas to guide their writing.
2. **Think-pair-share** Ask students to think about their chosen feeling and write as much as they can about it using their web. Then have students share their work with a partner. Tell pairs to help each other find rhyming words and include prepositional phrases.
3. **Multi-level options** See MULTI-LEVEL OPTIONS on p. 164.

Across Content Areas: Science

Learn About the Respiratory System

Define and clarify Pronounce and explain the meanings of *inhale, exhale, oxygen, carbon dioxide,* and *blood.* ***Say:*** *Name two gases in the air.* (oxygen, carbon dioxide) ***Ask:*** *When I breathe in, what do I do?* (inhale) *What gas do I breathe in?* (oxygen)

Answers
1. inhale; lungs
2. oxygen
3. blood
4. exhale

ASSESS

Give the definitions of *inhale, exhale, lungs,* and *oxygen* and have students say the correct words.

Chapter Materials

Activity Book: *pp. 89–96*
Audio: *Unit 3, Chapter 2*
Student Handbook
Student CD-ROM: *Unit 3, Chapter 2*
Teacher Resource Book: *Lesson Plan, Teacher Resources, Reading Summary, Activity Book Answer Key*
Teacher Resource CD-ROM
Assessment Program: *Quiz, pp. 41–42; Teacher and Student Resources, pp. 115–144*
Assessment CD-ROM
Transparencies
The Heinle Newbury House Dictionary/CD-ROM
Web Site: www.heinle.visions.com

Objectives

Prereading for vocabulary Ask students to look for specific words in the objectives. ***Ask:*** *What word means "a story about a person's life"?* (biography) *Is a biography about a real or made-up person?* (real) Continue with *role-play, interview,* and *character.*

Use Prior Knowledge

Prepare for a Trip to a Cold Climate

Gather and organize Brainstorm words to complete the chart. Students can share and explain their supply lists with the class.

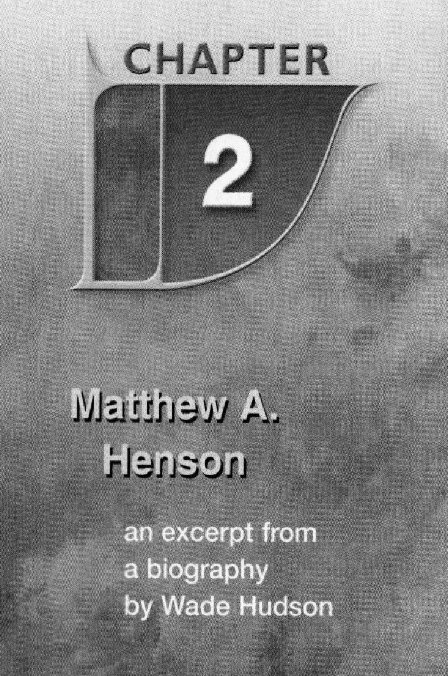

Into the Reading

Objectives

Reading Find the main idea and supporting details as you read a biography.

Listening and Speaking Role-play an interview with a character.

Grammar Identify two-word verbs.

Writing Write a short biography.

Content Science: Learn about temperature.

Use Prior Knowledge

Prepare for a Trip

Have you ever taken a trip? Where to? What did you take with you?

What would you take with you on a trip to a very cold place?

1. Copy the chart on a piece of paper.
2. With a partner, brainstorm what you would need to take with you on a trip to a very cold place where there is lots of ice and snow.
3. Share the information in your chart with the rest of the class.

A Trip to a Cold Place
1. Food
2. Sleds and dogs
3.
4.
5.

166 Unit 3 Courage

MULTI-LEVEL OPTIONS *Build Vocabulary*

Newcomer On the board, write *shut* and *close.* Close a door and ***say:*** *shut.* Close it again and ***say:*** *close.* ***Ask:*** *What else can you shut? What else can you close?* Point out suggestions such as a book, a drawer, and a cabinet. Have students demonstrate their responses using your suggestions.

Beginning Write these words in a column on the board: *bag, run, animal,* and *seat.* Write *jog, chair, sack,* and *beast* in a second column. Have students copy the lists. Ask them to work in pairs to match the synonym pairs by drawing lines to connect them.

Intermediate Write on the board: *run, jog, seat, chair, bag, sack, animal,* and *beast.* Have students work in pairs. Tell one student to use a word from the list in a sentence. Then have the other student restate the sentence, using the word's synonym. Tell students to alternate turns.

Advanced Have students work independently. Ask them to write a different sentence for each of the following words: *trip, voyage, journey,* and *expedition.* Challenge students to use a print or software thesaurus to find additional synonyms for *trip.* (trek, excursion, outing)

Build Background

The North Pole

The **North Pole** is the northern-most point of Earth. It is located near the center of the Arctic Ocean. It is made up entirely of frozen ocean. This area does not have any land.

Content Connection

The Inuit are a group of native people who live in Canada near the North Pole.

Build Vocabulary

Learn Synonyms with Reference Aids

In "Matthew A. Henson," the people in the story take a long and dangerous trip. Do you know any **synonyms** for the word *trip*? Remember, synonyms are words that have similar meanings.

1. Read the following sentences. The underlined words are synonyms for *trip*.
   a. They sailed on a long voyage from New York City to Canada.
   b. Peary selected Henson and four Inuit guides to make the last leg of the journey.
   c. Congress authorized a medal for all the men on the North Pole expedition.
2. Write the word *trip* and these synonyms in your Personal Dictionary.
3. A **thesaurus** is a reference book for synonyms. As you read, use a thesaurus or another synonym finder to find words with the same meaning as words you don't know. You can also use software such as an electronic or online dictionary or thesaurus. Record these words in your Personal Dictionary.

Personal Dictionary

Activity Book *p. 89*

Student CD-ROM

Home Connection

Build Vocabulary Have students ask family members or friends to help them complete additional synonym pairs. Give students these words: *car, road, song, advertisement, plan, shout, jump,* and *noise.* Have them compile their synonym pairs into a two-column chart.

Teacher Resource Book: *Two-Column Chart, p. 44*

Learning Styles *Mathematical*

Build Background Tell students to locate the North Pole in an atlas or on a map. Then have them use the map scale to estimate the distance from where they are to the North Pole.

Build Background

The North Pole

1. **Use a map** Direct students to a map or globe. Have them identify countries that border the North Pole, such as Canada, Russia, and Greenland.
2. **Analyze facts** *Ask: Why do you think there are no cities or roads near the North Pole?* (There is no land, only frozen ocean.)
3. **Content Connection** Bring in photos or books about the Inuit and other groups that live in the Arctic region. Ask students to speculate about life in such a remote place.

Build Vocabulary

Learn Synonyms with Reference Aids

Teacher Resource Book: *Web, p. 37; Word Square, p. 41; Personal Dictionary, p. 63*

1. **Use semantic mapping** *Say: Synonyms are words with similar meanings. The words* boat *and* ship *are synonyms.* Begin a semantic word map, such as a word square or a web. Ask students to suggest other synonyms.
2. **Use multiple reference aids** *Say: Synonyms are very close in meaning, but sometimes it's more appropriate to use one synonym rather than another. Dictionaries, thesauruses, and online or CD-ROM dictionaries and thesauruses often give information about when to use a particular word.* Have students use these reference aids to clarify the meaning and usage of the new words.
3. **Reading selection vocabulary** You may want to introduce the glossed words in the reading selection before students begin reading. Key words: *suffer, harsh, injure, give way, ignore, achievement.* Instruct students to write the words with correct spelling and their definitions in their Personal Dictionaries. Have them pronounce each word and divide it into syllables.
4. **Multi-level options** See MULTI-LEVEL OPTIONS on p. 166.

Have students write sentences using the new synonyms for *trip.*

Text Structure

Biography

Teacher Resource Book: *Reading Log, p. 64*

1. **Examine text features** Choose question words for the features: *When, What, How.* Ask questions and have students respond with the feature of a biography.
2. **Locate derivation** Have students locate the derivation of *description* in the glossary in the Student Handbook or other sources, such as online or CD-ROM dictionaries. Ask students to record the meaning and derivation in their Reading Logs.
3. **Multi-level options** See MULTI-LEVEL OPTIONS below.

Reading Strategy

Find the Main Idea and Supporting Details

Teacher Resource Book: *Reading Log, p. 64*

Define terms On the board, write: *main idea, details.* **Say:** *The main idea is the most important idea in a reading. Supporting details tell examples or information about the main idea.* Model filling in the chart.

ASSESS

On the board, write: *dates, actions and events,* and *descriptions.* Ask students to write one *wh-* question that asks about each feature.

Text Structure

Biography

"Matthew A. Henson" is a **biography.** A biography is the story of a person's life. It is written by another person. In a biography, you will find the distinguishing features shown in the chart.

As you read, record the events of Matthew Henson's life on a timeline in your Reading Log. Use a timeline like the one below.

Biography	
Dates	when important things happened in the person's life
Actions and Events	important or special things the person did
Descriptions	details about the people and places in the person's life

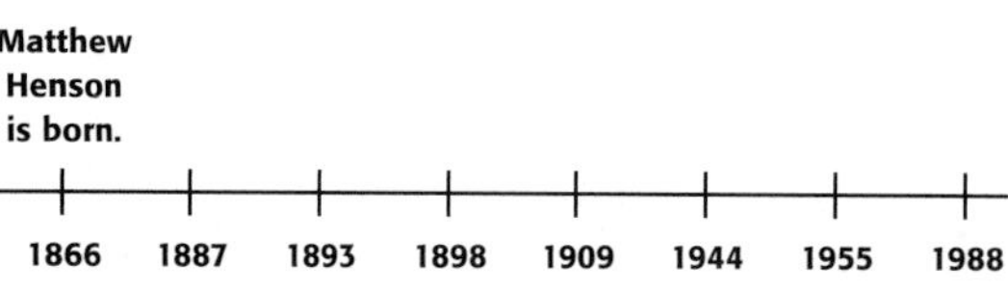

Student CD-ROM

Reading Strategy

Find the Main Idea and Supporting Details

The **main idea** of a paragraph (or of a longer part of a reading) is the most important thing that the writer wants you to understand. **Supporting details** are pieces of information that show you that the main idea is true. Here is an example:

> The weather outside was terrible. The temperature was 10°F. The wind was blowing very hard, and it was snowing. I did not want to go out!

Main Idea	Supporting Details
The weather was terrible.	10°F, windy, snowy

1. As you read "Matthew A. Henson," look for the main idea of each long paragraph. You can sometimes find the main idea in the first or last sentence of a paragraph.
2. Write the main ideas and supporting details in your Reading Log.

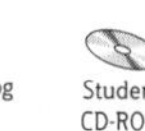

MULTI-LEVEL OPTIONS *Text Structure*

Newcomer Review dates with students. **Say:** *Today is (today's date).* **Ask:** *What is today's date? When is your birthday? In what year were you born?*

Beginning Remind students that a biography gives information about a person. **Ask:** *How would someone describe you?* Have students list adjectives and descriptive phrases about themselves. (funny, like to draw, good at math, tall, etc.)

Intermediate Tell students to list five important events in their lives. Remind students to include dates for each event. Ask student pairs to read their lists aloud to each other.

Advanced Ask students to pretend they are writing their own biographies. Have students write a paragraph about something important or special that they did. Remind students to include dates and descriptions of the event.

MATTHEW A. HENSON

an excerpt from a biography
by Wade Hudson

169

Reading Selection Materials

Audio: *Unit 3, Chapter 2*
Teacher Resource Book: *Reading Summary, pp. 87–88*

Preview the Selection

Teacher Resource Book: *Know/Want to Know/Learned Chart (KWL), p. 42*

1. **Interpret the image** ***Ask:*** *Who do you think this person is? What is he wearing? What is his coat made of? What does it tell you about the climate? Where do you think he is? Why do you think he is in this place? Do you think he has courage? Why do you think so?*
2. **Use a KWL chart** Have students suggest what they know about Matthew A. Henson based on this photo. Tell them to write questions about what they would like to know about him. List their ideas on a KWL chart. Remind students to use the questions on this chart to guide their reading of the selection. Have them complete the last column of the chart after they finish the reading.
3. **Connect** Remind students that the unit theme is *courage.* Ask them to predict the kinds of dangers or difficulties Matthew A. Henson might have faced near the North Pole.

Content Connection *The Arts*

Ask students to look at and think about the picture. ***Ask:*** *How does this picture make you feel? What kind of a person do you think this man was?* Have students write short rhymed or free-verse poems based on their responses to the picture.

Learning Styles *Natural*

Ask: *If you could make an expedition to anywhere in the world, where would you go? Why? Who would you take with you? What would you bring with you?* Then have students brainstorm the supplies that an explorer would need for an expedition to the North Pole.

Reading Selection

Read the Selection

1. **Use a map** Have students locate the labeled places on the map. Ask what they think the line from New York City to the North Pole represents. Remind students to use the map to help them understand the reading.
2. **Teacher read aloud** Read the selection aloud. Pause to check understanding and to identify features: dates, actions and events, descriptions.
3. **Summarize** *Ask: Why was the trip so difficult?* (The weather was very cold. The men got sick or were injured from the cold weather.)

Sample Answer to Guide Question

Main idea: The group began a trip to find the North Pole; supporting details: They traveled by ship from New York City to Columbia, Canada. They used dog sleds to carry food and supplies.

See Teacher Edition pp. 434–435 for a list of English-Spanish cognates in the reading selection.

1 The most northern part of the earth has below-freezing temperatures. Ice covers the area. This is the North Pole.

2 In 1893, no one had been to the North Pole. That year Admiral Robert E. Peary and Matthew Henson set out to reach the North Pole. But they were unsuccessful. They tried again in 1898, but failed. In 1909, they set out once more.

3 Peary, Henson, and a group that included explorer Robert Bartlett took off for the Pole. They sailed on a long voyage from New York City to Canada. Next, they set up a base camp at Camp Columbia, Canada. The camp was about 450 miles from the North Pole. In March 1909, the group packed dog sleds with food and supplies. Then they headed over the **polar** sea ice toward the North Pole.

Find the Main Idea and Supporting Details

What is the main idea of this paragraph? Give two supporting details.

4 Some of the men **suffered** from the **harsh** cold weather. They had to return to the camp. Finally, Peary selected Henson and four Inuit guides—Ootah, Seegloo, Egingwah, and Ooqueah—to make the last leg of the journey. It was early April 1909. They were closer than ever to really reaching the North Pole.

Audio

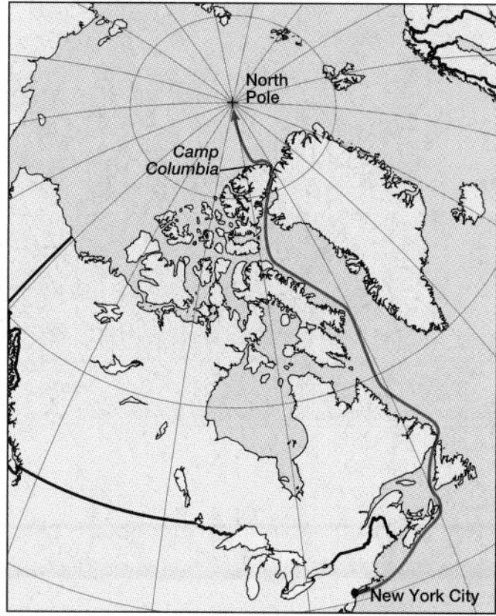

polar near one of Earth's poles
suffered felt pain or unhappiness
harsh extreme, very strong

MULTI-LEVEL OPTIONS *Read the Selection*

Newcomer Play the audio. Then reread pp. 170–171 aloud. Have students raise their hands when they hear a date. Then *ask: Is the North Pole covered with ice?* (yes) *Did the explorers take a plane to the North Pole?* (no) *Was the base camp in New York City?* (no) *Did Henson fall into the cold water?* (yes)

Beginning Read the Reading Summary aloud. Then do a paired reading of pp. 170–171. *Ask: What is the Admiral's name?* (Robert E. Peary) *Is the North Pole warm or cold?* (very cold) *Where was the base camp?* (Camp Columbia, Canada) *When did the group pack the dog sleds?* (March 1909)

Intermediate Have students do a paired reading of pp. 170–171. Then *ask: Why did some of the men return to camp?* (They suffered from the cold weather.) *Why couldn't Peary walk quickly?* (His feet were injured.) *Who saved Henson from the icy water?* (Ootah)

Advanced Have students read independently. Then *ask: How does Ootah save Henson's life?* (He pulls him from the icy water and helps him dry off.) *Why do you think these men made this dangerous voyage?* (They wanted to be the first to reach the North Pole.)

Pack ice near the North Pole.

5 Henson, Peary, and their guides traveled over the ice and snow. Peary's feet were **injured.** He could not walk as quickly as Henson. So Henson and his guides walked ahead—and disaster struck.

6 Along the way, Matthew Henson stepped out on a large cake of ice. *CRACK!* The ice **gave way.** Henson fell into the icy water below. The water temperature was **bitter** cold: **–15 degrees Fahrenheit.** In only a few minutes, Matthew Henson would have frozen to death.

7 Suddenly, there was a tug on Henson's hood. Someone was pulling him from the water. It was Ootah. Quickly, Ootah helped Henson pull off his wet boots and clothes and put on dry ones. Ootah shook the water from the furs Henson wore before the water turned to ice. Then Henson, Ootah, and Seegloo moved on. Admiral Robert E. Peary, Egingwah, and Ooqueah followed. The North Pole was less than thirty-five miles away.

Find the Main Idea and Supporting Details

The main idea of this paragraph can be stated as "Ootah saved Henson's life." Find two details that support this main idea.

Henson got closer and closer to 8
the Pole. Finally, he stopped. He looked around. Had he reached the North Pole? Henson set up camp there and waited for Peary.

---

injured hurt
gave way fell down; collapsed
bitter causing pain
–15 degrees Fahrenheit –26 degrees Celsius

Read the Selection

1. **Use the illustration** Ask students to describe the illustration. Point out the caption and have students guess what is going to happen in the reading.
2. **Understand terms** Ask students to find the meanings of the glossed words below the selection. Clarify meanings as needed.
3. **Paired reading** Read the Reading Summary aloud. Have students read the text in pairs.
4. **Identify cause and effect** *Ask: Why was it difficult for Peary to walk?* (His feet were hurt.) *Why did Henson fall into the water?* (The ice broke.)
5. **Multi-level options** See MULTI-LEVEL OPTIONS on p. 170.

Sample Answer to Guide Question

Ootah pulled Henson out of the water. He helped Henson take off the wet clothes and put on dry clothes.

Punctuation

Commas in a series

Tell students that commas separate words or phrases that are listed in a series. **Ask:** *What list of names is given in paragraph 4?* (Ootah, Seegloo, Egingwah, and Ooqueah) *Why are there commas between their names?* (Their names are listed in a series.) Ask students to find three more series lists with commas in paragraphs 5 (Henson, Peary, and their guides) and 7 (Henson, Ootah, and Seegloo; Admiral Robert E. Peary, Egingwah, and Ooqueah).

Apply Have students correct the comma errors in the following sentences. On the board, write: *Jack Elena and Tonia went to the park. I said hello to Pablo Sasha and Leon. She put on her hat gloves scarf and coat.*

Read the Selection

1. **Paired reading** Read paragraphs 9–11 aloud. ***Ask:*** *Why did Peary take a picture of Henson and the guides?* (to prove they made it to the North Pole) *How did they know they were at the North Pole?* (Peary made some observations.) Have students reread the selection in pairs.
2. **Summarize** ***Ask:*** *How do you know that Matthew A. Henson liked adventure?* (He started working on a ship when he was fourteen years old. Later he traveled with Peary to many different places.)

Sample Answer to Guide Question
Peary announced that they were at the North Pole.

Robert Peary's North Pole expedition.

9 When the Admiral arrived, he made **observations** from different points. He returned to the camp and made an **announcement.** The camp was at the exact point of the North Pole. He had Henson and the four guides stand on a ridge and he photographed them. Henson held the American flag. He felt proud. It had been an exciting adventure.

Find the Main Idea and Supporting Details

Read this detail: "He made observations from different points." What main idea does this detail support?

Matthew Henson was born in Charles County, Maryland, in 1866. After his mother died, he lived with an uncle in Washington, D.C. Henson always liked adventure. When he was fourteen years old, he signed on as a cabin boy on a ship called the *Katie Hines.* He was a member of the crew for five years. 10

Henson met Peary in 1887, when Henson was working in a clothing store in Washington, D.C. Peary liked Henson right away. Peary offered Henson a job . . . Henson . . . was interested in a trip Peary had planned to Nicaragua. It was a chance for him to travel again. For more than twenty years, the two men took many trips together. 11

observations things seen or measured

announcement something said in public

MULTI-LEVEL OPTIONS *Read the Selection*

Newcomer ***Ask:*** *Were the men at the North Pole?* (yes) *Were they happy and proud that they reached the North Pole?* (yes) *Did Henson hold the Canadian flag?* (no) *Did it take a long time for Henson to get a medal?* (yes)

Beginning ***Ask:*** *Where was the camp?* (at the North Pole) *Who got a gold medal for reaching the North Pole?* (Peary) *What kind of medal did Henson get?* (silver) *When did Matthew Henson meet Peary?* (in 1887)

Intermediate ***Ask:*** *Where did Henson go after his mother died?* (to live with an uncle in Washington, D.C.) *Why do you think Henson felt proud when he held the flag?* (He represented his country.) *Who recognized Henson's achievement first?* (the black community)

Advanced ***Ask:*** *Did other people think that Peary and Henson's North Pole expedition was important? Explain.* (Yes, the explorers were given medals and awards.) *Why did it take so long for the Congress of the United States to recognize Henson's achievement?* (because he was black)

12 On April 7, 1909, the great explorers began their journey back from the North Pole. They were very happy about their victory.

13 Robert E. Peary became famous. Peary was awarded a gold medal by the National Geographic Society. Robert Bartlett was also awarded a medal although he didn't even make the final trip to the North Pole. Matthew Henson was **ignored.**

14 For many years, the white world did not recognize Henson's great **achievement.** The black community, however, presented him with a number of awards. Finally, on January 28, 1944, Congress **authorized** a medal for all the men on the North Pole expedition. A year later, Henson was presented with a silver medal for **outstanding** service to the United States Government.

15 This great explorer died in 1955. On April 6, 1988, his **remains** were reburied with full military honors at Arlington National Cemetery. It was a most **suitable** honor for a great black American.

---

ignored not paid any attention to
achievement something you do that is difficult and important
authorized approved, agreed to
outstanding extra special, more than is expected
remains a dead body
suitable proper, fitting, correct

About the Author — Wade Hudson (born 1946)

Wade Hudson has written many books about African-American heroes for young readers. His wife, Cheryl Willis Hudson, also publishes books about African-Americans. Hudson was born and grew up in Louisiana. He worked for the equal rights of African-Americans before becoming a writer. When he writes, he wants to tell the true story of African-Americans.

➤ What is the author's purpose in writing this biography? Is it to entertain, to inform, or to influence?

A Capitalization

Places and abbreviations of names

Explain that the names of people and places are capitalized. Then explain that names can also be abbreviated, or shortened. Remind students that a one-letter abbreviation of a name (an initial) is always capitalized and followed by a period. ***Ask:*** *Why is the letter* E *capitalized in Robert. E. Peary?* (It is a one-letter abbreviation of a name.) *Why are the first letters of Arlington National Cemetery capitalized?* (It is a place.)

Evaluate Your Reading Strategy

Find the Main Idea and Supporting Details
Say: *You have practiced an important reading strategy. Now you can decide how well you have done. Does this statement describe how you read?*

> When I read, I look for the main idea and the details that support it. Finding the main idea and supporting details helps me understand and remember the reading later.

UNIT 3 • CHAPTER 2
Reading Selection

Read the Selection

1. **Identify main idea and supporting details** ***Ask:*** *How was Henson honored for his courage?* (He finally received some awards and he was buried in Arlington National Cemetery.)
2. **Multi-level options** See MULTI-LEVEL OPTIONS on p. 172.

About the Author

1. **Explain author background** Wade Hudson works for civil rights, black liberation, women's liberation, and the environment. He uses his writing skills to influence others and to persuade others to work for change.
2. **Interpret the facts** ***Ask:*** *Do you think Wade Hudson has courage?* (Yes, because he writes and works to make changes in the way people treat others. It takes courage to do that.)

Across Selections

Teacher Resource Book: *Two-Column Chart, p. 44*

Make comparisons Compare and contrast the problems and courage of Maya Angelou to the challenges and courage of Matthew A. Henson. ***Ask:*** *Which person needed more courage?* (Henson did. He could have been hurt or died looking for the North Pole.) *How are Angelou and Henson similar?* (They had courage to keep going and facing their problems.) Have students record their ideas on a two-column chart.

Reading Comprehension

Question-Answer Relationships

Sample Answers

1. It's at the top of the globe in the center of the Arctic Ocean.
2. Admiral Robert E. Peary
3. The black community, Congress, and the United States Government gave him awards. He was also buried in Arlington National Cemetery.
4. He fell into the icy water.
5. First, they took a ship to Columbia, Canada. Then they walked and used dog sleds. They set up camps along the way.
6. The National Geographic Society only gave awards to the leaders of the trip. They only gave awards to white participants.
7. They both liked to take risks and have adventures. I like some people because they like the same things I do.
8. Peary trusted Henson to continue the trip and to complete it if needed.
9. He probably felt angry and sad. But he was honored by the black community, and that was probably important to him.

Build Reading Fluency

Repeated Reading

Assessment Program: *Reading Fluency Chart, p. 116*

As students read aloud, time the reading and count the number of incorrectly pronounced words. Record results in the Reading Fluency Chart.

Beyond the Reading

Reading Comprehension

Question-Answer Relationships (QAR)

"Right There" Questions

1. **Recall Facts** Where is the North Pole?
2. **Recall Facts** Who led the trip that Matthew Henson took to the North Pole?
3. **Recall Facts** What honors did Matthew Henson receive for his journey?

"Think and Search" Questions

4. **Analyze Cause and Effect** What caused Matthew Henson to almost die on the trip?
5. **Recognize Sequence of Events** What steps did Henson's group have to take to reach the North Pole?
6. **Make Inferences** Why do you think that the National Geographic Society did not give Matthew Henson a medal after the 1909 trip?

"Author and You" Questions

7. **Compare Your Experiences** Why do you think that Matthew Henson and Robert Peary liked each other right away? What makes you like someone right away?
8. **Make Inferences** Peary sent Henson ahead after Peary hurt his feet. How do you think Peary felt about Matthew Henson?

"On Your Own" Question

9. **Speculate** How do you think Matthew Henson felt when he was not honored with the other North Pole explorers?

Activity Book p. 90

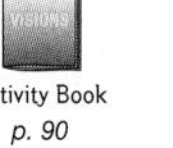
Student CD-ROM

Build Reading Fluency

Repeated Reading

Rereading one paragraph at a time can help increase your reading rate and build confidence.

1. With a partner, read aloud paragraph 1 in "Matthew A. Henson" three times.
2. Did your reading rate increase each time?
3. Next, read paragraph 2 three times.
4. Continue rereading each paragraph.
5. Stop after ten minutes.

174 Unit 3 Courage

MULTI-LEVEL OPTIONS *Elements of Literature*

Newcomer Prepare a blank storyboard with *First, Next, Then,* and *Last* in each square. On the board, write: *He received a silver medal. He got to Camp Columbia. Henson left New York. He found the North Pole.* Have small groups discuss and decide the order in which to write the sentences. Then have students read them aloud and fill in the storyboard.

Beginning Review transition words and phrases used to signal periods of time with students. *Say: Minute, hour, day, week, month . . . What comes next?* Ask students to locate and create a time line of all the years given in the selection.

Intermediate Have students brainstorm additional transition words and phrases for each category in the chart. Tell them to add their ideas to their Reading Logs.

Advanced Point out that transition words and phrases are often used to describe the steps in a process. Ask students to write simple directions for a process, such as folding a paper airplane or making a sandwich. Have students peer-edit with partners.

Listen, Speak, Interact 

Role-Play an Interview with a Character

Select one of the characters in the story you just read.

1. With a partner, role-play an interview. One of you will be the character in the story. The other will be a reporter for a magazine.
2. On a piece of paper, complete an Interview Preparation List like the one here.
3. Role-play the interview. Speak clearly and listen carefully.
4. Ask questions about anything you don't understand.

Interview Preparation List
Date: ______
Name of Character: ______
Name of Reporter: ______
Questions:
1. Why did you want to join the expedition to the North Pole?
2. ______
3. ______
4. ______
5. ______

Elements of Literature

Recognize Chronological Order and Transitions

Writers sometimes order events as they happen—starting with the first event and ending with the last. This is called **chronological order.**

Transitions are words or groups of words that connect ideas. They help readers follow the chronological order. Look at these transition words and phrases.

Time	Sequence	Periods of Time
in 1909	first	for five years
on Tuesday	second	in the summer
in the morning	next	last week
	then	
	finally	

1. Reread paragraph 3 of "Matthew A. Henson." Find three examples of transition words or phrases that signal time.
2. List the events in chronological order in your Reading Log.
3. Write three sentences of your own using time words.

Reading Log

Activity Book *p. 91*

Student CD-ROM

Cultural Connection

Remind students that Americans of all races and cultures have accomplished great things. Have small groups read biographies of other famous African-Americans, such as Harriet Tubman, Booker T. Washington, and George Washington Carver. Ask each group to prepare a short summary of the life and accomplishments of their subject. Have groups present their summaries to the class.

Learning Styles *Musical*

Tell students that some songs tell stories about people. Ask if they have heard the song "John Henry Was a Steel-Driving Man." Play a recording of the song, if available. Have small groups write and perform short songs that tell the story of Matthew Henson's life.

Listen, Speak, Interact

Role-Play an Interview with a Character

1. **Identify characters** Have students identify the main characters in the reading selection. Ask students to describe them and tell what they did.
2. **Brainstorm and organize** Brainstorm and record questions students can ask one of the main characters. Ask students to prioritize the questions.
3. **Ask and answer questions** Have students prepare and practice their interview in pairs. You may also want to model a role-play. Tell students to rely on their own personal experiences and knowledge to draw conclusions about the characters they are portraying.
4. **Newcomers** Help this group form simple interview questions. Provide a list of *wh-* question words (*who, what, when, where, why, how*) and other key words (*the North Pole, explore, camp, award, etc.*).

Elements of Literature

Recognize Chronological Order and Transitions

Teacher Resource Book: *Reading Log, p. 64*

1. **Use transitions** Review chronological order. Write some examples of transition words and phrases used in instructions and directions: *first, after that, repeat, then.*
2. **Multi-level options** See MULTI-LEVEL OPTIONS on p. 174.

Answers

1. Next; In March 1909; Then
2. They set up a base camp at Camp Columbia, Canada. The group packed dog sleds with food and supplies. They headed over the polar sea ice toward the North Pole.

ASSESS

Have students give examples of three different transition words or phrases.

Word Study

Recognize Proper Nouns

Teacher Resource Book: *Personal Dictionary, p. 63*

Make a vocabulary game Prepare index cards with several proper nouns for countries, regions, or continents. Ask students to give the proper nouns for people who are from those places. Write them on another set of cards to create a concentration game. Have students find the two proper nouns that go together.

Answers
Nicaraguan, Africa, Canada, European, Asia, Australia

Grammar Focus

Identify Two-Word Verbs

Explore parts of speech List other commonly used two-word verbs on the board: *give up, find out, look up.* Model using them in sentences. *Say: I give up. I can't win.* Have students create sentences using the two-word verbs.

Answers
1. took off 2. moved on 3. signed on

Say: Asia, Mexico, Canada, North America. Have students respond with the corresponding proper nouns for each. (Asian, Mexican, Canadian, North American)

Word Study

Recognize Proper Nouns

Proper nouns are the names of people (for example, *Matthew*); important places like cities, countries, and continents (for example, *Sacramento, California*); and some time words (for example, *Tuesday, January*).

The first letter of a proper noun is always written with a **capital letter** (the *t* in ***T****uesday* is a capital letter).

Some proper nouns refer to people who are from a certain place, for example: We are **Americans.** *Americans* are people from America.

Add **-n, -an,** or **-ian** to place names to make a proper noun that refers to a person. Copy the chart in your Personal Dictionary and complete it. Capitalize proper nouns.

Country, Region, or Continent	Person
Central America	Central American
Nicaragua	
	African
	Canadian
Europe	
	Asian
	Australian

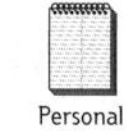
Personal Dictionary

Activity Book *p. 92*

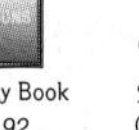
Student CD-ROM

Grammar Focus

Identify Two-Word Verbs

Two-word verbs use two words to explain an action.

> Matthew Henson set out to reach the North Pole.

The two-word verb *set out* means "left on a trip."

Find sentences with two-word verbs in the following paragraphs. Write the sentences on a piece of paper. Underline both words of the two-word verb.

1. In paragraph 3, find a two-word verb in the first sentence that means "left."
2. In paragraph 7, find a two-word verb that means "continued."
3. In paragraph 10, find a two-word verb that means "joined a group."

Activity Book *pp. 93–94*

Student Handbook

Student CD-ROM

176 **Unit 3** Courage

MULTI-LEVEL OPTIONS *From Reading to Writing*

Newcomer Have students draw a picture of someone they admire. Tell them to list five words that describe that person. Work with students to write descriptive sentences based on their lists.

Beginning Have students work in pairs to help each other complete the biography graphic organizer. Remind them to write complete sentences. Tell students to make sure their sentences have subjects and verbs.

Intermediate Ask students to select one sentence from their biography graphic organizer as a topic sentence for an expanded paragraph. Point out that the topic sentence only tells the main idea. Remind them to add details to the paragraph with additional sentences.

Advanced Have students exchange biographies with a partner. Reviewers should check for capitals, commas, and transitions. They may also suggest ideas for more descriptive writing. Remind students to be tactful. Also point out that final changes are up to the author.

From Reading to Writing 

Write a Short Biography

Write a biography about a famous person or someone in your family or community. Use "Matthew A. Henson" as a model for your writing. Research your biography at the school library, on the Internet, or by talking to people.

1. Introduce the person to the reader. Tell the person's story. Focus on important or special things the person did.
2. Include proper nouns to tell where the person comes from. Be sure to capitalize correctly.

Biography

______________ (title)

______________ (name) is important because ______________ (reason). On ______________ (date), ______________ (name) ______________ (did something).

Next ______________ (event).

Then ______________ (event).

Finally ______________ (event).

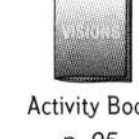
Activity Book p. 95

Across Content Areas 

Learn About Temperature

Temperature tells you how hot or cold something is. It is measured in degrees. The degrees are often shown with the symbol ° after the number, such as 75°.

There are two temperature systems, the **Celsius** and the **Fahrenheit** systems.

	Celsius	Fahrenheit
Water freezes	0°C	32°F
Water boils	100°C	212°F

To change from Fahrenheit to Celsius, use this formula:

$$^\circ C = (^\circ F - 32 \times 5/9)$$

Can you change 80°F to Celsius? For help with this problem, ask a math teacher or other expert.

Activity Book p. 96

Reteach and Reassess

Text Structure On the board, write: *Dates, Actions and Events,* and *Descriptions.* Have students provide an example from the selection of each feature.

Reading Strategy Have students select one paragraph from "Matthew A. Henson." Ask them to write the paragraph's main idea in their own words. Then have them list any supporting details.

Elements of Literature Write on the board: *in 1898, Next, Finally, for many years,* and *a year later.* Ask students to copy the list. Have them locate each of the transitions in the selection. Ask them to record the paragraph number of each example.

Reassess Write on the board: *Why do you think Wade Hudson wrote a biography about Matthew A. Henson?* Ask students to answer the question with one or two sentences.

From Reading to Writing

Write a Short Biography

1. **Make a picture** Have students suggest possible subjects for their biographies. List them on the board. Tell students to choose one and make pictures about the person's life.
2. **Think-quickwrite-pair-share** In pairs, have students explain their pictures or events for their biographies. Then have them write their biographies. Instruct them to identify the subject and to use transitions that show chronological order.
3. **Multi-level options** See MULTI-LEVEL OPTIONS on p. 176.

Across Content Areas: Science

Learn About Temperature

Connect Bring in thermometers and have students practice measuring temperatures of the air inside and outside of the school. Use the thermometers to explain the meaning of *degrees, Fahrenheit,* and *Celsius.* Ask students to suggest other times when people need to know the temperature of different things. Have students explain which temperature system is used in countries they have visited or lived in.

Answer

1. 26.67°C

ASSESS

Have students define key words: *temperature, degrees, Celsius, Fahrenheit.*

Into the Reading

Chapter Materials

Activity Book: *pp. 97–104*
Audio: *Unit 3, Chapter 3*
Student Handbook
Student CD-ROM: *Unit 3, Chapter 3*
Teacher Resource Book: *Lesson Plan, Teacher Resources, Reading Summary, Activity Book Answer Key*
Teacher Resource CD-ROM
Assessment Program: *Quiz, pp. 43–44; Teacher and Student Resources, pp. 115–144*
Assessment CD-ROM
Transparencies
The Heinle Newbury House Dictionary/CD-ROM
Web Site: www.heinle.visions.com

Objectives

Paired reading Have students work in pairs and take turns reading the objectives. ***Ask:*** *Is there an objective you already know?*

Use Prior Knowledge

Explore Differences

Share knowledge Describe how you and another teacher are different (age, interests, hair color, etc.). ***Ask:*** *In what ways are people different from one another?* Have students discuss differences between people and how people are treated differently because of these differences.

CHAPTER 3

Into the Reading

Anne Frank:

The Diary of a Young Girl

an excerpt from a diary
by Anne Frank

Objectives

Reading Use chronology to locate and recall information as you read a diary.

Listening and Speaking Act out a dialogue.

Grammar Use conjunctions to form compound sentences.

Writing Write a diary.

Content Social Studies: Describe social groups.

Use Prior Knowledge

Explore Differences

You will read a selection about a young girl who was treated badly because she was different. How are people different?

1. With a partner, make a web like the one here.
2. Complete your web with ways that people are different. Add ovals to your web if necessary.
3. As a class, talk about your webs. Discuss ways that people are sometimes treated because they are different.

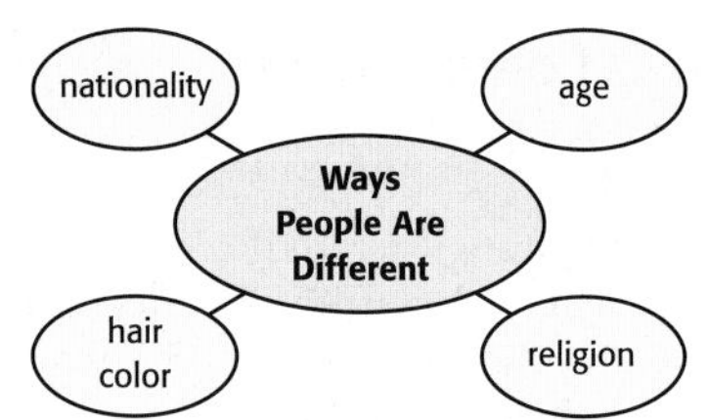

MULTI-LEVEL OPTIONS *Build Vocabulary*

Newcomer On the board, write: *belongings.* Demonstrate the word by showing students things in your desk or bag. Gesture and **say:** *These are my book, my pen, my comb, and my wallet. These are my belongings. They belong to me.* Then ask volunteers to tell the class about some of their belongings.

Beginning On the board, write: *belongings.* Demonstrate the word by showing students things in your desk or bag. Gesture and ***say:*** *These are my book, my pen, my comb, and my wallet. These are my belongings. They belong to me.* Then ask volunteers to tell the class about some of their belongings.

Intermediate ***Say:*** *Joe has heaps of homework. He has math, reading, science, and art. Does* heaps of *mean "a lot" or "a little"?* (a lot) ***Ask:*** *If there are heaps of papers on a desk, is the desk neat or messy?* (messy) Tell students to write a sentence that describes something they have *heaps of.* Have them share sentences in pairs.

Advanced Tell students to write a short paragraph using both *belongings* and *heaps of.* Have them share their paragraphs with a small group.

Build Background

World War II

Beginning in the late 1930s, Adolf Hitler, the Chancellor of Germany, invaded many neighboring countries, including Holland. Millions of people in Europe, most of them Jews, were taken to prison camps. Anne Frank, a teenage girl from Holland, and her family lived in a secret hiding place. One thing she took with her was her diary. Anne called her diary "Kitty."

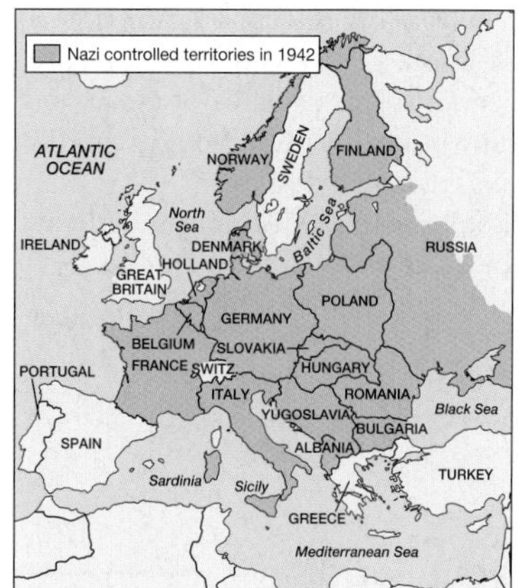

Content Connection

After Germany lost World War II in 1945, it was divided into two countries—East Germany and West Germany. Germany was finally reunited in 1990.

Build Vocabulary

Use Context

Sometimes you can learn the meanings of new words by using **context,** or nearby words and sentences.

Use the boldfaced words to help you choose the correct meaning for each underlined word.

1. Margot and I began to **pack** some of our most vital belongings . . . The first thing I put in was **this diary, then hair curlers, handkerchiefs, . . .**

   Belongings probably means
   a. clothes **b.** possessions

2. We put on heaps of clothes . . . I had on **two vests, three pairs of pants, a dress, on top of that a skirt, jacket, . . .**

   Heaps of probably means
   a. beautiful **b.** a lot of

Activity Book p. 97

Student CD-ROM

Content Connection ***Science***

Build Vocabulary Have students copy the following sentences: *Some craters may be the holes left by rocks that crashed into the moon. Many fish died after the factory dumped toxic waste in the river.* Ask students to use context clues to figure out the meanings of the underlined words. Tell students to use a dictionary to verify their definitions.

Learning Styles ***Intrapersonal***

Build Background Tell students to imagine having to move to a new place. ***Ask:*** *If you could only take one possession with you, what would it be? Why?* Have students write their answers in their Reading Logs.

Teacher Resource Book: *Reading Log, p. 64*

Into the Reading

Build Background

World War II

1. **Use a map** Have students locate Germany and Holland on the map. Ask them to share any information they know about these places. ***Ask:*** *What countries are near Germany?* Point out that this map gives the boundaries for countries in the 1930s. Have students compare this map to a current one of Europe.
2. **Content Connection** ***Ask:*** *Why do you think Germany was divided after the war?* (so Germany could not start wars again) *How do you think the German people felt when their country was reunited?* (very happy)

Build Vocabulary

Use Context

Teacher Resource Book: *Personal Dictionary, p. 63*

1. **Teacher think aloud** Write on the board: *Anne packed some of her most important belongings—*a diary, brushes, handkerchiefs, and some books. ***Say:*** *I know that packing is putting things into bags. So I guess the word* belongings *means "something that you have or own."*
2. **Reading selection vocabulary** You may want to introduce the glossed words in the reading selection before students begin reading. Key words: *concentration camp, doom, suspense, vital, inquire.* Instruct students to write the words with correct spelling and their definitions in their Personal Dictionaries. Have them pronounce each word and divide it into syllables.
3. **Multi-level options** See MULTI-LEVEL OPTIONS on p. 178.

Answers

1. b **2.** b

Have students write a sentence with a new word they learned on the page.

…cture

…iary

Recognize features Explain each of the features, giving examples as needed. Ask students to share about any diaries that they have kept.

Reading Strategy

Use Chronology to Locate and Recall Information

Teacher Resource Book: *Reading Log, p. 64*

1. **Share experience** *Say: Yesterday, I left school at 3:30. Then I took a bus to visit a friend. After dinner, I went home.* On the board, write the time phrases and events. Explain that time phrases can help you follow the order of events in a story.
2. **Multi-level options** See MULTI-LEVEL OPTIONS below.

Answers
1. Wednesday; Sunday

ASSESS

Ask: What are three features of a diary? (direct address, personal details, informal writing style)

Text Structure

Diary

The reading selection is an entry from Anne Frank's diary. A **diary** is a record of daily events. It is usually not meant to be read by others. Private thoughts and feelings are included.

Look for these distinguishing features as you read or listen to the audio recording of Anne Frank's diary.

Diary	
Direct Address	Diary entries sometimes address the diary as if it were a person; for example, "Dear Kitty."
Personal Details	Diary entries often tell how the writer feels.
Informal Writing Style	Diary entries are informal, so they may not always follow all of the rules of grammar or writing.

Student CD-ROM

Reading Strategy

Use Chronology to Locate and Recall Information

As you read, notice the **chronology**—the order in which events happen. This will help you follow the events in the story and find information in it.

1. Read the first two paragraphs. On which day is Anne writing? Which day is Anne going to tell us about?
2. Now look at the third paragraph. Phrases such as *at three o'clock* and *a bit later* can help you follow the chronology.
3. As you read the selection, notice the chronology. Record important events in your Reading Log.

Reading Log

Student CD-ROM

MULTI-LEVEL OPTIONS *Reading Strategy*

Newcomer On the board, draw a four-item timeline. Below it write: *store, bank, library, home. Say: First, I went to the store. Then, I went to the bank. Next, I went to the library. Last, I went home.* Have volunteers write: *First, Then, Next, Last* above the correct place.

Beginning Have students work in groups. Ask them to brainstorm words that can signal sequence, such as *first, next, before, after, last,* and *finally.*

Intermediate Have students work in pairs. Instruct one partner to describe a simple process, such as making a sandwich or building a snowman. Tell the other partner to record the steps using sequence words such as *first, next, after that,* and *finally.* Have partners switch roles and repeat the activity.

Advanced Have students write a brief diary entry for the day so far. Ask them to record the events of their day in order, using time words and transitions. Remind students to include the date at the top.

Anne Frank:
The Diary of a Young Girl

an excerpt from a diary
by Anne Frank

Reading Selection Materials

Audio: *Unit 3, Chapter 3*
Teacher Resource Book: *Reading Summary, pp. 89–90*

Preview the Selection

1. **Interpret the image** Have students examine and interpret the photo. ***Ask:*** *Who is the girl? How old do you think she is? What is she doing? What do you think she is writing about? Where is she? Does she look happy or sad? Do you think she has courage? Why or why not? How is she like you? How is she different from you?*
2. **Connect** ***Ask:*** *Is it easy or difficult to have courage when others don't like you because you are different?* Tell students they will read about the courage of a girl and her family during World War II.

Content Connection *Math*

Ask students to solve this problem: *Maria wrote in her diary every day. She wrote one entry each day, and each entry was two pages long. How many pages did she fill after three weeks of writing in her diary?* (42 pages) Ask students to work in pairs to create another word problem. Have them exchange and solve problems with another pair.

Learning Styles *Verbal*

Have students think about the picture. ***Ask:*** *What can you tell about this girl by looking at the picture? What kind of person do you think she was?* Tell students to present oral descriptions of the girl based on the picture and their imagination. Remind them to be imaginative and to use descriptive language.

UNIT 3 • CHAPTER 3
Reading Selection

Read the Selection

1. **Use features** Direct students to the date and greeting. Explain that Anne is writing to her diary. Call attention to the photo and caption below. Have students guess why Anne and her family hid in the building.
2. **Shared reading** Play the audio. Have volunteers read different paragraphs.
3. **Make predictions** *Ask: What do you think happened between Sunday and Wednesday?* (Anne's family went into hiding.)

Sample Answer to Guide Question
Sunday

See Teacher Edition pp. 434–435 for a list of English-Spanish cognates in the reading selection.

Audio

Wednesday, 8 July 1942

Dear Kitty,

1 Years seem to have passed between Sunday and now. So much has happened, it is just as if the whole world had turned upside down. But I am still alive, Kitty, and that is the main thing, Daddy says.

2 Yes, I'm still alive, indeed, but don't ask where or how. You wouldn't understand a word, so I will begin by telling you what happened on Sunday afternoon.

Use Chronology to Locate and Recall Information

What day was it when Margot told Anne that their father had received a call-up?

3 At three o'clock (Harry had just gone, but was coming back later) someone rang the front doorbell. I was lying lazily reading a book on the **veranda** in the sunshine, so I didn't hear it. A bit later, Margot appeared at the kitchen door looking very excited. "The **S.S.** have sent a call-up notice for Daddy," she whispered. "Mummy has gone to see

The building where Anne and her family hid.

veranda porch

S.S. Nazi police

MULTI-LEVEL OPTIONS *Read the Selection*

Newcomer Play the audio. Reread pp. 182–183 aloud. Have students raise their hands when they hear a person's name. Then ***ask:** Does Mummy go to see Mr. Van Daan?* (yes) *Is Mr. Van Daan a friend?* (yes) *Does Mr. Van Daan work with Daddy?* (yes) *Is Margot younger than Anne?* (no)

Beginning Read the Reading Summary aloud. Then play the audio. ***Ask:** When did the doorbell ring?* (at three o'clock) *What was Anne doing when the doorbell rang?* (reading a book) *Who will go into hiding with Anne's family?* (the Van Daans)

Intermediate Have students do a paired reading. Then ***ask:** What is the date of this diary entry?* (Wednesday, July 8, 1942) *What day is this entry mostly about?* (Sunday) *Why did Mummy go to talk with Mr. Van Daan?* (to decide whether to move to the hiding place)

Advanced Have students read independently. Then ***ask:** Why does Anne call her diary Kitty?* (It's like a friend.) *Did Anne think a call-up was a good thing or a bad thing?* (bad) *Why do you think the Franks and the Van Daans need a hiding place?* (to avoid being sent to a concentration camp)

Mrs. Frank and Anne

Mr. Van Daan already." (Van Daan is a friend who works with Daddy in the business.) It was a great shock to me, a **call-up;** everyone knows what that means. I picture **concentration camps** and lonely cells—should we allow him to be **doomed** to this? "Of course he won't go," declared Margot, while we waited together. "Mummy has gone to the Van Daans to discuss whether we should move into our hiding place tomorrow. The Van Daans are going with us, so we shall be seven in all." Silence. We couldn't talk any more, thinking about Daddy, who, little knowing what was going on, was visiting some old people in the Joodse Invalide; waiting for Mummy, the heat and **suspense** all made us very **overawed** and silent.

4 Suddenly the bell rang again. "That is Harry," I said. "Don't open the door." Margot held me back, but it was not necessary as we heard Mummy and Mr. Van Daan downstairs, talking to Harry, then they came in and closed the door behind them. Each time the bell went, Margot or I had to creep softly down to see if it was Daddy, not opening the door to anyone else.

Use Chronology to Locate and Recall Information

Who comes to the Franks' door? In what order do they arrive?

call-up an order to report to the police
concentration camps camps where the Nazis imprisoned and killed Jews
doomed likely to face harm or death
suspense worry about what will happen, especially while waiting
overawed too shocked to speak; frightened

UNIT 3 • CHAPTER 3
Reading Selection

Read the Selection

1. **Read aloud** Play the audio. Then have students reread in pairs.
2. **Identify events** Ask students to retell the events in order. You may want to list the events and model using time order words in the retelling: *first, then, after that, finally.*
3. **Share feelings** Ask questions to help students explain how the people in the story felt during these events.
4. **Multi-level options** See MULTI-LEVEL OPTIONS on p. 182.

Sample Answer to Guide Question
First, Anne's mother and Mr. Van Daan arrive. Then, Harry arrives.

Punctuation

Semicolons

Remind students that a complete sentence must have a subject and a verb and tell a complete thought. ***Say:*** *Sometimes, two related sentences can be connected. One way to connect them is with a semicolon.* Remind students that the word that follows a semicolon is not capitalized unless it is a proper noun. ***Say:*** *Find two examples of sentences connected with semicolons in paragraph 3* (lines 12 and 26). *Why are semicolons used in these sentences?* (to connect two complete, related sentences)

Apply Have students connect these sentence pairs with semicolons. On the board, write: *Finally, the bus arrived. I sat near the front. We didn't worry about the rain. There were plenty of umbrellas to share. I packed my lunch. It was a bologna and cheese sandwich, as usual.*

ddy says Yes, I'm still alive, indeed, but don't ask where or how. You wouldn't unde

Read the Selection

1. **Teacher read aloud** Read paragraphs 5–7 aloud to students. ***Ask:*** *Does Anne know where the family is going?* (no) *What types of things did she pack?* (a diary, hair curlers, handkerchiefs, schoolbooks, a comb, old letters)
2. **Analyze character feelings** Have students reread the selection in pairs. Tell students to list feelings Anne might have had. Ask students why she had those feelings. ***Ask:*** *Why was Anne frightened?* (She was worried about her sister.) *Why?* (She didn't want her sister to go away.)

Sample Answer to Guide Question
She knows the family is going into hiding. I think they will leave soon.

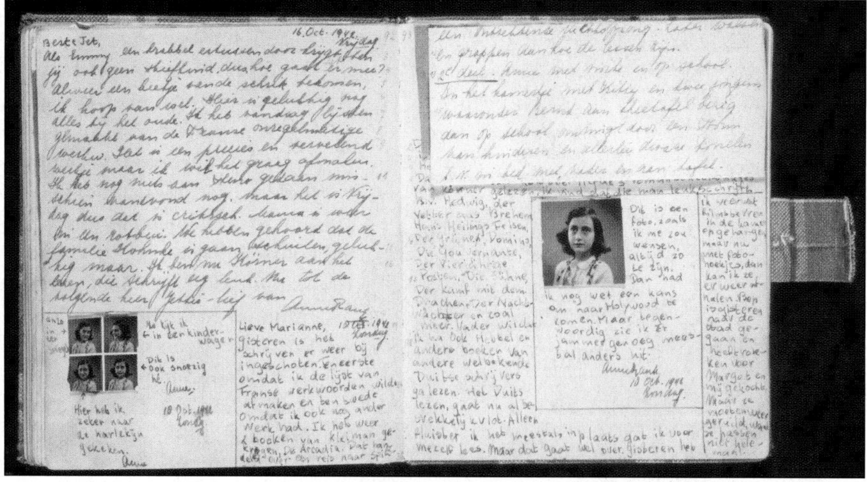

5 Margot and I were sent out of the room. Van Daan wanted to talk to Mummy alone. When we were alone together in our bedroom, Margot told me that the call-up was not for Daddy, but for her. I was more frightened than ever and began to cry. Margot is sixteen; would they really take girls of that age away alone? But thank goodness she won't go, Mummy said so herself; that must be what Daddy meant when he talked about us going into hiding.

6 Into hiding—where would we go; in a town or the country, in a house or a cottage, when, how, where. . . ?

7 These were questions I was not allowed to ask, but I couldn't get them out of my mind. Margot and I began to pack some of our most **vital** belongings into a school **satchel.** The first thing I put in was this diary, then hair curlers, handkerchiefs, schoolbooks, a comb, old letters; I put in the craziest things with the idea that we were going into hiding. But I'm not sorry, memories mean more to me than dresses . . .

Use Chronology to Locate and Recall Information

Why does Anne begin to pack? What will happen next?

vital important to life

satchel a small bag worn over the shoulder, larger than a purse

MULTI-LEVEL OPTIONS *Read the Selection*

Newcomer ***Ask:*** *Was the call-up for Daddy?* (no) *Did Anne begin to cry?* (yes) *Did Anne pack her diary?* (yes) *Did Anne go to the North Pole?* (no) *Did the family clean their house before they left?* (no)

Beginning ***Ask:*** *Who was the call-up for?* (Margot) *How old was Margot?* (sixteen) *What time did Anne wake up the next morning?* (at five-thirty) *What was the weather like when Anne woke up the next morning?* (warm and rainy; not as hot as Sunday)

Intermediate ***Ask:*** *Why did everyone wear so many clothes?* (They couldn't bring suitcases; they didn't want anyone to know they were leaving.) *Why did Anne pack her diary and old letters?* (They represented her memories; her memories were important to her.)

Advanced ***Ask:*** *How do you think Anne felt while she packed her things?* (scared, worried, excited, sad) *How would you have felt in a similar situation? For what reasons might Anne have been happy to go into hiding?* (She and her family would be safe.)

then hair curlers, handkerchiefs, schoolbooks, a comb, old letters; I put in the crazi

> **Use Chronology to Locate and Recall Information**
>
> What day of the week does Anne describe?

8 I was **dog-tired** and although I knew that it would be my last night in my own bed, I fell asleep immediately and didn't wake up until Mummy called me at five-thirty the next morning. Luckily it was not so hot as Sunday; warm rain fell steadily all day. We put on heaps of clothes as if we were going to the North Pole, the **sole** reason being to take clothes with us. No Jew in our situation would have dreamed of going out with a suitcase full of clothing. I had on two vests, three pairs of pants, a dress, on top of that a skirt, jacket, summer coat, two pairs of stockings, lace-up shoes, woolly cap, scarf, and still more; I was nearly **stifled** before we got started, but no one **inquired** about that . . .

9 There was one pound of meat in the kitchen for the cat, breakfast things lying on the table, stripped beds, all giving the impression that we had left helter-skelter. But we didn't care about impressions, we only wanted to get away, only escape and arrive safely, nothing else. Continued tomorrow.

Yours, Anne

---

dog-tired very tired; feeling like a tired dog
sole only
stifled feeling as if there is no air; overheated
inquired asked

About the Author

Anne Frank (1929–1945)

Anne Frank began her diary in 1942 on her 13th birthday. In 1944, Anne and her family were found by the Nazis. The entire family died in concentration camps except for Mr. Frank. Anne would have turned 16 on her next birthday. After the police took the Frank family, a friend found Anne's diary. Anne's father got it after the war and published it. Millions of people have read Anne's story of life in hiding. Even though Anne lived in fear of the Nazis, she wrote, "I still believe that people are really good at heart . . . I think it will all come right, that this cruelty too will end, and that peace . . . will return again."

➤ Do you admire Anne Frank? Why or why not?

A Capitalization

Opening and closing a letter or diary

Say: *Words that begin letters or diary entries are called* openings. *Words and phrases that end letters or diary entries are called* closings. On the board, write: *Dear* and *Yours.* ***Say:*** *Openings and closings are always capitalized.* Direct students to the opening on p. 182 and the closing on p. 185. Point out that an opening is followed by a person's name and a comma (or colon). Explain that a closing is followed by a comma and the writer's name.

Evaluate Your Reading Strategy

Use Chronology to Locate and Recall Information ***Say:*** *You have practiced an important reading strategy. Now you can decide how well you have done. Does this statement describe how you read?*

> When I read, I look for words such as *first* or *next* to help me determine the chronology. Understanding the chronology of a reading helps me to recall what happened. It also helps me locate information in a reading.

UNIT 3 • CHAPTER 3
Reading Selection

Read the Selection

1. **Shared reading** Complete the reading of the story as students follow along. Ask volunteers to join in for different parts.
2. **Use chronology to locate and recall information** Remind students of time phrases in the reading selection.
3. **Multi-level options** See MULTI-LEVEL OPTIONS on p. 184.

Sample Answer to Guide Question
She describes Monday.

About the Author

1. **Discuss author's point of view** Anne Frank was a victim of the Nazis. Have students consider if she understood what might happen to her and her family. Point out her optimism and feeling that people are basically good. Encourage students to give their opinions on the goodness of people and peace in the world.
2. **Interpret the facts** *Ask: How were Anne Frank and her family courageous?*

Answer
Example: Yes, because she was brave. She had a lot of courage in a dangerous situation.

Across Selections

Comparison and contrast Compare and contrast the features of a diary with a biography. Then *ask: Which character do you feel you know more about—Matthew Henson or Anne Frank? Why?*

Reading Comprehension

Question-Answer Relationships

Sample Answers

1. The events take place on July 5 (Sunday) and 6 (Monday), 1942.
2. She takes her diary, hair curlers, a comb, schoolbooks, handkerchiefs, and old letters.
3. Because someone in their family received a call-up notice.
4. A call-up means that someone will be sent to a concentration camp.
5. Margot
6. Because it would be suspicious for her to carry a suitcase. Jews would not carry a suitcase, because it would show they were trying to escape.
7. Because your memories cannot be replaced, but dresses can.
8. They were in a hurry to leave. Escaping and arriving safely were more important than the impressions their messy house left.
9. I think Anne felt sad, but she knew it would be more dangerous to stay.
10. If I had to leave home suddenly, I would take my photo album, some favorite books, and some special jewelry.

Build Reading Fluency

Reading Chunks of Words Silently

Assessment Program: *Reading Fluency Chart, p. 116*

When students have completed the reading fluency activity, record their progress in the Reading Fluency Chart.

Beyond the Reading

Reading Comprehension

Question-Answer Relationships (QAR)

"Right There" Questions

1. **Recall Facts** When do the events in this diary entry take place?
2. **Recall Facts** What are some things that Anne takes with her into hiding?

"Think and Search" Questions

3. **Analyze Cause and Effect** Why do the Franks decide to go into hiding when they do?
4. **Interpret** What does a call-up mean for the Frank family?
5. **Identify** Which member of the Frank family is called up by the police?
6. **Make Inferences** Why does Anne put on so many clothes instead of packing a suitcase? Why would a Jew "in our situation" not carry a suitcase?

"Author and You" Questions

7. **Interpret** Why does Anne say that memories are more important than dresses?
8. **Make Inferences** Why did the family leave their house so messy when they left?

"On Your Own" Questions

9. **Interpret** How do you think Anne felt leaving her home and many of her things behind?
10. **Compare Your Experiences** What things would you take with you if you had to leave home suddenly?

Activity Book *p. 98*

Student CD-ROM

Build Reading Fluency

Reading Chunks of Words Silently

Reading silently is good practice. It helps you learn to read faster.

1. Listen to paragraphs 1 and 2 of "The Diary of Anne Frank" on the Audio CD.
2. Listen to the chunks of words.
3. Silently reread paragraphs 1 and 2 two times.
4. Your teacher or a partner will time your second reading.
5. Raise your hand when you are finished.

MULTI-LEVEL OPTIONS *Elements of Literature*

Newcomer On the board, write: *serious* and *friendly.* Model a facial expression for each. Point to *serious* and ***say:*** *Show me your serious face.* Point to *friendly* and ***say:*** *Show me your friendly face.* Have students demonstrate a facial expression for each word.

Beginning ***Say:*** *I use a serious voice to tell a sad story.* Use a serious, formal voice. Have students imitate your tone and say: *This is my serious voice.* ***Say:*** *I use my friendly voice to tell a funny story.* Use a light, fun tone. Have students imitate your tone and say: *This is my friendly voice.*

Intermediate Tell students to work in pairs to find other examples of Anne's informal tone. Ask students to list the words and phrases that help make her tone informal. Have students repeat the exercise to identify examples of when Anne's tone is serious.

Advanced Have students work independently to rewrite the excerpts on p. 187 in a more formal tone. ***Ask:*** *What type of writing should have a formal tone?* (essay, business letter, research report, etc.) *What type of writing can have an informal tone?* (letter, e-mail, journal, etc.)

Listen, Speak, Interact 

Act Out a Dialogue

The **dialogue** of a selection is the exact words that people say to one another. In writing, dialogue is shown with quotation marks.

"That is Harry," I said.

The words *That is Harry* are the words that Anne said. If you write dialogue to act out, you do not need quotation marks.

Anne: That is Harry.

1. Work with a partner. Choose an event that Anne describes in her diary. Write a dialogue about the event to act out.
2. If there is any dialogue with quotation marks in the diary, include it.
3. Listen to the audio recording of the selection to help you learn to distinguish and produce the intonation (changing voice level) of words you will use.
4. Use clues from the text to guess what else the characters said during the event.
5. Perform your dialogue for the class.

Elements of Literature

Understand Tone

Tone is the attitude or feeling that a writer shows in a piece of writing. Tone can be serious or funny, formal or informal.

Copy the following sentences into your Reading Log. Underline the words and phrases (groups of words) that help make Anne's tone informal.

1. Yes, I'm still alive, indeed, but don't ask where or how. You wouldn't understand a word, so I will begin by telling you what happened on Sunday afternoon.
2. I put in the craziest things with the idea that we were going into hiding. But I'm not sorry, memories mean more to me than dresses.

Reading Log

Activity Book *p. 99*

Student CD-ROM

Community Connection

Have small groups choose an idea for a community improvement, such as building a park or cleaning up litter or graffiti. Then instruct groups to write a letter asking community leaders for help. Suggest that students begin the body of their letters with *We are writing to ask you to ______.* Remind students to include openings and closings and that the tone of their letters should be formal and serious.

Learning Styles *Musical*

Using music CDs or another source, play various instrumental selections for students. Select music that conveys an assortment of moods, including somber, celebratory, upbeat, playful, serious, sad, and silly. After each song, **ask:** *What was the tone of that song? How did it make you feel?*

Listen, Speak, Interact

Act Out a Dialogue

1. **Clarify terms** Direct attention to the examples of dialogue with quotation marks and dialogue for acting. Have students point out similarities and differences in the two forms.
2. **Use personal experience** Have students write and practice their dialogues in pairs. Remind them to draw on their own personal experiences and knowledge as they plan the lines for the characters.
3. **Newcomers** Point out lines with dialogue in the reading selection. Have pairs choose lines for their dialogues. Ask them to perform their dialogues and record them in their Reading Logs.

Elements of Literature

Understand Tone

Teacher Resource Book: *Reading Log, p. 64*

1. Point out and clarify the definition of tone. On the board, write: *serious, funny, formal, informal.* Have students guess the tone when you ***say:*** *Hi, Anne. What's up?* (informal) *Good afternoon, Mr. Jones. How are you today?* (formal) *This true story is sad and moving.* (serious) *This song is too much!* (funny)
2. **Multi-level options** See MULTI-LEVEL OPTIONS on p. 186.

Answers

1. I'm still alive; don't ask where or how; you wouldn't understand a word
2. The craziest things; but I'm not sorry

Have students write a statement that explains the tone of Anne Frank's diary.

Beyond the Reading

Word Study

Use the Suffix *-ion*

Teacher Resource Book: *Personal Dictionary, p. 63*

Use a word map On the board, write: *predict* + *-ion* = *prediction.* Direct students' attention to the suffix and its placement. Model sentences using the verb and noun. List other verbs and have students add *-ion* to create nouns: *suggest, communicate, connect.*

Answers
1. impression 2. situation

Grammar Focus

Use Conjunctions to Form Compound Sentences

Modeling On the board, write: *We have a lot of homework. The homework is easy.* Model combining the sentences using *but.* Have students find other sentences with *but* in the reading.

Answers
1. Paragraph 4: Margot held me back, but it was not necessary. Paragraph 7: These were questions I was not allowed to ask, but I couldn't get them out of my mind.

Write the verbs *select, locate, subtract* on the board. Have students add *-ion* to create nouns and use them in sentences.

Word Study

Use the Suffix *-ion*

The suffix ***-ion*** usually shows that a word is a noun (a person, a place, or a thing).

These were quest**ion**s I was not allowed to ask . . .

In some cases, you can add *-ion* to a verb to make a noun.

Suffix *-ion*		
Verb	**+ -ion**	**Noun**
impress	-ion	impression
situat~~e~~	-ion	situation

Notice that some verbs change their spelling when *-ion* is added.

Copy the following sentences in your Personal Dictionary. Fill in the blanks with a noun ending in *-ion.* Use the underlined word to make the noun.

1. The students impressed the teacher. They made a good ____ .
2. We are situated in a bad place. We don't like our ____ .

Personal Dictionary

Activity Book *p. 100*

Student CD-ROM

Grammar Focus

Use Conjunctions to Form Compound Sentences

A **conjunction** is a word like *and* or *but.* Conjunctions can join two sentences. Use a comma between the two sentences.

Compound Sentence
I'm still alive**,** but don't ask how.

Two Simple Sentences
I'm still alive.
Don't ask how.

Use *but* when you want to show contrast between two sentences. Use *and* to show a connection.

1. With a partner, reread paragraphs 4 and 7 of the selection.
2. Find two sentences that use the conjunction *but.* Write them on a piece of paper. Then write each one as two separate sentences.

Activity Book *pp. 101–102*

Student Handbook

Student CD-ROM

188 Unit 3 Courage

MULTI-LEVEL OPTIONS *From Reading to Writing*

Newcomer Have students create visual diaries. Tell them to draw pictures to represent the events in their days, including meals, school, sports, and other activities. Help students to write the appropriate day of the week at the top of each entry.

Beginning On the board, model this form for writing dates: *Monday, October 13, 2003.* Have students work in pairs. Ask one partner to point to a day on a calendar. Then ask the other partner to write the date, following the model on the board. Have partners switch roles.

Intermediate Ask pairs of students to list as many prepositions as they can. Have them use their lists as they write their diaries.

Advanced Have students review their diaries. Tell students to check for openings, closings, conjunctions, prepositional phrases, and words that show sequence. Also tell students to check punctuation, capitalization, and tone. Ask volunteers to share an entry.

From Reading to Writing 

Write a Diary

Write a diary every day for the next week.

1. Include dates in your diary.
2. Write in the first person, using the pronoun *I* for yourself and the pronoun *you* for the diary.
3. Describe something you did and how you felt each day.
4. Write in an informal tone.
5. Use the conjunctions *but* and *and* to join two sentences into one longer sentence.
6. Use prepositional phrases to tell where something happened.
7. End your diary entry with a closing such as *Yours, Your friend,* or *Love,* plus your name.

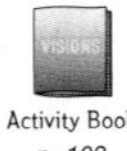

Activity Book *p. 103*

Across Content Areas 

Describe Social Groups

We can describe ourselves in many ways. One way is to describe the social groups that we belong to. Here are some examples:

Social Groups	
nationality	being a citizen of a country (for example, Mexican)
ethnicity	the culture that you feel you belong to (for example, Native American, Hispanic)
religion	your faith (for example, Christian, Buddhist, Muslim, Hindu)
gender	whether you are male or female

Copy the following sentences onto a piece of paper. Fill in the blanks with one of the social groups.

1. My family is from Thailand, so we enjoy eating Thai food and celebrating Thai holidays. Our ____ is Thai.
2. We are Buddhists. Our ____ is Buddhism.
3. Luis is a citizen of Cuba, so his ____ is Cuban.

Activity Book *p. 104*

Reteach and Reassess

Text Structure *Ask: How do many diary entries begin?* (direct address) *How do diary entries tell how the writer feels?* (personal details) *What is the writing style of a diary entry?* (informal)

Reading Strategy Ask students to read a short newspaper or magazine article. Have them locate key words that indicate sequence.

Elements of Literature Have students reread stanzas 1 and 2 of "Life Doesn't Frighten Me" on pp. 158–159. ***Ask:*** *What is the tone of the poem? How does it fit the meaning?*

Reassess Create a timeline with *Sunday, Monday,* and *Wednesday* marked on it. Have students review the selection. Ask them to complete the timeline by writing at least one key event for each day.

From Reading to Writing

Write a Diary

Teacher Resource Book: *Cluster Map, p. 38*

1. **Use a graphic organizer** Have students complete a cluster map before they write their diary entries. Ask them to share parts of their diaries in pairs. Tell partners to take notes on expressions of informal tone.
2. **Language experience story** Have less fluent students dictate their diaries as you write them. Then tell students to practice reading their diaries to partners and create pictures to illustrate them.
3. **Multi-level options** See MULTI-LEVEL OPTIONS on p. 188.

Across Content Areas: Social Studies

Describe Social Groups

1. **Connect** Direct students to the chart with definitions and examples of social groups. Have students suggest different examples of social groups represented in the local community.
2. **Create a form** Have students work in pairs to survey which social groups students in your school belong to. Have pairs collaborate to compose and organize a form for the four types of social groups. Tell pairs to use the form to survey ten students in the school. After they have gathered the information, have pairs revise their forms. Have pairs share their findings.

Answers
1. ethnicity **2.** religion **3.** nationality

Have students identify the social groups. ***Ask:*** *What are some groups identified by religion?* (Muslim, Christian) *What are some ethnic groups in our town?* (Mexican, Chinese) *What is the nationality of the U.S. president?* (American)

Chapter Materials

Activity Book: *pp. 105–112*
Audio: *Unit 3, Chapter 4*
Student Handbook
Student CD-ROM: *Unit 3, Chapter 4*
Teacher Resource Book: *Lesson Plan, Teacher Resources, Reading Summary, Activity Book Answer Key*
Teacher Resource CD-ROM
Assessment Program: *Quiz, pp. 45–46; Teacher and Student Resources, pp. 115–144*
Assessment CD-ROM
Transparencies
The Heinle Newbury House Dictionary/CD-ROM
Web Site: www.heinle.visions.com

Objectives

Offer observations Read the objectives aloud. *Say: A speech is a person speaking or talking.* Discuss when and why people give speeches. Ask if students have given or heard a speech.

Use Prior Knowledge

Discuss Ways to Treat Disease

Visualize *Say: Imagine your friend is sick. Who can help? What will they do to your friend?* Have students close their eyes and visualize the situation, people, and actions. Make a chart on the board and record the people and actions.

Lance Armstrong: Champion Cyclist

a speech
by President
George W. Bush

Into the Reading

Objectives

Reading Distinguish fact from opinion as you read a speech.

Listening and Speaking Listen to and discuss a speech.

Grammar Use superlative adjectives.

Writing Write a speech.

Content Social Studies: Read a chart.

Use Prior Knowledge

Discuss Ways to Treat Disease

The reading selection in this chapter is a speech addressed to Lance Armstrong. Armstrong is a champion cyclist (bike rider) who had cancer, a serious disease. He was very sick. His doctors did not think he would live.

When people get a disease, they can get help from doctors, from family, and from themselves.

1. Work with a partner. Brainstorm the kinds of help that sick people can get.
2. Copy the chart below on a piece of paper. List your ideas in your chart.
3. Share your information with the rest of the class.

Doctors and Nurses Can . . .	Family and Friends Can . . .	The Sick Person Can . . .
give medicine	visit	have courage

MULTI-LEVEL OPTIONS *Build Vocabulary*

Newcomer Show students a dictionary. Point to *dictionary* on the cover and say its name. Model looking up *speech* in the dictionary with small groups. Read the definition aloud. Have students work in pairs to locate *bicycle* in the dictionary.

Beginning Remind students that many reference aids list entries in alphabetical order. On the board, write: *speech, bicycle, cancer, cycling, France, president, race, winner,* and *mountain.* Ask pairs of students to work together to list the words in alphabetical order.

Intermediate *Ask: Where could I find the meaning of a word?* (dictionary, glossary) *Where could I find a lot of information about a topic or an event?* (encyclopedia, Internet, magazines, newspapers) Instruct students to find information on a topic using a reference aid.

Advanced Have students work in pairs. Ask students to look up *France* in as many different reference aids as they can. Instruct them to create a log to compare and contrast the type and amount of information they find in each source.

Build Background

The *Tour de France*

The *Tour de France* is a bicycle race held every summer in France. About 200 people enter the race. The race is more than 2,100 miles long (about 3,600 kilometers). The winner is the cyclist who covers the distance in the shortest time. Racers stop along the way to eat, sleep, and rest.

Content Connection

Cyclists in the *Tour de France* ride through the French Alps, mountains that reach a height of 15,771 feet (4,807 meters).

Build Vocabulary

Use Multiple Reference Aids

A **reference** is a source of information such as a dictionary. An **aid** is something that helps you. When you want help for reading, writing, revising, and editing, there are many reference aids that you can turn to.

1. **Glossary:** Some books have a **glossary** at the end that gives the meanings of difficult words.
2. **Encyclopedias:** These books are organized alphabetically and give more information than a dictionary. Many encyclopedias are also on CD-ROM.
3. **Newspapers and Magazines:** These contain current events. They are usually printed daily, weekly, and monthly.
4. **Internet:** This computer network allows you to find information using keywords.

Use two or more of these sources to look up these new vocabulary words: cancer, *Tour de France*, cycling.

Activity Book *p. 105*

Student CD-ROM

Build Background

The *Tour de France*

1. **Use a map** Have students locate France on a world map. Then direct them to the route of the *Tour de France* in their books. ***Ask:*** *Does the race start or end in Paris?*
2. **Content Connection** Have students locate the Alps on a map and identify other countries that the Alps cross.

Build Vocabulary

Use Multiple Reference Aids

Teacher Resource Book: *Personal Dictionary, p. 63*

1. **Identify reference aids** Bring in examples of the reference aids. Help students look up information in each one. Point out organizational features: index, alphabetical order, search engines. Tell students to use the aids to find information about the vocabulary words. Have students write the words and meanings in their Personal Dictionaries.
2. **Use a glossary or other sources** Have students skim the glossary of their science or social studies textbook and locate a word whose pronunciation is given. Ask them to use the pronunciation symbols to pronounce the word. Also have students locate the pronunciation of a word using an online or CD-ROM dictionary.
3. **Reading selection vocabulary** You may want to introduce the glossed words in the reading selection before students begin reading. Key words: *hazardous, determination, diagnose, champion, competitor.* Instruct students to write the words with correct spelling and their definitions in their Personal Dictionaries. Have them pronounce each word and divide it into syllables.
4. **Multi-level options** See MULTI-LEVEL OPTIONS on p. 190.

ASSESS

Have students write sentences using these words: *cancer, the Tour de France, cycling.*

Home Connection

Build Vocabulary Ask students to search for reference aids at home, the school library, the local public library, the classroom, and other places. Tell students to create a chart that shows which reference aids are available at each location. Have them ask family members or friends to help them.

Learning Styles *Intrapersonal*

Build Background Tell students to imagine racing a bicycle for more than 2,000 miles. *Ask: How would you feel right before the race starts? How would you feel during the race? How would you feel after the race? How would you feel if you won? Have you ever won a race? How did you feel?* Have students write their answers in their Reading Logs.

Teacher Resource Book: *Reading Log, p. 64*

Into the Reading

Text Structure

Speech

Teacher Resource Book: *Venn Diagram, p. 35; Two-Column Chart, p. 44*

Recognize features Direct attention to the feature chart. Give examples of the features. Ask students to compare the features of a speech with those of a diary and record similarities and differences on a chart or Venn diagram.

Reading Strategy

Distinguish Fact from Opinion

1. **Teacher think aloud** Draw a picture of a teenage boy on the board. ***Say:*** *This is John. He is five feet and eight inches tall. This is a fact. I can measure his height with a ruler to prove it. He weighs 150 pounds. This is a fact. I can measure his weight with a scale. He is good-looking. This is an opinion. I can't prove it.* Have students create their own statements of fact and opinion.
2. **Multi-level options** See MULTI-LEVEL OPTIONS below.

ASSESS

Ask: *What is a personal view—a fact or an opinion? What can you prove—a fact or an opinion?*

Text Structure

Speech

The reading selection is a speech given by President George W. Bush. A speech is written to present to an audience. Sometimes the writer prints the speech for others to read later. Look for the distinguishing features of a speech as you read.

Notice how President Bush uses humor or mentions people in the audience to help the audience feel involved with the topic.

Speech	
Personal Style	A speech may include casual or formal language.
Direct Address	A speech is spoken directly to the audience using the pronoun *you.*
Audience Reaction	A speech may have words in parentheses, such as "(Laughter)," to tell how the audience reacted.

Student CD-ROM

Reading Strategy

Distinguish Fact from Opinion

When you read, notice the difference between fact and opinion.

1. A **fact** can be proven. As you read, look for facts such as this: "The *Tour de France* takes place in France every summer." You can use reference aids to prove this fact.
2. An **opinion** is a personal view or an idea. It cannot be proven. As you read, look for opinions such as this: "The *Tour de France* is the best sporting event in the world."

Distinguish facts from opinions as you read and listen to the audio recording of the selection.

Student CD-ROM

192 Unit 3 Courage

MULTI-LEVEL OPTIONS *Reading Strategy*

Newcomer Write *apple* on the board. Beneath it, write *red* and *good.* Point to and say the words. Then point to *red* and ***say:*** *fact.* Point to *good* and ***say:*** *opinion.* Repeat with *bear, brown,* and *scary.* Then write *rain.* ***Say:*** *Tell me a fact.* (wet) *Tell me an opinion.* (fun)

Beginning Direct students to the picture on p. 193. ***Say:*** *This is a picture of President Bush and Lance Armstrong. Is that a fact or an opinion?* (fact) *This is a nice picture. Is that a fact or an opinion?* (opinion) Have students suggest and identify other facts and opinions about the picture.

Intermediate Direct students to the picture on p. 193. Have them work in pairs. Instruct partners to list three facts about the picture. Then tell them to list three opinions about the picture.

Advanced Have students review a newspaper or magazine article. Ask them to locate and list the facts and opinions in the article. Suggest that they organize their list in a two-column chart headed *Facts* and *Opinions.*

Lance Armstrong: Champion Cyclist

a speech by President George W. Bush

193

Reading Selection Materials

Audio: *Unit 3, Chapter 4*
Teacher Resource Book: *Reading Summary, pp. 91–92*

Preview the Selection

Teacher Resource Book: *Two-Column Chart, p. 44*

1. **Use the photograph** Have students describe and evaluate the purpose of the photograph. ***Ask:*** *Which person do you think is Lance Armstrong? Which person is President Bush? Who are the other people? Why is there a bicycle? Where do you think they are? Why is President Bush giving a speech about Lance Armstrong?*
2. **Identify facts and opinions** Help students state facts and give opinions about the people and events in the photograph. List them on a chart. Tell them to use the chart to guide their reading of the selection and to see if the statements are correct.
3. **Connect** Remind students that the unit theme is *courage.* ***Ask:*** *Why do you think Lance Armstrong has courage?*

Content Connection
Social Studies

Ask students to use a reference aid to find information about George W. Bush. Tell students to write down one fact and give one opinion about him. Have them share their facts and opinions with the class.

Learning Styles
Intrapersonal

Ask: *How do you think the people in this picture feel? What might they be thinking?* Have students choose one person in the picture and write a paragraph that describes what that person is feeling and thinking. Ask students to use evidence from the picture to support their ideas. Assure students that there are no right or wrong answers.

UNIT 3 • CHAPTER 4
Reading Selection

Read the Selection

1. **Use text features** Direct students to the prologue. Explain its purpose. Point out the main body of the speech. Then direct students to the glossed words. Have them check below for the meanings of these words.
2. **Reciprocal reading** Play the audio. Then arrange students in groups. Have a "leader" ask a question and summarize each paragraph.

Sample Answer to Guide Question
an opinion

See Teacher Edition pp. 434–435 for a list of English-Spanish cognates in the reading selection.

Audio

Prologue

People who achieve great things are often invited to the White House, where the U.S. President lives. Lance Armstrong won the *Tour de France.* The president made the following speech to introduce Lance Armstrong to guests of the White House.

1 THE PRESIDENT: Please be seated. It's my **privilege** to welcome you all to the White House, and to welcome my friend, a true champ, a great American, Lance Armstrong. (**Applause.**) America's incredibly proud of Lance, and I know two people who are really proud of him, as well, that's Kristen, his wife, and young Luke. Thank you all for coming, as well. (Applause.)

Distinguish Fact from Opinion

Is the statement "America's incredibly proud of Lance" a fact or an opinion?

2 We're also honored to have Chris Fowler of **ESPN** here. I'm so—thank you for coming, Chris. I was telling Chris a little earlier, it's one of the programs I can watch on TV that doesn't say anything about me at all. (Laughter.)

3 I want to thank the members of my **Cabinet** who are here. Thank you all for coming. I want to thank the members of the **United States Congress and the Senate** who are here. I see a lot from the Texas **delegation** here that are sure proud of you.

---

privilege honor
applause clapping
ESPN a television station that shows sports programs
Cabinet the group of people who advise the president most closely
United States Congress and the Senate the people elected to make U.S. laws
delegation a group of representatives

MULTI-LEVEL OPTIONS *Read the Selection*

Newcomer Play the audio. Then **ask:** *Did Lance Armstrong ride in a bicycle race?* (yes) *Is Lance with his parents?* (no) *Is Lance Armstrong courageous?* (yes) *Did Lance Armstrong have cancer?* (yes) *Does the* Tour de France *last three months?* (no)

Beginning Play the audio. ***Ask:*** *Who is giving the speech?* (President George W. Bush) *Where does the president live?* (in the White House) *How long do the racers ride up mountains?* (five days) *What disease did Lance Armstrong have?* (cancer) *How many weeks does the* Tour de France *last?* (three)

Intermediate Play the audio. ***Ask:*** *Why are people proud of Lance?* (He is a champion. He showed determination and courage.) *Was Lance's cancer dangerous? How do you know?* (Yes. He was told he had a 50 percent chance of dying.)

Advanced Play the audio. ***Ask:*** *What does George W. Bush think of Lance Armstrong? How can you tell? In what ways did Lance show courage?*

4 You all know the *Tour de France* is perhaps the most **physically demanding** event in sports. It lasts three weeks, stretches over 2,100 miles, and is often run in both **sweltering** heat and [really] cold weather. In the end, the race is won or lost in the mountains. During five days of climbs that are incredibly steep and **hazardous**—that's when the heart is tested, and that's when Lance Armstrong **excels.**

Distinguish Fact from Opinion

Find a fact in this paragraph.

5 In the hardest part of the race, Lance reveals an unbending will, uncommon **determination** and unquestioned courage. He has shown that courage [in] sport. He has also shown that courage in life.

6 Just a few years ago, Lance was **diagnosed** with cancer. He was weakened by **chemotherapy** treatments and told he had a 50-50 chance of living. He has done more than survive: He has **triumphed.** (Applause.)

physically demanding very difficult on your body
sweltering very hot
hazardous very dangerous
excels does the best job
determination the desire to continue even when the task is hard
diagnosed identified by a doctor that you have a disease
chemotherapy a treatment for cancer
triumphed succeeded greatly

Read the Selection

1. **Use the photograph** *Ask: Who are these people?* (racers in the *Tour de France*) *What are they doing?* (riding through the mountains) *Do you think it is easy or difficult to ride up mountains?* (difficult) *What qualities do these riders need to do this?* (strength, energy)
2. **Understand terms** Have students find the meanings of the glossed words at the bottom of the page. Clarify meanings as needed.
3. **Guided reading** Play the audio. Then have students reread each paragraph. Pause to clarify and ask comprehension questions.
4. **Discuss personal reaction** Use guiding questions to help students express their personal reactions to the information in paragraph 6.
5. **Multi-level options** See MULTI-LEVEL OPTIONS on p. 194.

Sample Answer to Guide Question
The *Tour de France* is 2,100 miles.

Spelling

To/two/too

Tell students that the words *to, two,* and *too* are words that sound the same but have different spellings and different meanings. Write *to* on the board. **Say:** *This word means "toward or in the direction of." Sometimes it is a word that introduces a verb, such as* to be *or* to have. Then write: *two.* **Say:** *This is the number after* one. Finally, write: *too.* **Say:** *This is a word that means* in addition to *or* also. *Read paragraph 1. Find* to, *T-O, and* two, *T-W-O.*

Apply Have students write the correct word (*to, two, too*) in each of the following sentences. On the board, write: *What did you bring ____ the party? I brought ____ big bowls of fruit. Alice brought a bowl of fruit, ____. There is going ____ be a lot of fruit!*

Read the Selection

Paired reading Have students reread the selection in pairs. ***Ask:*** *Which is more difficult—going through the French Alps or having cancer?* (having cancer) *When did Lance win the* Tour de France *a third time—before or after he was diagnosed with cancer?* (after) *Who was Lance Armstrong's chief competitor?* (Germany's Jan Ullrich) *Why did Lance slow down when Ullrich went off the road? Do you think you would slow down?*

Sample Answer to Guide Question
A fact. Jan Ullrich was the 1997 champion, so he won the race in 1997.

7 One observer commented that when you survive cancer, the French Alps start to look like speed bumps. (Laughter.)

8 Lance's story from cancer diagnosis to a third straight victory in the last *Tour de France* is one of the great human stories. It is a story of character and it is a story of class.

9 Germany's Jan Ullrich, the 1997 *Tour de France* **champion,** is Lance Armstrong's chief **competitor.** The two of them were leading during a critical stage of this year's *Tour de France* when Ullrich lost control of his bicycle, missed a turn and ended up in a ditch. When Lance saw what happened, he slowed down in order to allow his chief competitor to recover. It was, as Lance said, the right thing to do . . .

Distinguish Fact from Opinion

Is the statement that Jan Ullrich won the *Tour de France* in 1997 a fact or an opinion? Explain your answer.

champion a winner, especially of many prizes

competitor a person you race against

MULTI-LEVEL OPTIONS *Read the Selection*

Newcomer ***Ask:*** *Did Lance win the race three times in a row?* (yes) *Did Lance leave Jan in the ditch?* (no) *Are there sick children in the audience?* (yes) *Is Lance from Germany?* (no)

Beginning ***Ask:*** *What did Lance do when Jan Ullrich fell in the ditch?* (He slowed down and waited for Jan to recover.) *What disease do some children in the audience have?* (cancer) *What state is Lance Armstrong from?* (Texas)

Intermediate ***Ask:*** *Why does George W. Bush think people should be inspired by Lance?* (because he had courage and determination) *Has Lance won the* Tour de France *since George W. Bush gave this speech? When?* (yes, in 2002) *Do you admire Lance Armstrong? Why or why not?*

Advanced ***Ask:*** *Do you agree with George W. Bush that Lance Armstrong is an extraordinary human being? Is that a fact or an opinion?* (opinion) *Do you think Lance is a hero? Explain.*

10 Lance Armstrong is a vivid reminder that the great **achievements** of life are often won or lost in the mountains, when the climb is the steepest, when the heart is tested. There are many children in this audience who are showing similar determination in their fight with cancer and other serious illnesses. You face tough challenges and you **embrace** life day by day. You're showing courage on your own journey, and all of us are **inspired** by your example as well.

11 Ladies and gentleman, it is my honor to present to you a son of Texas, a great American champion, and an extraordinary human being: Lance Armstrong. (Applause.)

Epilogue

Lance Armstrong won his fourth *Tour de France* in 2002. After this win, he said, "Regardless of one victory, two victories, four victories, there's never been a victory by a cancer survivor. That's a fact that hopefully I'll be remembered for."

achievements successes
embrace put all your energy into
inspired given hope and energy to try hard

About the Author — George W. Bush (born 1946)

George W. Bush, the forty-third president of the United States, is the son of the forty-first president, George H. W. Bush. George W. Bush became president in 2000. He grew up in Texas and was governor of Texas from 1994 until he became president. Bush had an oil business and also owned part of the Texas Rangers baseball team before he began working in politics. Bush wants people to feel that he is someone like them: "I want the folks to see me sitting in the same kind of seat they sit in."

➤ Why did President Bush give this speech? To entertain, to inform, or to persuade people? Support your answer with a sentence from the speech.

Read the Selection

1. **Shared reading** Play the audio as students follow along in their books. Have groups of students join in for different sections. ***Ask:*** *Why does President Bush call Lance Armstrong a great American champion?* (He won the *Tour de France* many times and faced the challenge of cancer.) *What is your opinion of Lance Armstrong?* (I think he's a brave and strong person.) *How is fighting a disease like climbing the mountains?* (They both are difficult and take courage.)
2. **Multi-level options** See MULTI-LEVEL OPTIONS on p. 196.

About the Author

1. **Explain author background** George W. Bush was a businessman before he was governor of Texas. In 2002, he became the 43rd president of the United States.
2. **Analyze author motivation** *Ask: Why does George W. Bush want people to know about Lance Armstrong's courage and determination?* (He wants to give people a model of courage. He wants to encourage others to also have courage and determination.)

Across Selections

Compare text structure Compare and contrast the speech about Lance Armstrong and the diary by Anne Frank. ***Ask:*** *What is different about the stories of courage? Do you feel closer to Lance Armstrong or Anne Frank when you read the selections? Which do you like better—the speech or the diary? Why?*

9 Punctuation

Colons and dashes

Explain that a colon introduces a quotation, an example, an explanation, or a list. ***Say:*** *The written words of the speech are introduced by the speaker's name, followed by a colon.* Have students look at paragraph 1 of the reading. ***Ask:*** *Who is the speaker?* (the President) Tell students to locate additional colons in paragraphs 6 and 11. Then explain that dashes show an interruption. Have students locate the dashes in paragraphs 2 and 4.

Evaluate Your Reading Strategy

Distinguish Fact from Opinion ***Say:*** *You have practiced an important reading strategy. Now you can decide how well you have done. Does this statement describe how you read?*

> When I read, I decide whether a statement is a fact or an opinion. When I identify an opinion in the reading, I can ask myself, "Do I agree with this opinion? Why does the writer think this?"

Reading Comprehension

Question-Answer Relationships

Sample Answers

1. President George W. Bush
2. Lance Armstrong
3. Lance is a determined cyclist who works hard and succeeds on the mountain sections.
4. Armstrong wants to be a fair competitor.
5. I agree that Lance Armstrong is a great American. He doesn't give up. He's a good example for others.
6. It showed what a strong person Lance Armstrong is for winning after having cancer.
7. Lance Armstrong encourages others by his example. When people see him, they realize that they can overcome problems or difficulties with determination and courage.
8. I think presidents pay attention to people like Lance because they want to encourage and inspire other people in the country to be determined and not to give up.
9. Proud and happy. I felt that way when I received a ribbon for winning a math competition.

Build Reading Fluency

Adjust Your Reading Rate

Demonstrate to the students how you change your rate of reading depending on the purpose and type of reading material.

Beyond the Reading

Reading Comprehension

Question-Answer Relationships (QAR)

"Right There" Questions

1. **Recall Facts** Who is giving this speech?
2. **Recall Facts** Who is the speech about?

"Think and Search" Questions

3. **Interpret** How has Lance Armstrong shown his strengths as a cyclist?
4. **Character Traits** What does the story about Lance Armstrong waiting for Jan Ullrich tell you about Armstrong's character?

"Author and You" Questions

5. **Make Judgments** Do you agree with President Bush's opinion about Lance Armstrong? Why or why not?
6. **Make Inferences** Why does President Bush say that it was a triumph that Lance Armstrong won the *Tour de France*?
7. **Reflect** How does someone such as Lance Armstrong encourage other people?

"On Your Own" Questions

8. **Speculate** Why do you think that presidents pay attention to people like Lance Armstrong?
9. **Compare Your Experiences** How do you think Lance Armstrong felt as President Bush spoke? Think of a time when you have felt like that.

Activity Book *p. 106*

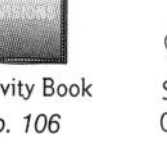
Student CD-ROM

Build Reading Fluency

Adjust Your Reading Rate

When you read a speech, you can learn to adjust your reading rate. Pause and read as if you are speaking to an audience.

1. Listen to paragraphs 1–3 of the speech on the Audio CD.
2. Silently read paragraphs 1–3.
3. With a partner, take turns reading aloud, as if you are giving the speech.
4. Did you adjust your reading rate?

MULTI-LEVEL OPTIONS *Elements of Literature*

Newcomer On the board, write: *happy, sad, angry, surprised,* and *proud.* Model facial expressions and body language for each. Point to *happy.* ***Ask:*** *How do you look when you are happy?* Have students use body language and facial expressions to demonstrate the mood. Repeat for each word.

Beginning Use exaggeration to show the difference between formal and informal language. Write *formal* on the board. ***Ask:*** *Would you be so kind as to approach my desk?* Write *informal* on the board. ***Say:*** *Please come here.* Ask students to work in pairs to say a sentence in a formal and an informal way.

Intermediate Have students practice formal and informal language in pairs. Tell one partner to say something using informal language. Have the other partner restate using formal language. Ask partners to switch roles and repeat the activity.

Advanced Remind students that tone is the way the writer feels about the subject. Tell students that writers choose specific words to help convey tone. Ask students to identify phrases in the speech that show George W. Bush's tone toward Lance (my friend, a true champ, a son of Texas).

Listen, Speak, Interact 

Listen to and Discuss a Speech

One way to understand a speech is to listen to it and discuss it with someone.

1. Listen to the recording of this speech. Focus on the speaker's message. Listen also to gain information about the subject of the speech. Ask your teacher to help you clarify words and ideas you do not understand.
2. Summarize your understanding of the speech for a partner. Then listen to your partner's summary. Compare your summary with your partner's.
3. Discuss the speech. Talk about the speaker's perspective. What are his opinions of Lance Armstrong? What facts support his opinions?

Elements of Literature

Identify Style, Tone, and Mood in a Speech

Style is the particular way something is written. For example, a style can be informal (using everyday words) or formal (using unusual words).

Tone is the writer's attitude toward the subject. For example, does the writer show respect, disapproval, or support of the topic?

Mood is the feeling the writer wants the audience to get from the speech. Happiness, sadness, and anger are examples of moods.

1. Make a chart like the one below in your Reading Log.
2. Read and listen to President Bush's speech again. Complete the chart with at least one description for each element.
3. What effect did the speech have on you as you read or listened to it? What mood or feeling did you have?

Reading Log

Activity Book p. 107

Student CD-ROM

Style, Tone, and Mood of President Bush's Speech		
The style is ______.	The mood is ______.	The tone is ______.

Content Connection *Technology*

Explain that one good way to prepare for public speaking is to record your presentation, listen to and review it, and then make changes. Ask students to select an appropriate passage to read aloud in class. Have them use tape or video recorders to record their speeches. Have students review, revise, and repeat their recordings until they feel comfortable. Then ask them to present their speeches to the class.

Learning Styles *Linguistic*

Have students listen to the audio of the speech. Then tell students to read the speech again. Ask them to write a paragraph that compares and contrasts the experience of hearing a speech with the experience of reading a speech.

Listen, Speak, Interact

Listen to and Discuss a Speech

1. **Reread** Play the audio. Then have groups summarize the speech.
2. **Analyze speaker's credibility** After listening to the audio of the speech, have pairs analyze the credibility of President Bush. *Ask: Did you believe President Bush? Did you trust his words? Why or why not? What might make him more credible?* (example: yes; used facts to support his opinions and spoke confidently; talking about some of his cycling experiences or personal relationship with Lance Armstrong)
3. **Newcomers** Reread with this group. Ask guiding questions to help them summarize. Write key words and phrases on the board. Students can write these expressions and summaries in their Reading Logs.

Elements of Literature

Identify Style, Tone, and Mood in a Speech

Teacher Resource Book: *Reading Log, p. 64*

1. **Define terms** Explain the meanings of *style, tone,* and *mood.* Provide examples and have students identify the style, tone, and mood of the speech. Have students look back through the speech for examples that support their decisions.
2. **Use personal experience** Have students describe a casual or formal style speech they have heard.
3. **Multi-level options** See MULTI-LEVEL OPTIONS on p. 198.

Answers

2. *Example:* The style is casual. The mood is happy. The tone is supportive.
3. *Example:* The speech made me feel inspired to work hard. I felt glad that someone survived some big challenges.

Have students define: *style, mood, tone.*

UNIT 3 • CHAPTER 4
Beyond the Reading

Word Study

Interpret Figurative Language

Teacher think aloud On the board, write: *The cyclists were flying down the hill.* **Say:** *I know that cyclists don't fly. Maybe the cyclists were going so fast they seemed to be flying.* Explain that this is an example of figurative language.

Answers
1. a 2. a 3. b

Grammar Focus

Use Superlative Adjectives

Explain and clarify Arrange three students in order of height. **Say:** *Tuan is the tallest.* On the board, write: *tall, tallest.* Use chairs and model which one is the *most comfortable.* Write: *comfortable, most comfortable.* Have students use other superlatives to describe people and objects in the room.

Answers
1. 4: most physically demanding, 5: hardest, 10: steepest

ASSESS

On the board, write: *fast, interesting.* Have students use the superlative forms in sentences.

Word Study

Interpret Figurative Language

Writers use **figurative language** to make writing vivid and exciting. In figurative language, meanings go beyond the usual definitions in a dictionary.

President Bush uses figurative language in his speech. The underlined words are figurative. What do they mean?

1. Lance Armstrong is a son of Texas.
   a. He was born and raised in Texas.
   b. He really likes Texas.
2. That's when the heart is tested.
   a. That's when you need courage.
   b. That's when you have a heart problem.
3. You embrace life day by day.
   a. You hug your friends every day.
   b. You love and enjoy your life.

Activity Book p. 108

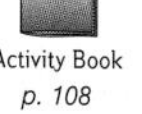
Student CD-ROM

Grammar Focus

Use Superlative Adjectives

Use **superlative adjectives** to compare three or more people, places, or things.

Ana thinks that science, math, and English are hard. But math is **the hardest** of the three.

There are two ways to form superlative adjectives.

Superlative Adjectives	
Most Short Adjectives: adjective + -est	**Long Adjectives: most + adjective**
hard + -est = the hardest	the most difficult

1. Find three examples of superlative adjectives using *-est* or *most* in paragraphs 4, 5, and 10.
2. Write one sentence using the superlative form of a short adjective and one sentence using the superlative form of a long adjective.

Activity Book pp. 109–110

Student Handbook

Student CD-ROM

MULTI-LEVEL OPTIONS *From Reading to Writing*

Newcomer Have students draw pictures of people they admire. Tell them to explain their pictures in pairs. Ask them to list five words that describe the person in the picture. Work with students to find adjectives and other descriptive terms.

Beginning Provide cloze sentences to assist students in writing simple speeches. On the board, write: *Ladies and gentlemen, I would like to tell you about _____. I think _____ has shown courage. This person showed courage when _____. This was courageous because* _____. Remind students that *courageous* means "brave."

Intermediate Suggest that students prepare notes for their speeches. Instruct students to practice their speeches until they can use their notes only for reference. Remind students that they do not have to memorize their speeches, but they should not read directly from their papers.

Advanced Have students practice their speeches with partners. Instruct partners to listen for tone, informal language, and mood. Ask them to suggest additional descriptive language.

From Reading to Writing 

Write a Speech

Write a three-paragraph speech about someone you know who has shown courage.

1. Use informal, everyday language. However, be sure you use correct grammar.
2. Address your audience directly using the word *you.*
3. Use words that set a tone. You can be humorous or serious, or both.
4. Use superlative adjectives, such as *smartest* or *most interesting,* to create a mood of appreciation for the subject of your speech.
5. Practice your speech aloud. Listen carefully for a smooth flow of ideas.
6. Present your speech to the class.

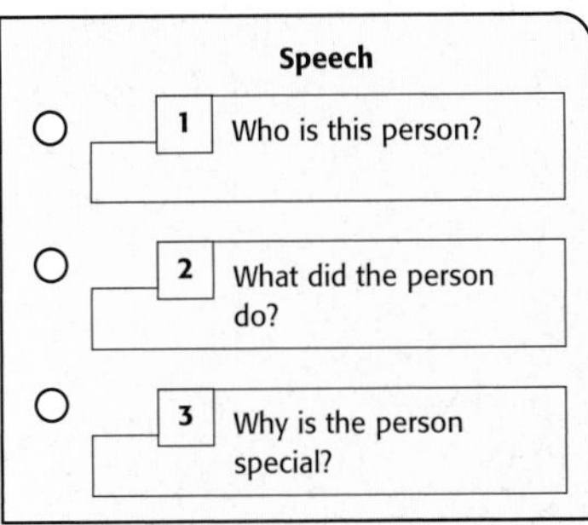

Activity Book p. 111

Across Content Areas 

Read a Chart

The chart below shows the **altitudes** (measures of height) of the highest mountains in four areas in the world.

In the **metric system,** height can be measured in *meters* (m.). In the **English system,** it can be measured in *feet* (ft.).

1. What are the names of the mountains on the chart? Where are they?
2. Find the name of the mountain in the U.S. How high is it?
3. How high is Mt. Blanc in meters? How high is it in feet?

Country	France	Argentina	Nepal	U.S.
Mountain Range	the Alps	the Andes	the Himalayas	the Rocky Mountains
Highest Mountain	Mt. Blanc	Mt. Aconcagua	Mt. Everest	Mt. Elbert
Altitude	4,807 m. 15,771 ft.	6,960 m. 22,028 ft.	8,848 m. 29,028 ft.	4,399 m. 14,433 ft.

Activity Book p. 112

Reteach and Reassess

Text Structure Review personal style, direct address, and audience reaction. Divide students into three groups. Assign one text feature to each group. Have groups review pp. 194–197 to find an example of their assigned feature.

Reading Strategy Tell students to write two facts about a current event. Have them exchange their facts with partners and write two opinions about the same event.

Elements of Literature Ask students to think about a speech they heard at school, in the community, or on television. Have them think about the style, tone, and mood of the speech. Ask students to share their thoughts in small groups.

Reassess Have students write one-paragraph reviews of the speech. Ask them to evaluate the content, language, tone, and mood.

From Reading to Writing

Write a Speech

1. **Brainstorm** Brainstorm a list of courageous people. Have students pick a person they know or admire.
2. **Think-quickwrite-pair-share** Tell students to think about their person. *Ask: Who is the person? What did the person do? Why is the person special?* Then direct them to write as much about their person as they can. In pairs, have students share their ideas. Tell students to use informal language and superlative adjectives.
3. **Multi-level options** See MULTI-LEVEL OPTIONS on p. 200.

Across Content Areas: Social Studies

Read a Chart

1. **Connect** Bring in a meter measuring stick and a 12-inch ruler. Have students compare the two measurement systems and tell which system is used in countries they have visited or lived in.
2. **Use a map** Have students locate the countries and mountain ranges on a world map.

Answers

1. Mt. Blanc, France; Mt. Aconcagua, Argentina; Mt. Everest, Nepal; Mt. Elbert, U.S.
2. Mt. Elbert; 14,433 feet
3. 4,807 meters; 15,771 feet

Have students measure themselves using the metric system (meters) and English system (feet). Then use the information to write two sentences about their height.

Chapter Materials

Activity Book: *pp. 113–120*
Audio: *Unit 3, Chapter 5*
Student Handbook
Student CD-ROM: *Unit 3, Chapter 5*
Teacher Resource Book: *Lesson Plan, Teacher Resources, Reading Summary, Activity Book Answer Key*
Teacher Resource CD-ROM
Assessment Program: *Quiz, pp. 47–48; Teacher and Student Resources, pp. 115–144*
Assessment CD-ROM
Transparencies
The Heinle Newbury House Dictionary/CD-ROM
Web Site: www.heinle.visions.com

Objectives

Make connections Read the objectives. ***Say:*** *What word does* memoir *look like?* (memory) *What other readings were about people's memories of events?* ("Anne Frank: The Diary of a Young Girl," "Mathew A. Henson") Explain that *memoir* is a French word that English has borrowed.

Use Prior Knowledge

Brainstorm Qualities of Natural Disasters

Connect with others' experiences Direct students to the list and sample cluster map. Read the examples. Clarify meanings of natural disasters. Ask students to share about natural disasters they have experienced. Have students compare similarities with others' experiences.

Into the Reading

Objectives

Reading Draw conclusions and give support as you read a memoir.

Listening and Speaking Discuss emergencies.

Grammar Identify pronoun referents.

Writing Write a memoir.

Content Social Studies: Read a map.

Use Prior Knowledge

Brainstorm Qualities of Natural Disasters

You are going to read a selection about an earthquake. An earthquake is a natural disaster. A disaster is an event that causes a lot of damage. A natural disaster happens by nature. It is not caused by people.

1. Look at this list of natural disasters.
2. Choose at least two of the natural disasters that you know about.
3. On a piece of paper, complete a cluster map like the one here. Add more ovals if necessary.
4. Share your ideas with the class.

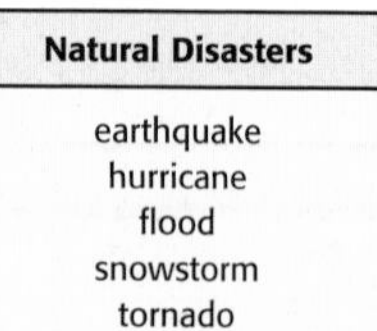

Natural Disasters
earthquake
hurricane
flood
snowstorm
tornado

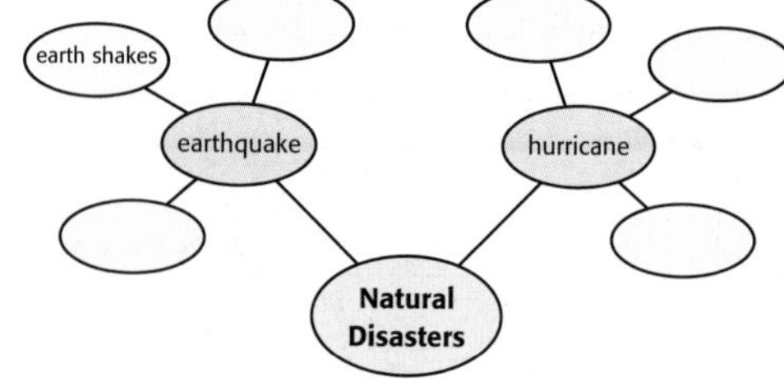

MULTI-LEVEL OPTIONS *Build Vocabulary*

Newcomer Show students a picture of a cow or bull. ***Ask:*** *Does it say "woof"?* (no) *What sound does it make?* When a volunteer makes the correct sound, write *bellow* on the board. ***Say:*** *This animal bellows.* Repeat using other animals. Have students draw different animals. Help them write key words to describe sounds the animals make.

Beginning Remind students that the first step in finding a word in the dictionary is turning to the section with the first letter of the word. On the board, write: *bellow.* Point to the *b.* ***Ask:*** *What is this letter?* Model finding the B section of the dictionary. Repeat for *net* and *whine.*

Intermediate Demonstrate finding *bellow* in the dictionary. Point out the guide words that help find the right page. Have a volunteer read the definition. Repeat for *frantically, net,* and *whine.*

Advanced Have students work in pairs. Tell one student to write a sentence, leaving a blank space for one of the words in the exercise. Then have the other student complete the sentence by filling in the correct missing word. Have students alternate turns until they have used all four words.

Build Background

Vietnam

Vietnam is a country in Southeast Asia. About 70 percent of the people in Vietnam are farmers. Most Vietnamese farmers grow rice as their main crop. In 1954, Vietnam was divided into two countries: North Vietnam and South Vietnam. The two countries went to war. The war ended in 1975, and Vietnam became one country again.

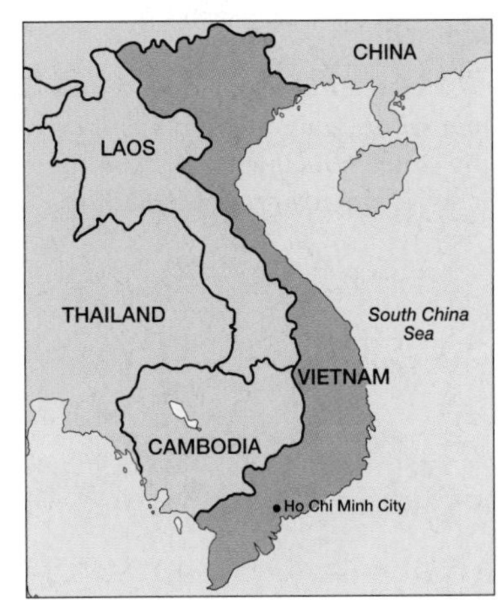

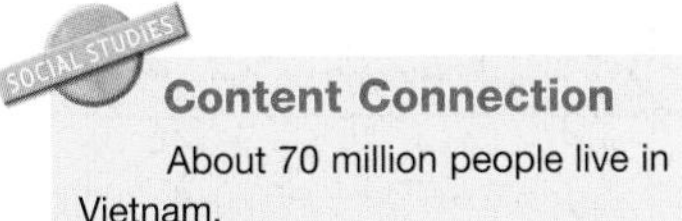

Content Connection

About 70 million people live in Vietnam.

Build Vocabulary

Use the Dictionary

In "Earthquake," some animals are frightened because they sense that an earthquake is coming. Find out how they acted.

1. Look up the underlined words below in a dictionary. Write the words and their definitions in your Personal Dictionary.
   - **a.** bellow
   - **b.** jump frantically in a net
   - **c.** whine
2. Match the parts of the sentences to describe what each animal did.

The buffalo (a large animal like a cow)	jumped frantically as if caught in a net.
The fish	bellowed fearfully.
The dog	whined.

Personal Dictionary

The Heinle Newbury House Dictionary

Activity Book p. 113

Student CD-ROM

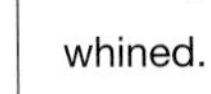

Build Background

Vietnam

1. **Use a map** Have students locate Vietnam on a world map. ***Ask:*** *What countries are near Vietnam? What's the name of the sea to the east of Vietnam? What are some cities in Vietnam?*
2. **Content Connection** Tell students that most people in Vietnam live along the coast. Bring in books or photos of Vietnam and Vietnamese people. Allow students to share information they know.

Build Vocabulary

Use the Dictionary

Teacher Resource Book: *Personal Dictionary, p. 63*

1. **Use experience** Ask students to act out how different animals might act when they are scared. Provide examples: a dog barks, a lion roars. List the animals and actions on the board.
2. **Use a dictionary** Have students look up the meanings of the new vocabulary words. Ask them to suggest types of animals that might do these actions.
3. **Reading selection vocabulary** You may want to introduce the glossed words in the reading selection before students begin reading. Key words: *instincts, debris, atmosphere, collapse, demolish, predator.* Instruct students to write the words with correct spelling and their definitions in their Personal Dictionaries. Have them pronounce each word and divide it into syllables.
4. **Multi-level options** See MULTI-LEVEL OPTIONS on p. 202.

Answers

2. The buffalo bellowed fearfully.
   The fish jumped frantically . . .
   The dog whined.

ASSESS

Have students write a sentence for each of the vocabulary words.

Content Connection *Science*

Build Vocabulary Have students work in small groups. Tell each group to select one of these animals: buffalo, fish, or dog. Ask groups to prepare short reports on their animals. Tell them to include information about where the animal lives, what it looks like, what it eats, and other important characteristics and behaviors. Ask groups to share their reports with the class.

Learning Styles *Natural*

Build Background Tell students that farmers in Vietnam also grow bananas, peanuts, and coffee. Provide samples of each. Give students seed peanuts and soil. Have them plant the seeds in cups. Tell students to use the Internet to find care instructions for their plants. Allow students to care for the plants and keep a journal describing their growth over time.

Text Structure

Memoir

Recognize features Direct attention to the chart of features. Guide students to compare features of a memoir with the features of a diary.

Reading Strategy

Draw Conclusions and Give Support

1. **Model drawing conclusions** On the board, draw three small circles with arrows pointing to a larger circle. ***Say:*** *I wake up. I walk outside. There are puddles of water on the sidewalk. There's a rainbow in the sky. Some drops of water fall onto my head. Puddles, rainbow, drops of water. I can draw the conclusion that it rained.* Use the circle chart to show the conclusion (large circle) with supporting details (small circles).
2. **Multi-level options** See MULTI-LEVEL OPTIONS below.

ASSESS

Ask: What are five features of a memoir? (personal pronouns, facts and memories, structure, feelings, setting)

Text Structure

Memoir

The reading selection is a **memoir.** A memoir tells about people and events that the writer remembers. Look at the chart. It shows the features of a memoir.

Memoir	
Personal Pronouns	*I, me, we,* or *us*
Interesting Facts and Memories	people and events
Structure	a beginning, a middle, and an end
Feelings	the writer's feelings and perspectives about the events and people in the memoir
Setting	usually a long time ago

Student CD-ROM

Reading Strategy

Draw Conclusions and Give Support

When you **draw a conclusion,** you make a true statement based on the information in the reading or from your own experience.

When you **give support,** you provide details and examples that explain your conclusion.

1. Read paragraph 1 of "Earthquake."
2. You can draw the conclusion that the animals and the people in the story lived closely together. You can support this because the animals "often warned" the people about danger. They had done this before.
3. As you read "Earthquake," continue to draw conclusions. Give support for your conclusions.

Student CD-ROM

MULTI-LEVEL OPTIONS *Reading Strategy*

Newcomer Help students to draw conclusions about the picture on p. 205. *Ask: Is this in the city?* (no) *Is this in the country?* (yes) *Is this a picture of a farm?* (yes)

Beginning Help students to draw conclusions about the boy in the picture on p. 205. ***Ask:*** *What do you see in the picture?* (a boy, some buffalo, a fence, and some houses) *What conclusion can you draw about the boy?* (He lives on a farm.)

Intermediate ***Ask:*** *What conclusions can you draw about the boy in the picture on p. 205?* (He lives or works on a farm.) *What support can you give for your conclusion?* (He's near some buffaloes, a fence, and some houses.)

Advanced Have students make up a story about the picture on p. 205. Tell them to draw conclusions in their story about who the boy is, what he is doing, and how he feels. Have them tell a partner their story and give support for their conclusions.

Earthquake

an excerpt from a memoir
by Huynh Quang Nhuong

205

Reading Selection Materials

Audio: *Unit 3, Chapter 5*
Teacher Resource Book: *Reading Summary, pp. 93–94*

Preview the Selection

Teacher Resource Book: *Know/Want to Know/Learned Chart, p. 42*

1. **Use the illustration** Have students describe the picture. ***Say:*** *The title of the selection is "Earthquake." Is the picture of the farm before the earthquake or after it? How do you know?*
2. **Use a KWL chart** Have students complete a chart with things they know about the story (title, information from the illustration). Direct them to write questions asking about the boy, the farm, and the earthquake. Students can use the chart to guide their reading of the memoir. Have them complete the last column after reading the selection.
3. **Relate to personal experiences** ***Ask:*** *Does this look like any farms you have seen? Why or why not? What is similar? What is different?*
4. **Connect** Remind students that the unit theme is *courage.* ***Ask:*** *When do you think this boy in the picture will need courage?*

Community Connection

Tell students that an earthquake is a kind of natural disaster. Tell students that some other natural disasters are hurricanes, tornadoes, blizzards, and floods. Explain to students that many communities have special plans to deal with disasters. Have students research local disaster plans.

Learning Styles *Verbal*

Explain to students that many writers use descriptive words and phrases that help readers picture ideas in their minds. Tell students that some examples of this kind of writing use animals, such as *He was as strong as an ox* or *The flutes sounded like birds singing.* Have students write three sentences that use animals to create images.

UNIT 3 • CHAPTER 5
Reading Selection

Read the Selection

Teacher Resource Book: *Web, p. 37*

1. **Use the illustration** Help students describe the farm in the picture. Provide appropriate vocabulary words.
2. **Teacher read aloud** Read aloud paragraphs 1 and 2 to students.
3. **Draw conclusions and give support** In pairs, have students reread the paragraphs. ***Ask:*** *What are the animals doing?* (The buffaloes were making loud noise, the chickens were hiding, the fish were jumping, and the dog was hiding.) *Why do you think they are doing that?* (Something bad is going to happen.) Use a graphic organizer, such as a web, to record the details that support the conclusions.

Sample Answer to Guide Question
The animals feel danger and are warning the people. The buffaloes were making loud noise, the chickens were hiding, the fish were jumping, and the dog was hiding.

See Teacher Edition pp. 434–435 for a list of English-Spanish cognates in the reading selection.

Audio

Draw Conclusions and Give Support

What conclusion can you draw about the animals? Give support for your conclusion.

1 **Domestic** animals living very close to the jungle often **preserve** their natural **instincts.** Most of the time our animals felt rather than saw danger and often warned us of the presence of enemies.

2 One afternoon we were not out in the field working because of the Lunar New Year holiday. The sky above our **hamlet** was clear, but the **atmosphere** became very heavy. Tank and our other buffaloes remained in the shed, eating. Suddenly they stamped their feet very hard and bellowed fearfully. We looked around and saw chickens and ducks run into bamboo bushes to hide, and in the ponds, fish of all sizes jumped frantically as if they were caught in a net. Our watchdog crawled under a bed and whined.

domestic kept in the house or for the family's use
preserve keep, still have
instincts ways of acting that an animal or person can do without learning or thinking about
hamlet a small village
atmosphere the air

MULTI-LEVEL OPTIONS *Read the Selection*

Newcomer Write on the board and ***say:*** *buffaloes, chickens, ducks, fish, dog.* Then play the audio. Have students raise their hands when they hear the animals. ***Ask:*** *Did the buffaloes run away?* (no) *Did the chickens and ducks hide?* (yes) *Did the fish jump?* (yes) *Did the dog bark?* (no)

Beginning Read the Reading Summary aloud. ***Ask:*** *What did the buffaloes do?* (stamp their feet and bellow) *Where did the ducks and chickens hide?* (in the bamboo bushes) *What kind of animal is Tank?* (a buffalo) *Where did the family hide?* (in a bomb shelter)

Intermediate Have students do a paired reading. ***Ask:*** *Why weren't the people working in the field?* (It was a holiday.) *How did the animals act?* (frightened) *Why did the people run into the bomb shelter?* (The animals were warning them of danger.)

Advanced Have students read silently. Then ***ask:*** *When did you first think that something bad might happen? Explain. At what point were you sure that something bad was about to happen? Why?*

Draw Conclusions and Give Support

What is Tank's role in the herd of buffalo? What support is there for this conclusion?

3 We quickly opened the door of the shed and let Tank and the other buffaloes out. At first Tank led his small herd to the garden; then he changed his mind and moved them to the banana grove behind the house. We then ran to the **bomb shelter,** and the watchdog followed us. About three minutes later a powerful earthquake shook the whole area.

4 The **deafening** noise made by trees falling, rocks crashing down the mountains, and houses **collapsing** was terrifying. When it was over and we **emerged** from our shelter, we saw that both the house and the shed were **demolished.** Most of the fruit trees in the garden were either broken or **uprooted** by fallen boulders. We realized that if Tank and the other buffaloes had stayed in the

---

bomb shelter a building or an underground cave made to keep people safe during a bomb explosion

deafening loud enough to make you deaf or hurt your hearing

collapsing falling down

emerged came out of

demolished destroyed, broken

uprooted torn out of the ground with the roots

Spelling

Plurals

Explain that *plural* means "more than one." On the board, write: *1 rock, 2 rocks; 1 house, some houses; 1 buffalo, 6 buffaloes.* Tell students that we form most plurals by adding an *s.* When a word ends in *o, s, x, ch,* or *sh,* we add *es* to form a plural. Point out that some words ending in *o* take an *s* in the plural (e.g. *mangos*) and that *fish* has the irregular plural *fish.*

Apply Write these words: *animal, enemy, buffalo, chicken, duck, bush, pond, minute, tree, rock, boulder.* Have students work in pairs to write the plural form of each word. Then have students find each plural word on pp. 206–207.

Read the Selection

1. **Understand terms** Have students find the meanings of the glossed words at the bottom of the page. Clarify meanings as needed.
2. **Reciprocal reading** After students listen to the audio, arrange them in groups for reciprocal reading. Assign each student a different section of the reading selection. A "leader" should read his/her section aloud, answer questions, and summarize the section.
3. **Multi-level options** See MULTI-LEVEL OPTIONS on p. 206.

Sample Answer to Guide Question

Tank is the leader of the herd. Tank led the herd to the garden and then moved them to the banana grove behind the house.

Read the Selection

Teacher read aloud Read paragraph 5 aloud. *Ask: Why are they going to stay in the garden?* (The house and shed were destroyed, and the garden was protected by a hedge.) *How do you know they live near the forest or jungle?* (There are wild animals nearby.) *What did the family do in the evening?* (They cleared part of the garden.)

Sample Answer to Guide Question

The hedge is very important. It is a kind of shelter that protects people and farm animals from wild animals. The narrator says that after other earthquakes, wild animals caused damage where there were no shelters.

garden, they could easily have been killed, because five of our eight huge mango trees had been knocked down. All the houses on the southern side of the hamlet were gone, but nobody got hurt. The **casualties** were limited to a few cattle that had been crushed by falling rocks.

Draw Conclusions and Give Support

What conclusion can you draw about the importance of the hedge? What support can you give?

5 That evening we cleared part of the garden of broken branches to make a place for our family and cattle to spend the night. It was **relatively** safe for us and for them to be in the garden, because a thick **hedge** surrounded it. Earthquakes like this one had struck our village before. But after those disasters, people had not built shelters for themselves or their domestic animals. Then wild beasts, attracted by the smell of **unburied** dead animals, had come to the hamlet and caused much damage.

---

casualties injuries
relatively fairly, mostly
hedge a tall border of thick plants
unburied not yet put under the ground

MULTI-LEVEL OPTIONS *Read the Selection*

Newcomer *Ask: Did anybody get hurt?* (no) *Did the family spend the night in the shed?* (no) *Was this the first earthquake in their village?* (no) *Did they build a bonfire?* (yes)

Beginning *Ask: Where did the family spend the night?* (in the garden) *Who barricaded the entrance?* (the boy's father and cousin) *Where were the buffaloes, goats, and watchdog?* (in the garden) *Where did the hogs go?* (back to their sty)

Intermediate *Ask: Why was the garden a safe place?* (It was protected by a thick hedge.) *Why wasn't there much space in the garden?* (There were fallen trees, buffaloes, goats, and a watchdog.) *What were two reasons for building the bonfire?* (for warmth and to keep wild animals away)

Advanced *Ask: How do you think the boy and his family felt after the earthquake?* (worried, afraid, and glad they were all safe) *Do you think they felt lucky? Explain.*

Draw Conclusions and Give Support

Is the family comfortable in the garden? What conclusion can you draw? What support can you give?

6 While my father and my cousin **barricaded** the entrance of the garden with broken branches, my mother and I built a **bonfire.** The fire would help keep **predators** away and at the same time keep us warm—all our blankets were buried under heavy **debris.** There wasn't much space in the garden. We were **hemmed in** by enormous fallen trees, three water buffaloes, five goats, and a watchdog. There would also have been several hogs, but they determinedly made holes in the hedge and went back to their **half-demolished** sty.

barricaded covered, closed up
bonfire a large fire
predators animals that eat other animals or people
debris remains of something broken
hemmed in surrounded by
half-demolished partly destroyed

UNIT 3 • CHAPTER 5
Reading Selection

Read the Selection

1. **Guided reading** Play the audio, pausing to ask comprehension questions and to clarify vocabulary. ***Ask:*** *What did the father and cousin do?* (They put branches to block the entrance to the garden.) *What did the writer and his mother do?* (They started a fire.)
2. **Visualize** Have pairs of students reread the selection. Ask students to describe what the garden looked like with the family and animals in there.
3. **Make predictions** Use guiding questions to help students make predictions about what will happen that night and the next day.
4. **Multi-level options** See MULTI-LEVEL OPTIONS on p. 208.

Sample Answer to Guide Question

No. They try to make the garden safe and to protect themselves and their animals, but it was not comfortable. They needed a fire to keep warm. There was little room to move because of fallen trees. The animals were also in the garden with the family.

th Spelling

Adding *-ed* and doubling final consonants

Write on the board and ***say:*** *Today I play. Yesterday I played.* Ask students which tense the verb in the second sentence is in. (simple past tense) ***Say:*** *To make most verbs in the simple past tense, add* -ed. Write: *jump/jumped.* ***Say:*** *To make a verb that ends with* -e *in the simple past tense, drop the* -e *and add* -ed. Write: *bake/baked.* ***Say:*** *For one-syllable verbs that end with a consonant, a vowel, and another consonant, double the last letter and add* -ed. Write: *slip/slipped.*

Apply Write these words: *crush, clear, cause, hem.* Have students work in pairs to write the simple past tense form of each verb. Then have students find each simple past tense verb on pp. 208–209.

Read the Selection

1. **Identify text structure** Remind students that one feature of a memoir is feelings. *Ask: What feelings does the author have that night?* (He enjoys sleeping outside, but he is also worried about the future.)
2. **Paired reading** Have students reread the selection with partners. *Ask: Why was it hard for the family to sleep?* (They were worried.) *What did the father, mother, and cousin talk about?* (They discussed building a new house and getting money for it.)

Sample Answer to Guide Question
I think he enjoys sleeping outdoors because it's different. He could see the stars and enjoy the fresh air. I know that many young people enjoy camping or sleeping outside in the summer.

Draw Conclusions and Give Support

Why does the author enjoy sleeping outdoors? Give support from what you know about young people.

7 This was the first time I had slept in the open air, and despite **circumstances,** I thoroughly enjoyed it. Tank and the other **domestic** animals, unlike wild **beasts,** liked the fire very much. They lay down as close as possible to it and stayed awake, while we people tried to sleep to escape the terrible day. But worry kept us **wakeful,** so my father, my mother, and my cousin sat up near the fire and talked about what they would do in the next few days. While they discussed how to build a new house and where to get the money to **finance** their project, I stayed with Tank.

circumstances the situation
domestic related to home life
beasts animals
wakeful unable to sleep
finance pay for

MULTI-LEVEL OPTIONS *Read the Selection*

Newcomer *Ask: Does Tank like the fire?* (yes) *Did the adults sleep?* (no) *Did the boy feel safe near Tank?* (yes)

Beginning *Ask: Who sat near the fire to talk?* (the boy's parents and cousin) *What did they talk about?* (what to do in the next few days) *Where did the boy stay?* (near Tank) *What did he count in the sky?* (fruit bats)

Intermediate *Ask: Why did the people want to go to sleep?* (so they could stop thinking about the terrible day) *Why couldn't the adults sleep?* (They were too worried.) *Did the boy like sleeping outside?* (yes) *How did the boy finally fall asleep?* (Tank made him feel safe.)

Advanced *Ask: How does the boy think the world inside the garden compares with the world outside the garden? Explain.*

Draw Conclusions and Give Support

How does the author feel about Tank? Give support for your conclusion.

8 I leaned against Tank's shoulder and gazed into the sky to count the number of giant fruit bats passing by. The warmth of his shoulder, the **regularity** of his breathing, the beat of his heart, and the **enormity** of his body made me feel safe and comfortable. The lonely call of **nocturnal** birds, the occasional roaring of tigers in the nearby jungle—these belonged to the **insecure** and **unpredictable** dark world outside our garden. Little by little I drifted into a gentle sleep.

---

regularity evenness, in a regular pattern
enormity very large size
nocturnal awake and active at night; sleeping in the day
insecure unsafe
unpredictable unsure, impossible to know what to expect

About the Author — Huynh Quang Nhuong (born 1946)

Huynh Quang Nhuong writes about his boyhood in Mytho, Vietnam, in his book *The Land I Lost.* He tells about the place where he grew up. Mr. Huynh served in the South Vietnamese army. After the war, he came to the United States and became a citizen. He now lives in Missouri. Mr. Huynh wants his books to please people in both of his homelands: Vietnam and the United States. He says, "I am the first Vietnamese to write fiction and nonfiction in English. I hope my books will make people from different countries happy . . . Good literature unites people."

➤ What challenges do you think the author faced in writing *The Land I Lost?*

th Spelling

Past tense of words ending in *-y*

Remind students that many simple past tense verbs are formed by adding *-ed.* **Say:** *For most words that end with* -y, *drop the* -y *and add* -ied. Have students locate the simple past tense of *try* in paragraph 7. **Ask:** *How do you form the* simple *past tense of* try*?* (Drop the *-y* and add *-ied.*)

Apply Write *cry, worry, fry, pry* on the board. Have students work in pairs to write the simple past tense form of each verb.

Evaluate Your Reading Strategy

Draw Conclusions and Give Support *Say: You have practiced an important reading strategy. Now you can decide how well you have done. Does this statement describe how you read?*

> When I read, I draw conclusions by considering the information in the reading and my own knowledge. Drawing conclusions helps me think better about what I am reading.

Read the Selection

1. **Paired reading** After pairs of students read the selection, ask them to contrast inside the garden and outside in the jungle.
2. **Multi-level options** See MULTI-LEVEL OPTIONS on p. 210.

Sample Answer to Guide Question
He likes Tank and feels safe with him. He leans against Tank because he is warm and comfortable.

About the Author

1. **Explain author's background** Huynh Quang Nhuong received gold and silver medals for his military service. His memoirs paint pictures of people dealing with terrible events with courage and calmness.
2. **Interpret the facts** *Ask: What challenges did Huynh face in his life?* (earthquakes, wild animals, a war, moving to a new country, learning a new language)

Across Selections

Compare Discuss tone and mood. ***Ask:*** *How is this memoir similar to Anne Frank's diary?* (They use a calm tone. The mood is sad, but there's a feeling of hope.) *How are they different?* (Anne writes about events when they happen. Huynh writes about experiences that happened long ago.)

Reading Comprehension

Question-Answer Relationships

Sample Answers

1. The animals are all hiding outside.
2. The family spends the night in the garden.
3. Before the earthquake, all the animals act strangely and make a lot of noise.
4. Tank was looking for a safe place for the herd.
5. All of the houses on the southern side were completely destroyed after the earthquake.
6. It is about how a family survived an earthquake and made a safe place for themselves and their animals for the night.
7. The family needs shelter.
8. Tank makes him feel safe. The buffalo is his friend.
9. I think the family will sell something to get money for a new house.
10. I think I would feel uncomfortable. It's too big and would smell.

Build Reading Fluency

Rapid Word Recognition

Rapid word recognition is an excellent activity for students who struggle with irregular spelling patterns. Time students for 1 minute as they read the words in the squares aloud.

Beyond the Reading

Reading Comprehension

Question-Answer Relationships (QAR)

"Right There" Questions

1. **Recall Facts** Where are the animals during the earthquake?
2. **Recall Facts** Where does the family spend the night after the earthquake?

"Think and Search" Questions

3. **Recognize Sequence of Events** What happens before the earthquake?
4. **Make Inferences** Why does Tank take the buffaloes to the garden and then to the banana grove?
5. **Compare and Contrast** How is the southern side of the hamlet different after the earthquake?
6. **Paraphrase Text** How would you tell someone what the selection is about in your own words?

"Author and You" Questions

7. **Make Connections** Why does the author's family want to rebuild their home?
8. **Analyze Cause and Effect** Why do you think Tank's presence makes the author feel better?

"On Your Own" Questions

9. **Predict** What do you think the author's family will do now?
10. **Understand Characters' Experiences** How would you feel sleeping next to a buffalo?

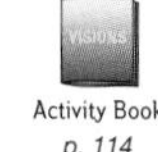

Activity Book p. 114

Build Reading Fluency

Rapid Word Recognition

It helps to practice reading words with silent letters. Rapidly recognizing these words will help increase your reading speed.

1. With a partner, review the words in the box.
2. Next, read the words aloud for one minute. Your teacher or partner can time you.

often	heavy	were	one	were
rather	one	heavy	were	one
one	sky	rather	often	sky
were	were	each	rather	often
sky	rather	heavy	sky	heavy

3. How many words did you read in one minute? Was it more than on page 98?

MULTI-LEVEL OPTIONS *Elements of Literature*

Newcomer *Say: You are looking for clues or hints in the story. The animals give the boy clues. Raise your hands when the animals do something strange or surprising.* Then read paragraph 2. ***Ask:*** *What are the animals showing the boy?* (Something dangerous is going to happen.)

Beginning Explain to students that writers give clues or hints about something that will happen. To model foreshadowing, sit down with a dictionary, as if you are about to look up a word. ***Say:*** *This is a clue. What will I do next?* Then reread paragraph 2 with the group and help them identify examples of foreshadowing.

Intermediate Tell students that foreshadowing helps them make predictions about what might happen later in a story. Have small groups make and discuss predictions for what might happen if "Earthquake" continued.

Advanced Have students write opening paragraphs of an event that happened to them. Ask them to include at least one clue that foreshadows what is going to happen later. Have pairs exchange paragraphs and try to guess what will happen in their partners' stories.

Listen, Speak, Interact 

Discuss Emergencies

"Earthquake" describes an emergency that Huynh Quang Nhuong and his family faced. An emergency is a bad or dangerous situation that requires immediate attention.

1. What kinds of emergencies do you know about?
2. With a partner, choose one kind of emergency, for example, a car accident, a fire in a house, or a person getting sick suddenly.
3. Create a list of steps to take in this kind of emergency. Practice reading your list aloud to your partner. Speak clearly and with an informative, or helpful, tone to describe each step. Share your list with the rest of the class.

In Case of Fire
Step 1: *Get out of the building.*
Step 2: ______
Step 3: ______
Step 4: ______

Elements of Literature

Recognize Foreshadowing

Foreshadowing gives clues about what is going to happen in a narrative. In "Earthquake" Huynh Quang Nhuong uses foreshadowing to show that something bad is going to happen. For example, in the sentence "Our watchdog crawled under a bed and whined," the dog's behavior is foreshadowing.

1. Find two more examples of foreshadowing in paragraph 2. Hint: Look for foreshadowing in the descriptions of the weather and the behavior of the animals.
2. Write the examples in your Reading Log.

Reading Log

Activity Book *p. 115*

Student CD-ROM

Content Connection *The Arts*

Show an appropriate mystery movie in class. Before viewing the movie, ask students to keep track of any clues or foreshadowing. Remind them that in movies, foreshadowing can happen with dialogue, music, sound effects, or visual images or effects. Ask students to make predictions about what will happen as they watch the movie. After the movie ends, have students evaluate their predictions.

Learning Styles *Visual*

Have students choose an animal described in "Earthquake." Ask them to draw a picture that shows the animal as it is described in the story. Then have groups work together to create a picture of the garden before and after the earthquake.

Listen, Speak, Interact

Discuss Emergencies

1. **Brainstorm emergencies** Have students suggest different emergency situations. Ask students to work in pairs to choose an emergency and describe what they would do.
2. **Newcomers** List students' ideas on the board. Have them act out what they would do in the emergencies. List key words and phrases on the board. Have pairs complete storyboards with captions to share with the class.

Elements of Literature

Recognize Foreshadowing

Teacher Resource Book: *Reading Log, p. 64*

1. **Teacher think aloud** Write *foreshadow* on the board. ***Say:*** *I see the words* fore *and* shadow. Fore *reminds me of something that happens before. A shadow is a shape or figure of something. So* foreshadowing *is some shape or idea that tells about something before it happens.* Then, in pairs, have students look for and describe foreshadowing in the story.
2. **Personal experience** Ask students to suggest examples of foreshadowing in movies or television shows.
3. **Multi-level options** See MULTI-LEVEL OPTIONS on p. 212.

Answers

1. *Sample answers:* the atmosphere became very heavy; buffaloes suddenly stamped their feet and bellowed

Have students list four emergencies and one important action to take in each.

Beyond the Reading

Word Study

Form Compound Words

Make a vocabulary game Write words that form compound words on sets of cards. Use the cards for a game of compound-word concentration.

Answers

1. *Sample answer: up + rooted* = the pulling up of a plant so the roots are out of the ground
2. *Examples: after + noon* = daytime after 12 o'clock; *watch + dog* = a dog that watches the family or house
3. snowstorm; homework; textbook

Grammar Focus

Identify Pronoun Referents

Apply Review and list subject pronouns on the board. Say sentences with noun subjects and have students substitute subject pronouns.

Answers

1. they—fish
2. he—Tank
3. they—Tank and the other buffaloes

ASSESS

On the board, write: *My sister is eight years old. Andy and Sam like to watch movies. The fish were jumping in the lake.* Have students rewrite the sentences using subject pronouns for the underlined nouns.

Word Study

Form Compound Words

Compound words are formed by combining two words into one larger word. For example, the word *earthquake* is made of two words: *earth* + *quake*.

You can sometimes learn the meaning of a compound word by looking at the meanings of the smaller words. Look at the chart.

Word	Word	Compound Word
earth: the planet we live on	quake: to shake	earthquake: a shaking of the earth

1. Use the chart to figure out the meaning of *uprooted*.
2. Find another example of a compound word in paragraph 2 of the reading. Can you guess its meaning? Look it up in a dictionary to check your guess.
3. What other compound words do you know? Match up the words to make compound words.

snow	work
home	book
text	storm

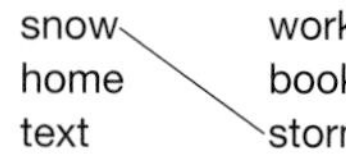

The Heinle Newbury House Dictionary

Activity Book p. 116

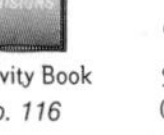
Student CD-ROM

Grammar Focus

Identify Pronoun Referents

Pronouns stand for nouns.

My father, my mother, and my cousin sat near the fire and talked about what they would do.

In the sentence above, *they* stands for the nouns *my father, my mother, and my cousin*. We can also say that *my father, my mother, and my cousin* is the **referent** for *they*.

Read each sentence and find the referent for each underlined pronoun.

1. Fish of all sizes jumped frantically as if they were caught in a net.
2. Tank led his herd to the garden; then he changed his mind.
3. If Tank and the other buffaloes had stayed in the garden, they could easily have been killed.

Activity Book pp. 117–118

Student Handbook

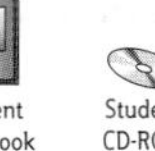
Student CD-ROM

MULTI-LEVEL OPTIONS *From Reading to Writing*

Newcomer Ask students to draw a picture of an important event in their life. Have them tell three details about the event. Help them write three words that describe their feelings about the event.

Beginning Have students list three important events in their lives. Ask students to pick the most important event from their lists. Tell them to draw self-portraits that show their thoughts and feelings about the event.

Intermediate Instruct students to write topic sentences for each paragraph of their memoirs. Ask students to select one sentence to expand into a paragraph. Remind them that they must add details to the paragraph with additional sentences. Have them share paragraphs in pairs.

Advanced Have pairs of students exchange memoirs for peer review. Reviewers should check for plurals, past tense verbs, topic sentences, and supporting details. Have students use the comments to revise their writing.

From Reading to Writing

Write a Memoir

Write a three-paragraph memoir that describes an event from your past.

1. In the first paragraph, tell about an event and why it is interesting to your audience.
2. In the second paragraph, give details that make this event interesting.
3. In the third paragraph, tell your audience about your thoughts and feelings about the event.

My Memoir

1 Event and why it is important

2 Interesting details and facts

3 Your thoughts and feelings about the event

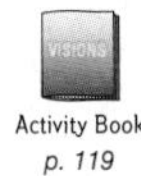

Activity Book p. 119

Across Content Areas

Read a Map

There are many earthquakes in a part of the world called the Ring of Fire. Look at the map of the Ring of Fire and answer the questions below.

1. The blue area in the middle of the map is an ocean. Which ocean is it?
2. Which continents do you see to the east?
3. Which continents do you see to the west?
4. Which continents does the Ring of Fire touch?

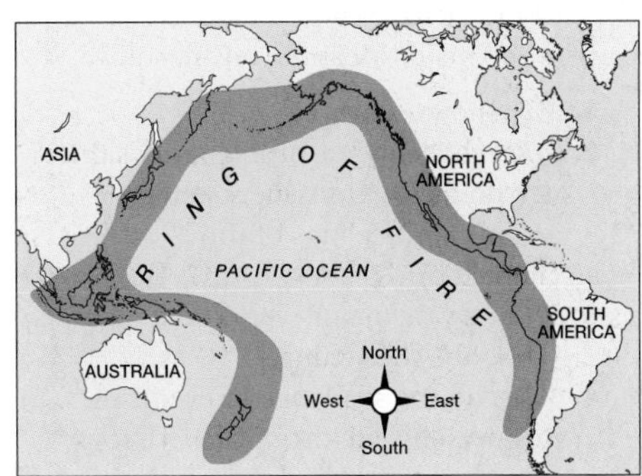

Activity Book p. 120

Reteach and Reassess

Text Structure Write *MEMOIR* vertically on the board. Work with students to make an acrostic of the features of a memoir. (me**M**ories; fe**E**lings; **M**emories; pers**O**nal pronouns; sett**I**ng; st**R**ucture)

Reading Strategy Ask students to write three facts about themselves. Have pairs exchange lists. Tell them to use the facts to draw conclusions about each other.

Elements of Literature Read six sentences from "Earthquake," three of which contain foreshadowing. Ask students to identify the sentences that foreshadow.

Reassess Create a chart with three rows labeled *Features, Conclusions,* and *Foreshadowing.* Have students complete the chart with examples from the selection.

From Reading to Writing

Write a Memoir

Teacher Resource Book: *Outline, p. 59*

1. **Use an outline** Have students suggest events for their memoirs. List ideas on the board. Model using an outline to organize ideas. Discuss the content of each of the paragraphs. Ask students to choose events and create outlines.
2. **Think-quickwrite-pair-share** Ask students to use their outline and write as much as they can. Have them share with a partner and add details about thoughts and feelings.
3. **Multi-level options** See MULTI-LEVEL OPTIONS on p. 214.

Across Content Areas: Social Studies

Read a Map

1. **Define and clarify** Explain meanings of the directions (north, south, east, west), *ocean, continent.* Direct students to the map on this page. Have them point out oceans and continents and the compass rose with the directions. Explain that the Ring of Fire is also a zone for volcanoes.
2. **Connect** Provide students with a world map or an atlas. Have students name countries that are located on the Ring of Fire.

Answers

1. Pacific Ocean
2. North America, South America
3. Australia, Asia
4. Asia, North America, South America

Have students write a checklist for writing a memoir. Students can use it after they complete their writing.

UNIT 3
Apply and Expand

Materials

Student Handbook
CNN Video: *Unit 3*
Teacher Resource Book: *Lesson Plan, p. 18; Teacher Resources, pp. 35–64; Video Script, pp. 165–166; Video Worksheet, p. 175; School-Home Connection, pp. 133–139*
Teacher Resource CD-ROM
Assessment Program: *Unit 3 Test, pp. 49–54; Mid-Book Exam, pp. 55–60; Teacher and Student Resources, pp. 115–144*
Assessment CD-ROM
Transparencies
The Heinle Newbury House Dictionary/CD-ROM
Heinle Reading Library
Web Site: www.heinle.visions.com

Listening and Speaking Workshop

Present a Biographical Narrative

Teacher Resource Book: *Sunshine Organizer, p. 40*

Use sequential order Review transition words and phrases to sequence events.

Step 1: Use a timeline to get organized.
Focus on the sequence of events. Then add supporting facts and details.

Step 2: Be specific and present facts.
Have students work in pairs to help each other present the major ideas.

UNIT 3 Apply and Expand

Listening and Speaking Workshop

Present a Biographical Narrative

> **Topic**
> Choose someone you read about or know about who showed courage. Focus on the sequence of events in the person's life and how the person found courage. Tell why you admire the person.

Step 1: Use a timeline to get organized.

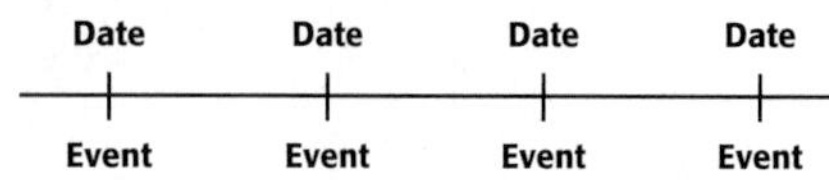

Step 2: Be specific and present facts.

Answer the following questions to present the major ideas of your narrative.

1. *Who* shows courage?
2. *What* challenge or problem does this person face? (Describe specific actions and feelings of the character.)
3. *Where* do the main events take place? (Describe the setting.)
4. *When* do the sequence of events in this person's life take place? (Use dates and times.)

Step 3: Use an attention-grabbing opening.

Use one of these suggestions for your opening:

1. Ask a question.
2. Say something funny.
3. Make a dramatic statement.
4. Refer to an authority and use quotations.

Step 4: Prepare some visuals to add interest.

1. Use a timeline on a poster, a picture from the Internet, or a drawing of your own to show information you found. Help your listeners interpret the visuals.
2. If possible, use a computer presentation to help you sequence the events.

Step 5: Practice your biographical narrative.

1. After you have one idea for an opening, put each group of additional ideas on a note card.
2. Practice with a partner.
3. Answer the questions on the Active Listening and Speaking Checklists.
4. Revise your report based on feedback.
5. Practice your talk to include stops or pauses to show visuals.

216 **Unit 3** Courage

MULTI-LEVEL OPTIONS *Listening and Speaking Workshop*

Newcomer Have students create illustrated timelines for the life of someone famous or someone they know. Suggest that students use original drawings or pictures from magazines to illustrate their timelines. Help students add dates and captions to their timelines.

Beginning Have students tell partners one or two autobiographical sentences, such as *I was born in Guatemala in 1988; I like to play soccer;* or *I have two dogs.* Then tell students to present biographies of their partners in small groups by retelling the information they learned.

Intermediate Instruct students to write several choices for opening statements. Have small groups evaluate one another's openings. Tell them to select and refine their opening statements based on their peers' comments. Remind students to be tactful and constructive.

Advanced Have students practice their speeches in pairs. Direct reviewers to check for the following: an attention-grabbing opening; details about who, what, when, and where; information that tells how the subject showed courage; an organized sequence of events.

Active Listening Checklist

1. I liked ____ because ____ .
2. I want to know more about ____ .
3. You stayed on the topic. Yes / No
4. I understood the major ideas of your narrative. Yes / No
5. Your nonverbal messages helped me to understand ____ .

Speaking Checklist

1. Did I speak too slowly, too quickly, or just right?
2. Did I speak loudly enough?
3. Was my voice too high, too low, or just right?
4. Did I use visuals to make the speech interesting?
5. Did I look at the audience?

Step 6: Present.

Use nonverbal messages such as gestures and body language. This will help listeners understand your presentation. Speak slowly and clearly. Smile!

Viewing Workshop

Compare and Contrast Visual and Electronic Media with Written Stories

Compare Points of View

View a video, a television, or an Internet biography about someone you read about in this unit.

1. What information did you learn about the subject of the biography? Where was the person born? What was the challenge? How was the person courageous?
2. Compare and contrast the video, television, or Internet version with the reading selection in this unit. Were the attitudes toward the person the same or different in the two presentations?
3. Evaluate which presentation gives you the most information about the subject of the biography. Explain your ideas.
4. Find out two new facts about the person.

Further Viewing

Watch the *Visions* CNN Video for Unit 3. Do the Video Worksheet.

CNN Video

Home Connection

Instruct students to ask family members to talk about unfamiliar relatives, such as great-grandparents or distant cousins. Have students take notes about their relatives. Remind students to record information that answers *Who*, *What*, *When*, and *Where* questions.

Learning Styles *Kinesthetic*

Have students review their biographies. Ask them to choose one event to silently act out for the class, using facial expressions, body language, and props. Have class members guess the event.

Step 3: Use an attention-grabbing opening.
Brainstorm a list of ideas and suggestions for possible openings.

Step 4: Prepare some visuals to add interest.
Help students exchange timelines with a partner and suggest visuals that will help listeners understand.

Step 5: Practice your biographical narrative.
Go over the procedure and checklists before students practice in pairs. Demonstrate effective gestures and body language.

Step 6: Present.
Have students invite friends or family to the presentations.

ASSESS

Have students write a sentence telling the most important thing they learned about preparing and presenting.

Portfolio

Students may choose to record or videotape their speeches to place in their portfolios.

Viewing Workshop

Compare and Contrast Visual and Electronic Media with Written Stories

Teacher Resource Book: *Venn Diagram, p. 35; Two-Column Chart, p. 44*

1. **Make observations** Pause occasionally for comments. List ideas on the board.
2. **Use graphic organizers** Use a two-column chart or Venn diagram to help students as they compare and contrast the video version and the reading selection.
3. **Compare and evaluate media** Have students use the diagrams to make comparisons.
4. **Take notes** Students can check their notes or view the video again to identify new information about the person.

Writer's Workshop

Response to Literature

Write a definition Have students create their own definitions based on what they have read. Ask students to share their definitions in pairs.

Step 1: Research.
Help prepare good interview or research questions. Have students read through their note cards and circle the most important ideas and details.

Step 2: Write a draft.
Explain and clarify the meanings of the items on the checklist. Model examples as needed. Help students prepare their list of sources.

Writer's Workshop

Response to Literature

Writing Prompt

Decide what *you* think courage means. Write a definition of courage in response to the selections that you have read and the material that you have viewed.

Step 1: Research.

1. Create a list of questions about courage.
2. Gather information from books that you have read or from TV shows and movies that you have viewed. Discuss with family and friends their experiences with courage. Write your ideas on note cards.
3. Evaluate your research to check if you found answers to your questions. Frame new questions you would like to research answers to.

What is courage?

What is courage?

Step 2: Write a draft.

1. Review your ideas and plan the order of your definition.
2. Use the Definition Checklist below to help you.

Definition Checklist

1. Include an introduction that states your definition of courage.
2. Write at least three main paragraphs that include a supporting idea about courage.
3. Give two or three details such as facts or examples to support the main idea in each paragraph.
4. End with a conclusion that summarizes your thoughts on courage.

3. Use superlative adjectives to make comparisons. For example, compare the courage of people you know about.
4. Write a list of sources (places where you gathered information). For example, write the titles of books, TV shows, and movies you used.
5. Use the correct format for citing your sources. See your Student Handbook.

MULTI-LEVEL OPTIONS *Writer's Workshop*

Newcomer Have students draw a picture of a real person or fictional character who they think showed courage. Assist students in labeling their pictures with adjectives and captions. Have students share their drawings in small groups.

Beginning Provide this cloze sentence for students: *I think ____ is brave because ____.* Have students share their completed sentences with partners.

Intermediate Have students write a first draft. Remind them that superlative adjectives are formed either by adding *-est* to the end of an adjective or by placing *most* before an adjective.

Advanced Have students "test" their definitions. Ask small groups to brainstorm a list of courageous real and fictional people. Then have students apply their definitions to each person to evaluate whether they qualify as courageous based on their definitions.

Step 3: Revise your work.

1. Use a resource such as the Editing Checklist in your Student Handbook to check your work.
2. Refer to reference sources you used for research to help you clarify ideas and revise text. Also ask your teacher to help you clarify and revise your work.
3. Reread your draft and ask yourself these questions:
   a. Is my definition of courage clear?
   b. Do my transitions lead readers from one paragraph to the next?
   c. Is my main point convincing?
4. Collaborate with a partner. Read each other's work. Note on a piece of paper any strong and weak points in your partner's draft. Give your partner ideas about how to revise and organize the definition.
5. Give the notes to your partner. Use the Peer Editing Checklist in your Student Handbook. Discuss the strong and weak points in each of your papers. Make any changes you feel are necessary.

Step 4: Edit and proofread.

1. Proofread your revised definition. Make sure you have used correct punctuation, spelling, and grammar.
2. Use the Editor's Checklist in your Student Handbook.
3. If possible, use a computer to write your paper. Use software such as an online dictionary or thesaurus to check your work.
4. Ask your teacher to help you edit your work for correct punctuation, spelling, and grammar. Use the spelling and grammar checks on your computer.

Step 5: Publish.

Make an anthology, or collection, of the class's work. Follow these steps:

1. Collect everyone's work. Write a table of contents listing each paper's title, author, and page number.
2. Title the collection *Visions of Courage.* Design an illustrated cover with your class drawings or photos that show courage.
3. Analyze your classmates' published work as models for writing. Review them for their strengths and weaknesses.
4. What strategies did you and your classmates use to write? How did you and your classmates express ideas?
5. Set goals as a writer based on your writing and the writing of your classmates.

The Heinle Newbury House Dictionary

Student Handbook

UNIT 3
Apply and Expand

Step 3: Revise your work.
Review the questions for students to use as they evaluate their own work and then participate in peer conferencing. Have students share their stories and give one another feedback and suggestions on their drafts.

Step 4: Edit and proofread.
Have students work on improving their definitions by adding and elaborating as needed. Remind students about the editing and proofreading points. Point out various resources for proofreading and editing, including the Editor's Checklist in the Student Handbook.

Step 5: Publish.
As a group, compile the definitions of *courage.* Allow time for students to read and enjoy the different ways of expressing ideas and supporting their statements.

Have students compile a collection of the class's writing. Guide students to create a cover with a visual and a title. Add the collection to the classroom library.

Portfolio

Students may choose to include their writing in their portfolios.

Community Connection

Have students search local newspaper articles for someone who has shown courage. Ask students to briefly report their findings, using evidence from the articles to support their choices.

Learning Styles *Interpersonal*

Ask: *Did you ever show courage? When? What did you do that was courageous or brave? Did your actions fit your definition of courage? How?* Have students discuss in small groups.

UNIT 3
Apply and Expand

Projects

Project 1: Give a Speech

1. **Choose a topic** Brainstorm a list of today's situations where people need courage. After students choose a topic, have them prepare questions for gathering information.
2. **Speak to communicate ideas** Help students prepare their speeches. Direct attention to tone, gestures, visuals, and word choice to add impact and clarity. Allow time for students to practice before presenting to the class.

Project 2: Design a Web Page or an Art Exhibit

Organize and synthesize information To provide ideas to students, direct them to visuals in this unit that illustrate courage, such as the unit opener art. Suggest different ways to arrange student pictures and quotes before deciding on the final form for their exhibit or presentation.

Portfolio 

Students may choose to include their projects in their portfolios.

Projects

These projects will help you develop your ideas about courage. Work alone, with a partner, or with a group of classmates. If you need help, ask a teacher, a parent, or your librarian.

Project 1: Give a Speech

What are some reasons why people today need to have courage? Choose a topic, such as saying "No" to smoking, and prepare a speech to your class about why people would need courage to face this situation. Write five questions about the topic and courage.

1. Gather information.
   a. Talk to the school librarian and five other adults. Ask each of them the five questions.
   b. Visit some Internet news sites. Read articles on the topic you have chosen.
2. Write a speech about what you learn. Make visuals to help your listeners understand your points. Refer to Chapter 4 and use George W. Bush's speech as a model.
3. Check your written speech for word choice and tone. Does your speech explain why we need courage?
4. Give your speech to the class. If possible, make an audio or a video recording of it so that you can share your speech with your family.

Project 2: Design a Web Page or an Art Exhibit

Think about what you have learned about courage in this unit. Use that information to make a Web page, an art exhibit, or a technology presentation.

1. Find pictures that show courage. Use the Internet or look in art books from the school library.
2. Gather speeches that people have made about courage. Look in books of collected speeches. Use tables of contents and headings to find speeches about courage.
3. Find short quotes about courage. Look in books or CD-ROMs that include quotes (such as *Bartlett's Familiar Quotations*). Use the keyword *courage* to search the index.
4. For a Web page or technology presentation, design the quotes you found in special type.
5. For an art exhibit, write the speech or quotation text on a poster board. Label each image and include where you found it. You may also record the text on audio. Play the audio as viewers look at the images.
6. Share your presentation with the class or other classes in your school.
7. Compare and contrast your work with the reading selections. How does your presentation show courage in a similar or different way to the selection?

MULTI-LEVEL OPTIONS *Projects*

Newcomer Have students create posters about courage. On one half, have students illustrate scary situations. On the other half, have them write names or show people who have shown courage. They can draw, use magazine clippings, or download images from the Internet.

Beginning Have students view a video of *Charlotte's Web.* Then *ask: Who showed courage? How did this character show his or her courage?* Tell students to draw a picture of an event in the movie where a character showed courage.

Intermediate Have small groups brainstorm situations that call for courage. Ask students to select and list the five best ideas. Tell students to use the list as a springboard for speech ideas.

Advanced Have students compile their projects into a class exhibit. Ask them to submit ideas for a name for the exhibit. Tell them to vote to select a name. Then have students create flyers that invite parents, friends, and members of the community to view their exhibit.

Further Reading

The books below tell how people have shown courage in their lives. Read one or more of them. In your Reading Log, record how courage was displayed in the books you read. Write your thoughts and feelings about what you read. Answer these questions:

1. How do the characters show courage?
2. Do the characters show similar or different types of courage?

The Diary of Anne Frank: The Definitive Edition
by Anne Frank, Bantam Books, Inc., 1997. Anne describes her life in hiding during World War II. This newly published edition includes 30 percent more material than the original.

Lance Armstrong
by Kimberly Garcia, Mitchell Lane Publishers, Inc., 2002. Being the four-time champion of the *Tour de France* is only one of Lance Armstrong's accomplishments. In this biography, Garcia describes Armstrong's battle against cancer.

Out of the Dust
by Karen Hesse, Scholastic Inc., 1999. Fifteen-year-old Billie Jo lives on a wheat farm in Oklahoma during the Great Depression. She struggles to rebuild her relationship with her father after an accident kills her mother. Billie Jo finds the courage to repair her life in this unique story told completely in free-verse poetry.

A Single Shard
by Linda Sue Park, Clarion Books, 2002. This book takes place in twelfth-century Korea. In a journey against great odds, Tree-Ear, an orphan boy, pursues his dream of becoming a potter. He learns how courage helps achieve a goal.

The Unknown Shore: The Lost History of England's Arctic Colony
by Robert Ruby, Henry Holt & Co., Inc., 2001. England first attempted to settle the New World on an island off the coast of the Canadian Arctic known as Meta Incognita ("Unknown Shore"). This book tells the story.

Charlotte's Web
by E. B. White, HarperTrophy, 1999. In this classic barnyard book, small but valiant Charlotte uses courage and her sharp wit to save Wilbur from being killed.

Miracle's Boys
by Jacqueline Woodson, Penguin Putnam, 2000. Tyree, Charlie, and Lafayette are three orphaned brothers raising themselves after their father drowns and their mother dies of diabetes.

Reading Log

Heinle Reading Library

UNIT 3
Apply and Expand

Further Reading

Teacher Resource Book: *Reading Log, p. 64*

Respond to literature Have students select a book and prepare a five-minute talk about the courage of the characters. Tell them to decide the main points of their talk and organize their information. Have them make an outline. Remind students to use an attention-grabbing introduction and to support their main idea with details. Instruct them to explain their personal reaction by telling how they feel, why they feel that way, and what they learned from the person's courage.

Assessment Program: *Unit 3 Test, pp. 49–54; Mid-Book Exam, pp. 55–60.*

Introduce the Unit

Unit Materials

Activity Book: *pp. 121–152*
Audio: *Unit 4*
Student Handbook
Student CD-ROM: *Unit 4*
CNN Video: *Unit 4*
Teacher Resource Book: *Lesson Plans, Teacher Resources, Reading Summaries, School-Home Connection, Video Script, Video Worksheet, Activity Book Answer Key*
Teacher Resource CD-ROM
Assessment Program: *Quizzes and Test, pp 61–74; Teacher and Student Resources, pp. 115–144*
Assessment CD-ROM
Transparencies
The Heinle Newbury House Dictionary/CD-ROM
More Grammar Practice workbook
Heinle Reading Library
Web Site: www.heinle.visions.com

Heinle Staff Development Handbook

Refer to the Heinle Staff Development Handbook for more teacher support.

Unit Theme: Discoveries

Define and discuss discoveries *Ask: What is a discovery? Who makes discoveries? Where? What types of things do they discover?* Record student suggestions on a cluster map.

Unit Preview: Table of Contents

1. **Use the table of contents to locate information** Read the chapter titles and authors of the selections. ***Ask:*** *Who is the author of the poem in Chapter 1? What page does Chapter 3 begin on?* Continue with other examples.
2. **Connect** *Ask: Which titles interest you?*

UNIT 4

Discoveries

CHAPTER 1 *page 224* — **The Library Card** — an excerpt from a novel by Jerry Spinelli

At the Library — a poem by Nikki Grimes

CHAPTER 2 *page 238* — **Discovering the Inca Ice Maiden** — a nonfiction narrative by Johan Reinhard

CHAPTER 3 *page 252* — **The Art of Swordsmanship** — a folktale by Rafe Martin

CHAPTER 4 *page 264* — **Mae Jemison, Space Scientist** — a biography by Gail Sakurai

222

UNIT OBJECTIVES

Reading

Compare and contrast as you read an excerpt from a novel and a poem • Use graphic sources of information as you read a nonfiction narrative • Use dialogue to understand character as you read a folktale • Find the main ideas and supporting details as you read a biography

Listening and Speaking

Take notes, organize, and summarize
- Describe personal accomplishments
- Participate in a dramatic read-aloud
- Discuss your goals

Louis Pasteur experimenting for the cure of hydrophobia in his laboratory, Adrien Emmanuel Marie, print. 1885.

View the Picture

1. What could the person in this picture be discovering?
2. What are some discoveries you have made?

In this unit, you will read a story, a poem, a nonfiction narrative, a tale, and a biography that center on people and their discoveries. You will share their excitement. You will learn about the features of these writing forms and how to write them yourself.

223

Grammar
Identify sentences with relative clauses • Identify *be* + adjective + infinitive • Use adverbs to show time • Use and punctuate dependent clauses with *although* and *when*

Writing
Write a story • Write a first-person nonfiction narrative • Write a folktale • Write a short biography

Content
Language Arts: Use the library • Social Studies: Understand the atmosphere and altitude • The Arts: Learn about art in everyday objects • Science: Understand gravity

UNIT 4
Introduce the Unit

View the Picture

1. **Art background** Louis Pasteur (1822–1895) was a French scientist who developed a process that stopped milk from spoiling and causing disease. The process was called pasteurization in his honor. Pasteur also developed vaccines to protect against deadly anthrax and rabies.
2. **Art interpretation** *Ask: Does this look like a modern laboratory? Can you name any of the equipment? How do the colors, shapes, and lines in this illustration influence its message and tell a story?*
   a. **Describe choice of style** Have students describe the style of the illustration. Ask them to explain how the realistic presentation of scientific equipment connects observers to the scientist's discovery.
   b. **Use personal experience** *Ask: Do you like to do science experiments?* Help students describe experiments they have done.
   c. **Speculate** Have students suggest how the scientist has been working and how he feels right now in the picture.
   d. **Connect to theme** *Say: The theme of this unit is* discoveries. *Pasteur is trying to discover a cure for hydrophobia* (rabies). *Do you think that he did eventually find a cure?* (In 1885, Pasteur did discover a vaccine for rabies.)

ASSESS

Teacher Resource Book: *Cluster Map, p. 38*

Have students draw pictures of themselves discovering something new. ***Say:*** *Try to use a part of the art on this page in your drawing, such as the realistic images and colors.* Display drawings on a cluster map or other graphic organizer on discoveries.

UNIT 4 • CHAPTER 1
Into the Reading

Chapter Materials

Activity Book: *pp. 121–128*
Audio: *Unit 4, Chapter 1*
Student Handbook
Student CD-ROM: *Unit 4, Chapter 1*
Teacher Resource Book: *Lesson Plan, Teacher Resources, Reading Summary, Activity Book Answer Key*
Teacher Resource CD-ROM
Assessment Program: *Quiz, pp. 61–62; Teacher and Student Resources, pp. 115–144*
Assessment CD-ROM
Transparencies
The Heinle Newbury House Dictionary/CD-ROM
Web Site: www.heinle.visions.com

Objectives

Preview *Say: These objectives are what we will learn in Chapter 1. Is there an objective you already know?*

Use Prior Knowledge

Explore Sources of Information

Use a roundtable Have students work in groups. Give each group a piece of paper titled: *Library, Internet,* or *Expert.* Tell students to write information from their sources on the group's list. Have groups share their responses with the class.

Answer

3. *Example:* Yes. I've been there. Our class went to find books about trees.

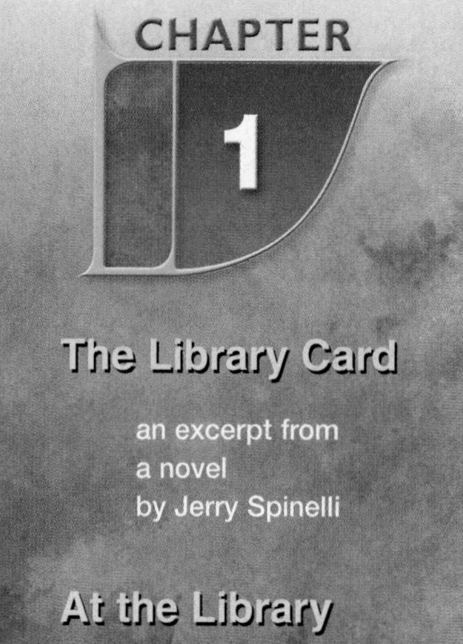

The Library Card

an excerpt from
a novel
by Jerry Spinelli

At the Library

a poem
by Nikki Grimes

Into the Reading

Objectives

Reading Compare and contrast as you read an excerpt from a novel and a poem.

Listening and Speaking Take notes, organize, and summarize.

Grammar Identify sentences with relative clauses.

Writing Write a story.

Content Language Arts: Use the library.

Use Prior Knowledge

Explore Sources of Information

Where do you go when you need answers to questions? How do you know which source to use for certain questions?

1. Make a chart like the one shown. List the kinds of information you can find from each source.
2. Talk as a group about what information you can find in each of these sources.
3. Is there a library in your school or community? Have you been there? Tell your class about it.

Library	
Internet	
Teacher/Expert	

MULTI-LEVEL OPTIONS *Build Vocabulary*

Newcomer Write on the board: *The enormous house had many rooms.* Point to and ***say:*** *enormous.* Point to and ***say:*** *many rooms.* ***Say:*** Enormous *means "very big."* Repeat with *The miniature book fit in my pocket.* (*Miniature* means "very small.")

Beginning Have students work in groups. Ask groups to review earlier selections in the book. Have each group find an example of a word that is defined in context with repetition. Ask each group to write a definition for the word and share the definition with the other groups.

Intermediate Write on the board: *bug/cicada/locust.* Have students work in pairs to find another synonym for these words. (insect) Tell pairs to write a new sentence using repetition to explain meaning. Do the same with *boggled/tingly/goosebumps* and *spinning/woozy.* Have students share sentences with another pair.

Advanced On the board, write: *insect, boggled,* and *faint.* Ask students to look up each word in a dictionary. Instruct students to write a sentence using repetition for each word. Have students add the words and definitions to their Personal Dictionaries.

Build Background

Public Libraries

Hundreds of years ago, books were rare and expensive. Only wealthy people owned books and had libraries. Today, almost every town or city in the United States has at least one public library. If you live in the town, you can get a library card. With a library card, you can borrow books, videos, and other materials for free.

A Library Card

Content Connection

Librarians are people who work in libraries. They help you find the book or information that you are looking for.

Build Vocabulary

Use Repetition to Find Meaning

Writers often say something and then mention it again using different words. You can use this repetition to learn words.

1. Copy the following sentences in your Personal Dictionary.
   a. The bug was called cicada, also seventeen-year locust.
   b. The whole idea made him tingly. He looked at his arm. He had goosebumps.
   c. The ceiling was spinning, he was woozy.
2. Circle the part of the sentence that repeats the meaning of the underlined word.
3. Look up any words that you do not know in a dictionary. Write the words and their definitions in your Personal Dictionary.

Personal Dictionary

The Heinle Newbury House Dictionary

Activity Book p. 121

Student CD-ROM

Content Connection
Science

Build Vocabulary Have students work in small groups. Tell each group to use the Internet or other reference aids to research the cicada. Ask groups to prepare short reports on the insect. Tell them to include where it lives, what it looks like, what it eats, and other important characteristics and behaviors. Ask groups to share their reports with the class.

Learning Styles
Visual

Build Background Ask small groups of students to visit the school library or local library. Have them create maps of the library. Ask them to use a key to show the different areas of the library and where different types of books are kept.

Build Background

Public Libraries

1. **Relate to personal experiences** Bring in a library card. Ask students to share experiences they have had at a library or getting a library card.
2. **Content Connection** Ask if students have ever asked a librarian for help. Have them share their experiences with the class. Familiarize students with the school librarian. Have the school librarian meet with the class.

Build Vocabulary

Use Repetition to Find Meaning

Teacher Resource Book: *Personal Dictionary, p. 63*

1. **Use context clues** Tell students that writers often explain difficult words with examples or simpler words. Write on the board: *Maria was boggled when she saw the huge bug. It surprised and frightened her.* Have students identify other words that help explain *boggled.* (surprised, frightened) ***Ask:*** *Where can I check if I'm not sure?* (ask the teacher, look in a dictionary)
2. **Reading selection vocabulary** You may want to introduce the glossed words in the reading selections before students begin reading. Key words: *vanish, waistband, ambush, pirate, paradise, wise.* Instruct students to write the words with correct spelling and their definitions in their Personal Dictionaries. Have them pronounce each word and divide it into syllables.
3. **Multi-level options** See MULTI-LEVEL OPTIONS on p. 224.

Answers

1. **a.** locust; **b.** goosebumps; **c.** spinning

ASSESS

Have students write three sentences using the new words.

Text Structure

Fiction

Define and explain features Copy the feature chart for "Fiction" on the board. Have students give examples of character, plot, and sequence of events from fictional selections they have read in previous chapters.

Reading Strategy

Compare and Contrast

Teacher Resource Book: *Venn Diagram, p. 35; Reading Log, p. 64*

1. **Use a Venn diagram** Create a Venn diagram. Explain *compare.* Ask students to compare, or identify things that are the same about the two libraries. Then ask them to *contrast,* or identify differences. Record them on the diagram.
2. **Multi-level options** See MULTI-LEVEL OPTIONS below.

ASSESS

Ask for "student definitions" of: *character, plot, sequence of events.*

Text Structure

Fiction and Poem

"The Library Card" is a work of **fiction.** It tells a made-up story about made-up people.

Look for these elements of fiction as you read "The Library Card."

Fiction	
Characters	the people in the story
Plot	the events that happen in the story
Sequence of Events	the order of the events; there is a beginning, a middle, and an end

"At the Library" is a **poem.**

Poem	
Rhyme	the last words of some lines have the same ending sound
Vivid Language	expressive nouns, verbs, and adjectives help the reader form images
Repetition	sentence structures are repeated

Look at these elements of a poem as you read "At the Library."

Student CD-ROM

Reading Strategy

Compare and Contrast

To **compare** is to see how two or more things are the same. To **contrast** is to see how they are different. For example, think about a public library and a school library.

Compare: Both libraries have books.
Contrast: The public library is for everyone. The school library is only for the students at the school.

1. As you read "The Library Card," look for things to compare and contrast in the selection. Look at the descriptions of different animals and insects that the main character reads about. How are they the same or different?
2. As you read "At the Library," look for things to compare and contrast with "The Library Card." For example, "Who is the main character? How does the character feel about books?"
3. Write your ideas in your Reading Log.

Reading Log

Student CD-ROM

MULTI-LEVEL OPTIONS *Reading Strategy*

Newcomer Display a dictionary and a paperback novel. Hold up both and ***say:*** *books.* Open each book and ***say:*** *words.* Tap the dictionary and ***say:*** *hard.* Bend the novel and ***say:*** *soft.* Help pairs of students express their similarities and differences. (hair color, height, gender, etc.)

Beginning ***Say:*** *When you compare, you see how things are alike. When you contrast, you see how things are different.* Hold up a pencil and pen. ***Ask:*** *How are these alike?* (Both are for writing.) *How are they different?* (color; ink vs. graphite; erasable vs. non-erasable; etc.)

Intermediate Ask pairs of students to choose two objects in their book bags or from their desks. Have pairs discuss the similarities and differences between the two objects. Then instruct pairs to write sentences that compare and contrast the two objects. Offer these starters: *Both are ______. One is ______, but the other is ______.*

Advanced Have students review two earlier selections in the book. Ask students to write a paragraph that compares and contrasts the two selections. Suggest that students compare and contrast genre, topic, writing style, point of view, and text structure.

THE LIBRARY CARD

an excerpt from a novel
by Jerry Spinelli

AT THE LIBRARY

a poem
by Nikki Grimes

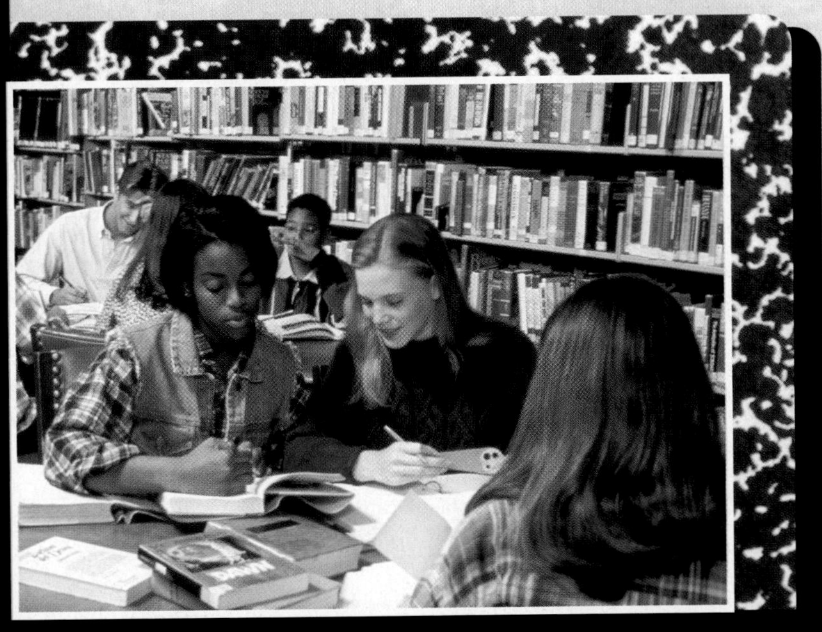

227

Reading Selection Materials

Audio: *Unit 4, Chapter 1*
Teacher Resource Book: *Reading Summary, pp. 95–96*

Preview the Selections

1. **Speculate** Tell students that the picture relates to both the novel excerpt and the poem that they will read. ***Ask:*** *What is happening in this picture? What inference can you make about the selections from this picture?*
2. **Connect** Remind students that the unit theme is *discoveries.* Ask them how the library relates to discoveries. Point out that in some discoveries, people find something that no one has ever seen or realized before. Other discoveries are something new that a person learns for himself or herself. Have students guess if the discoveries in this chapter are going to be new for everyone or new for an individual person.

Community Connection

Have students create a poster about community libraries. Ask students to use the telephone book or other resources to find local libraries. Tell them to list the libraries' names, addresses, and telephone numbers. Also have students include the hours of operation for each library. Hang the poster in the classroom or around the school for student reference.

Learning Styles *Intrapersonal*

Remind students that, whereas some discoveries may seem more significant than others, all discoveries are important. Tell students that the simple act of learning something new is as valuable a discovery as finding a new planet. ***Ask:*** *What important discovery have you made recently? If you could make any discovery, what would it be? Why?* Have students write their answers in their Reading Logs.

Teacher Resource Book: *Reading Log, p. 64*

Reading Selection

Read the Selection

1. **Use text features** Point out the prologue and explain its purpose. Direct students to the numbered paragraphs in the reading selection. Remind students to use the illustration to help them understand.
2. **Teacher read aloud** Read the selection aloud. Pause to check understanding. Ask students to identify character, plot, and sequence of events.
3. **Compare and contrast** *Ask: What did the library card look like?* (It was blue and blank.) *What did Mongoose remember seeing on the card before?* (Library Card)

Sample Answer to Guide Question

It's different because he remembers it saying *Library Card.*

See Teacher Edition pp. 434–435 for a list of English-Spanish cognates in the reading selection.

Audio

The Library Card

an excerpt from a novel by Jerry Spinelli

Prologue

In this excerpt you will read about a boy named Mongoose. He is a street-smart teenager who lives in New York City. One day he finds the shell of a bug called a locust. He also finds a mysterious blue library card. Mongoose goes to the library that same day to find out more about the strange insect.

Compare and Contrast

How is the card in the boy's hand the same as or different from the way he remembers it being?

1 He had passed the library so many times in his life, hundreds, but he had never gone inside. He was not even sure it was for kids.

2 He pulled the blue card from his pocket. He had put it there after picking it up from the floor that morning. For the first time he took a good look at it. One side was blank. The other side was . . . blank too! He kept turning it over and over. He could have sworn it said LIBRARY CARD when he had looked at it on the roof.

3 It was just a blue, blank scrap.

4 And yet still, somehow, he knew it was a library card.

5 Problem was, he wasn't sure how it worked. He thought maybe it was like a ticket, giving the holder **admittance,** as to a basketball game. Finding no ticket-taker at the door, he entered, walked up three steps, turned a corner, and found himself facing a counter with a lady behind it.

6 When the lady looked up and saw him coming, she smiled as if she knew him. Was he supposed to know her? He walked up to the counter and showed her the card. He felt silly showing a blank card. "You collecting tickets?" he said.

admittance the right to enter

MULTI-LEVEL OPTIONS *Read the Selection*

Newcomer Play the audio. Read the selection again. *Ask: Was the card blue?* (yes) *Was there writing on the card?* (no) *Did Mongoose take the book home?* (yes) *Did he read the book?* (yes) *Was the bug called a cicada?* (yes)

Beginning Read the Reading Summary aloud. Then *ask: What color was the card?* (blue) *What was written on the card?* (nothing) *When did he pick up the card from the floor?* (that morning) *Who was behind the counter?* (a lady) *Where did she put the card?* (in his pocket)

Intermediate Have students do a paired reading. *Ask: How did Mongoose think the card worked?* (like a ticket) *What did the lady do when she saw Mongoose?* (She smiled at him.) *How did Mongoose feel when he showed her the card?* (silly)

Advanced Have students read independently. Then *ask: What was the lady's job?* (librarian) *Why did Mongoose feel silly when he showed the lady the blue card?* (He didn't know what it was for.) *What did he learn about the bug?* (It was a seventeen-year locust, it buries itself in the ground for seventeen years, it sheds its skin.) *How did Mongoose feel about what he learned?* (He was boggled.)

Compare and Contrast

How is using a library card the same as or different from using a ticket to get into a basketball game?

7 She took the card. She looked at it, then into his eyes. The silly feeling **vanished.** "No," she said, "this is not to let you in. It's to let a book out." She reached across the counter and slid the card into his coat pocket. "Now, how may I help you?"

8 Mongoose told the lady about the big bug.* She nodded and went away for a minute. She returned with a book.

9 "You'll find what you need in here," she said. She handed him the book. She smiled. "Good reading."

10 As he left the library, he stuck the book under his coat and in his **waistband.** He sprinted home.

11 Only behind the closed door of his room did he take out the book. It was called the *I Wonder.* He found what he wanted on page twenty-three. The bug was called cicada, also seventeen-year locust. Mongoose read on. He learned that this cicada bug comes down from the tree as a baby worm and buries itself in the ground for seventeen years. And when it comes out—**presto!** It's a big bug that sheds its skin—eyes and all—and that's what Mongoose had found.

12 Amazing.

13 Imagine being in the dark—underground—for seventeen *years.*

14 And when you come out you're different than when you went in.

* The shell of a strange insect Mongoose found that day.

vanished disappeared

waistband the part of a skirt or pair of pants that fits around the waist

presto quickly, suddenly

Read the Selection

1. **Use the illustration** Ask students to describe the characters. Have students suggest what the librarian and the boy are talking about.
2. **Use text features** Direct students to the asterisk in paragraph 8. Explain its use and have students find the information to which it refers.
3. **Paired reading** After students listen to the audio or to you read the selection, have students reread it with partners.
4. **Summarize** Ask questions to help students summarize the events. Students can act out the story.
5. **Multi-level options** See MULTI-LEVEL OPTIONS on p. 228.

Sample Answer to Guide Question

Both a library card and a ticket allow a person to do something. A library card lets a person take something out. A ticket lets a person in to watch a game.

A Capitalization

Direct quotations

Tell students that, in a piece of writing, what the people or characters say is called *dialogue.* Remind students that dialogue is often shown by enclosing words in quotation marks. Tell students that when dialogue is shown this way, it is called a *direct quotation.* Point out that the first word of a direct quotation is always capitalized. Direct students to paragraph 1 on p. 229. ***Ask:*** *Why is the word* you *capitalized?* (It is the first word of a direct quotation.)

Apply Have students find and copy three more examples of direct quotations in paragraphs 7 and 9. Ask students to circle the first word in each quotation and the quotation marks. Then have students underline the initial capitalization.

UNIT 4 • CHAPTER 1
Reading Selection

Read the Selection

1. **Analyze character** *Ask: What is the boy discovering?* (what a cicada is, how to use a library card, how to use books) *How do you think he feels?* (surprised, interested, amazed, excited) *Why do you think so?* (He sounds excited about what he learned.)
2. **Paired reading** Read the selection aloud. *Ask: Why does the boy feel strange?* (He's learning so much.) *Have you ever felt that way?* Have students reread the selection with partners.

Sample Answer to Guide Question
In the beginning, he was unsure about what to do. Now, he's amazed by the many new things he found in the book.

15 And then you crawl out of your own skin!

16 The whole idea **boggled** him, made him tingly. He looked at his arm. He had goosebumps.

17 The chair he sat in no longer felt safe. He moved to the floor, his back against the wall. He started paging back to the start of the book—he knew books should be read from beginning to end—but he kept getting **ambushed.** Pictures and words and numbers drew his eyeballs to them like flies to flypaper.

18 He read about a bird that stays in the air for up to four years.

19 And a bird, called the tickbird, that **hitches** a ride on the back of a rhino.

20 And an insect—none other than the common old cockroach—that can walk around for two weeks with its head cut off.

21 And a fish that climbs trees.

22 And another bird that fights its enemies by vomiting on them.

Compare and Contrast

How are Mongoose's feelings different from his feelings at the beginning of the story?

---

boggled amazed, confused

ambushed attacked from a hidden position; in the reading *ambushed* is used to mean *distracted*

hitches hitchhikes, or asks for a ride

MULTI-LEVEL OPTIONS *Read the Selection*

Newcomer *Ask: Does Mongoose get goosebumps?* (yes) *Does he read about a bird that rides on a rhino?* (yes) *Does Mongoose eat dinner?* (no)

Beginning *Ask: Where does Mongoose move?* (to the floor) *Which insect can live with its head cut off?* (cockroach) *Which animal can turn on a lightbulb?* (electric eel) *What was Mongoose holding when his mother came into his room?* (the book)

Intermediate *Ask: Why did Mongoose get goosebumps?* (He's amazed by what he's reading.) *What did the book say about the mole rat?* (It's the world's ugliest animal.) *Why did Mongoose miss dinner?* (He was so interested in the book, he lost track of time)

Advanced *Ask: Why did Mongoose have trouble starting at the beginning of the book?* (Everything he saw interested him.) *Did Mongoose read often?* (no) *How do you know?* (It was a rare sight, according to his mother.)

23 And an eel that's electric, that can turn on a lightbulb.

24 And the mole rat. The book called it the world's ugliest animal, and it was right. He had to spend an hour on the picture of the mole rat alone.

25 And a worm that can stretch itself up to ninety feet.

26 Mongoose slid full-body to the floor. The ceiling was spinning, he was woozy.

27 His mother came in. She frowned down at him. "How long have you been in here?"

28 "Don't know," said Mongoose truthfully.

29 "You know you missed dinner four hours ago? You know it's nine o'clock?"

30 "You know there's a fish that climbs trees?"

31 Mrs. Hill looked down at her son, on his back on the floor, eyes closed, a look on his face she could not recall ever seeing before. And a book in his hand. About tree-climbing fish she knew nothing, but she did know that if there were such a thing, it surely was not as rare as the sight of her youngest son holding a book. And missing a meal.

Compare and Contrast

How are Mrs. Hill's feelings about Mongoose the same as or different from her feelings about him before she came into the room?

About the Author — Jerry Spinelli (born 1941)

Jerry Spinelli has been writing since he was a teenager. He has written many novels that use his own experiences as a child growing up. Spinelli's books often look at the difficult choices young adults have to make. Spinelli says, "Don't tell my English teachers, but not much planning goes into my novels. . . . There's no outline telling me how to get from here to there, because I have found that there is no way to know what is inside the story until I am in there myself."

➤ What strategies does the author use to compose his novels?

Spelling

Long vowel sounds

Tell students that adding the letter *e* to words that end in a consonant, a vowel, and a consonant makes the vowel sound long. Review the long /a/, /i/, and /o/ sounds. Write on the board and ***say:*** *rat, win,* and *hop.* Add *e* to each word, then say the new words. As you say each word, underline the vowel and the silent *e.* Ask students to look at paragraph 19. Write *rid* on the board. ***Ask:*** *How do you say this word?* Then add *e* to make *ride.* ***Ask:*** *How do you say this word? Why does this word have the long /i/ sound?*

Apply On the board, write: *pin, pine, hat, hate, lob, lobe, Sam, same, Tim, time, cod, code.* Have students copy the words. Ask pairs to say the words to each other and circle the words with long vowel sounds.

Read the Selection

1. **Shared reading** Continue the reading of the story as students follow along. Ask students to join in for direct quotations. ***Ask:*** *Why is his mother surprised?* (He missed dinner and is looking at a book.) *Do you think the boy read many books before?* (no) *Why or why not?* (His mother is so surprised.)
2. **Summarize** Ask questions to help students summarize and act out the events of the story.
3. **Multi-level options** See MULTI-LEVEL OPTIONS on p. 230.

Sample Answer to Guide Question

Before she came into the room, she was upset that Mongoose had missed dinner. After she learned he missed dinner because he was reading, she was surprised and pleased.

About the Author

1. **Explain author background** Read the author biography to students. Explain that Jerry Spinelli has won many awards, such as the Newbury Award and the Boston Globe-Horn Book Award. Some of his popular books are *Maniac Magee, Wringer,* and *Space Station Seventh Grade.*
2. **Interpret facts** ***Ask:*** *What kind of experiences do you think Jerry Spinelli had at the library when he was young?* (I think he really liked to read books and learn new things.) ***Ask:*** *Do you think his books are serious or funny? Why?* (Funny, because of the titles)

Answer

Sample answer: The author does not plan. He lets the story develop as he writes.

Read the Selection

1. **Use text features** Have students identify features of the poem. (stanzas, rhyming words) Then ask students to find the meanings of the glossed words.
2. **Choral reading** Read the poem to the students. Have different groups do choral readings of different lines of the stanza. *Ask: What does the writer see as she reads?* (seas, pirates, talking birds, children flying, and trees walking)
3. **Identify figurative language** *Ask: Can the writer really go into the book?* (no) *Can children fly or trees walk?* (no) *What do you think it means?* (She can pretend she's in different places as she reads.)

Sample Answer to Guide Question
The speaker read about things that really can't happen. Mongoose read about things that were real.

See Teacher Edition pp. 434–435 for a list of English-Spanish cognates in the reading selection.

Audio

At the Library

a poem by Nikki Grimes

Compare and Contrast
How are the speaker's reading experiences similar to or different from Mongoose's in "The Library Card"?

I flip the pages of a book and slip inside,
where **crystal** seas await and **pirates** hide.
I find a **paradise** where birds can talk,
where children fly and trees prefer to walk.
Sometimes I end up on a city street.
I recognize the brownskin girl I meet.
She's skinny, but she's strong, and brave, and **wise.**
I smile because I see *me* in her eyes.

crystal clear and sparkling
pirates people who steal ships and planes and the cargo they carry
paradise a perfect place where everything is just the way you want it to be
wise having good judgment

MULTI-LEVEL OPTIONS *Read the Selection*

Newcomer *Ask: Is this a poem about books?* (yes) *Are there pirates in the book?* (yes) *Can the children in the book fly?* (yes) *Is the skinny girl afraid?* (no)

Beginning *Ask: What is this poem about?* (books) *Where do the birds talk?* (paradise) *What can the trees do in paradise?* (walk) *Where does she see the skinny girl?* (on a city street)

Intermediate *Ask: What kind of books does the girl like to read?* (fiction) *How do you know?* (She talks about books where birds talk, children fly, and trees walk.) *Why does she smile at the skinny girl?* (because she sees herself in her eyes)

Advanced *Ask: What does she mean when she says "I see* me *in her eyes?"* (The character reminds her of herself.) *Would "Imagination" be a good title for this poem? Explain.*

About the Author — Nikki Grimes (born 1950)

Nikki Grimes moved around a lot as a child. Her family faced difficult times. During this challenging period, she always discovered a friend in books. But Grimes felt unhappy that very few books contained girls like herself—African-American girls from families with problems. She decided to write some herself. Grimes said, "'When I grow up,' I thought, 'I'll write books about children who look and feel like me.'"

➤ Do you think that Nikki Grimes is the girl in the poem? What challenges did Nikki Grimes face to become a writer?

Punctuation

Italics for emphasis

Explain italic print to students. Tell students that when they read words in italics, they should say those words with emphasis. Read the second stanza of the poem aloud, placing emphasis on the word *me.* Then read the stanza again, without emphasis on *me.* ***Ask:*** *How was that different?* Direct students to the last line of the poem. ***Ask:*** *Why is the word* me *written in italic print?*

Evaluate Your Reading Strategy

Compare and Contrast ***Say:*** *You have practiced an important reading strategy. Now you can decide how well you have done. Does this statement describe how you read?*

> I make comparisons and contrasts as I read. Making comparisons and contrasts helps me understand and evaluate information that I read.

Read the Selection

Teacher Resource Book: *Two-Column Chart, p. 44*

1. **Choral reading** Play the audio. Then have students reread the poem chorally.
2. **Summarize** Ask questions to help students summarize the poem. *Who is the speaker?* (a girl) *What does she look like?* (She has brown skin.) *Where does she live?* (in a city) *Why does she smile when she sees the brownskin girl?* (It's a girl who reminds the speaker of herself.)
3. **Compare and contrast** *Ask: How is the speaker's city different from the world she read about?* List ideas on a two-column chart.
4. **Multi-level options** See MULTI-LEVEL OPTIONS on p. 232.

About the Author

1. **Explain author background** Nikki Grimes has written many award-winning books about growing up in an urban environment. Her writing includes poetry, fiction, and biographies.
2. **Interpret the facts** *Ask: Why do you think Nikki Grimes writes about girls like herself? What kind of people do you like to read about?*

Across Selections

Teacher Resource Book: *Venn Diagram, p. 35*

Use a Venn diagram Discuss the ways the two readings in this chapter are alike and different. For example, both of the selections tell about a young person reading a book, but one is reading about real facts and the other is reading fiction. Have students record their ideas on a Venn diagram.

UNIT 4 • CHAPTER 1
Beyond the Reading

Reading Comprehension

Question-Answer Relationships

Sample Answers

1. No, Mongoose has never been inside a library before.
2. The librarian smiles at him and asks how she can help him.
3. He checks out a book about science facts called *I Wonder.*
4. Mongoose wants to find out the name of a bug.
5. Mongoose never had his own library card and never went to the library before, so he doesn't know how it works.
6. Both of the reading selections are about books that a boy and a girl read from the library. The boy reads about a book with real facts. The girl reads a book about fantasy and imaginary things.
7. Mongoose felt that the librarian was friendly and would help him.
8. Mongoose realizes that there are so many interesting things to learn from books that he is dizzy from all the thinking he is doing.
9. The speaker knows that there are other people like herself.
10. Most students will say that they also have had similar situations.

Build Reading Fluency

Reading Chunks of Words Silently

Assessment Program: *Reading Fluency Chart, p. 116*

When students have completed the reading fluency activity, record their progress in the Reading Fluency Chart.

Beyond the Reading

Reading Comprehension

Question-Answer Relationships (QAR)

"Right There" Questions

1. **Recall Facts** Has Mongoose ever been inside the library before?
2. **Recall Facts** What does the librarian do?
3. **Recall Facts** What kind of book does Mongoose check out?

"Think and Search" Questions

4. **Make Inferences** What information does Mongoose most want to get from the library book?
5. **Connect** Why does Mongoose not understand how a library card works?
6. **Compare and Contrast** In what ways are the two reading selections in this chapter the same and different?

"Author and You" Questions

7. **Make Inferences** Why does Mongoose's silly feeling vanish when the librarian looks into his eyes?
8. **Understand Figurative Language** Why does Mongoose feel "ambushed" by the information in the book?
9. **Evaluate** In "At the Library," why do you think the speaker smiles about seeing a young girl who seems like her?

"On Your Own" Question

10. **Compare Your Experiences** Mongoose did not know how to behave in a library. Have you ever been in a similar situation? Describe it.

Activity Book *p. 122*

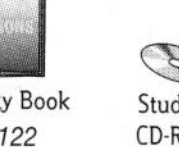
Student CD-ROM

Build Reading Fluency

Reading Chunks of Words Silently

Reading silently is good practice. It helps you to learn to read faster.

1. Listen to the audio recording of paragraphs 1–2 of "The Library Card."
2. Listen to the chunks of words.
3. Silently reread paragraphs 1–2 two times.
4. Your teacher or a partner will time your second reading.
5. Raise your hand when you are finished.

234 **Unit 4** Discoveries

MULTI-LEVEL OPTIONS *Elements of Literature*

Newcomer Write on the board: *Sam ate a sandwich, a salad, a bowl of soup, a baked potato, and three apples for lunch.* Remind students that a comma is often used in place of *and.* Rewrite the sentence: *Sam ate a sandwich and a salad and a bowl of soup and a baked potato and three apples for lunch.* Read the sentence aloud as students join in for *and.* **Say:** *This style makes Sam's lunch seem very big.*

Beginning Write on the board: *Sam ate a sandwich, a salad, a bowl of soup, a baked potato, and three apples for lunch.* **Ask:** *What word can replace a comma?* (and) Rewrite the sentence: *Sam ate a sandwich and a salad and a bowl of soup and a baked potato and three apples for lunch.* Have students read the sentence aloud. Tell them to place emphasis on *and.* **Say:** *This style makes Sam's lunch seem very big.*

Intermediate Ask pairs of students to work together. Have pairs think about interesting things they have learned from books. Ask students to create a list of four or five items. Then ask students to write sentences that imitate the style of paragraphs 19–25. Remind students to begin sentences with *And.*

Advanced Ask students to write a simple narrative paragraph about something they did recently. Then ask them to revise the narrative to use a style that expresses an emotion. Have pairs exchange paragraphs and try to guess the emotion their partners wanted to express.

Listen, Speak, Interact 

Take Notes, Organize, and Summarize

Both selections in this chapter are about the joy of reading.

1. Choose something that you really enjoyed reading. Tell your partner about it. What was it about? Why did you like it?
2. As your partner speaks, listen carefully to gain information. Take notes.
3. Organize your notes in outline form.
4. Write a summary of your partner's talk.

Outline
Book: "Strange Animals" I. What it was about: A. Frogs B. Worms that can stretch II. Why she liked it: A. She likes science. B. It had great pictures. C. She learned a lot.

Elements of Literature

Recognize a Writing Style

Writers use **style** (the way they use language) to express themselves.

1. Look at paragraphs 19–25 of "The Library Card." Notice that the writer begins several sentences with the word *and.* Each *and* that the writer uses suggests "And there's more!" This lets us know that Mongoose feels amazed and excited.
2. Skim the reading (read quickly) to find another place in the selection where the author does the same thing.
3. With a partner, read paragraphs 19–25. Use an excited tone of voice to match the writer's style.
4. Make a section in your Reading Log called "Uses of style to show emotion." Write some of the *and* sentences from paragraphs 19–25 in your log. As you discover other similar uses of style write them in this section of your Reading Log.

Reading Log

Activity Book *p. 123*

Student CD-ROM

Content Connection *The Arts*

Show a documentary or a theatrical movie in class or have students view a school or community play. Ask students to take notes on the production as they view it. Tell them to use the outline form on this page. Then have students use their notes to write a brief summary of what they viewed.

Learning Styles *Natural*

Ask students to spend 15–30 minutes viewing an outdoor scene, either outside or through a window. Have students take notes as they observe. Tell them to include information on everything that they see, hear, feel, smell, and think. Ask students to organize their notes in outline form. Have them use their outlines to write a descriptive paragraph.

Beyond the Reading

Listen, Speak, Interact

Take Notes, Organize, and Summarize

1. **Make an outline** Talk about something you enjoyed reading. Demonstrate making an outline to include the name of the reading, what it was about, and why you liked it. Direct attention to the main points of the outline and the supporting facts or details. Have students create outlines for books or stories they enjoyed.
2. **Newcomers** Use questions to help students identify their favorite readings. Write their answers and the reasons they liked them. Have students use these to create their own simple outlines.

Elements of Literature

Recognize a Writing Style

Teacher Resource Book: *Reading Log, p. 64*

1. **Explain writing style** Point out words in the selection and have students guess if the author's style is casual or formal, serious or entertaining, adult-like or child-like. Model reading with pauses and stress appropriate for the style.
2. **Personal experience** Have students share examples of times when people were excited about what they were talking about.
3. **Multi-level options** See MULTI-LEVEL OPTIONS on p. 234.

Answers

2. Paragraph 11: And when it . . .
Paragraph 14: And when you come out . . .
Paragraph 15: And then you crawl . . .

ASSESS

Have students write a summary statement about Mongoose's first trip to the library.

Word Study

Understand Historical Influences on English Words

Teacher Resource Book: *Personal Dictionary, p. 63*

1. **Discuss cognates** Have students share cognates in English and other languages, such as *computer/computadora.*
2. **Use a dictionary** Demonstrate finding etymologies of words in the dictionary.

Answers

3. *insectum, vomitus, implicare, autumnus*

Grammar Focus

Identify Sentences with Relative Clauses

Explain relative clauses Write the sample on the board. Point out the subjects and verbs in each clause.

Answers

2. He read about a <u>bird</u> that stays . . .
   And a <u>bird</u> . . . that hitches a ride . . .
   And an <u>insect</u> . . . that can walk . . .
   And a <u>fish</u> that climbs . . .
   And another <u>bird</u> that fights . . .
   And an <u>eel</u> that's electric . . . that can turn . . .

ASSESS

Write on the board: *I like books that* ______. Have students complete the relative clause.

Word Study

Understand Historical Influences on English Words

English often has two words for the same idea. One word is often scientific or formal and is often from Latin. The other is usually informal and is from Old English.

1. Read each of these sentences from "The Library Card." Look at the underlined word. The word after the sentence means the same thing.
   a. Mongoose told the lady about the big <u>bug</u>. (insect)
   b. The bug was called <u>cicada</u>. (seventeen-year locust)
   c. And another bird that fights its enemies by <u>vomiting</u> on them. (throwing up)
2. Copy the chart in your Personal Dictionary.
3. Use the dictionary to locate the origin of the words in the first column. Find the Latin root for each word. Write it next to the English word.

From Latin	From Old English
insect	bug
vomit	throw up
employer	boss
autumn	fall (the season)

Personal Dictionary

The Heinle Newbury House Dictionary

Activity Book *p. 124*

Student CD-ROM

Grammar Focus

Identify Sentences with Relative Clauses

A **clause** is a group of words that has a subject and a verb. In a complex sentence, there is more than one clause. One of the clauses can be a **relative clause.**

A relative clause is introduced by a relative pronoun such as *that.* This kind of clause describes something in the main clause. Relative clauses are *not* complete sentences.

He read about a **bird** <u>that stays in the air for up to four years.</u>

1. Look in paragraphs 18–23 on pages 230–231 for relative clauses starting with *that.*
2. Identify the relative clause and tell which word it describes.
3. Write your own sentence containing a relative clause beginning with *that.*

Activity Book *pp. 125–126*

Student Handbook

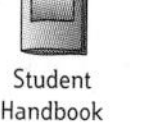
Student CD-ROM

236 **Unit 4** Discoveries

MULTI-LEVEL OPTIONS *From Reading to Writing*

Newcomer Have students draw self-portraits that show how they feel about reading. Around the portraits, students can draw or glue pictures of things that can be read, such as books, magazines, signs, menus, newspapers, and greeting cards.

Beginning Have students brainstorm words and phrases that describe how they feel about reading, such as *excited* and *learn new things.* Help students use these ideas to write sentences that begin with *When I read, I* ______.

Intermediate Have students create a pre-writing chart with the labels *characters, setting, plot,* and *style.* Ask them to complete the chart by describing the character's feelings, setting, several plot events, and the style they will use. Have them use their charts to write their story.

Advanced Have pairs exchange stories for peer review. Reviewers should check for style, structure (beginning, middle, end), and relative clauses. They should also check that the main character's feelings about reading are clear.

From Reading to Writing 

Write a Story

Write a story to show what reading can mean to a person.

1. Make sure your story has a beginning, a middle, and an end.
2. Base your story on one main character. This can be a made-up person.
3. In the story, tell how the person feels about reading. Use the character's actions and words to help you show this. Use your writing style to show the character's feelings.
4. Include relative clauses with *that* to describe.

Activity Book
p. 127

Across Content Areas 

Use the Library

Most libraries have a computerized **catalogue,** which is a list of all the books in a library. You type in a search word, for example, *insects.* All the books that are about that word come up in a list.

This information tells you where to find the book. If you need help, ask a librarian. Librarians are there to help you.

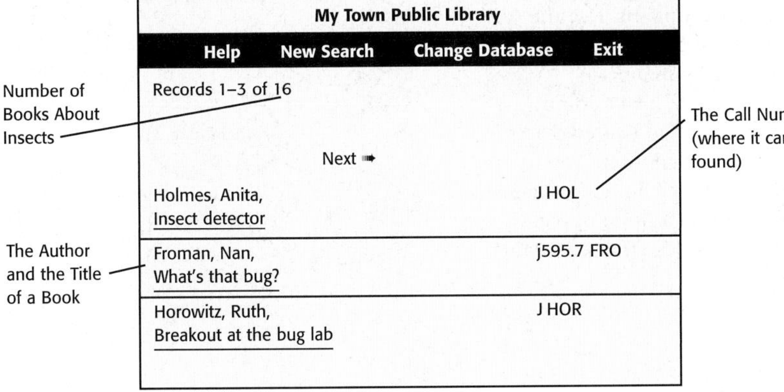

Activity Book
p. 128

Reteach and Reassess

Text Structure Have students review the plot of "The Library Card." ***Ask:*** *What happens at the beginning? What happens in the middle? What happens at the end?*

Reading Strategy Divide students into two groups. Name one *Compare* and the other *Contrast.* Display two objects. Have the groups take turns comparing and contrasting the two items.

Elements of Literature Ask groups of students to evaluate the styles of earlier selections in the book.

Reassess Create a chart with two columns labeled *"The Library Card"* and *"At the Library."* Label two rows *Features* and *Style.* Have students complete the chart with examples from the selections.

From Reading to Writing

Write a Story

1. **Create a story chart** Have students choose a character and complete a story chart including: character and feelings; setting; beginning, middle, and end.
2. **Think-quickwrite-pair-share** Ask students to write as much as they can about the person and his/her feelings about reading. Then, in pairs, have students share their stories. Tell them to consider how their words and writing style help show the character's feelings.
3. **Multi-level options** See MULTI-LEVEL OPTIONS on p. 236.

Across Content Areas: Language Arts

Use the Library

1. **Define and clarify** Explain the meaning of *catalogue.* Point out the types of information available in catalogue listings: authors, titles, call numbers, number of books. If possible, have the class go to the library and practice looking for books on particular topics using a computerized catalogue. Have students locate books in the library from the catalogue listings.
2. **Create a form** Point out that some libraries allow you to print out the results of a catalogue search but many do not. Have pairs collaborate to compose and organize a form they can use for the catalogue information as they look for books on the shelves. Tell pairs to use the illustration of catalogue search results as they organize the form. Have pairs use their form to record catalogue information and find books in the school library. Then have pairs revise their forms based in this experience.

ASSESS

Have students generate a list of steps for using a computerized catalogue in the library.

UNIT 4 • CHAPTER 2
Into the Reading

Chapter Materials

Activity Book: *pp. 129–136*
Audio: *Unit 4, Chapter 2*
Student Handbook
Student CD-ROM: *Unit 4, Chapter 2*
Teacher Resource Book: *Lesson Plan, Teacher Resources, Reading Summary, Activity Book Answer Key*
Teacher Resource CD-ROM
Assessment Program: *Quiz, pp. 63–64; Teacher and Student Resources, pp. 115–144*
Assessment CD-ROM
Transparencies
The Heinle Newbury House Dictionary/CD-ROM
Web Site: www.heinle.visions.com

Objectives

Preread for vocabulary Read the objectives. Explain *accomplishments, atmosphere,* and *altitude.* For example, **say:** *Accomplishments are difficult things you do and finish. Reading a long book is an accomplishment. What are your accomplishments?*

Use Prior Knowledge

Share Knowledge About Mountains

Brainstorm Have students discuss mountains they know or have visited. In groups, brainstorm words to describe mountains and complete a semantic word map.

Answers
1. **a.** a high part of the earth; **b.** Mt. McKinley, Mt. Everest; **c.** to reach the top

CHAPTER 2

Discovering the Inca Ice Maiden

a nonfiction narrative
by Johan Reinhard

Objectives

Reading Use graphic sources of information as you read a nonfiction narrative.

Listening and Speaking Describe personal accomplishments.

Grammar Identify *be* + adjective + infinitive.

Writing Write a first-person nonfiction narrative.

Content Social Studies: Understand the atmosphere and altitude.

Use Prior Knowledge

Share Knowledge About Mountains

What do you know about mountains?

1. With a partner, discuss what you know about mountains. Use the following questions as a guide:
   a. What is a mountain?
   b. Look at a map. Name some mountains in the United States or in another country.
   c. Why do people climb mountains?
2. Copy the web on a piece of paper. Add words that describe mountains.

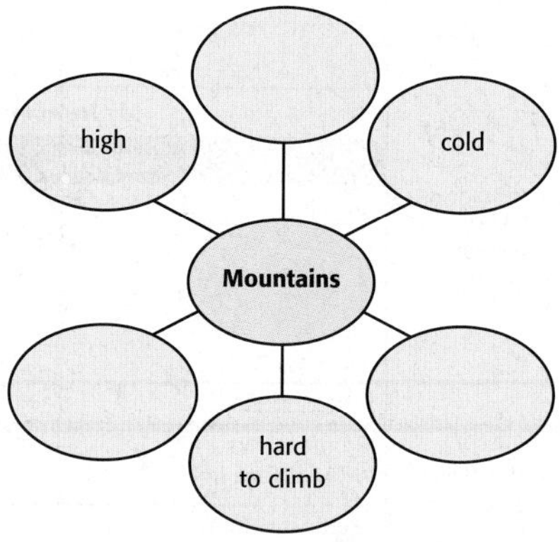

MULTI-LEVEL OPTIONS *Build Vocabulary*

Newcomer Write on the board and **say:** *mountain* and *volcano.* Find pictures of mountains and volcanoes in magazines, encyclopedias, or other resources. As you display each picture, point to and say the appropriate word. Use non-verbal and simple verbal cues to contrast the differences. Have students echo each word.

Beginning Write on the board and **say:** *mountain* and *volcano.* Find pictures of mountains and volcanoes in magazines, encyclopedias, or other resources. As you display each picture, **ask:** *Is this a mountain or a volcano?*

Intermediate Have pairs select a key word and its related word from the chart. Ask pairs to look up the words in the dictionary. Tell pairs to write definitions for their words. Ask pairs to share their definitions in groups.

Advanced Ask students to select a key word and its related word from the chart. Have each student write a sentence using the selected words. Tell students that they can look up words in a print or electronic dictionary if necessary. Ask them to share their sentences in small groups.

Build Background

Inca Culture

The Inca people lived in the Andes Mountains in South America. They formed the Inca empire. An empire is a group of nations ruled by an emperor, or leader. The Inca empire grew strong until the Spanish took control in 1532. The Incas were known for their beautiful arts and crafts as well as buildings and temples. Today, we still find items left behind by the Incas, such as jewelry, clothing, and pottery.

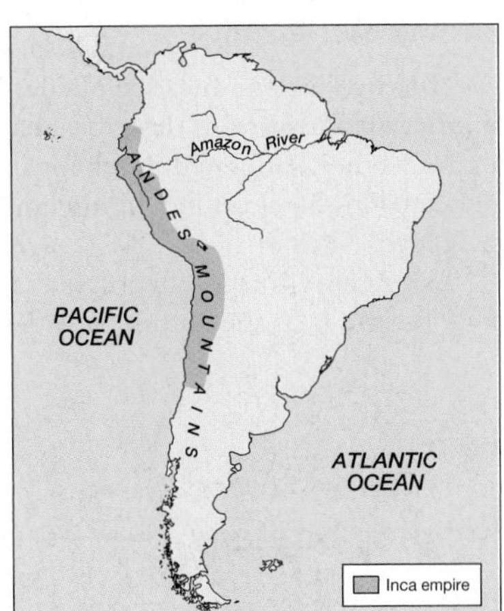

Content Connection

Anthropologists are scientists who study people and their culture.

Build Vocabulary

Understand Key Words and Related Words

Key words are the most important words in a narrative. **Related words** are words or phrases that are connected to the key words.

1. Copy the chart in your Personal Dictionary.
2. As you read "Discovering the Inca Ice Maiden," write additional related words that are associated with the key words in the chart.

Key Words	Related Words
volcano	erupting
mountain	summit
mountain climbing	ice ax

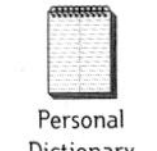
Personal Dictionary

Activity Book p. 129

Student CD-ROM

Content Connection
Math

Build Vocabulary Tell students that the largest volcano on earth is Mauna Kea in Hawaii. This volcano rises 13,678 feet above sea level, but the entire height, measured from its base at the ocean floor, is 33,476 feet. Have students calculate how much of Mauna Kea is underwater. (19,798 ft; 59%) Challenge interested students to calculate Mauna Kea's height in meters and miles. (10,203 m; 6.34 mi)

Learning Styles
Verbal

Build Background Ask students to work in groups to research the history and culture of the Inca people. Instruct each group member to focus on one topic, such as government, culture, religion, art, science, or architecture. Have groups prepare oral reports to present the information they gathered.

Build Background

Inca Culture

Teacher Resource Book: *Know/Want to Know/Learned (KWL) Chart, p. 42*

1. **Locate information on a map** Direct students to the map. Have them find important bodies of water in the Inca empire. (Pacific Ocean, Lake Titicaca, and the Amazon River)
2. **Use a KWL chart** Bring in materials on the Incas. List things students know about the culture and also information they would like to know. Refer to the chart while reading the selection. Complete the last column after reading the selection.
3. **Make guesses** *Ask: What would it be like to live in the Andes Mountains in the 1500s?*
4. **Content Connection** Ask students to identify what an anthropologist might want to study, such as clothing, tools, buildings.

Build Vocabulary

Understand Key Words and Related Words

Teacher Resource Book: *Personal Dictionary, p. 63*

1. **Use a semantic word map** Direct attention to the semantic word map students prepared for *mountains.* Point out the key word: *mountains.* Explain the surrounding words and related terms.
2. **Reading selection vocabulary** You may want to introduce the glossed words in the reading selection before students begin reading. Key words: *erupt, crater, route, erosion, mummy, circumstances.* Instruct students to write the words with correct spelling and their definitions in their Personal Dictionaries. Have them pronounce each word and divide it into syllables.
3. **Multi-level options** See MULTI-LEVEL OPTIONS on p. 238.

Have students define *empire, emperor, key words,* and *related words.*

Text Structure

Nonfiction Narrative

Recognize features Point out the question words in the chart. Have students suggest complete questions to add to their KWL charts using these question words.

Reading Strategy

Use Graphic Sources of Information

1. **Draw on experience** *Say: I want to drive from our town to New City. What can I use to show me the way?* (a map) Help students to identify sources of information they see every day, such as icons, subway maps, and directions on telephones and other machines. If possible, show students an Internet-based map system.
2. **Multi-level options** See MULTI-LEVEL OPTIONS below.

Answer
Example: The story is about an Inca girl in the mountains.

ASSESS

Ask: What question words do you ask about a nonfiction narrative? (who, what, when, where, why, how)

Text Structure

Nonfiction Narrative

"Discovering the Inca Ice Maiden" is a **nonfiction narrative.** It describes real events as they happened. Look for the elements in the chart in a nonfiction narrative.

As you read this nonfiction narrative, look for the facts the author provides.

Nonfiction Narrative	
Facts answer the following questions:	
• Who? • What? • When?	• Where? • Why? • How?

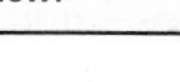
Student CD-ROM

Reading Strategy

Use Graphic Sources of Information

In this selection, there are several **graphic sources of information.** There are illustrations, a map, and a timeline. Graphic sources of information can help you understand a reading. They can also give information that is *not* in the reading.

1. Look at the illustration on page 241. What does it tell you about the story? Where does it take place? Can you guess what the story is about?
2. As you read the selection, use the graphics as a source of information. Use them to locate and learn information.

Student CD-ROM

MULTI-LEVEL OPTIONS *Reading Strategy*

Newcomer Display a map of the world. Point to the United States and *say: We are in the United States.* Then display a map of the United States. Point to your state and *say: We live in (state).* Ask students to name other countries they know. Help them locate the countries on the map.

Beginning Display a map of the world. ***Ask:** Where were you born?* Have students point out the countries on the map. Display a map of the United States. ***Ask:** What is the name of this country? What is the name of this state?* Have students locate their state on the map.

Intermediate Direct students to the map on p. 239. ***Ask:** What continent is this?* (South America) *What things can you learn about this continent by looking at this map?* (There are mountains. There is a lake and a river. The Atlantic Ocean is to the east. The Pacific Ocean is to the west.)

Advanced ***Ask:** What kind of information can you learn from a map?* (places; setting; geography; etc.) *From a timeline?* (sequence; events; history) *From pictures?* (what people, places, and things look like) Have students respond by writing complete sentences.

Discovering the Inca Ice Maiden

a nonfiction narrative
by Johan Reinhard

241

UNIT 4 • CHAPTER 2
Reading Selection

Reading Selection Materials

Audio: *Unit 4, Chapter 2*
Teacher Resource Book: *Reading Summary, pp. 97–98*

Preview the Selection

1. **Teacher think aloud** *Say: I can see in the picture a girl walking in the mountains. She isn't wearing clothes like we do, so I think she belongs to a different cultural group or she lived at a different time. The title is "Discovering the Inca Ice Maiden." So, maybe the girl is from the Inca empire. I know Incas lived in the Andes, so maybe those are the mountains.*
2. **Student think aloud** Have students add to the think aloud. Use guiding questions to have them make suggestions about who the Ice Maiden is, where she is going, what is going to happen to her. Students can draw on information from the illustration, vocabulary, and other previous activities from this chapter.
3. **Connect** Remind students that the unit theme is *discoveries.* Ask who or what will be discovered.

Cultural Connection

Remind students that scientists often learn about ancient cultures by studying artifacts. Tell students that art, toys, and tools can tell scientists a lot about the people who made and used them. Have students select objects from home that they think tell a lot about their culture. Ask students to bring in the objects for informal presentations in which they explain why they chose their objects. Have students compare and contrast their objects.

Learning Styles *Intrapersonal*

Tell students that the study of volcanoes is called volcanology. ***Ask:*** *What kind of person would enjoy volcanology?* Ask students to write a paragraph describing a person who might be interested in volcanology and the reasons someone might decide to study it. Remind students that there are no "right" answers when they give opinions.

Read the Selection

1. **Use text features** Point out the italicized paragraphs and explain their purpose. Direct students to the glossed words. Remind students to use the illustration to help understanding.
2. **Teacher read aloud** Read the selection aloud. Pause to check understanding and to identify facts about the narrative: who, where, and when. Have students reread the selection in pairs.
3. **Analyze characters** *Ask: Why is the writer climbing a volcano?* (Maybe he is a scientist who studies volcanoes.)

Sample Answer to Guide Question
It shows the ash from the active volcano blowing toward the inactive volcano.

See Teacher Edition pp. 434–435 for a list of English-Spanish cognates in the reading selection.

1 *Sabancaya became increasingly active during 1990,* ***erupting*** *about half a dozen times a day—every day of the year. The erupting volcano* ***spewed*** *clouds of dark ash up into the sky. Wind carried the ash over Sabancaya's higher neighbor, the volcano Ampato, which is inactive. Eventually Ampato's snow-capped summit was covered with dark ash, which slowly began absorbing the sun's rays, causing the snow to melt.*

2 *After four years the weight of the melting snow caused a section of Ampato's highest summit to collapse into its* ***crater.***

Use Graphic Sources of Information

How does the illustration on this page help you understand the collapse of Mt. Ampato?

3 *Within this mix of falling ice and rock was a cloth-wrapped bundle.*

4 *When the bundle smashed against an icy outcrop about 200 feet below, an outer cloth was torn open—and 500-year-old Inca artifacts were strewn over the rugged landscape.*

Audio

5 *But the most important part of the bundle remained intact as it came to rest on top of the ice . . .*

6 I'd climbed more than a hundred volcanoes in the Andes mountains without ever seeing an active volcano up close. From the top of Ampato, I would be able to look down and see Sabancaya erupting. I was as excited as my Peruvian assistant, Miguel Zárate, and I started our climb out of the village of Cabanaconde, heading toward Ampato. On September 5, we made a small base camp at 16,300 feet.

erupting exploding
spewed pushed out with force
crater a large hole in a volcano

MULTI-LEVEL OPTIONS *Read the Selection*

Newcomer Play the audio. Discuss the illustrations. ***Ask:*** *Did Sabancaya erupt?* (yes) *Did Ampato erupt?* (no) *Was there ice on the mountain?* (yes) *Was there grass on the mountain?* (yes) *Did they reach the summit on the first day?* (no)

Beginning Read the Reading Summary aloud. ***Ask:*** *Which volcano erupted every day?* (Sabancaya) *Which volcano did they climb?* (Ampato) *Where are the volcanoes?* (in the Andes Mountains) *What was the summit like?* (rounded and covered with grass)

Intermediate Have students do a paired reading. ***Ask:*** *Why was their route difficult?* (Ice pinnacles blocked their way.) *Why were they puzzled when they saw the grass?* (Grass doesn't grow at that altitude.) *Why didn't they reach the summit on the first day?* (They ran out of time before dark.)

Advanced Have students read silently. ***Ask:*** *How did the narrator feel about climbing Ampato?* (excited) *Why?* (He'd never seen an active volcano up close.) *How are ice and snow important to this story?* (Melting snow caused the summit to collapse. Ice made the climb difficult.)

7 During our first **ascent** of Ampato on September 6, we made our way up the northern slope. We thought this would be a fairly simple **route,** but, as we neared the top, ice **pinnacles** blocked our way. They had been formed by **erosion** caused by the sun and wind.

8 We had to break through a mile of ice pinnacles to reach one of the lower summits at 20,400 feet. Much to our surprise, just as we were about to reach it, we saw a long layer of grass **encased** in the ice. We were puzzled. How did so much grass get here? Grass could not grow at this altitude!

9 We climbed the rest of the way to the summit and found that it was rounded and covered with grass, the "grass site." Pieces of Inca pottery and textiles, rope, chunks of wood, and even leather and wool sandals were scattered about. Flat **slabs** of rock had been carried from over a thousand feet below to make flooring. One slab still had a rope around it. The rock floor had been covered with thick layers of grass, to make a resting place.

Use Graphic Sources of Information

Look at the illustration. What kinds of things did the Inca people use?

10 [The climbers were unable to reach the summit that day because it was too late. They went back to their camp.]

11 . . . The next morning we crossed over the "grass site" at 20,400 feet and made our way through and around ice pinnacles inside Ampato's crater until we were about 200 feet below the summit . . . The frozen rock was steep and slippery . . . Finally I was just able to get over the worst part by pulling myself up with my ice ax.

ascent going upward
route a path of travel
pinnacles pointed formations on a mountain peak
erosion a natural process in which material is moved on Earth's surface
encased enclosed
slabs thick, flat pieces of something

UNIT 4 • CHAPTER 2
Reading Selection

Read the Selection

1. **Use graphic sources of information** Ask students to describe the objects in the illustration.
2. **Paired reading** After students listen to the audio or to you read the selection, have them reread it in pairs.
3. **Summarize** ***Ask:*** *What did they find at 20,400 feet?* (grass) *What other items did they find?* (pottery, textiles, rope, wood, leather, and wool sandals) *Was it easy or difficult to climb in the crater?* (difficult)
4. **Multi-level options** See MULTI-LEVEL OPTIONS on p. 242.

Sample Answer to Guide Question

They used sandals, rope, pottery, and wood.

Capitalization

Proper adjectives

Explain that adjectives that describe nationalities or ethnic groups are *proper adjectives.* Tell students that proper adjectives are always capitalized, just like the places they describe. Direct students to paragraph 4. ***Ask:*** *Why is* Inca *capitalized?* (It is a proper adjective.) *Can you find another proper adjective that is capitalized in paragraph 6?* (Peruvian)

Apply Have students correct the capitalization errors in the following sentences. Write on the board: *We ate dinner at a portuguese restaurant. He bought two loaves of french bread. Her dress was made of chinese silk. Our class learned about hispanic artists.*

Read the Selection

1. **Use the illustration** Ask students to guess where the climbers are and what they are looking at.
2. **Shared reading** Continue the reading of the narrative as students follow along. Read aloud or ask volunteers to read parts as students join in when they can. ***Ask:*** *What do they think the feathers are?* (an Inca statue or headdress) *How many statues did they find?* (three) *How long had the statues been uncovered?* (only a few days) *What else do they see on the ice?* (a mummy bundle)

Sample Answer to Guide Question
I can see the slope is slippery and it is hard to climb down it.

12 I pulled Miguel up, too, and the rest of the way was a simple scramble up over ice and rock to the **ridge** top . . .

13 I stopped to take notes while Miguel continued along the ridge. He whistled, and I looked up to see him with his ice ax raised.

14 When I reached him, he pointed without saying a word: Even from 40 feet away, it was possible to see reddish feathers sticking out near the top of the ridge. We had both seen feathers like this on Inca statues at other sites, and so we knew instantly they would most likely be from a feathered headdress.

15 Although the feathers were only about 10 feet down from the top, the slope was steep and slippery—a mix of gravel and sand over ice. A slip would have meant certain death. Miguel . . . climbed down to uncover a statue made of a rare seashell, with a reddish feathered headdress. Nearby, also covered with gravel, were two more statues, one gold and one silver.

Use Graphic Sources of Information

How does the illustration help you understand the danger that Miguel was in?

16 Their **textiles** were so well **preserved,** they looked new. The feathers that had been exposed were still in good condition. This meant that the gravel in which the statues had been buried had fallen away only days before. Indeed, the statues could have fallen farther down the slope at any moment . . . We then climbed down off the ridge and scrambled our way around beneath it . . . A little farther we saw what looked to us like a **mummy bundle** lying on the ice.

ridge a long, narrow, high piece of land
textiles cloths, fabrics made by weaving
preserved kept in good condition
mummy a dead body that has been kept in very good condition
bundle things close together, usually tied

MULTI-LEVEL OPTIONS *Read the Selection*

Newcomer ***Ask:*** *Did Miguel take notes?* (no) *Were the feathers red?* (yes) *Was the slope steep and slippery?* (yes) *Did Miguel uncover three statues?* (yes) *Did they find maize, llama bones, and pottery?* (yes) *Was the frozen mummy a boy?* (no)

Beginning ***Ask:*** *What did Miguel do when he saw the feathers?* (He whistled and raised his ax). *What were the three statues made of?* (seashell, gold, silver) *What was in the two cloth bags?* (food, bones, pottery) *Was the mummy a boy or a girl?* (a girl)

Intermediate ***Ask:*** *Why did Miguel whistle?* (to get Johan's attention; to show him the feathers) *How did they know the feathers would be a headdress?* (They'd seen feathers like that before.) *Why did he think the bundle was a mummy?* (the stripes on the cloth)

Advanced ***Ask:*** *How did they know that the area where the statues had been buried had fallen away recently?* (The statues were in good condition.) *Why were they excited to find a mummy?* (Only three frozen mummies had ever been found in South America.)

17 It seemed so unlikely to find a mummy out in the open, we literally couldn't believe our eyes. Miguel said, "Maybe it's a climber's backpack . . ." As we drew closer, I knew from the stripes on the cloth that it was probably a mummy bundle . . . The bundle containing the victim had been buried in the structure that had collapsed when part of the summit ridge crashed into the crater . . . I grew more excited as I remembered that only three frozen mummies had been recovered in all of South America.

18 Descending toward it, we found fragments of a torn textile. A seashell, two cloth bags containing food offerings (**maize** kernels and a maize cob), **llama** bones, and pieces of Inca pottery were **strewn** about on the slope above the bundle.

Use Graphic Sources of Information

Use the text and the illustration to summarize what Reinhard and Miguel found.

After I photographed these items, Miguel used his ice ax to cut loose the bundle from the ice. 19

He turned it on its side for a better grip. Both of us were momentarily stunned as the body turned. 20

We looked straight into the face of a young girl. 21

She was the first *frozen* female mummy found in South America! 22

maize corn
llama a South American animal, like a small camel, used to carry loads
strewn scattered

Read the Selection

1. **Use the illustration** Ask students to describe the mummy bundle.
2. **Shared reading** Continue the reading of the story as students follow along. Read aloud or ask volunteers to read parts. ***Ask:*** *How does the writer know it is probably a mummy bundle?* (the stripes on the cloth) *Why did he take photos of these things?* (to remember where they found these things and what they looked like)
3. **Multi-level options** See MULTI-LEVEL OPTIONS on p. 244.

Sample Answer to Guide Question
Reinhard and Miguel found some cloth and a mummy bundle.

 Spelling

Forming words with double consonants

Tell students that before adding suffixes to most C-V-C words, the final consonant is doubled. Write on the board and ***say:*** *slip.* Then write and ***say:*** *slippery.* Ask students to look at paragraph 14. Write: *red/reddish.* ***Ask:*** *Why are there two* ds *in reddish?* (The suffix *-ish* was added to the C-V-C word *red.*)

Apply On the board, write: *pot* and *stun.* Ask students to find these base words with suffixes added in paragraphs 18 and 20. (pottery, stunned) Have students form the correct words in the following sentences: *He told a (fun + -y) joke. He was (run + -ing) up the slope. Don't get (bit + -en) by a snake!*

Read the Selection

1. **Summarize and make predictions** Ask students to restate the main events of the narrative and then guess what Miguel and Reinhard will do next.
2. **Shared reading** Continue the reading of the narrative as students follow along. Read aloud or ask volunteers to read parts. ***Ask:*** *Why do Miguel and Reinhard want to take the artifacts with them?* (So others don't steal them and so they don't get damaged.)

Sample Answer to Guide Question
She lived sometime between 1438 and 1532. It shows the time of the Inca empire.

23 I wondered what to do next. If we left the mummy behind in the open, the sun and the volcanic ash would cause further damage. Climbers might find her and take her and the other **artifacts** as souvenirs or to sell. The ground was frozen rock hard, and it was impossible to bury the mummy. A heavy snowfall could cover the summit and make recovery impossible . . .

24 I decided that we should try to carry the mummy and the statues down the mountain. This would be difficult under the best **circumstances.** Unfortunately, we were both feeling weak, and I had an upset stomach . . .

25 Brushing aside a feeling of **dread,** we wrapped the bundle in plastic and attached it to my backpack. We had to scramble for a mile around the ice pinnacles inside the crater to link up with the route back to camp.

This was one of the hardest things I've ever done. My backpack was so heavy that any slip meant a hard fall, and I crashed to the ground a dozen times. I could only get back on my feet by propping myself against the ground with my ice ax and lunging upward. Every fall meant precious minutes lost. 26

Instead of its getting easier once we were out of the crater, the way became more dangerous . . . Finally I realized it was foolish to continue. We left the mummy **amidst** some ice pinnacles at 19,900 feet. 27

It took us two hours to descend to our tent 700 feet below and crawl exhausted into our sleeping bags. 28

Use of Graphic Sources of Information

Read and interpret (to understand) the timeline. Around what time did the Ice Maiden live? How does the timeline help you know this?

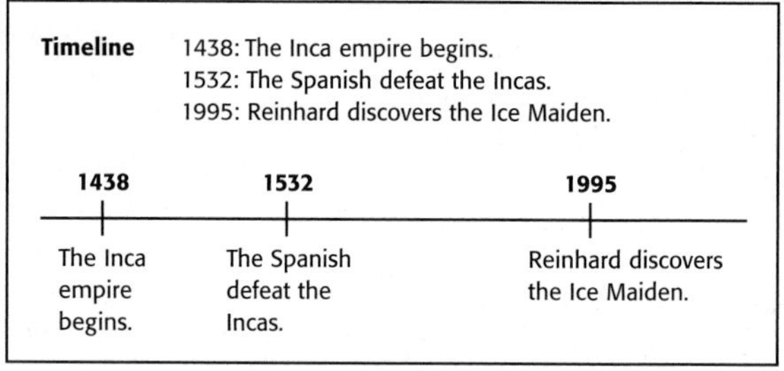

artifacts objects produced by human workmanship
circumstances conditions that affect something else
dread a strong fear of something in the future
amidst surrounded by

MULTI-LEVEL OPTIONS *Read the Selection*

Newcomer ***Ask:*** *Was the ground easy to dig?* (no) *Was his backpack heavy?* (yes) *Did they leave the mummy behind?* (yes) *Did they go back to get the mummy?* (yes) *Was the girl sick when she died?* (no)

Beginning ***Ask:*** *Where did they leave the mummy?* (among ice pinnacles at 19,900 feet) *How long did it take to get down to their tent?* (two hours) *When did they retrieve the mummy?* (the next day) *Where did they bring it?* (Arequipa) *When was the mummy sent to the United States?* (1996)

Intermediate ***Ask:*** *Why didn't they want to leave the mummy in the open?* (It could be damaged or stolen.) *Why couldn't they bury the mummy?* (The ground was frozen.) *What did they do with the mummy that day?* (They carried it part of the way down the mountain.) *Why was the mummy sent to the United States?* (for further study)

Advanced ***Ask:*** *Why did they decide to try to carry the mummy?* (to protect it from weather and climbers) *What made carrying the mummy so difficult?* (They were sick; it was heavy.) *What was learned about the mummy?* (She was 14 years old, healthy, and lived around 1470.)

Epilogue

29 The next day, Reinhard went back to get the mummy. He and Zárate took it to the city of Arequipa where specialists gathered to study it. In 1996, the mummy was sent to the United States for further study. The Ice Maiden is now back in Arequipa, and scientists continue to learn from her. For example, they have discovered that:

30 The girl lived around A.D. 1470. She was about 14 years old when she died. She had normal skeletal growth, no bone disease, and she had no **malnutrition.**

malnutrition a sick condition caused by lack of food

About the Author

Johan Reinhard (born 1943)

Johan Reinhard was born in Joliet, Illinois. He studied anthropology at the University of Arizona and at the University of Vienna in Austria. Since 1980, Reinhard has worked in the mountains of South America. He has discovered more than 50 burial sites there. Reinhard has written five books and has published many articles about his adventures.

➤ Why do you think Johan Reinhard wrote about his discovery of the Inca Ice Maiden? To entertain, to inform, or to persuade?

Punctuation

Commas within large numbers

Explain that commas are used in numbers above 999. Tell students to insert a comma before every third digit from the right. Write on the board and ***say:*** *19,900.* Remind students that commas aren't used when writing a year, such as *2004.*

Apply Have students correct the following sentences: *The base camp was 16300 feet high. One of the summits was at 20400 feet.*

Evaluate Your Reading Strategy

Use Graphic Sources of Information *Say: You have practiced an important reading strategy. Now you can decide how well you have done. Does this statement describe how you read?*

When I see graphic information in a reading, I use it to help me understand the reading. Graphic information can also tell me new things about the reading.

Read the Selection

1. **Paired reading** Read the epilogue aloud. Have students read it again in pairs. ***Ask:*** *Why do scientists want to study the Ice Maiden?* (They want to know more about the Inca people and culture.)
2. **Multi-level options** See MULTI-LEVEL OPTIONS on p. 246.

About the Author

1. **Explain author background** Johan Reinhard combines his love of mountain climbing with his anthropological research. He is currently studying sacred beliefs and cultural practices of mountain people. He has worked in many countries and speaks six languages.
2. **Interpret the facts** ***Ask:*** *Why do you think Reinhard speaks so many languages?* (so he can talk with the people in different countries where he works)

Across Selections

Make comparisons Compare the discovery of the Ice Maiden to the discovery the boy and girl in Chapter 1 made. ***Ask:*** *How did the people who made the discoveries feel? What was similar about the discoveries? How were they different?*

Reading Comprehension

Question-Answer Relationships

Sample Answers

1. Sabancaya
2. Miguel Zárate is Johan Reinhard's assistant from Peru.
3. ice axes
4. Because there were many ice formations to go around or over.
5. They found grass growing; grass doesn't grow so high on the mountain.
6. Ampato was covered with dark ashes that made the ice melt. This heavy, wet snow made the top of the mountain collapse into the crater.
7. It might have become more damaged by the sun and air. The mummy might have been found by other people who would not have taken care of it.
8. It helps you understand how cold and dangerous it was on the mountain.
9. surprised, excited
10. The tone of the text is excited. The author is very proud.
11. The Inca lived high in the mountains and volcanoes. There were different animals there. I live in a city far from the mountains with lots of stores and other buildings.

Build Reading Fluency

Read to Scan for Information

Explain that students need to adjust their reading to quickly scan the text to locate key words. Have them read the question then quickly scan to find the answer and identify key words.

Beyond the Reading

Reading Comprehension

Question-Answer Relationships (QAR)

"Right There" Questions

1. **Recall Facts** What active volcano is near Ampato?
2. **Recall Facts** Who is Miguel Zárate?
3. **Recall Facts** What tool helped the climbers reach the summit?

"Think and Search" Questions

4. **Explain** Why was it difficult for the climbers to continue up the northern slope?
5. **Identify** What did the climbers find growing near the summit? Why was this strange?
6. **Analyze Cause and Effect** What happened to Ampato when Sabancaya erupted?
7. **Analyze Cause and Effect** What might have happened to the mummy if Reinhard and Zárate had left it on the mountain?

"Author and You" Questions

8. **Explain** Explain how the author's description of the mountain helps you understand the setting of the narrative.
9. **Describe** Describe how you think the author felt after finding the mummy.
10. **Analyze Tone** What is the tone of the text? Humorous, serious, or excited? What do you think is the author's attitude toward the events in the text?

"On Your Own" Question

11. **Find Differences** Identify several differences between where the Inca lived and where you live.

Activity Book p. 130

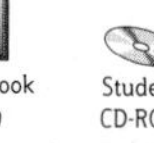
Student CD-ROM

Build Reading Fluency

Read to Scan for Information

You must adjust your reading rate to read fast when you scan. Scan to look for the title and boldfaced (darkened) key words in "Discovering the Inca Ice Maiden." Write the answers to these questions on a piece of paper.

1. What is the title of the reading?
2. What are the key words?

MULTI-LEVEL OPTIONS *Elements of Literature*

Newcomer Play the audio. Pause at each first-person pronoun. Write on the board and *say: I, me, we,* and *us.* Play the audio again. Have students raise their hands each time they hear one of the words on the board.

Beginning Write on the board: *I, me, we,* and *us.* Say each word. Point to yourself when you *say: I* and *me.* Indicate yourself and the students when you *say: we* and *us.* Ask students to pronounce each word and mimic your gestures. Have pairs locate sentences in the selection with these words.

Intermediate Ask students to copy three sentences from the selection with the pronouns *I, me, we,* or *us,* leaving blanks for each pronoun. Have pairs exchange sentences and fill in the correct pronouns. Ask students to write one original sentence using one of the pronouns.

Advanced Ask students to locate an earlier selection in the book that is written in third-person point of view, such as "The Library Card" or "Arctic Adventure." Have students rewrite one paragraph of the selection in first-person point of view. Have pairs of students peer-edit the paragraphs.

Listen, Speak, Interact 

Describe Personal Accomplishments

In "Discovering the Inca Ice Maiden," Johan Reinhard describes his accomplishments. He explains how he climbed a mountain and how he discovered the mummy.

1. Work with a partner. Discuss how you accomplished something in the past. Clarify your ideas with examples: *I got an A in math. I studied hard.* Then answer the following questions:
   a. What did you learn from this accomplishment?
   b. What difficulties did you face?
   c. How did it change you?
2. Discuss something you would like to accomplish in the future. Answer the following questions:
   a. Why would you like to accomplish this?
   b. Has it been done before?
   c. How are you going to accomplish this?

Elements of Literature

Understand First-Person Point of View

Johan Reinhard, the author of the reading selection, is the narrator (teller) of the story. He uses the pronouns *I, me, we,* and *us.* This kind of story is written in **first-person point of view.**

In grammar, the pronouns *I, me, we,* and *us* are called *first-person pronouns.* That is why we call this point of view *first person.*

There are two people in "Discovering the Inca Ice Maiden," Johan Reinhard and Miguel Zárate.

1. Read paragraph 6 of the story. Notice the use of the pronouns *I* and *we.*

	Johan Reinhard	Miguel Zárate	Both
Author			
Character			
Narrator			
I			
We			

2. Copy the chart. Which words on the left refer to Johan Reinhard, Miguel Zárate, or both? Put an "X" in the correct column.

Activity Book p. 131

Student CD-ROM

Content Connection *Social Studies*

Have students work in groups to find a first-person account of an exploration or a discovery. Suggest that students look in their social studies texts or in newspapers or magazines. Ask groups to present the article by doing a group read aloud (one paragraph per student).

Learning Styles *Kinesthetic*

Ask students to work in groups of three to write skits based on the selection. Group members should play the roles of Johan, Miguel, and a narrator. Have pairs present their skits to the class. Encourage students to use props. Remind students that they should act out the scenes in addition to speaking the dialogue.

Listen, Speak, Interact

Describe Personal Accomplishments

Teacher Resource Book: *Reading Log, p. 64*

1. **Brainstorm** Have students suggest accomplishments they are proud of. List them on the board.
2. **Organize ideas** Review the questions, telling students to answer first about a past personal accomplishment and then a future accomplishment they hope to achieve. Have students record details about their accomplishments in their Reading Logs and then share with a partner.

Answers

1. *Example:* I learned I can read directions. It was difficult because the questions used different words each time. It made me look at the words and sentences more carefully.
2. *Example:* I would like to travel on a space shuttle to learn more about space. It's been done before, but I'd do different science experiments there. I'm going to finish school, and then learn how to fly airplanes.

Elements of Literature

Understand First-Person Point of View

1. **Personal experience** Have students use first-person pronouns by asking guiding questions such as *What did you . . . ?* List the pronouns on the board. Use the same procedure to review third-person pronouns, such as *What did she . . . ?*
2. **Multi-level options** See MULTI-LEVEL OPTIONS on p. 248.

Answers

Johan Reinhard: Author, Character, Narrator, I, We
Miguel Zárate: Character, We

Have students write sentences using four first-person pronouns: *I, my, we, our.*

Word Study

Spell *-ed* Forms of Verbs

Make flash cards Write some regular verbs. Ask students to identify the *-ed* verb ending for each. Have students create flash cards with the verb on one side and the *-ed* form on the other for individual or pair review.

Answers

1. & 2. preserved, looked, exposed, buried, climbed, scrambled, looked

Grammar Focus

Identify *Be* + Adjective + Infinitive

Define and explain Write on the board: *It is fun to read.* Point out the form of *be* + an adjective + an infinitive. Ask students to substitute adjectives and infinitives in the sentence to express their own ideas.

Answers

1. It was foolish to continue.
2. was (be) + foolish (adjective) + to continue (infinitive)

ASSESS

Write on the board: *walk, carry, stop, learn.* Ask students to write the words and add the correct *-ed* ending to them.

Word Study

Spell *-ed* Forms of Verbs

You know that you can add *-ed* to regular verbs to make the past tense.

erupt + ed → erupt**ed**

Look at the chart. Sometimes you need to make a spelling change before adding *-ed.*

If the verb ends in a vowel, add **-d.** describe → describe**d**
If the verb ends in *consonant* + **y,** change the **y** to **i** and add **-ed.** carry → car**ried**
For a one syllable verb that ends in *consonant* + *vowel* + *consonant,* double the final consonant and add **-ed.** slip → sli**pped**

1. Reread paragraph 16. Find four examples of past tense verbs that end with *-ed.*
2. Write the verbs on a piece of paper. Circle the endings.

Activity Book p. 132 | Student CD-ROM

Grammar Focus

Identify *Be* + Adjective + Infinitive

You can sometimes use a form of *be* + an adjective + an infinitive to describe the infinitive's action. An **infinitive** is the word *to* followed by the simple form of a verb.

The ground was frozen rock hard, and it was impossible to bury the mummy.

Subject	*Be*	Adjective	Infinitive
It	is was	impossible difficult	to bury.
We	are were	puzzled	to see it.

1. Reread paragraph 27. Find a sentence that uses *be* + adjective + infinitive.
2. Write the sentence on a piece of paper. Label the form of *be,* the adjective, and the infinitive.

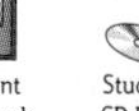

Activity Book pp. 133–134 | Student Handbook | Student CD-ROM

MULTI-LEVEL OPTIONS *From Reading to Writing*

Newcomer Have students draw pictures of places they have visited. Help them to write captions for their pictures. Use these sentence starters: *My name is _____. I went to _____. I saw _____.*

Beginning Help students make first-person statements. Provide these sentence starters: *My name is _____. I am _____ years old. I like to _____. I can _____. I went to _____ with _____. We saw _____.*

Intermediate Have students write first-person sentences to respond to the questions. Tell them to trade sentences with a partner. Direct partners to check that the questions have been answered. Also have partners ask questions about additional details they would like to know.

Advanced Have students review their narratives. Ask them to underline all first-person pronouns. (I, me, my, mine, we, us, our, ours) Have partners check that pronouns were used correctly.

From Reading to Writing 

Write a First-Person Nonfiction Narrative

Write a first-person nonfiction narrative about a place you have visited. Write three paragraphs. Use "Discovering the Inca Ice Maiden" as a model.

1. Answer these six questions before you begin:
   a. Where is the place?
   b. When were you there?
   c. Who was there?
   d. What was there?
   e. Why did you go there?
   f. How did you react to it?
2. Provide details. Describe some of your activities during the trip. Describe some of your thoughts and feelings during the trip. Discuss how you felt after the trip was over.
3. Use the past tense form of verbs.

Activity Book p. 135

Across Content Areas 

Understand the Atmosphere and Altitude

The **atmosphere** is the air that surrounds Earth. The atmosphere changes depending on how high you are.

At **sea level** (the height of the land right by the ocean), the atmosphere is thick. There is a lot of oxygen to breathe. On a high mountain, the atmosphere gets thinner. There is less oxygen in the air.

We use sea level as a starting point to measure **altitude** (the height of land or a flying airplane). Sea level is at 0 meters (0 feet) altitude. Mt. Everest, the highest mountain in the world, has an altitude of 8,848 meters (29,028 feet) above sea level. When people climb Mt. Everest, they take bottles of oxygen with them.

Copy these sentences on a piece of paper. Complete each one with the word *atmosphere, sea level,* or *altitude.*

1. A city on a mountain has a higher ____ than a city by the ocean.
2. The ____ was so thin that it was hard to breathe.
3. Denver, Colorado, is 5,280 feet above ____ .

Activity Book p. 136

From Reading to Writing

Write a First-Person Nonfiction Narrative

Teacher Resource Book: *Sunshine Organizer, p. 40*

1. **Think-pair-share** Have students decide on their topic. Tell them to explain the details of their trip in pairs. Then have students write their narratives. Remind them to include details about the place and events from the trip. Students may want to prepare an illustration to accompany their narratives.
2. **Multi-level options** See MULTI-LEVEL OPTIONS on p. 250.

Across Content Areas: Science

Understand the Atmosphere and Altitude

Connect Explain the meanings of *atmosphere, sea level,* and *altitude.* ***Ask:*** *What was the altitude of the mountains Johan Reinhard and Miguel Zárate climbed?* (20,000 feet) *Why was it difficult for them to carry heavy backpacks and to climb?* (There wasn't much air for them to breathe.) Have students find the altitudes of other mountains.

Answers
1. altitude 2. atmosphere 3. sea level

ASSESS

Say definitions and have students respond with the correct word: *atmosphere, altitude, sea level.*

Reteach and Reassess

Text Structure *Ask: What kinds of questions are answered in a nonfiction narrative?* (Who? What? When? Where? Why? How?)

Reading Strategy Assign one graphic feature (maps, timelines, pictures) to three groups. Have them choose an example from this selection or an earlier selection. Ask each group to describe the information provided by the graphic and how it helps readers to understand the selection.

Elements of Literature Ask students to review samples of their writing. Have students offer examples of first-person writing. ***Ask:*** *How do you know this is first-person writing?*

Reassess Write on the board: *Who? What? Where? When? Why? How?* Have students write a question and answer for facts in the selection.

Chapter Materials

Activity Book: *pp. 137–144*
Audio: *Unit 4, Chapter 3*
Student Handbook
Student CD-ROM: *Unit 4, Chapter 3*
Teacher Resource Book: *Lesson Plan, Teacher Resources, Reading Summary, Activity Book Answer Key*
Teacher Resource CD-ROM
Assessment Program: *Quiz, pp 65–66; Teacher and Student Resources, pp. 115–144*
Assessment CD-ROM
Transparencies
The Heinle Newbury House Dictionary/CD-ROM
Web Site: www.heinle.visions.com

Objectives

Paired reading Have student pairs take turns reading the objectives. Explain and point out key words. *Ask: Is there an objective you can already do?*

Use Prior Knowledge

Evaluate Learning Experiences

1. **Brainstorm** *Ask: What have you learned in school? What have you learned on your own?*
2. **Think-pair-share** Have students share experiences in pairs.

CHAPTER 3

The Art of Swordsmanship

a folktale
by Rafe Martin

Into the Reading

Objectives

Reading Use dialogue to understand character as you read a folktale.

Listening and Speaking Participate in a dramatic read-aloud.

Grammar Use adverbs to show time.

Writing Write a tale.

Content The Arts: Learn about art in everyday objects.

Use Prior Knowledge

Evaluate Learning Experiences

Think about how you learn math. Then think about how you learn to ride a bicycle. How are these learning experiences the same or different?

1. Choose one skill from each list in the chart. Think about how you learned each skill.
2. Tell a partner how you learned the skills.
3. As a class, discuss the difference between skills you learn by someone explaining them to you and skills you learn through practice.

Learn how to:	Learn how to:
• find your way around town • organize your schoolbooks • throw a ball • ride a bicycle	• add fractions • tell a verb from a noun • cook • tie your shoes

MULTI-LEVEL OPTIONS *Build Vocabulary*

Newcomer Prepare index cards with the root word *side* and the affixes *-s, a-, in-, be-, -ways,* and *-walk.* Show students how to combine them into new words. ***Say:*** *When you know the meaning of a root word, you can figure out the meaning of a new word with the root word in it.*

Beginning Write *covering* on the board. Ask students to identify its root. (cover) Then write: *uncover, discover, covered, discovery, undiscovered, recover.* Guide students to definitions by discussing the meanings of the other parts of the words. ***Say:*** *When you know the meaning of a root word, you can figure out the meaning of a new word with the root word in it.*

Intermediate ***Ask:*** *What shorter word do you see in* uncover? (cover) ***Say:*** Cover *is a root. A root is the main part of a word. Knowing the meaning of roots can help you guess the meanings of new words.* Have pairs think of and write additional words with the root *cover.*

Advanced Have students complete the activity and share their work with a partner. Then ask students to repeat the activity with the following words: *artifact, artist, defendable, defensive, defender.*

Build Background

Swordfighting

For hundreds of years, people used swords as weapons. Swords are metal and have sharp edges that make them dangerous weapons. Today, fencing is an Olympic sport based on swordfighting.

Content Connection

The different types of fighting arts that came from Asia are called the **martial arts.** Some popular forms are karate, judo, kung fu, and tai chi. Many of the martial arts are practiced without using any weapons.

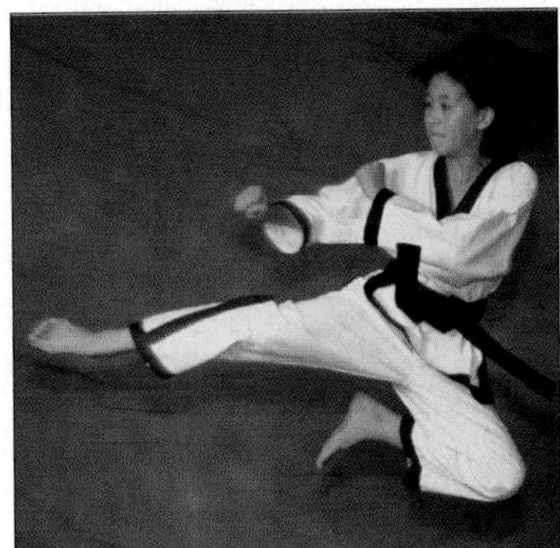

Build Vocabulary

Identify Related Words

Sometimes a group of unfamiliar words will share a root word. If you know the meaning of the root word, you can guess the meaning of the larger words. In this reading selection, several words are about swords and using swords.

1. Write the following sentences on a piece of paper:
   a. Once a young man named Manjuro sought out the greatest swordmaster in the country.
   b. How long will it take me to become a master swordsman?
   c. Time went on but Manjuro received no training in swordsmanship.
2. Circle the root word that is shared by all of the underlined words.
3. Then use the remaining part of the word to tell what you think each underlined word means. Check your work in a dictionary.

The Heinle Newbury House Dictionary

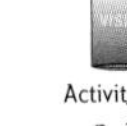
Activity Book p. 137

Student CD-ROM

Home Connection

Build Vocabulary Have students create root-word charts. Ask students to list words that contain the following root words: *photo, vision, room, bath, paper, pot, bake, book,* and *eye.* Suggest that students look around the house for ideas. Students can ask family members to help them complete their charts.

Learning Styles ***Kinesthetic***

Build Background Tell students that sword fights they see in movies or on TV are choreographed. Explain that choreography is a series of planned movements. Ask pairs of students to choreograph and mime a duel. Alternatively, ask students who have studied martial arts to present brief examples of their art.

Build Background

Swordfighting

1. **Use resources** Bring in pictures of swordfighting. *Ask: Have you seen swordfighting in the movies? Is it dangerous or safe? Why did people use swords for fighting?*
2. **Content Connection** Martial arts are popular for exercise and for self-defense. Ask if students have ever seen or learned some martial arts. Allow volunteers to demonstrate some of the moves.

Build Vocabulary

Identify Related Words

Teacher Resource Book: *Personal Dictionary, p. 63*

1. **Analyze words** Write *swordfighting* on the board. Ask students to identify the root word. Ask them to explain the meaning by using what they know about *swords* and *fighting.* Remind students to look for related words for clues to meaning.
2. **Reading selection vocabulary** You may want to introduce the glossed words in the reading selection before students begin reading. Key words: *master, impatience, dismay, alert, gradually, extraordinary.* Instruct students to write the words with correct spelling and their definitions in their Personal Dictionaries. Have them pronounce each word and divide it into syllables.
3. **Multi-level options** See MULTI-LEVEL OPTIONS on p. 252.

Answers

2. sword
3. a. A swordmaster is a great teacher or master with a sword.
   b. A swordsman is a man who uses a sword.
   c. Swordsmanship is the skill of fighting with swords.

ASSESS

Have students use the vocabulary words in sentences.

Text Structure

Folktale

Share examples Ask students to share tales they know from other cultures. Have them identify the features of a folktale in the tales that they know.

Reading Strategy

Use Dialogue to Understand Character

1. **Recognize dialogue** Have students point out examples of dialogue. Call attention to the use of quotation marks. Explain that dialogue is the words of a speaker, but it also gives you information *about* the speaker.
2. **Multi-level options** See MULTI-LEVEL OPTIONS below.

Answers

3. Manjuro is young and impatient. He wants to learn quickly.
4. "I can't wait that long." "That's still too long."

ASSESS

Ask: What are three features of folktales? (time-related beginning, a lesson, simple plots and settings)

Text Structure

Folktale

"The Art of Swordsmanship" is a **folktale.** It tells a special kind of story. Folktales were originally told orally (out loud). Folktales are usually passed down to us by word of mouth. This is called the *oral tradition.* Look at the chart. It shows some features of a folktale.

Many folktales come from different regions and cultures. Read or listen to the selection. Compare and contrast the selection to other folktales you have heard from different regions and cultures.

Folktale	
A Time-Related Beginning	Folktales come from a long time ago. The story usually begins, "Once upon a time" or "Once."
Simple Plots and Settings	The events in a folktale might have taken place anywhere and at any time.
A Lesson	Folktales teach something or show how to behave.

Student CD-ROM

Reading Strategy

Use Dialogue to Understand Character

The **dialogue** of a story is the exact words the characters say. In a story, you can identify dialogue by the quotation marks ("...") around the words. Dialogue can tell you something about the speaker's **character.** Character is the combination of features that make a person different from others. This includes how he or she thinks, feels, and acts.

1. Listen as your teacher reads aloud the first page.
2. Pay special attention to what the characters say to each other.
3. Describe Manjuro's character by what he says.
4. Take notes on words he says that support your opinion.

Student CD-ROM

254 Unit 4 Discoveries

MULTI-LEVEL OPTIONS *Reading Strategy*

Newcomer *Say: I wonder if it is going to rain today.* Write on the board and *say: I said, "I wonder if it is going to rain today."* Indicate the words inside each set of quotation marks. *Say: I said these words.* Have students work in pairs. Direct them to look at paragraphs 7–9 of "The Library Card" (p. 229) and identify three quotations.

Beginning On the board, write: *The teacher said, "I wonder if it is going to rain today." Ask: What did the teacher say?* Write: *"May I borrow your pencil?" John asked. Ask: What did John say? Say: The quotation marks show you the exact words people say.*

Intermediate Have students work in pairs. Tell them to review earlier selections to find examples of dialogue. Tell them to choose a dialogue they like and perform it for another pair. Remind students that they should only speak the words inside quotation marks.

Advanced On the board, write: *I asked my mother if I could go to the party. She told me that I couldn't go. Then I asked her why, and she said that I had to finish my homework.* Have students rewrite the sentences as dialogue. Remind students to use quotation marks and speaker tags.

The Art of Swordsmanship

a folktale

by Rafe Martin

255

UNIT 4 • CHAPTER 3
Reading Selection

Reading Selection Materials

Audio: *Unit 4, Chapter 3*

Teacher Resource Book: *Reading Summary, pp. 99–100*

Preview the Selection

1. **Teacher think aloud** Have students examine the illustration as you ***say:*** *The title of the story is "The Art of Swordsmanship." I see a young man walking with a stick. He probably wants to learn how to use a sword. I wonder what he will discover. I know that folktales have a lesson in them. Will this young man discover a great teacher? Will he discover that swordfighting is easy or difficult?*
2. **Connect** Use questions to help students share their thoughts about the title, the illustration, and the content of the folktale. Ask what discoveries the young man will make about swordsmanship. Tell students they will read about his learning experiences and the discoveries he makes.

Content Connection
Technology

Ask pairs of students to enter the key word *swordsmanship* into an Internet search engine. Have students check 3–5 of the results. Ask students to write short summaries of the sites they found. Remind students to include the name of the site, the kind of site it is (sales, news, informational, etc.), and what kind of information is available on the site. Have students share their summaries with the class.

Learning Styles
Verbal

Have students find additional folktales. Suggest that they search textbooks, the library, or the Internet. Tell students that most folktales were passed orally throughout a culture until they were written down. Ask students to choose folktales to present orally within small groups. Remind them to practice good speaking and listening behaviors.

Reading Selection

Read the Selection

1. **Use text features** Direct students to the illustration. Ask them to make guesses about the characters. Then direct students to glossed words and have them find their meanings at the bottom of the page. Point out the amount of dialogue on the page. Remind students to think carefully about what the characters say and what it tells about them.
2. **Shared reading** Play the audio or read the selection to the students. Have students join in for direct quotations. Ask volunteers to act out parts of the dialogue between Manjuro and Banzo.
3. **Make predictions** *Ask: Do you think Manjuro will be a good student? Why or why not?*

Sample Answer to Guide Question
Manjuro is not a patient student. "I can't wait that long."

See Teacher Edition pp. 434–435 for a list of English-Spanish cognates in the reading selection.

Audio

Use Dialogue to Understand Character

Describe Manjuro's character. What does he say to support your description?

1 Once a young man named Manjuro sought out the greatest **swordmaster** in the country, a man named Banzo, wanting to become his student.

2 "How long," Manjuro asked, "will it take me to become a **master** swordsman?"

3 Banzo replied, "Your entire life."

4 "I can't wait that long," said Manjuro. "What if I become your **devoted** servant, how long then?"

5 "Maybe ten years," said Banzo.

6 "That's still too long," said Manjuro. "What if I work even harder, day and night? How long then?"

7 "Thirty years, then," Banzo said.

8 "Thirty years!" exclaimed Manjuro. "First you tell me ten, and then thirty. How can that be?"

swordmaster a person very skilled in using a sword
master an expert
devoted loyal

MULTI-LEVEL OPTIONS *Read the Selection*

Newcomer Play the audio. Then read the story again. Tell students to join in whenever they can. ***Ask:*** *Is Banzo the greatest swordmaster in the country?* (yes) *Does Manjuro want to wait to become a master swordsman?* (no) *Is Manjuro impatient?* (yes) *Does Manjuro become Banzo's servant?* (yes)

Beginning Read the Reading Summary aloud. Then play the audio. Tell students to join in when they see direct quotations. ***Ask:*** *Who does Manjuro ask for help?* (Banzo) *What does Manjuro want?* (to become a master swordsman) *What does Manjuro do for the first three years?* (chores)

Intermediate Have students do a paired reading. ***Ask:*** *Why does Manjuro look for Banzo?* (Banzo is the greatest swordsman.) *Why did Manjuro suggest becoming Banzo's servant?* (to learn faster) *How did Manjuro feel about his first three years of service?* (unhappy)

Advanced Have students read silently. ***Ask:*** *What characteristic does Banzo value?* (patience) *How do you know?* (That is the first lesson he teaches Manjuro.) *Does Manjuro possess this quality? Explain.* (Manjuro is not patient at first, but he learns to be in his first three years of service.)

9 "A man in such a hurry seldom learns quickly," said Banzo.

10 Understanding that he was being **reprimanded** for **impatience,** Manjuro agreed to become Banzo's servant. "However long it takes," he **vowed,** "I will become a great swordsman!"

11 But to his **dismay,** for the first year he did nothing but sweep and clean, chop wood, wash dishes, cook, carry water, and other such household tasks. He never got a chance to even look at a sword, much less handle one! "I will be patient," Manjuro said to himself. "Surely Banzo is just testing my determination." But the second year was the same as the first. As was the third. Time went on but Manjuro received no training in swordsmanship.

Use Dialogue to Understand Character

What words tell you that Manjuro's attitude has changed?

---

reprimanded criticized, scolded
impatience a lack of patience; an inability to wait
vowed promised
dismay disappointment

Read the Selection

1. **Paired reading** Have students listen to the audio or to you read the selection. Then have students read it again in pairs.
2. **Analyze character motivation and development** Ask students to explain why Manjuro agreed to be Banzo's servant. ***Ask:*** *How is Manjuro different from the beginning of the story?*
3. **Make predictions** *Ask: When do you think Manjuro will learn swordfighting?*
4. **Multi-level options** See MULTI-LEVEL OPTIONS on p. 256.

Sample Answer to Guide Question
"However long it takes," he vowed . . . "I will be patient," Manjuro said to himself.

Punctuation

Commas within quotes

Explain that when dialogue is written with quotation marks, the speaker is named before or after the spoken words. Tell students that when the speaker is named after the words, a comma comes after the words but inside the closing quotation mark. Direct students to paragraph 2. ***Ask:*** *Where else on this page do you see a comma at the end of a line of dialogue?* (paragraphs 4, 5, 6, 7)

Apply Have students add commas to correct the punctuation errors in the following sentences. Write on the board: *"A man in such a hurry seldom learns quickly" said Banzo. "However long it takes" he vowed, "I will become a great swordsman!" "I will be patient" Manjuro said to himself.*

UNIT 4 • CHAPTER 3
Reading Selection

Read the Selection

1. **Teacher read aloud** Read paragraph 12 aloud. *Ask: Why is Manjuro upset?* (He's not learning what he wants to learn.) *What did Banzo hit Manjuro with?* (a wooden sword) *Why do you think he did that?* (Maybe he was angry at Manjuro.)
2. **Role-play** Have students reread the selection in pairs. Ask volunteers to act out the scene using a foam sword. *Ask: How do you think Manjuro felt when Banzo hit him?* (surprised) *What would you do if you were Manjuro?* (I'd jump up and yell at him.)

Sample Answer to Guide Question
Manjuro feels disappointed and upset.

Use Dialogue to Understand Character

How does Manjuro feel at this point?

12 Finally Manjuro became quite upset. "I'd better leave," he thought. "I'm not learning a thing and time is going by." A short time later, while Manjuro was working in the garden, Banzo quietly approached him and thwacked him with a wooden sword. Whack! The next day Banzo again surprised Manjuro and whack! hit him again. Soon Manjuro became **alert** at all times—cooking, cleaning, chopping wood—for, whack! he never knew when Banzo might strike again with the **blunt** wooden sword.

---

alert watchful

blunt not sharp

MULTI-LEVEL OPTIONS *Read the Selection*

Newcomer *Ask: Did Manjuro want to leave?* (yes) *Did Banzo hit Manjuro with a wooden sword?* (yes) *Did Manjuro know when Banzo would strike him with the sword?* (no) *Did Manjuro learn to block the blows from the sword?* (yes) *Did Manjuro become a great swordsman?* (yes)

Beginning *Ask: When did Banzo hit Manjuro?* (when Manjuro was working in the garden) *What did he hit him with?* (a blunt wooden sword) *How did Manjuro block the sword?* (with a pot lid, a broom, a piece of wood) *What did Manjuro learn?* (to block the sword; to be a great swordsman)

Intermediate *Ask: Why did Manjuro want to leave?* (He didn't think he was learning anything.) *Why did Manjuro become alert?* (He never knew when Banzo would hit him.) *What was the result of Banzo's unexpected attacks?* (Manjuro learned to block; he became a talented swordsman.)

Advanced *Ask: How did Banzo's attacks teach Manjuro to be a master swordsman?* (Manjuro learned to be alert at all times and to block the attack.) *What does Manjuro learn from Banzo?* (swordsmanship, patience, alertness) *What lesson does this folktale teach?* (Learning takes time and hard work.)

13 **Gradually,** something **extraordinary** began to happen. As the sword descended, Manjuro instantly and **instinctively** blocked the oncoming blow with a pot lid, a broom, or a piece of wood. **Sharpened** naturally by the constant and unexpected attacks of Banzo, Manjuro had become a talented swordsman! No one could overcome him now—not even the great swordsman Banzo himself.

14 And so, Manjuro went on to become even greater than his teacher.

gradually a little at a time
extraordinary unusual, special
instinctively naturally, as if by instinct
sharpened made very skilled

About the Author

Rafe Martin (born 1946)

Rafe Martin's mother read folktales to him before he could read himself. At that time, many people in Martin's large family had recently come to the United States. He heard all of their stories whenever the family gathered. He noticed that each person added a special piece to the stories. Martin says, "Those who hear or read . . . words [in a story] can see, can feel and live, a whole life in their minds."

➤ What was the author's purpose in writing this folktale? To entertain? To inform? To persuade? To teach a lesson?

Read the Selection

1. **Shared reading** Complete the reading of the folktale as students follow along. Ask volunteers to join in for different parts. ***Ask:*** *What did Manjuro have to learn before he could be a great swordsman?* (patience, alertness)
2. **Multi-level options** See MULTI-LEVEL OPTIONS on p. 258.

About the Author

1. **Explain author's background** Rafe Martin takes part in many conferences and storytelling festivals. He works with all age groups and helps them to develop their own creative abilities. Martin has received numerous awards.
2. **Interpret the facts** ***Ask:*** *How do you think Rafe Martin learned to tell stories? What kind of stories would you like to tell?*

Across Selections

Make comparisons and contrasts Think about Manjuro and Mongoose. Compare and contrast what each one discovered and how they discovered it. ***Ask:*** *What did each learn? How did they learn it? Who helped them learn? Did they know they were learning at the time?*

Spelling

Silent *k*

Say: *In some words, the letter* k *is silent. Words that begin with* kn *are pronounced like* n. Direct student to the last sentence in paragraph 12. ***Ask:*** *What word begins with* kn*?* (knew) *How do you say it?* (new)

Apply Have students circle the silent *k* in these sentences. On the board, write: *Did you know that I hurt my knee? She is knocking on the kitchen door.* Then have them read the sentences in pairs.

Evaluate Your Reading Strategy

Use Dialogue to Understand Character

Say: *You have practiced an important reading strategy. Now you can decide how well you have done. Does this statement describe how you read?*

> When reading a story, I read dialogue carefully. Paying attention to dialogue helps me understand the characters better.

Reading Comprehension

Question-Answer Relationships

Sample Answers

1. Manjuro was a young man who wanted to learn swordsmanship.
2. Banzo was the greatest swordmaster in the country.
3. Manjuro works as Banzo's servant, cleaning and doing household chores.
4. He offers to become Banzo's devoted servant and to work day and night.
5. Manjuro's impatience will make it take a longer time to learn. More work in a shorter time doesn't make you learn faster.
6. Banzo whacks Manjuro to teach Manjuro to have quick reflexes and to respond to attacks.
7. I agree because if you are in a hurry, you don't usually stop to think and analyze everything completely.
8. I don't think his teaching method is a good one. It's not good for teachers to hit students. Also, students like to know when and what exactly they are learning.

Build Reading Fluency

Repeated Reading

Assessment Program: *Reading Fluency, Chart, p. 116*

As students read aloud, time the reading and count the number of incorrectly pronounced words. Record results in the Reading Fluency Chart.

Beyond the Reading

Reading Comprehension

Question-Answer Relationships (QAR)

"Right There" Questions

1. **Recall Facts** Who is Manjuro?
2. **Recall Facts** Who is Banzo?
3. **Recall Facts** What does Manjuro do for the first years that he works for Banzo?
4. **Analyze Cause and Effect** What is one thing that Manjuro offers to do in order to shorten his training time as a swordmaster?

"Think and Search" Questions

5. **Interpret** What does Banzo mean when he says that working harder will make Manjuro's lesson take longer?
6. **Make Inferences** Why does Banzo whack Manjuro with the wooden sword?

"Author and You" Question

7. **Evaluate** Do you agree with the statement that a man in a hurry seldom learns as quickly?

"On Your Own" Question

8. **Make Judgments** Do you think that Banzo's teaching method is a good one? What could be some bad results of this method?

Activity Book *p. 138*

Student CD-ROM

Build Reading Fluency

Repeated Reading

Rereading one paragraph at a time can help increase your reading rate and build confidence in reading dialogue.

1. With a partner, read paragraph 1 in "The Art of Swordsmanship" two times.
2. Did your reading rate increase the second time you read?
3. Next, read paragraph 2 two times.
4. Continue rereading each paragraph.
5. Stop after ten minutes.

260 **Unit 4** Discoveries

MULTI-LEVEL OPTIONS *Elements of Literature*

Newcomer Ask students to draw a picture of Manjuro at the beginning of the folktale. Then have them draw a second picture that shows Manjuro at the end of the folktale. Help them choose one piece of dialogue to add to each picture.

Beginning Have students work with partners to draw one scene from the story. Help them write one-sentence captions that tell what is happening in their pictures.

Intermediate Ask pairs of students to create comic strips of the folktale. Tell them to include important dialogue in speech bubbles. Remind students that their comic strips should illustrate any ways that Manjuro and Banzo change over the course of the folktale.

Advanced Have students use their completed charts to write an analysis of one of the characters. Tell them that their analyses should describe the character, tell about any changes, and explain what caused the changes. Ask them to include direct quotations that show special traits.

Listen, Speak, Interact 

Participate in a Dramatic Read-Aloud

A dramatic read-aloud helps you understand a selection. You can gain confidence by dramatically using **pitch, tone,** and **volume** as you read aloud.

1. Form groups of three. Decide who will be the narrator and the two characters.
2. Practice reading the story aloud with expression.
3. Take turns reading aloud in front of your classmates.

Use Your Voice
Pitch—low or high
Volume—loud or soft
Tone—angry, sad, happy, or friendly

Elements of Literature

Examine Character Traits and Changes

Authors create characters through what the characters say, think, and do. These actions show **character traits**—what the characters are like. Some traits are intelligence, kindness, and honesty. Authors also often cause their characters to change in a story.

1. Use dialogue and details in the folktale to understand the character traits of Manjuro and Banzo.
2. Create a chart like the one here in your Reading Log. Choose one character and complete the chart.

The Art of Swordsmanship	
Character	
Dialogue Words	
Actions	
Thoughts	
Appearance	
Change	

Reading Log

Activity Book *p. 139*

Student CD-ROM

Cultural Connection

Have pairs research martial arts. Ask pairs to choose kung fu, karate, jujitsu, tae kwon do, tai chi, judo, or another martial art. Ask them to find general information as well as the answers to the following questions: *In what country did this art originate? How old is this art? What are the basic beliefs and principles of this art?* Have students present their findings orally.

Learning Styles *Visual*

Some students find it helpful to use visual character maps. Have pairs create simple stick figures to represent Manjuro and Banzo. Have them connect text boxes to the figures. (Dialogue—mouth; Actions—feet; Thoughts—head; Appearance—body; Change—heart) Have them transfer the information from their charts to the boxes in their drawings.

Listen, Speak, Interact

Participate in a Dramatic Read-Aloud

Teacher Resource Book: *Reading Log, p. 64*

1. **Reread in small groups** Direct students to the chart on voice. Model examples of pitch, volume, and tone. Have students repeat after you. Arrange students into groups of three. Have them reread the story aloud.
2. **Use reference aids** Tell students that being confident about how words are pronounced will help them focus on reading dramatically. Have students list unfamiliar words and find their pronunciations using an online or a CD-ROM dictionary. Ask students to practice pronouncing the words with a partner. Check for correct pronunciation.
3. **Newcomers** Reread with this group. Have them practice reading aloud the dialogues using appropriate intonation and gestures.
4. **Evaluate** Have students write a critique of their own dramatic reading in their Reading Logs.

Elements of Literature

Examine Character Traits and Changes

Teacher Resource Book: *Reading Log, p. 64*

1. **Record information** Direct students to the chart on character change. Point out the row titles and explain as needed. Have students choose one of the characters and record details that describe their traits and examples of how they changed.
2. **Personal experience** Point out that character changes occur in movies and television shows. Allow students to share how characters change in other forms of media.
3. **Multi-level options** See MULTI-LEVEL OPTIONS on p. 260.

Have students use their notes to describe one of the characters and explain how he changed.

Word Study

Find Word Origins and Prefixes

Teacher Resource Book: *Personal Dictionary, p. 63*

1. **Teacher think aloud** On the board, write: *extraordinary. Say: I see* ordinary *in this word. I know that means "something normal, not special."* Extra- *is a prefix. I can find its meaning in the dictionary and then figure out the meaning of* extraordinary.
2. **Use a dictionary** Demonstrate finding etymologies and meanings of words and prefixes in the dictionary.

Answers

2. *in-:* Latin; "in" or "upon"; instantly, instinctively
un-: Latin; "not"; unexpectedly

Grammar Focus

Use Adverbs to Show Time

1. **Brainstorm and list** On the board, write: _____ *we played soccer. Ask: What can I add to show when this happened?*

Answers

2. Finally Manjuro became quite upset.
A short time later, while Manjuro was working . . .
The next day Banzo surprised Manjuro . . .
Soon Manjuro became alert . . .

ASSESS

Have students write sentences using three adverbs or adverb phrases to show time.

Word Study

Find Word Origins and Prefixes

Many English words have their **origins** (where they come from) in other languages. To find out the origins of words, look in a large dictionary.

Prefixes are word parts added to the beginnings of words. Some prefixes also come from other languages.

Prefix	Origin	Meaning	Prefix + Root
1. extra-	Latin	outside of or beyond	extraordinary
2. im-	Latin	not	impatience
3. in-			
4. un-			

1. Copy the chart into your Personal Dictionary. Complete it with two more words from paragraph 13.
2. Use a large dictionary to locate the origins of the prefixes.

Personal Dictionary

Activity Book *p. 140*

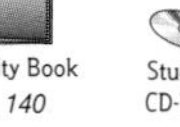
Student CD-ROM

Grammar Focus

Use Adverbs to Show Time

When writers want to tell the reader *when* something happened, they often use **adverbs** or **adverb phrases** near the beginning of a sentence.

Once a young man named Manjuro sought out the greatest swordmaster.

The word *once* places Manjuro's story in the past.

1. Here is a list of some adverbs and adverb phrases that tell *when* something happened:

once ten years ago finally
the next day soon

2. Find the adverbs showing time in paragraph 12. Write the sentences on a piece of paper.
3. For each example, underline the adverb or adverb phrase.

Activity Book *pp. 141–142*

Student Handbook

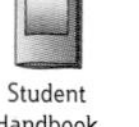
Student CD-ROM

MULTI-LEVEL OPTIONS *From Reading to Writing*

Newcomer Pair newcomer students with advanced students. Have newcomers draw a picture of a character doing something extraordinary.

Beginning Pair beginning students with intermediate students. Have beginners draw a picture of a character doing something extraordinary. Ask them to explain their pictures to their partners.

Intermediate Pair intermediate students with beginning students. Ask intermediate students to think about what their partners have drawn and said. Have partners work together to write a folktale.

Advanced Pair advanced students with newcomer students. Ask advanced students to think about the pictures drawn by their partners. Have advanced students base their folktales on their partners' pictures.

From Reading to Writing 

Write a Folktale

Write a folktale about something extraordinary that has happened to you or to someone else. Use the questions in the box to help you collect information.

1. Make sure your folktale has a beginning, a middle, and an end.
2. Use dialogue to show the character traits of the people.
3. Start your folktale with "Once upon a time . . ." Start sentences with adverbs or adverb phrases to show time.
4. Draw a visual, such as a picture, to go with your story.
5. Read your tale to the class.

> Where did the events happen?
> When did the events happen?
> Who is the main character?
> What does the character look like?
> How does the character act?
> What does the character do?
> What lesson does the character learn?

Activity Book
p. 143

Across Content Areas 

Learn About Art in Everyday Objects

Many useful objects are also works of art. Read the sentences. They tell about other objects that can be works of art.

1. The museum had **pottery.** People used the pottery to carry water.
2. The floors of the king's palace were covered with **carpets** from Persia.
3. Much of the **furniture** in the palace was made of wood that was carved by hand.
4. The dress was made of special **fabric.** The fabric had pictures painted on it.

Now match each word with the correct photo.

a. carpet
b. furniture
c. fabric
d. pottery

Activity Book
p. 144

UNIT 4 • CHAPTER 3
Beyond the Reading

From Reading to Writing

Write a Folktale

Teacher Resource Book: *Storyboard, p. 43*

1. **Use a graphic organizer** Have students suggest topics for their folktales. Students can prepare storyboards or other graphic organizers to plan their tales. Have students work in pairs to help add dialogue and adverbs to show time.
2. **Language experience story** For less fluent students, have them dictate their folktales as you write them. Then tell students to create illustrations and practice reading their tales.
3. **Multi-level options** See MULTI-LEVEL OPTIONS on p. 262.

Across Content Areas: The Arts

Learn About Art in Everyday Objects

Share cultural examples Have students find or create pictures of designs and patterns used to decorate everyday objects. If possible, have them explain the significance of colors and designs.

ASSESS

Have students draw or bring in examples of pottery, carpet, fabric, and furniture.

Reteach and Reassess

Text Structure *Ask: What kind of a beginning does a folktale have?* (time-related) *What does a folktale teach?* (a lesson) *What kind of plot does a folktale have?* (simple) *What kind of setting does a folktale have?* (simple)

Reading Strategy Divide students into groups. Ask each group to select one paragraph with dialogue. Have groups explain what the dialogue tells about the character that says it.

Elements of Literature Have students work in pairs. Ask each pair to choose an earlier selection in the book. Then have them complete a chart like the one on p. 261.

Reassess Have students write a one-paragraph summary of the story. Remind them to include descriptions of the characters, how they change, and the lesson that the folktale teaches.

Chapter Materials

Activity Book: *pp. 145–152*
Audio: *Unit 4, Chapter 4*
Student Handbook
Student CD-ROM: *Unit 4, Chapter 4*
Teacher Resource Book: *Lesson Plan, Teacher Resources, Reading Summary, Activity Book Answer Key*
Teacher Resource CD-ROM
Assessment Program: *Quiz, pp. 67–68; Teacher and Student Resources, pp. 115–144*
Assessment CD-ROM
Transparencies
The Heinle Newbury House Dictionary/CD-ROM
Web Site: www.heinle.visions.com

Objectives

Paired Reading Have pairs take turns reading the objectives section. Explain the objectives to students. ***Ask:*** *Which objectives from the list can you do already?*

Use Prior Knowledge

Discuss Astronauts

Gather and organize Arrange students in pairs to list facts they know about astronauts and outer space. ***Ask:*** *What do astronauts do? Where do they go? Do they need any special equipment? What can you find in outer space? Can we visit outer space?*

CHAPTER 4

Into the Reading

Mae Jemison,
Space Scientist

a biography
by Gail Sakurai

Objectives

Reading Find the main ideas and supporting details as you read a biography.

Listening and Speaking Discuss your goals.

Grammar Use and punctuate dependent clauses with *although* and *when*.

Writing Write a short biography.

Content Science: Understand gravity.

Use Prior Knowledge

Discuss Astronauts

An astronaut is a person who goes into outer space. What do you know about astronauts and outer space?

1. With a partner, brainstorm answers to this question. Record your ideas on a chart.
2. As a class, make a list of everyone's ideas on the board.
3. Ask a science teacher to visit your classroom. Find out which ideas on your list are correct.

Astronauts	Outer Space
train for a long time	no air

MULTI-LEVEL OPTIONS *Build Vocabulary*

Newcomer Display a picture of an astronaut. ***Say:*** *astronaut.* Point to the picture and repeat. Have students echo the word. Point to the picture a third time and encourage students to say *astronaut.* Repeat the process with pictures of a space shuttle, a doctor, a frog, and Earth.

Beginning Write on the board: *The space shuttle thundered into the morning sky above the Kennedy Space Center. Higher and higher it soared over the Atlantic Ocean.* Read the sentences once at a fairly rapid rate, then again, more slowly. ***Say:*** *I can read slowly to understand the words.*

Intermediate Have small groups create reading-rate posters. Ask students to design posters with tips for adjusting reading rate. Tell students to include the name of each method, how to do it, and why it is helpful. Post their work for students to refer to as they read.

Advanced Ask students to work in groups of three. Have each group member explain one method of adjusting reading rate. Ask students to use their own words and to provide examples. Remind students that they can also use a dictionary to find the meanings of new words.

Build Background

The United States Space Shuttle

A space shuttle is a vehicle that carries astronauts into space. Space shuttles take off like rockets but land on Earth like airplanes. In 1981, the United States sent up its first space shuttle. The space shuttle carries astronauts into space to do scientific studies. These astronauts study outer space, Earth's weather, and how the human body responds to weightlessness.

Content Connection

The space shuttle carries materials for the construction of a permanent International Space Station, where scientists will live and work.

Build Vocabulary

Adjust Reading Rate

Adjusting your reading rate (changing how fast you read) can help you understand the meanings of new words.

1. **Unfamiliar Words** Read more slowly. Take time to read each word in a sentence carefully. Reread sentences that have unfamiliar words.
2. **Familiar Words and Sentences** Use the text you already understand to help you find the meanings of unfamiliar words.
3. **Glosses** Use glosses if they are included. A gloss gives a short definition of an unfamiliar word. Glosses in this book appear at the bottom of the selection pages.

Activity Book *p. 145*

Student CD-ROM

Build Background

The United States Space Shuttle

1. **View a launching** Show a video of a shuttle launching or landing. ***Ask:*** *Where is the shuttle? What are the people doing? Why do you think they are doing that?*
2. **Content Connection** Bring in pictures of space stations. Explain that the first space station was launched in 1971 by the Russians followed by eight temporary stations, including *Mir* (Russian) and *Skylab* (American).

Build Vocabulary

Adjust Reading Rate

Teacher Resource Book: *Personal Dictionary, p. 63*

1. **Share experiences** *Say: Sometimes I see a new word when I read. I think the word is important, so I read the sentence again slowly for clues.*
2. **Relate to personal experience** Have students tell what they do when they encounter new words in a reading selection.
3. **Reading selection vocabulary** You may want to introduce the glossed words in the reading selection before students begin reading. Key words: *spacecraft, encourage, discourage, refugee, investigate.* Instruct students to write the words with correct spelling and their definitions in their Personal Dictionaries. Have them pronounce each word and divide it into syllables.
4. **Multi-level options** See MULTI-LEVEL OPTIONS on p. 264.

ASSESS

Have students describe two strategies to deal with unfamiliar words.

Content Connection *Science*

Build Vocabulary Tell students that science material often has unfamiliar information, new words, and complicated ideas. Explain that reading slowly and rereading can help them better understand this material. Provide a science article. Have students apply these reading strategies as they read. Ask students to evaluate the effectiveness of the strategy.

Learning Styles *Mathematical*

Build Background Tell students that scientists aboard the *International Space Station* can do long-term experiments because they stay in the station for a long time. Have students design long-term experiments that they would do on the *ISS.* Tell them to include a theory to be tested and a description of the experiment, as well as a prediction about the results.

Text Structure

Inductive Organization

Recognize features Direct attention to the chart of inductive organization. Explain that facts are used to draw conclusions.

Reading Strategy

Find the Main Ideas and Supporting Details

1. **Model finding the main idea** *Say: I went shopping yesterday. I drove my car to the mall. I went to two department stores. I bought a sweater for $25 and a hat for $15. Ask: What is the main idea?* (I went shopping yesterday.) *What are the details?* (drove car, mall, two department stores, etc.)
2. **Multi-level options** See MULTI-LEVEL OPTIONS below.

ASSESS

Ask: What is inductive organization? (specific facts that lead to a conclusion)

Text Structure

Inductive Organization

"Mae Jemison, Space Scientist" is a biography that organizes information **inductively. Inductive** texts begin with specific facts that lead to a general conclusion. They are organized the following way:

Inductive Organization

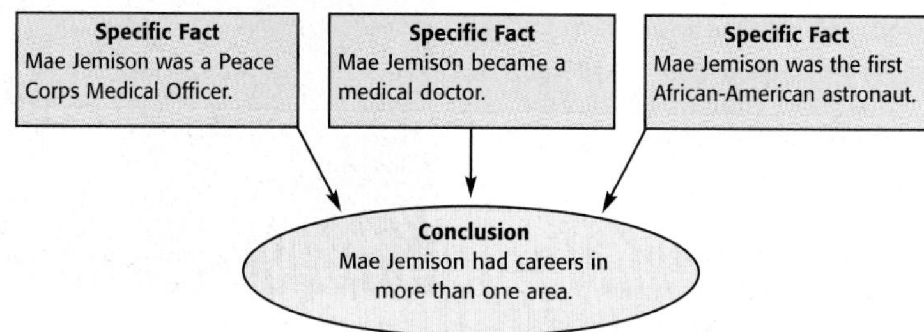

Student CD-ROM

Reading Strategy

Find the Main Ideas and Supporting Details

The **main ideas** in a biography are the important parts of a person's life. The **supporting details** include all the information that helps you understand the main idea.

Main Idea	The space shuttle *Endeavour* thundered into the morning sky above Kennedy Space Center.
Supporting Detail	Higher and higher it soared over the Atlantic Ocean.

1. As you read each paragraph, ask yourself what it is mostly about. If you are not sure, try this. Take a sentence out of the paragraph. If the paragraph is unclear without it, you have found the main idea. It is the sentence you took out.
2. Look for supporting details in the rest of the paragraph. Each detail will answer a question such as *how, what, who, when, where,* or *why.*

Student CD-ROM

MULTI-LEVEL OPTIONS *Reading Strategy*

Newcomer Write on the board: *We went to the carnival.* Ask students to draw a picture about the sentence. Tell them to include details in their pictures. *Say:* We went to the carnival *is the main idea.* Point out specific supporting details in each picture.

Beginning Show a picture of a soccer game. ***Ask:*** *Is this picture about a ball?* (no) *That is a detail. Is this a picture about a cheering crowd?* (no) *That is a detail. Is this picture about a soccer game?* (yes) *That is the main idea.* Tailor questions to your picture.

Intermediate Ask students to select a paragraph from a previous selection. Have them apply the sentence-removal strategy to find the main idea of the paragraph. Ask students to write the main idea and then to summarize the supporting details in a list.

Advanced Tell students to select a paragraph from an earlier writing assignment. Have them work in pairs. Ask students to try to identify their partner's main idea. If it is difficult, remind students to use the sentence-removal strategy to find it. Have partners discuss ways to clarify main ideas.

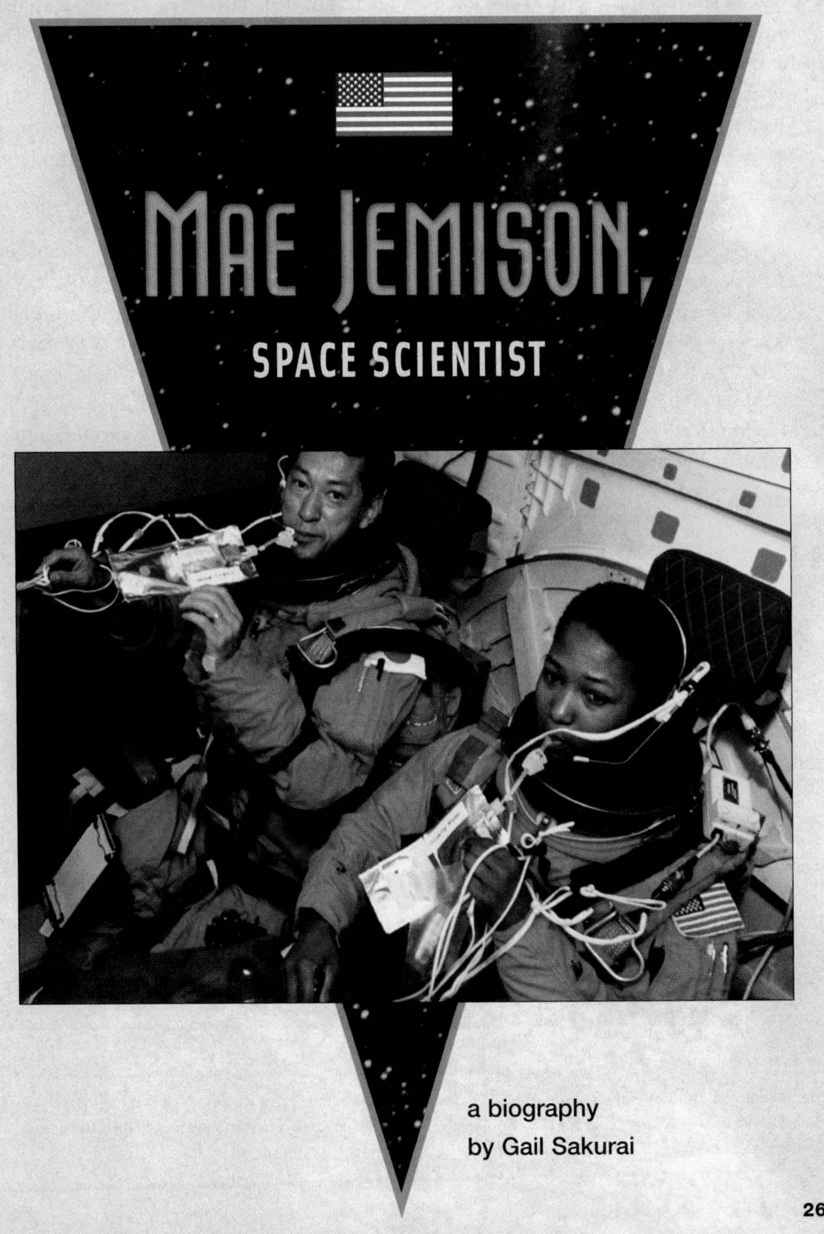

Reading Selection Materials

Audio: *Unit 4, Chapter 4*
Teacher Resource Book: *Reading Summary, pp. 101–102*

Preview the Selection

Teacher Resource Book: *Know/Want to Know/Learned Chart (KWL), p. 42*

1. **Use the photograph** Have students describe the picture. ***Ask:*** *Who are the people? Where are they? What are they doing? What do you think a space scientist does? What do they need to know? How do you think they feel in space?*
2. **Use a KWL chart** Have students complete a chart with things they know about the reading selection (title, information from the illustration). Ask them to write questions about what they want to learn about Mae Jemison, the space shuttle, and the work of a space scientist. Students can use the chart to guide their reading of the biography. Have them complete the chart after reading the selection.
3. **Relate to personal experiences** ***Ask:*** *What type of machines and equipment do you use? Do you think space scientists use some of these?*
4. **Connect** Remind students that the unit theme is *discoveries.* ***Ask:*** *What are things that scientists can discover in space?*

Content Connection *Math*

Ask students to solve the following problem. On the board, write: *The space probe* Pioneer 10 *was launched on March 3, 1972. It passed Jupiter on December 3, 1973. Jupiter is approximately 390,400,000 miles from Earth. Assuming that the probe traveled at a constant speed, about how many miles did* Pioneer 10 *travel each day?* (640 days; 610,000 miles per day) Allow students to use calculators.

Learning Styles *Intrapersonal*

Ask students to think about whether they would like to travel into space. ***Ask:*** *Would you like to be an astronaut? Why or why not? If you spent a long time in space, what would you miss the most? What would be the most exciting part of being an astronaut or traveling into space? What would frighten you?* Have students write their answers in their Reading Logs.

Teacher Resource Book: *Reading Log, p. 64*

Reading Selection

Read the Selection

1. **Use the photograph** Help students describe the launch scene.
2. **Use text features** Explain the use of italicized words in the reading selection for the proper name of the space shuttle.
3. **Teacher read aloud** Read the selection aloud. Then have students reread the paragraphs in pairs. ***Ask:*** *What is* Endeavor*?* (a space shuttle) *What did it do?* (It left the Kennedy Space Station.)

Sample Answer to Guide Question
A few minutes later, *Endeavor* was in orbit around the Earth.

See Teacher Edition pp. 434–435 for a list of English-Spanish cognates in the reading selection.

1 The space shuttle *Endeavour* **thundered** into the morning sky above Kennedy Space Center. Higher and higher it soared over the Atlantic Ocean. A few minutes later, *Endeavour* was **in orbit** around the Earth.

Find the Main Ideas and Supporting Details

What is the main idea of this paragraph?

2 Aboard the **spacecraft,** astronaut Mae Jemison could feel her heart pounding with excitement. A wide, happy grin split her face. She had just made history. She was the first African-American woman in space. The date was September 12, 1992 . . .

3 Mae's dream didn't come true overnight. It happened only after many long years of hard work, training, and preparation . . . Her parents, Charlie and Dorothy Jemison, were helpful and **supportive** of all of Mae's interests. "They put up with all kinds of stuff, like science projects, dance classes, and art lessons," Mae said. "They **encouraged** me to do it, and they would find the money, time, and energy to help me be involved."

Audio

thundered made a noise like thunder
in orbit on a path in space that leads around Earth
spacecraft a machine that flies in space
supportive giving support; helping to make happen
encouraged acted in ways that helped something happen

MULTI-LEVEL OPTIONS *Read the Selection*

Newcomer Play the audio. ***Ask:*** *Is* Endeavor *the name of a space shuttle?* (yes) *Is Mae Jemison an astronaut?* (yes) *Was she the first African-American woman in space?* (yes) *Did people stop Mae from following her dream?* (no) *Did she go to college and medical school?* (yes)

Beginning Read the Reading Summary aloud. ***Ask:*** *Who was the first African-American woman in space?* (Mae Jemison) *Did Mae reach her goal quickly and easily?* (no) *Who supported Mae?* (her parents) *Who thought she should be a nurse?* (her teacher)

Intermediate Read the Reading Summary aloud. Have students do a paired reading. ***Ask:*** *Why was Mae excited?* (She was the first African-American woman in space.) *How did Mae's parents help her realize her dream?* (They always supported her interests.) *What did Mae do after going to college?* (She went to medical school.)

Advanced Have students do a jigsaw reading. Assign groups to be responsible for teaching different paragraphs. ***Ask:*** *Do you think Mae was ever discouraged about reaching her goal? What words would best describe Mae's personality? Explain your answer with examples.*

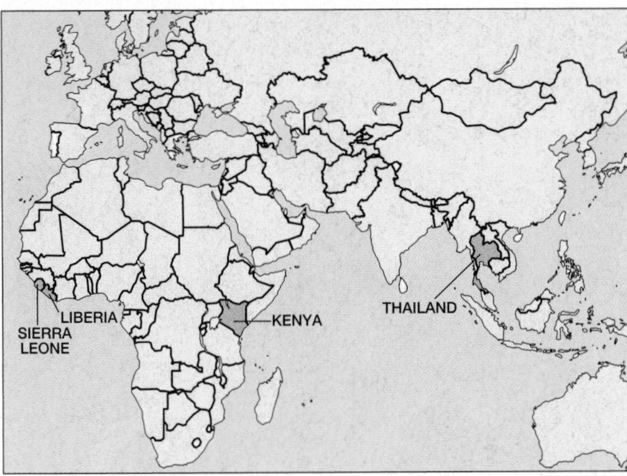

4 Other adults were not as encouraging as Mae's parents. When Mae told her kindergarten teacher that she wanted to be a scientist, the teacher said, "Don't you mean a nurse?" In those days, very few African-Americans or women were scientists. Many people, like Mae's teacher, couldn't imagine a little black girl growing up to become a scientist. But Mae refused to let other people's limited imaginations stop her from following her dreams.

5 Mae loved to work on school science projects. She spent many hours at the public library, reading books about science and space . . . She knew that she wanted to be an astronaut. Although all the astronauts at that time were white and male, Mae wasn't **discouraged** . . .

Find the Main Ideas and Supporting Details

How does the detail that Jemison spent many hours at the public library reading about science and space support the main idea of this paragraph?

Mae went to college, and then to medical school. She traveled to several countries as part of her medical training . . . She helped provide basic medical care for people in rural Kenya and at a Cambodian **refugee** camp in Thailand . . . 6

discouraged likely to give up

refugee a person who has left his or her homeland because of war, poverty, or hunger

Read the Selection

1. **Use a map** Have students identify the labeled countries on the map. Ask students to guess why they might be important.
2. **Reciprocal reading** Play the audio. Then arrange students in groups for reciprocal reading. Assign each student a different portion of the selection. One student should read aloud his/her portion, answer questions of others in the group, and help summarize the portion.
3. **Analyze character traits and motivation** Ask questions to help students describe Mae Jemison and her reasons for studying science and medicine.
4. **Multi-level options** See MULTI-LEVEL OPTIONS on p. 268.

Sample Answer to Guide Question

This detail shows that Mae loved reading and learning about science.

A Capitalization

Proper nouns

Explain to students that nouns that name a particular person, place, or thing are called proper nouns. Tell students that proper nouns are always capitalized. ***Ask:*** *Why does Mae Jemison's name start with capital letters?* (It is a proper noun.) *Can you find two more names in paragraph 3 that begin with capital letters?* (Charlie and Dorothy Jemison)

Apply Have students correct the capitalization errors in the following sentences. Write on the board: *The space shuttle endeavor rose above the kennedy space center. It soared over the atlantic ocean. Dr. jemison helped provide medical care for people in kenya and thailand.*

Read the Selection

Student read aloud Ask volunteers to read aloud. ***Ask:*** *Where did Mae work as Medical Officer in the Peace Corps?* (in Sierra Leone and Liberia) *What types of classes did she begin?* (engineering) *What is NASA?* (The National Aeronautics and Space Administration, the program that does U.S. space exploration) *Do you think it was easy or difficult to be accepted in the astronaut program?* (Difficult; there were 2,000 applicants.)

Sample Answer to Guide Question
Mae was accepted into the astronaut program in June 1987.

7 Although she had settled into a career as a doctor, . . . Mae decided to join the Peace Corps, an organization of volunteers who work to improve conditions in **developing nations.**

8 She spent more than two years in West Africa as the Peace Corps Medical Officer for Sierra Leone and Liberia . . .

9 When her **tour of duty** in the Peace Corps was over, Mae returned home and **resumed** her medical practice. She also started taking engineering classes.

Mae had not forgotten her dream 10
of traveling in space . . . She applied to the National Aeronautics and Space Administration (NASA), which is responsible for U.S. space exploration . . . She was accepted into the astronaut program in June, 1987. She was one of only fifteen people chosen from nearly two thousand **qualified applicants!** . . .

Find the Main Ideas and Supporting Details

What is the main idea of this paragraph?

developing nations countries with less wealth and technology
tour of duty time you have agreed to serve
resumed started again
qualified trained in the correct way
applicants people who want and apply for a job

MULTI-LEVEL OPTIONS *Read the Selection*

Newcomer ***Ask:*** *Was Mae a doctor?* (yes) *Did Mae join the Peace Corps?* (yes) *Did Mae forget her dream of traveling in space?* (no) *Was Mae accepted into the astronaut program?* (yes) *Did Mae go right into space?* (no) *Did Mae do an experiment about motion sickness?* (yes)

Beginning ***Ask:*** *Where did Mae go after the Peace Corps?* (home) *What government agency trains astronauts?* (NASA) *What kind of an astronaut did Mae become?* (a mission specialist) *What did Mae investigate?* (a new way to control motion sickness)

Intermediate ***Ask:*** *What did Mae do after her Peace Corps duty ended?* (She returned home and practiced medicine.) *Why did Mae apply to NASA?* (She remembered her dream of space travel.) *How did Mae earn a place in history books?* (She became the first African-American woman in space.)

Advanced ***Ask:*** *Why is it significant that Mae was accepted into the astronaut program?* (Over 2,000 people applied, but only 15 were accepted.) *What does Mae Jemison believe about equality among different people of the world? Explain.* (She believes that all peoples of the world can be and do anything they want.)

11 At the end of her training, . . . Mae officially became a mission **specialist** astronaut. "We're the ones people often call the scientist astronauts," Mae explained. "Our responsibilities are . . . to do the experiments once you get into orbit . . . and . . . do . . . space walks . . ."

Although Mae was a **full-fledged** 12
astronaut, she still had to wait four more years before she went into space . . . But on September 12, 1992, the long wait was over . . . On that day Dr. Mae Jemison earned her place in the history books as the first African-American woman in space. Mae said, "My participation in the space shuttle mission helps to say that all peoples of the world have astronomers, physicists, and explorers."

Find the Main Ideas and Supporting Details

What is one detail that supports the main idea that Mae Jemison finally made it into space?

Endeavour's mission was **devoted to** 13
scientific research. Mae was responsible for several key experiments . . . She **investigated** a new way of controlling space motion sickness. Half of all astronauts experience space sickness during the first few days in space. They often feel dizzy and nauseated. Astronauts can take medicine to control space sickness, but the medicine can make them tired.

---

specialist someone with special training in a particular area

full-fledged completely trained

devoted to focused on

investigated explored, studied

Read the Selection

1. **Guided reading** Continue the reading of the selection as students follow along. Read aloud or ask volunteers to read. Pause to ask comprehension questions and to clarify vocabulary. ***Ask:*** *What does a mission specialist astronaut do?* (They do experiments in space.) *What types of experiments did Mae do in space?* (She studied a new way to control motion sickness.)
2. **Find main ideas** Use guide questions to help students identify the main ideas.
3. **Analyze character** Ask students to describe how Mae felt when she finally went on the space shuttle into space. Have them consider if they would like to go into space and how they would feel.
4. **Multi-level options** See MULTI-LEVEL OPTIONS on p. 270.

Sample Answer to Guide Question

But on September 12, 1992, the long wait was over. . . .

A Capitalization

Acronyms as proper nouns

Write *NASA* on the board. Tell students that *NASA* is an acronym for the National Aeronautics and Space Administration. Point out that the acronym is made from the first letters, or initials, of each word. ***Say:*** *When a proper noun is abbreviated as an acronym, all the letters are capitalized.*

Apply Ask students to write the acronyms for these proper nouns. Write: *North Atlantic Treaty Organization* (NATO); Public Broadcasting Service (PBS); *Strategic Arms Limitation Talks* (SALT); *United States Air Force* (USAF); *Scholastic Aptitude Test* (SAT). Challenge students to think of and write more acronyms for proper nouns.

Read the Selection

Reciprocal reading Read paragraphs 14–15 aloud. Then arrange students in groups for reciprocal reading. Assign each student a different portion of the selection. Students should read aloud the portion, answer questions of others in the group, and help summarize it.

Sample Answer to Guide Question
The first sentence is the main idea.

14 To carry out the space sickness experiment, Mae used "biofeedback" techniques. Biofeedback uses **meditation** and relaxation to control the body's functions. Mae wore special **monitoring** equipment to record her heart rate, breathing, temperature, and other body functions. If she started to feel ill, she would meditate . . . The purpose of the experiment was to see if Mae could avoid space sickness without taking medication. The results of the experiment were not **conclusive,** but space researchers still hope to use biofeedback in the future.

Find the Main Ideas and Supporting Details

Is the main idea of this paragraph in the first or last sentence?

15 Mae was also in charge of the frog experiment. Early in the flight, she **fertilized** eggs from female South African frogs. A few days later, tadpoles **hatched.** She then watched the tadpoles carefully. Her goal was to find out if the tadpoles would develop normally in the **near-zero gravity** of space.

"What we've seen is that the eggs were fertilized and the tadpoles looked pretty good," said Mae. "It was exciting because that's a question that we didn't have any information on before."

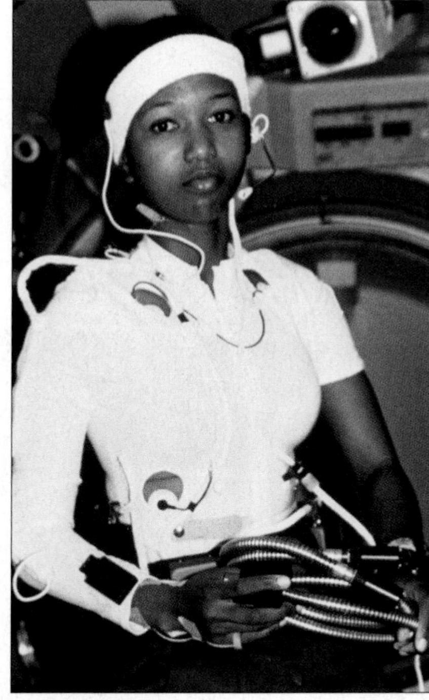

meditation a period of focused deep thought and quiet thinking
monitoring keeping track of, watching
conclusive sure, complete, final
fertilized started the development of new life
hatched came out of an egg
near-zero gravity almost no gravity

MULTI-LEVEL OPTIONS *Read the Selection*

Newcomer *Ask: Did Mae wear special equipment?* (yes) *Did the equipment record her heart rate and temperature?* (yes) *Did her experiments prove biofeedback always works?* (no) *Was she in charge of the frog experiment?* (yes) *Is she still an astronaut?* (no) *Does she still travel?* (yes)

Beginning *Ask: What did Mae wear to record her body functions?* (monitoring equipment) *What did Mae do if she started to feel ill?* (She meditated.) *What other experiment did Mae do?* (a frog experiment) *What did Mae do after retiring from NASA?* (She formed her own company.)

Intermediate *Ask: What was the goal of the space sickness experiment?* (to find out how to prevent space sickness) *What were the results?* (Biofeedback may help.) *What was the goal of the frog experiment?* (to find out if tadpoles develop normally in the near-zero gravity of space)

Advanced *Ask: How did Mae make her childhood dreams come true?* (She studied medicine, worked hard, and stayed focused.) *What "new challenges" did Mae confront?* (helping to make life better in poor and developing countries)

16 On September 20, 1992, at 8:53 A.M., *Endeavour* landed at Kennedy Space Center. The crew had spent more than 190 hours (almost eight days) in space. They had traveled 3.3 million miles and had completed 127 orbits of Earth! . . .

17 Mae Jemison had made her childhood dream come true. She was ready for new challenges . . . On March 8, 1993, she permanently **resigned** from the astronaut corps.

18 Mae formed her own company called The Jemison Group, Inc. The Jemison Group's goal is to develop ways of using science and technology to improve the quality of life. Mae's company makes a special effort to improve conditions in poor and developing countries . . .

Find the Main Ideas and Supporting Details

Name a detail that supports the main idea about The Jemison Group, Inc.

Besides her work with The Jemison Group, Mae spends much of her time traveling around the country, giving speeches, and encouraging young people to follow their dreams. Mae Jemison believes in the motto: 19

"Don't be limited by others' limited imaginations." 20

resigned gave up her job

About the Author

Gail Sakurai (born 1952)

Gail Sakurai started to write stories because she loved to read. She was only eight when she wrote her first story. Many of Sakurai's books are nonfiction books about people or important parts of history. She also enjoys retelling folktales. Sakurai feels that it is hard to find the time for writing. Yet she does not let that stop her. Sakurai says, "My childhood dream came true with the publication of my first book in 1994—only twenty-nine years later than originally planned."

➤ What challenges did Gail Sakurai face in writing and publishing her books?

Read the Selection

1. **Student read aloud** Ask volunteers to read aloud. ***Ask:*** *Why do you think Mae began her company, the Jemison Group, Inc.?* (She wants to discover new ways to improve the quality of life.)
2. **Summarize** Have students work in groups to summarize the events in Mae's life.
3. **Multi-level options** See MULTI-LEVEL OPTIONS on p. 272.

Sample Answer to Guide Question
The company tries to improve conditions in poor and developing countries.

About the Author

1. **Explain author's background** Gail Sakurai was a big fan of *Star Trek,* a TV series and series of movies about travels in space.
2. **Interpret the facts** ***Ask:*** *Why do you think Gail Sakurai chose to write a biography of Mae Jemison?* (Gail is interested in space travel, and Mae is a true hero in space history.)

Across Selections

Contrast Have students point out differences between a first-person narrative, such as "Discovering the Inca Ice Maiden," and this third-person biography. ***Ask:*** *Do you feel you know more about the subject of a reading in the first-person or the third-person?*

Punctuation

Parentheses for information

Explain that when writers want to include extra information in a sentence, they can put the information in parentheses. Tell students that the information inside the parentheses explains, describes, or renames. Direct students to paragraph 16. ***Ask:*** *Why is* almost eight days *in parentheses?* (It is extra information.) *What does this information do?* (It renames *190 hours.*)

Evaluate Your Reading Strategy

Find the Main Ideas and Supporting Details ***Say:*** *You have practiced an important reading strategy. Now you can decide how well you have done. Does this statement describe how you read?*

I look for the main idea and supporting details when I read. Finding the main idea and supporting details helps me understand and recall what I read.

Reading Comprehension

Question-Answer Relationships

Sample Answers

1. She did experiments on space sickness and frog development.
2. The biography focuses on her job as an astronaut.
3. Her work as an astronaut is important because she was the first African-American woman to go into space.
4. Before she became an astronaut, she was a doctor.
5. To get into space she had to apply to NASA, be chosen, go through astronaut training, and wait for a place on a shuttle flight.
6. I think she set up a company so that she can continue to use her knowledge of science and medicine to help solve problems around the world.
7. I would ask her what problems are the most important right now for scientists to solve. I would also ask her if she thinks that science can find all the answers to world problems.
8. I feel very happy and proud when I reach a goal.
9. I like her motto because it makes me realize that I can try to reach any goal even if others haven't done it before me.

Build Reading Fluency

Reading Silently

Assessment Program: *Reading Fluency Chart, p. 116*

When students have completed the reading fluency activity, record their progress in the Reading Fluency Chart.

Beyond the Reading

Reading Comprehension

Question-Answer Relationships (QAR)

"Right There" Questions

1. **Recall Facts** What experiments does Mae Jemison do in space?
2. **Recall Facts** Which of Mae Jemison's jobs does the biography focus on?

"Think and Search" Questions

3. **Find the Main Idea** Why is Mae Jemison's work as an astronaut especially important?
4. **Recognize Sequence of Events** What was Mae Jemison's job before she became an astronaut?
5. **Note Steps in a Process** What steps did Mae Jemison have to take to get into space?

"Author and You" Questions

6. **Draw Conclusions** Why do you think Mae Jemison set up a company that uses science to help people living in developing countries?
7. **Form Questions** Based on the information and knowledge you have, what additional questions would you ask Mae Jemison?

"On Your Own" Questions

8. **Compare Your Own Experiences** Mae Jemison reached an important goal. How do you feel when you reach a goal?
9. **Evaluate** Do you agree with Mae Jemison's motto? Why or why not?

Activity Book p. 146

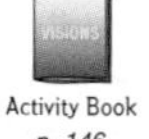
Student CD-ROM

Build Reading Fluency

Reading Silently

Reading silently is good practice. It helps you learn to read faster.

1. Listen to the audio recording of paragraphs 1 and 2 of "Mae Jemison, Space Scientist."
2. Listen to the chunks of words as you follow along.
3. Reread paragraphs 1 and 2 silently two times.
4. Your teacher or partner will time your second reading. Raise your hand when you are finished.

MULTI-LEVEL OPTIONS *Elements of Literature*

Newcomer Draw a time line with four cross marks. Play the audio. Pause at each event from the list and write it at the appropriate mark. (b, d, c, a) Point to each event. *Say: This happened when Mae was a little girl. Then this happened. This happened later. This happened last.*

Beginning Have students work in pairs. Tell each pair to copy the four sentences onto strips of paper. Ask them to think about approximately how old Mae was when each event happened. Have them put the strips in order.

Intermediate Have students work in pairs to put the events in order. Then ask individuals to list three more events from the story. Have partners exchange lists. Ask students to add their partners' new items to their lists, putting them in chronological order.

Advanced Have students put the events in order. Then ask them to write a paragraph about each event. Tell them that their paragraphs should tell the events in chronological order. Suggest that they use transition words such as *first, next, then,* and *finally.*

Beyond the Reading

Listen, Speak, Interact 

Discuss Your Goals

When you set a goal for yourself, you choose something that you want to happen in the future, and you work to make it happen. For example, getting a good job is a goal for many young people.

Mae Jemison worked hard for a long time to reach her goal of becoming an astronaut. The author tells about what Jemison studied and what jobs she had to prepare her for space.

1. With a partner, reread the biography aloud. Record ways Jemison worked to reach her goal.
2. Talk about goals each of you has worked hard to reach. List them in a chart like the one below.
3. Share your goals with your partner and the steps you took to reach your goals.

Goals	*Steps to Reach the Goals*
learn to skateboard	ask my friend for help practice every day

Elements of Literature

Recognize Flashbacks

The biography "Mae Jemison, Space Scientist" begins when Mae Jemison is an adult. Then the selection goes back in time to tell stories about Jemison's childhood. In a **flashback,** the author describes earlier events.

In your Reading Log, put the following events in chronological (time) order—the order in which they happened.

a. Jemison goes into space on September 12, 1992.
b. Jemison's kindergarten teacher tells her to become a nurse.
c. Jemison goes to medical school.
d. Jemison works on school science projects.

Reading Log

Activity Book p. 147

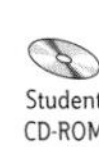
Student CD-ROM

Listen, Speak, Interact

Discuss Your Goals

1. **Think-pair-share** Brainstorm and list goals students have met. Model describing a goal and explaining the steps you took to reach the goal. Have students think about a goal they achieved. Then in pairs, ask them to explain the steps they took to meet it.
2. **Newcomers** List students' ideas on the board. Have them act out the steps for achieving the goal. List key words and phrases on the board. Have pairs complete storyboards with captions to share with the class.

Answers

1. *Example:* She studied science and space; went to medical school; joined the Peace Corps; took engineering classes; applied to NASA.

Elements of Literature

Recognize Flashbacks

Teacher Resource Book: *Reading Log, p. 64*

1. **Teacher think aloud** Write *flashback* on the board. ***Say:*** *I see the words* flash *and* back. Flash *reminds me of something that happens quickly and suddenly.* Back *is "something behind." So a flashback is an event where someone suddenly looks back in the past.* Then in pairs, have students arrange the story events in proper chronological order.
2. **Personal experience** Ask students for examples of flashbacks in movies or television shows.
3. **Multi-level options** See MULTI-LEVEL OPTIONS on p. 274.

Answers

b., d., c., a.

ASSESS

Have students write their own definition of a flashback.

Content Connection *The Arts*

Ask students to think about flashbacks they have seen in films, television shows, or plays. Have students select an example and write a paragraph that summarizes the plot. Then have students write a paragraph that explains how the flashback was used. Ask students to explain the purpose of the flashback in the plot.

Learning Styles *Intrapersonal*

Have students think of goals they have not yet reached. ***Ask:*** *What is the best way to reach your goal? What things will you have to do to reach your goal?* Ask students to create step-by-step plans for reaching their goals. Have them write their plans in narrative or list form. Tell them to include dates they hope to reach each step. Instruct students to include at least three steps in their plans.

UNIT 4 • CHAPTER 4

Beyond the Reading

Word Study

Identify Greek and Latin Word Origins

Teacher Resource Book: *Personal Dictionary, p. 63*

Use cognates Have students suggest cognates in other languages with these roots.

Answers

3. *Sample answers: phys -:* Greek; "nature"; "a person who studies nature"
tele -: Greek; "far off" + *vision:* Latin; "to see"; "a device used to see far away events"
cover: Latin; "to hide"; "to find something hidden or unknown"

Grammar Focus

Use and Punctuate Dependent Clauses with *Although* and *When*

Review clauses Write on the board: *Although it's raining, we are outdoors.* Help students identify the subject and verb in the main and dependent clause.

Answers

1. Although she had settled into a career . . . , Mae decided to join . . . (7); When her tour of duty in the Peace Corps was over, Mae returned home and resumed her medical practice (9); Although Mae was a full-fledged astronaut, she still had to wait . . . (12)
2. Example: When I watch the stars, I think about going on the space shuttle.

ASSESS

Have students write complex sentences using *although* and *when.*

Word Study

Identify Greek and Latin Word Origins

Many English words and spellings come from other languages and cultures. Knowing the meanings of some Greek and Latin word forms, or **roots,** can help you figure out English words.

1. Copy a chart like the one below into your Personal Dictionary.
2. Look up the word origins and their meanings in the dictionary.
3. Complete the chart.

Word	Root	Origin	Root Meaning	English Definition
astronaut	astro	Latin	star	person who flies into space (to the stars)
	naut	Latin	sailor	
physicist	phys			
television	tele			
	vision			
discover	cover			

Personal Dictionary

The Heinle Newbury House Dictionary

Activity Book *p. 148*

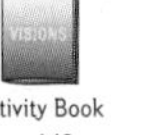

Student CD-ROM

Grammar Focus

Use and Punctuate Dependent Clauses with *Although* and *When*

Gail Sakurai begins several sentences with a clause that starts with **although** or **when.**

Although all of the astronauts at that time were white and male,
(dependent clause)

Mae wasn't discouraged.
(main clause)

Dependent clauses are not complete sentences. They must be used with a main clause.

You must always use a comma after a dependent clause when it comes at the beginning of a sentence.

1. Find other sentences in the selection that include dependent clauses with *although* or *when.*
2. Write a sentence that begins with a clause containing *although* or *when.* Use correct punctuation.

Activity Book *pp. 149–150*

Student Handbook

Student CD-ROM

276 Unit 4 Discoveries

MULTI-LEVEL OPTIONS *From Reading to Writing*

Newcomer Have students draw pictures of people who are important to them. Ask them to draw one picture for each of these periods in the person's life: childhood, adolescence, and adulthood.

Beginning Have students draw pictures of a person who is important to them. Ask them to draw one picture for each of these periods in the person's life: a special moment in the person's life, his/her childhood, and adulthood. Ask students to make simple statements based on their pictures.

Intermediate Help students complete the outline. Then have them write a paragraph about each item in the outline. Have them read their biographies to a partner.

Advanced Ask pairs of students to peer-edit the biographies. Reviewers should check for spelling, punctuation, and word choice. They should also check for a flashback and important dates, facts, and events. Remind students to be tactful. Also point out that final changes are up to the author.

From Reading to Writing 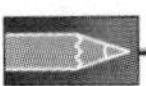

Write a Short Biography

1. Choose a person who is important to you in some way.
2. Gather information by talking to the person or by using reference materials and resources in the library and on the Internet.
3. Make sure all facts, dates, and details are correct.
4. Begin your biography with a moment from the person's adult life. Then use a flashback to explore how that person grew up and was educated.
5. Include important parts of the person's life. Do not describe everything that the person ever did. Show your readers the most important parts of the person's life.

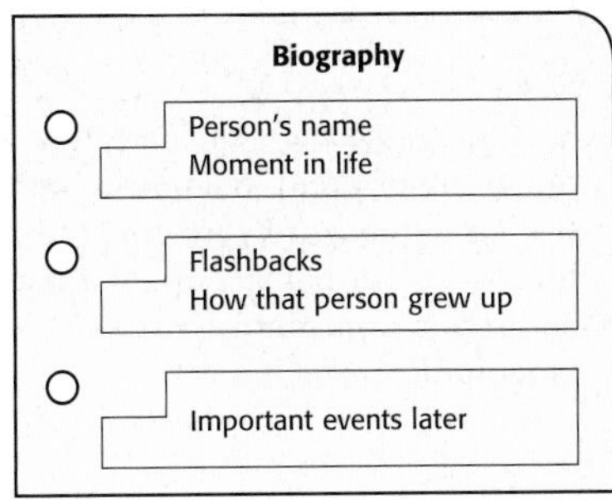

Activity Book
p. 151

Across Content Areas 

Understand Gravity

When you read scientific texts, look for **definitions, explanations,** and **examples.** Read the following article. Then find an example of each.

Gravity

Gravity is the force that attracts one object to another. If an object is very large, like Earth, its attraction is very strong. If you jump into the air, you fall back down because Earth's gravity pulls you down.

The larger an object is, the greater its gravitational pull is. The sun is much larger than Earth, so it has much more gravity.

Astronauts in space float in the air. This is because the astronauts do not have the same gravitational force pulling them to Earth as when they are on (or closer to) Earth.

Activity Book
p. 152

From Reading to Writing

Write a Short Biography

Teacher Resource Book: *Outline, p. 59*

1. **Use an outline** Have students gather information about a person for their biography assignment. Model using an outline to organize ideas. Discuss the content of each of the paragraphs. Ask students to choose events and create outlines.
2. **Think-quickwrite-pair-share** Ask students to use their outlines and write as much as they can about the person they chose. As students share with a partner, they can add details about the person's life.
3. **Multi-level options** See MULTI-LEVEL OPTIONS on p. 276.

Across Content Areas: Science

Understand Gravity

Define and clarify Explain: *definition, explanation,* and *example.* Direct students to the article in their textbook. Have them point out a definition (the force that attracts one object to another), an explanation (if an object is large, its attraction is strong), and an example of gravity (When you jump into the air, you fall back because Earth's gravity pulls you down.).

Have students prepare a timeline of the individual they wrote about for the short biography. Have them label the flashback they used.

Reteach and Reassess

Text Structure Draw an inductive organization chart. Ask students to supply facts from the selection to support this conclusion: *Mae Jemison is determined and hardworking.*

Reading Strategy Divide students into small groups. Assign one paragraph from the selection to each group. Have each group find the main idea of the paragraph and any supporting details.

Elements of Literature Ask students to search previous selections or other sources for examples of flashbacks. Have students discuss their findings in pairs.

Reassess Instruct groups to create a timeline of the important events in Mae Jemison's life. Ask students to use another color to number the events in the order they are presented in the selection.

UNIT 4 Apply and Expand

Materials

Student Handbook
CNN Video: *Unit 4*
Teacher Resource Book: *Lesson Plan, p. 23; Teacher Resources, pp. 35–64; Video Script, pp. 167–168; Video Worksheet, p. 176; School-Home Connection, pp. 140–146*
Teacher Resource CD-ROM
Assessment Program: *Unit 4 Test, pp. 69–74; Teacher and Student Resources, pp. 115–144*
Assessment CD-ROM
Transparencies
The Heinle Newbury House Dictionary/CD-ROM
Heinle Reading Library
Web Site: www.heinle.visions.com

Listening and Speaking Workshop

Report a Biographical Sketch About a Person's Hobby

Teacher Resource Book: *Interview, p.54*

Ask and answer questions Review question words and question formation.

Step 1: Prepare a list of questions. Remind students how to form *wh*-questions. Model asking the questions. Have students practice asking the questions.

Step 2: Conduct your interview. Arrange students in pairs to interview each other. Remind them to take notes on their partners' responses.

UNIT 4 Apply and Expand

Listening and Speaking Workshop

Report a Biographical Sketch About a Person's Hobby

Topic

A biographical sketch is about one thing or event in a person's life, such as a hobby. You are going to interview your partner about a hobby and report your findings as a biographical sketch.

Step 1: Prepare a list of questions.

1. *Who* are you? (Get your partner's name, age, and grade in school.)
2. *Where* do you live? (City, state, neighborhood)
3. *What* do you like to do? (Hobby—could be a sport, singing, collecting something)
4. *With whom* do you do the hobby? (Family and friends, alone)
5. *What* do you like most about your hobby?

Step 2: Conduct your interview.

1. Make sure your partner knows the questions ahead of time.
2. Use note cards for each question to help you stay on track. Make notes about what your partner says.
3. Allow your partner enough time to answer without interruption.
4. Ask for more details if necessary.
5. State the purpose of the interview before you begin.
6. If possible, record your interview on audio or video.

Active Listening Checklist

1. I liked ____ because ____.
2. I understood the purpose of the biographical sketch. Yes / No
3. I understood the major ideas. Yes / No
4. I needed you to clarify ____.

Speaking Checklist

1. Did I speak too slowly, too quickly, or just right?
2. Did I speak loudly enough for the audience to hear me?
3. Did I produce the correct intonation patterns? (Was my voice too high, too low, or just right?)
4. Did I show respect and act politely?

MULTI-LEVEL OPTIONS *Listening and Speaking Workshop*

Newcomer *Say: I like to ____. My hobby is ____.* Mime doing your hobby. ***Ask:*** *What do you like to do?* Have students draw pictures of themselves doing their hobbies. Help them label their activities. Ask students to mime their favorite hobby.

Beginning Tell students to ask partners questions, such as *What is your name? What is your hobby? Why do you like it?* Have partners answer the questions. Then divide students into small groups and have them retell the information they learned about their partners' hobbies. Make a class chart of hobbies.

Intermediate Have students work in pairs to develop the questions for their interviews. Tell them to practice asking questions and taking notes. Then ***ask:*** *What did you have difficulty with? What can you do to make that easier?*

Advanced Have students ask their partners: *Do you have a funny or interesting story about your hobby? Did anything funny or interesting ever happen when you were doing your hobby?* Instruct students to use the responses to add interest-grabbing openers to their biographical sketches.

Step 3: Be attentive and polite.

1. Look at your partner when he or she is speaking.
2. Show interest in the answers.
3. Thank the person when you are finished.

Step 4: Prepare and give your biographical sketch.

1. Review the notes you took and organize the information in a logical way. If you recorded the interview, listen to it to be sure that your information is correct.
2. Ask your teacher to help you distinguish your intonation patterns. This will help you determine if your voice is too low or too high.
3. On a new set of note cards, write the three or four key points that you want to make.
4. Practice your report. Give it to your partner. Ask him or her to check your facts. Use the Presentation Checklist in your Student Handbook.
5. Give your biographical sketch to the class.

Viewing Workshop

Interpret Important Ideas from Maps

View a Historical Atlas

At the school library, find a historical atlas. View maps from different time periods. Use the Internet or CD-ROM encyclopedias to view exploration maps. Choose two maps to study further. For each map, answer the following questions:

1. What does the map show? What is its title?
2. What time period does the map cover?
3. How are the places on the map different?
4. What kind of special information does the map explain? It might explain exploration routes, crops grown in certain places, where and when battles were fought.
5. Does the legend help you understand the map?

Further Viewing

Watch the *Visions* CNN Video for Unit 4. Do the Video Worksheet.

CNN Video

Step 3: Be attentive and polite.

Model appropriate behavior and expressions for acknowledging responses. Remind students to ask for clarification as needed.

Step 4: Prepare and give your biographical sketch.

Review procedures and checklists before students practice in pairs. Demonstrate effective gestures and body language.

ASSESS

Have students write a sentence telling the most important thing they learned in preparing and presenting their sketch.

Portfolio

Students may choose to record or videotape their biographical sketches to place in their portfolios.

Viewing Workshop

Interpret Important Ideas from Maps

1. **Use an atlas** Help students find atlases and other sources with historical maps in the library. Point out time periods and implications. Call attention to map keys and legends.
2. **Take notes** Compare the historical maps to current maps. Students can answer the questions as they study their maps.

Content Connection *Math*

Have students work in pairs to select two locations on one of their maps. Ask students to use the scale and a calculator to figure out the distance between the two locations. Ask students to find the distance in miles and kilometers.

Learning Styles *Natural*

Have students view maps with exploration routes. Ask students to imagine that they are explorers. Tell them to plan a route for their expedition. Ask them to make a list of the supplies they think they will need for their journey. Have them present their plans to the class.

UNIT 4
Apply and Expand

Writer's Workshop

Write to Inform: Write an E-mail

Write an e-mail Point out that an e-mail is a letter that is sent electronically.

Step 1: Brainstorm.
Have students choose their books. In groups or individually, have students brainstorm a list of everything they liked in their books.

Step 2: Arrange your ideas in logical order.
Have students read through their lists and circle the most important ideas and details. Then ask them to number the ideas in a logical order.

Step 3: Write a draft.
Model examples as needed. Review the purpose and content of each of the paragraphs.

Writer's Workshop

Write to Inform: Write an E-mail

Writing Prompt

You want to tell a friend about the best book you have ever read. Write an e-mail message to recommend it to him or her.

Step 1: Brainstorm.

1. What book interests you?
2. Make a short list of specific things about the book that interest you.
3. What effect did it have on you?

Step 2: Arrange your ideas in logical order.

1. What is the most important idea?
2. What is the least important idea?

Step 3: Write a draft.

Paragraph 1: The Opening

1. Tell your friend that you are writing to tell about a great book.
2. Name the title and the author, and tell why you like the book.
3. Use a tone and a style to show why you like this book best.

Paragraph 2: The Body

1. State your main idea clearly and add details for support.
2. Use "first" for your first detail.

Paragraph 3: The Closing

1. The last paragraph is the closing.
2. Repeat the opening with new words.
3. Write your name at the end.

```
To: Julie
Cc:
Subject: A Great Book

Julie,

I wanted to tell you about a
great book. It's about ________
and the title is ____________
by __________. I liked it because
____________________________.
I think you'll like it too.

The book has wonderful characters
and a great plot. First
____________________________
____________________________.

I hope you'll get this book out
of the library and tell me what
you think.

Miguel
```


MULTI-LEVEL OPTIONS *Writer's Workshop*

Newcomer Show students the covers of several fiction or nonfiction novels from the school library. Ask them to think about books they have read. Then ask them to pick their favorite. Have them draw a cover for the book. Help them write the title and author's name.

Beginning Have students work with partners to complete the brainstorming step. Tell partners to ask each other the questions and help each other write their answers. Have pairs collaborate to compose their letters together.

Intermediate Have students write drafts of a body paragraph. Tell them to begin by writing a topic sentence. Remind students that a topic sentence tells the main idea of a paragraph. Have students complete their paragraphs with sentences that contain supporting details.

Advanced Ask students to share their e-mails. After each one, ***ask:*** *Has anyone else read this book? Do you agree with this recommendation? Why or why not?* Then ask students who haven't read the book: *Did this letter make you want to read the book?*

Step 4: Revise your e-mail.

1. Use resources such as the Editor's Checklist in your Student Handbook to check your work.
2. Refer to the book you are writing about to clarify ideas and details. Ask your librarian or teacher if you need help.
3. Be sure your main idea and supporting details are clear. Include details that support your opinion of the book.
4. Collaborate with a partner. Read and review each other's work. Can you organize and combine sentences better?

Step 5: Edit your e-mail

1. Use your software's spelling and grammar checks.
2. Edit spelling mistakes and typing errors. Make sure you correctly spell words that sound the same but are spelled differently. For example, *there, their,* and *they're.*
3. Check for capitalization, apostrophes, and punctuation.
4. Can you combine any of your sentences with *although* or *when?*
5. Can you combine any of your sentences with relative clauses?

Step 6: Send your e-mail.

1. Ask your teacher to help you send your e-mail. If possible, send it to a classmate.
2. Did you receive any e-mail messages from your classmates? What did you learn about the books they have read?

UNIT 4
Apply and Expand

Step 4: Revise your e-mail.
Have students share their drafts and give one another feedback. Then have them collaborate to organize and revise their e-mails.

Step 5: Edit your e-mail.
Have students work on adding and refining as needed. Point out various resources for proofreading and editing.

Step 6: Send your e-mail.
Allow time for students to send and respond to their e-mails.

Have students generate individual checklists that focus on special areas they want to work on.

Portfolio

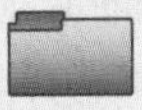

Students may choose to include their writing in their portfolios.

Home Connection

Have students interview a family member about his/her favorite book. Then have students present their findings to the class. Provide these sentence frames: *My _____ told me that his/her favorite book is _____. It is a book about _____. He/she liked it because _____.*

Learning Styles *Musical*

Have students work in pairs. Have partners give recommendations about the best songs or CDs they have ever heard. Ask them to follow the format of the book recommendation.

UNIT 4
Apply and Expand

Projects

Project 1: Make a Future-Discovery Poster

1. **Brainstorm and list** Brainstorm as a group and list ideas for a future discovery, considering the possible benefits and uses for each discovery. Have students choose one as the topic of their poster.
2. **Use graphic organizers** Have students decide on the best form of graphics to illustrate their discovery and its benefit.

Project 2: Make Discoveries About Your Community

1. **Choose a category** Brainstorm a list of community resources. Have students explain what they might discover from each one. If possible, take a trip to the school or a neighborhood library. Have students choose categories and prepare questions to research.
2. **Gather and organize** Allow time for students to use resources to find answers to their questions and to prepare a chart to present their findings to the class.

Portfolio

Students may choose to include their projects in their portfolios.

Projects

These projects will help you further explore what you know about discoveries. Work alone, with a partner, or with a group. Remember to ask adults for help when you need it.

Project 1: Make a Future-Discovery Poster

Think of discoveries that would make life easier, safer, healthier, or more enjoyable. Make a poster of one of your ideas.

1. Choose the discovery that you like best. Think of a name or a short phrase to describe your discovery.
2. Write reasons why this discovery helps people. These are the benefits of the discovery.
3. Ask your partner to tell you if your ideas are clear.
4. For your discovery, list its name and its benefits.
5. Illustrate your discovery. You can show what the discovery looks like, you can show its benefit, or you can show someone using it.
6. Talk about the items and why you think they would be important.

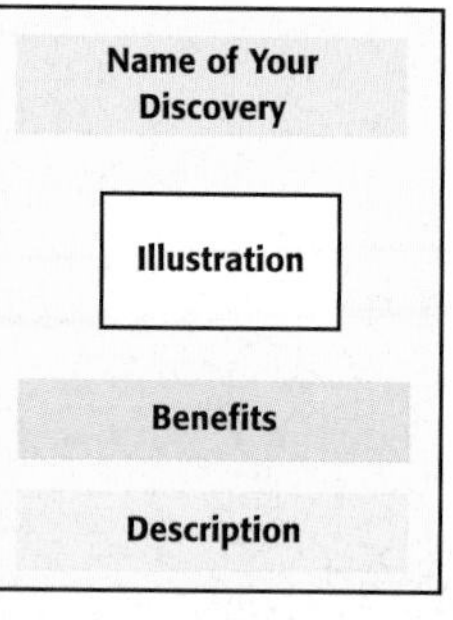

Project 2: Make Discoveries About Your Community

1. Work with a group. Divide the research into categories such as community history, services, sports, arts, buildings, and ways to have fun. Each person or pair should choose one of the categories. Think of two questions to answer for each category.
2. Brainstorm ways to get information. For example, you might scan the phone book, look at your community's Web site, talk to a town official, or read books about local history.
3. Revise your questions if you need to. Then continue to research answers.
4. Look for the information. Organize and summarize what you find in a chart like the one shown.
5. Send the chart to a chamber of commerce in your community or region. What is their reaction?

Category	Information
sports	baseball team plays four nights a week at Newtown Stadium

MULTI-LEVEL OPTIONS *Projects*

Newcomer Ask students to think of and draw a useful invention. Work with students to write labels and captions.

Beginning Ask a member of the local historical society to give a short presentation about your community's history. Have students draw one interesting aspect of the presentation. Help students write a brief explanation to include with the illustration.

Intermediate Ask a member of the local historical society to give a short presentation about your community's history. Have students take notes and ask questions to the guest speaker. Tell pairs of students to write one-paragraph summaries of the presentation. Have them share their summaries in pairs.

Advanced Have students work in pairs to complete the Project 2. Instruct them to collaborate to compose a news report of their findings. Ask students to use their chart to organize their reports. Have them practice their reports with another pair. Then instruct them to revise their news reports based on feedback. Have them give their reports to another class.

Further Reading

The books listed below explore the theme of discovery. Read one or more of them. In your Reading Log, record the discoveries described in each book. Write your thoughts and feelings about what you read. Take notes on your answers to these questions:

1. What new discoveries did this book describe?
2. What similar discoveries have you made in your life?

The Library Card
by Jerry Spinelli, Scholastic, Inc., 1998. This book includes four short stories about four different teenagers who find a mysterious blue library card. The main characters in the stories discover the joy of reading—a discovery that changes their lives.

Find Where the Wind Goes: Moments from My Life
by Dr. Mae Jemison, Scholastic, Inc., 2001. In her autobiography, Dr. Mae Jemison tells about her experience in becoming the first African American woman in space.

Tuck Everlasting
by Natalie Babbitt, Farrar, Straus & Giroux, Inc., 1986. The Tuck family has the secret to eternal life. Winnie, a girl in their town, discovers their secret. Through her discovery, Winnie learns the true meaning of life and death and why eternal life may not be as desirable as she once believed.

The Tiger Rising
by Kate DiCamillo, Candlewick Press, 2001. Rob Hurton and his friend Sistine discover a tiger trapped inside of a cage in the woods behind the motel where Rob lives. Rob and Sistine's attempt to free the tiger starts the emotional healing process for Rob, who has just recently lost his mother.

Jason's Gold
by Will Hobbs, HarperTrophy, 2000. In 1897, gold was discovered in Canada's Yukon Territory. This story mixes fiction and facts about the Klondike gold rush to tell the story of 15-year-old Jason and his dog King as they make an incredible 10,000-mile journey.

Travels with a Tangerine: A Journey in the Footnotes of Ibn Battutah
by Tim Mackintosh-Smith, Welcome Rain Publishers, 2002. In 1325, Ibn Battutah began a 29-year pilgrimage from his home in Tangiers to Mecca. This book describes the first stage of his pilgrimage as he travels from Tangiers to Constantinople.

Popular Science: Science Year by Year: Discoveries and Inventions from the 20th Century That Shape Our Lives
by Popular Science Magazine, Scholastic, Inc., 2001. The nation's leading science magazine has compiled a book of the greatest scientific inventions of the twentieth century. Inventions include electric guitars, toasters, television, computers, and bubble gum.

Reading Log

Heinle Reading Library

UNIT 4
Apply and Expand

Further Reading

Teacher Resource Book: *Reading Log, p. 64*

Respond to literature Instruct students to select a book about a discovery and prepare a composition about the person and the discovery. Have students decide on the main points of the book and organize their information. Tell them to choose supporting details. Remind them to use an attention-grabbing introduction. Ask students to explain their personal reactions by sharing a personal discovery that is similar or different.

Assessment Program: *Unit 4 Test, pp. 69–74*

UNIT 5

Introduce the Unit

Unit Materials

Activity Book: *pp. 153–184*
Audio: *Unit 5*
Student Handbook
Student CD-ROM: *Unit 5*
CNN Video: *Unit 5*
Teacher Resource Book: *Lesson Plans, Teacher Resources, Reading Summaries, School-Home Connection, Video Script, Video Worksheet, Activity Book Answer Key*
Teacher Resource CD-ROM
Assessment Program: *Quizzes and Test, pp. 75–88; Teacher and Student Resources, pp. 115–144*
Assessment CD-ROM
Transparencies
The Heinle Newbury House Dictionary/CD-ROM
More Grammar Practice workbook
Heinle Reading Library
Web Site: www.heinle.visions.com

Heinle Staff Development Handbook

Refer to the Heinle Staff Development Handbook for more teacher support.

Unit Theme: Communication

Use personal experience *Ask: What languages do you use to communicate? How else do you communicate with people?* (pictures, symbols, gestures, facial expressions)

Unit Preview: Table of Contents

1. **Use text features** *Ask: Which chapter is about hearing?* (3) *Which chapter is about drawing and writing?* (4) *Which chapter has two reading selections?* (2) *What types of reading selections are they?* (a biography and a play)
2. **Connect** *Ask: Which types of readings interest you? Which reading selections do you think you will enjoy most?*

UNIT 5

Communication

CHAPTER 1 *page 286* — **How Tía Lola Came to ~~Visit~~ Stay** an excerpt from a novel by Julia Alvarez

CHAPTER 2 *page 302* — **Helen Keller** an excerpt from a biography by George Sullivan

The Miracle Worker an excerpt from a play by William Gibson

CHAPTER 3 *page 316* — **Hearing: The Ear** an excerpt from a textbook

CHAPTER 4 *page 328* — **The Art of Making Comic Books** an illustrated "how-to" book by Michael Morgan Pellowski

284

UNIT OBJECTIVES

Reading

Predict what will happen in a narrative • Compare and contrast as you read a biography and a play • Represent text information in an outline as you read an excerpt from a textbook • Make inferences as you read an illustrated "how-to" book

Listening and Speaking

Role-play dialogue • Interpret lines from a play • Discuss how sound waves travel • Explain a concept for a character

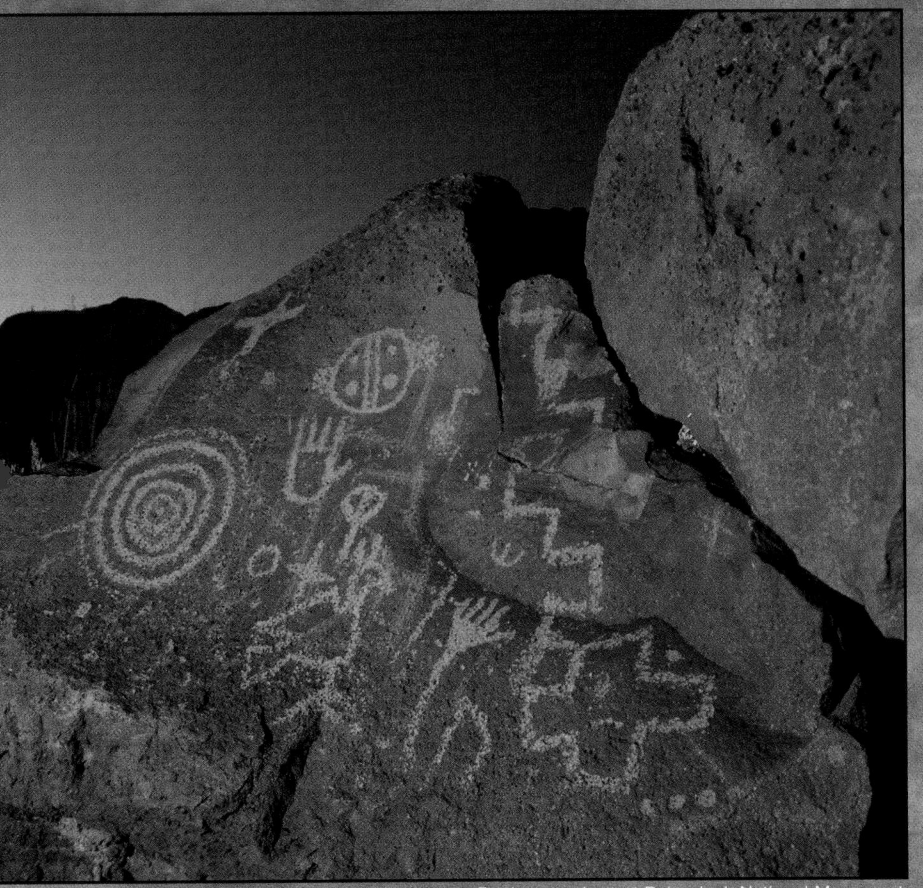

Rock engravings at Petroglyph National Monument, Danny Lehman, Photographer. ca. 1000–1600.

View the Picture

1. How does this picture show communication?
2. How do you communicate with other people?

In this unit, you will read a story, biography, play, textbook article, and pictorial narrative. Each reading selection focuses on communication. You will learn about the features of these writing forms and how to write them yourself.

285

Grammar
Recognize present perfect tense • Recognize and use past progressive verbs • Recognize subject and verb agreement in the present tense • Understand the present conditional

Writing
Write a narrative with dialogue • Write a scene from a play • Write to inform • Write an illustrated "how-to" article

Content
Social Studies: Read a weather map • Science: Learn about some causes of diseases • The Arts: Learn about the voice • The Arts: Learn about art forms

UNIT 5
Introduce the Unit

View the Picture

1. **Art background** Petroglyphs are ancient and stylized rock carvings that have been found throughout the Western Hemisphere. Although no one knows for sure who made these carvings or why, researchers have suggested that petroglyphs may have had religious significance, provided directions to travelers, or recorded important local events.
2. **Art interpretation** Have students describe the petroglyphs and guess what they might mean. ***Ask:*** *Are these carvings realistic? What do you think the lines and patterns represent?*
   a. **Interpret message** *Ask: What message do you think the people who drew the petroglyphs wanted to communicate? What makes you think that?*
   b. **Use personal experience** *Ask: What symbols do you see around you that communicate ideas?* (safety symbols, directions) Have students show or explain signs and symbols they use.
   c. **Speculate** Have students suggest reasons why the petroglyph artist used pictures to communicate instead of words.
   d. **Connect to theme** *Say: The theme of this unit is* communication. *What do you think was communicated in these petroglyphs?*

ASSESS

Have students brainstorm a list of methods of communication used today. Allow three minutes. Then have students share their ideas with the class.

Chapter Materials

Activity Book: *pp. 153–160*
Audio: *Unit 5, Chapter 1*
Student Handbook
Student CD-ROM: *Unit 5, Chapter 1*
Teacher Resource Book: *Lesson Plan, Teacher Resources, Reading Summary, Activity Book Answer Key*
Teacher Resource CD-ROM
Assessment Program: *Quiz, pp. 75–76; Teacher and Student Resources, pp. 115–144*
Assessment CD-ROM
Transparencies
The Heinle Newbury House Dictionary/CD-ROM
Web Site: www.heinle.visions.com

Objectives

Paired reading Have students work in pairs to read the objectives. *Ask: Are there any objectives that we can do already?*

Use Prior Knowledge

Discuss Different Cultures and Languages

Gather and organize Divide students into groups. Have each group make a list of languages that they speak. As groups share their responses with the class, create a tally chart. Point out that students who speak two languages (e.g., English and Spanish) are bilingual and those who speak three are trilingual.

CHAPTER 1

How Tía Lola Came to ~~Visit~~ Stay

an excerpt from a novel by Julia Alvarez

Into the Reading

Objectives

Reading Predict what will happen in a narrative.

Listening and Speaking Role-play dialogue.

Grammar Recognize the present perfect tense.

Writing Write a narrative with dialogue.

Content Social Studies: Read a weather map.

Use Prior Knowledge

Discuss Different Cultures and Languages

The people of a culture are often connected through language. Research how many different languages the students in your class can speak.

1. Make a chart like the one below.
2. Ask students, "Which languages do you speak?" Record the answers on your chart.
3. Make a class chart with everyone's answers. Take turns interpreting the chart: "Six people speak Chinese."
4. Discuss what you know about the languages and the countries where they are spoken.

Name	Chinese	English	Hmong	Spanish	______
Sergio	x	x			

MULTI-LEVEL OPTIONS *Build Vocabulary*

Newcomer Write *adios* and *goodbye* on the board. Ask students to tell you words in other languages for *goodbye.* Have students create large, colorful, decorative signs with their words. Ask them to teach you or other students how to pronounce the words. Display the signs in the classroom.

Beginning Write *adios* and *goodbye* on the board. Brainstorm a list of English synonyms and words in other languages for *goodbye.* Have students create pages for a "Goodbye Book." Instruct them to choose a word and draw a picture or decorate the word. Display the book in the classroom library.

Intermediate On the board, write: *gazing, frosty, sliver, mutters,* and *swarm.* Have pairs look up each word in the dictionary. Then have the pairs work together to write sentences for each word. Tell students to use context clues in their sentences.

Advanced On the board, write: *gazing, frosty, sliver, mutters,* and *swarm.* Ask students to look up each word in the dictionary. Then have students write a sentence, using context clues, for each word. Tell them to add the words and definitions to their Personal Dictionaries.

Build Background

The Dominican Republic

The Dominican Republic is a country on the Caribbean island of Hispaniola. Hispaniola is between the Caribbean Sea and the Atlantic Ocean. The weather in the Dominican Republic is warm and tropical.

The people of the Dominican Republic speak Spanish. Almost half of the Dominican population works on farms.

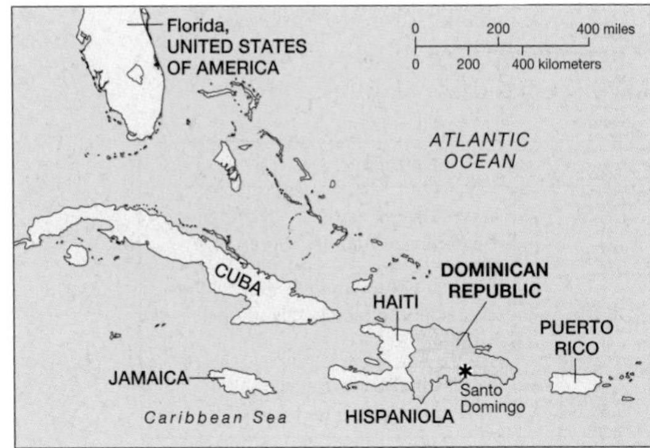

Content Connection

The Dominican Republic shares Hispaniola with Haiti. Haitians speak Creole and French.

Build Vocabulary

Use Context Clues

You can learn the meaning of a new word by looking for clues in the same sentence or the next sentence. For example, you will find in the reading selection that *tía* is the Spanish word for *aunt*.

Use context clues to guess the meanings of the underlined words in the following sentences.

1. I won't have much to say to her except "¡*Adiós*!" Goodbye!
2. "*Te quiero mucho*," she closes, just as Miguel has done. I love you lots.
3. Juanita blubbers tearfully and follows their mother out of the room.

Activity Book
p. 153

Student
CD-ROM

Build Background

The Dominican Republic

1. **Use a map** Have students find the Dominican Republic on a map or globe. ***Ask:*** *What bodies of water are around the Dominican Republic? What other island nations are near it?*
2. **Content Connection** Mention that the Dominican Republic was discovered by Christopher Columbus in 1492. ***Ask:*** *Do you know anyone famous from the Dominican Republic?* (baseball stars Sammy Sosa, Pedro Martinez)

Build Vocabulary

Use Context Clues

1. **Teacher think aloud** *Say: I see* Tía Lola *in the title of the story. I don't know what* tía *means, but when I start to read on page 290, someone asks, "Why can't we just call her Aunt Lola?" I guess that* tía *means "aunt."*
2. **Reading selection vocabulary** You may want to introduce the glossed words in the reading selection before students begin reading. Key words: *unpack, memory, get divorced, tease, recognize, boast.* Instruct students to write the words with correct spelling and their definitions in their Personal Dictionaries. Have them pronounce each word and divide it into syllables.
3. **Multi-level options** See MULTI-LEVEL OPTIONS on p. 286.

Answers

1. *Adios* means "goodbye."
2. *Te quiero mucho* means "I love you a lot."
3. *Blubbers* means "cries very hard."

Home Connection

Build Vocabulary Have students create trees for family words. Display a simple family tree with the words *me, mother, father, brother, sister, aunt, uncle, cousin, grandmother,* and *grandfather* in the appropriate places. Ask students to create similar trees with words in other languages. Have students share their trees with the class.

Learning Styles ***Natural***

Build Background Tell students that the main crops farmed in the Dominican Republic are sugarcane, coffee, cocoa, cotton, and rice. Bring in examples of each product. Have students work in groups. Give a small portion of each product to each group. Ask groups to collaborate to compose and organize a record that tells how each crop looks, feels, tastes, and smells. After recording information, have groups revise their records.

ASSESS

Have students write sentences using the new words.

Text Structure

Narrative

Use a graphic organizer to define and explain features Write the features chart on the board. Have students give examples of structure, dialogue, and details from other narrative selections they have read in the book.

Reading Strategy

Predict

Teacher Resource Book: *Reading Log, p. 64*

1. **Model the strategy** Talk about current weather conditions. Model making predictions about tomorrow's weather based on what you see and know. Ask students to make predictions about upcoming sports events or school activities.
2. **Multi-level options** See MULTI-LEVEL OPTIONS below.

ASSESS

Ask for "student definitions" of: *structure, dialogue,* and *details.*

Text Structure

Narrative

"How Tía Lola Came to ~~Visit~~ Stay" is **narrative** writing. It tells a story. A narrative has these features:

Narrative	
Structure	A narrative is made up of a beginning, a middle, and an end.
Dialogue	Dialogue in a narrative shows how characters speak directly to one another.
Details	Details make a narrative real, interesting, and entertaining.

1. As you read or listen to the recording of the selection, notice what you learn about the characters from the dialogue. Notice what you learn from the story details.
2. How do the characters use language to reflect their culture or region?

Student CD-ROM

Reading Strategy

Predict

As you read or listen to the audio recording of the selection, **predict** what will happen next. When you predict, you make a guess about the future. You can do this based on your knowledge of what has already happened.

1. Read the title and look at the pictures. What do you think the selection is about? Write your prediction in your Reading Log.
2. Read page 290. What will happen next? Why do you think so? Write your prediction in your Reading Log.
3. Check your prediction after you read page 291. Is it answered there? Were you correct?
4. Continue to predict as you read the selection.

Reading Log

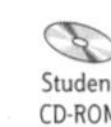

Student CD-ROM

MULTI-LEVEL OPTIONS *Reading Strategy*

Newcomer On the board, write: *"How Tía Lola Came to Visit"* and, after a brief pause, cross out *Visit* and write *Stay* next to it. *Say: The author changed the title. She wrote* visit *first. Then she wrote* stay. *What do you think will happen in this story?* Ask students to draw pictures of their predictions.

Beginning Have students look at the title and picture on p. 289. Ask them to predict what this story might be about. Tell them to draw pictures of their predictions. Help them to write captions for their pictures. Have students review their pictures with a partner.

Intermediate Have students look at the title and picture on p. 289 and predict what they think this story will be about. Ask them to write a prediction in complete sentences. Offer this sentence starter: *I predict that* ______.

Advanced *Ask: Have you ever made a prediction? Were you correct?* Have students write a paragraph about a prediction they made. Tell them to include the prediction, why they made it, and whether or not it turned out to be correct.

How Tía Lola Came to ~~Visit~~ Stay

an excerpt from a novel by Julia Alvarez

289

Reading Selection Materials

Audio: *Unit 5, Chapter 1*
Teacher Resource Book: *Reading Summary, pp. 103–104*

Preview the Selection

1. **Predict from an image** Have students study the picture and the title. Ask them to make predictions about the story based on what they know. Use questions to guide them as needed. ***Ask:*** *Who is Tía Lola? Where do you think she is from? What do you think she is like? What language do you think she speaks? Who do you think Tía Lola is going to visit or stay with? What do you think the children will think about Tía Lola? Will they like her?*
2. **Background knowledge** Point out the flower border around the picture to students. ***Ask:*** *Have you seen flowers like these before? Where do you think they grow? What do these flowers make you think of?* (Hibiscus flowers grow in tropical countries, and in the states of Florida and Hawaii.)
3. **Connect** Remind students that the unit theme is *communication.* Ask them how the people in the story might communicate. Have students guess if it will be easy or difficult for the people in the story to communicate with one another. Ask them what the correction in the title communicates.

Cultural Connection

Explain to students that many families live with extended family members such as cousins, grandparents, aunts, or uncles. Ask students to talk to their own families, friends, or neighbors who live with extended families. Instruct students to write informational paragraphs about what it is like to live with extended family.

Learning Styles *Interpersonal*

Tell students that body language includes gestures, facial expressions, and touching motions such as handshakes, hugs, and pats on the back. Ask groups to create and define a list of terms, expressions, or emotions that can be communicated through body language. Give these examples: waving = "Hello"; stomping your foot = "I'm frustrated and angry!"; smiling = "I'm happy."

UNIT 5 • CHAPTER 1
Reading Selection

Read the Selection

1. **Use text features** Point out the prologue and remind students of its purpose. Direct students to italicized words and phrases in the selection and explain that these are Spanish words or phrases. Remind students to use the illustration and map to help understanding.
2. **Teacher read aloud** Read the selection aloud. Pause to check understanding and to identify characters, setting, and events.
3. **Analyze character relationships** *Ask: Why does Juanita like to use Spanish words?* (She wants to make her mother happy.) *Why doesn't Miguel like to use Spanish?* (It makes him feel different and uncomfortable.)

Sample Answer to Guide Question
He will probably say, "Adiós, Tía Lola." Miguel will call her Aunt Lola.

See Teacher Edition pp. 434–435 for a list of English-Spanish cognates in the reading selection.

Audio

Prologue

Miguel and his younger sister, Juanita, are dealing with two big changes in their lives: their parents have ended their marriage, and they have moved with their mother from New York City to Vermont. Their mother is sad about ending the marriage, but she is happy that her Tía (Aunt) Lola is coming to visit. Miguel is not sure that he likes the idea.

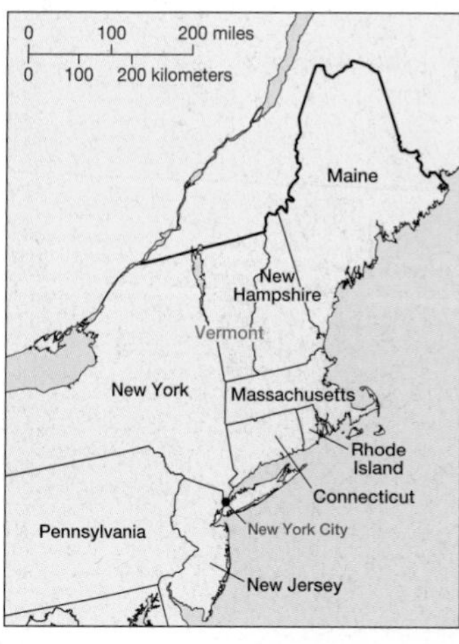

1 "Why can't we just call her *Aunt* Lola?" Miguel asks his mother. Tomorrow their aunt is coming from the Dominican Republic to visit with them in their new home in Vermont. Tonight they are **unpacking** the last of the kitchen boxes before dinner.

2 "Because she doesn't know any English," his mother explains.

3 "*Tía* is the word for aunt in Spanish, right, Mami?" Juanita asks. When their mother's back is turned, Juanita beams Miguel a know-it-all smile.

4 Their mother is gazing sadly at a blue bowl she has just unpacked. "So you see, Miguel, if you call her Aunt, she won't know you're talking to her."

5 That's fine, Miguel thinks, I won't have much to say to her except "*¡Adiós!*" Goodbye! But he keeps his mouth shut. He knows why his mother is staring at the blue bowl, and he doesn't want to upset her in the middle of a **memory.**

6 "So, please, Miguel," his mother is saying, "just call her Tía Lola. Okay?"

Predict
How do you think Miguel will greet Tía Lola? Make a prediction based on what Miguel is saying here.

unpacking taking things out of a box or suitcase

memory thoughts about something from the past

MULTI-LEVEL OPTIONS *Read the Selection*

Newcomer Play the audio. Then read the selection aloud. ***Ask:*** *Does* tía *mean "aunt"?* (yes) *Does Tía Lola know any English?* (no) *Does it make their mother happy to talk about Tía Lola?* (yes) *Does Juanita speak Spanish?* (yes) *Does anybody know how old Tía Lola is?* (no)

Beginning Read the Reading Summary aloud. Then do a partner read aloud of the text. ***Ask:*** *Where does Miguel live?* (Vermont) *Where is Tía Lola from?* (the Dominican Republic) *When is Tía Lola coming to visit?* (tomorrow) *Who is Juanita?* (Miguel's younger sister)

Intermediate Have students do a partner read aloud. ***Ask:*** *Why is their mother happy?* (Tía Lola is coming to visit.) *How does Miguel feel about Tía Lola's visit?* (He's not sure he likes it.) *Why does Juanita speak to her mother in Spanish?* (She knows it makes her mother happy.)

Advanced Have students read silently. ***Ask:*** *Has Miguel's family lived in Vermont for a long time? How can you tell?* (No; they are still unpacking.) *Why is Miguel's mother sad when she looks at the blue bowl?* (It brings back memories of life before the divorce.)

7 Miguel kind of nods, kind of just **jerks** his head to get his hair out of his eyes. It can go either way . . .

8 [Juanita] begins asking questions about Tía Lola because it makes their mother happy to talk about her favorite aunt back on the island where she was born. "How old is she, Mami?"

9 "Who?"

10 "Tía Lola, Mami, *Tía Lola que viene mañana,*" Juanita says in Spanish. It also makes their mother happy when they use Spanish words. *Tía* for "aunt." *Mañana* for "tomorrow." Tía Lola who comes tomorrow. "Is she real old?"

11 "Actually, nobody knows how old Tía Lola is. She won't tell," their mother says. She is smiling again. Her eyes have a **faraway** look. "She's so young at heart, it doesn't matter. She'll be fun to have around."

12 "Is she married?" Juanita asks. Mami has told them they have **tons** of cousins back on the island, but are any of them Tía Lola's kids?

Predict

Make a prediction about how Tía Lola will look and what she will be like. What clues does Juanita's mother give you to make a prediction?

---

jerks moves quickly
faraway from a long distance
tons a lot

UNIT 5 • CHAPTER 1
Reading Selection

Read the Selection

1. **Use the illustration** Ask students to describe the characters. Have students suggest what the mother and Juanita are talking about. ***Ask:*** *What does it mean that Miguel's arms are folded across his chest? How does this help tell the story?*
2. **Understand terms** Have students find the meanings of the italicized phrases in the selection. Clarify meanings as needed.
3. **Use text features** Direct students to the dialogue. Point out the use of quotation marks. Remind students to look for clues about the characters and details about the story within the dialogue.
4. **Paired reading** After students listen to the audio or to you read the selection, have them reread with partners and check if their predictions were correct.
5. **Summarize** Ask questions to help students summarize the selection and point out more clues about the characters. Students can act out the dialogue.
6. **Multi-level options** See MULTI-LEVEL OPTIONS on p. 290.

Sample Answer to Guide Question
Tía Lola will be old with gray hair. She will be smiling. The mother says no one knows how old Tía Lola is, but she is fun to have around.

Spelling

Words with two spellings

Tell students that a few words in English can be correctly spelled in different ways. Say that *goodbye* and *goodby* are both correct. Also point out that the abbreviation *OK* is acceptable for the word *okay.*

Apply Have students use a dictionary to look up *catalogue/catalog; gray/grey; T-shirt/tee shirt; catsup/ketchup; hiccough/hiccup;* and *dialog/dialogue.* Ask which words can be spelled both ways? (all of them)

Read the Selection

Paired reading Play the audio. Have students reread the selection in pairs. ***Ask:*** *Why did the mother begin to cry?* (Miguel said something that upset her.) *Did you ever say anything to upset someone? How did you feel when that happened?* Have students act out the dialogue in small groups.

Sample Answer to Guide Question
I think now he would say, "Hola, Tía Lola."

13 "I'm afraid Tía Lola never did get married," Mami sighs. "But, kids, do me a favor. Just don't ask her about it, okay?"

14 "Why not?" Juanita wants to know.

15 "It's a **sensitive issue,**" her mother explains.

16 Juanita is making her I-don't-understand-this-math-problem face. "But why didn't she get married?"

17 Miguel speaks up before his mother can answer. He doesn't know how the thought has popped into his head, but it suddenly pops out of his mouth before he can stop it. "She didn't get married so she wouldn't have to **get divorced** ever."

18 Mami blinks back tears. She stands quickly and leaves the room.

19 Miguel studies the beans pictured on the outside of the can his mother has picked for dinner. One little bean has on a Mexican hat.

20 "You made Mami cry!" Juanita **blubbers** tearfully and follows their mother out of the room.

21 Miguel finds himself alone in a drafty kitchen with all the dirty bowls and plates to wash and the table to wipe. As he cleans up at the sink, he glances out the window at the frosty world outside. Up in the sky, the moon is just the tiniest silver sliver. It looks as if someone has gobbled up most of it and left behind only this bit of light for Miguel to see by.

Predict

Check your prediction about Miguel. Predict how he will greet her.

22 For the first time since he heard the news, he is glad his aunt is arriving tomorrow. It might be nice to have a fourth person—who is still talking to him—in the house, even if her name is Tía Lola.

---

sensitive issue a topic that is hard to talk about
get divorced end a marriage
blubbers cries loudly

MULTI-LEVEL OPTIONS *Read the Selection*

Newcomer ***Ask:*** *Did Tía Lola ever get married?* (no) *Does Miguel make his mother cry?* (yes) *Does Juanita leave the room?* (yes) *Does Miguel decide he is happy that Tía Lola is coming?* (yes) *Does Miguel have a driver's license?* (no)

Beginning ***Ask:*** *What is pictured on the can Miguel looks at?* (beans; one is wearing a Mexican hat.) *Who makes Juanita and her mother cry?* (Miguel) *When do they go to the airport?* (in the morning) *Who goes in the airport to look for Tía Lola?* (Miguel and Juanita)

Intermediate ***Ask:*** *Why does Mami cry?* (Miguel talks about divorce.) *Why is Miguel glad that Tía Lola is coming?* (It will be nice to have someone in the house who isn't mad at him.) *Why does Miguel agree to go inside to look for Tía Lola?* (Mami's sweet voice is impossible to resist.)

Advanced *Why does Miguel's comment make Mami cry?* (She's still sad about the divorce.) *Why does Juanita cry?* (because Mami is crying) *Why does Miguel think he might not mind jail?* (He's nervous about all the changes in his life; jail doesn't seem as unpleasant.)

✧✧✧✧

23 The next morning at the airport, Miguel's mother cannot find a parking space. "You kids, go in so we don't miss your aunt. I'll join you as soon as I find a spot."

24 "I'll help you," Miguel offers.

25 "Miguel, *amor,* how can you help me? You don't have a license. The **cops'll** take you in if they catch you driving," his mother **teases.**

26 As nervous as Miguel is feeling about his aunt's visit and his new school and their move to Vermont, he thinks he wouldn't mind spending the next year all by himself in jail.

27 "*Por favor,* honey, would you go inside with your sister and look for Tía Lola?" His mother's **sweetened-up** voice is like a handful of chocolate chips from the package in the closet. Impossible to resist.

Predict

Will Miguel go inside with his sister to find Tía Lola?

28 "*¡Los quiero mucho!*" she calls out to both children as they clamber out of the car.

29 "Love you, too," Juanita calls back.

30 The crowd **swarms** around them in the small but busy terminal.

---

cops'll cops (police officers) will
teases makes fun of
sweetened-up very sweet
swarms moves in a large group

Read the Selection

1. **Paired reading** Play the audio. Have students reread the selection in pairs. ***Ask:*** *Why doesn't Miguel want to go look for his aunt?* (He doesn't know her and has never seen her.) *What would you do if you were Miguel?*
2. **Summarize** Ask questions to help students summarize the scene. Have volunteers act out the dialogue.
3. **Multi-level options** See MULTI-LEVEL OPTIONS on p. 292.

Sample Answer to Guide Question

I think he will go inside.

Punctuation

Commas after introductory time clauses

Explain that a clause is a group of words with a subject and a verb. ***Say:*** *A clause at the beginning of a sentence that tells when something happens is an introductory time clause.* Tell students that an introductory time clause is usually followed by a comma. Direct students to the first sentence of paragraph 22. ***Say:*** For the first time since he heard the news *is an introductory time clause. It tells* when *Miguel is glad.* Ask students to find an introductory time clause in paragraph 3. (When their mother's back is turned) ***Ask:*** *What does it tell?* (when Juanita beams Miguel a know-it-all smile)

Apply Write on the board: *Before Mami can answer Miguel speaks.* Have students correct the sentence by adding a comma after the introductory time clause. (Before Mami can answer, Miguel speaks.)

Read the Selection

1. **Use the illustration** *Ask: How do Juanita and Miguel feel?* (scared) *Is there anyone who might help them?* (Everyone in the picture is busy, but there probably are other people who might help.) *What other things do you see and hear at an airport?* (You see airport workers and information counters. You hear announcements and people being paged.)
2. **Paired reading** Read aloud to students. Have students reread the selection in pairs. *Ask: Who do Miguel and Juanita ask for help?* (a lady working at a counter) *Can she help them?* (No, but she says they can page their aunt.) Have students reread the selection in small groups and act out the dialogue.

Sample Answer to Guide Question
I think they will ask someone for help.

31 Juanita slips her hand into Miguel's. She looks scared, as if all that Spanish she has been showing off to their mother has just left on a plane to South America. "You think we'll **recognize** her?" she asks.

Predict
How do you think Miguel and Juanita will find Tía Lola?

32 "We'll wait until somebody who looks like *she's* looking for *us* comes out of the plane," Miguel says. He sure wishes his mother would hurry up and find a parking spot.

33 Several businessmen rush by, checking their watches, as if they are already late for whatever they have come for. Behind them, a grandma puts down her shopping bag full of presents, and two little boys run forward and throw their arms around her. A young guy turns in a slow circle as if he has gotten off at the wrong stop. A girl hugs her boyfriend, who kisses her on the lips. Miguel looks away.

34 Where is this aunt of theirs?

35 The crowd **disperses,** and still their aunt is nowhere in sight. Miguel and Juanita go up to the counter and ask the lady working there to please page their aunt. "She doesn't know any English," Miguel explains, "only Spanish."

36 The woman in the blue suit has so many **freckles,** it looks as if someone has spilled a whole bag of them on her face. "I'm sorry, kids. I took a little Spanish back in high school, but that was ages ago. I'll tell you what. I'll let you **page** your aunt yourself."

recognize see someone and know who it is
disperses moves away in different directions
freckles brown spots on a person's skin
page use a loudspeaker to call someone or make an announcement

MULTI-LEVEL OPTIONS *Read the Selection*

Newcomer *Ask: Does Juanita hold Miguel's hand?* (yes) *Does she look scared?* (yes) *Do they see Tía Lola right away?* (no) *Do they ask the lady at the counter to page Tía Lola?* (yes) *Does the lady speak Spanish?* (no)

Beginning *Ask: Who do the children ask to page Tía Lola?* (the lady behind the counter) *What is on the lady's face?* (freckles) *Where does the lady take the children?* (to an office behind the counter) *Who is in the office?* (a bald man) *What is he doing?* (turning dials on a machine)

Intermediate *Ask: Why does Juanita hold Miguel's hand?* (She's scared; she's afraid they won't recognize Tía Lola.) *Why do the kids go to the counter?* (to ask the lady to page Tía Lola) *Why does the lady suggest that Miguel page his aunt?* (She doesn't know Spanish; Juanita is scared.)

Advanced *Ask: How do the kids feel when they are in the airport?* (nervous, scared) *What else could Miguel and Juanita have done to find Tía Lola?* (hold up a sign; call out her name) *Why does Miguel say he doesn't speak Spanish?* (He doesn't feel comfortable speaking it in public.)

Predict

Do you think Juanita will page her aunt? What do you know about Juanita that can help you make this prediction?

37 "She'll do it," Miguel **nudges** his sister forward. Even though he is older, Juanita is the one who is always showing off her Spanish to their father and mother.

38 Juanita shakes her head. She looks scared. She looks about to cry.

39 "There's nothing to be scared of," Miguel **encourages,** as if he himself has paged his aunt every day of his life.

40 "That's right, sweetie," the woman agrees, nodding at Juanita. But Juanita won't **budge.** Then, turning to Miguel, the woman suggests, "Seeing as she's scared, why don't you do it instead?"

41 "I don't speak Spanish." It isn't **technically** a lie because he doesn't know enough to speak Spanish in public to a whole airport terminal.

42 "You do, too," Juanita **sniffles.** "He knows but he doesn't like to talk it," she explains to the airline lady.

43 "Just give it a try," the freckled lady says, opening a little gate so they can come behind the counter to an office on the other side. A man with a bald head and a tired face and earphones sits at a desk turning dials on a machine. The lady explains that the children need to page a lost aunt who does not speak any English.

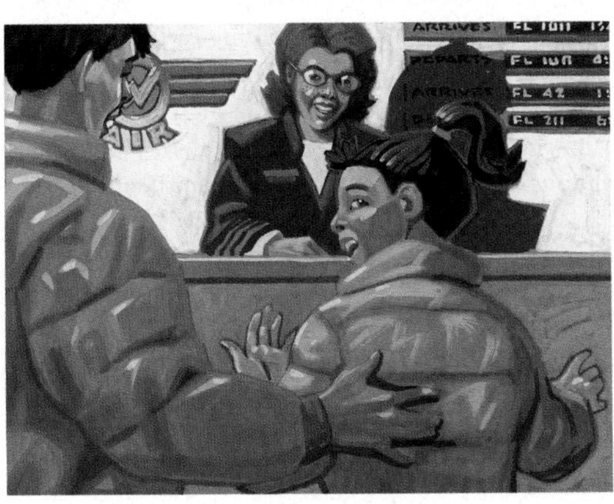

44 "Come here, son." The man beckons to Miguel. "Speak right into this microphone. Testing, testing." He tries it out. The man adjusts some knobs and pushes his chair over so Miguel can stand beside him.

---

nudges pushes gently
encourages helps someone to do something
budge move
technically exactly
sniffles speaks while crying

Read the Selection

1. **Paired reading** Have students reread the selection in pairs. ***Ask:*** *Do you think Miguel often speaks Spanish?* (no) *Why or why not?* (He doesn't like to.)
2. **Summarize** Ask questions to help students summarize the events. Have volunteers act out the dialogue of the story.
3. **Make predictions** Ask students to describe Miguel. Have them predict if he will speak in Spanish or English and what he will say. Ask students to consider what they would do if they were Miguel looking for a relative in a busy airport.
4. **Multi-level options** See MULTI-LEVEL OPTIONS on p. 294.

Sample Answer to Guide Question

I think Juanita will do it because she likes to show off speaking Spanish to her mother.

th Spelling

Their, there, they're

Tell students that *their, there,* and *they're* are three words that sound the same but have different spellings and different meanings. Write *their* on the board. ***Say:*** Their *is a possessive pronoun that answers* whose? *It means "belonging to them."* Write: *there.* ***Say:*** There *is a word that answers* where? *It means "in that place."* Write: *they're.* ***Say:*** They're *is a contraction of the words* they are. *It tells who is doing something.* Tell students that they can decide which word to use by asking themselves: *Do I need to tell* whose *or* where, *or do I need to say* they are*?*

Apply Have students write the correct word in each of the following sentences. Write on the board: *Miguel and Juanita are looking for ____ aunt. ____ going to ask the lady for help. "Is that her over ____?" asked Miguel.*

Read the Selection

1. **Use text features** Direct attention to glossed words and have students find the meanings below. Point out italicized phrases and help students find their meanings in context.
2. **Paired reading** Read aloud to students. Have students reread the selection in pairs. *Ask: What did Miguel say?* (Miguel said, "Hi, Tía Lola. I love you a lot.") *Did Tía Lola hear their messages?* (yes) Have students work in small groups to act out the dialogue.

Sample Answer to Guide Question
I think she will hear and understand it. I think she will be very happy and pleased.

45 Miguel looks down at the microphone. He can feel his stomach getting **queasy** and his mind going blank. All he can remember of his Spanish is Tía Lola's name and the word for "hello."

46 "*Hola, Tía Lola,*" Miguel says into the microphone. Then, suddenly, the **corny** words his mother says every night when she tucks him into bed, the ones she has just called out when he and Juanita climbed out of the car, **pop out.** "*Te quiero mucho.*"

47 Juanita is looking at him, surprised. Miguel scowls back. "It's the only thing I remember," he mutters. With all the stuff popping out these days, he's going to have to get a **brake** for his mouth.

Predict

Do you think Tía Lola will hear or understand Juanita's language? How will Tía Lola react? Make predictions based on what you know about Tía Lola.

48 "I remember more!" Juanita **boasts.** She steps forward, her fears forgotten, and speaks into the microphone. "*Hola, Tía Lola,*" she says in a bright voice as if she is on TV announcing sunny weather tomorrow. "*Te esperamos por el mostrador.*" She and Miguel will be waiting by the counter. "*Te quiero mucho,*" she closes, just as Miguel has done. I love you lots.

49 As Miguel and his sister walk out of the office, they hear a **tremendous** shout. It isn't a shout in Spanish, and it isn't a shout in English. It's a shout anyone anywhere would understand.

50 Someone is **mighty** pleased to see them.

51 On the other side of the counter stands their aunt Lola. You can't miss her! Her skin is the same soft brown as theirs. Her black hair is piled up in a bun on her head with a pink **hibiscus** on top. She wears bright red lipstick and above

---

queasy sick to one's stomach
corny too obvious, not sophisticated
pop out come out on its own
brake the part of a machine that makes it stop
boasts brags, makes oneself look good
tremendous very big or loud
mighty very, in a strong way
hibiscus a bright, tropical flower

MULTI-LEVEL OPTIONS *Read the Selection*

Newcomer *Ask: Does Miguel page Tía Lola?* (yes) *Does Juanita remember more Spanish?* (yes) *Does Tía Lola shout in Spanish?* (no) *Does Tía Lola have soft, brown skin like the children?* (yes) *Does their mother wait in the car?* (no) *Is Tía Lola happy they welcomed her in Spanish?* (yes)

Beginning *Ask: What Spanish words does Miguel remember at first?* (hello; Tía Lola) *Where does Juanita say they will wait?* (by the counter) *What do the kids hear as they walk out of the office?* (a shout) *Who shouted?* (Tía Lola) *How does Tía Lola greet them?* (with hugs)

Intermediate *Ask: Why is Miguel queasy?* (He's nervous; he can't remember any Spanish.) *What does Miguel finally say?* (I love you lots.) *Why is it hard to miss Tía Lola?* (the hibiscus; bright red lipstick; a beauty mark; a colorful dress) *How does Miguel respond to the hug?* (He hugs her back.)

Advanced *Ask: Why does Miguel say his mouth needs a brake?* (He knows he speaks without thinking first.) *What does Lola's appearance suggest about her personality?* (colorful; glamorous; outgoing) *How is Lola similar to Mami?* (voice) *How is she different?* (clothing) *Does Miguel change during the story?* (yes) *Explain.*

her lips she has a big black beauty mark. On her colorful summer dress, parrots fly toward palm trees, and flowers look ready to **burst** from the fabric if they can only figure out how.

52 Behind their aunt, their mother is approaching in her hiking boots and navy-blue parka, her red hat and mittens. "Tía Lola!" she cries out. They hug and kiss and hug again. When Tía Lola pulls away, the beauty mark above her upper lip is gone!

53 "Those two," Tía Lola is saying in Spanish to Miguel's mother as she points to him and Juanita, "those two gave me my first welcome to their country. *¡Ay Juanita! ¡Ay Miguel!*" She **spreads** her arms for her niece and nephew. "*Los quiero mucho.*"

Predict

How do you think Tía Lola will like living with them?

54 It is a voice impossible to resist. Like three handfuls of chocolate chips from the package in the closet . . . For the moment, Miguel forgets the recent move, his papi and friends left behind in New York. When Tía Lola wraps her arms around him, he hugs back, just as hard as he can.

---

burst come out, break open

spreads opens wide

About the Author

Julia Alvarez (born 1950)

Julia Alvarez came to the United States from the Dominican Republic when she was ten years old. She liked to read so that she would not feel alone. When she was in high school, she knew she wanted to be a writer. She said, "What made me into a writer was coming to this country . . . losing a culture, a homeland, a language, a family . . . I wanted a portable homeland. And that's the imagination."

➤ What do you think Julia Alvarez's purpose was in writing this story? What challenges did she face? What strategies did she use?

Read the Selection

1. **Paired reading** Have students reread the selection in pairs. ***Ask:*** *Do you think Miguel and Juanita will enjoy being with Tía Lola?* (I think they will.)
2. **Multi-level options** See MULTI-LEVEL OPTIONS on p. 298.

Sample Answer to Guide Question
I think she will like being with her relatives.

About the Author

1. **Explain author background** Julia Alvarez was born in New York City but grew up in the Dominican Republic. She went to an American school there and learned English. ***Ask:*** *Do you think it was easy or difficult for Julia Alvarez to come to the United States when she was 10?* (Easy, because she spoke English.)
2. **Interpret facts** ***Ask:*** *Why are some people uncomfortable speaking a foreign language in the United States? When do you speak English? When do you like to use another language?*

Across Selections

Teacher Resource Book: *Reading Log, p. 64*

Compare and Contrast Have students compare this story to another narrative, such as "Discovering the Inca Ice Maiden" or "Antarctic Adventure." Ask questions to help students identify similarities and differences. Have students record their observations in their Reading Logs.

Punctuation

Italics for words in other languages

Explain that italics are slanted print. Tell students that when words from other languages appear in texts, they are usually printed in italics. Direct students to paragraph 46. ***Ask:*** *Why are the words* Hola, Tía Lola *written in italics?* (They are Spanish words.) *What other words in this paragraph are written in italics?* (Te quiero mucho.) *In what other paragraphs do you see Spanish words?* (48, 53)

Evaluate Your Reading Strategy

Predict *Say: You have practiced an important reading strategy. Now you can decide how well you have done. Does this statement describe how you read?*

> When I read, I use my knowledge of what has happened to predict what will happen next. Predicting gets me involved in the story and makes reading more enjoyable.

Reading Comprehension

Question-Answer Relationships

Sample Answers

1. She is Mami's favorite aunt.
2. the Dominican Republic
3. Mami, Juanita, and Miguel
4. Tía Lola doesn't speak English.
5. They are afraid to page their aunt because they have never done anything like that before; Miguel only knows a little bit of Spanish; they may also be afraid of what other people might think.
6. It was the only Spanish that he could remember right then.
7. It reminded her of her own divorce.
8. The world looked "frosty" because his mother and sister were mad at him and were "cold," not talking to him.
9. He has never met this aunt and doesn't think he will enjoy being with her because she doesn't speak English.
10. I think he will like her because she seems very friendly and happy.
11. I think Miguel doesn't like to speak Spanish because it makes him different from the other kids in his school and in his neighborhood.

Build Reading Fluency

Reading Silently

Assessment Program: *Reading Fluency Chart, p. 116*

When students have completed the reading fluency activity, record their progress in the Reading Fluency Chart.

Beyond the Reading

Reading Comprehension

Question-Answer Relationships (QAR)

"Right There" Questions

1. **Identify** Who is Tía Lola?
2. **Recall Facts** Where is Tía Lola from?
3. **Recall Facts** Who went to the airport to meet Tía Lola?

"Think and Search" Questions

4. **Draw a Conclusion** Why would Tía Lola not understand the word *aunt* in English?
5. **Draw a Conclusion** Why are Miguel and Juanita afraid to page their aunt in the airport?
6. **Understand Motivation** Why did Miguel say, "*Te quiero mucho!*" over the microphone when he was trying to find his aunt?

"Author and You" Questions

7. **Draw an Inference** Why do you think Miguel's words in paragraph 17 make his mother cry?
8. **Draw an Inference** Why does the world look "frosty" to Miguel on page 292?

"On Your Own" Questions

9. **Draw an Inference** Why do you think Miguel is nervous about his aunt's visit?
10. **Speculate** Do you think that Miguel will like Tía Lola? Why or why not?
11. **Speculate** Why do you think that Miguel doesn't like to speak Spanish?

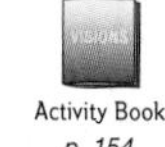

Activity Book
p. 154

Build Reading Fluency

Reading Silently

Reading silently is good practice. It helps you learn to read faster. This is an important way to become a fluent reader.

1. Listen to the audio recording of paragraph 1 of "How Tía Lola Came to ~~Visit~~ Stay."
2. Listen to the chunks of words as you follow along.
3. Reread paragraph 1 silently two times.
4. Your teacher or partner will time your second reading.

MULTI-LEVEL OPTIONS *Elements of Literature*

Newcomer Play the audio. Pause at each third-person pronoun. Write on the board and *say: they, them, their, she, her, he, him,* and *his.* Play the audio again. Have students raise their hands each time they hear one of the words on the board.

Beginning On the board, write: *they, them, their, she, her, he, him,* and *his.* Point to a girl student. Use *she* and *her* in sentences. Point to a boy student. Use *he, him,* and *his* in sentences. Point to a group of students. Use *they, them,* and *their* in sentences. Have pairs locate sentences in the selection with these words.

Intermediate Ask students to copy three sentences from the story with *they, them, she, he,* or *him* leaving a blank for each pronoun. Have pairs exchange sentences and fill in the correct pronouns. Ask students to write an original sentence using one of the pronouns.

Advanced Ask students to locate an earlier selection in the book that is written in first-person point of view, such as "Discovering the Inca Ice Maiden" or "Earthquake." Have students rewrite one paragraph of the selection in third-person point of view. Have pairs of students peer-edit the paragraphs.

Listen, Speak, Interact 

Role-Play Dialogue

The characters in "How Tía Lola Came to ~~Visit~~ Stay" use **dialogue.** Dialogue is the words that the characters speak. Quotation marks go around what the people say. Look at this example of dialogue:

"Why not?" Juanita wants to know.

"It's a sensitive issue," her mother explains.

1. With two partners, read aloud the dialogue in paragraphs 1–6, on page 290. Role-play the characters. One person reads Miguel's dialogue, one reads Juanita's dialogue, and one reads Mami's dialogue.
2. Perform your dialogue for the class. Use this checklist to help you.

Speaking Checklist

1. Speak loudly enough for the audience to hear.
2. Speak slowly and clearly.
3. Produce the correct intonation patterns of words and sentences.
4. Speak with feeling.
5. Look at the audience.
6. ______________________

Elements of Literature

Recognize Point of View

Every story has a **point of view.** The point of view is the way the person narrates (tells) the story. "How Tía Lola Came to ~~Visit~~ Stay" is told from the **third person** point of view. Who tells the story in third person point of view? Study the chart to find out. Copy the chart into your Reading Log.

Point of View	
First Person	A character tells the story using the words *I, me, we,* and *us.*
Third Person	Someone else tells the story using the words *he, she,* and *they.*

Reading Log

Activity Book *p.155*

Student CD-ROM

Content Connection *Math*

Supply the following data: *New York City is 250 miles from Burlington, Vermont. Santo Domingo is 1,500 miles from New York City.* Ask students to solve these problems: *If you fly from Burlington to New York to Santo Domingo, how many miles will you travel?* (1,750 miles) *How long would the trip take on a plane flying at 500 miles per hour?* (3.5 hours)

Learning Styles *Intrapersonal*

Ask students to imagine what it was like for Tía Lola to be in a place where she didn't speak the same language as most of the other people. ***Ask:*** *What things might be difficult for Tía Lola in Vermont? How may her personality make things easier or harder? What do you think Miguel and his family did to make things easier for her?* Have students write their answers in their Reading Logs.

Teacher Resource Book: *Reading Log, p. 64*

Listen, Speak, Interact

Role-Play Dialogue

1. **Reread in small groups** Replay the audio or read aloud the reading selection. Arrange students in groups of three, grouping beginning, intermediate, and advanced students together. Have them read the parts of the dialogue.
2. **Newcomers** Reread with this group. Model appropriate inflection and have students repeat their parts. Model how to add gestures and facial expressions. Have students assess their role-play in their Reading Logs.

Elements of Literature

Recognize Point of View

Teacher Resource Book: *Reading Log, p. 64*

1. Explain *point of view, first person,* and *third person.* Point out words in the selection and have students determine if the story is told in the first or third person. Ask students to look back at other reading selections and identify the point of view.
2. **Personal experience** Have students share an experience they had using the first person and then tell about an experience a friend or relative had using the third person.
3. **Multi-level options** See MULTI-LEVEL OPTIONS on p. 298.

ASSESS

Write on the board: *Miguel met his aunt at the airport. I love my aunt.* Have students copy the sentences and tell the point of view: first person or third person.

Beyond the Reading

Word Study

Use the Prefixes *un-* and *im-*

Teacher Resource Book: *Personal Dictionary, p. 63*

Make a word map Write *unhappy* on the board. Point out the prefix and the word it was added to. Ask students to use it in a sentence. Repeat with *impolite.*

Answers

2. *un-, packed, unpacked; im-, possible, impossible*

Grammar Focus

Recognize the Present Perfect Tense

Use the present perfect tense *Ask: Who has visited Boston? Who has traveled on a train?* Write answers on the board. Point out the verb *have/has* and the past participle.

Answers

paragraph 4: . . . she has just unpacked . . .
paragraph 12: Mami has told them . . .
paragraph 17: . . . how the thought has popped into his head . . .
paragraph 21: . . . as if someone has gobbled up . . . and left behind . . .

ASSESS

Write on the board: *un-, im-; true, finished, proper.* Have students make words meaning: "not proper," "not complete," and "not true."

Word Study

Use the Prefixes *un-* and *im-*

Prefixes are word parts added to the beginning of words. They change the meaning of a word. Two common prefixes are:

un-: means "not" or the "opposite of"

Example: The kids were unhappy about the move to Vermont.

im-: means "not"

Example: Juanita thought Miguel was impolite.

1. Make a chart like the one here in your Personal Dictionary.
2. Read paragraphs 4 and 27 of the reading selection and find other words with the prefixes *un-* and *im-*. Write the words in your chart.

Prefix	Word	New Word
un-	happy	unhappy
im-	polite	impolite

3. Look up other words starting with *un-* and *im-* in your dictionary. You can also use an electronic dictionary on a CD-ROM. Write the words and their meanings in your Personal Dictionary.

Personal Dictionary

The Heinle Newbury House Dictionary

Activity Book *p. 156*

Student CD-ROM

Grammar Focus

Recognize the Present Perfect Tense

Writers use the **present perfect tense** when they describe a past action that has an effect on the present. It is formed with *has* or *have* and the past participle of a verb.

Mami has cooked lunch for Miguel and Juanita.

The effect is on the present: Lunch is ready for them to eat now.

Find sentences in paragraphs 4, 12, 17, and 21 that use the present perfect tense.

Activity Book *pp. 157–158*

Student Handbook

Student CD-ROM

MULTI-LEVEL OPTIONS *From Reading to Writing*

Newcomer Have students draw pictures of people who have come to visit them. Help students write captions and labels for their drawings. Ask them to share their pictures in small groups.

Beginning Create and provide a two-column chart with spaces to answer the questions on the list. Have students work in pairs to complete their charts.

Intermediate Have students create a pre-writing chart with the labels *characters, setting, plot,* and *details.* Ask them to use their answers to the list of questions to complete their charts. Instruct them to use their charts to write their stories.

Advanced Have pairs exchange stories for peer review. Reviewers should check for structure (beginning, middle, end), dialogue punctuation, third-person point of view, and the correct spelling of homophones. They should also check that the details of the story answer the questions in the list.

From Reading to Writing 

Write a Narrative with Dialogue

Write a story about someone coming to visit your family. Use the list of questions to plan the main parts of your story. Answer each question on the list.

1. Include details about your family, your home, and your visitor.
2. Use quotation marks to show dialogue.
3. Be sure your story has a beginning, a middle, and an end.
4. Use the third person point of view.
5. Be sure you have correctly spelled words that sound the same but are spelled differently. For example, *they're*, *there*, and *their*.

The Visitor
• **Who** is coming to visit? • **How** is the visit special? • **Why** is the visitor coming? • **When** is the visitor coming? • **What** happens? • **Where** is your home and **where** is the visitor coming from?

Activity Book
p. 159

Across Content Areas 

Read a Weather Map

A **weather map** gives information about the weather on a specific day.

A **legend** tells you how to read a map. Find the legend at the bottom of the map. Find the **symbols** (pictures that stand for ideas) for rain and snow.

1. What color is used for the hottest temperature?
2. What color is used for the coldest temperature?
3. Name one state where it is raining.

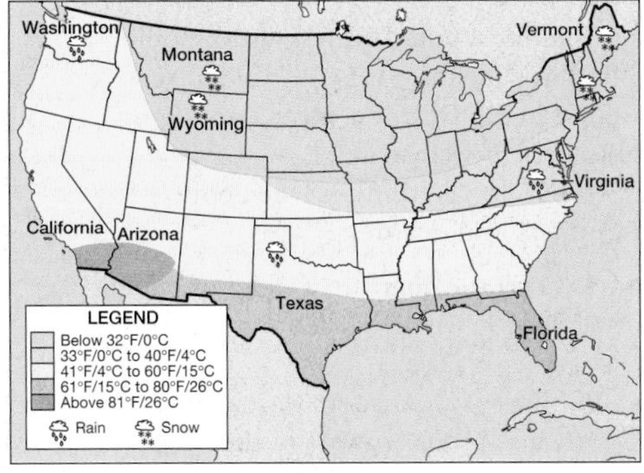

Activity Book
p. 160

Reteach and Reassess

Text Structure Have students review the plot of the story. ***Ask:*** *What happens at the beginning?* (Miguel and Juanita talk to Mami about Tía Lola.) *What happens in the middle?* (They can't find Lola in the airport, so they page her.) *What happens at the end?* (They find Tía Lola; everyone hugs.)

Reading Strategy Have students review the predictions they made. Ask them to choose one prediction, briefly explain it, tell why they made it, and tell whether it was correct.

Elements of Literature Ask students to review samples of their writing. Have students offer examples of third-person writing. ***Ask:*** *How do you know this is third-person writing?*

Reassess Ask students to work in pairs to write and present brief reviews of the story. Tell them to include a summary, interesting details, and whether they would recommend the story to another reader.

From Reading to Writing

Write a Narrative with Dialogue

1. **Paired discussion** After students have thought about the questions in the box, arrange them in pairs. Have them ask each other the questions and discuss the people and events of their narratives.
2. **Write a draft** During writing, tell students to use dialogue and third-person point of view.
3. **Multi-level options** See MULTI-LEVEL OPTIONS on p. 300.

Across Content Areas: Social Studies

Read a Weather Map

1. **Define and clarify** Explain *legend* and *symbols.* Point out information pictured on the weather map: temperature ranges and weather conditions. Remind students of the two systems for temperature: Fahrenheit and Celsius. Have students find local weather maps in newspapers or on the Internet.
2. **Create a record** Have students work in pairs to record the local temperature for a week. Tell them to measure the temperature at the same time each day. Have pairs collaborate to compose and organize a record for these temperatures. After recording information, have pairs revise their records.

Answers

1. red **2.** blue **3.** Washington

ASSESS

Have students write a quiz question about the weather map on p. 301 or one from a local newspaper. Tell them to exchange questions and answer one another's question.

Chapter Materials

Activity Book: *pp. 161–168*
Audio: *Unit 5, Chapter 2*
Student Handbook
Student CD-ROM: *Unit 5, Chapter 2*
Teacher Resource Book: *Lesson Plan, Teacher Resources, Reading Summary, Activity Book Answer Key*
Teacher Resource CD-ROM
Assessment Program: *Quiz, pp. 77–78; Teacher and Student Resources, pp. 115–144*
Assessment CD-ROM
Transparencies
The Heinle Newbury House Dictionary/CD-ROM
Web Site: www.heinle.visions.com

Objectives

Preread for vocabulary Read the objectives. *Ask: What is a biography? What is a play?*

Use Prior Knowledge

Recall Facts About Blindness and Deafness

Share Knowledge Have students describe experiences they have had with blindness or deafness. Make a list of special tools blind and deaf people use, such as canes, Braille, or closed captioning (on television).

Answers
1. True 2. False 3. True 4. False 5. True

CHAPTER 2

Helen Keller

an excerpt from a biography
by George Sullivan

The Miracle Worker

an excerpt from a play
by William Gibson

Into the Reading

Objectives

Reading Compare and contrast as you read a biography and a play.

Listening and Speaking Interpret lines from a play.

Grammar Recognize and use past progressive verbs.

Writing Write a scene from a play.

Content Science: Learn about some causes of diseases.

Use Prior Knowledge

Recall Facts About Blindness and Deafness

Blindness and deafness are disabilities. Blindness means not being able to see well or at all. Deafness means not being able to hear well or at all.

What do you think is true about blindness and deafness?

1. Copy the chart on a sheet of paper.
2. Decide whether each statement is true or false.
3. Share your answers with a partner. Check your answers in the school library or on the Internet.

Blindness and Deafness	True	False
1. People who are blind can read books.		
2. People who are blind or deaf cannot go to school.		
3. People who are deaf can learn to speak a language.		
4. People who are blind cannot have jobs or live alone.		
5. Some people who are deaf communicate by using a hand language.		

MULTI-LEVEL OPTIONS *Build Vocabulary*

Newcomer Write *turn* and *whirl* on the board. Turn and *say: turn.* Repeat for *whirl.* Write: *groping* and *reaching.* Demonstrate the words in the same way. Point to the words and have volunteers demonstrate the actions. Then have students say and demonstrate the words in pairs.

Beginning Write these words in a column on the board: *run, throw, trip,* and *raise.* Write *stumble, trot, lift,* and *toss* in a second column. Have students copy the lists. Ask students to work in pairs to match the synonym pairs by drawing lines to connect them.

Intermediate On the board, write: *douses, groping, whirls, soaks, reaching,* and *turns.* Have students work in pairs. Instruct one student to use a word from the list in a sentence. Then tell the other student to restate the sentence, using the word's synonym. Have partners alternate turns.

Advanced Have students work independently. Ask students to write a different sentence for each of the following words: *douses, groping, whirls.* Challenge students to find additional synonyms for each word. (splashes, saturates; feeling, handling; rotates, spins)

Build Background

Helen Keller

Helen Keller was born in Tuscumbie, Alabama, in 1880. She was a smart and friendly child who learned to speak very early. When Helen was one and a half years old, she became very sick. Doctors think she may have had scarlet fever. Helen got better from her fever but lost her sight and hearing. She lived in darkness and silence. Helen struggled very hard to tell others what she needed and what she was feeling. The struggle often made her angry, and she became a difficult child.

Content Connection

People who get scarlet fever today usually take penicillin. Penicillin is an **antibiotic** that kills **bacteria** (tiny living things that can cause diseases).

Build Vocabulary

Find Synonyms for Action Verbs

"The Miracle Worker" includes **action verbs** to describe what is happening.

1. With a partner, look at the underlined words in the following sentences. Choose the **synonym** (a word with a similar meaning) for each word from the box.

turns	reaching	breaks	soaks

a. The water tumbling half into and half around the pitcher douses Helen's hand.
b. Helen scrambles back onto the porch, groping, and finds the bell string.
c. Helen whirls to the pump, pats it, holds up her palm, and Annie spells into it.
d. Helen drops the pitcher on the slab under the spout, it shatters.

2. Check your work in a dictionary or synonym finder.
3. Write the words and their synonyms in your Personal Dictionary.

Personal Dictionary

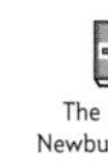
The Heinle Newbury House Dictionary

Activity Book *p. 161*

Student CD-ROM

Content Connection
Technology

Build Vocabulary Have students use computer aids, such as an electronic thesaurus or synonym finder, or the thesaurus feature of word processing software, to find more synonyms. Give students these words: *miracle, transform, mystery,* and *reveal.* Ask students to find one or more synonyms for each word. Have them compile their synonyms into a two-column chart.

Teacher Resource Book: *Two-Column Chart, p. 44*

Learning Styles
Musical

Build Background Tell students that although deaf people cannot hear music, they can still enjoy it. Explain that deaf people can detect rhythm by feeling the vibrations made by sound waves. Ask students to place their hands on a speaker while you play a piece of music. Suggest that they cover their ears or use earplugs. Ask students to describe what they feel.

Build Background

Helen Keller

1. **Experience blindness and deafness** Bring in a blindfold and headphones and have volunteers wear them. Ask others to communicate simple tasks for the volunteers to do. Discuss how people felt trying to communicate.
2. **Make guesses** *Ask: What would it be like to grow up without being able to see or hear?*
3. **Content Connection** Bring in some pictures of bacteria or have students look at bacteria through a microscope.

Build Vocabulary

Find Synonyms for Action Verbs

1. **Teacher think aloud** Write on the board: *The baseball hit the window and the glass shattered.* ***Say:*** *I can visualize the ball hitting the window. I know the baseball is going to break the glass, so I guess* shattered *means "broke into pieces and made noise."*
2. **Reading selection vocabulary** You may want to introduce the glossed words in the reading selections before students begin reading. Key words: *miracle, transform, mystery, reveal, frantic, tremble, gestures, unsteady.* Instruct students to write the words with correct spelling and their definitions in their Personal Dictionaries. Have them pronounce each word and divide it into syllables.
3. **Multi-level options** See MULTI-LEVEL OPTIONS on p. 302.

Answers
a. soaks **b.** reaching **c.** turns **d.** crashes

ASSESS

Have students use the vocabulary words in sentences.

UNIT 5 • CHAPTER 2

Into the Reading

Text Structure

Biography and Drama

Recognize features Point out features, reminding students of a biography ("Mae Jemison, Space Scientist") and a play ("And Now Miguel") they have read.

Reading Strategy

Compare and Contrast

Teacher Resource Book: *Reading Log, p. 64*

1. **Teacher think aloud** *Say: When I go to the store, I compare things. I look to see if the sizes are the same. I contrast the things, too. I look to see if the prices are different.* Ask students to name qualities or information they compare and contrast as they shop.
2. **Multi-level options** See MULTI-LEVEL OPTIONS below.

Answers

1. "Helen Keller" looks like a regular narrative with text in paragraphs. "The Miracle Worker" looks like a play with characters' dialogues introduced by colons and directions in parentheses.
2. The narrative describes a past event; the play shows the event as it happens. The event is the same in both selections.

Ask students to define *stage direction, acts,* and *scenes.*

Text Structure

Biography and Drama

The first reading selection, "Helen Keller," is a **biography** (a story of a person's life). The second selection, "The Miracle Worker," is a **drama** (a play).

As you read, look for the features of a biography and a drama.

Biography	
Events	Biographies describe important events in the person's life.
Point of View	Biographies are usually told in the third-person point of view.
Facts	Biographies include information and facts that are true.

Drama (Play)	
Playwright	The author of a play is called a playwright.
Stage Directions	Stage directions tell actors where to move, what actions to make, and how to speak.
Characters	The name of the character who is speaking is before each line of dialogue.
Acts	Plays are divided into sections called acts.
Scenes	Acts can be divided into scenes. Each scene is a different place or time.

Reading Strategy

Compare and Contrast

You are going to read two selections. Both describe the same moment in Helen Keller's life. As you read, compare and contrast the selections.

1. View the pages of both selections. How do they look different?
2. Read the first paragraph of each selection. How are they the same? Do they include the same facts? Do they have different information?
3. Make a Venn Diagram in your Reading Log to record the similarities and differences you find in the two selections.

MULTI-LEVEL OPTIONS *Reading Strategy*

Newcomer Write *same* and *different* on the board. Display a CD and a cassette. Hold up both and ***say:*** *music* and *sounds.* Point to *same.* Show the CD and ***say:*** *circle.* Show the cassette and ***say:*** *rectangle.* Point to *different.* Help pairs of students express similarities and differences between them. (hair color, height, gender, clothing, etc.)

Beginning ***Say:*** *When you compare, you see how things are alike. When you contrast, you see how things are different.* Hold up a fork and a spoon. ***Ask:*** *How are these alike?* (Both are for eating.) *How are they different?* (Fork has tines; fork is pointy; spoon is smooth and round; etc.)

Intermediate Ask pairs of students to choose objects in the classroom. Have pairs discuss the similarities and differences between their two objects. Then have pairs write sentences that compare and contrast their objects. Offer these starters: *Both are _____. One is _____, but the other is _____.*

Advanced Have students look at the photograph of Mae Jemison on p. 271. Ask students to write a paragraph that compares and contrasts that photograph with the one of Helen Keller on p. 305. Tell them that the differences are clearer than the similarities. Challenge them to find as many similarities as they can.

Helen Keller

an excerpt from a biography by George Sullivan

The Miracle Worker

an excerpt from a play by William Gibson

305

Reading Selection Materials

Audio: *Unit 5, Chapter 2*
Teacher Resource Book: *Reading Summary, pp. 105–106*

Preview the Selections

Teacher Resource Book: *Venn Diagram, p. 35*

1. **Use the photograph** Ask students to describe the girl in the picture. ***Ask:*** *What is her name? How old does she look? When do you think she lived? What is she wearing? What games and activities do you think she liked to do? What is she thinking about?*
2. **Compare and contrast** Have students draw on information from the photograph to compare and contrast the life of the girl to their lives. Use a Venn diagram to record their responses and ideas.
3. **Connect** Remind students that the unit theme is *communication.* ***Ask:*** *Does it look like the girl is communicating with anyone? Why do you think so? Who do you think will communicate with her? How will they be able to communicate?*

Content Connection *Science*

Ask students to work in small groups to create diagrams of the eye and the ear. Have groups use the library or the Internet to research the human eye and ear. Tell students to include labels and captions that name the various parts of the eye and ear and describe the parts' functions.

Learning Styles *Kinesthetic*

Have students use library books, Internet sources, or other reference aids to find diagrams that show sign language. Have students work in pairs to learn to sign the alphabet. Ask pairs to practice signing the alphabet and their names. Have pairs present what they learned to the class.

Read the Selection

1. **Use text features** Read the prologue together. Have students identify the people in the photo and describe what they are doing.
2. **Teacher read aloud** Read the selection aloud. Pause to check understanding and to have students identify features of the biography: events, point of view, and facts. Have students reread the selection in pairs.
3. **Analyze relationships** *Ask: Why do you think Annie is happy? What do you think Helen has learned from Annie?*

Sample Answer to Guide Question
Helen's behavior has changed. Before she was wild, but now she is happy and gentle.

See Teacher Edition pp. 434–435 for a list of English-Spanish cognates in the reading selection.

Audio

Helen Keller
an excerpt from a biography by George Sullivan

Prologue

When Helen Keller was seven years old, her parents brought Annie Sullivan to their home. Annie came to teach Helen. She had studied at a school for the blind. When Annie first came to the Keller's home, she taught Helen the manual alphabet. This means she formed the letters of the alphabet with her fingers. She did this in the palm of Helen's hand so that Helen could feel the letters. For a long time, Helen enjoyed this game, but she did not understand that the letters Annie formed made words. She did not realize that words stood for things, people, and feelings.

Compare and Contrast

What has happened to Helen's behavior? How does it compare to how she acted before?

1 About two weeks after Helen and Annie had moved into "The Little House," Annie wrote a joyful letter to a friend at the Perkins Institution. "My heart is singing for joy this morning. A miracle has happened! . . . The wild little creature of two weeks ago has been **transformed** into a gentle child. She is sitting by me as I write, her face serene and happy, **crocheting** a long red chain of Scotch wool.

2 "She lets me kiss her now," Annie's letter continued, "and when she is in a particularly gentle mood, she will sit in my lap for a minute or two . . .

3 "The great step—the step that counts—has been taken."

4 The "great step" would soon lead to an event that some people would call a miracle.

5 Day after day, Annie spelled words into Helen's hand. Helen would then take Annie's hand and spell each word back. It was like a

transformed changed in an important way

crocheting making cloth by looping thread with a hooked tool

306 Unit 5 Communication

MULTI-LEVEL OPTIONS *Read the Selection*

Newcomer Play the audio. Read the pages again. ***Ask:*** *Was Annie Helen's teacher?* (yes) *Did Helen know that letters made words?* (no) *Does Annie spell words into Helen's hand?* (yes) *Did Helen know that words named things?* (no)

Beginning Read the Reading Summary aloud. Then ***ask:*** *Who came to teach Helen?* (Annie) *Where did Annie form letters?* (in Helen's hand) *Where did Annie take Helen for a break?* (the water pump) *What was the first word Helen learned the meaning of?* (water)

Intermediate Have students do a paired reading. ***Ask:*** *Why did Annie form letters in Helen's hand?* (so Helen could feel them) *Why was the day at the water pump a "real" miracle?* (Helen understood the mystery of language.)

Advanced Have students read independently. Then ***ask:*** *What was the first miracle?* (Helen was sitting quietly; she was no longer "wild"; she let Annie kiss her; she sat in Annie's lap.) *What was the second miracle?* (Helen connected the finger spelling of *water* with its actual meaning.)

game to Helen, and she enjoyed it. But she did not **link** the words to the things they stood for. B-R-E-A-D was just a series of letters to Helen. She did not know that it meant a baked food.

6 "She has no idea yet," Annie Sullivan wrote, "that everything has a name."

7 One day, Helen and Annie began their daily spelling lesson. Helen was in a restless mood. She was being difficult that day. Annie decided that they should take a break. They headed for the water pump at the back of the main house.

8 Helen described what then happened in *The Story of My Life.* "Someone was drawing water and my teacher placed my hand under the spout. As the cool stream **gushed** over one hand, she spelled into the other the word water, first slowly, then rapidly. I stood still, my whole attention fixed upon the motions of her fingers.

9 "Suddenly, I felt [as if] somehow the **mystery** of language was **revealed** to me. I knew then that W-A-T-E-R meant the wonderful cool something that was flowing over my hand."

10 After Helen had spelled out "water" several times, she dropped to her knees and pointed to the ground and asked for its name. She pointed to the pump and asked for its name. Suddenly, she pointed to Annie and asked for her name. Annie slowly spelled out T-E-A-C-H-E-R. From that time on, Annie was "Teacher" to Helen.

Compare and Contrast

What did Helen know at the beginning of this page? What did she know at the end?

---

link connect
gushed flowed quickly and in a large stream
mystery something hard to understand
revealed shown

Read the Selection

1. **Use text features** Ask students to describe the object in the illustration. Ask what it shows about the time and place of the reading.
2. **Understand terms** Have students examine the meanings of the glossed words below the selection. Clarify as needed.
3. **Paired reading** After students listen to the audio or to you read the selection, have them reread it in pairs.
4. **Summarize** ***Ask:*** *What words did Helen learn?* (water, ground, pump, teacher) *What were Helen and Annie doing when Helen first understood language?* (They were getting water from a pump.)
5. **Share personal experiences** Have students think of a time when they learned a word or expression that was important to them. ***Ask:*** *What word did you learn? How did you learn it? Why was it important to you? How did you feel?*
6. **Multi-level options** See MULTI-LEVEL OPTIONS on p. 306.

Sample Answer to Guide Question

At the beginning of the page, Helen knew a series of letters. At the end of the page, she knew that the series of letters meant words and things.

Punctuation

Hyphens

Explain to students that, in writing, the letters that represent the spelling of a word are written in capital letters and separated with hyphens. ***Ask:*** *Why are there hyphens between the letters* B, R, E, A, *and* D *in paragraph 5?* (The letters are spelling out the word *bread.*) *What other words are spelled out on page 307?* (water, teacher)

Apply Have students correct the following sentences by adding hyphens where necessary. Write on the board:

"D I C T I O N A R Y," said the spelling-bee contestant. "How do you spell your last name?" he asked. "S U L L I V A N," she replied.

Read the Selection

1. **Shared reading** Read aloud or play the audio. Have students join in for Helen's writing and thoughts. ***Ask:*** *What other words did Helen learn?* (mother, father, sister) *How did she feel?* (very happy)

Sample Answer to Guide Question
At the end, Helen is happy and eager. She's excited about what she has learned and wants to learn more.

About the Author

Interpret the facts ***Ask:*** *Why do you think George Sullivan chose Helen Keller for a biography?* (He thought the way she learned to speak and communicate was very interesting. He thought her story would inspire other people with disabilities, too.)

Compare and Contrast

In Build Background you read that Helen was angry and difficult. Compare and contrast this to her mood at the end.

11 Now Helen was eager to learn. "Everything had a name," she wrote, "and each name gave birth to a new thought.

12 "I learned a great many new words that day," Helen continued. "I do not remember what they all were. But I do know that mother, father, sister, teacher were among them. . . .

13 "It would have been difficult to find a happier child than I was as I lay in my crib at the close of that **eventful** day and lived over the joys it had brought me, and for the first time longed for a new day to come."

---

eventful worth remembering, important

About the Author — George Sullivan (born 1927)

George Sullivan has written more than 250 books, mostly for young readers. He has written about sports and history. Sullivan has written biographies about interesting people. He enjoys taking photographs and includes these in many of his books. Sullivan said, "I'm always being asked where I get the ideas for my books. That's never been a problem for me. The ideas spring from my curiosity about people, places, and events."

➤ Why do you think George Sullivan wrote this book? To entertain, to inform, or to persuade? What strategies does he use to write?

MULTI-LEVEL OPTIONS *Read the Selection*

Newcomer Play the audio. Have students join in when they can. ***Ask:*** *Is Annie pleased with Helen?* (no) *Does Annie make Helen work the pump handle?* (yes) *Does Helen drop the pitcher?* (yes) *Does Annie spell* water *on Helen's hand?* (yes)

Beginning Play the audio. Put students into groups of three. Assign a narrator to read stage directions and the other two students to read Annie's and Helen's dialogues aloud. ***Ask:*** *How does Annie feel at the beginning of the scene?* (She's upset with Helen.) *What does Helen carry outside?* (a pitcher) *What word does Helen understand?* (water)

Intermediate Play the audio. In groups of three, have students read the stage directions, and Annie's or Helen's dialogues aloud. ***Ask:*** *What does Annie make Helen do?* (work the pump; pump water) *Why does Helen's face change?* (She suddenly understands that the word Annie spells in her hand has a meaning.)

Advanced Have students read silently. Tell groups of three to read the stage directions, Annie's dialogue, and Helen's dialogue aloud. ***Ask:*** *How does Annie feel when she takes Helen to the pump?* (upset) *Why does Helen say "water" like a baby?* (She hasn't spoken since she lost her hearing as a baby.)

The Miracle Worker

an excerpt from a play by William Gibson

1 (ANNIE *has pulled* HELEN *downstairs again by one hand, the pitcher in her other hand, down the porch steps, and across the yard to the pump. She puts* HELEN'S *hand on the pump handle,* ***grimly***.)

2 **Annie:** All right. Pump.

3 (HELEN *touches her cheek, waits uncertainly.*)

4 No, she's not here. Pump!

5 (*She forces* HELEN'S *hand to work the handle, then lets go. And* HELEN *obeys. She pumps till the water comes, then* ANNIE *puts the pitcher in her other hand and guides it under the spout, and the water tumbling half into and half around the pitcher douses* HELEN'S *hand.* ANNIE *takes over the handle to keep water coming, and does automatically what she has done so many times before, spells into* HELEN'S *free palm:*)

6 Water. W, a, t, e, r. *Water.* It has a—*name*—

Compare and Contrast

How is this description of Helen's discovery different from the description in the first reading, "Helen Keller"?

7 (*And now the miracle happens.* HELEN *drops the pitcher on the* ***slab*** *under the spout, it shatters. She stands transfixed.* ANNIE *freezes on the pump handle: there is a change in the sundown light, and with it a change in* HELEN'S *face, some light coming into it we have never seen there, some struggle in the depths behind it; and her lips tremble, trying to remember something the muscles around them once knew, till at last it finds its way out, painfully, a baby sound buried under the* ***debris*** *of years of dumbness.*)

8 **Helen:** Wah. Wah.

9 (*And again, with great effort*)

10 Wah. Wah.

11 (HELEN *plunges her hand into the* ***dwindling*** *water, spells into her own palm. Then she gropes* ***frantically***, ANNIE *reaches for her hand, and* HELEN *spells into* ANNIE'S *hand.*)

12 **Annie** [whispering]: Yes.

13 (HELEN *spells it again.*)

---

grimly unhappily, perhaps a little angrily
slab a large, flat piece of stone or concrete
debris garbage
dwindling getting smaller and smaller
frantically in a panic, hurrying

Punctuation

Colons

Explain that a colon can come before a quotation, an example, an explanation, or a list. ***Say:*** *In a play, the dialogue is introduced by the speaker's name, followed by a colon.* Have students look at line 2 on p. 309. ***Ask:*** *Who is the speaker?* (Annie) Then tell students that in a dialogue, the first word after a colon is capitalized because it is a new sentence.

Reading Selection

Read the Selection

1. **Use the text features** Ask students to find the names of the characters and stage directions. Point out that the stage directions are in parentheses and italicized.
2. **Understand terms** Call attention to the glossed words and their meanings.
3. **Shared reading** Play the audio or read aloud as students join in for different parts. Assign one student to be the narrator (giving the stage directions), and divide the rest into two groups reading the parts of Helen and Annie. ***Ask:*** *Why do you think Annie is pulling Helen down the stairs?* (Helen doesn't want to go with her.) *How do you think Annie is feeling?* (frustrated or angry) *Do you think that Annie has spelled a few words or many words for Helen before?* (many words; it seems like she's tired and frustrated that Helen hasn't learned.) *What do you think Helen was thinking about as the water poured over her hands?* (Maybe she remembered a word, *water,* that she knew before she was sick.)
5. **Multi-level options** See MULTI-LEVEL OPTIONS on p. 308.

Sample Answer to Guide Question

This description gives more details of Helen with the water and Annie talking and spelling the words into her hand. I can visualize the characters and the scene more.

See Teacher Edition pp. 434–435 for a list of English-Spanish cognates in the reading selection.

UNIT 5 • CHAPTER 2
Reading Selection

Read the Selection

1. **Summarize and make predictions** Ask students to restate the main events of the scene and then guess what Helen will do next with what she learned.
2. **Paired reading** Have students reread the selection with partners. *Ask: How does Helen feel?* (excited) *Why is Helen running around?* (She wants to know the names of all the things around her.)

Sample Answer to Guide Question
Helen was very demanding in this play, but she sounded more gentle and quiet in the biography. Yes, she was surprised when she realized what language was.

14 Yes!

15 (HELEN *grabs at the handle, pumps for more water, plunges her hand into its* **spurt** *and grabs* ANNIE'S *to spell it again.*)

16 *Yes!* Oh, my dear—

17 (*She falls to her knees to clasp* HELEN'S *hand, but* HELEN *pulls it free, stands almost* **bewildered,** *then drops to the ground, pats it swiftly, holds up her palm,* **imperious,** ANNIE *spells into it:*)

18 Ground.

19 (HELEN *spells it back.*)

20 Yes!

21 (HELEN *whirls to the pump, pats it, holds up her palm, and* ANNIE *spells into it.*)

22 Pump.

23 (HELEN *spells it back.*)

24 Yes! Yes!

25 (*Now* HELEN *is in such an excitement she is* **possessed,** *wild,* **trembling,** *cannot be still, turns, runs, falls on the porch steps, claps it, reaches out her palm, and* ANNIE *is at it instantly to spell:*)

26 Step.

27 (HELEN *has no time to spell back now, she whirls groping, to touch anything,* **encounters** *the* **trellis,** *shakes it, thrusts out her palm, and* ANNIE *while spelling to her cries wildly at the house.*)

28 Trellis. Mrs. Keller! Mrs. Keller!

29 (*Inside,* KATE *starts to her feet.* HELEN *scrambles back onto the porch, groping, and finds the bell string, tugs it; the bell rings, the distant chimes begin tolling the hour, all the bells in town seem to break into speech while* HELEN *reaches out and* ANNIE *spells* **feverishly** *into her hand.* KATE *hurries out, with* KELLER *after her;* AUNT EV *is on her feet, to peer out the window; only* JAMES

Compare and Contrast

Compare this description of Helen to what you learned about Helen in the first reading. Do you know more about her?

spurt a big burst
bewildered confused
imperious having an attitude; acting superior or better than someone else
possessed held by, unable to get away from the feeling
trembling shaking
encounters finds
trellis a wooden structure for plants
feverishly with excitement

MULTI-LEVEL OPTIONS *Read the Selection*

Newcomer *Ask: Does Helen learn the words for* ground, pump, *and* step*?* (yes) *Does Annie call Helen's mother?* (yes) *Does Helen's mother ring the bell?* (no) *Does Helen know that Annie is her teacher?* (yes)

Beginning *Ask: How does Helen tell Annie she wants to know another word?* (She pats the ground.) *What words does Helen learn after* water*?* (ground, step, trellis) *Where is the bell string?* (on the porch) *What does Annie do when Helen pats her cheek?* (She spells t-e-a-c-h-e-r.)

Intermediate *Ask: Why does Helen pat the ground and the pump?* (to show that she wants to learn those words) *Why does Annie call Mrs. Keller?* (to show her what Helen has learned) *What does Helen find to pull?* (the bell string) *What do you think the characters are feeling?* (surprise, excitement) *What name does Helen learn for Annie?* (teacher)

Advanced *Ask: What is the mood of the play once Helen understands that words have meaning?* (feverish; excited) *Who does Annie call for?* (Mrs. Keller) *Why does Annie back away from Helen and her parents?* (It's a family moment; she's not a family member.)

*remains at the table, and with a napkin wipes his damp brow. From up right and left the servants—*VINEY, *the two Negro children, the other servant—run in, and stand watching from a distance as* HELEN, *ringing the bell, with the other hand encounters her mother's skirt; when she throws a hand out,* ANNIE *spells into it:)*

30 Mother.

31 (KELLER *now* ***seizes*** HELEN'S *hand, she touches him,* ***gestures*** *a hand, and* ANNIE *again spells:)*

32 Papa–she *knows!*

33 (KATE *and* KELLER *go to their knees,* ***stammering,*** *clutching* HELEN *to them, and* ANNIE *steps* ***unsteadily*** *back to watch the threesome,* HELEN *spelling wildly into* KATE'S *hand, then into* KELLER'S, KATE *spelling back into* HELEN'S; *they cannot keep their hands off her, and rock her in their clasp.*

Compare and Contrast

How is the mood or feeling at the end of the play the same or different from the biography?

34 *Then* HELEN *gropes, feels nothing, turns all around, pulls free, and comes with both hands groping, to find* ANNIE. *She encounters* ANNIE'S *thighs,* ANNIE *kneels to her,* HELEN'S *hand pats* ANNIE'S *cheek impatiently, points a finger, and waits; and* ANNIE *spells into it:)*

35 Teacher.

36 (HELEN *spells it back, slowly;* ANNIE *nods.)*

37 Teacher.

---

seizes grabs

gestures makes a motion that suggests a particular meaning, such as a wave

stammering unable to complete words, usually from being full of strong feelings

unsteadily as if shaky on one's feet or likely to fall over, perhaps moving from side to side or stumbling

About the Author — William Gibson (born 1914)

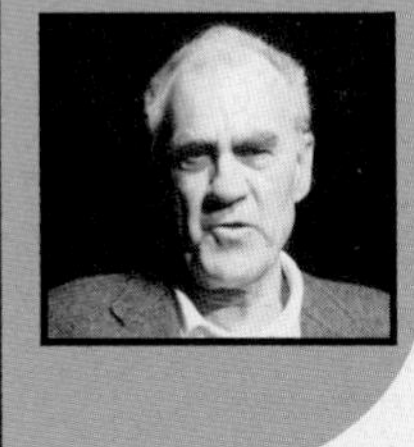

William Gibson is best known for his drama about Helen Keller and Annie Sullivan. He wrote *The Miracle Worker* in 1957 as a script for television. The script was later changed to work as a stage play and a film.

➤ Why do you think that William Gibson gave the title *The Miracle Worker* to this play?

Read the Selection

Paired reading Read the play aloud. Then have pairs of students read it again and act out the scene. ***Ask:*** *Who does Annie call?* (Mr. and Mrs. Keller) *How did Helen's parents feel about Helen's learning?* (They were very happy.)

Sample Answer to Guide Question

At the end of the play, both Annie and Helen are calm, positive, and ready for teaching and learning; at the end of the narrative, Helen is excited, joyous, and thinking about the future.

About the Author

1. **Explain author background** William Gibson helped plan the Broadway version and film version of his play. He became upset when the directors and producers wanted to make some changes in the script.
2. **Interpret the facts** ***Ask:*** *Why do you think Gibson included so many stage directions with so much detail?* (He had an image of the scene and wanted others to see it that way, too.)

Across Selections

Teacher Resource Book: *Reading Log, p. 64*

Make comparisons Have students work in groups. Ask them to compare and contrast the biography and the play. ***Ask:*** *What was similar about them? What differences were there? Which did you enjoy more? Why?* Have them take notes in their Reading Logs.

Punctuation

Italics for stage direction

Tell students that when a play is written, the parts that tell what the characters do and how they move are called *stage directions.* Briefly review italic print with students. Tell them that when they read a play, the stage directions are usually written in italics. Direct students to paragraph 17. ***Ask:*** *Why is this paragraph written in italics?* (It gives stage directions.) Tell students that italics help readers distinguish the directions from the dialogue. See Elements of Literature on p. 313.

Evaluate Your Reading Strategy

Compare and contrast ***Say:*** *You have practiced an important reading strategy. Now you can decide how well you have done. Does this statement describe how you read?*

When I want to compare, I ask, "How are these two things the same?" When I want to contrast, I ask, "How are these two things different?"

When I compare and contrast as I read, I understand more about the author's message.

Reading Comprehension

Question-Answer Relationships

Sample Answers

1. Annie is Helen's teacher.
2. Annie has a problem because Helen didn't realize that the letters represented words.
3. The first word that Helen connects is *water.*
4. She feels the water as Annie spells the word into her hand.
5. The biography is told in the third-person point of view.
6. KELLER now seizes HELEN'S hand, she touches him, gestures a hand, and ANNIE again spells.
7. I think she was a good teacher. She kept trying until her student learned.
8. I think Helen felt amazed and surprised, but then excited.
9. I think she was excited that she could communicate with others and they could communicate with her.
10. I was excited when I learned how to ride a bicycle. My older brother helped me, and he was very proud of me.

Build Reading Fluency

Adjust Your Reading Rate

Demonstrate to the students how you change your rate of reading depending on the purpose and type of reading material.

Beyond the Reading

Reading Comprehension

Question-Answer Relationships (QAR)

"Right There" Questions

1. **Recall Facts** What is the relationship between Helen and Annie?
2. **Recall Facts** In "Helen Keller," what problem does Annie have with Helen?
3. **Recall Facts** In both reading selections, what is the first word that Helen connects to the thing it names?

"Think and Search" Questions

4. **Connect** How does Helen learn that W-A-T-E-R spells *water?*
5. **Recognize Distinguishing Features** Name one feature from "Helen Keller" that helps you identify it as a biography.
6. **Understand Literary Terms** In "The Miracle Worker," what is an example of stage directions?

"Author and You" Questions

7. **Evaluate** Do you think Annie Sullivan was a good teacher? Why or why not?
8. **Make an Inference** How did Helen feel as she learned her first words?
9. **Draw Conclusions** Why do you think Helen was so excited by her discovery?

"On Your Own" Question

10. **Connect with Your Own Experiences** Tell about a time when you have been very excited about learning something.

Activity Book
p. 162

Build Reading Fluency

Adjust Your Reading Rate

When you read a play, you can learn to adjust your reading rate. Pause and read like you are speaking to a person.

1. With a partner, choose parts in "The Miracle Worker."
2. Read the parts with expression.
3. Choose your favorite part of the play.
4. Read it aloud in front of the class.
5. Did you adjust your reading rate?

MULTI-LEVEL OPTIONS *Elements of Literature*

Newcomer Write on the board and *say: upset.* Read an "upset" line of dialogue from the exercise ("All right. Pump!"). Write and *say: happy.* Read the "happy" lines of dialogue from the exercise. ("Papa—she knows!") ***Ask:*** *How do you look and sound when you're upset? How do you look and sound when you're happy?*

Beginning Ask student pairs to role-play the dialogue (Jennifer: line b; Mom: line a) from the exercise. Ask them to follow the stage directions as written.

Intermediate Ask student pairs to role-play the dialogue (Jennifer: line b; Mom: line a) from the exercise. Ask them to follow the stage directions as written. Then ask them to read the alternate lines of dialogue. Tell them to speak and act in a way that matches the dialogue.

Advanced Have students write stage directions to match the second set of dialogue. (Jennifer: line a; Mom: line b) Ask pairs to perform the dialogue with their new stage directions.

Listen, Speak, Interact 

Interpret Lines from a Play

"The Miracle Worker" tells the actors what to do through dialogue and stage directions.

1. With a partner, reread the play. Choose two examples of stage directions and the dialogue that goes with them.
2. Act out (perform) the dialogue. One of you will play Annie, and the other will play Helen.
3. Videotape your performance, if possible.
4. Share your interpretation with the class. Talk about how you acted out the dialogue and stage directions.

Elements of Literature

Analyze Stage Directions

Stage directions are an important part of a play. They tell readers how the characters act. Most of the text in "The Miracle Worker" is stage directions. Look at the following text from the reading:

> 5 (. . . ANNIE takes over the handle to keep water coming, and does automatically what she has done so many times before, spells into HELEN'S free palm:)
>
> 6 Water. W, a, t, e, r. *Water*. It has a—*name*—

The stage directions in paragraph 5 show what Annie does as she says the words in paragraph 6.

Look at the following examples. Choose the correct dialogue to go with the stage directions.

1. (JENNIFER *is sad. She walks toward her mother with her head down.*)
   a. **Jennifer:** Mom, guess what? I won the essay contest!
   b. **Jennifer:** I didn't have a good day today. I lost the essay contest.
2. (MOM *wipes* JENNIFER's *tears and hugs her. She speaks softly.*)
   a. **Mom:** That's OK. You still did a good job. You can try again next year.
   b. **Mom:** That's great! We should celebrate!

Activity Book *p. 163*

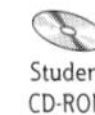
Student CD-ROM

Listen, Speak, Interact

Interpret Lines from a Play

1. **Reread in pairs** Pair beginning and advanced students. Have them read and act out the parts.
2. **Newcomers** Reread with this group. Have them identify each character's feelings and actions as you read. Write these feelings on the board. Have students demonstrate appropriate gestures and facial expressions to help interpret the lines. Have students record these interpretive ideas in their Reading Logs.

Elements of Literature

Analyze Stage Directions

1. **Offer observations** Read the explanation about stage directions. Have volunteers demonstrate Annie's actions as described in the example. Point out differences between the performances but remind students that the general actions are similar.
2. **Multi-level options** See MULTI-LEVEL OPTIONS on p. 312.

Answers
1. b 2. a

ASSESS

Read different stage directions and have students show the appropriate gesture or expression.

Community Connection

Have students to work in small groups. Instruct groups to research amateur and professional theater groups and dance companies in the community. Ask students to compile a schedule of upcoming local events. Suggest that students attend free events and write reviews to share in class.

Learning Styles *Linguistic*

Ask students to write journal entries as Annie or Helen. Tell them that their entries should be for the day described in the biography and the play. Remind students to use the first person and describe their thoughts and feelings as well as the events.

Word Study

Use the Suffix *-ly*

Teacher Resource Book: *Personal Dictionary, p. 63*

Make a word map Write *slow* on the board. Then add the suffix *-ly* and pronounce it. Have students demonstrate standing up slowly. ***Say:*** *They stand up slowly. What verb does it describe?* (stand up) Repeat with *quickly.*

Answers

1. slowly, rapidly; automatically; painfully; frantically; swiftly
2. spelled; spelled; does; finds; gropes; pats

Grammar Focus

Recognize and Use Past Progressive Verbs

Clarify terms Write on the board: *I was listening to music last night.* Point out the helping verb *was* and the *-ing* form of the main verb. Have students say what they were doing last night.

Answers

1. was being; was drawing
2. *Example:* I was walking to school when I saw you. Helping verb: was. Past progressive verb: walking.

ASSESS

On the board, write: *careful, nice, quick.* Tell students to add the suffix *-ly* to the words and then use them in sentences.

Word Study

Use the Suffix *-ly*

You learned earlier that one common suffix is **-ly.** It makes an adjective into an adverb. **Adverbs** describe a verb and tell more precisely *how* an action happened.

> **grimly** means "in a grim way"
>
> She puts Helen's hand on the pump handle, grimly.

The word *grimly* answers the question: How did Annie put Helen's hand on the pump? She did it in a grim (serious) way. Both of the selections in this chapter have examples of vivid and precise adverbs ending in *-ly.*

1. In your Personal Dictionary, make a chart and list other words ending in *-ly* from paragraph 8 of "Helen Keller" and paragraphs 5, 7, 11, and 17 of "The Miracle Worker."
2. Write the verb that each *-ly* word describes.

Adverb	Verb It Describes
grimly	puts

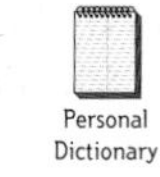
Personal Dictionary

Activity Book p. 164

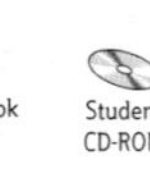
Student CD-ROM

Grammar Focus

Recognize and Use Past Progressive Verbs

The **past progressive tense** describes an action from the past that was in progress. Here is an example from the first reading selection:

> W-A-T-E-R meant the wonderful cool something that was flowing over my hand.

The water continued to flow. Notice that the past progressive verb has a helping verb. The helping verb can be *was* or *were.*

1. Find two more examples of past progressive verbs from paragraphs 7 and 8 of "Helen Keller."
2. On a piece of paper, write your own sentence using a past progressive verb. Underline the past progressive verb. Circle the helping verb.

Activity Book pp. 165–166

Student Handbook

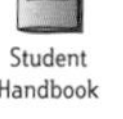
Student CD-ROM

MULTI-LEVEL OPTIONS *From Reading to Writing*

Newcomer Have students think about things they have found or learned. Ask students to draw pictures of their discovery. Then have them act it out in small groups.

Beginning Have students create a pre-writing chart with the labels *characters, setting,* and *plot.* Tell groups to use the charts to organize their ideas. Help them plot the scene, develop the characters, and draft the dialogue. Have groups perform their scenes for the class.

Intermediate Have students work in groups. Instruct them to create a pre-writing chart with the labels *characters, setting,* and *plot.* Tell them to use the charts to organize their ideas. Have them use their charts to write their scenes.

Advanced Have students exchange their completed scenes with partners. Ask partners to extend the play by writing a second scene.

From Reading to Writing

Write a Scene from a Play

Write a **scene** from a play. Focus your scene on a discovery you have made.

1. Show what happens in the story through the characters' actions.
2. Use past continuous verbs.
3. Use adverbs to describe *how* actions are completed.
4. Share your written scene with a partner. Read your scene aloud, with each of you taking different roles.

Scene 1

Carlos: *Hey! Let's turn down this street and see if we can find our way home.*

(CARLOS points down the street and looks at his friend, BEN.)

Ben: *I don't know what the street is on the other side.*

Activity Book
p. 167

Across Content Areas

Learn About Some Causes of Diseases

Microorganisms are very small living things. Some can cause diseases.

Bacteria are single cell microorganisms. Bacteria can cause diseases like scarlet fever and cholera. Medicines called **antibiotics** can kill bacteria.

Viruses are another type of microorganism. They can cause flu and chicken pox. Scientists have developed **vaccines** that prevent some viruses from making us sick.

Write the answers to these sentences on a piece of paper.

1. Antibiotics can be used to cure diseases caused by ____ .
   a. bacteria **b.** viruses
2. An example of a disease caused by a virus is ____ .
   a. cholera **b.** flu
3. How could you find more information about one of the diseases listed in the article? Look ____ .
   a. in an encyclopedia
   b. on the Internet
   Both **a** and **b**

Activity Book
p. 168

Reteach and Reassess

Text Structure Draw a tree with three branches. Then draw a tree with five branches. Label the "roots" of the first tree *Biography* and the second tree, *Drama*. Have students name and describe one text feature for one of the trees. Repeat until the trees are completed.

Reading Strategy Display two items, such as a map and an atlas. Have students compare and contrast them.

Elements of Literature Have students review "And Now Miguel" on p. 206. Ask them to point out stage directions. *Ask: How do stage directions help you understand a play?*

Reassess Ask students to think about the similarities and differences between the biography and the play. Have students write paragraphs that explain which selection they preferred and why.

From Reading to Writing

Write a Scene from a Play

1. **Make a plan** Have students suggest things they discovered. List ideas on the board. Have students identify characters, setting, and actions for their writing.
2. **Perform a scene** In pairs, have students say and act out the lines of dialogue for their scene. Later, have students add clear stage directions for others to act out the same scene.
3. **Multi-level options** See MULTI-LEVEL OPTIONS on p. 314.

Across Content Areas: Science

Learn About Some Causes of Diseases

Define key vocabulary Explain the meanings of *microorganisms, bacteria, viruses,* and *antibiotics. Ask: What are some examples of microorganisms?* (bacteria and viruses) *Are microorganisms large or small?* (very small) *What types of medicines are used for microorganisms?* (antibiotics and vaccines)

Answers
1. a **2.** b **3.** Both a and b.

Write on the board: *Bacteria can cause the flu. Antibiotics can kill bacteria. Vaccines are the same as antibiotics.* Have students write *True* or *False* for each statement. (False; True; False)

Chapter Materials

Activity Book: *pp. 169–176*
Audio: *Unit 5, Chapter 3*
Student Handbook
Student CD-ROM: *Unit 5, Chapter 3*
Teacher Resource Book: *Lesson Plan, Teacher Resources, Reading Summary, Activity Book Answer Key*
Teacher Resource CD-ROM
Assessment Program: *Quiz, pp. 79–80; Teacher and Student Resources, pp. 115–144*
Assessment CD-ROM
Transparencies
The Heinle Newbury House Dictionary/CD-ROM
Web Site: www.heinle.visions.com

Objectives

Pair reading Have students work in pairs and take turns reading the objectives section. Explain and point out key words. ***Ask:*** *What textbooks do you read?*

Use Prior Knowledge

Listen to Learn

Preview ***Ask:*** *What sounds do you hear at night when you close your eyes? Are they the same sounds you hear when you are awake and doing things? Why or why not?* List students' responses.

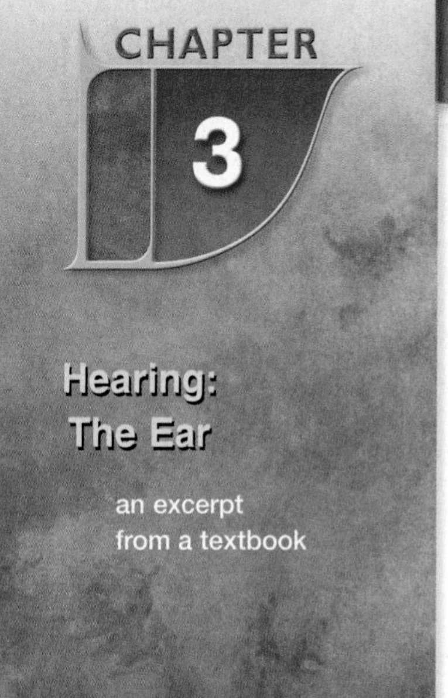

Into the Reading

Objectives

Reading Represent text information in an outline as you read an excerpt from a textbook.

Listening and Speaking Discuss how sound waves travel.

Grammar Recognize subject and verb agreement in the present tense.

Writing Write to inform.

Content The Arts: Learn about the voice.

Use Prior Knowledge

Listen to Learn

1. Close your eyes and sit quietly for one minute. Listen to all of the sounds you hear. Make a mental list of the sounds. A mental list is a list that is in your mind and not written down.
2. Open your eyes. Copy the chart below on a piece of paper. Write down the sounds you heard.
3. Compare your list with your classmates'. Did everyone hear the same things?
4. Discuss what helps you to listen better.

Sounds in the Classroom	Sounds in the School	Sounds Outdoors
foot tapping	door closing	siren

MULTI-LEVEL OPTIONS *Build Vocabulary*

Newcomer Demonstrate how to use glosses to find the meaning of unknown words. Use an earlier selection as an example. Remind students that glossed words are usually highlighted with boldfaced print.

Beginning Remind students that many reference aids list entries in alphabetical order. Write on the board: *vibrate, vocal chords, passage, vibrations, cochlea, engineers, balance,* and *molecules.* Ask pairs of students to work together to write the words in alphabetical order.

Intermediate ***Say:*** *Dictionary entries are listed in alphabetical order. Glossed words can be highlighted with boldfaced print, with a small, star-shaped symbol called an asterisk, or with a number.* Ask students to find examples of glossed words in their other textbooks.

Advanced Ask students to work in pairs to write brief explanations of how to use a dictionary, a gloss, and a textbook to find the meanings of new science words. Remind students that an index can help them find terms in a textbook. Have students share their explanations in groups.

Build Background

The Ear

The human ear is made up of three main parts: the outer ear, the middle ear, and the inner ear. The outer ear is what you see on the outside of your head plus the ear canal. The ear canal connects the outer ear to the middle ear. A tube in the middle ear opens when your ears "pop" in an airplane or elevator. Hearing occurs in the inner ear.

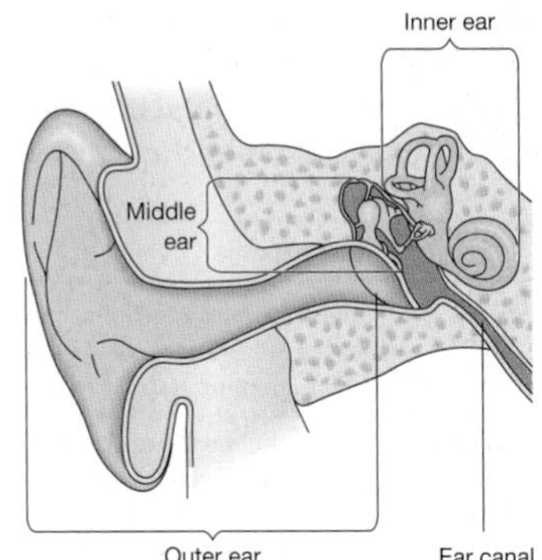

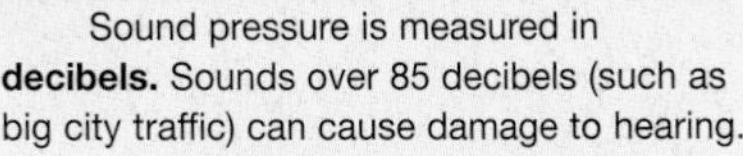

Content Connection

Sound pressure is measured in **decibels.** Sounds over 85 decibels (such as big city traffic) can cause damage to hearing.

Build Vocabulary

Identify Science Vocabulary

As you read "Hearing: The Ear," you will see words that you may not know. Here are ways to learn new science words.

1. **Glosses** Check the glosses at the bottom of each page to find definitions.
2. **Dictionary** Check a dictionary for definitions.
3. **Graphics in a Science Textbook** Check the drawings, photographs, and labels. Important terms are used as headings so you can find them.

As you read, write definitions for the science vocabulary in your Personal Dictionary.

Personal Dictionary

The Heinle Newbury House Dictionary

Activity Book *p. 169*

Student CD-ROM

Content Connection ***Technology***

Build Vocabulary Ask students to think of ways they can use technology to understand science vocabulary and concepts. Brainstorm with students to create a list of electronic reference aids, including the Internet, electronic dictionaries and encyclopedia, and science-content CD-ROMS. Have students arrange these ideas in a chart that describes how each source can help them to understand science material.

Learning Styles ***Mathematical***

Build Background Help students understand the functions of the parts of the ear and the process of hearing. Ask students to draw a flowchart with six boxes connected with arrows. In the boxes, write: *inner ear, ear canal, sound in, middle ear, hearing occurs, outer ear.* Have students write the terms in the flowchart in the correct order. (sound → outer ear → ear canal → middle ear → inner ear → hearing)

Build Background

The Ear

1. **Use the illustration** Have students point to the three main parts of the ear. ***Ask:*** *Which part of the ear is the largest? Which parts can't you see? Did you ever have a doctor or nurse look inside your ear? What do you think they were looking at?* (eardrum, signs of infection)
2. **Content Connection** Have students guess the number of decibels of: a washing machine (75); typical speech (55–65); rustling leaves (near 0); a walkman at mid-volume (100); a rock concert (110).

Build Vocabulary

Identify Science Vocabulary

Teacher Resource Book: *Personal Dictionary, p. 63*

1. **Use a glossary or other sources** Point out that it is often difficult to figure out the pronunciation of science vocabulary based on its spelling. Have students skim the glossary of their science textbook and locate a word whose pronunciation is given. Ask them to use the pronunciation symbols to pronounce the word. Also have students locate the pronunciation of a word using an online or CD-ROM dictionary.
2. **Reading selection vocabulary** You may want to introduce the glossed words in the reading selection before students begin reading. Key words: *rapid, siren, interpret, tilt.* Instruct students to write the words with correct spelling and their definitions in their Personal Dictionaries. Have them pronounce each word and divide it into syllables.
3. **Multi-level options** See MULTI-LEVEL OPTIONS on p. 316.

ASSESS

Tell students to name three places they can find information about new scientific vocabulary.

Text Structure

Textbook

Recognize features Direct students to "Antarctic Adventure" (p. 32) and "Why Do Leaves Change Color in the Fall?" (p. 84). Ask what textbook features they find in those selections. (headings, graphics) Have students find and share other examples in their textbooks.

Reading Strategy

Represent Text Information in an Outline

Teacher Resource Book: *Outline, p. 59*

1. **Analyze an outline** Read and explain the organization and use of outlines. Have students look at paragraphs 2–4 on p. 320. Ask them to compare the information in the outline to the information in the paragraphs. Call attention to the use of the subheadings and glossed words.
2. **Multi-level options** See MULTI-LEVEL OPTIONS below.

ASSESS

Ask: What are four features of textbooks? (headings, subheadings, graphics, specific details and examples)

Text Structure

Textbook

"Hearing: The Ear" comes from a science **textbook,** a book written specifically to teach students. Look for these features of a textbook as you read:

Textbook	
Headings	"titles" of major sections; capital letters are used for the first word and important words
Subheadings	"titles" that divide major sections into smaller sections; capital letters are used for the first word and important words
Graphics	ways of showing information with drawings, charts, and other features
Specific Details and Examples	information that helps you understand the points the textbook is making

The Parts of the Ear

The Outer Ear

The Middle Ear

The Inner Ear

Student CD-ROM

Reading Strategy

Represent Text Information in an Outline

One way to learn as you read a textbook is to write an **outline** of the information. In an outline, you list the major parts of what you are reading. Then you list the important facts about that part.

You can use the subheadings and the words in **bold** in a text to help you with your outline. Use **Roman numerals** (I, II, III) for the major parts.

As you read "Hearing: The Ear," write an outline of the information.

Outline

I. Sound Waves
- **A.** Vibrations produce sounds.
- **B.** Vocal cords vibrate to produce voice.
- **C.** etc.

II. Ears for Hearing and Balance
- **A.** Outer ear funnels sound waves to eardrum.
- **B.** etc.

Student CD-ROM

MULTI-LEVEL OPTIONS *Reading Strategy*

Newcomer Ask students to copy the diagram of an ear from p. 317. As they read the selection, have them gather information from the text and graphic features to add labels and captions to their picture.

Beginning Review Roman numerals with students. Have them create a two-column chart with the headings *Numbers* and *Roman Numerals.* Have them write the numbers 1–10 in the first column. Help them write the Roman numeral equivalents in the second column.

Intermediate Ask pairs to exchange outlines for peer review. Have reviewers check for correct numbering with Roman numerals and that the details are lettered correctly. Also have reviewers check that their partners have included important details from each section.

Advanced Have students work in pairs to review "Antarctic Adventure" (p. 32) or "Why Do Leaves Change Color in the Fall?" (p. 84). Ask them to outline two pages of their selection, creating headings or subheadings as needed. Tell students to use the outline on p. 318 as a model.

Hearing: The Ear

an excerpt
from a textbook

319

Reading Selection Materials

Audio: *Unit 5, Chapter 3*
Teacher Resource Book: *Reading Summary, pp. 107–108*

Preview the Selection

Teacher Resource Book: *Know/Want to Know/Learned Chart (KWL), p. 42*

1. **Use the photograph** Have students describe the photograph. Ask them to speculate what the boy is listening to. Have students share what they enjoy listening to.
2. **Use a KWL chart** Create a KWL chart. Have students share what they know about the ear and the sense of hearing. Tell them to use the information from previous parts of this chapter along with their own personal experiences and knowledge. List the items on the board. Then encourage students to create questions about what they would like to know about how people hear. Include these on the KWL chart. Remind students to use their questions on this chart to guide their reading of the selection.
3. **Connect** Remind students that the unit theme is *communication*. ***Ask:*** *Why is listening important for communication?*

Content Connection *Social Studies*

Ask students to work in small groups to research a hearing-related topic. Have them choose from this list or find their own topic: hearing aids through history; cochlear implants; noise and hearing loss; the history of radio; Alexander Graham Bell; and the Search for Extraterrestrial Intelligence (SETI). Ask students to work together to write brief reports on their topics. Tell students to include drawings or other visual aids.

Teacher Resource Book: *Web, p. 37*

Learning Styles *Visual*

Ask pairs of students to brainstorm words, terms, and ideas that relate to hearing and the ear. Have pairs arrange their ideas on a semantic word map (or web). Suggest that they use *Hearing* or *The Ear* as their center term. Provide an example of a semantic word map for students to use as a model.

Read the Selection

1. **Use text features** Call attention to the heading, subheading, and illustration. Then direct students to glossed words and their meanings at the bottom of the page. Remind students to use these features to guide their reading.
2. **Do a jigsaw reading** Play the audio. Have groups read and prepare one paragraph to teach to the class.
3. **Use examples** *Ask: What example helps you understand what sound is?* (plucking a rubber band) *What examples help you understand vibrations and sounds?* (drums and radio parts)

Sample Answer to Guide Question
Sound Waves

See Teacher Edition pp. 434–435 for a list of English-Spanish cognates in the reading selection.

Hearing: The Ear

How do your ears work?

1 Next time you watch television, close your eyes and listen. What do you hear? Besides the sounds from the television, you might hear people talking in the kitchen and cars on the street. But what exactly are these sounds? And how do you hear them?

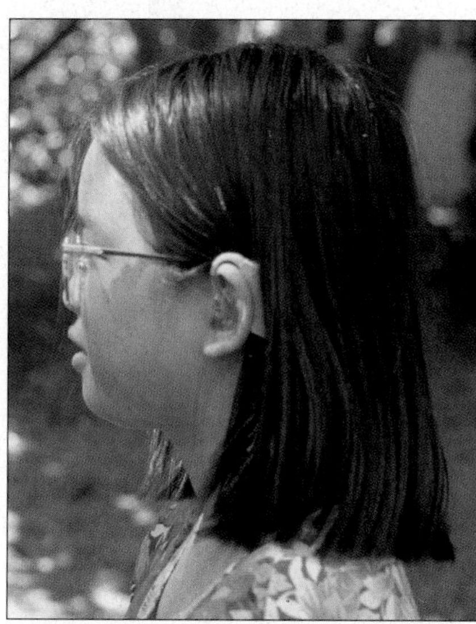

Audio

Sound Waves

You can find out what sound is by carefully stretching a rubber band tightly and plucking it with your finger. The plucking causes the rubber band to move back and forth, or vibrate, very quickly. At the same time, the rubber band makes a humming sound. If you touch the rubber band to keep it from vibrating, the hum stops, too. 2

Represent Text Information in an Outline

What is the name of the subheading for this section?

Vibrations produce sounds. You hear the sound of a drum when you hit a drum head and make it vibrate. You hear sounds from a TV or radio when parts inside the speakers vibrate. People hear your voice when the **vocal cords** in your throat vibrate. 3

Some things vibrate, or move back and forth, very slowly. Slow vibrations make low sounds, like the boom of a bass drum or a fog horn. **Rapid** vibrations make high sounds, like the sound of a guitar string or a high note in music. 4

vibrations the movement created when something moves back and forth very quickly

vocal cords the part of the throat that vibrates to help a person speak

rapid very quick

MULTI-LEVEL OPTIONS *Read the Selection*

Newcomer Play the audio. Read the pages again. ***Ask:*** *Do vibrations make sounds?* (yes) *Is sound a form of energy?* (yes) *Does sound move in waves?* (yes) *Can sounds travel through liquids and solids?* (yes) *Do you hear the same sounds in each ear?* (no)

Beginning Read the Reading Summary aloud. Then do a paired reading. ***Ask:*** *What produces sound?* (vibrations) *What sounds do slow vibrations make?* (low) *How does sound move?* (in waves) *Besides air, what can sound waves travel through?* (liquids and solids)

Intermediate Have students do a paired reading. ***Ask:*** *How do vocal chords produce sound?* (They vibrate.) *How does vibration speed affect sound?* (slow = low, rapid = high) *Why can you hear underwater and when you eat?* (Sound travels through liquids and solids.)

Advanced Have students read silently and work to complete their outlines. ***Ask:*** *How can you use a rubber band to prove vibration produces sound?* (If you stop the vibration, the hum stops.) *How do sound waves travel?* (Molecules bump against each other.) *What is the effect of hearing differently in each ear?* (You can tell that sounds are coming from different places.)

5 Sound is a form of energy that moves in waves. For example, you give the strings of a guitar energy when you pluck them. This energy makes the strings move back and forth. Then, gas **molecules** in the air next to the strings begin to vibrate too. They bump against other molecules, and make them vibrate. In this way, sound waves move through the air.

6 Many of the sounds you hear travel through the air. But sound waves also travel through **liquids** and **solids.** When you go swimming, you can hear sounds underwater because sound waves move through water. You can even hear yourself crunch foods such as celery because sound waves move through the bones in your head!

7 The sounds you hear in one ear are a little different from the sounds you hear in the other ear. Because you have two ears, you can tell that sounds are coming from different places.

8 **Sound engineers,** who make compact discs and tapes, record music and other sounds in **stereo.** The engineers use at least two differently placed **microphones** to record the music. When you play the music through two stereo speakers, sounds for the left ear come through one speaker, and sounds for the right ear come through the other speaker.

Represent Text Information in an Outline

What important fact from this paragraph should you include in your outline?

molecules tiny particles of material such as water or air
liquids matter that is fluid and is not a gas or a solid; water is an example of a liquid
solids matter that is not a liquid or a gas; a piece of wood is a solid
sound engineers people who record music using machines to blend and control the sounds
stereo using two or more channels
microphones small machines that make sounds louder

Read the Selection

1. **Understand terms** Have students find the meanings of the glossed words below the selection. Use pictures or examples to clarify meanings.
2. **Partner read aloud** After students listen to the audio or to you read the selection, have them read it aloud in pairs.
3. **Represent text information in an outline** Help students add information from this section to their outlines. Have them pick out the subheadings for the Roman numerals. For each subheading, ask guiding questions to help students pick out key facts and information.
4. **Clarify** Bring in stereo headphones and have students listen using one, then the other, then both. Guide discussion of differences they noticed in the sounds they heard.
5. **Multi-level options** See MULTI-LEVEL OPTIONS on p. 320.

Sample Answer to Guide Question
Sounds can travel through the air, through liquids, and through solids.

A Capitalization

Titles and headings

Remind students that the title tells the topic of a selection. Tell students that nonfiction selections often have headings and subheadings. Explain that subheadings break the selection into pieces and tell the main idea of each piece. Then tell students that subheadings are often printed in larger or darker type than the selection itself. Point out that the title is usually in larger type than the subheadings. Explain to students that the main words in titles, headings, and subheadings are always capitalized. Remind students that most prepositions and words like *a, an,* and *the* are usually not capitalized. Tell students that the first word of a title or subheading is *always* capitalized.

Read the Selection

1. **Use the diagram** Direct attention to the diagram and labels. Have students point out the various parts of the ear and the arrows that indicate the direction of the sound waves.
2. **Paired reading** Play the audio. Then have students read it again in pairs. ***Ask:*** *Through which part of the ear do the sound waves travel first?* (the eardrum) *What animal is the cochlea shaped like?* (a snail)

Sample Answer to Guide Question
Roman numeral II

Ears for Hearing and Balance

9 Your ears are much more than flaps on the sides of your head. The most important parts of your ears are inside your head. Find the ear parts in the picture, as you read about how the ear works.

Represent Text Information in an Outline

Should this subheading be Roman numeral II or III in your outline?

10 A **shrieking siren** sends sound waves through the air. The flaps on the sides of your head—your outer ears—catch the sound waves as they pass by. Each outer ear **funnels** the sound waves into a tubelike passage inside your head that leads to the eardrum.

Your eardrum stretches across the 11
tube like a skin stretched over a drum. When sound waves hit the eardrum, the eardrum vibrates. These vibrations travel through three connected bones that are smaller than a matchhead.

The bones create a new set of 12
waves that enter the **cochlea.** You can see that the cochlea is shaped like a **snail shell.** It's filled with a liquid and lined with tiny, hairlike cells. As the waves pass through the liquid, the hairlike cells begin to wiggle.

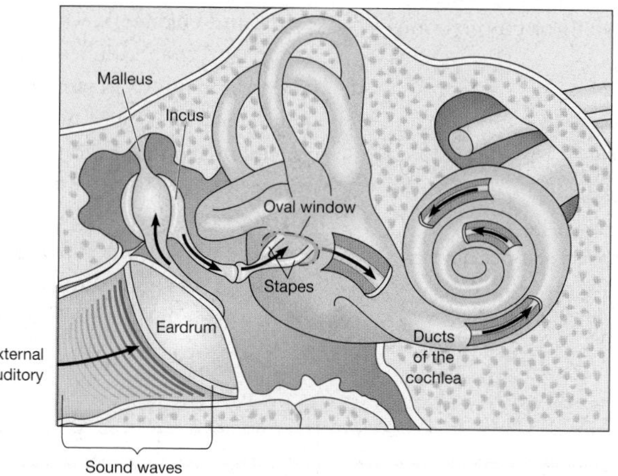

shrieking high-pitched and whining
siren a machine used on ambulances, police cars, and fire trucks to make a loud sound and warn others
funnels directs from a larger opening to a smaller opening
cochlea a part of the inner ear shaped like a spiral
snail shell a spiral-shaped shell of the small soft animal called a snail

MULTI-LEVEL OPTIONS *Read the Selection*

Newcomer ***Ask:*** *Does your outer ear funnel sound?* (yes) *Is your eardrum outside your head?* (no) *Does the eardrum vibrate when sounds hit it?* (yes) *Are there bones inside your ear?* (yes) *Does your brain interpret sounds?* (yes) *Do your ears help you keep your balance?* (yes)

Beginning ***Ask:*** *Where are the most important parts of your ears?* (inside your head) *What is the cochlea shaped like?* (a snail) *What is inside the cochlea?* (fluid and tiny, hairlike cells) *Where are sounds interpreted?* (brain) *What two things do ears help?* (hearing and balance)

Intermediate *What happens when sounds hit the eardrum?* (It vibrates.) *What happens when waves pass through the cochlea?* (Hairlike cells wiggle.) *What happens in the nerve cells?* (Waves become electric signals; they go to the brain.) *Why do you need balance?* (to prevent falling)

Advanced ***Ask:*** *What do outer ears do?* (They funnel sounds in.) *Why would a torn eardrum cause hearing loss?* (can't detect vibrations; vibrations can't move through normal processes) *How do the ears, brain, and muscles work together to keep you upright?* (Ears tell the brain your position; brain tells muscles how to keep you upright.)

13 Notice that the sound of the siren has traveled through air, solid, and liquid. That's quite a trip, and it's a fast one too! In the cochlea, the journey's almost over because the wiggling cells excite tiny nerve cells.

14 In the nerve cells, the sound waves change to electric signals that race along nerve cells to the brain. It's up to your brain to **interpret** the signals and tell you that you hear a siren!

15 Your ears also help you keep your balance. You need your sense of balance to keep from falling. The parts of the inner ear that look like loops help you stay upright—whether you're sitting, standing, walking, running, or spinning like the dancer in the picture.

Represent Text Information in an Outline

What important fact from this paragraph should you include in your outline?

16 As you move, your inner ears pick up changes in the position of your body and of your head. If you **tilt** or turn your head, these parts of your ear send signals to your brain. Then your brain sends out signals that tell your muscles what to do to keep you from falling.

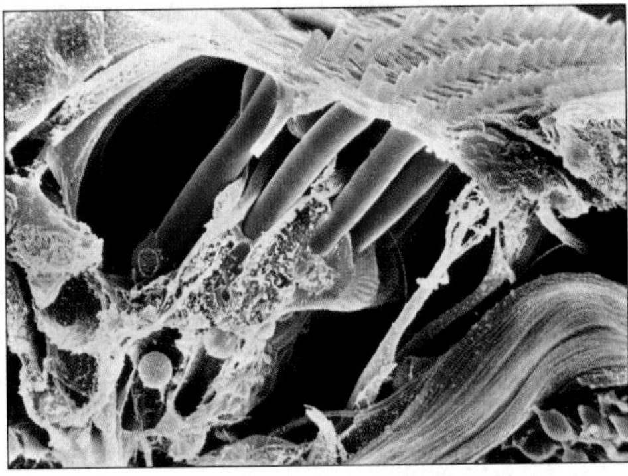

Inside the inner ear.

interpret understand

tilt tip to the side

Read the Selection

1. **Shared reading** Read the article aloud as students follow along. Ask volunteers to join in for different parts. ***Ask:*** *In the nerve cells, what happens to the sound waves?* (They change to electric signals and go to the brain.) *What part of your body interprets the electric signals?* (the brain) *What is balance?* (It is keeping steady so you don't fall.)
2. **Summarize** Have pairs of students reread the selection. Guide students to pick out key facts and information to summarize the main points of the selection.
3. **Multi-level options** See MULTI-LEVEL OPTIONS on p. 322.

Sample Answer to Guide Question
Your ears help you stay balanced, so you don't fall over.

Across Selections

Connect subject matter and content Have students fill in the last column of the KWL chart they started. ***Ask:*** *What is the most important thing you learned about hearing? Why do you think it is important to learn about hearing and the ear? What kinds of problems with parts of the ear might make it difficult for people to hear? Does this text help you understand the problems that Helen Keller and other deaf people face? Why or why not?*

Spelling

Words ending in *-ing*

Remind students that *-ing* is added to the end of verbs to show continuing action. Tell students that when a verb ends with *e*, the *e* is dropped before adding *-ing*. Then mention that in a one-syllable word ending in C-V-C, the final consonant is doubled before adding *-ing*. Have students look at p. 323. Write on the board: *wiggle / wiggling; spin/spinning*. ***Ask:*** *Why is there no* e *in* wiggling*?* (drop *e* before adding *-ing*) *Why is the* n *doubled in* spinning*?* (C-V-C word)

Evaluate Your Reading Strategy

Represent Text Information in an Outline

Say: *You have practiced an important reading strategy. Now you can decide how well you have done. Does this statement describe how you read?*

When I read textbooks, I look for headings and subheadings and make an outline. Making an outline helps me remember the facts from a textbook. I can also use my outline to review before a test.

Reading Comprehension

Question-Answer Relationships

Sample Answers

1. Sound is caused by vibrations—things moving back and forth.
2. Sound travels in waves through air, liquids, and solids.
3. in the nerve cells
4. Your ears help you hear and help you stay balanced.
5. The outer ear funnels the sound into a tubelike passage.
6. Anything that vibrates makes sounds.
7. The ear (and all its smaller parts), the nerves, and the brain.
8. If I could not hear well, I would have to use my eyes more (for reading or watching).
9. How do hearing aids help people hear better? What types of problems of the ear make people deaf? Why can animals hear sounds that people can't hear? How much noise is dangerous for our ears?
10. I think they use an illustration because it would be difficult to take a picture of the real inside of the ear. Also, in the illustration, you can color the different parts to make it clearer and add lines to show the direction of the sounds.

Build Reading Fluency

Read to Scan for Information

Explain that students need to adjust their reading to quickly scan the text to locate key words. Have them read the question then quickly scan to find the answer and identify key words.

Beyond the Reading

Reading Comprehension

Question-Answer Relationships (QAR)

"Right There" Questions

1. **Recall Facts** What causes sound?
2. **Recall Facts** How does sound travel?
3. **Recall Facts** Where do sound waves change to electric signals?

"Think and Search" Questions

4. **Connect** What two main jobs do your ears perform?
5. **Sequence** What is the first thing to happen when a sound wave reaches your ear?
6. **Analyze Cause and Effect** What makes sounds?

"Author and You" Question

7. **Summarize** What parts of your body help you hear properly?

"On Your Own" Questions

8. **Speculate** How would your life change if you could not hear well?
9. **Raise Questions** What unanswered questions would you research about hearing and the ear? Use your knowledge to think of questions.
10. **Interpret Visual Images** Why do you think page 322 uses an illustration to support the text instead of a photo? How do the different parts of the illustration help you understand the text?

Activity Book p. 170

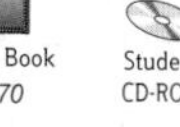
Student CD-ROM

Build Reading Fluency

Read to Scan for Information

You must adjust your reading rate to read fast when you scan. Scanning is looking for the title, headings, subheadings, and key words in a text. With a partner answer these questions.

1. What is the title of the reading?
2. What are the headings?
3. What are the subheadings?
4. What are the key words?

MULTI-LEVEL OPTIONS *Elements of Literature*

Newcomer Write on the board and *say: play.* Play *is a general verb.* Display pictures of specific types of play, such as sports, board games, and musical instruments. Have students write *play* in the center of a piece of paper. Have them add drawings of specific types of play.

Beginning Write *eat, move,* and *make* on the board. Ask students to work in groups to create word trees for each word. Tell students that their words should get more specific as they move down the tree. Model an example with *eat, bite, nibble.*

Intermediate Ask students to write simple sentences using general verbs. Then have students exchange sentences with partners. Ask partners to rewrite each sentence using a more specific verb. Have pairs discuss the differences between the two sentences.

Advanced Ask students to write paragraphs using general verbs. Then have them rewrite their paragraphs using specific verbs. Ask students to evaluate the benefits of using more specific verbs in their writing.

Listen, Speak, Interact 

Discuss How Sound Waves Travel

Participate in a shared reading, which will show you how to use clues to get meaning from the reading.

1. With a partner, scan the selection for descriptions of sound waves. To scan the selection, look through the selection quickly.
2. Take turns reading one of the descriptions aloud. First read in your normal voice. Then read in a whisper, or a very quiet voice.
3. Was it more difficult to hear your partner read in a quiet voice? When you read in a quiet voice, do you think the sound waves travel differently than when you read in a louder voice? Use words from the selection to explain your answer.

Elements of Literature

Recognize Descriptive Language

Scientific writing must be very precise (exact). Science writers use descriptive language to help you picture actions. Descriptive language is very precise. It tells you exactly what is happening and helps you form a picture in your mind.

1. Copy the chart in your Reading Log.
2. Use a dictionary to find the meanings of the specific verbs *pluck, vibrate,* and *crunch.* Write the definitions in the chart.
3. How do the specific verbs give you more information than the general verbs?

General Verbs	Specific Verbs
pull	pluck definition: ______
move	vibrate definition: ______
bite	crunch definition: ______

Reading Log

The Heinle Newbury House Dictionary

Activity Book p. 171

Student CD-ROM

Listen, Speak, Interact

Discuss How Sound Waves Travel

Teacher Resource Book: *Reading Log, p. 64*

1. **Scan for information** Direct students to the table of contents or index in their textbook. Have them practice scanning by themselves to find pages for various reading selections or subjects. Then have them work in pairs and ask each other to scan for specific information.
2. **Newcomers** Reread with this group. Demonstrate whisper reading. Then have volunteers read aloud in normal voices as you whisper the examples.
3. **Evaluate** Have students write their own explanations of how sound waves travel in their Reading Logs.

Elements of Literature

Recognize Descriptive Language

Teacher Resource Book: *Reading Log, p. 64*

1. **Clarify terms** Give examples to explain *precise.* On the board, write: *Our school is in the United States of America.* Guide students to give more precise statements by narrowing down the place: region, state, city, street.
2. **Multi-level options** See MULTI-LEVEL OPTIONS on p. 324.

Answers

2. *Possible definitions:*
   pluck: to stretch and release (a string of an instrument)
   vibrate: to move back and forth quickly
   crunch: to chew with a noisy sound
3. *Possible answer:* The specific verbs give clues about the sound, speed, and manner of the action.

Content Connection *The Arts*

Provide several recorded samples of the sounds made by different musical instruments or ask a music teacher or music students to perform brief samples on several different instruments. Ask students to explain the differences between the sounds made by each instrument, such as pitch (e.g., high), which part vibrates (e.g., reed), what causes vibration (e.g., blowing), etc.

Learning Styles *Visual*

Ask students to find the words *vibrate, pluck,* and *crunch* in paragraphs 3, 5, and 6. Then ask students to use the paragraphs to form mental images. Ask students to draw pictures of what they see in their minds for each paragraph.

Have students use the three specific words in sentences.

Word Study

Identify Words with Greek Origins

Teacher Resource Book: *Personal Dictionary, p. 63*

1. **Teacher think aloud** *Say:* Tele- *means "far" in Greek.* Vision *is seeing pictures or images. So, a television "lets you see pictures from far away."*
2. **Use analogies** *Say: A television sends pictures just like a _____ sends voices.* (telephone) Have students create their own analogies.

Answers

2. *Possible words:* telegram, telegraph
3. *Possible definitions:* a written message sent from far away; a device that allows communication using codes from far away

Grammar Focus

Recognize Subject and Verb Agreement in the Present Tense

Say: I like milk. You like milk. He _____ milk. Have students supply the missing verb.

Answers

1. This energy makes . . .; A shrieking siren sends . . .; Each outer ear funnels . . .; Your eardrum stretches . . .; . . . the eardrum vibrates.

ASSESS

Have students write sentences in the present tense using: *we, he, you, she, they,* and *it.*

Word Study

Identify Words with Greek Origins

Many words in English come from Greek words. Understanding word origins can help you learn new words. For example, the prefix *tele-* means "far" in Greek. How does this help you understand the word *television*?

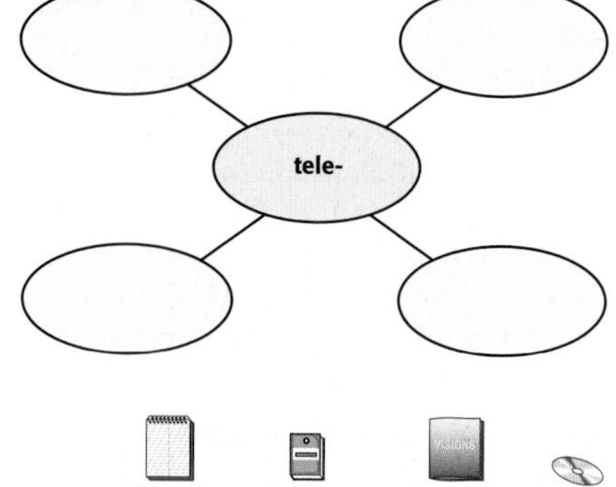

1. On a piece of paper, make a web like the one shown.
2. Look up words starting with the Greek prefix *tele-* in a dictionary. Write them in your web.
3. What do each of these words mean? Write the words and their definitions in your Personal Dictionary.

Personal Dictionary · The Heinle Newbury House Dictionary · Activity Book *p. 172* · Student CD-ROM

Grammar Focus

Recognize Subject and Verb Agreement in the Present Tense

A verb in the present tense must *agree* with its subject. If the subject of the sentence is *he, she, it,* or a singular noun, the verb ends in *s*. This is called third-person singular.

Sound	moveS	in waves.
third-person singular subject	present tense verb	

1. Look for three examples of third-person singular subjects and verbs. Look in paragraphs 5, 10, and 11 of the selection.
2. Write one sentence with a third-person singular subject and verb.

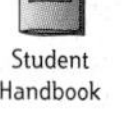

Activity Book *pp. 173–174* · Student Handbook · Student CD-ROM

326 Unit 5 Communication

MULTI-LEVEL OPTIONS *From Reading to Writing*

Newcomer Have students illustrate the steps in a simple process, such as unlocking a door or buying an item in a store. Provide key words. (e.g., doorknob, lock, turn) Help them to add a title and captions that identify the main parts of the process.

Beginning Ask students to list the main steps in a simple process, such as preparing a sandwich. Help them write their steps on index cards. (e.g., *Gather cheese, bread, lettuce, and mustard; toast the bread;* etc.) Have students explain the process in groups using index cards to show each step.

Intermediate Have students create a pre-writing flowchart. Ask them to organize their ideas in their flowcharts. Suggest that students write their headings in boxes and their details in circles. Have students use the information in their flowcharts to write their instructions.

Advanced Have students exchange their writing with partners. Ask partners to evaluate whether the process is described in order and includes enough details to complete the process described.

From Reading to Writing 

Write to Inform

Write about how to do something that you know. For example, you might explain how to research something on the Internet.

1. Use a heading and subheadings to organize information. This will help readers identify the parts of the process. Be sure to capitalize the first word and important words.
2. Address the reader directly, using the pronoun *you*.
3. Add specific details and real-life examples to make it easier for readers to understand the process.
4. Illustrate your entry to help explain difficult parts of the process.

How to Research Something on the Internet

The Internet Service Provider
First, you must have an Internet Service Provider. Some examples are . . .

Logging On
In order to log on, first . . .

Key Words
For every topic you research . . .

Activity Book
p. 175

Across Content Areas 

Learn About the Voice

The vocal cords in your **larynx** (voice box) make sound. Men's vocal cords are thicker and vibrate more slowly than women's. Therefore, men have lower voices.

In music, men usually sing the lower notes. Some men can sing higher or lower notes than other men. The same is true for women. There are four main categories of voices, two for men and two for women: **soprano, alto, tenor,** and **bass.**

Copy the chart. Complete it with the four voice categories. Here are some clues.

1. *Alto* is a woman's part, and *tenor* is a man's part.
2. *Soprano* is the highest part, and *bass* is the lowest part.

	Men	*Women*
Higher		
Lower		

Activity Book
p. 176

From Reading to Writing

Write to Inform

1. **Model the steps** Ask a volunteer to demonstrate researching on the Internet. Have others suggest phrases to describe the actions.
2. **Think-quickwrite-pair-share** Ask students to write as much as they can to explain the steps. Remind them to use details and examples to clarify the steps. As students share with a partner, have the partners do the actions to see if they make sense.
3. **Multi-level options** See MULTI-LEVEL OPTIONS on p. 326.

Across Content Areas: The Arts

Learn About the Voice

1. **Explore music and singing voices** Bring in CDs or cassettes of vocal music. Have students describe the voices as high, low, loud, soft, male, female.
2. **Relate to personal experiences** If possible, have students bring in samples of music or instruments from other cultures to share and describe to the class. Ask volunteers to sing their favorite songs in English or another language. Have the class decide if the singers have a bass, tenor, alto, or soprano voice.

Answers
Men: lower (bass); higher (tenor)
Women: lower (alto); higher (soprano)

ASSESS

Ask students to name their favorite singer. Have them identify him/her as a *soprano, alto, tenor,* or *bass.*

Reteach and Reassess

Text Structure *Ask: What does the subheading on p. 322 tell you?* (how the ears help with hearing and balance) *Which graphic helps you "see" inside the ear?* (diagram on p. 322) *What specific examples help you understand* high sounds*?* (guitar string, high note, on p. 320)

Reading Strategy Ask groups of students to review an earlier informational selection, such as "Matthew A. Henson" (p. 169) or "Discovering the Inca Ice Maiden" (p. 241). Have students create an outline that includes the title and headings.

Elements of Literature Ask students to review the selection to find other examples of specific verbs. Have students list the verbs they find.

Reassess Ask students to summarize one section of the reading. Tell students to briefly restate the most important ideas in their own words.

Chapter Materials

Activity Book: *pp. 177–184*
Audio: *Unit 5, Chapter 4*
Student Handbook
Student CD-ROM: *Unit 5, Chapter 4*
Teacher Resource Book: *Lesson Plan, Teacher Resources, Reading Summary, Activity Book Answer Key*
Teacher Resource CD-ROM
Assessment Program: *Quiz, pp. 81–82; Teacher and Student Resources, pp. 115–144*
Assessment CD-ROM
Transparencies
The Heinle Newbury House Dictionary/CD-ROM
Web Site: www.heinle.visions.com

Objectives

Teacher think aloud *Say: I know illustrations are pictures, so the pictures will probably be important. But what is* "how-to"*? I know how to ride a bicycle and how to use a computer. Maybe this book will explain the steps of how to do something.* Explain and point out key words in the other objectives.

Use Prior Knowledge

Discuss Comic Books

Bring in sample comic books. Then have students discuss their answers to the questions in pairs.

CHAPTER 4

The Art of Making Comic Books

an illustrated "how-to" book
by Michael Morgan Pellowski

Objectives

Reading Make inferences as you read an illustrated "how-to" book.

Listening and Speaking Explain a concept for a character.

Grammar Understand the present conditional.

Writing Write an illustrated "how-to" article.

Content The Arts: Learn about art forms.

Use Prior Knowledge

Discuss Comic Books

What do you know about comic books? Ask and answer these questions with a partner.

1. Do you have any comic books? Which ones?
2. Do you know any comic book heroes? What special powers do they have?
3. What movies have you seen that are based on comic book heroes?
4. Where can you find comic books?
5. How do you think that a comic book is made? Is it made by one person or a team of people?

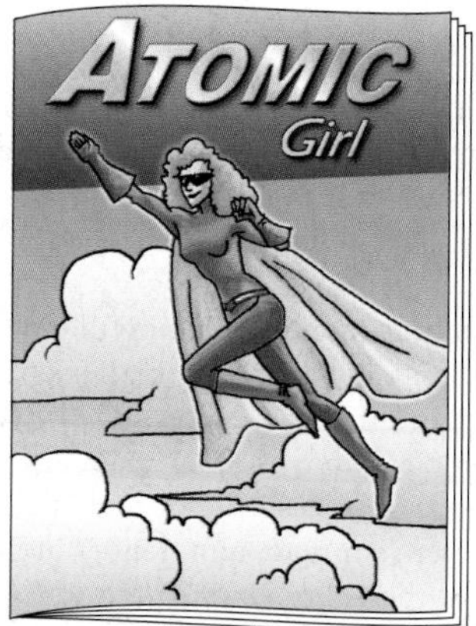

MULTI-LEVEL OPTIONS *Build Vocabulary*

Newcomer Write *art* on the board. Ask students to draw pictures of different tools that artists use, such as paint, brushes, clay, etc. Help students write labels for their drawings. Have students "teach" these words in groups.

Beginning Write *art* on the board. Ask students to draw pictures of different tools that artists use, such as paint, brushes, clay, etc. Have students work in pairs to find ways to group their tools into categories, such as painting or pottery. Help students label their categories and share them in groups.

Intermediate Write *art* on the board. Have students brainstorm a list of words they know about art. Then have pairs group the words into categories. Have them share their categories with another pair.

Advanced On the board, write: *artisan* and *portrait.* Ask students to look up each word in a dictionary. Then have students write sentences using the words. Ask them to provide context clues in each sentence. Have students read their sentences in pairs.

Build Background

The History of Comic Books

A comic book tells a story mostly through pictures and dialogue. The words of the characters are written in balloons above their heads.

Comic books had their origins in newspaper comics. In the 1930s these comics were sometimes reprinted in book form. The comic book characters were often funny (the word *comic* means *funny*).

In the mid 1930s, a new kind of comic book appeared. These books had original stories, not stories reprinted from newspaper comics, and they were about a specific adventure.

In 1938, the comic book world changed when Superman, a superhero, appeared. Since then, superheroes have been the main characters of comic books.

Content Connection

Several popular movies have been based on comic book superheroes.

Build Vocabulary

Learn Words About Art

You can use your own knowledge and context clues to learn words about art.

1. Work with a partner. Read the following sentences. Match the underlined words with their definitions.

Definitions
• person or animal in a story
• special clothing
• an idea

   a. You can't begin to write or draw stories until you have a concept.
   b. Creating a character is like fitting together the pieces of a puzzle.
   c. The rule for costumes is the same as for body type.
2. Check your answers in a dictionary.
3. Write the words and definitions in your Personal Dictionary.

Personal Dictionary

The Heinle Newbury House Dictionary

Activity Book *p. 177*

Student CD-ROM

Home Connection

Build Vocabulary Have students build a list of words about art. Ask them to brainstorm words about art with family members and record their results in lists. Have students use a dictionary to find the meaning of any words they don't know. Use their lists to compile a class list.

Learning Styles *Linguistic*

Build Background Provide students with a variety of comic strips with pictures only. Delete any dialogue. Have them work in pairs to create their own dialogues. Remind them to write the dialogues on paper first and check for spelling and punctuation. Compile the strips into a class comic book for the class library.

Build Background

The History of Comic Books

1. **Use a newspaper** Have students find examples of comics in newspapers. ***Ask:*** *What characters do you see? What do they look like? Do they look real or imaginary? Which comics do you like?*
2. **Content Connection** Ask students if they have seen any of the comic book superheroes in movies. ***Ask:*** *What do they look like? What do they wear that is special? What do they do?*

Build Vocabulary

Learn Words About Art

Teacher Resource Book: *Personal Dictionary, p. 63*

1. **Use a semantic word map** Have students suggest words associated with comics. Use guiding questions as needed. Include *concept, character,* and *costume.*
2. **Reading selection vocabulary** You may want to introduce the glossed words in the reading selection before students begin reading. Key words: *alien, dimension, absurd, best-seller, sketch.* Instruct students to write the words with correct spelling and their definitions in their Personal Dictionaries. Have them pronounce each word and divide it into syllables.
3. **Multi-level options** See MULTI-LEVEL OPTIONS on p. 328.

Answers

1. a. an idea
   b. person or animal in a story
   c. special clothing

ASSESS

Have students define *concept, character,* and *costume.* Then ask them to write one sentence with each word.

Text Structure

Illustrated "How-to" Book

Discuss purpose of illustrations Have students find examples of illustrations and captions in a textbook. ***Say:*** *Illustrations are an important part of a book. In some books, such as a narrative, illustrations tell a story. Many times, illustrations support written text. They help readers visualize written text and they sometimes add more detail.* Remind students of the role of illustrations in "Why Do Leaves Change Color in the Fall?"

Reading Strategy

Make Inferences Using Text Evidence

Teacher Resource Book: *Reading Log, p. 64*

1. **Teacher think aloud** ***Say:*** *I see everyone in the class laughing. I can infer that they are having a good time.* Give other statements (a sports team is jumping up and down and smiling; a student is in the principal's office; students are going into the auditorium). Have students make inferences.
2. **Multi-level options** See MULTI-LEVEL OPTIONS below.

ASSESS

Ask: *What are illustrations?* (drawings) *What are captions?* (words next to pictures) *What is a step-by-step explanation?* (information that tells you what to do)

Text Structure

Illustrated "How-to" Book

Illustrations are drawings or other artwork that help you understand a text. "The Art of Making Comic Books" is a **"how-to"** book. It tells how to make comic books. It also uses illustrations to show parts of the process. Here are some special features of an illustrated "how-to" book.

Look for these distinguishing features as you read. Focus on the information in the pictures.

Illustrated "How-to" Book	
Illustrations	drawings and other artwork that explain and add detail
Captions	words next to the pictures that explain what is happening
Step-by-Step Explanation	information that tells you exactly what to do

Student CD-ROM

Reading Strategy

Make Inferences Using Text Evidence

As you read, you need to **make inferences** to understand. You make inferences by using **text evidence** (words and details) that gives you information.

1. Read the first paragraph of "The Art of Making Comic Books." What evidence tells you that the characters in comic books are made up?
2. In your Reading Log, make a chart like the one shown. Write the inference you can make from the text evidence.

Text Evidence	*Inferences*
humans fly like birds	*characters are made up*
teenagers stay young forever	
let your imagination run wild	

Reading Log

Student CD-ROM

330 Unit 5 Communication

MULTI-LEVEL OPTIONS *Reading Strategy*

Newcomer Help students make inferences about the picture on p. 331. ***Ask:*** *Is the woman sad?* (no) *Are you going to read a story about climbing a mountain?* (no) *Is this woman using her imagination?* (yes)

Beginning Direct students to the picture on p. 331. ***Ask:*** *Will this story have mountain climbers? How do you know?* (No; there are none in the picture.) *How can you tell this woman is imagining and not remembering?* (Dragons are not real.) Explain that their answers are inferences, or guesses.

Intermediate Ask students to work in pairs. Have them write three inferences, or guesses, they can make about the woman in the picture on p. 331. Tell them to compare their inferences with another pair.

Advanced Have students make up a story about the picture on p. 331. Instruct them to make inferences in their stories about who the woman is, what she is thinking about and why, and how she is feeling. Ask them to share their stories with partners.

The Art of Making Comic Books

an illustrated "how-to" book
by Michael Morgan Pellowski

331

UNIT 5 • CHAPTER 4
Reading Selection

Reading Selection Materials

Audio: *Unit 5, Chapter 4*
Teacher Resource Book: *Reading Summary, pp. 109–110*

Preview the Selection

1. **Use the illustration** Have students identify and describe the different people and creatures in the illustration. ***Ask:*** *Who are they? Do they look real or imaginary? Does the woman look real or imaginary? Why do you think so? Why is she thinking about these people and creatures? What types of stories would these people and creatures be in?*
2. **Brainstorm** Have students brainstorm a list of meanings for the title of the selection. Write their ideas on the board. Tell them to use the vocabulary and information from previous parts of this chapter along with their own personal experiences and knowledge.
3. **Connect** Remind students that the unit theme is *communication.* ***Ask:*** *Are comic books a means of communication? What is the purpose of comic books—to inform, entertain, or persuade?*

Content Connection
The Arts

Provide samples of school-appropriate comic books. Divide students into small groups and give each group a comic book. Ask each group to assume the roles of the characters in their comic book and act out one scene from the book. Have students use props when necessary. Suggest that students select and use appropriate background music to enhance their performance.

Learning Styles
Intrapersonal

Ask: *Have you ever read a comic book? Do you like comic books? Do you think comic books can be considered "real" books? What can you learn from a comic book? Is there a comic book hero you can relate to or identify with?* Ask students to write brief essays about their opinions of comic books. Tell students to include details and examples that support their opinions.

Reading Selection

Read the Selection

1. **Use the illustration** Use the illustration to guide a discussion of *real* vs. *imaginary*. ***Ask:*** *Is this picture realistic or imaginary? What types of stories are in comic books—real or imaginary? What types of imaginary people and creatures may be in the stories?*
2. **Paired reading** Play the audio. Point out and find the meanings of glossed words. Have students work in pairs to reread the selection.
3. **Use context clues** Guide students to guess the meanings of idioms and expressions by pointing out context clues. For example, point students to the phrase ". . . and anything else overactive imaginations . . ." to guess the meaning of "conjure up."

Sample Answer to Guide Question

The words (*aliens, mutants, barbarians, avenging, predicaments*) make me think the characters are not real and that some of them are very bad or strange.

See Teacher Edition pp. 434–435 for a list of English-Spanish cognates in the reading selection.

Audio

Make Inferences Using Text Evidence

Look at the boldfaced words only. How can you use them to make an inference about the characters in comic books?

1 Biff! Zap! Ka-pow! Welcome to the world of comic books. It's a place where animals walk, talk, and think like people and marvelously well-muscled humans fly like birds. It's a world populated by heroes, villains, and tough **antihero** good guys who act like bad guys.

2 In the timeless universe of comic books, teenagers stay young forever and get in and out of wild **predicaments** in the blink of an eye. The comic book world is filled with **aliens,** monsters, superheroes, detectives, pirates, robots, **mutants,** magicians, **avenging** soldiers, fearless **barbarians,** and anything else overactive imaginations can conjure up.

antihero a hero who does not have the usual qualities of a hero, such as courage or physical strength

predicaments troubling situations

aliens beings from outer space

mutants creatures whose features have changed from normal to strange

avenging getting revenge

barbarians characters who are brutal and do not follow any rules

MULTI-LEVEL OPTIONS *Read the Selection*

Newcomer Play the audio. Then reread the selection aloud. Have students join in when they can. ***Ask:*** *Do comic books have heroes and villains?* (yes) *Is imagination the key to the comic book industry?* (yes) *Are some comic books based on real-life situations?* (yes) *Do giant turtles and talking ducks exist in real life?* (no)

Beginning Read the Reading Summary aloud. ***Ask:*** *Where do animals walk, talk, and think like people?* (comic books) *What happens to teenagers in comic books?* (They stay young forever; they get in and out of wild predicaments.) *What is the key to the world of comic books?* (imagination)

Intermediate Have students do a paired reading. ***Ask:*** *What are antiheroes?* (good guys who act like bad guys) *What kinds of characters can you find in comic books?* (aliens, robots, superheroes, mutants, etc.) *How do most successful comic books use reality?* (as a springboard into fantasy)

Advanced Have students read silently. ***Ask:*** *What kind of fiction are comic books?* (fantasy) *What limit is there on the content of comic books?* (None; anything you can imagine can happen.) *Can anyone produce comic books?* (yes, if you use your imagination)

3 Imagination! That's the key to unlocking the gateway into the comic book industry. Some comic book stories build on real-life situations of war, crime, history, politics, technology, science, or romance. But most successful comic books use reality only as a **springboard** into a **dimension** beyond belief. When was the last time you bumped into a half-human robot **terminator** or a hairy mutant at the mall? In real life you won't encounter six-foot-tall turtles in the sewers or millionaire ducks who speak with Scottish accents.

4 If you want to be a comic book writer and/or artist, let your imagination run wild. When your imagination shifts into overdrive, you can capture that creative power to produce your own comics . . .

Make Inferences Using Text Evidence

What is the most important quality for a comic book writer to have? Use text clues to help you answer.

springboard a place to start
dimension (here) another world
terminator a character who hunts other characters on command

Read the Selection

1. **Use the illustration** Have students point out realistic and imaginary components of the illustration. ***Ask:*** *What does this picture tell you about comic books?* (There is a combination of real and imaginary.)
2. **Paired reading** Read the selection aloud. Then, have students read it again in pairs.
3. **Make inferences** Ask questions to help students make inferences about real-life comic stories and imaginary stories. ***Ask:*** *If a comic book is about history, will the characters probably be real or imaginary?* (real) *If a six-foot-tall turtle is the hero, is the book about real situations or imaginary ones?* (imaginary)
4. **Clarify terms and expressions** Call attention to figurative and idiomatic expressions in the selection, such as "key to unlocking the gateway" and "imagination shifts into overdrive." Explain meanings as needed.
5. **Multi-level options** See MULTI-LEVEL OPTIONS on p. 332.

Sample Answer to Guide Question

The most important qualities of a comic book writer are imagination and creativity. The text says, ". . . let your imagination run wild" and "When your imagination shifts into overdrive, you can capture that creative power . . . ."

Punctuation

Hyphens

Tell students that hyphens are dashes used to connect two or more words. Explain that when two or more words are connected with hyphens, they become one word or term. ***Ask:*** *What words are connected with hyphens in paragraph 3?* (real, life; half, human; six, foot, tall) Explain that each word has its meaning, but the hyphenated words together have a new meaning.

Apply Write on the board: real; life; *real-life; six; foot; tall; six-foot-tall; half; human; half-human; well; muscled; well-muscled.* Have students copy the list and write definitions for each word or term.

UNIT 5 • CHAPTER 4

Reading Selection

Read the Selection

1. **Use the heading and illustration** *Ask: What is the heading for this section?* (Comic Book Characters) *How does it connect to the illustration?* (The illustration is steps to drawing a character.) Ask students to make predictions about the content.
2. **Paired reading** Have students listen to the audio or to you read the selection. Then, have students reread in pairs.
3. **Analyze words** Call attention to hyphenated words and expressions. Tell students to examine the individual words to guess the meanings of the hyphenated forms.

Sample Answer to Guide Question

Imagination is a good thing to use when you make a character. You can have the character be and do anything.

Comic Book Characters

5 To produce a successful comic book, you need a star if the book revolves around a main character, or an interesting **premise** if the book focuses on a theme like horror, UFOs, or crime. If it's a theme book, you may also want to develop a host to introduce stories.

6 Creating a character is your chance to let your imagination run wild. Over the years, comic book stars have ranged from polite **do-gooders** to **off-the-wall** or imperfect folks with acne, **hang-ups,** and even money problems. Experiment with the **absurd.** Go one step beyond. The comic book field knows no boundaries where heroes and stars are concerned.

Make Inferences Using Text Evidence

Draw an inference about the role that imagination plays in creating comic book characters.

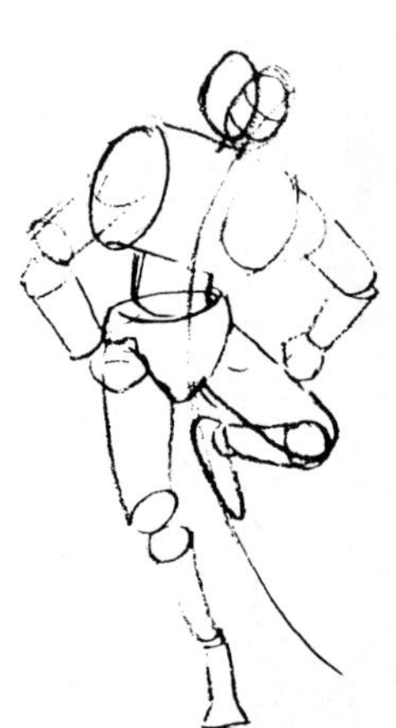

premise an idea
do-gooders people who always try to do good things
off-the-wall somewhat crazy or different
hang-ups difficulties
absurd foolish, ridiculous

MULTI-LEVEL OPTIONS *Read the Selection*

Newcomer *Ask: Do all comic books have a star?* (no) *Does a host introduce the stories in a theme comic book?* (yes) *Can a comic book character be absurd?* (yes) *Is defining a hero or concept the first step in creating a comic book?* (yes) *Does a comic book character have to be realistic?* (no)

Beginning *Ask: What does a successful comic book need?* (a star or an interesting premise) *When can you let your imagination run wild?* (when you create a character) *What do you need before you begin writing or drawing a comic book?* (a solid concept)

Intermediate *Ask: When would you need a host?* (for a theme book) *What does a host do?* (introduce stories) *What might be a result of having an outrageous character?* (a best-selling comic book) *What can distinctive features do for a character?* (set that character apart from others)

Advanced *Ask: How can a good imagination lead to a successful comic book?* (A character's features can be anything you imagine; more unusual characters mean a more interesting comic book.) *What is the first aspect of a character that you should consider?* (physical appearance)

Make Inferences Using Text Evidence

The text says to "take the time to define and refine your hero." What does this phrase suggest about the importance of characters in comics?

7 You can't begin to write or draw stories until you have a solid concept, so take the time to define and refine your hero. Who knows? The next comic book **best-seller** might be the outrageous character you come up with . . .

Drawing New Characters

8 . . . A number of important issues come into play as a new character takes shape. Some questions to ask yourself are: How realistic do I want this character to look? What kind of body type do I want the hero to have? Slender? **Stocky?** Muscular? Is the character ugly or handsome? Tall or short? Young or old? What **distinctive features** can I create that will set my character apart from others?

---

best-seller a very popular work that many people buy
stocky strongly built
distinctive features characteristics that identify a person

UNIT 5 • CHAPTER 4
Reading Selection

Read the Selection

1. **Use the heading and illustration** Direct students to the heading and illustration. Have students predict what this section is about
2. **Paired reading** After students listen to the audio or to you read the selection, have them reread in pairs.
3. **Clarify terms and expressions** Ask students to name comic book heroes and characters that have different body types. Have them describe any other distinctive features about their favorite characters.
4. **Use analogies** Call attention to examples of opposites used in the selection. Make a list of opposites and have students create their own analogies for others to complete. ***Say:*** Ugly *is to* handsome *as* weak *is to* _____. (strong, muscular)
5. **Multi-level options** See MULTI-LEVEL OPTIONS on p. 334.

Sample Answer to Guide Question
It is important that the characters are clear and well-defined because the whole story is centered around the characters.

Spelling

Silent *w*

Tell students that when words begin with *wr,* the initial *w* is silent. Write on the board and *say: write.* ***Ask:*** *What sound do you hear at the beginning of this word?* (the /r/ sound) *What sound does the* w *make?* (None; it's silent.)

Apply Write on the board: *wrap, wrong, wrestle,* and *wring.* Ask students to copy the list and circle the silent *w* in each word. Then ask students to look in a dictionary to find additional words that begin with a silent *w.* (wrap, wreath, wreck, wren, wrench, wrinkle, wrist, etc.)

Read the Selection

1. **Use the illustration** *Ask: Are these good characters or bad characters?* (probably bad) *Why do you think so?* (Their eyes look mean. They look scary.) *Which one do you like the best? Why?*
2. **Paired reading** Read aloud or have volunteers read aloud portions of the selection. Then, have students reread in pairs.
3. **Brainstorm characteristics** Have students identify different characteristics used in the illustrations, such as hair, build, facial features (eyes, chins, noses). Make a list of descriptive words and phrases for each characteristic.

Sample Answer to Guide Question
You should draw a lot of features and make them all different.

9 Creating a character is like fitting together the pieces of a jigsaw puzzle. You take a bunch of characteristics (hair, build, **facial** features, body type, and so on) and fit them together until you find just the right look for the character.

10 Sometimes it is a good idea to **sketch** a series of heads and faces first and then do a series of various body types. You can even break that process down further into a variety of eyes, noses, chins, and so on. Once you have a wide variety of choices, you can mix and match your sketches until your character has just the correct combination of features.

Make Inferences Using Text Evidence
What can you conclude about how many features you should draw before creating your character?

facial of the face

sketch draw quickly without giving many details

MULTI-LEVEL OPTIONS *Read the Selection*

Newcomer *Ask: Is creating a character like solving a puzzle?* (yes) *Is it a good idea to sketch heads and faces first?* (yes) *Does a character have to wear a mask and a cape?* (no)

Beginning *Ask: What pieces do you fit together to find the right look for a character?* (physical characteristics) *What should you sketch first?* (heads, faces) *When can you mix and match your sketches?* (once you have a wide variety) *What rule is the same as the rule for costumes?* (rule for body types)

Intermediate *Ask: How is creating a character like putting together a puzzle?* (You mix and match pieces until you have a good combination.) *What process should you follow to choose costumes and clothing?* (The same as body types; try different looks until you find the right one.)

Advanced *Ask: How could you summarize the main idea of these two pages?* (Try combinations of costumes and faces until you find the right look for your character.) *Why might it be important to break down the face-sketching process?* (to have a wider variety of choices of facial features)

Costumes/Clothing

11 The rule for costumes and clothing is the same as for body type. Try several different looks on your characters. What kind of mask should your superhero wear, if any? Should he or she wear boots and a cape? If you're doing an animal character, does the animal dress in human clothes? Experiment with a number of looks before making any final choices.

About the Author — Michael Morgan Pellowski (born 1949)

Michael Pellowski was born in New Jersey. He had many other jobs before writing books for young people. For example, he taught art and physical education. He also played football with the New England Patriots. Pellowski started writing in 1975 and has written numerous books. He writes under his own name and also as Ski Michaels. He created and hosted his own television show for children. Pellowski explained, "I'm interested in three major topics—humor, children, and sports . . . I close my weekly television show with the words 'Don't grow up too fast, because it's great to be a kid.' That sums up my cause in life."

➤ Do you think Michael Pellowski likes or dislikes comic books? Find evidence in the reading and in his biography above to support your opinion.

UNIT 5 • CHAPTER 4
Reading Selection

Read the Selection

1. **Shared reading** Complete the reading of the selection as students follow along. Ask students to join in when they can.
2. **Make inferences** *Ask: Can you make an inference about how important costumes and clothing are for a comic book character?* (very important) Ask students to point out supporting text details.
3. **Multi-level options** See MULTI-LEVEL OPTIONS on p. 336.

About the Author

1. **Evaluate information about the author** Read the author biography aloud. *Ask: What three topics is Michael Pellowski interested in?* (humor, children, and sports)
2. **Interpret the facts** *Ask: How do you think Michael Pellowski included these three topics in his book?* (Comic books are usually for children and they are fun to read and include a lot of action.)

Across Selections

Teacher Resource Book: *Venn Diagram, p. 35*

Compare and contrast text structure Have students compare and contrast the text structure of "The Art of Making Comic Books" to "Hearing: The Ear." Have them comment on illustrations, tone, and point of view. Help students point out similarities and differences and to record ideas on a Venn diagram.

A Capitalization

Exclamations

Explain that an exclamation point indicates that a sentence should be read with strong emotion or emphasis. *Ask: What do the exclamation points in the first line on page 332 tell you?* (to read those words loudly, with emphasis) Tell them that a one-word exclamation is always capitalized. Then remind students that the first word in any sentence is always capitalized. *Ask: Why is the word* imagination *capitalized in paragraph 3?* (It is a one-word exclamation.)

Evaluate Your Reading Strategy

Make Inferences Using Text Evidence

Say: You have practiced an important reading strategy. Now you can decide how well you have done. Does this statement describe how you read?

I look for evidence in the text that helps me make inferences.

Making inferences based on evidence lets me go beyond what the author says directly.

Reading Comprehension

Question-Answer Relationships

Sample Answers

1. It's about how to plan or create characters for a comic book.
2. Decide on a main character or an interesting idea for the story.
3. monsters, aliens, and superheroes
4. Some features are based on real people and some features are made up.
5. You need imagination and creativity.
6. You can try lots of ideas and then decide which features you like best for the character.
7. I think creating comic books is hard because you need to try lots of ideas and sometimes you run out of ideas.
8. I think I would be good because I have lots of wild ideas, and I like to draw.
9. I would make a character who is really smart. He would look normal, but he discovers a potion that makes him so fast you cannot see him move. He'd solve lots of crimes and prevent lots of accidents.

Build Reading Fluency

Repeated Reading

Assessment Program: *Reading Fluency Chart, pp. 116*

As students read aloud, time the reading and count the number of incorrectly pronounced words. Record results in the Reading Fluency Chart.

Beyond the Reading

Reading Comprehension

Question-Answer Relationships (QAR)

"Right There" Questions

1. **Recall Facts** What is this selection about?
2. **Recall Facts** What is the first step in creating a comic book?
3. **Recall Facts** Name three characters found in comic books.

"Think and Search" Questions

4. **Make Inferences** What can you infer about the characters in comic books? Do they have features based on real people or are the features all made up?
5. **Find the Main Idea** What do you need to make a successful comic book?
6. **Analyze Cause and Effect** How does first sketching different faces and heads help you create a character?

"Author and You" Question

7. **Make Observations** Do you think that creating comic books is hard or easy? Explain.

"On Your Own" Questions

8. **Speculate** Do you think you would be good at creating comic books? Why or why not?
9. **Speculate** If you created a comic book character, what would he or she look like?

Activity Book *p. 178*

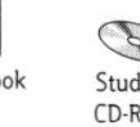
Student CD-ROM

Build Reading Fluency

Repeated Reading

"The Art of Making Comic Books" has difficult words. You can learn to read and understand faster if you read one paragraph at a time. Rereading builds confidence.

1. With a partner, read paragraph 1 on page 334 three times.
2. Next, read paragraph 2 three times.
3. Continue rereading each paragraph.
4. Stop after ten minutes.

MULTI-LEVEL OPTIONS *Elements of Literature*

Newcomer Use exaggeration to demonstrate the difference between formal and informal language. Write *formal* on the board. ***Say:** How do you do? It is my greatest pleasure to make your acquaintance.* Then write *informal.* ***Say:** Nice to meet you.* Have students point out the differences. (length of words, sentences, tone)

Beginning Have students practice using complete sentences in pairs. Write on the board: *What did you do today? Got up. Went to school. Took a test. Played soccer. Did homework. Ate dinner.* Have pairs change the phrases into complete sentences. Ask them to decide which set of answers is less formal.

Intermediate Have students work in pairs to find other examples of informal writing in the selection. Ask students to list the words and phrases or informal sentence structures that help make the writing informal.

Advanced Have students work in pairs to rewrite paragraph 3 in a formal style. ***Ask:** What types of writing should have a formal style?* (research report, essay, business letter, etc.) *What type of writing can have an informal style?* (letter, e-mail, journal, etc.)

Listen, Speak, Interact 

Explain a Concept for a Character

"The Art of Making Comic Books" provides details about making comic book characters.

1. Reread the selection with a partner. Discuss the different features and types of comic book characters.
2. Brainstorm your own character. As you speak, use evidence and examples to support your ideas. Make a list of characteristics, special powers, and how the character will look.
3. Clarify your ideas. Explain why you want to give your character these qualities.
4. Draw the character with your partner. Make sure each feature is based on your list of ideas.
5. Present your character to the class. Explain each feature. Also explain your reasons for including it.

Elements of Literature

Recognize Writing Style

Remember, **style** is the way writers use language to express themselves.

Michael Pellowski uses an informal writing style in "The Art of Making Comic Books." He does not always use complete sentences.

> What kind of body do I want the hero to have? Slender? Stocky? Muscular?

Now look at the example written in a more formal style:

> What kind of body do I want the hero to have? Should he be slender? Should he be stocky? Should he be muscular?

1. Discuss the informal and formal examples with a partner. How do you feel when you read each one? Which one sounds "friendlier"?
2. Read paragraph 3 and pay attention to the question near the end of the paragraph. What is your reaction to the question? Do you think that this question shows formal or informal style?

Activity Book p. 179

Student CD-ROM

Cultural Connection

Have students work in small groups. Tell groups to research folk heroes from another culture. Ask groups to create comic book characters based on the folk heroes they researched. Have groups present their ideas to the class. As a class, create a plot summary for a comic book with all of the folk-hero characters.

Learning Styles *Natural*

Have students add animal-like characteristics to their comic book characters. Ask them to observe a pet, an animal on television or in a movie, or an animal in the wild, such as a squirrel or a bird. Have students list the interesting natural abilities of the animal, such as flying, tree climbing, or night vision. Tell them to add any combination of these abilities to their characters.

Listen, Speak, Interact

Explain a Concept for a Character

1. **Reread in pairs** Arrange students into pairs for reading and creating characters. As they present, remind them to explain why the features and qualities are important.
2. **Newcomers** Reread with this group. Help them identify features and types of characters. Write key words and qualities on the board. After students draw their own characters, have them record their ideas in their Reading Logs.

Elements of Literature

Recognize Writing Style

1. **Clarify terms** Review the concept of *style.* Remind them of the writing style they learned using *and* in "The Library Card." Ask students to explain the difference between complete and incomplete sentences.
2. **Use personal experiences** Have students suggest other formal and informal things, such as parties, clothing, or letters.
3. **Multi-level options** See MULTI-LEVEL OPTIONS on p. 338.

Answers

1. *Possible answer:* The first one makes me feel like I'm talking with friends. The second one makes me feel like I'm in a classroom. The first one sounds "friendlier."
2. *Possible answer:* I think it's funny, so I laugh at the question. The question shows informal style.

ASSESS

Write on the board: *Have fun. I sincerely hope you enjoy the activities.* Have students identify sentence styles as formal or informal.

Beyond the Reading

Word Study

The Suffix *-ian*

Teacher Resource Book: *Personal Dictionary, p. 63*

Make a word map Write on the board and *say: Mexico.* Add *-an* (dropping the final *o*) and pronounce it. Ask volunteers to explain the connection between *Mexico* and *Mexican.* Provide other examples, such as *Canada/Canadian; Russia/Russian; Iran/Iranian; Brazil/Brazilian.*

Answers

2. magician, barbarian 3. a person who uses magic; a cruel or uncivilized person 5. a person who works with books; a person who works with machines; a person who tells jokes and is funny.

Grammar Focus

Understand the Present Conditional

Write on the board: *If it rains, we can't play outside.* Point out the main clause (*we can't play outside*) and the dependent clause (*If it rains*). Explain that the main clause depends on the dependent clause. The main clause "happens" if the dependent clause "happens."

Answers

1. Needing a star depends on if the book revolves around a main character.

ASSESS

Have students tell about these types of people: *Canadian, historian, musician.*

Word Study

The Suffix *-ian*

The suffix **-ian** is often used to tell where a person is from.

She's a Californian.

The suffix **-ian** can also give you other kinds of information about people.

1. Copy the chart in your Personal Dictionary.
2. Reread paragraph 2 of the reading selection and find two examples of words with the suffix *-ian.* Write the words in the chart.
3. Look the words up in the dictionary and write them in your chart.
4. Add these words to your chart:

   librarian technician comedian

5. If you know their meanings, write them in the chart. If not, look them up and then write them in.

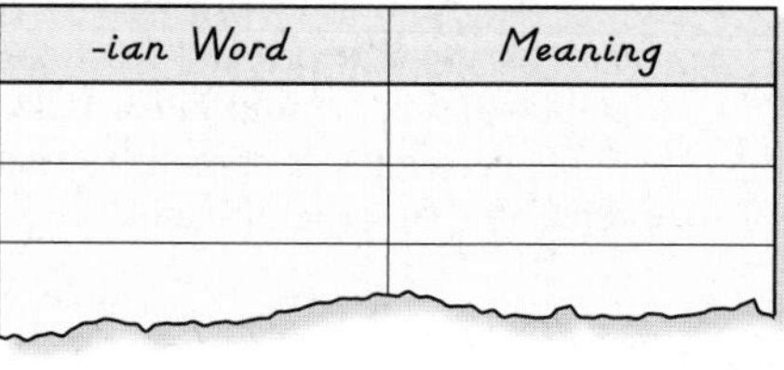

-ian Word	Meaning

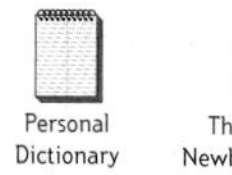
Personal Dictionary

The Heinle Newbury House Dictionary

Activity Book *p. 180*

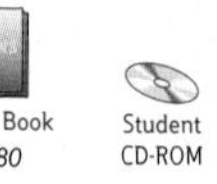
Student CD-ROM

Grammar Focus

Understand the Present Conditional

A present conditional sentence has a dependent clause beginning with *if.*

In the present conditional sentence, one action depends on another.

If I study hard, I make good grades.

Making good grades *depends on* studying hard.

Note that when the dependent clause comes first, it is followed by a comma.

1. Read this sentence:

   You need a star if the book revolves around a main character.

2. Decide which of the two phrases above depends on the other.

Activity Book *pp. 181–182*

Student Handbook

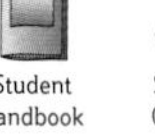
Student CD-ROM

340 Unit 5 Communication

MULTI-LEVEL OPTIONS *From Reading to Writing*

Newcomer Have students illustrate the steps in a simple process. Help them to add a title and captions that identify the main steps in the process.

Beginning Ask students to list the main steps in a simple process, such as making a salad. Help students write and illustrate the steps on index cards. (For example: *Buy vegetables, wash vegetables, cut them into small pieces,* etc.) Have students explain the process to newcomers, using the index cards as notes and as visual aids.

Intermediate Have students brainstorm a list of transitions and sequence words they can use in their articles. (first, next, then, finally, etc.) Have students refer to their lists when writing. Remind students that using transitions will help their writing flow smoothly between sentences and paragraphs.

Advanced Have students exchange their articles with partners. Ask partners to evaluate whether the process is explained correctly, has helpful illustrations, and is written in an informal writing style.

From Reading to Writing 

Write an Illustrated "How-to" Article

Write an illustrated "how-to" article. Use the chart to plan.

	Text	Illustrations
Step 1		
Step 2		
Step 3		

1. Tell what you are going to explain.
2. Use a step-by-step approach. Start at the beginning and move to the end of the process. Record the steps from first to last.
3. Use illustrations and captions.
4. Use an informal writing style.

Activity Book
p. 183

Across Content Areas 

Learn About Art Forms

People who create art are called artists. There are many different forms of art.

To learn more about these art forms, do an Internet search. Use the key words *painting, sculpture, photography,* or *graphic design.* You can also look for a book on art in your school library. Ask your librarian to help you.

Art Form	Artist	More About the Art Form
painting	painter	The type of paint can make a painting look very different. Some examples are oil paints and watercolors.
sculpture	sculptor	A sculpture is a three-dimensional representation of an object. Sculptors use materials such as clay, wood, wax, stone, or metal.
photography	photographer	A photographer uses a camera. It can be a still camera or a video camera.
graphic design	graphic designer	Graphic designers use technology such as computer programs to create pictures, illustrations, and other visual images.

Activity Book
p. 184

Student
Handbook

From Reading to Writing

Write an Illustrated "How-to" Article

1. **Brainstorm ideas** Have students brainstorm a list of topics. Remind them to write down all their ideas. Then tell them to pick the best idea.
2. **Think-pair-share** Ask students to record the steps on a chart, noting illustrations and text needed. Have them share their ideas in pairs and give each other suggestions and feedback before making a final copy.
3. **Multi-level options** See MULTI-LEVEL OPTIONS on p. 340.

Across Content Areas: The Arts

Learn About Art Forms

1. **Explore art forms** Bring in art books or pictures of art forms. Ask students to describe them and decide what materials were used to make them. Have students share what they know about these forms of art.
2. **Relate to personal experiences** Have students research art forms from other cultures they know. Ask them to share and describe the art forms to the class.

ASSESS

Have students write a question-and-answer quiz about the art forms and artists. For example: *Who uses a camera to take pictures?* (a photographer) *What does a sculptor make?* (objects from clay or stone)

Reteach and Reassess

Text Structure Divide students into three groups. Assign one text feature to each group. (illustrations, captions, step-by-step explanation) Tell each group to compose a definition of their assigned text feature. Have a volunteer from each group write their group's definition on the board.

Reading Strategy Tell students to write three facts about themselves. Have them exchange lists with a partner. Ask students to write at least one inference about their partners.

Elements of Literature Have students review a previous selection. ***Ask:*** *Is this formal or informal writing? Why do you think the author chose this style?*

Reassess Ask students to work in pairs to summarize the main idea of the selection. (creating comic book characters) Remind students that this is an excerpt. Ask pairs to write a one-sentence prediction of what they think the next part of the book will be about.

UNIT 5
Apply and Expand

Materials

Student Handbook
CNN Video: *Unit 5*
Teacher Resource Book: *Lesson Plan, p. 28; Teacher Resources, pp. 35–64; Video Script, pp. 169–170; Video Worksheet, p. 177; School-Home Connection, pp. 147–153*
Teacher Resource CD-ROM
Assessment Program: *Unit 5 Test, pp. 83–88; Teacher and Student Resources, pp. 115–144*
Assessment CD-ROM
Transparencies
The Heinle Newbury House Dictionary/CD-ROM
Heinle Reading Library
Web Site: www.heinle.visions.com

Listening and Speaking Workshop

Present an Oral Summary of a Reading

Teacher Resource Book: *Sunshine Organizer, p. 40*

Step 1: Use the Sunshine Organizer to plan your summary.
Arrange students in pairs to help each other get the facts for their organizers.

Step 2: Plan your summary.
Tell students to brainstorm a list of opening and concluding statements. Have groups discuss their strengths and weaknesses.

UNIT 5 Apply and Expand

Listening and Speaking Workshop

Present an Oral Summary of a Reading

> **Topic**
> Choose the reading selection that you liked best from this unit. Prepare and present a summary of the reading.

Step 1: Use the Sunshine Organizer to plan your summary.

Answer these questions. Be specific.

1. *What* is the title of the story?
2. *Who* are the characters? Did you like them? Why or why not?
3. *Where* do the main events take place?
4. *When* do the main events take place?
5. *What* was the problem or conflict?
6. *How* did the character resolve the problem?
7. *Why* is it your favorite story?

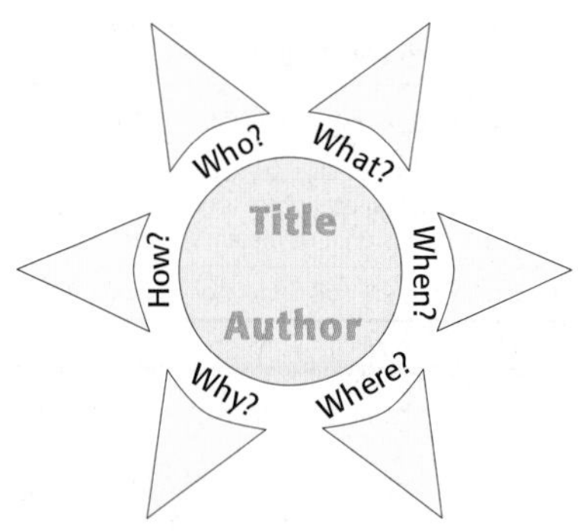

Step 2: Plan your summary.

1. Use one of these ideas for a strong opening.
   a. Ask a question.
   b. Say something funny.
   c. Make a dramatic statement.
   d. Refer to an authority and use quotes.
2. Make note cards on your key points.
3. Write an ending that states why you liked the story.

Step 3: Practice your presentation with a partner.

1. Stay on the topic.
2. Be confident so that your listeners will believe that you know what you are talking about.
3. Use your note cards.
4. Ask your partner to fill out the Active Listening Checklist.
5. Fill out the Speaking Checklist.
6. Evaluate the feedback from the checklists and revise your summary.

342 **Unit 5** Communication

MULTI-LEVEL OPTIONS *Listening and Speaking Workshop*

Newcomer Have students think about each of the selections in this unit. ***Ask:*** *Which selection in this unit was your favorite? Why?* Then ask them to draw pictures to represent the selections they chose.

Beginning Help students summarize their selections by creating flowcharts or timelines. Tell them to organize key events or ideas in the order in which they were presented. Remind students that they should restate information in their own words.

Intermediate Tell students to write several choices for opening statements. Ask small groups to evaluate one another's openings. Have students select and refine their opening statements based on their peers' comments. Remind them to be tactful and constructive as they give feedback.

Advanced Have students complete self-evaluations. Ask them to rate their own presentations based on the following criteria: 1) answered *wh*-questions; 2) strong opening; 3) summary; 4) good speaking behavior. Tell students to give themselves a score from 1–5 for each category.

Active Listening Checklist

1. I liked ____ because ____ .
2. I want to know more about ____ .
3. I thought the opening was interesting / not interesting.
4. You stayed on the topic. Yes / No
5. I did not understand ____ . I needed for you to repeat or clarify ____ .

Speaking Checklist

1. Did I speak too slowly, too quickly, or just right?
2. Did I speak loudly enough for the audience to hear me?

Step 4: Present your summary to the class.

You may want to record your summary on audio or video to share with your family.

Viewing Workshop

View and Think

Evaluate Visual Media

Visual media include signs, posters, television, videos, technology presentations, and movies.

1. Record all the types of visual media you have seen this week in a journal. Tell what important events were shown in each.
2. Evaluate the purpose of each type of media. Is it for entertainment? Does it try to persuade you? Does it give information?
3. Decide the effect of each type of media and how it influences you. If you had to choose only one form of media to view, which one would you choose? Why? Record your ideas.
4. What nonverbal messages do the types of media show? What do nonverbal messages such as gestures and body language tell you?
5. Share your ideas with the class.

Further Viewing

Watch the *Visions* CNN Video for Unit 5. Do the Video Worksheet.

CNN Video

Step 3: Practice your presentation with a partner.
Review the checklists before students practice in pairs. If possible, have them practice with those summarizing the same reading selection.

Step 4: Present your summary to the class.
Have students analyze the checklist responses and make notes about changes and adjustments to their oral presentations. Invite another class or parents to see the presentations.

ASSESS

Have students write two sentences telling what they liked the best about their own presentations and what they would like to do better next time.

Portfolio

Students may choose to record or videotape their oral presentations to place in their portfolios.

Viewing Workshop

View and Think

Teacher Resource Book: *Three-Column Chart, p. 45*

1. **List examples** As you go over the instructions for the project, allow students to give examples of the different types of media. Keep a list on the board for reference.
2. **Use graphic organizers** Create a chart to help students as they record types of media, content, and purpose. Clarify the meanings of *entertainment* and *persuade.*
3. **Analyze effect** Use questions to guide students as they analyze the effect of media and how the media affects them.

Content Connection *Math*

Create a chart that lists different types of visual media in the first column. (signs, posters, television, movies) One at a time, have students place a tally mark in the second column for each type of media they saw during the week. Distribute copies of the chart to small groups. Tell groups to use the totals to create bar graphs. Ask them to evaluate the data shown in the graph. ***Ask:*** *Which type of visual media was seen by the most students? By the fewest?*

Learning Styles *Musical*

Have small groups vote to choose a selection from this unit. Ask groups to write jingles about their selections. Have them select a well-known song for the tune of their jingle. Remind them that their jingles should tell the title, give a brief summary, and "advertise" the selection by telling why other readers would like it. Allow interested groups to sing their jingles for the class.

UNIT 5
Apply and Expand

Writer's Workshop

Write a Persuasive Editorial

Teacher Resource Book: *Persuasive—Debate and Writing, p. 51*

Use a graphic organizer Have students analyze the organization of the story chart as a model for their own writing.

Step 1: Brainstorm.
Remind students to label the lists. After completing the lists, tell students to circle the most important items and formulate their opinions on the cell phone question.

Step 2: Organize your ideas.
Reinforce the purpose of the letter. Write on the board: *Make others believe that your views are correct.* Have students keep this in mind as they choose supporting facts and examples.

Step 3: Write a draft.
Review the suggested order: introduction, paragraphs for each major idea, and conclusion. Remind students to use the various verb tenses and correct forms when appropriate.

Writer's Workshop

Write a Persuasive Editorial

Writing Prompt

You have been reading about the theme of communication. Your school board is deciding whether to allow students to carry cell phones in school. Write an editorial for your school newspaper. (Newspapers print editorials to give opinions on important topics.)

Your goal is to persuade your audience that your position is correct.

Step 1: Brainstorm.

1. Make a list of all the reasons *for* and *against* cell phones in school.
2. Decide on your opinion. Do you believe students should be allowed to carry cell phones in school? Write your opinion in one or two sentences.
3. List your best reasons for your position.

For	Against
You can stay in touch with your parents.	Phones ringing in class are distracting.

Step 2: Organize your ideas.

1. Put your ideas in order of importance. List the most important idea first.
2. For each idea, list the facts, examples, and evidence that support it.

Step 3: Write a draft.

1. Write an introductory paragraph.
   a. State why you are writing this editorial.
   b. Briefly state your position.
2. Write a paragraph about each of your major ideas. State the idea and give its supporting details.
3. Write a paragraph to conclude your letter. Briefly restate why you are for or against cell phones in school.
4. Make grammar work for you.
   a. Use the present perfect tense to talk about past actions that are important in the present: *I have had a cell phone for six months. It helps me stay in touch with my parents.*
   b. Use the past progressive tense to describe an important action from the past that was in progress: *Last year, many students were using the pay phone down the street. This was dangerous because . . .*
   c. Use present conditional sentences to express results: *If students have cell phones, they stay in better touch with their parents.*
   d. If you use the simple present tense, be sure to add *-s* to verbs with third-person singular subjects: *My cell phone helps me let people know if I am late.*

344 **Unit 5** Communication

MULTI-LEVEL OPTIONS *Writer's Workshop*

Newcomer Tell students to think about reasons to allow cell phones in school and good reasons to prohibit them. Ask them to fold a piece of paper in half and draw pictures that illustrate one reason for each opinion. Help students write *For* and *Against* above each picture and to add captions.

Beginning Have students work in pairs to complete the brainstorming step. Tell them to try to contribute ideas for both columns.

Intermediate Have students write drafts of their main paragraphs. Tell them to begin by writing topic sentences. Remind students that a topic sentence tells the main idea of a paragraph. Have them complete their paragraphs with sentences that contain supporting details.

Advanced Divide students into two groups based on the position they argued in their editorials. Ask students to use their notes to conduct an informal debate on the topic of allowing cell phones in school.

> *Our school board is now deciding whether students may use cell phones in school. I am* ______________________________ .
>
> *First, cell phones are* ______________________________ .
>
> *For example,* ______________________________ .
>
> *Another important point is that* ______________________________ .
>
> *This is true because* ______________________________ .
>
> *For these reasons, I firmly believe that* ______________________________ .

Step 4: Revise and edit your editorial.

1. Do you have support for all of your main ideas?
2. Does your editorial make sense?
3. Proofread your editorial to find errors in spelling, capitalization, punctuation, and paragraph indentation.

If you use a computer, use the spelling check or other features to check your work.

4. Collaborate with a partner to organize and revise your editorial. Ask a partner to read your editorial and give you feedback.
5. Revise your draft. Add or delete text as needed. Elaborate on your main ideas (provide more support for them).
6. Review how you have organized your draft. Reorganize or rearrange text so the order makes sense.

Step 5: Publish.

1. Prepare a final draft. If you write your editorial by hand, use your best handwriting. If you use a computer or a typewriter, be sure to check for typing errors.
2. Write a brief cover letter to the editor of your school newspaper. Explain that you would like to have your editorial published. Tell the editor how to get in touch with you.
3. Put your editorial and the cover letter in an envelope and mail or take it to the newspaper. Be sure to keep a copy of the editorial for yourself.
4. Read the newspaper to see if your editorial and your classmates' editorials are published.
5. Read the published editorials. Identify challenges you and your classmates had in writing to persuade.

The Heinle Newbury House Dictionary

Student Handbook

Step 4: Revise and edit your editorial.

Point out the different editing and proofreading points. Give clarification and explanation as needed. Then, in pairs, have students share their editorials and give each other feedback on their drafts.

Step 5: Publish.

Encourage students to make their editorials interesting so others will want to read them and pay attention to their ideas. Allow time for students to read one another's editorials. If possible, submit the editorials to the school newspaper.

ASSESS

Have students write a sentence explaining what was the most difficult part of writing a persuasive editorial.

Portfolio

Students may choose to include their writing in their portfolios.

Community Connection

Have students review local newspapers to find editorial articles that focus on community issues. Instruct pairs of students to select one article and write a brief summary. Tell them to restate the writer's opinion and provide facts, details, and examples that the writer uses to support his/her opinion.

Learning Styles *Visual*

Remind students that writers express their opinions with words, but artists express their opinions with pictures or other visual means. Display some examples of editorial cartoons. Review some common symbols, such as Uncle Sam (who represents the U.S. government) and the donkey and elephant (which represent political parties). Ask students to choose current issues and draw editorial cartoons that express their opinions.

UNIT 5
Apply and Expand

Projects

Project 1: List Types of Foreign-Language Communication

Teacher Resource Book: *Business Letter, p. 57*

1. **Gather and organize** Discuss how and where to find information about community foreign media resources. Direct students to the chart and discuss how to analyze the results.
2. **Language experience editorial** Work with students to write a letter suggesting a new type of media that would help the community. Remind them to use ideas about communication connecting people across cultures.

Project 2: Design Your Own Media

1. **Communicate an idea through media** Brainstorm a list of possible ideas about the reading selections. Have students choose another form of media for communicating the same idea.
2. **Compare and contrast** Have students prepare a visual presentation of their media example. Tell them to point out similarities and differences in information and purpose compared with the original readings.

Portfolio 

Students may choose to include their projects in their portfolios.

Projects

These projects will help you learn more about communication. Work alone or with a partner.

Project 1: List Types of Foreign-Language Communication

Does your community have forms of communication (media) in other languages?

1. List types of communication in your community that exist in other languages. For example, is there a television station with programs in Korean? Which Web sites can be viewed in Spanish or other languages?
2. List the kinds of communication you could not find in your community. For example, there may be no radio programs in Polish.
3. List your findings in a chart like the one below.
4. Discuss foreign language communication with a partner. Explain how these types of communication connect people across cultures.

Foreign Language Communication in My Community	Foreign Language Communication Not in My Community

5. Of the missing media, which ones do you recommend be started? Write an editorial about your idea and send it to your community newspaper for publication.

Project 2: Design Your Own Media

Have you ever thought about starting a newspaper? Would you like to draw cartoons or make posters? Would you like to host a radio program?

1. Think about the kinds of media you studied in this unit. What types of media do you use each day? Choose a form that you enjoy.
2. Create an example of this media based on one of the selections in the unit. For example, make a newspaper, draw a cartoon, or record a radio program to show something that happens in the selection.
3. Compare and contrast your media to the reading selection.
   a. How is the information the same? How is it different?
   b. What is the purpose of your media? To inform, to entertain, or to persuade? What was the author's purpose in writing the selection?
4. Share your media with the class. Evaluate how your classmates' media influence you. What effect do they have on your feelings and ideas?

MULTI-LEVEL OPTIONS *Projects*

Newcomer Discuss different types of media with students. Write on the board: *radio, television, newspapers, Internet, books.* Display images to represent each type of media. For each image, ***ask:*** *In our community, what languages can you (read/see/hear) this in?*

Beginning Have students brainstorm a list of different types of media. Then have them brainstorm a list of foreign languages spoken in the community. Display the lists for students to use as they complete their charts for Project 1.

Intermediate Suggest that students use a computer to create their own media for Project 2. For example, have them use drawing software, a clip art package, a newsletter template of a word processing program, or recording software to complete their projects.

Advanced Have students use the Internet, library, or other source to find data on how many people in your community speak certain languages. Ask students to compare this with what they learned in Project 1 and evaluate whether the community's media meets the needs of its residents.

Further Reading

Listed below are some books about communication. Read one or more of them. Write your thoughts and feelings about what you read. In your Reading Log, take notes on your answers to these questions:

1. Make connections between different texts. How are all types of communication similar? How are they different?
2. What is the most interesting thing you learned about communication from the books you read?
3. What question would you ask each author?
4. How can you use a book you read as a model for writing? What goals would you set as a writer after reading this book?

How Tía Lola Came to ~~Visit~~ Stay
by Julia Alvarez, Alfred A. Knopf, 2001. Tía Lola comes from the Dominican Republic to visit Miguel's family in Vermont. At first his aunt, who cannot speak English, embarrasses Miguel. Then Tía Lola helps Miguel discover his heritage.

Helen Keller
by George Sullivan, Scholastic Trade, 2001. In this book, the author uses Helen Keller's own writings to tell her life story. We learn about Keller's struggles with being blind and deaf, how she learned to overcome these physical challenges, and how she was able to help others do the same.

Dear Dr. Bell . . . Your Friend, Helen Keller
by Judith St. George, William Morrow & Co., 1993. Alexander Graham Bell, the inventor of the telephone, and Helen Keller were lifelong friends. Bell met Keller when she was six years old and helped her parents find her teacher, Annie Sullivan. This book describes the friendship shared by these people.

Speech and Hearing: Encyclopedia of Health
by Billy Alstetter, Chelsea House Publishers, 1991. This book discusses the connection between speech and hearing and how the brain interprets speech. The book also discusses speech and hearing disorders.

Manga Mania: How to Draw Japanese Comics
by Christopher Hart and Chris Hart, Watson-Gutpill Publications, Inc., 2001. This book shows how to draw in the distinct style of Japanese animation.

Communications and Broadcasting
by Harry Henderson with Lisa Yount, Facts on File, Inc., 1997. This book discusses the history of telecommunications dating back to Samuel Morse's telegraph.

Ancient Communications: From Grunts to Graffiti
by Michael B. Woods and Mary B. Woods, The Lerner Publishing Group, 2000. Ancient civilizations had their own particular ways of communicating. This book discusses the ancient civilizations of India, China, Egypt, the Middle East, Greece, and Rome.

Reading Log

Heinle Reading Library

Further Reading

Teacher Resource Book: *Reading Log, p. 64*

Respond to literature Have students select a book about communication and prepare a five-minute talk. Tell them to identify the type(s) of communication mentioned in the book. Ask students to consider how the author communicated his/her ideas. ***Ask:*** *Was the style formal or informal? Were pictures or illustrations important? Was dialogue an important feature? Can you use any of these in your own writing to become a better communicator of ideas?* Have students formulate goals to improve their own writing based on what they learn from other authors.

Assessment Program: *Unit 5 Test, pp. 83–88*

Unit Materials

Activity Book: *pp. 185–216*
Audio: *Unit 6*
Student Handbook
Student CD-ROM: *Unit 6*
CNN Video: *Unit 6*
Teacher Resource Book: *Lesson Plans, Teacher Resources, Reading Summaries, School-Home Connection, Video Script, Video Worksheet, Activity Book Answer Key*
Teacher Resource CD-ROM
Assessment Program: *Quizzes, Test, and End-of-Book Exam, pp. 89–108; Teacher and Student Resources, pp. 115–144*
Assessment CD-ROM
Transparencies
The Heinle Newbury House Dictionary/CD-ROM
More Grammar Practice workbook
Heinle Reading Library
Web Site: www.heinle.visions.com

Unit Theme: Frontiers

Describe mental images Tell students that a frontier is an undeveloped area or an area beyond a settled place. ***Ask:*** *What do you think a frontier looks like?* Have students express their thoughts and images of a frontier.

Unit Preview: Table of Contents

1. **Use text features** ***Ask:*** *Which chapter is about a frontier in space?* (Chapter 2) *Which chapter has speeches?* (Chapters 3, 4)
2. **Connect** ***Ask:*** *Which of these frontiers or people do you know? Which seem interesting?*

UNIT 6

Frontiers

CHAPTER 1 *page 350* **The Lewis and Clark Expedition**
an excerpt from a textbook

CHAPTER 2 *page 362* **A Wrinkle in Time**
an excerpt from a science fiction novel by Madeleine L'Engle

CHAPTER 3 *page 380* **I Have a Dream**
an excerpt from a speech by Martin Luther King Jr.

CHAPTER 4 *page 392* **Lyndon Baines Johnson: Our Thirty-Sixth President**
an excerpt from a biography by Melissa Maupin

Speech to the Nation: July 2, 1964
an excerpt from a speech by Lyndon Baines Johnson

348

UNIT OBJECTIVES

Reading

Use chronology to locate and recall information as you read an informational text • Describe mental images as you read science fiction • Draw conclusions with text evidence as you read a speech • Distinguish fact from opinion as you read a biography and a speech

Listening and Speaking

Use inference to act out a story • Present a story • Present a speech • Conduct an interview

The Rocky Mountains: Emigrants Crossing the Plains, N. Currier and J.M. Ives, lithograph. 1866.

View the Picture

1. A frontier is a place where something new begins. What kind of frontier is shown here?

2. What other kinds of frontiers do you know about?

In this unit, you will read excerpts from a textbook, a novel, two speeches, and a biography. Each selection focuses on people who have explored new frontiers. You will learn about the features of these writing forms and how to write them yourself.

349

Grammar

Use appositives • Identify the past perfect tense • Use dependent clauses with *that* • Use the conjunction *yet* to show contrast

Writing

Write an informational text • Write a science fiction narrative • Write a persuasive speech • Write a biography

Content

Social Studies: Use headings as you read • Science: Learn about the speed of light • Social Studies: Learn about the United States Constitution • Social Studies: Learn about the branches of government

UNIT 6

Introduce the Unit

View the Picture

1. **Art background** This lithograph was published by the famous New York printers, Currier and Ives. It was one of a series of prints, lithographs, and engravings of the American wilderness from the last half of the 19th century. The original was hand colored by Frances F. Palmer on stone plates, a process that produces softer lines and colors than the typical steel-plate lithograph.
2. **Describe choice of style** *Ask: Does this picture look realistic or imaginary? Do you think this was a real scene from history? How do the colors make this frontier seem—scary, exciting, beautiful?*
3. **Evaluate the images** Have students describe the illustration and tell how they would feel in one of the wagons driving across the plains. ***Ask:*** *Do you think you would like to cross the Rocky Mountains in a covered wagon? Why or why not? What is the artist trying to express about frontiers and people who explore frontiers?*
4. **Use personal experience** *Ask: What frontiers are there in the world today?*
5. **Connect to theme** *Say: The theme of this unit is* frontiers. *How does this lithograph show frontiers?*

ASSESS

Have students agree on a summary statement about frontiers.

Chapter Materials

Activity Book: *pp. 185–192*
Audio: *Unit 6, Chapter 1*
Student Handbook
Student CD-ROM: *Unit 6, Chapter 1*
Teacher Resource Book: *Lesson Plan, Teacher Resources, Reading Summary, Activity Book Answer Key*
Teacher Resource CD-ROM
Assessment Program: *Quiz, pp. 89–90; Teacher and Student Resources, pp. 115–144*
Assessment CD-ROM
Transparencies
The Heinle Newbury House Dictionary/CD-ROM
Web Site: www.heinle.visions.com

Objectives

Make observations Read aloud and explain the objectives. Help students recall vocabulary from earlier units. ***Say:*** *I remember the word* nonfiction. *Is that about a real story or a make-believe story? What other reading selections were nonfiction?*

Use Prior Knowledge

Explore Ideas About Frontiers

Compare and contrast Have students compare responses in pairs. Ask volunteers to explain their responses.

Answers
Possible answers: **1.** T **2.** T **3.** T **4.** F **5.** T **6.** T

CHAPTER 1

Into the Reading

The Lewis and Clark Expedition

an excerpt from a textbook

Objectives

Reading Use chronology to locate and recall information as you read an informational text.

Listening and Speaking Use inference to act out a story.

Grammar Use appositives.

Writing Write an informational text.

Content Social Studies: Use headings as you read.

Use Prior Knowledge

Explore Ideas About Frontiers

Read the following statements and record your responses on a piece of paper. If you think that a statement is true, write *T.* If you think that a statement is false, write *F.*

1. I would like to be one of the first people to see a new place.
2. I would keep a journal if I explored a new land.
3. When exploring a new place, it is useful to have partners with different skills.
4. It would be easy to explore an unknown land.
5. We can learn many things from people who explore new places.
6. People can have different purposes for exploring a new land.

Discuss your answers with a partner.

MULTI-LEVEL OPTIONS *Build Vocabulary*

Newcomer Write on the board: *expedition = trip.* Hold up a picture of people hiking. ***Ask:*** *What are these people doing?* Write a list of synonyms for *expedition.* Then look up *expedition* in the dictionary.

Beginning On the board, write: *expedition = trip.* ***Say:*** *Words that mean the same thing are called synonyms.* Hold up a thesaurus. ***Say:*** *You can look for synonyms in here.* Have pairs list additional synonyms for *expedition.*

Intermediate ***Ask:*** *Where can you find synonyms for a word?* (thesaurus) Have students work in pairs to list synonyms for *expedition, goal, supplies,* and *attack.* List them on the board in a two-column chart.

Advanced Ask pairs to look up *expedition* in the thesaurus. Have them add as many synonyms as they can to their word wheels.

Build Background

The Louisiana Purchase

In 1803, the United States bought the Louisiana Territory from France. The Louisiana Purchase added 828,000 square miles of land to the United States. It nearly doubled the size of the United States. At that time, the land only cost about four cents per acre.

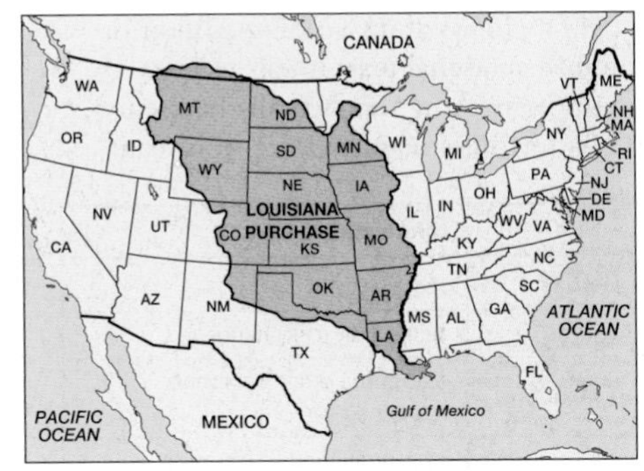

Content Connection

Miles and **acres** are measurements in the U.S. system. Here are the amounts in the metric system:

1 mile = 1.61 kilometers
1 acre = 0.4 hectares

Build Vocabulary

Use a Word Wheel

Brainstorm ideas about a vocabulary word to help you understand it.

1. Brainstorm what you know about the word *expedition.* If necessary, look up the word in a dictionary. You may also use a thesaurus or synonym finder to find words with meanings that relate to *expedition.*
2. Write three words that help you remember the meaning of *expedition.* Write them in a Word Wheel like the one here.

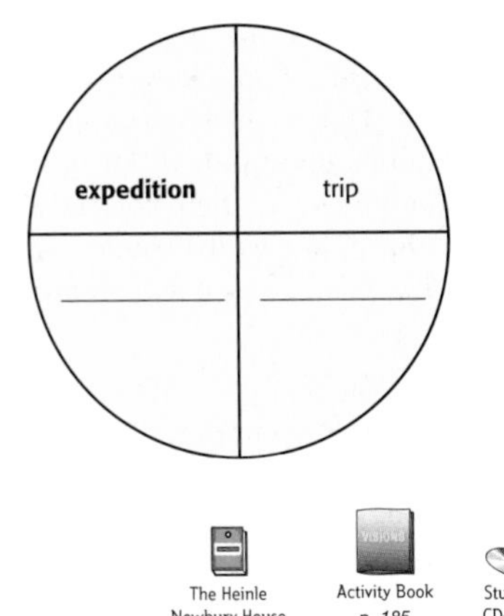

The Heinle Newbury House Dictionary
Activity Book p. 185
Student CD-ROM

Content Connection *Social Studies*

Build Background Ask students to work in small groups. Have them use the library or the Internet to research other American land purchases. Suggest that they find information on the purchase of Alaska, Manhattan, or California. Have groups take notes on what they find. Ask students to use their notes to present their information to the class.

Learning Styles *Kinesthetic*

Build Vocabulary Have students "be" word wheels. Ask students to form groups of four. Assign each group an action verb, such as *run, write,* or *search.* Have groups use a dictionary and glossary to find synonyms for their assigned words. Ask groups to stand in circles and act out their synonyms.

Build Background

The Louisiana Purchase

1. **Use a map** Have students compare the map to a current U.S. map. ***Ask:*** *What states were in the United States in 1803? What states did the area of the Louisiana Purchase become?* (AR, CO, IA, KS, LA, MN, MO, MT, NE, ND, OK, SD, WY)
2. **Relate to personal experience** Ask students to share any knowledge or experiences they have of this area.
3. **Content Connection** Miles and kilometers measure length; acres and hectares measure area. ***Ask:*** *Where do you see miles and kilometers?* (road signs) *Where do you see acres?* (land sale signs)

Build Vocabulary

Use a Word Wheel

Teacher Resource Book: *Personal Dictionary, p. 63*

1. **Teacher think aloud** *Say: I remember "Antarctic Adventure" and "Matthew A. Henson" were both about expeditions, or long trips.*
2. **Use multiple reference aids** *Say:* Expedition *and* trip *are very close in meaning, but sometimes it's more appropriate to use one rather than the other. Reference aids often give information about when to use a particular word.* Have students look up the words in a dictionary, thesaurus, and online or CD-ROM dictionary and thesaurus to clarify meaning and usage.
3. **Reading selection vocabulary** You may want to introduce the glossed words in the reading selection before students begin reading. Key words: *fascinate, relationship, records, previous, supplies, equipment, vast.* Instruct students to write the words with correct spelling and their definitions in their Personal Dictionaries. Have them pronounce each word and divide it into syllables.
4. **Multi-level options** See MULTI-LEVEL OPTIONS on p. 350.

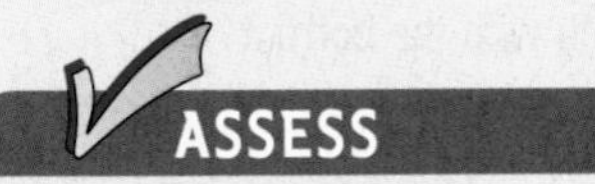

Have students write sentences using the words from their word wheels.

Into the Reading

Text Structure

Informational Text

Teacher Resource Book: *Reading Log, p. 64*

1. **Use a graphic organizer to define and explain features** Write the feature chart on the board. Have students give examples of the features from other selections they have read.
2. **Multi-level options** See MULTI-LEVEL OPTIONS below.

Reading Strategy

Use Chronology to Locate and Recall Information

Teacher Resource Book: *Reading Log, p. 64*

Use personal experiences Ask students to recall events from the previous week using chronology and time-sequence words.

ASSESS

Ask students to create their own definitions of *setting, events, chronology,* and *time sequence.*

Text Structure

Informational Text

"The Lewis and Clark Expedition" is an **informational text.** It tells us facts about something that actually happened. Look for these features when you read:

	Informational Text
Setting	real places
Events	things that really happened
Chronology	told in the order the events happened
Time Sequence	uses time words such as *before, after, finally* to help the reader follow what happened

As you read "The Lewis and Clark Expedition," note important events in your Reading Log.

Student CD-ROM

Reading Strategy

Use Chronology to Locate and Recall Information

As you read, notice that the story is told in the order that the events actually happened. This is called **chronological order.** Remembering the order in which events happened can help you recall information. Time words (such as days, dates, *then, finally*) can help you identify chronology.

1. Read the first page. What is the first important event described on this page? What is the next? Write these events in your Reading Log.
2. Continue listing events in chronological order until you finish the selection.

page 354

1. *Jefferson chooses Meriwether Lewis to lead expedition.*
2. *Lewis chooses William Clark.*

MULTI-LEVEL OPTIONS *Text Structure*

Newcomer Prepare pictures of a student waking up, eating breakfast, and leaving for school. Write on the board: *first, next, last.* Hold up the pictures in sequence as you point to and say the words. Have volunteers come up and repeat. Then have them make three drawings of their afternoons and label each with the correct word.

Beginning Add a third column for examples to the chart above. *Ask: Where do you spend your days? What things happen during the day? In what order do these events happen? Can you describe the order of these events using time words?* Have each student make his/her own chart.

Intermediate Create and distribute blank charts like the one on p. 352. Include headings and the left-column labels. Have pairs complete charts to describe the first day of school. Remind them to use the correct time sequence words. Have pairs compare charts with other pairs.

Advanced Ask pairs to review a newspaper article and complete an Informational Text chart with information from the article. Instruct them to list the events in chronological order using time words. Have them share their charts in small groups.

The Lewis and Clark Expedition

an excerpt from a textbook

353

Reading Selection Materials

Audio: *Unit 6, Chapter 1*
Teacher Resource Book: *Reading Summary, pp. 111–112*

Preview the Selection

Teacher Resource Book: *Sunshine Organizer, p. 40*

1. **Use a graphic organizer** Have students examine the picture and the title. Ask questions to help students make predictions about the expedition. ***Ask:*** *Who are these men? Where do you think they are going? How did they travel? When and for how long do you think they traveled? Why are they going to this frontier? What do you think they will see and find there?* Have students fill in their predictions on a Sunshine Organizer.
2. **Connect** Remind students that the unit theme is *frontiers.* ***Ask:*** *Why do you think the Lewis and Clark expedition was important for people in the United States?*

Content Connection
The Arts

Have pairs discuss and evaluate the illustration. Tell them to create a word web to organize their thoughts. Ask them to include ideas that answer the following questions: *When did this expedition take place? What can you tell about the main characters? Do you think this art is a good choice to introduce the selection?*

Learning Styles
Natural

Provide a map of Lewis and Clark's exploration route. Ask students to work in small groups to imagine that they will be guiding Lewis and Clark on the expedition. Tell them to plan the best route. Then ask them to make a list of supplies they think they will need for the journey. Have groups present their plans.

UNIT 6 • CHAPTER 1
Reading Selection

Read the Selection

1. **Use text features** Point out the map and have students identify states, territories, and other areas of land. Ask them to find names of rivers and other geographical features. Remind students to use the illustration and map to help understanding.
2. **Teacher read aloud** Read the selection aloud. Pause to check understanding and to identify setting and events. Point out that Thomas Jefferson was president when the Louisiana Purchase was made.
3. **Use chronology to locate and recall information** Have students identify the key events in the selection and arrange them in chronological order on a timeline.

Sample Answer to Guide Question
Lewis and Clark had been captains in the army. Thomas Jefferson had wondered about the lands in the west. The United States acquired the Louisiana Territory.

See Teacher Edition pp. 434–435 for a list of English-Spanish cognates in the reading selection.

1 Long before the Louisiana Purchase, Thomas Jefferson had been **fascinated** by lands in the West. Who lived there, he wondered? What was the land like? Could the Missouri River possibly lead to a water **route** to the Pacific Ocean? Jefferson wanted to know the answers to these questions.

To find the answers, Jefferson sent an expedition to the newly **acquired** land, now called the Louisiana Territory. Jefferson chose Meriwether Lewis, who was an army captain, to lead the expedition. Lewis chose a fellow army captain, his friend William Clark, to share command.

Use Chronology to Locate and Recall Information

What happened before Lewis and Clark were chosen to lead the expedition?

Audio

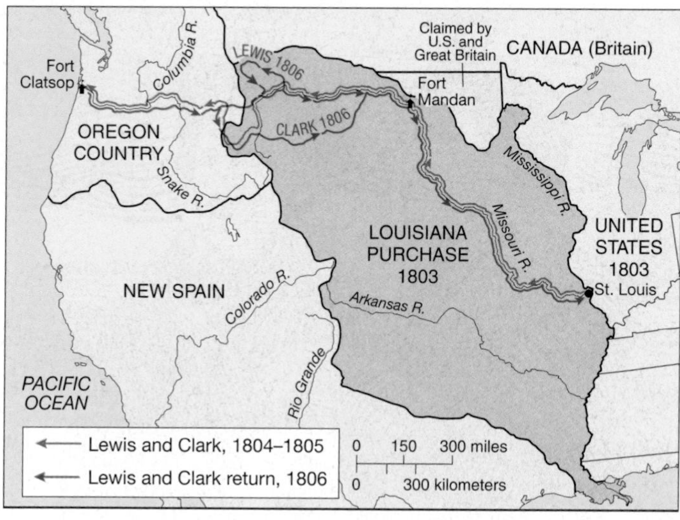

fascinated greatly interested
route a path along which one travels
acquired bought or gotten

MULTI-LEVEL OPTIONS *Read the Selection*

Newcomer Play the audio. Reread the pages aloud. ***Ask:*** *Did Jefferson know a lot about the West?* (no) *Did Jefferson send an expedition to the West?* (yes) *Did Lewis and Clark lead the expedition?* (yes) *Were Lewis and Clark the only members of the group?* (no) *Was York a slave?* (yes)

Beginning Read the Reading Summary aloud. ***Ask:*** *Who wondered about the West?* (Jefferson) *Who led the expedition?* (Lewis and Clark) *What area were they going to explore?* (Louisiana Territory) *When did they start their journey?* (May 1804) *Where did they start?* (St. Louis)

Intermediate Have students do a paired reading. ***Ask:*** *Why did Jefferson send Lewis and Clark west?* (He wondered about that area.) *What were the three goals of the expedition?* (find water route to Pacific; build relationships with Native Americans; note geological/geographical data)

Advanced Have students read silently. ***Ask:*** *Why do you think Lewis chose Clark?* (They were both army captains and friends.) *Why were hunters and boatmen brought along?* (for their skills with water travel; to provide food) *Was Clark a good friend to York? Why or why not?* (No, he wouldn't free him.)

The Native American Sacagawea guiding the Lewis and Clark expedition. Painting by Alfred Russel.

3 Jefferson told the two captains they had three goals. One was to search for a water route to the Pacific Ocean. The second was to establish **relationships** with the Native Americans they met. Jefferson wanted the Indians to know his "wish was to be neighborly, friendly, and useful to them." The third goal was to pay close attention to "the soil and face of the country," to its plants, animals, minerals, **climate,** and to keep careful, written **records** of their findings. Today, the journals of Lewis and Clark are the main source of information about their expedition.

4 In May 1804, Lewis and Clark and other members of the expedition set out westward from St. Louis, Missouri, along the Missouri River. Follow their route on the map on the **previous** page. The expedition included soldiers, river boatmen, hunters, and York, Clark's slave and childhood friend. During the expedition, York worked at Clark's side much of the time, and had shown he was ready to **sacrifice** his life to save Clark's. Nevertheless, when York later asked to be freed as a reward for his **contributions** to the expedition, Clark refused.

Use Chronology to Locate and Recall Information

If the Louisiana Purchase took place in April 1803, how long did it take Jefferson, Lewis, and Clark to organize the expedition?

relationships connections between people
climate the type of weather a place has
records things (usually written) that prove an event happened
previous coming before something else
sacrifice give up something valuable
contributions helpful participation

Read the Selection

1. **Use the illustration** Ask students to describe the picture and suggest why a guide might be important when exploring a new area or frontier.
2. **Paired reading** Read the selection aloud. Have students reread it with partners. ***Ask:*** *What were the goals of the expedition?* (to find a water route to the Pacific Ocean; make connections with the Native Americans; and learn about the plants, animals, and climate of the area)
3. **Use chronology to locate and recall information** *Ask: When did they begin their trip?* (in May 1804) Ask other questions to help students summarize important events of the selection and add them to the list in their Reading Logs.
4. **Multi-level options** See MULTI-LEVEL OPTIONS on p. 354.

Sample Answer to Guide Question

It took over a year for Jefferson, Lewis, and Clark to organize the expedition.

Punctuation

Commas after introductory phrases

Tell students that introductory phrases, or groups of words that come at the beginning of a sentence, are usually followed by a comma. Explain that introductory phrases often tell *when, where, why,* or *how.* Direct students to sentence 1. ***Say:*** *"Long before the Louisiana Purchase" is an introductory phrase. It tells* when *Jefferson was fascinated.* Ask students to look at paragraph 2. ***Ask:*** *What is the introductory phrase?* (To find the answers) *What does it tell?* (why Jefferson sent an expedition)

Apply Have students find and copy the two sentences from paragraph 4 with introductory phrases. Tell students to underline the introductory phrase and circle the comma in each sentence. (sentence 1: In May 1804; sentence 3: During the expedition)

Read the Selection

1. **Use the illustration** Ask students to describe the woman in the picture and suggest how she might be connected to the expedition.
2. **Paired reading** Read the selection aloud. *Ask: Who was Sacagawea?* (the wife of a French-Canadian guide) *Why was she important on the trip?* (She could interpret some of the Indian languages and she showed that this was a peaceful trip.) Have students reread the selection in pairs and add events to their timelines.

Sample Answer to Guide Question
They faced hardships throughout the whole trip.

5 Three boats carried expedition members, equipment, and **supplies.** They did not know it then, but they would not return for another 28 months.

6 During their first winter, they hired a French Canadian fur trapper and his Soshone wife, Sacagawea (sah KAH gah way ah), to act as **interpreters** and guides. Sacagawea helped Lewis and Clark establish good relations with Native Americans along the way. She helped translate Indian languages for the expedition. The baby she carried on her back signaled the peaceful purposes of the expedition.

Throughout the expedition, its 7
members faced many **hardships.** They had to paddle their boats against strong river currents. Every now and then, a boat would turn over, sending **equipment** splashing into the water. And there was always the danger of being attacked by dangerous animals, like 900-pound grizzly bears.

Use Chronology to Locate and Recall Information

When did the members of the expedition face hardships?

supplies goods necessary for an operation
interpreters people who translate one language into another
hardships difficulties in living conditions
equipment items needed for a purpose

MULTI-LEVEL OPTIONS *Read the Selection*

Newcomer *Did the trip take 28 months?* (yes) *Did Sacagawea carry a baby?* (yes) *Was the trip easy?* (no) *Did they see bison?* (yes) *Did they cross the Rocky Mountains?* (yes) *Did they find a water route to the Pacific Ocean?* (no)

Beginning *How long was the group gone?* (28 months) *Whom did they hire as guides and interpreters?* (Sacagawea and a fur trapper) *What difficulties and dangers did they face?* (strong currents; falling into the water; bears) *When did they finally return?* (September 1806)

Intermediate *Why did they hire Sacagawea and her husband?* (to interpret and guide; to establish good relations with Native Americans) *What were some bad things that happened?* (overturned boats, dangerous animals) *What was a good thing?* (fabulous views)

Advanced *What did Sacagawea's baby signify?* (that the group was peaceful) *Why was this important?* (so Native Americans wouldn't be afraid) *Was the trip a success? Explain.* (yes and no; they reached the Pacific and made many observations, but they didn't find a water route.)

8 But Lewis and Clark were rewarded with some **fabulous** views. They saw a herd of 20,000 bison stretching across the plain and fast deerlike animals called pronghorns racing by. They crossed the tall, **spectacular** Rocky Mountains. Finally their eyes were filled with the sight of the great Pacific Ocean—"Ocean in view! Oh the joy!" wrote Clark.

The explorers finally returned to St. Louis in September 1806. They had not found a water route to the Pacific. But they had recorded and described thousands of varieties of plants and animals, and even brought some back for Jefferson to examine. They had also mapped a **vast** area, opening it to future exploration and new settlers from the United States. 9

Use Chronology to Locate and Recall Information

If the expedition took 28 months total, in what year would Lewis and Clark likely have arrived at the Pacific Ocean?

fabulous great, wonderful
spectacular wonderful, exciting
vast wide

UNIT 6 • CHAPTER 1
Reading Selection

Read the Selection

1. **Use text features** Have students describe the animal and guess its significance in the selection. Review meanings of glossed words.
2. **Paired reading** Continue reading the selection as students follow along. Read aloud or ask volunteers to read parts. Then have students reread in pairs. ***Ask:*** *Why do you think they were happy to see the Pacific Ocean?* (They had completed the trip.)
3. **Use a timeline** Ask questions to help students summarize key events. Have them use the information to make a timeline.
4. **Multi-level options** See MULTI-LEVEL OPTIONS on p. 357.

Sample Answer to Guide Question
1805

Across Selections

Compare and contrast Have students compare this informational text to another narrative, such as "Matthew A. Henson" or "Antarctic Adventure." Ask questions to help students identify similarities and differences.

Spelling

th and t; thr and tr

Write on the board: *ten/then* and *tree/three.* ***Say:*** *The letter* t- *sounds like /t/ in* top. *The letters* tr *sound like* /tr/ *in tree.* Ask students to find and say two words in paragraph 6 that start with *tr-*. (trapper, translate) ***Say:*** *The letters* th- *sound like* /th/ *in* they. *The letters* thr- *sound like* /thr/ *in* throw. Ask students to find and say two words in paragraphs 5 and 7 that start with *thr-*. (three, throughout)

Evaluate Your Reading Strategy

Use Chronology to Locate and Recall Information *Say: You have practiced an important reading strategy. Now you can decide how well you have done. Does this statement describe how you read?*

I pay attention to the chronological order of events as I read. If I know the chronology of events, I can recall information better. I can also find information more quickly.

UNIT 6 • CHAPTER 1
Beyond the Reading

Reading Comprehension

Question-Answer Relationships

Sample Answers

1. members of the expedition and their equipment and supplies
2. She was the wife of a French-Canadian fur trapper; she and her husband worked as guides and interpreters; she was Shoshone.
3. for almost two and a half years
4. to see if there was an all-water route to the Pacific Ocean, to make friends with Native Americans, and to learn about the plants, animals, minerals, and climate of the area
5. She translated some of the Indian languages; she showed that it was a peaceful trip.
6. Clark was very happy to see the ocean. It meant they had reached their goal and now they could start going home.
7. When I first moved to this town, it was new. I explored it, going a little bit farther each time. I learned good places to go and other places to avoid.
8. How did they travel over the Rocky Mountains? (They couldn't use boats there.) How many different Native American languages did Sacagawea speak?

Build Reading Fluency

Reading Silently

Assessment Program: *Reading Fluency Chart, p. 116*

When students have completed the reading fluency activity, record their progress in the Reading Fluency Chart.

Beyond the Reading

Reading Comprehension

Question-Answer Relationships (QAR)

"Right There" Questions

1. **Recall Facts** What did Lewis and Clark's three boats carry?
2. **Identify** Who was Sacagawea?
3. **Recall Facts** For how long did Lewis and Clark travel?

"Think and Search" Questions

4. **Identify Main Ideas** What did President Jefferson want the two captains to do when they explored the Louisiana Purchase?
5. **Explain** How did Sacagawea help Lewis and Clark?

"Author and You" Question

6. **Analyze Cause and Effect** Why did Clark write "Oh the joy!" when he saw the Pacific Ocean?

"On Your Own" Questions

7. **Compare Events to Your Own Experiences** Have you ever explored a place that was new to you? Describe your experiences.
8. **Ask Questions** What unanswered questions do you have about the selection after reading it? Use what you have learned and your own knowledge to think of these questions.

Activity Book *p. 186*

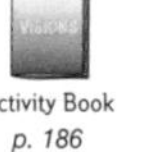
Student CD-ROM

Build Reading Fluency

Reading Silently

Reading silently is good practice. It helps you learn to read faster.

1. Listen to the audio recording of paragraph 1 of "The Lewis and Clark Expedition."
2. Listen to the chunks of words as you follow along.
3. Reread paragraph 1 silently two times.
4. Your teacher or partner will time your second reading. Raise your hand when you are finished.

MULTI-LEVEL OPTIONS *Elements of Literature*

Newcomer Have students draw pictures of Lewis, Clark, or Jefferson. Help them write three words or phrases that describe the person. Ask students to share their drawings with a partner.

Beginning Have students draw pictures of Lewis, Clark, Jefferson, York, or Sacagawea. Ask them to write five words or phrases that describe the person. Help students with adjectives and other descriptive terms. Have them refer to the selection if necessary.

Intermediate Have students work in pairs to write descriptive paragraphs about one of the characters in the selection. Tell them to include traits given in and inferred from the selection. Help students confirm their descriptions by providing additional information.

Advanced Have students work in pairs to research one of the five main characters in this selection. Encourage them to use outside resources for research. Ask them to use their research to prepare an oral report to share with the class. Encourage them to rehearse their speeches.

Listen, Speak, Interact 

Use Inference to Act Out a Story

The reading selection does not include any dialogue, but we can assume that the people talked to each other.

Jefferson: I want to find out what the land to the west is like.

Lewis: What do you want to know?

Jefferson: Well, who lives there?

1. Read the first two paragraphs of "The Lewis and Clark Expedition." With a partner, write down a conversation between Jefferson and Lewis or between Lewis and Clark.
2. Act out your conversation for the class. Adapt your word choice, diction, and usage to reflect the time when Lewis and Clark lived. They spoke formally.

Elements of Literature

Analyze Characters

Informational texts often discuss **characters** who were historical figures. The two main characters in this account are Lewis and Clark. Other important figures are Sacagawea and York. By reading carefully, you can find out what they were like.

1. Look back in the selection to find information about these people.
   a. What kind of person do you think Lewis was?
   b. What kind of friendship did Lewis and Clark have?
   c. What kind of relationship did Clark and York have?
   d. How would you describe Sacagawea's character?
2. With a small group, explain your answers.
3. Look through "The Lewis and Clark Expedition" to find more traits about the historical figures. Find examples that support your ideas. Also look for evidence in facts and details that tell about the characters.
4. List these people and their traits in your Reading Log.
5. Form three questions about the figures. How would you research answers to your questions?

Reading Log

Activity Book p. 187

Student CD-ROM

Listen, Speak, Interact

Use Inference to Act Out a Story

1. **Reread in pairs** Read the first two paragraphs aloud. As pairs create and act out their dialogues, remind them that Jefferson was president and the characters should use polite and formal language.
2. **Newcomers** Reread with this group. As students suggest lines, list them on the board. Help them add formal gestures and expressions. Have students assess their role-play in their Reading Logs.

Elements of Literature

Analyze Characters

Teacher Resource Book: *Reading Log, p. 64*

1. **Teacher think aloud** *Say: In the first paragraph, I read that Thomas Jefferson was fascinated with the West. I think Jefferson was curious and liked to learn about new places and things.* Ask students to make their own analyses of characters.
2. **Multi-level options** See MULTI-LEVEL OPTIONS on p. 358.

Answers

1. **a.** Lewis was a good leader and organizer. He was brave and intelligent. **b.** Lewis and Clark were good friends who worked well together. **c.** Clark depended on York and had confidence in him. York was a good servant and a reliable person. **d.** Sacagawea was probably friendly and respectful of other people. She was strong and intelligent.

ASSESS

Have students choose a favorite character in the reading and write two sentences describing the person.

Home Connection

Ask students to take notes during a family meal or other family event. Tell them to use their notes to write dialogue for the conversation. Ask students to enlist family members to act out the conversation, using the script they've written. Tell students to ask their family members to evaluate the accuracy of the script.

Learning Styles *Musical*

Have students add music to their character analyses. Tell students to think about one of the characters from the selection. Ask them to select a song or other piece of music that they think matches the character. For example, students may choose the theme from "Indiana Jones" for Lewis, since he was an adventurer. Have students present their song selections to the class.

UNIT 6 • CHAPTER 1
Beyond the Reading

Word Study

Use a Thesaurus and a Synonym Finder to Find Synonyms

Teacher Resource Book: *Personal Dictionary, p. 63*

Use multiple reference aids Have students use a print, online, and CD-ROM thesaurus or synonym finder to clarify the meaning and usage of: *lead, goal, supplies, attack.*

Answers
Examples: supplies: provisions, food; attack: assault, start a fight

Grammar Focus

Use Appositives

Explain terms Write on the board: *Mr. Lima, the art teacher, likes to draw and paint.* Point out the appositive and explain its function. Have students create sentences with appositives about people in class or the school.

Answers
1. The author can use appositives to give an explanation.
2. During their first winter, . . . and his Shoshone wife, Sacagawea, to act . . .

ASSESS

Have students write two sentences about friends using appositives.

Word Study

Use a Thesaurus and a Synonym Finder to Find Synonyms

Synonyms are words that have similar meanings. A **thesaurus** and a **synonym finder** list synonyms for words. These resources are arranged in alphabetical order. Synonyms are listed after the key word that you look up.

Jefferson chose Meriwether Lewis to lead the expedition.

The entry for the word *lead* in a thesaurus or a synonym finder might be:

lead guide, show the way, direct, escort, pilot, go in front, head

The chart below lists words in the reading that you could replace with synonyms.

1. Find synonyms for each word in a thesaurus or a synonym finder.
2. Write the words and their synonyms in your Personal Dictionary.

Word in Reading	Synonyms
goal	aim, target
supplies	
attack	

Personal Dictionary

Activity Book p. 188

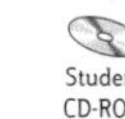
Student CD-ROM

Grammar Focus

Use Appositives

An **appositive** is a word or phrase that follows a noun in order to give extra information about it.

Lewis chose a fellow army captain, his friend William Clark, to share command.

The expedition included York, Clark's childhood friend.

You use a comma before and after an appositive if it is in the middle of a sentence. If an appositive comes at the end of a sentence, use a comma at the beginning of the appositive and a period at the end.

1. Why do you think it is helpful for the author to use appositives?
2. Find another example of an appositive in paragraph 6.

Activity Book pp. 189–190

Student Handbook

Student CD-ROM

MULTI-LEVEL OPTIONS *From Reading to Writing*

Newcomer On the board, write: *trip. Say: When you visit another city, you take a* trip. Display images of a boat, airplane, train, and car. Point to each picture. ***Ask:*** *Who has been on one of these?* Have students draw a picture of the last place they visited with their family.

Beginning Write on the board: *I took a trip to _____.* Have students fill in the blank. ***Ask:*** *What did you see and do?* Help students list their responses. Have them put the events in order. Ask them to write sentences describing their trip, using time words such as *first, next,* and *finally.*

Intermediate Have students create a pre-writing graphic organizer, such as a timeline, flowchart, or story map. Ask students to use the information in their organizer as they write.

Advanced Have students exchange papers for peer editing. Partners should check for time words, adjectives, adverbs, punctuation, capitalization, and tone. Ask students to revise their stories as necessary.

From Reading to Writing 

Write an Informational Text

Write about a trip you have taken.

1. List the order of events on a piece of paper.
2. Choose the five most important events to include, and write a short paragraph about each.
3. Use chronological order to put the events in the order that they happened. Use time words to help readers understand the chronology.
4. Don't use dialogue. Simply summarize what happened.
5. Exchange your work with a partner after you write a draft. Proofread each other's writing.
6. Discuss how you and your partner can improve your work. Edit and revise your writing as needed.

Activity Book p. 191

Across Content Areas 

Use Headings as You Read

Headings are words in large type. The first word and all important words are capitalized. They are titles for a section of text. You can use headings to locate information as you research.

Read the headings on this page. What do you think the page is about?

On a piece of paper, match the sentences with the heading under which they would go.

1. The earliest European visitors were the Spanish.
2. These people lived in all regions of North America before Europeans arrived.
3. One major French area was called Louisiana.
4. The English established colonies on the east coast of the continent.

People in the Americas

Native Americans

Xxx xx xxxxxx x xxx xxxxx. Xxxx xxx, xx xxx. X xxxx x xxx xxxxxx, xxx x xx xxxxx.

The Spanish

Xxx xx xxxxxx x xxx xxxxx. Xxxx xxx, xx xxx. X xxxx x xxx xxxxxx, xxx x xx xxxxx.

The English

Xxx xx xxxxxx x xxx xxxxx. Xxxx xxx, xx xxx. X xxxx x xxx xxxxxx, xxx x xx xxxxx.

The French

Xxx xx xxxxxx x xxx xxxxx. Xxxx xxx, xx xxx. X xxxx x xxx xxxxxx, xxx x xx xxxxx.

Activity Book p. 192

From Reading to Writing

Write an Informational Text

Teacher Resource Book: *Timelines, p. 39; Chronological Order, p. 50*

1. **Use a graphic organizer** Have students create a timeline to record the events of their trip. Arrange students in pairs to tell each other about their trips. Instruct them to ask each other questions to learn more details about their partners' trips.
2. **Write a draft** During the writing process, remind students to use time expressions.
3. **Multi-level options** See MULTI-LEVEL OPTIONS on p. 360.

Across Content Areas: Social Studies

Use Headings as You Read

Share experiences Have students recall what headings are and how they have used them before (p. 31 "Antarctic Adventure, " or p. 319 "Hearing: The Ear"). Direct attention to the examples in the book, pointing out the boldface, capital letters, and large type.

Answers

1. The Spanish; 2. Native Americans; 3. The French; 4. The English

ASSESS

Ask: What is a heading? How can you use headings?

Reteach and Reassess

Text Structure Have students form four groups. Assign each group a text feature (setting, events, chronology, time sequence). Ask each group to prepare and present a definition or description of their assigned feature and provide examples from the selection.

Reading Strategy Ask groups of students to create timelines that show the chronology of the selection.

Elements of Literature Ask students to choose one of the characters from the selection. Have students present oral analyses of their characters. Tell them to complete and ***say:*** *My name is _____. On the expedition, I _____. I would describe myself as _____.*

Reassess Ask students to summarize each section of the selection (Jefferson forms expedition; the journey; results). Tell students to briefly restate the most important ideas in their own words.

Chapter Materials

Activity Book: *pp. 193–200*
Audio: *Unit 6, Chapter 2*
Student Handbook
Student CD-ROM: *Unit 6, Chapter 2*
Teacher Resource Book: *Lesson Plan, Teacher Resources, Reading Summary, Activity Book Answer Key*
Teacher Resource CD-ROM
Assessment Program: *Quiz, pp. 91–92; Teacher and Student Resources, pp. 115–144*
Assessment CD-ROM
Transparencies
The Heinle Newbury House Dictionary/CD-ROM
Web Site: www.heinle.visions.com

Objectives

Use personal knowledge Read the objectives aloud. **Ask:** *Is fiction about a real or made-up story? What is science fiction? What books, movies, or television programs are science fiction? Do you like it?*

Use Prior Knowledge

Record Ideas About Space Travel

Teacher Resource Book: *Know/Want to Know/Learned Chart (KWL), p. 42*

Gather and organize Have students begin a space travel KWL chart using what they already know from Unit 4 and other sources.

CHAPTER 2

Into the Reading

A Wrinkle in Time

an excerpt from a science fiction novel by Madeleine L'Engle

Objectives

Reading Describe mental images as you read science fiction.

Listening and Speaking Present a story.

Grammar Identify the past perfect tense.

Writing Write a science fiction narrative.

Content Science: Learn about the speed of light.

Use Prior Knowledge

Record Ideas About Space Travel

In Unit 4, you read about astronaut Mae Jemison's travels in space aboard the space shuttle. However, she did not travel to other planets, as the characters in "A Wrinkle in Time" do. What do you know about traveling in space?

1. Copy the Know/Want to Know/Learned Chart on a piece of paper.
2. Fill in the chart. In the first column, list what you know about travel to other planets. In the second column, list what you would like to know. When you learn something new about space travel, write it in the third column.

Space Travel		
Know	**Want to Know**	**Learned**
Astronauts have gone to the moon.	Will astronauts ever go to another planet?	Scientists are developing technology to take people to Mars.

MULTI-LEVEL OPTIONS *Build Vocabulary*

Newcomer Write on the board and **say:** *I get annoyed when my brother hides my books. It really makes me mad.* Point to each word in the sentence as you say it aloud. Then write the sentence on the board without the word *annoyed.* **Ask:** *What word could you use here?* Make a list of familiar synonyms.

Beginning Write on the board and **say:** *I get frustrated when my little brother hides my school bag.* Then **ask:** *What do you think* frustrated *means? How would you feel if your brother or sister took your books?* List their ideas on the board. **Say:** *You can often find the meaning of a word by using context clues.*

Intermediate Ask students to explain to partners how they can use context clues to find the meaning of a word in a sentence. Have pairs brainstorm different kinds of context clues (definitions, examples, explanation, synonyms, etc.). Then have each pair write a definition for *context clues.*

Advanced Write on the board: *evaporate* and *thrust.* Have students look up the definitions of these words and write sentences using the words. Ask them to provide context clues in each sentence. Have students read their sentences to a partner.

Build Background

Travel in Science Fiction

Science fiction stories usually tell about discoveries and inventions that do not exist. For example, people might travel through space in a way that we do not understand today. In this reading, the main character travels through a fifth dimension.

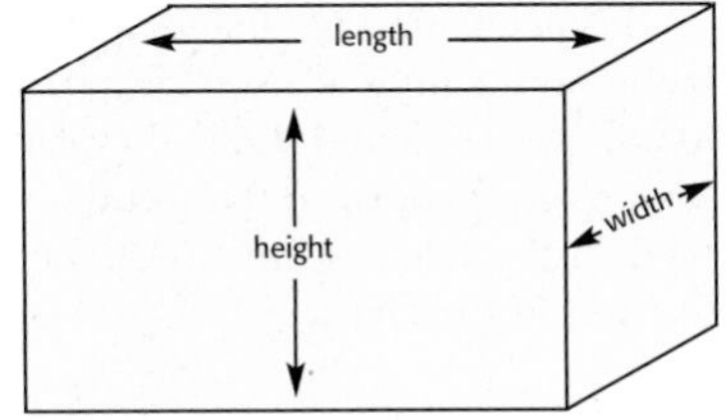

Three dimensions

Content Connection

A **dimension** is a measurement in one direction. In everyday life, we think of three dimensions: length, width, and height. The fourth dimension, studied by the scientist Albert Einstein, is time.

Build Vocabulary

Use Context Clues

You can often guess the meaning of a new word by using **context clues.** Context clues are familiar words in a sentence or nearby sentences that help you understand a new word.

Read the following sentences. There are clues that can help you determine the meaning of the underlined word. In your Personal Dictionary, write the meaning you guess for each underlined word. Check your definitions in a dictionary.

1. Mrs. Who seemed to evaporate until there was nothing but the glasses, and then the glasses, too, disappeared.
2. There was a gust of wind and a great thrust and a sharp shattering as she was shoved through—what?

Personal Dictionary

The Heinle Newbury House Dictionary

Activity Book *p. 193*

Student CD-ROM

Content Connection
Science

Build Vocabulary Ask students to use a science text or other resource to understand the concept of evaporation. ***Ask:*** *Could a human being evaporate? Why not?* Help students understand that liquid evaporates, but some parts of the body, like bones and teeth, are solid, not liquid. Challenge groups to find out what portion of the human body is water. (approximately 2/3 or 66%)

Learning Styles
Visual

Build Background Explain to students that the first three dimensions—length, width, and height—can be represented visually by drawing a shape like the cube on p. 363. ***Ask:*** *If you drew something to represent "time," what would it look like?* Have students create images to represent the idea of time.

Build Background

Travel in Science Fiction

1. **Relate to personal experience** Have students discuss space travel they have seen in movies or TV shows. ***Ask:*** *Where did the people travel? How did they travel? What was different between the movies and real space travel?*
2. **Content Connection** Have students name measurements for the first dimension (inch, foot, meter), second dimension (square inches, square centimeters), third dimension (cubic centimeters, cubic feet). Explain that at this time, fourth and fifth dimensions are theories and cannot be visually represented.

Build Vocabulary

Use Context Clues

Teacher Resource Book: *Personal Dictionary, p. 63*

1. **Teacher think aloud** Write on the board: *With a blast,* the rocket shot into the sky. ***Say:*** *Sometimes I can guess the meanings of new words by looking at the rest of the sentence for clues. I know that a shot makes a lot of noise, so I guess that* blast *means the same thing.*
2. **Reading selection vocabulary** You may want to introduce the glossed words in the reading selection before students begin reading. Key words: *despair, confident, civilization, brief, dissolve, expand and contract, visible, amusement, on purpose.* Instruct students to write the words with correct spelling and their definitions in their Personal Dictionaries. Have them pronounce each word and divide it into syllables.
3. **Multi-level options** See MULTI-LEVEL OPTIONS on p. 362.

Answers
1. to disappear **2.** a big push

Have students write sentences using the vocabulary words.

Text Structure

Science Fiction

1. **Use a graphic organizer to define and explain features** Copy the feature chart. Have students contrast science fiction and other types of fiction they have read.
2. **Multi-level options** See MULTI-LEVEL OPTIONS below.

Reading Strategy

Describe Mental Images

Visualize Remind students that they use mental images and visualize in math class by making models or pictures. Point out they can use this same process in reading literature.

ASSESS

Have students describe a scene to show happiness without using the word *happy.*

Text Structure

Science Fiction

Science fiction is a made-up story based on scientific ideas. Using these ideas, science fiction shows the reader what might happen in the future. As you read "A Wrinkle in Time," look for the features in the chart.

Science Fiction	
Characters	may have special powers
Setting	a time and place in the future or where no one has ever been
Scientific Ideas	imaginary ideas and events based on scientific information

Student CD-ROM

Reading Strategy

Describe Mental Images

Writers often try to make you "see" what you are reading about. These **mental images** are part of the pleasure of reading. Mental images also help you remember the characters and events in a story.

In "A Wrinkle in Time," Meg and her friend, Calvin, are going to do something that frightens Meg. The author writes:

> "Could we hold hands?" Meg asks.
>
> Calvin took her hand and held it tightly in his.

What mental image do you see when you read these lines? As you read the selection, pay attention to the mental images that you see.

Student CD-ROM

MULTI-LEVEL OPTIONS *Text Structure*

Newcomer Using visuals and gestures to illustrate, ***say:*** *The spaceship landed on my front lawn. The door slowly opened and strange-looking people came out. All of a sudden, one pointed a finger at me and I lifted up off the ground.* ***Ask:*** *Could this really happen or is it science fiction?*

Beginning Ask small groups to brainstorm words and ideas that might be used in a science fiction story. Provide blank Science Fiction Charts. Have students use their ideas to complete the charts. Then ask the groups to orally improvise brief science fiction plots.

Intermediate Have partners describe science fiction TV shows, movies, or books they've experienced. Have students evaluate their partners' descriptions using the Science Fiction Chart on p. 364. ***Ask:*** *Did your partner's example contain the features of science fiction?*

Advanced Have students use the chart to brainstorm ideas they can use to write plot summaries for science fiction stories. Have them peer edit the summaries for transitions and time words. Remind students that science fiction does use real scientific information.

A Wrinkle in Time

an excerpt from a science fiction novel
by Madeleine L'Engle

Reading Selection Materials

Audio: *Unit 6, Chapter 2*
Teacher Resource Book: *Reading Summary, pp. 113–114*

Preview the Selection

1. **Use the illustration** Have students describe the scene. Use guiding questions to help students make predictions about the picture and the people in it. ***Ask:*** *What are the children looking at? Why do you think they are looking at the stars? Do you think they will go to the stars or other planets? Why or why not? Are they old enough to travel like that by themselves?*
2. **Connect** Remind students that the unit theme is *frontiers.* ***Ask:*** *Why do you think space is called a frontier?*

Content Connection *Technology*

Tell students that many books, movies, and television shows have plots about space travel. Long ago, the topic was considered science fiction, but it is now a reality. Ask students to think of other ideas that were once science fiction but now exist. (cell phones, personal computers, etc.) Then ask what technologies may become reality in their lifetimes. ("warp" speed space travel; moon colony; etc.)

Learning Styles *Intrapersonal*

Ask: *Have you ever read a science fiction book or story? Have you ever watched a science fiction movie or television show? Did you like it? Why or why not? In general, do you like science fiction stories? Why or why not?* Ask students to write brief essays about their opinions of the science fiction genre. Tell students to include facts and examples that support their opinions.

UNIT 6 • CHAPTER 2
Reading Selection

Read the Selection

1. **Use text features** Direct students to the prologue. Ask them to describe the images in the illustration. Remind students to use the glossed words and the other features to help understanding.
2. **Teacher read aloud** Read the selection aloud. Pause to check understanding and to identify characters, setting, and problem.
3. **Describe mental images** Ask volunteers to act out how Meg and the others would look if they had no hope and if they were afraid.

Sample Answer to Guide Question
I think Meg's eyes would be wide open and she would try to move back from the others.

See Teacher Edition pp. 434–435 for a list of English-Spanish cognates in the reading selection.

Audio

Prologue

Meg and her brother Charles Wallace are looking for their father, who is a scientist. He disappeared while doing top secret work on something called a tesseract, which is a way to travel through dimensions. Three mysterious women appear, who call themselves Mrs. Which, Mrs. Who, and Mrs. Whatsit. They take Meg, Charles Wallace, and their friend Calvin across space and time to look for the missing man. Meg is losing hope. Note Mrs. Which's speech: She repeats sounds in words.

1 "My child, do not **despair.** Do you think we would have brought you here if there were no hope? We are asking you to do a difficult thing, but we are **confident** that you can do it. Your father needs help, he needs courage, and for his children he may be able to do what he cannot do for himself."

2 "Nnow," Mrs. Which said. "Aare wee rreaddy?"

3 "Where are we going?" Calvin asked.

Describe Mental Images

Imagine how Meg looked as she felt her fear.

4 Again Meg felt an actual physical tingling of fear as Mrs. Which spoke.

5 "Wwee musstt ggo bbehindd thee sshaddow."

6 "But we will not do it all at once," Mrs. Whatsit comforted them. "We will do it in short **stages.**" She looked at Meg. "Now we will **tesser,** we will wrinkle again. Do you understand?"

7 "No," Meg said flatly.

---

despair feel hopeless
confident with strong belief in one's ability or that something will definitely happen
stages periods of time
tesser use a tesseract to travel

MULTI-LEVEL OPTIONS *Read the Selection*

Newcomer Play the audio. Read the pages aloud. ***Ask:*** *Does their father need help?* (yes) *At first, does Meg understand what they are going to do?* (no) *Does Mrs. Who speak in Spanish?* (yes)

Beginning Read the Reading Summary aloud. Then ***ask:*** *Who needs the children's help?* (Charles and Meg's father) *Where are they going to go?* (behind the shadow) *Who felt a tingling of fear?* (Meg) *What does Mrs. Who use to explain the trip?* (her skirt)

Intermediate Have students do a paired reading. ***Ask:*** *Why are the children upset?* (their father is missing) *Why is it hard for Mrs. Whatsit to explain tessering?* (There are no words for what she is talking about.) *How does tessering compare to moving at light speed?* (faster)

Advanced Have students read silently. ***Ask:*** *What do you learn in paragraph 1?* (Mr. Wallace has to do something he's afraid to do, but he might find the courage if it would help his children.) *How did the skirt explanation help you understand?* (I could picture the idea in my mind.)

8 Mrs. Whatsit sighed. "Explanations are not easy when they are about things for which your **civilization** still has no words. Calvin talked about traveling at the speed of light. You understand that, little Meg?"

9 "Yes," Meg nodded.

10 "That, of course, is the **impractical,** long way around. We have learned to take short cuts wherever possible."

11 "Sort of like math?" Meg asked.

12 "Like in math." Mrs. Whatsit looked over at Mrs. Who. "Take your skirt and show them."

13 "*La experiencia es la madre de la ciencia.* Spanish, my dears. Cervantes. *Experience is the mother of knowledge.*" Mrs. Who took a **portion** of her white robe in her hands and held it tight.

14 "You see," Mrs. Whatsit said, "if a very small insect were to move from the section of skirt in Mrs. Who's right hand to that in her left, it would be quite a long walk for him if he had to walk straight across."

15 Swiftly Mrs. Who brought her hands, still holding the skirt, together.

16 "Now, you see," Mrs. Whatsit said, "he would *be* there, without that long trip. That is how we travel."

Describe Mental Images

What image of Mrs. Who do you have in this paragraph?

civilization a high level of government, laws, written language, art, music, and so on, within a society or culture

impractical not practical, not sensible

portion a small piece of a larger thing

Spelling

The f sound using f, ph, gh

Explain to students that the *f* sound can be spelled **f** or **ph.** Write on the board and ***say:*** *telephone.* ***Ask:*** *What letters spell the* f *sound in this word?* (ph) Write and ***say:*** *after.* ***Ask:*** *What letter spells the* f *sound in this word?* (f) Remind students that sometimes the *f* sound is spelled **gh,** as in *cough, laugh, enough,* and *rough.*

Apply Ask students to find and list the words that have the *f* sound in paragraphs 1–4. Tell them to underline the letter or letters that spell the *f* sound in each word. (if, difficult, confident, father, for, felt, physical, fear)

Read the Selection

1. **Understand terms** Have students find the meaning of the italicized phrase in the selection. Clarify meanings of glossed words as needed.
2. **Use the illustration** Remind students to use the illustration to clarify understanding.
3. **Provide background** Miguel de Cervantes was a Spanish author. He wrote the first modern novel, *Don Quixote,* in 1605.
4. **Paired reading** Play the audio. Then have students reread in pairs. ***Ask:*** *What is a shortcut?* (a short, quicker way to do something) *How does Mrs. Who make the insect's long trip into a short trip?* (by moving her robe so it doesn't have to walk the whole way)
5. **Draw conclusions** ***Ask:*** *Are the women from the same civilization or place as Meg and the two boys?* (no) *How do you know?* (Mrs. Whatsit says, ". . . your civilization. . . ." She also talks about how "we travel," which is different from the children's way of traveling.)
6. **Multi-level options** See MULTI-LEVEL OPTIONS on p. 366.

Sample Answer to Guide Question

I think Mrs. Who is a very smart person who likes to explain difficult ideas and concepts by demonstrating them with everyday items.

Read the Selection

1. **Use the illustration** Ask students to describe the people in the picture and predict what Charles and Meg are talking about.
2. **Shared reading** Play the audio. Have volunteers read aloud portions.
3. **Make predictions** Have students reread the selection in small groups. Review the dimensions that Charles Wallace explains. *Ask: What do you think he will explain now?* (the fourth dimension)

Sample Answer to Guide Question
He puts his head down a little and maybe turns a little bit red.

17 Charles Wallace accepted the explanation **serenely.** Even Calvin did not seem **perturbed.** "Oh, *dear,*" Meg sighed. "I guess I *am* a moron. I just don't get it."

18 "That is because you think of space only in three dimensions," Mrs. Whatsit told her. "We travel in the fifth dimension. This is something you can understand, Meg. Don't be afraid to try. Was your mother able to explain a tesseract to you?"

19 "Well, she never did," Meg said. "She got so upset about it. Why, Mrs. Whatsit? She said it had something to do with her and Father."

20 "It was a **concept** they were playing with," Mrs. Whatsit said, "going beyond the fourth dimension to the fifth. Did your mother explain it to you, Charles?"

Describe Mental Images

Charles is embarrassed. How does he look?

21 "Well, yes," Charles looked a little embarrassed. "Please don't be hurt, Meg. I just kept at her while you were at school till I got it out of her."

22 Meg sighed. "Just explain it to me."

23 "Okay," Charles said. "What is the first dimension?"

24 "Well—a line: ————"

25 "Okay. And the second dimension?"

26 "Well, you'd square the line. A flat square would be in the second dimension."

27 "And the third?"

28 "Well, you'd square the second dimension. Then the square wouldn't be flat any more. It would have a bottom, and sides, and a top."

serenely very calmly, peacefully
perturbed upset, flustered
concept a general idea

MULTI-LEVEL OPTIONS *Read the Selection*

Newcomer *Did Meg understand Mrs. Whatsit's explanation?* (no) *Do the women travel in the fifth dimension?* (yes) *Is time the fourth dimension?* (yes) *Is the fifth dimension a tesseract?* (yes) *Does Charles think the shortest distance between two points is always a line?* (no)

Beginning *Who understands Mrs. Whatsit's explanation?* (Charles, Calvin) *Who doesn't understand?* (Meg) *How does Meg think of space?* (in three dimensions) *Who explained a tesseract to Meg?* (Charles) *What is the fourth dimension?* (time)

Intermediate *Why did Meg call herself a moron?* (Charles and Calvin understood the explanation, but she didn't.) *Who explained a tesseract to Charles?* (his mother) *What happens when you add a tesseract to the first four dimensions?* (time travel)

Advanced *Does Meg discover why a tesseract upset her mother?* (no) *How did Charles learn what a tesseract is?* (He bugged his mother until she told him.) *Why did Meg get excited?* (For a brief moment, she understood the concept of tesseracting.)

29 "And the fourth?"

30 "Well, I guess if you want to put it into mathematical terms you'd square the square. But you can't take a pencil and draw it the way you can the first three. I know it's got something to do with Einstein and time. I guess maybe you could call the fourth dimension Time."

31 "That's right," Charles said. "Good girl. Okay, then, for the fifth dimension you'd square the fourth, wouldn't you?"

32 "I guess so."

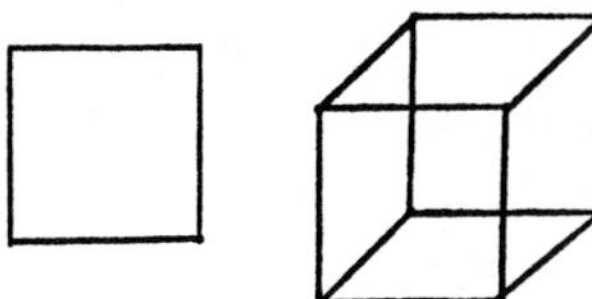

33 "Well, the fifth dimension's a tesseract. You add that to the other four dimensions and you can travel through space without having to go the long way around. In other words, to put it into Euclid, or old-fashioned plane **geometry,** a straight line is *not* the shortest distance between two points."

34 For a **brief illuminating** second Meg's face had the listening, probing expression that was so often seen on Charles's. "I see!" she cried. "I got it! For just a moment I got it! I can't possibly explain it now, but there for a second I saw it!" She turned excitedly to Calvin. "Did you get it?"

Describe Mental Images

What image of Meg do you have in this paragraph?

geometry the mathematical study of lines, angles, shapes, and so on

brief short

illuminating giving light to

UNIT 6 • CHAPTER 2
Reading Selection

Read the Selection

1. **Understand terms** Have students find the meaning of the glossed words in the selection. Clarify as needed.
2. **Use the illustration** Have students explain which of the dimensions are pictured. (second dimension and third dimension)
3. **Provide background** Euclid of Alexandria was the most prominent mathematician of ancient times. He was born around 325 B.C. In his book, *The Elements,* he explained the basic properties of triangles, parallels, rectangles, and squares.
4. **Shared reading** Play the audio and have volunteers read portions of the selection aloud. Pause occasionally to ask comprehension questions. Explain who Albert Einstein (created the Theory of Relativity, $E = MC^2$) and Euclid (father of modern geometry) were. Then have students reread the selection in pairs. ***Ask:*** *What did Einstein call the fourth dimension?* (time) *What is a tesseract?* (the fifth dimension)
5. **Analyze characters** ***Ask:*** *Do you think Charles Wallace and Meg have studied a lot of math and science?* (yes) *Why do you think so?* (They know about Albert Einstein, Euclid, geometry, and other things in math. Also, their father is a scientist.)
6. **Multi-level options** See MULTI-LEVEL OPTIONS on p. 368.

Sample Answer to Guide Question

I think Meg looks happy because she understands. She's smiling and her eyes are wide open with happiness.

Spelling

Ordinal numbers

Review the spellings of the words *one, two, three, four,* and *five.* Write on the board and ***say:*** *1st, 2nd, 3rd, 4th,* and *5th.* Tell students that these are called ordinal numbers and that they have their own words to name them. Write and ***say:*** *first.* Repeat for *second, third, fourth,* and *fifth.*

Apply Have students spell the ordinal numbers to complete the following sentences. Write: **1.** *(3rd) That's the _____ time I told you!* **2.** *(1st) Pélé won a trophy for _____ place at the science fair.* **3.** (2nd) *Elena got a ribbon for _____ place.* **4.** (4th, 5th) *Is the assembly during _____ or _____ period today?*

Read the Selection

1. **Use the illustration** Ask students to describe Meg and guess what she is feeling and why she might feel that way.
2. **Shared reading** Play the audio and have volunteers read aloud portions.
3. **Summarize** Have students reread the selection in small groups. Ask questions to help them summarize the events and to make suggestions about what will happen next.

Sample Answer to Guide Question
I see them slowly disappearing, like a ghost or a shadow that is very clear but then gets lighter and lighter.

35 He nodded. "Enough. I don't understand it the way Charles Wallace does, but enough to get the idea."

36 "Sso nnow wee ggo," Mrs. Which said. "Tthere iss nott all thee ttime in the worrlld."

37 "Could we hold hands?" Meg asked.

38 Calvin took her hand and held it tightly in his.

39 "You can try," Mrs. Whatsit said, "though I'm not sure how it will work. You see, though we travel together, we travel alone. We will go first and take you afterward in the backwash. That may be easier for you." As she spoke the great white body began to **waver,** the wings to **dissolve** into **mist.** Mrs. Who seemed to **evaporate** until there was nothing but the glasses, and then the glasses, too, disappeared. It reminded Meg of the **Cheshire Cat.**

Describe Mental Images

What do you "see" in your mind as Mrs. Whatsit and Mrs. Who disappear?

waver become unsteady
dissolve disappear slowly
mist a cloudy haze
evaporate change into a gas
Cheshire Cat a character in the story *Alice in Wonderland;* the Cheshire Cat faded slowly until the only thing left was his smile

MULTI-LEVEL OPTIONS *Read the Selection*

Newcomer *Does Calvin understand?* (yes) *Does Meg want to hold hands because she is afraid?* (yes) *Did Mrs. Whatsit disappear first?* (yes) *Did Mrs. Who remind Meg of the Cheshire Cat?* (yes) *Was Meg surprised by the nothingness?* (no)

Beginning *Who wanted to hold hands?* (Meg) *Who held Meg's hand?* (Calvin) *Who disappeared first?* (Mrs. Whatsit) *What part of Mrs. Who disappeared last?* (her glasses) *What did it remind Meg of?* (the Cheshire Cat) *What did Meg feel after her journey?* (Calvin's hand in hers)

Intermediate *What does Mrs. Whatsit say about holding hands?* (They can try, but everyone travels alone.) *Why are the women going to take the children in the backwash?* (It may be easier for them.) *How did Meg know when the journey was almost over?* (She felt Calvin's hand again.)

Advanced *How well does Calvin understand tessering?* (not as well as Charles) *Why do you think Meg wants to hold hands?* (She's still a little afraid.) *Was that the first time Meg tessered? How do you know?* (No; the phrase "this time she was prepared")

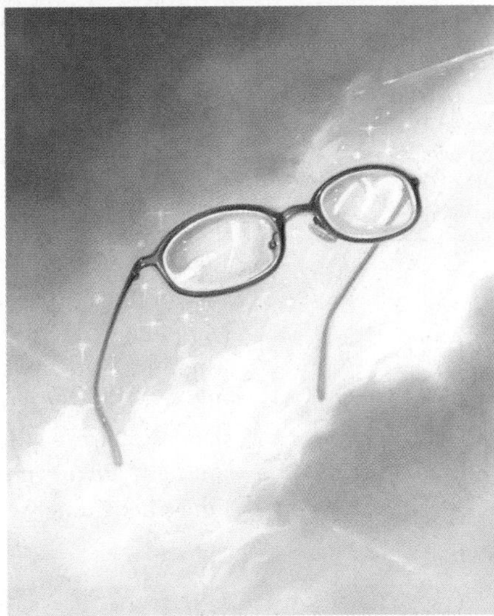

40 —I've often seen a face without glasses, she thought—but glasses without a face! I wonder if I go that way, too. First me and then my glasses?

41 She looked over at Mrs. Which. Mrs. Which was there and then she wasn't.

Describe Mental Images

What do you "see" happening to Meg in the first sentence of this paragraph?

42 There was a gust of wind and a great thrust and a sharp shattering as she was shoved through—what? Then darkness; silence; nothingness. If Calvin was still holding her hand she could not feel it. But this time she was prepared for the sudden and complete **dissolution** of her body. When she felt the tingling coming back to her fingertips she knew that this journey was almost over and she could feel again the pressure of Calvin's hand about hers.

---

dissolution slow disappearance

Read the Selection

1. **Use the illustration** Have students explain the illustration, reminding them to look back at p. 370 as needed. Ask them how they would feel if they saw a pair of glasses hanging in the air.
2. **Paired reading** Play the audio. Then have students reread in pairs.
3. **Identify character feelings** Have students consider how they would feel if suddenly everything were dark and there were no noise and they couldn't feel anything. ***Ask:*** *Would you feel worried? Nervous? Scared? How do you think Meg felt when this happened to her?*
4. **Multi-level options** See MULTI-LEVEL OPTIONS on p. 370.

Sample Answer to Guide Question

I see Meg starting to fade and then moving very quickly like a leaf in the wind.

A Capitalization

Titles

Write on the board and ***say:*** *Mr., Ms., Mrs.,* and *Miss.* Tell students that these are called titles and they come before people's names. Remind students that titles are part of names, and so they must always be capitalized. Direct students to paragraph 36. ***Ask:*** *Why is* Mrs. *capitalized?* (It's a title and part of a name.) Do you see any other titles on this page? (paragraph 39: Mrs. Whatsit and Mrs. Who)

Apply Have students correct the following sentences by capitalizing any titles. Write on the board:

My math teacher's name is ms. Qwan.

My soccer coach, mr. Ramirez, says that I am a good goalie.

After miss Ross gets married, her name will be mrs. Bellamy.

Read the Selection

1. **Use the illustration** Direct students to the illustration. Ask them to describe the people. *Ask: Do they look like real people or flat pictures?*
2. **Shared reading** Play the audio and have volunteers read portions aloud. *Ask: How does Meg feel?* (strange) *Why?* (She is flat because she's become two-dimensional.)
3. **Analyze facts** Have students reread the selection in small groups. Ask them to find different parts of the body that could not function correctly on the two-dimensional planet.

Sample Answer to Guide Question
I see her being pressed down like a paper doll, and she can't breathe.

Describe Mental Images

What do you "see" happening to Meg in the first two sentences of this paragraph?

43 Without warning, coming as a complete and unexpected shock, she felt a **pressure** she had never imagined, as though she were being completely flattened out by an enormous steamroller. This was far worse than the nothingness had been; while she was nothing there wa no need to breathe, but now her lungs were squeezed together so that although she was dying for want of air there was no way for her lungs to **expand and contract,** to take in the air that she must have to stay alive. This was completely different from the thinning of atmosphere when they flew up the mountain and she had had to put flowers to her face to breathe. She tried to gasp, but a paper doll can't gasp. She thought she was trying to think, but her flattened-out mind was as unable to **function** as he lungs; her thoughts were squashed along with the rest of her. Her heart tried to beat; it gave a knifelike, sidewise movement, but it could not expand.

44 But then she seemed to hear a voice, or if not a voice, at least words, words flattened out like printed words on paper: "Oh no! We can't stop here! This is a *two*-dimensiona planet and the children can't manage here!"

pressure weight
expand and contract take air in and out
function work

MULTI-LEVEL OPTIONS *Read the Selection*

Newcomer *Did Meg feel flat?* (yes) *Could the children manage on the two-dimensional planet?* (no) *Did they stop there?* (no) *Was Meg relieved when they left the two-dimensional planet?* (yes) *When the trip was over, was Calvin still holding Meg's hand?* (yes)

Beginning *How did Meg feel on the two-dimensional planet?* (like she was being flattened by a steamroller) *How did Meg feel when they left the two-dimensional planet?* (relieved) *Who did Meg think she heard talking?* (Charles Wallace) *Who was standing beside Meg when the trip was over?* (Calvin)

Intermediate *Why couldn't they stop at the two-dimensional planet?* (The children couldn't survive.) *Why was Meg relieved when they left the two-dimensional planet?* (She didn't feel flattened.) *How did Meg know that the women were there?* (She could feel their presence.)

Advanced *Why couldn't the children survive on the two-dimensional planet?* (They are three-dimensional beings.) *How does Calvin feel by the time the trip is over? How do you know?* (afraid; he's holding Meg's hand tightly.) *Why is Charles angry?* (He knows the danger they faced.)

45 She was whizzed into nothingness again, and nothingness was wonderful. She did not mind that she could not feel Calvin's hand, that she could not see or feel or be. The relief from the **intolerable** pressure was all she needed.

46 Then the tingling began to come back to her fingers, her toes; she could feel Calvin holding her tightly. Her heart beat regularly; blood **coursed** through her veins. Whatever had happened, whatever mistake had been made, it was over now. She thought she heard Charles Wallace saying, his words round and full as spoken words ought to be, "*Really*, Mrs. Which, you might have killed us!"

47 This time she was pushed out of the frightening fifth dimension with a sudden, immediate **jerk.** There she was, herself again, standing with Calvin beside her, holding on to her hand for dear life, and Charles Wallace in front of her, looking **indignant.** Mrs. Whatsit, Mrs. Who, and Mrs. Which were not **visible,** but she knew they were there; the fact of their presence was strong about her.

Describe Mental Images

Meg's trip is over. What mental image do you have?

intolerable difficult or painful
coursed flowed
jerk a quick, sharp movement
indignant angry because of unfairness
visible able to be seen

Read the Selection

1. **Understand terms** Have students find the meanings of the glossed words. Clarify as needed.
2. **Use the illustration** Ask students if the characters are still two-dimensional or if they look normal again.
3. **Shared reading** Play the audio and have volunteers read the paragraphs aloud.
4. **Draw conclusions** Ask students to explain why the three women are invisible. ***Ask:*** *How do the children know the three women are there?* (Charles Wallace is talking to them.) *Why do you think they can't see the women?* (Maybe people cannot see things in the fifth dimension because it cannot be drawn on paper.)
5. **Multi-level options** See MULTI-LEVEL OPTIONS on p. 372.

Sample Answer to Guide Question

I think Meg is glad the trip is over and she feels normal again.

Spelling

Silent h

Tell students that for many words that begin with *wh-*, the *h* is silent. Write on the board and ***say:*** *who, what, where.* ***Ask:*** *What sound do you hear at the beginning of each of these words?* (the *w* sound) *What sound does the h make in each word?* (None; it's silent in each word.)

Apply Write on the board: *when, why, whether, whatever, whenever, whoever, which, wheel, white, whale, whip, whisper,* and *whistle.* Ask students to copy the list and circle the silent *h* in each word. Then ask students to look in the dictionary to find additional words that begin with *wh-* where the *h* is silent. (whimper, while, whirl, etc.)

UNIT 6 • CHAPTER 2 Reading Selection

Read the Selection

1. **Use the illustration** Ask students to describe the women and their expressions. Have students suggest what they are saying.
2. **Provide background** Prospero is the lead character in *The Tempest,* a play by William Shakespeare, written in 1611. The phrase "We are such stuff as dreams are made on" is from the end of the play.
3. **Shared reading** Read the selection aloud. Have volunteers read aloud portions. ***Ask:*** *What is Mrs. Whatsit wearing?* (shawls, scarves, old coat, and hat) *Do the women have bodies like the children?* (no)
4. **Summarize** Have students reread the selection in small groups and summarize up to this point. ***Say:*** *Mrs. Who talks about dreams. Do you think the children are dreaming all this?*

Sample Answer to Guide Question

She's very kind looking, motioning for them to take it easy. She's soft and gentle.

Describe Mental Images

What image do you have of Mrs. Whatsit?

48 "Cchilldrenn, I appolloggize," came Mrs. Which's voice.

49 "Now, Charles, calm down," Mrs. Whatsit said, appearing not as the great and beautiful beast she had been when they last saw her, but in her familiar wild garb of shawls and scarves and the old tramp's coat and hat. "You know how difficult it is for her to **materialize.** If you are not substantial yourself, it's *very* difficult to realize how limiting **protoplasm** is."

50 "I *ammm* ssorry," Mrs. Which's voice came again; but there was more than a hint of **amusement** in it.

51 "It is *not* funny." Charles Wallace gave a childish stamp of his foot.

52 Mrs. Who's glasses shone out, and the rest of her appeared more slowly behind them. "*We are such stuff as dreams are made on.*" She smiled broadly. "Prospero in *The Tempest.* I *do* like that play."

materialize appear in solid form
protoplasm a sticky liquid found in all living things
amusement entertainment, fun

MULTI-LEVEL OPTIONS *Read the Selection*

Newcomer *Did Mrs. Which apologize?* (yes) *Does Mrs. Whatsit appear as a great and beautiful beast?* (no) *Does Charles stamp his foot?* (yes) *Did they take the children to the two-dimensional planet on purpose?* (no) *Do they go to Orion's Belt?* (yes)

Beginning *Who is dressed in wild clothing?* (Mrs. Whatsit) *Who gets angry with the women?* (Charles) *What part of Mrs. Who reappears first?* (her glasses) *Where do they end up?* (Orion's Belt)

Intermediate *Why does Mrs. Which apologize?* (for taking them to the two-dimensional planet) *What do the women think of the two-dimensional planet?* (pleasant and amusing) *Why do they go to Orion's Belt?* (to see a friend and to look at Earth)

Advanced *How do the women explain their mistake?* (Because they do not have real bodies, they forget that the children are three-dimensional and can only survive in a three-dimensional place.) *Why is Charles angry?* (He thinks the women were trying to hurt them intentionally.)

53 "You didn't do it **on *purpose?*"** Charles demanded.

54 "Oh, my darling, of course not," Mrs. Whatsit said quickly. "It was just a very understandable mistake. It's very difficult for Mrs. Which to think in a **corporeal** way. She wouldn't hurt you **deliberately;** you know that. And it's really a pleasant little planet, and rather amusing to be flat. We always enjoy our visits there."

55 "Where are we now, then?" Charles Wallace demanded. "And why?"

56 "In **Orion's Belt.** We have a friend here, and we want you to have a look at your own planet."

---

on purpose intentionally
corporeal with a body
deliberately on purpose
Orion's Belt part of a constellation of stars visible from Earth

About the Author — Madeleine L'Engle (born 1918)

Madeleine L'Engle was born in New York City. Although L'Engle claims not to know exactly how many books she has written, the number is at least 60, including fiction for children, young adults, and adults. L'Engle is best known for combining fantasy and science fiction. "A Wrinkle in Time" was written in 1962. This book was the first book of three about Meg and her family and friends. Madeleine L'Engle has said, "I have written since I could hold a pencil, much less a pen, and writing for me is an essential function, like sleeping and breathing."

➤ If you could ask Madeleine L'Engle a question about this story, what would it be?

Read the Selection

1. **Use text features** Have students describe the constellation (a group of stars) and guess its significance in the selection. Review meanings of glossed words.
2. **Shared reading** Continue reading the selection. Ask volunteers to read parts. Then have students reread the selection in pairs. *Ask: Are they on Earth?* (no) *Where are they?* (in space, in Orion's Belt)
3. **Make inferences** Ask questions to help students explain why the women enjoy visiting the two-dimensional planet and why the children could not visit there.
4. **Multi-level options** See MULTI-LEVEL OPTIONS on p. 374.

About the Author

Interpret facts Madeleine L'Engle won the Newbury Medal in 1962 and the Lewis Carroll Shelf Award for *A Wrinkle in Time.* ***Ask:*** *What references to science did Madeleine L'Engle use in this story?* (the four dimensions, Orion's Belt) *What are some examples of fantasy in the story?* (traveling by tesseract, people disappearing)

Across Selections

Compare and contrast Have students compare and contrast the expedition of Lewis and Clark with the travels of Meg, Charles Wallace, and Calvin. Ask questions to help students identify similarities and differences.

Punctuation

Italics for emphasis

Review italics with students. Remind students that italics are sometimes used to show emphasis. ***Say:*** *When you read words in italics, say those words with emphasis.* Read paragraph 49 aloud, placing emphasis on the word *very.* Then read the paragraph again, without emphasis. ***Ask:*** *How was that different?* ***Say:*** *Look at paragraph 51. Why is the word* not *written in italics?* Elicit from students that the writer wanted to emphasize the word.

Evaluate Your Reading Strategy

Describe Mental Images ***Say:*** *You have practiced an important reading strategy. Now you can decide how well you have done. Does this statement describe how you read?*

> As I read a story, I pay attention to the mental images that I get from the reading. Mental images can help me enjoy reading, and they can help me remember a story.

Reading Comprehension

Question-Answer Relationships

Sample Answers

1. Meg didn't understand at first, but then she understood for a minute.
2. The second dimension has only length and width—it is flat. The third dimension has depth, so it has volume.
3. in Orion's Belt
4. Meg feels and sees nothing.
5. The tesseract helps them travel long distances in a very short time through shortcuts.
6. This is about some children learning about a new way to travel (tesseract) and then going to a planet far away in an incredibly short time.
7. She fears getting lost by herself in these travels and not knowing exactly where she is.
8. The author had to explain how to travel in space in short time spans. She needed to know a lot about math, geometry, dimensions, and science.
9. The illustrations show the fading and changing that happens during the traveling, or tesseracting.

Build Reading Fluency

Echo Read Aloud

Model reading aloud with expression. Read one line at a time. Ask the class to read (echo) the same line you just read before going on to the next line or sentence.

Beyond the Reading

Reading Comprehension

Question-Answer Relationships (QAR)

"Right There" Questions

1. **Recall Facts** Does Meg understand how they are going to travel?
2. **Recall Facts** What is the difference between the second and the third dimensions?
3. **Recognize Sequence** Where are the children at the end of the selection?

"Think and Search" Questions

4. **Support with Detail** How does Meg feel when she is in the fifth dimension?
5. **Explore the Main Idea** How is a tesseract helpful to the women and children?
6. **Paraphrase Text** How would you tell someone what the selection is about in your own words?

"Author and You" Question

7. **Draw Conclusions** What do you think is Meg's greatest fear?

"On Your Own" Questions

8. **Speculate** What challenges do you think the author faced in writing this story? What do you think she might have needed to know about to write the story?
9. **Analyze Illustrations** How does the style of the illustrations help you to understand the text? (The style of an illustration is how it looks.)

Activity Book p. 194

Student CD-ROM

Build Reading Fluency

Echo Read Aloud

Echo reading helps you learn to read with expression. This is an important characteristic of effective readers. Your teacher will read a line. Then the class reads the same line.

1. Listen to your teacher read a line from "A Wrinkle in Time."
2. Then, read the same line with expression.
3. Continue listening, then reading.

MULTI-LEVEL OPTIONS *Elements of Literature*

Newcomer Turn off the lights to make the classroom dark. Play scary music and read a ghost story. Then ***ask:*** *How did you feel while you listened? What was the mood? Was it scary? Why?* Make a list on the board of things that made the mood scary.

Beginning Use a serious voice and ***say:*** *I use serious words to tell a sad story. What kind of words can be used to tell a funny story? This is called "setting the mood."*

Intermediate Have students work in pairs to find other examples of the mood in the story. ***Ask:*** *How is the mood revealed through the conversation between characters?* Have students list words and phrases that show the mood of the story.

Advanced Have students work independently to rewrite a passage from the story to have a different mood. ***Ask:*** *What words or phrases help to show the mood of your passage?* Have them underline these words or phrases.

Listen, Speak, Interact 

Present a Story

Prepare and present a Reader's Theater performance of a part of the selection.

1. Work in a group of seven students. Six of you will take the role of one of the characters from the reading (Charles, Meg, Calvin, Mrs. Who, Mrs. Which, and Mrs. Whatsit). Group members should read the words that their characters speak. These are the words in quotation marks (" . . . ").
2. The seventh member of the group will be the narrator. The narrator reads the parts between the dialogues.
3. Listen to the audio recording of the part of the selection you will perform. This will help you with pronunciation.
4. Speak loudly enough so that everyone can hear. Use good pitch—not too high or too low. Don't speak too fast. Show feeling.
5. Practice your reading several times.
6. Present your Reader's Theater performance to the class.

Elements of Literature

Understand Mood

An author sometimes sets a **mood** that affects the reader's feelings. The mood may be full of suspense. The reader may not know what is going to happen next. In "A Wrinkle in Time," Madeleine L'Engle sets a mood that makes the reader uneasy (not comfortable) and a little frightened. How does she do this?

1. Read the first two sentences of the selection. What do they tell about Meg's feelings?
2. Notice how different characters talk. Which character in particular seems to make Meg uneasy? Why? How can you tell?
3. Look in the text for other words or phrases that set an uneasy mood in the story. Write them in your Reading Log.
4. Compare your list with your classmates.

Reading Log

Activity Book
p. 195

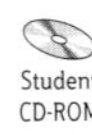
Student CD-ROM

Listen, Speak, Interact

Present a Story

1. **Reread in small groups** Play the audio. Then have students practice their parts. Point out words and expressions that are stressed. Encourage students to add gestures and facial expressions to add to their presentation.
2. **Newcomers** Reread with this group. Have them choose a particular portion of the reading selection for their presentation. Allow time for students to practice and tape record their parts, then listen to and assess their parts before presenting to the entire class.

Elements of Literature

Understand Mood

Teacher Resource Book: *Reading Log, p. 64*

1. **Clarify terms** Review *mood.* Have students suggest different types of feelings and identify the mood set by the author in this story. Have students work in pairs to find words and phrases from the story that show mood.
2. **Multi-level options** See MULTI-LEVEL OPTIONS on p. 376.

Answers

1. Meg thought there was no hope. She felt sad and hopeless.
2. Mrs. Which makes Meg uneasy probably because she speaks differently with the repeated sounds in her words. Meg feels afraid when Mrs. Which speaks.

ASSESS

Have students generate a checklist for presenting stories orally.

Content Connection *Science*

Ask students to use the library or the Internet to research the topic of time travel. Have students locate specific theories related to time and the possibility of time travel. Ask them to write paragraphs that summarize their findings and give their opinions about the likelihood of time travel in their lifetime.

Learning Styles *Linguistic*

Ask students to write journal entries as one of the main characters in the story. Tell them that their entries should describe one of the main events in the story. Remind students to describe their thoughts and feelings as well as the setting and the event.

Word Study

Understand the Prefixes *un-*, *in-*, and *im-*

Teacher Resource Book: *Personal Dictionary, p. 63*

Use a list-group-label Have students brainstorm a list of words with the prefixes. Have students group the words by prefix and label the groups with the prefixes.

Answers
2. un-; expected
3. intolerable
4. in-; tolerable; not tolerable

Grammar Focus

Identify the Past Perfect Tense

Recognize past participles Write on the board: *I had visited the city before we moved here.* Point out *had* and the past participle. Explain that most verbs add *-ed* to make the past participle. Review common irregular forms. Have students use the model on the board to talk about past events.

Answers
paragraph 43: . . . she had had to put . . .
paragraph 49: . . . she had been . . .

ASSESS

Say definitions and have students respond with words using the prefixes *un-*, *in-*, and *im-*.

Word Study

Understand the Prefixes *un-*, *in-*, and *im-*

A **prefix** is a word part added to the beginning of a word. It changes the word's meaning. The prefixes *un-*, *in-*, and *im-* can be added to a word to give it the opposite meaning.

1. In your Personal Dictionary, make a chart like the one shown.
2. Complete the chart for the words shown from "A Wrinkle in Time."
3. Find another word in the selection with one of the prefixes. Look in paragraph 45.
4. Fill in the new word, its prefix, the root word, and the meaning.

Word in Text	Prefix	Root Word	Meaning
impractical	im-	practical	not practical
unexpected	______	______	not expected
______	in-	tolerable	______
______	______	______	______

Personal Dictionary

The Heinle Newbury House Dictionary

Activity Book *p. 196*

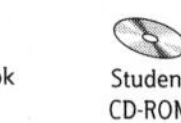
Student CD-ROM

Grammar Focus

Identify the Past Perfect Tense

When authors tell a story that happened in the past, they use different past tenses. The **past perfect tense** is used to talk about actions that have already happened in the story. Here are some examples from the reading selection:

She felt a pressure she had never imagined.

This was far worse than the nothingness had been.

The author uses the word *had* with a past participle form of the verb. It describes feelings Meg had before this point in the story.

Find other examples of the past perfect tense in the story. Look at paragraphs 43 and 49.

Activity Book *pp. 197–198*

Student Handbook

Student CD-ROM

378 **Unit 6** Frontiers

MULTI-LEVEL OPTIONS *From Reading to Writing*

Newcomer Reread the ending of the story aloud. Write on the board: *first* and *next*. ***Ask:*** *What happened first? What might happen next?* Brainstorm ideas for events that could happen next.

Beginning Draw a blank sequence timeline like the one on p. 379. ***Ask:*** *What might happen next if the story continued?* Fill in the sequence timeline as a class. Help students begin a narrative using these ideas. Have small groups continue the narrative. Ask groups to share their endings.

Intermediate Ask pairs of students to list the past and past perfect tenses of as many verbs as they can think of. Have them refer to their lists as they write their science fiction narratives.

Advanced Have students review their science fiction narratives. Tell them to check for openings, closings, mood, dialogue, main ideas, actions, and words and phrases that show sequence. Also tell students to check punctuation, capitalization, and tone. Ask students to revise their stories as necessary.

From Reading to Writing 

Write a Science Fiction Narrative

Suppose that you are Madeleine L'Engle. What would you make happen next in the story?

1. Reread the end of the reading selection. Make a list of things that might happen next. Select the one that you think will make the best story.
2. Make a sequence timeline like the one shown. Write down what you think will happen next. First, write only the main ideas for each board.
3. Use your storyboard to write your narrative.
4. Set the mood by carefully choosing dialogue and actions.
5. Use the past and past perfect tense when appropriate.

Sequence Timeline

1. Meg and Charles Wallace meet Mr. Hunter in Orion.	→	2. Mrs. Whatsit shows them Earth.	→	3. Meg is homesick.	→	4. Meg and Charles Wallace . . .

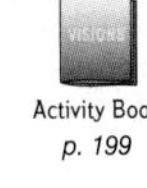

Activity Book p. 199

Across Content Areas 

Learn About the Speed of Light

Physicists are scientists who study the nature of the universe. They say that light always travels at the same speed if it is in a **vacuum.** A vacuum is where nothing exists, as in space.

Physicists have measured the speed of light in a vacuum at 299,792,458 meters per second. Most physicists say that nothing can travel at a speed faster than this.

In July of each year, the sun is about 152,500,000,000 meters from Earth. How many seconds does it take light to get from the sun to Earth in July? Use a calculator or a computer program to help you.

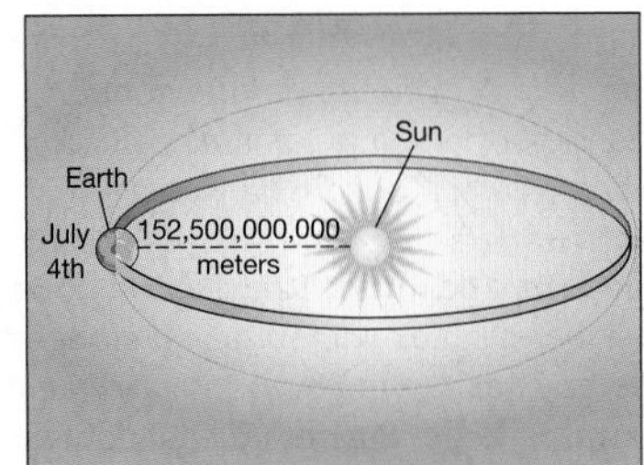

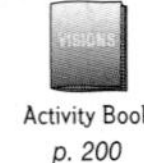

Activity Book p. 200

From Reading to Writing

Write a Science Fiction Narrative

1. **Organize information** Have students create a sequence timeline for the main events in their story. Arrange students in pairs to share their story ideas. Have them ask each other questions to learn more details about the characters, setting, and events.
2. **Write a draft** Remind students to use dialogue.
3. **Multi-level options** See MULTI-LEVEL OPTIONS on p. 378.

Across Content Areas: Science

Learn About the Speed of Light

Explain terms Read the information aloud. Clarify the meanings of boldfaced words. Call attention to the illustration to help understanding. Help students with the numbers.

Answer

152,500,000,000 meters ÷ 299,792,458 meters/second = approx. 509 seconds

ASSESS

Round off the speed of light to the nearest hundred million. (300,000,000 meters per second)

Reteach and Reassess

Text Structure Draw a two-column chart on the board. Label the rows: *Characters, Setting,* and *Scientific Ideas.* Ask students to suggest examples from the story to complete the chart.

Reading Strategy Ask students to draw pictures of the mental images they formed when they read about the two-dimensional planet.

Elements of Literature Have pairs review an earlier selection in the book, such as "The Miracle Worker" (p. 209) or "The Library Card" (p. 228). Ask pairs to describe the mood of the selection and to list words and phrases the author used to create that mood.

Reassess Ask students to present brief critiques of the story. Tell them to include a summary, interesting details, and whether they would recommend the story to another reader.

Chapter Materials

Activity Book: *pp. 201–208*
Audio: *Unit 6, Chapter 3*
Student Handbook
Student CD-ROM: *Unit 6, Chapter 3*
Teacher Resource Book: *Lesson Plan, Teacher Resources, Reading Summary, Activity Book Answer Key*
Teacher Resource CD-ROM
Assessment Program: *Quiz, pp. 93–94; Teacher and Student Resources, pp. 115–144*
Assessment CD-ROM
Transparencies
The Heinle Newbury House Dictionary/CD-ROM
Web Site: www.heinle.visions.com

Objectives

Paired reading Have students work in pairs and take turns reading the objectives section. Explain and point out key words. ***Ask:*** *What speeches have we read?*

Use Prior Knowledge

Explore Freedom

1. **Brainstorm** Ask students to read the definitions. Then have them brainstorm a list of U.S. constitutional freedoms. (speech, press, assembly, religion)
2. **Compare and contrast** Have students complete freedom charts. Then ask them to compare their ideas in pairs.

Into the Reading

CHAPTER 3

I Have a Dream

an excerpt from a speech by Martin Luther King Jr.

Objectives

Reading Draw conclusions with text evidence as you read a speech.

Listening and Speaking Present a speech.

Grammar Use dependent clauses with *that*.

Writing Write a persuasive speech.

Content Social Studies: Learn about the United States Constitution.

Use Prior Knowledge

Explore Freedom

Read the pronunciations and definitions of **free** and **freedom.**

free /fri/ *adj.* **1** not under the control of another person or institution: *After twenty years in prison, he was a free man.*
freedom /ˈfridəm/ *n.* **1** having the power to act and speak without being stopped: *The boy has the freedom to go where he wants to go.* **2** a set of legal rights protected by the government, such as freedom of speech or religion: *Our various freedoms are the bases of our nation.*

1. Make a chart like the one shown. Fill in the chart with your ideas. How do you think freedom is expressed at home, at work, and at school?
2. Exchange charts with a partner. Compare your ideas.

Freedom	
at school	can ask lots of questions
at home	
at work	

MULTI-LEVEL OPTIONS *Build Vocabulary*

Newcomer Write on the board: *warm, home,* and *dream.* Read a dictionary definition of each word. ***Say:*** *Warm can also mean a good* feeling. *A dream can be a wish someone hopes for. Home can also mean family. Many English words have a dictionary meaning and a meaning that is a feeling.*

Beginning On the board, write: *warm.* ***Say:*** *I feel warm inside when my mom hugs me.* Provide a dictionary definition for *warm.* ***Ask:*** *Is this meaning right for this sentence?* Write: *denotative* and *connotative.* Point to *denotative* and ***say:*** *This is the dictionary meaning.* Point to *connotative* and ***say:*** *This is the "feeling" meaning.*

Intermediate Write on the board: *dream, warm,* and *home.* Have students work in pairs. Ask one student to say the denotative meaning of one word. Have the other student give the connotative meaning of the word. Have students alternate turns.

Advanced Ask students to write sentences with the following words: *heat, oasis, table, dream, home, warm.* Then have them work in pairs to decide whether each sentence is using the denotative or connotative meaning for each word.

Build Background

Segregation and Martin Luther King Jr.

In the 1950s, African-Americans did not enjoy the same rights as white Americans. In some places African-Americans were legally segregated from (separated from) whites. For example, African-Americans had to sit in the back of public buses or trains.

In 1955, Martin Luther King Jr. started a political movement in Montgomery, Alabama, to protest against segregated city buses in that city. King's ideas about resisting segregation spread throughout the nation. His nonviolent methods of making change led to new laws and new freedoms for African-Americans.

Content Connection

From the beginning of the history of the United States in the 1600s to the 1860s, many African-Americans were **slaves.** They were owned by other people and they had no rights.

Build Vocabulary

Distinguish Denotative and Connotative Meanings

A **denotative meaning** is what a word usually means. *Home* usually means the place where you live. A word also often has a **connotative meaning,** which is about the images or feelings that the word can give. For example, *home* can also make us think of family, comfort, and safety.

1. Look up the first meaning of the word *dream* in the dictionary. This is the denotative meaning of *dream.* Write it in your Personal Dictionary.
2. In the first paragraph of the reading, Martin Luther King Jr. says, "I have a <u>dream</u> that one day this nation will rise up and . . ." Is he asleep?
3. Describe the connotative meaning of *dream* in this sentence.
4. In paragraph 1, look for these additional examples of using connotative meanings for words. Use your dictionary to find the denotative meanings. Then describe the connotative meanings.
   a. the <u>heat</u> of injustice
   b. an <u>oasis</u> of freedom
   c. the <u>table</u> of brotherhood

Activity Book p. 201

Student CD-ROM

Cultural Connection

Build Vocabulary Provide blank three-column charts with the headings *Word, Denotative Meaning,* and *Connotative Meaning.* Ask students to fill in the charts with words from other languages and their English equivalents.

Teacher Resource Book: *Three-Column Chart, p. 45*

Learning Styles ***Intrapersonal***

Build Background Ask students to consider the actions and beliefs of Martin Luther King Jr. ***Ask:*** *Do you think he was brave? Do you think you could have done what he did?* Then ask students to write paragraphs that explain whether or not they would have acted as King did and why or why not.

Build Background

Segregation and Martin Luther King Jr.

1. **Use illustrations** Bring in photos and resources on the civil rights movement to clarify the meaning of *segregation.* ***Ask:*** *With segregation, did all people have the same freedoms? Why or why not?*
2. **Content Connection** Slaves were used on many of the large plantations in the South. Slaves were freed after the Civil War, but it has been an ongoing process for African-Americans to achieve all the freedoms promised.

Build Vocabulary

Distinguish Denotative and Connotative Meanings

1. **Teacher think aloud** On the board, write: *flower.* ***Say:*** *If I look in the dictionary, I see that a flower is a part of a plant. When I think about a flower, I see something pretty and I feel happy and cheerful.* Have students find denotative meanings of other words in the dictionary and explain their feelings about or connotative meanings of the words.
2. **Reading selection vocabulary** You may want to introduce the glossed words in the reading selection before students begin reading. Key words: *self-evident, injustice, vicious, racist, crooked, transform, allow.* Instruct students to write the words with correct spelling and their definitions in their Personal Dictionaries. Have them pronounce each word and divide it into syllables.
3. **Multi-level options** See MULTI-LEVEL OPTIONS on p. 380.

Answers

Sample answers: **1.** images or ideas during sleep **2.** no **3.** It's something he wishes and hopes for. **4. a.** anger; **b.** rest and refreshment; **c.** open communication, good relations

ASSESS

Have students write two sentences using the denotative and connotative meanings of *segregation.*

Text Structure

Speech

Teacher Resource Book: *Web, p. 37*

1. **Make a semantic** Have students suggest words associated with speeches. Ask who gives speeches, why, when, where, and to whom. Use the words to create a web. Point out the speech feature chart. Give examples of the features.
2. **Multi-level options** See MULTI-LEVEL OPTIONS below.

Reading Strategy

Draw Conclusions with Text Evidence

Use personal knowledge Point out to students that they often draw conclusions in science labs. They observe an experiment and then draw conclusions about what they saw. Ask students about a science experiment they did and the conclusions they drew.

ASSESS

Ask: What are four features of a speech? (personal style, direct address, repetition, compares and contrasts)

Text Structure

Speech

"I Have a Dream" is a speech that was given in 1963 by Martin Luther King Jr. Speeches are written and read aloud by someone who wants to present a strong message.

Before you read the speech, listen to the audio recording. Listen for the features that often appear in speeches.

As you read, write examples of these features in your Reading Log.

Speech	
Personal Style	emotional and exciting; tries to persuade the audience to do something
Direct Address	is presented directly to the audience; uses first person *(I)*
Repetition	repeats key words to help the audience remember
Compares and Contrasts	talks about the past, present, and future

Reading Log

Student CD-ROM

Reading Strategy

Draw Conclusions with Text Evidence

To understand a speech, the listener or reader must **draw conclusions** about what was happening at the time the speech was given. As you listen to or read "I Have a Dream," look for **text evidence** about what life was like for some Americans in 1963. In your Reading Log, record the evidence you find and the conclusions you draw from it.

Quotation:

I have a dream that one day this nation will rise up and live out the true meaning of its creed, "We hold these truths to be self-evident; that all men are created equal."

Conclusion:

The United States was not living up to its creed.

Reading Log

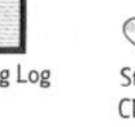
Student CD-ROM

382 **Unit 6** Frontiers

MULTI-LEVEL OPTIONS *Text Structure*

Newcomer Display the text of a speech. Recite some of the speech. *Say: A speech is words that are said aloud for you to hear.* Write *repetition* on the board. Play a recording of a speech. Have students raise their hands each time they hear words repeated.

Beginning Display the text of a speech. Recite some of the speech. *Say: A speech is words that are read aloud for others to hear. Sometimes a speech is written down.* Write *repetition* on the board. ***Say:*** *Listen for words that are repeated when you listen to the speech.*

Intermediate Pair intermediate and advanced students to listen to another famous speech (e.g., President Kennedy's inaugural "Ask Not What Your Country Can Do for You" address). Ask students to write examples of each text feature listed in the chart on p. 382. ***Ask:*** *Did the speech you reviewed contain all of the features in the chart?*

Advanced See Intermediate Multi-level Option.

I HAVE A DREAM

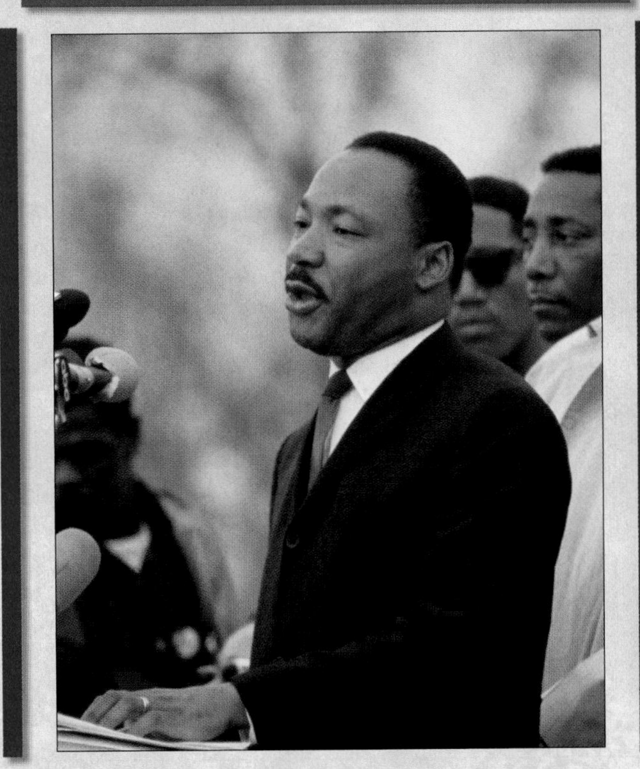

an excerpt from a speech
by Martin Luther King Jr.

383

Reading Selection Materials

Audio: *Unit 6, Chapter 3*
Teacher Resource Book: *Reading Summary, pp. 115–116*

Preview the Selection

1. **Use the photo** Have students suggest who is speaking and what he is speaking about. Ask them why they think he is pointing.
2. **Connect the art to the theme** *Ask: Why do you think this is a photo and not a painting or drawing?* Use questions to help students comment on the posture and expression of Martin Luther King Jr. Point out the title of the speech and have students suggest what the dream might be about. Make a list of predictions about the speech and have students check back at the end of the reading selection.
3. **Connect** Remind students that the unit theme is *frontiers*. ***Ask:*** *How is a dream like a frontier? What types of difficulties do you think Martin Luther King Jr. faced at this "frontier/dream"?*

Community Connection

Remind students that King protested against segregation. Explain that while segregation is officially illegal today, it still exists in some forms. Tell students that some clubs and organizations restrict membership. Ask groups to research local clubs and organizations to find out about their membership policies.

Learning Styles *Interpersonal*

Help students practice tolerance skills. Have them work in small groups. Ask members to take turns talking about themselves. Tell them to describe their cultural and ethnic backgrounds, things they believe and feel, things they like and dislike, and things that make them happy and sad. After each student speaks, ask the other members to take turns completing this sentence: *I am like _____ because I _____, too.*

Read the Selection

1. **Use text features** Call attention to the photograph. Direct students to glossed words and their meanings at the bottom of the page. Remind students to use these features to guide their reading.
2. **Summarize** Play the audio to students with books closed. Repeat the audio and have students follow along. Help summarize key points and clarify vocabulary.
3. **Analyze tone and mood** *Ask: Does Martin Luther King Jr. sound angry or hopeful? Do you think he wants other people to have this same dream?*

Sample Answer to Guide Question
"I say to you today, my friends, even though we face the difficulties of today and tomorrow, I still have a dream."

See Teacher Edition pp. 434–435 for a list of English-Spanish cognates in the reading selection.

Audio

Draw Conclusions with Text Evidence

What quotation helps you draw a conclusion about King's message?

1 I say to you today, my friends, even though we face the difficulties of today and tomorrow, I still have a dream. It is a dream deeply rooted in the American dream. I have a dream that one day this nation will rise up and live out the true meaning of its **creed,** "We hold these truths to be **self-evident;** that all men are created equal." I have a dream that one day on the red hills of Georgia, the sons of former slaves and the sons of former slave owners will be able to sit down together at a table of brotherhood. I have a dream that one day even the state of Mississippi, a state **sweltering** with the heat of **injustice,** sweltering with the heat of **oppression,** will be transformed into an oasis of freedom and justice. I have a dream that my four children will one day live in a nation where they will not be judged by the color of their skin but by the content of their character.

2 I have a dream today!

creed beliefs
self-evident speaking for themselves, obvious
sweltering suffering from heat
injustice lack of justice; unfairness
oppression the act of governing or treating harshly

MULTI-LEVEL OPTIONS *Read the Selection*

Newcomer Play the audio. Read the pages aloud. ***Ask:*** *Did King dream of freedom and justice in Georgia, Mississippi, and Alabama?* (yes) *Did King have four children?* (yes) *Did King talk about the governor of New York?* (no)

Beginning Play the audio. Then read the Reading Summary aloud. ***Ask:*** *What did King believe about all men?* (They are created equal.) *Where did he want the sons of slaves and slaveholders to sit together?* (Georgia) *What did he hope Alabama would be transformed into?* (an oasis of freedom and justice)

Intermediate Have students read the Reading Summary silently. Then play the audio. ***Ask:*** *What did King say his dream was rooted in?* (the American dream) *How did King feel about Mississippi?* (It was sweltering with injustice and oppression.) *Who did King believe was a racist?* (the governor of Alabama)

Advanced Have students read the speech silently. Then play the audio. ***Ask:*** *How is King's dream rooted in the American dream?* (He quotes the Declaration of Independence.) *Did he think his dream would come true for himself in his lifetime? How can you tell?* (No, he kept referring to children.)

Draw Conclusions with Text Evidence

What does King's description of the governor of Alabama tell you about the tension between people at this time? Give evidence for your conclusion.

3 I have a dream that one day down in Alabama—with its **vicious racists,** with its Governor having his lips dripping with the words of **interposition** and **nullification***—one day right there in Alabama, little black boys and black girls will be able to join hands with little white boys and white girls as sisters and brothers.

4 I have a dream today!

5 I have a dream that one day every valley shall be **exalted,** and every hill and mountain shall be made low. The rough places will be plain, and the **crooked** places will be made straight, and the glory of the Lord shall be revealed, and all **flesh** shall see it together.

* At this time, some southern states threatened to disobey any federal laws that allowed more rights for African-Americans.

vicious cruel, hostile

racists people who believe that their race is better than other races

interposition the idea that a state may not follow a federal order

nullification the refusal of a state to enforce a federal law

exalted highly raised

crooked bent, not straight

flesh living things

UNIT 6 • CHAPTER 3
Reading Selection

Read the Selection

1. **Locate information on a map** Have students locate the different states and places mentioned in the speech on a map of the United States. Point out that the Washington Monument in the photograph is in Washington, D.C.
2. **Paired reading** Play the audio. Then have students read it again in pairs.
3. **Draw conclusions with text evidence** ***Say:*** *Martin Luther King talks about black children and white children joining hands in his dream. Do you think that black children and white children were friendly toward one another at the time of this speech? What conclusion can you draw?* (They were not friendly.)
4. **Identify repetition** Have students point out examples of repetition in the speech. ("I have a dream that one day . . . I have a dream today!")
5. **Multi-level options** See MULTI-LEVEL OPTIONS on p. 384.

Sample Answer to Guide Question

The governor sounds very mean and cruel, so I think there was a lot of tension and problems between black and white people at this time.

Spelling

Irregular plurals

Remind students that many words are made plural by adding *-s* or *-es*. Then explain that some words have irregular plural forms. Write on the board and ***say:*** *child, man, children,* and *men.* **Ask:** *Which words are singular?* (child, man) *Which words are plural?* (children, men)

Apply Have students correct the following sentences by circling the correct plural forms. Write: ***1.*** *How many persons/people attended the meeting?* ***2.*** *More than twenty mans/men came to the meeting.* ***3.*** *Only nine women/womans attended.* ***4.*** *The meeting was disrupted when three mice/mouses scurried across the floor.* ***5.*** *At last year's meeting, two gooses/geese flew in the window!* (people, men, women, mice, geese)

Read the Selection

1. **Paired reading** Play the audio. Then have students read it again in pairs. *Ask: Do people need to work hard to achieve the change and dream that King is speaking about? How do you know?*
2. **Identify figurative language** Have students find examples of figurative language in the speech. (changes in the physical landscape, "a mountain of despair," "a symphony of brotherhood," "let freedom ring")

Sample Answer to Guide Question
The struggle was difficult because King calls it a Mountain of despair.

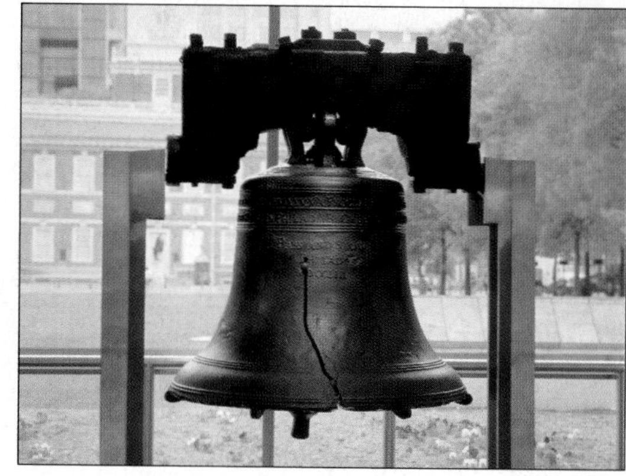
The Liberty Bell

Draw Conclusions with Text Evidence

How can you describe the struggle for freedom at this time? Which of King's words support your conclusion?

6 This is our hope. This is the faith that I go back to the South with. With this faith we will be able to **hew** out of the mountain of **despair** a stone of hope. With this faith we will be able to **transform** the jangling **discords** of our nation into a beautiful symphony of brotherhood. With this faith we will be able to work together, to pray together, to struggle together, to go to jail together, to stand up for freedom together, knowing that we will be free one day. And this will be the day. This will be the day when all of God's children will be able to sing with new meaning, "My country, 'tis of thee, sweet land of liberty, of thee I sing. Land where my fathers died, land of the pilgrims' pride, from every mountainside, let freedom ring."* And if America is to be a great nation, this must become true.

7 So let freedom ring from the **prodigious** hilltops of New Hampshire. Let freedom ring from the **mighty** mountains of New York. Let freedom ring from the

* King quotes from the words to "My Country 'Tis of Thee," a patriotic song.

hew chop or cut
despair sadness without hope
transform change
discords disagreements
prodigious marvelous or amazing
mighty having great strength or power

MULTI-LEVEL OPTIONS *Read the Selection*

Newcomer *Did King think his dream could happen?* (yes) *Did King think his dream would make America a great nation?* (yes)

Beginning *What did King think people could transform the nation into?* (a symphony of brotherhood) *Where did King want freedom to ring?* (many states and places; all of America) *Who did King think could join hands and sing?* (everyone; all of God's children)

Intermediate *What did King believe would help transform the nation?* (hope and faith) *Why did King say the ideas in the song had to become true?* (so America could become a great nation) *Why did King name specific places?* (to personalize his message for different listeners)

Advanced *Why do you think King quoted the song "My Country, 'Tis of Thee"?* (to reinforce the idea that freedom and equality are American beliefs) *What was King's message about freedom?* (No one is truly free without equality.)

heightening Alleghenies of Pennsylvania! Let freedom ring from the snowcapped Rockies of Colorado! Let freedom ring from the curvaceous slopes of California! But not only that. Let freedom ring from Stone Mountain of Georgia! Let freedom ring from Lookout Mountain of Tennessee! Let freedom ring from every hill and every molehill of Mississippi. From every mountainside, let freedom ring.

8 And when this happens, and when we **allow** freedom to ring, when we let it ring from every village and every hamlet, from every state and every city, we will be able to speed up that day when all of God's children—black men and white men, Jews and Gentiles, Protestants and Catholics—will be able to join hands and sing in the words of the old Negro spiritual, "Free at last. Free at last. Thank God Almighty, we are free at last."

Draw Conclusions with Text Evidence

What conclusion can you make about how King wanted this speech to make people feel?

heightening rising, growing taller

allow let, permit

About the Author — Martin Luther King Jr. (1929–1968)

Martin Luther King Jr. was born in 1929 in Atlanta, Georgia. As a child, he was angry at the segregation that he saw around him. He helped win equal rights for African-Americans, including the right to vote. In 1964, he was awarded the Nobel Peace Prize. In 1968, King was shot and killed in Memphis, Tennessee.

➤ Why do you think Martin Luther King Jr. wrote this speech? Was it to entertain, to inform, or to persuade? What was the effect on the listener? What was the effect on you as you listened?

Punctuation

Apostrophes for singular and plural possessives

Review apostrophes to show possession. ***Say:*** *To show possession for singular nouns add -'s.* Write on the board: *girl's* and *bus's.* ***Say:*** *To show possession for plural nouns that ends in -s, only add the apostrophe.* Direct students to paragraph 6. ***Ask:*** *Can you find a plural possessive?* (pilgrims') *Can you find a singular possessive in paragraph 8?* (God's)

Evaluate Your Reading Strategy

Draw Conclusions with Text Evidence

Say: *You have practiced an important reading strategy. Now you can decide how well you have done. Does this statement describe how you read?*

I use facts and details from my reading to draw conclusions about the meaning of the text. Drawing conclusions as I read helps me understand more of the author's meaning.

Read the Selection

1. **Choral reading** Play the audio. Then do a choral reading of the whole speech. Assign two students to lead two groups that alternate paragraphs.
2. **Identify repetition and contrast** ***Ask:*** *What phrases are repeated?* (Let freedom ring; Free at last.) *What contrasts does King use?* (blacks and whites, Jews and Gentiles, Protestants and Catholics)

Sample Answer to Guide Question
He wanted people to feel ready to work and struggle to make his dream come true.

About the Author

1. **Evaluate information about the author** Martin Luther King Jr. began his nonviolent protest in 1955 and led many protests, boycotts, and marches. ***Ask:*** *Why do you think he was given the Nobel Peace Prize?* (He worked for equal rights through peaceful means.)
2. **Interpret the facts** ***Ask:*** *Why do you think he was shot?* (Not everyone liked his ideas and the changes that he worked for.)

Across Selections

Connect to theme Have students discuss how Martin Luther King Jr.'s dream was a frontier. Point out that integration would create a new view of the country/world. It would require a struggle to get there, just as Lewis and Clark struggled and faced many problems to reach their goal.

Reading Comprehension

Question-Answer Relationships

Sample Answers

1. To live in a place where they aren't judged by their skin color but by their character.
2. Everyone would be free.
3. Everyone will work and struggle together to make a country where everyone is free and treated equally.
4. They can change the angry voices to beautiful singing voices with everyone singing together.
5. He includes the words because it is a traditional American song that many students sing in school.
6. He wanted people to keep working toward freedom and equality in the future and not to give up faith and hope.
7. King is hopeful that people will work together and his dream will come true.
8. I think I would have agreed. He makes me feel like I would want to follow what he says.
9. The author wanted to persuade people to feel the way he does. He wanted people to believe in and work for his dream with him.

Build Reading Fluency

Adjust Your Reading Rate

Demonstrate to the students how you change your rate of reading depending on the purpose and type of reading material.

Beyond the Reading

Reading Comprehension

Question-Answer Relationships (QAR)

"Right There" Questions

1. **Recall Facts** What does Martin Luther King Jr. say his dream is for his four children?
2. **Find the Main Idea** What does King say will happen when Americans "allow freedom to ring"?
3. **Paraphrase** Paraphrase King's dream.

"Think and Search" Question

4. **Find Details** What does King say can be done if people have faith and hope?

"Author and You" Questions

5. **Identify Symbolism** Why does King include the words of "My Country 'Tis of Thee"?
6. **Understand Author's Purpose** What do you think King wanted people to do after they heard his speech?
7. **Distinguish Opinion** What does "I Have a Dream" tell you about King's opinions?

"On Your Own" Questions

8. **Infer** After hearing this speech, do you think you would have agreed with King? Why or why not?
9. **Draw Conclusions** How do you think the author intended people to respond to this speech? Why?

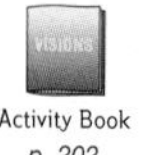

Activity Book p. 202 Student CD-ROM

Build Reading Fluency

Adjust Your Reading Rate

When you read a speech, you can learn to adjust your reading rate. Pause and read like you are giving the speech, "I Have a Dream."

1. Listen to the audio recording of paragraph 7 on pages 386–387.
2. Read paragraph 7 silently two times.
3. Read paragraph 7 aloud to a partner.
4. Read with expression, as if you were giving the speech to an audience.

388 Unit 6 Frontiers

MULTI-LEVEL OPTIONS *Elements of Literature*

Newcomer Pair newcomer students with advanced students. Have advanced students tell simple, acceptable jokes to the newcomer students. ***Ask:*** *Who was the audience?* Have newcomers raise their hands. ***Say:*** *The audience is the group of people that are listening.*

Beginning Pair beginners with intermediate students. Have intermediate students tell simple, acceptable jokes to their partners. ***Ask:*** *What was the purpose of the jokes?* (to entertain) ***Say:*** *A writer must know the audience and purpose for writing.* List different purposes on the board. (to inform, entertain, persuade)

Intermediate Pair intermediate students with beginners. ***Say:*** *Work together to write a paragraph. The purpose of your paragraph is to persuade.* Have students exchange paragraphs with another pair. ***Ask:*** *Did the paragraph persuade you? Did the writer meet his or her purpose?* Then ***ask:*** *Who was the audience?*

Advanced Pair advanced students with newcomers. Have the advanced students tell jokes to their partners. ***Ask:*** *Who is your audience?* (newcomers) *What is your purpose?* (to entertain) *What else could you tell to entertain your audience?* (a funny story, etc.)

Listen, Speak, Interact 

Present a Speech

It is important for people giving speeches to speak clearly and expressively.

1. Choose one paragraph from the speech to present to the class.
2. Listen to the audio recording of the speech. This will help you distinguish sounds of words. Say words out loud to practice making the correct sounds.
3. Also listen to the audio recording to distinguish intonation (how your voice rises and falls). Say sentences out loud to practice intonation.
4. Make a speech evaluation checklist.
5. Perform the speech for the class. Ask your classmates to fill out the evaluation.

Speech Evaluation Checklist		
Did I:	Yes	No
speak clearly?	____	____
stand up straight?	____	____
use gestures and body language to communicate?	____	____
____	____	____

Elements of Literature

Identify Audience and Purpose

Every piece of writing should have an audience and a purpose.

To write effectively, you need to know your **audience**—the people you are writing to. Who is the audience for King's speech? How do you know? Record your answers in your Reading Log.

It is also important to have a **purpose**—your reason for writing. Speeches might have one of these purposes:

1. To **inform** (to give new information).
2. To **persuade** (to try to influence the audience's actions or beliefs).
3. To **entertain** (to give people pleasure).

What is the purpose of King's speech? Support your answer by noting evidence from the speech. Record your answers in your Reading Log.

Reading Log

Activity Book p. 203

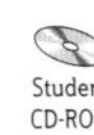
Student CD-ROM

Content Connection
Social Studies

Ask groups to research Martin Luther King Jr. Have each group research one subtopic: childhood, family, marriage and children, parents, siblings, education, awards or honors. Ask students to prepare brief reports on their topics. Have groups present their reports orally. Encourage students to include photos, drawings, and other visual aids.

Learning Styles
Visual

Provide graphic organizers to help visual learners plan and prepare their oral reports on Martin Luther King Jr.

Listen, Speak, Interact

Present a Speech

Teacher Resource Book: *Reading Log, p. 64*

1. **Reread in small groups** Have small groups choose portions to read aloud. Point out how King used pauses to help his audience understand his message.
2. **Newcomers** Reread with this group. Have them practice reading aloud their selections.
3. **Evaluate** Have students write an evaluation of their own presentations in their Reading Logs.
4. **Analyze speaker's credibility** In pairs, have students analyze the credibility of their partner. ***Ask:*** *Did you believe your partner? Did you trust their words? Why or why not? What suggestions would you give your partner to be more credible?* (example: be more confident, use stronger emotion, etc.)

Elements of Literature

Identify Audience and Purpose

Teacher Resource Book: *Reading Log, p. 64*

1. **Clarify terms** Give examples of audience and purposes. Have students suggest when they hear people talking to inform, persuade, or entertain.
2. **Analyze persuasive techniques** Play the audio of the speech. ***Ask:*** *What is the purpose of King's speech?* (persuade) *What techniques did he use to persuade his audience?* (emotional, exciting style; connotative meanings to evoke images and feelings; reminders of past and present; vision for future) Have pairs list techniques. ***Ask:*** *What effect did the speech have on you? Do you agree with King more after listening to the speech? Why?*
3. **Multi-level options** See MULTI-LEVEL OPTIONS on p. 388.

ASSESS

Write on the board: *inform, persuade, entertain.* Have students give definitions.

Word Study

Recognize Figurative Language

Teacher Resource Book: *Word or Concept Wheel, p. 36; Personal Dictionary, p.63*

Use a Word Wheel Help students make a Word Wheel. Have them include both denotative and connotative meanings for the underlined words. Students can use their wheels as they describe their pictures of the figurative expressions.

Answers

2. *Examples:* **a.** mountain: a large part of Earth's surface; a large obstacle; **b.** valley: a long, narrow region of land; the lower or worse places to be made better

Grammar Focus

Use Dependent Clauses with *That*

Write on the board: *I have a dream that my children will be free.* Call attention to the two clauses. Have students identify the subject and verb in each clause.

Answers

2. *Examples:* I have a dream that the teacher will not give us homework. I have a dream that children everywhere will have enough to eat and good schools to go to.

ASSESS

Have students find an example of figurative language in the speech.

Word Study

Recognize Figurative Language

In **figurative language,** words mean more than their dictionary definitions. When Martin Luther King Jr. writes "a symphony of brotherhood," he is not really talking about music.

Figurative language often uses the connotative meaning of words instead of denotative meanings. Recall that a connotative meaning is about the images or feelings a word gives. A denotative meaning is what a word means most of the time.

1. Choose one of the following examples of figurative speech:
   a. Hew out of the <u>mountain</u> of despair a stone of hope.
   b. Every <u>valley</u> shall be exalted, and every <u>hill</u> and mountain shall be made low.
2. Use a dictionary to find the denotative meaning of the underlined word. Then determine the connotative meaning of the word.
3. On a piece of paper, draw a picture of what the words actually say. Then write a short description of what you think is King's figurative meaning.

Personal Dictionary

The Heinle Newbury House Dictionary

Activity Book p. 204

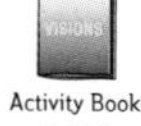
Student CD-ROM

Grammar Focus

Use Dependent Clauses with *That*

Clauses are parts of sentences that have a subject and a verb. Many sentences in "I Have a Dream" by Martin Luther King Jr. begin with, "I have a dream that . . ." The sentence "I have a dream" can stand alone. It is a main clause. However, King adds a **dependent clause** beginning with *that.* It makes what he is dreaming of more specific.

1. Find sentences that begin "I have a dream that . . ." in the reading.
2. Write three sentences about your dreams. Use dependent clauses with *that.* Be sure to use correct punctuation.

Activity Book pp. 205–206

Student Handbook

Student CD-ROM

MULTI-LEVEL OPTIONS *From Reading to Writing*

Newcomer Help students brainstorm things they wish they were allowed to do. Ask students to choose one activity and draw pictures of themselves doing it. Help students add captions and titles.

Beginning Have small groups brainstorm topics for their speeches. Tell each group to select one topic. Ask groups to work together to complete their webs. Have students use the webs to write their speeches.

Intermediate Have students create a pre-writing chart with the headings *Pros* and *Cons.* Ask students to use the ideas in their webs to complete their charts. Have students use their charts as they write their speeches. Remind them to consider their audience and purpose as they write.

Advanced Have pairs exchange their speeches for editing. Ask reviewers to use the chart on p. 382 to make sure all the features are in the speech. Also have them consider the following: *Is it convincing? Does it persuade? If not, what needs to be added?* Have students revise as necessary and present their final speeches to the class.

'rom Reading to Writing

Vrite a Persuasive Speech

Write a speech about a dream you ave to solve a problem in your school r community. You must persuade your udience that the dream is a good one.

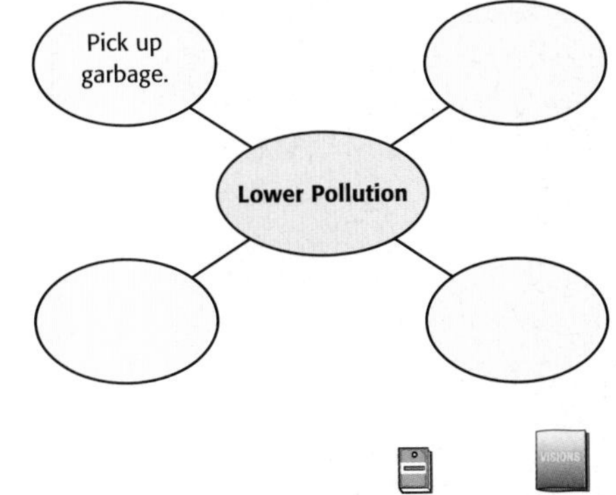

1. Make a web like the one shown. Use it to organize your ideas for reaching your dream.
2. Identify your audience and purpose.
3. Use figurative language. Use a dictionary to help you distinguish the denotative and connotative meanings of words.
4. Repeat important words to help your audience remember what you say.

The Heinle Newbury House Dictionary

Activity Book *p. 207*

Across Content Areas

.earn About the United States Constitution

The **Constitution of the United States** vas written in 1787. It tells what the government can do and what kinds of aws the government can pass.

The Constitution has to be **amended** (changed) from time to time. For example, he 13th Amendment made slavery illegal. The 19th Amendment gave women the right to vote.

An important part of the Constitution is the **Bill of Rights.** This lists the first ten amendments to the Constitution. These amendments give Americans basic freedoms such as freedom of speech.

Copy these sentences on a piece of paper. Decide if each one is *true* or *false*.

1. The Constitution cannot be changed.
2. The right to freedom of religion is in the Bill of Rights.
3. The Constitution says how fast you can drive.

Check your answers with your social studies teacher.

Activity Book *p. 208*

Reteach and Reassess

Text Structure Divide students into four groups. Assign one text feature of a speech to each group. (personal style, direct address, repetition, compare and contrast) Ask groups to find examples in the selection of their assigned features.

Reading Strategy Have students write three facts about themselves. Have pairs exchange lists and use the information to draw conclusions about each other.

Elements of Literature Have students review an earlier selection in the book. ***Ask:*** *What was the author's purpose for writing?* (inform, entertain, or persuade) *Who is the author's audience?*

Reassess Ask students to write personal responses to the selection. Ask them to describe how the speech made them feel, what they liked and disliked about it, and what they learned from it.

From Reading to Writing

Write a Persuasive Speech

1. **Gather and organize** Help students brainstorm ideas and solutions for the problem they choose. Then have them organize their ideas on a web.
2. **Think-quickwrite-pair-share** Ask students to write as much as they can to persuade others of their solutions to the problems. Remind them to repeat key words and ideas in their speeches. Have students share their ideas with a partner before making a final copy.
3. **Multi-level options** See MULTI-LEVEL OPTIONS on p. 390.

Across Content Areas: Social Studies

Learn About the United States Constitution

1. **Use resource materials** Bring in copies of the Constitution and Bill of Rights. Have students look at the language and organization of the documents.
2. **Relate to personal experiences** Ask students to share information about the Constitution and other important U.S. government documents, such as the Declaration of Independence, the Emancipation Proclamation, etc. If possible, have students compare and contrast some of the basic ideas and freedoms included in the U.S. Constitution with those in constitutions of other countries.

Answers
1. false **2.** true **3.** false

Have students write a quiz question about the Constitution for others in the class to answer.

Chapter Materials

Activity Book: *pp. 209–216*
Audio: *Unit 6, Chapter 4*
Student Handbook
Student CD-ROM: *Unit 6, Chapter 4*
Teacher Resource Book: *Lesson Plan, Teacher Resources, Reading Summary, Activity Book Answer Key*
Teacher Resource CD-ROM
Assessment Program: *Quiz, pp. 95–96; Teacher and Student Resources, pp. 115–144*
Assessment CD-ROM
Transparencies
The Heinle Newbury House Dictionary/CD-ROM
Web Site: www.heinle.visions.com

Objectives

Paired reading Have students work in pairs and take turns reading the objectives section. Explain and point out key words. ***Ask:*** *Are there any objectives that you can already do?*

Use Prior Knowledge

Talk About What United States Presidents Do

Bring in a picture of the President and the White House. Have students share information they know.

CHAPTER 4

Lyndon Baines Johnson: Our Thirty-Sixth President

an excerpt from a biography by Melissa Maupin

Speech to the Nation: July 2, 1964

an excerpt from a speech by Lyndon Baines Johnson

Into the Reading

Objectives

Reading Distinguish fact from opinion as you read a biography and a speech.

Listening and Speaking Conduct an interview.

Grammar Use the conjunction *yet* to show contrast.

Writing Write a biography.

Content Social Studies: Learn about the branches of government.

Use Prior Knowledge

Talk About What United States Presidents Do

The president of the United States is the leader of the country. He has many important duties (jobs that he has to do).

1. With a partner, make a list of the duties of the president of the United States that you know about.
2. Work with the class to put together a chart with all the duties that everyone has listed.
3. Do you know about leaders in other countries? What duties do they have? Compare and contrast them.

President's Duties
signs new laws
command the armed forces

MULTI-LEVEL OPTIONS *Build Vocabulary*

Newcomer Use an earlier selection as an example. Point to the words in boldface in the text. Remind students that glossed words are usually highlighted with boldfaced print. Demonstrate using the glosses to find the meanings of new words.

Beginning Remind students that many reference aids list entries in alphabetical order. Write on the board: *nominate, biography, opinion, President,* and *discrimination.* Ask pairs of students to work together to write the words in alphabetical order.

Intermediate ***Say:*** *Dictionary entries are listed in alphabetical order. Glossed words are highlighted with boldfaced print or an annotation, such as a number or a symbol.* Have students tell you if glossed words are alphabetized on the page. (no)

Advanced Ask students to write brief explanations of how to use a dictionary, a gloss, and a textbook to find the meanings of new government words. Remind students that an index can help them find terms in a textbook. Have students share their definitions with partners.

Build Background

Presidential Elections

In the United States, presidential elections are held every four years. First, political parties nominate (choose) candidates to represent them and run for office. Candidates for president and vice president run for office as a team. Then, in the presidential election, citizens vote for the person they want to take office. If the president dies, the vice president becomes president.

See page 401 to learn more about how "Vice President" Johnson also served later as "President" Johnson.

Content Connection

You can vote in a presidential election if you are at least 18 years old and a citizen of the United States. You must **register** (sign up) before voting.

Build Vocabulary

Identify Key Words About Government

Every text has **key words** (important words) you should know in order to understand the text. Identifying these key words is an essential skill.

1. Reread the Build Background section above. As you read, write down any unfamiliar words that you think are important to know.
2. Select one word from your list to define. Try using context clues to find the meaning of the word. Then check your ideas for the definition in a dictionary.
3. Teach your vocabulary word to a partner. Explain why you think the word is important to know and how you found the definition. Then ask your partner to explain a word.
4. As you read the selection, continue to identify key words. Define and record them in your Personal Dictionary.

Personal Dictionary

The Heinle Newbury House Dictionary

Activity Book *p. 209*

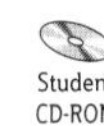
Student CD-ROM

Content Connection
Math

Build Background Have students use an almanac, the Internet, or other source to find statistical data for presidential elections. Ask students to work in groups to create charts and graphs to illustrate their data. Suggest that they create pie graphs that show percentages of voters for different candidates; tables that show data about voter turnout; bar graphs that compare political party membership across regions; or other appropriate graphics.

Learning Styles
Visual

Build Vocabulary Many students find it easier to understand and remember vocabulary and concepts by creating visual aids. Ask pairs of students to gather government-related vocabulary from multiple sources, including this text, social studies texts, magazines, and newspapers. Have pairs organize their terms logically in word wheels, semantic word maps, or webs.

Teacher Resource Book: *Word or Concept Wheel, p. 36; Web, p. 37*

Build Background

Presidential Elections

Teacher Resource Book: *Timelines, p. 39*

1. **Use a graphic organizer** Create a flow chart to illustrate the steps in a presidential election.
2. **Relate to personal experience** Have students talk about candidates they have seen or heard about. Ask students to compare U.S. presidential elections to how leaders are chosen in other countries.
3. **Content Connection** The first Tuesday in November is Election Day. ***Ask:*** *Do you know where people vote? Have you ever been to a voting site?*

Build Vocabulary

Identify Key Words About Government

Teacher Resource Book: *Personal Dictionary, p. 63*

1. **Use LINK (Listen, Inquire, Note, Know)** Have students listen as you read the Build Background text and choose an unfamiliar word. Remind students to try using context clues before checking in a dictionary for the meaning. Ask students to explain the word's meaning to a partner and demonstrate knowledge of it by using it in a sentence.
2. **Reading selection vocabulary** You may want to introduce the glossed words in the reading selections before students begin reading. Key words: *discrimination, plead, reserve, occasion, ideal, eliminate, opportunity, deny, ability.* Instruct students to write the words with correct spelling and their definitions in their Personal Dictionaries. Have them pronounce each word and divide it into syllables.
3. **Multi-level options** See MULTI-LEVEL OPTIONS on p. 392.

ASSESS

Ask: How often are the presidential elections held? (every four years)

Into the Reading

Text Structure

Biography

1. **Recognize features** Review the features and explanations. ***Ask:*** *What other readings have been biographies?* ("Helen Keller," "Mae Jemison, Space Scientist," and "Matthew A. Henson")
2. **Multi-level options** See MULTI-LEVEL OPTIONS below.

Reading Strategy

Distinguish Fact from Opinion

Teacher think aloud Write on the board: *The students in this class are seventh graders. They are the best students in the school.* ***Ask:*** *The first sentence is a fact that can be checked. The second sentence is my opinion. It's what I think. It's harder to prove.* Have students offer other facts and opinions about the school and the weather.

Answers

Facts: "Lyndon Baines Johnson: Our Thirty-Sixth President" Opinions: "Speech to the Nation: July 2, 1964"

ASSESS

Have students write one fact and one opinion about the photograph on p. 395.

Text Structure

Biography

Both of the selections in this chapter relate to Lyndon B. Johnson, the thirty-sixth president of the United States. The first selection is a **biography.** Biographies tell the story of a person's life. Look for features of a biography as you read.

As you read "Lyndon Baines Johnson: Our Thirty-Sixth President," notice which events and details the author thinks are important for you to know.

The second selection is a **speech.** Review the features of a speech on page 382.

Biography	
Third-Person Point of View	The story is told by someone other than the biography's subject, using the words *he, she,* and *they.*
Chronology	Chronology tells important events in the person's life and when they happened.
Important Details	Details show what the person was like and why the person's life was important.

Reading Strategy

Distinguish Fact from Opinion

A **fact** is something that can be proven. An **opinion** is a belief that may be true, but cannot be proven.

Our classroom has five windows.
This is a fact.

Our classroom is very comfortable.
This is an opinion.

It is important to understand the difference between fact and opinion.

1. Read the titles of the two readings in this chapter. Which do you think is more likely to contain facts? Which do you think may contain opinions? Why?
2. Read and listen to the audio recording of the two selections. Distinguish between the facts and opinions in each. Opinions sometimes begin with "I believe" or "we believe."

Student CD-ROM

MULTI-LEVEL OPTIONS *Text Structure*

Newcomer Ask students to draw self-portraits. ***Ask:*** *What can you tell us about yourself?* Help students add captions based on their responses. Explain that true stories about people are called *biographies.* Remind them a biography tells important information about someone's life.

Beginning ***Say:*** *A biography tells about a person's life.* Have students list presidents they would like to read about. Tell them to find a biography to read or read Internet sites and report on their choices in small groups.

Intermediate Have students list famous people they want to know about. Instruct them to read and share a biography by reporting to the class. Remind them that biographies tell factual information about a person.

Advanced Have students find a biography on a United States president. Have them read and report on him. Ask students to exchange reports for peer editing.

Lyndon Baines Johnson:

Our Thirty-Sixth President

an excerpt from a biography by Melissa Maupin

Speech to the Nation:

July 2, 1964

an excerpt from a speech by Lyndon Baines Johnson

395

UNIT 6 • CHAPTER 4
Reading Selection

Reading Selection Materials

Audio: *Unit 6, Chapter 4*
Teacher Resource Book: *Reading Summary, pp. 117–118*

Preview the Selections

Teacher Resource Book: *Know/Want to Know/Learned Chart (KWL), p. 42*

1. **Use the photo** Have students describe the man and the room in the photo. ***Ask:*** *Who do you think he is? Where is he? What is he doing?* Read the titles of the reading selections to help identify the man.
2. **Use a KWL** Have students brainstorm things they know about President Johnson and questions they have about him. Record these on a KWL chart. Refer back to the chart as students complete the reading selections.
3. **Connect** Remind students that the unit theme is *frontiers.* ***Ask:*** *Do presidents explore new frontiers? How and when might that happen?*

Community Connection

Arrange for a federal, state, or local official to give a speech on a topic the students will find interesting. Allow for a question and answer session following the speech. Ask students to take notes during the speech and Q & A. Have students use their notes to write "thank you" letters to the speaker. Remind students to include why they enjoyed the speech and what they learned from it.

Learning Styles ***Linguistic***

Ask students to study the photo of Lyndon Johnson. Have them write a descriptive paragraph about Johnson, based on the photograph and what they already know. Ask them to describe both physical characteristics and personality traits. Remind students to draw conclusions and make inferences. For example, they know that Johnson was a president, so they can infer that he had strong political opinions.

Reading Selection

Read the Selection

1. **Use text features** Direct attention to the prologue and photo. Have students find the meanings of the glossed words at the bottom of the page.
2. **Reciprocal reading** Read the selection aloud. Have students work in groups. Assign one student from each group to reread a paragraph and ask the group questions about it.
3. **Distinguish fact from opinion** Point out the names, dates, and specific time references. Remind students that these are often used with facts.

Sample Answer to Guide Question
It's a fact. It can be proved that Johnson took the oath of office at a certain time. This statement is not someone's belief or opinion about it.

See Teacher Edition pp. 434–435 for a list of English-Spanish cognates in the reading selection.

Audio

Lyndon Baines Johnson: Our Thirty-Sixth President
an excerpt from a biography by Melissa Maupin

Prologue

In 1960, John F. Kennedy was elected president of the United States, and Lyndon B. Johnson was his vice president. When Kennedy **was assassinated** in 1963, Johnson became president.

Distinguish Fact from Opinion
Is the first sentence a fact or an opinion? How do you know?

1 Just hours after Kennedy's death, Johnson took the **oath of office** as president of the United States. Five days later, he addressed the nation on television. He vowed to carry out all of Kennedy's programs. One important goal was civil rights for all Americans. Kennedy wanted to end **discrimination** against blacks and other minorities in the country. President Johnson **pleaded** with the country to put their differences aside in the memory of the late President Kennedy. "Let us put an end to the teaching and preaching of hate and evil and violence," he said.

was assassinated was murdered; usually describes the murder of someone important
oath of office a formal promise to do something
discrimination unfair treatment of someone, especially because of race, gender, religion, and so on
pleaded requested urgently

396 Unit 6 Frontiers

MULTI-LEVEL OPTIONS *Read the Selection*

Newcomer Play the audio. Read the pages aloud. ***Ask:*** *Was Lyndon Johnson the 36th president?* (yes) *Did Johnson become president when Kennedy died?* (yes) *Did Kennedy like discrimination?* (no) *Was the Civil Rights Act passed in 1964?* (yes) *Did discrimination end in 1964?* (no)

Beginning Read the Reading Summary aloud. ***Ask:*** *Who was the 36th president?* (Johnson) *When did Johnson take office?* (in 1963) *When was the Civil Rights Act passed?* (in 1964) *What did the Civil Rights Act make illegal?* (segregation laws) *Who still struggled for equal rights?* (African-Americans)

Intermediate Have students do a paired reading. ***Ask:*** *What did Johnson want Americans to end?* (discrimination against minorities; hate, evil, violence; segregation laws) *Whom did segregation laws discriminate against?* (African-Americans and other minorities)

Advanced Have students read independently. ***Ask:*** *How did Johnson become president?* (was vice-president; became president when Kennedy was killed) *How did the Civil Rights Act of 1964 affect discrimination and segregation?* (made segregation illegal but didn't end discrimination)

President Johnson signs the Civil Rights Act.

Distinguish Fact from Opinion

What are the facts of the Civil Rights Act of 1964? What did this act achieve?

2 Next, Johnson pushed through the Civil Rights Act of 1964. This ended segregation laws that discriminated against African-Americans. Segregation laws kept blacks from entering certain public places that were **reserved** for whites only, such as restrooms, hotels, and restaurants. The Civil Rights Act made such laws illegal. But even with this act, problems with discrimination continued. African-Americans still struggled for equal rights.

reserved set aside for use by someone

About the Author

Melissa Maupin (born 1958)

Melissa Maupin has written many biographies of United States presidents, including Franklin D. Roosevelt, William Howard Taft, Calvin Coolidge, and Lyndon B. Johnson. She has also written a biography of Benjamin Banneker, the famous astronomer and mathematician.

➤ Why do you think the author wrote this biography? Was it to persuade, to inform, or to entertain?

What question would you like to ask Melissa Maupin?

Read the Selection

1. **Reciprocal reading** Read the selection aloud. Have students continue to work in the same groups. Assign new students from each group to reread a paragraph and ask questions about it.
2. **Clarify terms and expressions** Review the meaning of *segregation*. Remind students to use context clues to guess the meanings of new words before checking in a dictionary.
3. **Distinguish fact from opinion** Have students identify various statements as facts or opinions.
4. **Multi-level options** See MULTI-LEVEL OPTIONS on p. 396.

Sample Answer to Guide Question

The act ended segregation laws. It made the segregation laws illegal. The act gave equal rights to African-Americans, but some discrimination still continued.

About the Author

Evaluate information about the author Read the author biography to students. ***Ask:*** *What types of people does Melissa Maupin often write about?* (presidents) *Why do you think she writes about them?* (Maybe she likes history or leaders of countries.)

Spelling

***qu* for the *kw* sound**

Remind students that the letters *qu* are usually pronounced */kw/.* Write on the board and ***say:*** *quick.* Have students repeat the word aloud. ***Say:*** *These letters make the* kw *sound.* Repeat for *request.* Direct students to read the last line on p. 397. ***Ask:*** *What word is spelled with the letters* qu? (equal) *What sound do they make in this word?* (kw)

Apply Have students list as many words as they can think of that have the *kw* sound spelled with the letters *qu.*

UNIT 6 • CHAPTER 4
Reading Selection

Read the Selection

1. **Use text features** Ask students to point out text features and explain their importance. Read and discuss the prologue. Discuss the photograph and the glossed words.
2. **Guided reading** Play the audio. Pause to check comprehension. Then have students read again in pairs.
3. **Analyze words** Have students suggest what "frontier" President Johnson is discussing.

Sample Answer to Guide Question

It is an opinion because it is his personal statement. Not everyone would agree with it. It can't be proven.

See Teacher Edition pp. 434–435 for a list of English-Spanish cognates in the reading selection.

Audio

Speech to the Nation: July 2, 1964

an excerpt from a speech by Lyndon Baines Johnson

Prologue

After a long and difficult **struggle** to get Congress to approve the Civil Rights Act of 1964, President Johnson wanted to tell all Americans about the new law. His speech was heard on television and radio from the White House on the evening of July 2, 1964.

1 My fellow Americans:

2 I am about to sign into law the Civil Rights Act of 1964. I want to take this **occasion** to talk to you about what that law means to every American.

3 One hundred and eighty-eight years ago this week a small band of **valiant** men began a long struggle for freedom. They **pledged** their lives, their fortunes, and their sacred honor not only to found a nation, but to **forge** an **ideal** of freedom—not only for political independence, but for personal liberty—not only to **eliminate** foreign rule, but to establish the rule of justice in the affairs of men.

4 That struggle was a turning point in our history. Today in far corners of distant continents, the ideals of those American patriots still shape the struggles of men who hunger for freedom.

Distinguish Fact from Opinion

Is it a fact or an opinion that the struggle for civil rights "was a turning point in our history"?

---

struggle a fight
occasion a special time or event
valiant brave
pledged formally promised to do something
forge make, create
ideal high standard
eliminate remove, exclude

MULTI-LEVEL OPTIONS *Read the Selection*

Newcomer Play the audio. *Did Johnson give this speech?* (yes) *Did he give the speech to tell about the Civil Rights Act?* (yes) *Did he think people should fight to protect freedom?* (yes) *Did he believe everyone should be treated equally?* (yes) *Did he believe that everyone was?* (no)

Beginning *Who gave this speech?* (Johnson) *When?* (July 2, 1964) *When did he say the long struggle for freedom began in America?* (188 years before) *What kinds of Americans did he say died in battles to protect freedom?* (all races and colors)

Intermediate *Why did Johnson give this speech?* (to tell Americans about the Civil Rights Act) *What did he say was the turning point in American history?* (the struggle for freedom) *What did he believe all Americans must have?* (equality, rights, liberty) *Why were millions of Americans being denied liberty?* (skin color)

Advanced *What event of 188 years ago was Johnson referring to?* (American Revolution; independence from England) *How do you think he felt as he gave this speech? Explain.* (proud, happy, because the Act finally passed; sad, angry because so many people still didn't have equality)

5 This is a proud **triumph.** Yet those who founded our country knew that freedom would be secure only if each **generation** fought to renew and enlarge its meaning. From the minutemen at Concord to the soldiers in Viet-Nam, each generation has been equal to that trust.

6 Americans of every race and color have died in battle to protect our freedom. Americans of every race and color have worked to build a nation of widening **opportunities.** Now our generation of Americans has been called on to continue the unending search for justice within our borders.

Distinguish Fact from Opinion

What words show that this is an opinion?

7 We believe that all men are created equal. Yet many are **denied** equal treatment.

8 We believe that all men have **unalienable** rights. Yet many Americans do not enjoy those rights.

9 We believe that all men are entitled to the blessings of **liberty.** Yet millions are being deprived of those blessings—not because of their own failures, but because of the color of their skin.

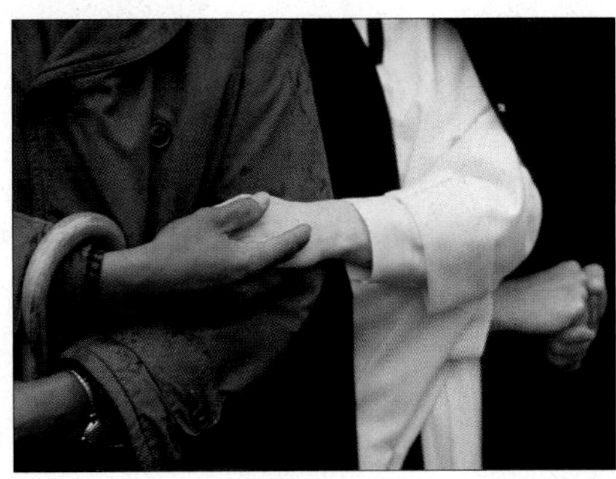

triumph a great success, victory
generation a group of people of approximately the same age
opportunities good times to do something
denied refused, rejected
unalienable not able to be taken away; permanent
liberty freedom from control

Read the Selection

1. **Use visuals and resource materials** If possible, bring in pictures and books about the American Revolution and the Vietnam War. Explain briefly when and why these wars were fought.
2. **Paired reading** After students listen to the audio or to you read the selection, have them read it again in pairs.
3. **Summarize** Ask students to restate the main points of the speech.
4. **Distinguish fact from opinion** As students summarize, have them identify facts and opinions used in the speech.
5. **Multi-level options** See MULTI-LEVEL OPTIONS on p. 398.

Sample Answer to Guide Question
"We believe" shows that this is an opinion.

Punctuation

Commas in dates

Write on the board:

July 2, 1964
She was born on July 2, 1964.
She was born on July 2, 1964, in Ohio.

Say: *When writing a complete date, place a comma between the day of the month and the year. If a sentence continues, put another comma after the year.* Remind students that no comma is needed before a year unless a day is included. Write:

July 1964
She was born in July 1964.
She was born in 1964.
She was born in July 1964, in Ohio.
She was born in 1964, in Ohio.

Then ***ask:*** *Why is there a comma after the 2 in the title?* (It's a complete date.) Direct students to paragraph 2. ***Ask:*** *Why is there no comma before 1964?* (There's no day.)

Reading Selection

Read the Selection

1. **Use text features** Direct students to the glossed words. Have them share information they may know about the political parties and debates. Remind students to use the features as they read the selection.
2. **Guided reading** Read the selection aloud. Ask comprehension questions and clarify meaning as needed after each paragraph.
3. **Summarize the main points** Have pairs of students summarize the main points and compare their summaries with those of other pairs.

Sample Answer to Guide Question
It reflects an opinion because everyone may not describe it the same way.

10 The reasons are deeply imbedded in history and tradition and the nature of man. We can understand—without **rancor** or hatred—how this all happened.

11 But it cannot continue. Our Constitution, the foundation of our Republic, **forbids** it. The principles of our freedom forbid it. Morality forbids it. And the law I wi sign tonight forbids it.

12 That law is the product of months of the most careful **debate** and discussion. It was **proposed** more than one yea ago by our late and beloved President John F. Kennedy. It received the **bipartisan** support of more than two-thirds of the Members of both the House and the Senate. An overwhelming **majority** of **Republicans** as well as **Democrats** voted for it.

13 It has received the thoughtful support of tens of thousands of civic and religious leaders in all parts of this Nation. And it is supported by the great majority of the American people.

Distinguish Fact from Opinion

President Johnson says, "That law is the product of months of the most careful debate and discussion." Does the underlined part of this sentence reflect fact or opinion?

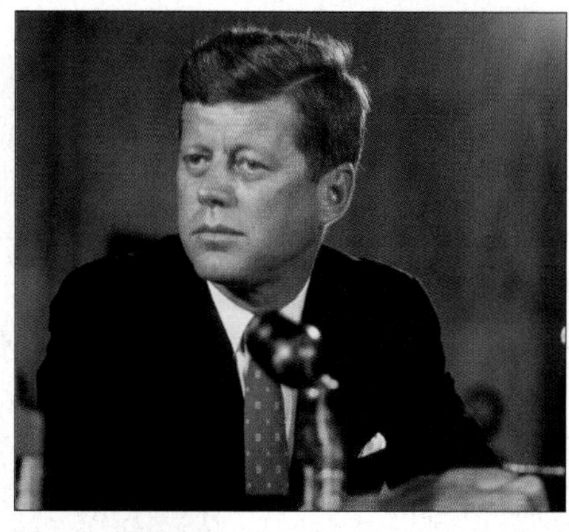

President John F. Kennedy

rancor deep, long-lasting, and bitter hatred
forbids does not permit
debate consideration and discussion
proposed suggested, recommended
bipartisan involving two political parties
majority more than half, but not all, of something
Republicans members of the Republican Party, one of the two main political parties in the United States
Democrats members of the Democratic Party, one of the two main political parties in the United States

MULTI-LEVEL OPTIONS *Read the Selection*

Newcomer *Does the Constitution forbid freedom?* (no) *Did Kennedy propose the law?* (yes) *Did most Americans support the law?* (yes) *Did the law restrict freedom and give some people special treatment?* (no) *Did it say that everyone had equal rights to vote and get public services?* (yes)

Beginning *What is the foundation of our Republic?* (Constitution) *Who proposed the law?* (Kennedy) *Who supported the law?* (politicians, civic and religious leaders, most Americans) *What kind of equality did the law provide?* (voting and access to businesses, public places)

Intermediate *What does Johnson say caused discrimination?* (history, tradition, the nature of man) *Why does he say discrimination cannot continue?* (forbidden by Constitution, principles of freedom, morality, and the new law) *What does the law provide?* (equality in voting, in access to public services)

Advanced *What was Johnson's opinion of Kennedy?* (beloved) *How does he show that the law is popular with Americans?* (He lists many of its supporters.) *Why do you think he explained that the law doesn't restrict freedoms or give anyone special treatment?* (to persuade people to support it)

14 The purpose of the law is simple.

15 It does not **restrict** the freedom of any American, so long as he respects the rights of others.

16 It does not give special treatment to any citizen.

17 It does say the only limit to a man's hope for happiness, and for the future of his children, shall be his own **ability.**

18 It does say that those who are equal before God shall now also be equal in the **polling booths,** in the classrooms, in the factories, and in hotels, restaurants, movie theaters, and other places that provide service to the public.

Distinguish Fact from Opinion

President Johnson mentions specific places where the law will apply. Is this opinion or fact?

---

restrict limit
ability the skill and power to do something
polling booths places where people vote

About the Author — Lyndon Baines Johnson (1908–1973)

Lyndon Baines Johnson was born near Stonewall, Texas. His father was a state legislator and often took him to see the state government at work. When he was in college, Johnson decided to go into politics, and he worked his way up through Congress. In 1960, John F. Kennedy asked Johnson to run for vice president with him. Kennedy and Johnson won the election, and Johnson began his duties as vice president. In 1963, President Kennedy was assassinated. Johnson became the president of the United States. He is especially remembered for the many civil rights laws that he helped pass.

➤ Sometimes presidents believe very strongly in the laws that they sign. Other times, they are not very enthusiastic about them. Based on your reading of the speech, do you think that President Johnson strongly believed in the Civil Rights Act, or not? Explain.

Read the Selection

1. **Shared reading** Complete the reading of the selection as students follow along. Ask volunteers to read aloud.
2. **Draw conclusions** Have students use clues in the text to draw a conclusion about the main point of the speech. Ask them to point out supporting details.
3. **Multi-level options** See MULTI-LEVEL OPTIONS on p. 400.

Sample Answer to Guide Question
It is a fact that the law will apply in all those places for everyone.

About the Author

Evaluate information about the author *Ask: What work did Johnson do before he was vice-president and president?* (He was in Congress and in other government positions.)

Across Selections

Teacher Resource Book: *Venn Diagram, p. 35; Two-Column Chart, p. 44*

Compare and contrast points of view Have students compare and contrast President Johnson's speech with Martin Luther King Jr.'s speech. Help them find similarities and differences in point of view, tone, persuasiveness, and images. Record ideas on a Venn diagram or a two-column chart.

A Capitalization

Proper names

Say: The words that name a government body, an act, a law, or a document are proper names. Proper names are always capitalized. Direct students to paragraph 11. *Ask: Why is* Constitution *capitalized?* (It's the name of a government document.)

Apply Have students correct capitalization errors. Write on the board: *the declaration of independence He served in congress for twenty years. The civil rights act was passed in 1964.*

Evaluate Your Reading Strategy

Distinguish Fact from Opinion *Say: You have practiced an important reading strategy. Now you can decide how well you have done. Does this statement describe how you read?*

> When I read, I think about whether a statement can be proven and is a fact or if the statement is the opinion of the author. Distinguishing fact from opinion helps me to be a more careful reader.

Reading Comprehension

Question-Answer Relationships

Sample Answers

1. Johnson was vice-president and became president when John F. Kennedy was assassinated in 1963.
2. He gave the speech on July 2, 1964.
3. voting booths, schools, workplaces, and public places
4. It promised equal rights to all citizens and an end to segregation laws.
5. by signing the act to make it a law
6. People in America have always struggled and fought for freedom and their rights. This new law will help more citizens realize equal rights.
7. Because some people were opposed to giving African-Americans equal rights, and the act made it a law.
8. To point out that the struggle and desire for personal rights and equality have always been part of the history of the country.
9. Yes, because it made people aware that discrimination and injustice needed to be corrected.
10. Both speeches point out the desire for everyone to have equal rights and justice. Johnson's speech gives a historical view to support equal rights. King's speech is more of a personal and emotional appeal.

Build Reading Fluency

Choral Read Aloud

Ask students to read aloud with you for 5–10 minutes daily. Remind them to keep their eyes on the words. This will help students with phrasing, intonation, and pronunciation.

Beyond the Reading

Reading Comprehension

Question-Answer Relationships (QAR)

"Right There" Questions

1. **Recall Facts** How did Lyndon B. Johnson become president of the United States? When?
2. **Recall Facts** When did President Johnson give his speech about the Civil Rights Act of 1964?
3. **Recall Facts** In what places did the new law make all citizens equal?

"Think and Search" Questions

4. **Find Main Ideas** What did the Civil Rights Act of 1964 promise?
5. **Find Main Ideas** How did President Johnson believe that he could continue the struggle for freedom?
6. **Paraphrase** Explain Johnson's speech in your own words.

"Author and You" Question

7. **Identify Cause and Effect** Why wa the Civil Rights Act necessary?

"On Your Own" Questions

8. **Draw Conclusions** Why do you think that President Johnson discussed American history in his speech?
9. **Support Opinions** Do you think that the Civil Rights Act was important? Why or why not?
10. **Compare and Contrast** Compare and contrast Johnson's speech with that of Martin Luther King Jr. in Chapter 3. How are they the same? How are they different?

Activity Book p. 211

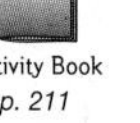
Stud CD-R

Build Reading Fluency

Choral Read Aloud

A choral read aloud means the teacher reads aloud together with the class. This helps improve your listening and reading skills.

1. Read aloud paragraphs 7–9, on page 399, with your teacher.
2. Try to keep up with the class.
3. You may point to the text as you rea

MULTI-LEVEL OPTIONS *Elements of Literature*

Newcomer Direct students to paragraphs 7–9 on p. 399. Read the paragraphs aloud and pause each time you say "We believe" so students can repeat the phrase aloud. ***Ask:*** *Why do you think that phrase is repeated?*

Beginning Direct students to paragraphs 7–9 on p. 399. Read the paragraphs aloud. Then ask students to say something important that they believe in. Record their responses. Create a class "speech" by having the class say "We believe" followed by individuals stating their response.

Intermediate Ask students to find repetition in "I Have a Dream" (pp. 383–387). Have them list the repeated words and phrases. ***Ask:*** *What do you believe in?* Have them use their responses to write short speeches with repetition. ***Ask:*** *Why is it important to repeat words and ideas in a speech?*

Advanced Ask students to write persuasive speeches that have sentences beginning with *We Believe. . . .* Remind students of the features of persuasive writing and the importance of repetition. Have them practice their speeches and then present them to the class.

isten, Speak, Interact 

onduct an Interview

In the first selection, Melissa Maupin
lls a story from President Johnson's life.
he story is told in the third person and
lls important facts from his life.

1. You will interview a classmate. Think of five questions you would like to ask him or her. The questions should include facts about his or her life, goals, and so forth.
2. Write your questions on paper or index cards. Interview the person and record the person's answers.
3. Save these questions and answers for the From Reading to Writing section of this chapter.

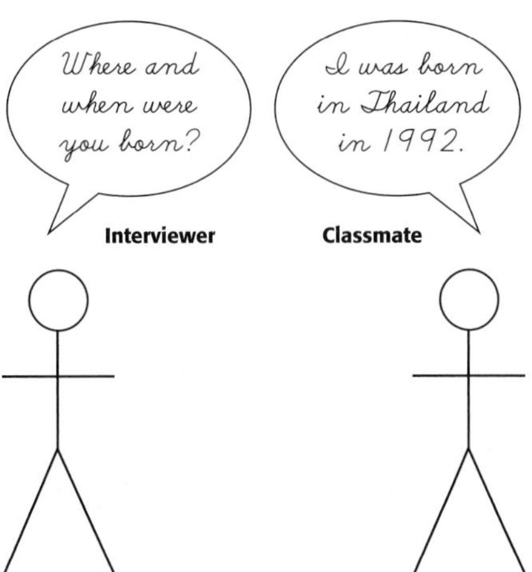

lements of Literature

ecognize Repetition in a Speech

Speechwriters sometimes use
epetition of a word or a phrase to help
e listeners understand. Repetition can
so make the speech sound powerful.

1. Reread paragraphs 7–9 on page 399. What phrase is used at the beginning of each paragraph?
2. Find another example of repeated phrases on page 401.
3. Recall Martin Luther King Jr.'s "I Have a Dream" speech. Can you remember the repeated words? If not, go back to page 384 and reread the speech.
4. Choose three of the sentences with repetition that you like best and record them in your Reading Log.

Reading Log

Activity Book p. 211

Student CD-ROM

Home Connection

Ask students to write five informational questions to ask a family member or a neighbor. Help students edit and revise their questions as necessary. Have them copy their final questions onto index cards. Tell students to conduct their interviews and to write their subjects' responses on the backs of the appropriate index cards. Ask students to share their findings in small groups.

Learning Styles *Musical*

Have students listen to the audio of the speech again. Then have students reread the speech. Ask students to write paragraphs that compare and contrast the experience of hearing a speech with the experience of reading a speech. Have students also tell which experience they prefer and to explain why.

Listen, Speak, Interact

Conduct an Interview

Teacher Resource Book: *Interview, p. 54*

1. **Prepare questions** Model interviewing a volunteer. Review question words and question formation. Have students prepare their own interview questions.
2. **Compose an interview form** Ask students to create a form for their interview. Instruct them to organize the form into questions and answers. Have pairs of students practice the interview using the form. Then have groups revise the form based on the practice.
3. **Newcomers** Ask students to suggest possible questions. List them on the board and have students practice asking them. Tell them to choose five of the questions and conduct their interview. Review how to ask for clarification and repeat an answer. Have students record their partner's responses.

Elements of Literature

Recognize Repetition in a Speech

1. **Use personal experiences** Have students think of other times when people repeat things, such as a sports coach, a teacher, a parent. Ask them if they remember better things they hear once or several times.
2. **Multi-level options** See MULTI-LEVEL OPTIONS on p. 402.

Answers

1. I believe
2. It does (not) say
3. I have a dream . . . Let freedom ring

ASSESS

Have students decide on a statement that summarizes the effectiveness of using repetition in speeches.

Beyond the Reading

Word Study

Identify Adjectives

Teacher Resource Book: *Personal Dictionary, p. 63*

Clarify terms Remind students that an adjective needs to refer to a person, place, or thing and is placed before the noun. Ask volunteers for examples of adjectives.

Answers

2. proud triumph; unending search; careful debate; bipartisan support; overwhelming majority

Grammar Focus

Use the Conjunction *Yet* to Show Contrast

Write on the board: *We won the game, yet I don't feel happy.* Point out the contrast between the two clauses and the connection between them with *yet.*

Answers

1. proud triumph. Yet those . . .; are created equal. Yet many . . .; blessings of liberty. Yet millions . . .
2. **a.** Yet my parents make me go to bed at 9:00.
   b. Yet I still don't understand it.

Have students brainstorm a list of adjectives about a favorite teacher.

Word Study

Identify Adjectives

People often use **adjectives** to make their sentences more interesting. An adjective is a word that describes a noun.

> One hundred and eighty-eight years ago this week a small band of valiant men began a long struggle for freedom.

The underlined words are all adjectives: *small* describes the size of the band of men, *valiant* describes the men themselves, and *long* describes the struggle. The sentence would not be as interesting if the adjectives were taken out.

1. Look at pages 399–401 and find these nouns.

triumph	search	debate
support	majority	

2. Find the adjective that describes each noun.
3. Look up the adjectives in a dictionary to find their meanings.

Personal Dictionary

The Heinle Newbury House Dictionary

Activity Book p. 212

Stude CD-RC

Grammar Focus

Use the Conjunction *Yet* to Show Contrast

In his speech, President Johnson contrasts people's opinions and facts. To do so, he uses the conjunction *yet.*

1. Find the sentences in President Johnson's speech where he uses *yet* to show differences. Look in paragraphs 5, 7, and 9 on page 399.
2. The conjunction *yet* shows contrast in the following sentences. Copy them on a piece of paper, and fill in the blanks.
   a. I think I am old enough to stay up late. Yet my parents ____ .
   b. I studied all day for my math test. Yet I ____ .

Activity Book pp. 213–214

Student Handbook

Stude CD-RC

MULTI-LEVEL OPTIONS *From Reading to Writing*

Newcomer Pair with advanced students. Have newcomers illustrate the biography of a classmate, family member, or neighbor. Ask advanced students to help add captions. Have partners work together to write and illustrate their biographies.

Beginning Pair with intermediate students. Ask beginners to list the main steps in writing a biography. Have partners work together to write and illustrate their biographies.

Intermediate Pair with beginners. Ask intermediate students to list the main events in their subjects' lives. Have them organize their ideas in pre-writing flowcharts. Have pairs use their flowcharts to write their biographies.

Advanced Pair with newcomers. Have partners work together to write and illustrate their biographies. Ask students to exchange their writing with other pairs for peer-review. Tell reviewers to evaluate mechanics, details, point of view, pronoun use, and verb tenses.

·om Reading to Writing

·rite a Biography

Use the questions and answers you ·ked a partner in the Listen, Speak, ·teract activity to write a short biography. ·you prefer, research information about ·lifferent person.

1. Evaluate your information. If you are unsure about a fact, ask the person you are writing about or do further research.
2. Use the biography of Lyndon Johnson as a model.
3. Use third-person point of view. Use the pronouns *she, he, it,* and *they.*
4. Use the past perfect tense when appropriate. (See page 378.)

Activity Book
p. 215

·cross Content Areas

·arn About the Branches of Government

The government of the United States ·s three **branches** (main parts).

The **legislative branch** makes the laws. ·consists of the House of Representatives ·d the Senate.

The **executive branch** approves and ·forces the laws. The president of the ·nited States heads this branch.

The **judicial branch** interprets the laws ·ays what they mean). The Supreme ·ourt makes up this branch of ·vernment.

Which branch of government does each · these newspaper headlines refer to?

1. **New Transportation Law Passed**
2. **Court Says Schools Must Get More Money**
3. **President Announces New Rules for Workplace Safety**

Activity Book
p. 216

From Reading to Writing

Write a Biography

1. **Think-pair-share** Have students review their notes and write a draft of a biography. Students can use the biography in the book as a model. Then have students share their drafts in pairs.
2. **Revise and add** Ask students to consider changes and additions to their biographies. Remind them to use adjectives to add interest and to use the past perfect tense when appropriate.
3. **Multi-level options** See MULTI-LEVEL OPTIONS on p. 404.

Across Content Areas: Social Studies

Learn About the Branches of Government

1. **Use a graphic organizer** Create a circle graph divided into thirds to illustrate the equal branches of the government. Ask students to explain what they know about the branches and their functions.
2. **Use newspapers and magazines** If possible, bring in local newspapers and have students look for articles about the different branches of government. Have them find the names of local representatives and senators.

Answers
1. legislative **2.** judicial **3.** executive

Have students match the names of the three branches with their duties.

Reteach and Reassess

Text Structure Draw a tree with three branches. Label the "roots" *Biography.* Have volunteers name and describe text features for the tree.

Reading Strategy Write on the board: *school lunch, homework,* and *school uniforms.* Have students select one topic and write two facts and two opinions about it in random order. Tell pairs to exchange lists and identify the facts and the opinions.

Elements of Literature Have students review "I Have a Dream." (p. 384) ***Ask:*** *Did the speaker use repetition? What words or phrases were repeated? What was the effect of the repetition?*

Reassess Ask students to write a paragraph comparing the two speeches. Remind students to evaluate the text structure and content.

UNIT 6
Apply and Expand

Materials

Student Handbook
CNN Video: *Unit 6*
Teacher Resource Book: *Lesson Plan, p. 33; Teacher Resources, pp. 35–64; Video Script, pp. 171–172; Video Worksheet, p. 178; School-Home Connection, pp. 154–160*
Teacher Resource CD-ROM
Assessment Program: *Unit 6 Test and End-of-Book Exam, pp. 97–108; Teacher and Student Resources, pp. 115–144*
Assessment CD-ROM
Transparencies
The Heinle Newbury House Dictionary/CD-ROM
Heinle Reading Library
Web Site: www.heinle.visions.com

Listening and Speaking Workshop

Give a Persuasive Speech

Teacher Resource Book: *Persuasive—Debate and Writing, p. 51*

Present an opinion Tell student to reread the speeches in this unit (“I Have a Dream” p. 380; “Speech to the Nation” p. 396) to recall features used in effective speeches.

Step 1: Plan your speech.

Arrange students in pairs to list reasons for and against.

UNIT 6 Apply and Expand

Listening and Speaking Workshop

Give a Persuasive Speech

Topic

In this unit, you read about people who helped others. Your school is thinking about requiring students to do community work. Examples of community work are helping the elderly and tutoring children. Is this a good idea? Present your opinion in a speech to the class.

Persuasive Speech

Introduction
State one issue and your position.
Give one argument from the other position and tell why it is not good.
Reason 1 with example and detail
Reason 2 with example and detail
Reason 3 with example and detail
Conclusion
Restate your position. Call for action.

Step 1: Plan your speech.

1. Make a list of reasons for and against the topic.
2. Decide if you are for or against community work.

Step 2: Write your speech.

Introduction

1. State the issue and your position.
2. State a reason on the other side of the issue. Then explain why that reason is not a good one. Give facts and examples to clarify your ideas.
3. Explain that there are many good reasons to support your position.

Reasons and Examples

1. Give three good reasons to support your position. This will help your listeners understand the major ideas of your speech.
2. Use phrases like “I am in favor of . . .” “I do not agree that . . .”
3. Support each of your reasons with facts and examples. This is your supporting evidence.
4. Be careful not to exaggerate or be disrespectful.

Conclusion

1. Tell what the issue means to you.
2. Urge your listeners to join you in taking action.

Step 3: Practice your speech.

1. Use note cards for each main point.
2. Use the Presentation Checklist.
3. Ask a partner to listen to you and give you feedback.
4. Revise your speech based on your partner’s feedback.

MULTI-LEVEL OPTIONS *Listening and Speaking Workshop*

Newcomer Ask students to draw pictures of different kinds of community service. Help them write key words to label each drawing.

Beginning Have students work with partners to make their *For* and *Against* lists. Tell students to try to contribute ideas for both columns.

Intermediate Tell students to write several choices for their opening statements. Ask small groups to evaluate one another’s openings. Have students select and refine their opening statements based on their peers’ comments. Remind students to be tactful and constructive.

Advanced Divide students into two groups based on the position they took in their speeches. Ask students to use their notes to conduct an informal debate on the topic of requiring students to perform community work.

Active Listening Checklist

1. I liked ____ because ____ .
2. I want to know more about ____ .
3. I thought the opening was interesting / not interesting.
4. You stayed on the topic. Yes / No
5. I understood the major ideas of your speech. Yes / No
6. I understood the facts you used as supporting evidence. Yes / No

Presentation Checklist

Did you:

1. have a good opening?
2. support your reasons with facts as evidence?
3. support your reasons with examples?
4. tell listeners what the issue means to you?
5. use interesting, specific words?
6. look at the audience?
7. speak so everyone could hear you?

Step 4: Present your speech.

1. Speak clearly and loudly enough for everyone to hear you.
2. Use expression to show that you respect the audience, but you are convinced of your opinion.

Viewing Workshop

View and Think

View Videos of Speeches

Find videos of the two speeches in this unit. Compare and contrast the printed and video versions of the speech.

1. How are the printed and video speeches the same or different?
2. What did you learn from the video that you did not know from the printed speech?
3. Which version most influences how you feel about the speech? What effect does it have on you?
4. How do you interpret the nonverbal messages in the video? For example, what does the speaker's gestures and body language tell you?
5. What do you like and not like about the videos of the speeches?

Further Viewing

Watch the *Visions* CNN Video for Unit 6. Do the Video Worksheet.

CNN Video

Step 2: Write your speech.
Point out the three main parts of a speech: introduction, reasons and examples, conclusions.

Step 3: Practice your speech.
Go over the checklists before students practice in pairs. After practicing their speeches, have students analyze the credibility of their partners. *Ask: Did you believe your partner? Did you trust their words? Why or why not? What suggestions would you give your partner to be more credible?* (example: be more confident, use stronger emotion, include more facts to support opinions, etc.) Allow time for students to revise and make adjustments in their speeches based on their partner's feedback.

Step 4: Present your speech.
Invite another class or parents to the class to see the presentations.

ASSESS

Have pairs choose the speech they thought was most effective and list the persuasive techniques used by the speaker. Tell them to make two suggestions to make the speaker more persuasive.

Portfolio

Students may choose to record or videotape their oral presentations to place in their portfolios.

Viewing Workshop

View and Think

Teacher Resource Book: *Two-Column Chart, p. 44*

Go over the instructions for the project.

1. **Use graphic organizers** Create a two-column chart to help students as they record similarities and differences they notice between the written and video versions of their selected speeches.
2. **Analyze effect** Use questions to guide students as they analyze the effect and influence of the versions on the audience.

Content Connection
Math

Help students to create a survey about school-required community work. Ask students to poll friends, classmates, and family members. Have them ask each person whether they support the idea of schools requiring community work. Then have students discuss their findings and use their data to create graphs that illustrate the numbers of and percentages of people that are for or against the idea.

Learning Styles
Mathematical

Tell students that the best way to persuade others is with a logical argument. Remind students that a logical argument makes sense and is supported by facts. Tell students that a good argument also addresses and refutes the opposing position. Ask students to evaluate whether their classmates' persuasive speeches offer logical arguments.

Writer's Workshop

Write a Research Report

Teacher Resource Book: *Know/Want to Know/Learned Chart (KWL), p. 42; Note-Taking, p. 58*

Brainstorm ideas. Have students suggest different famous people to research.

Step 1: Research.
Students can use a KWL to list questions and information they want to research.

Step 2: Revise questions.
After students have done some research, have them make adjustments in their report questions and plans.

Step 3: Record information.
Remind students to list sources.

Step 4: Organize your ideas.
Have students organize their ideas in chronological order.

Point out that they should include all information related to the person's accomplishment.

Writer's Workshop

Write a Research Report

> **Writing Prompt**
> Write a report about a famous person who was the first to do something.

Step 1: Research questions like:

1. *Who* was the first to . . . ? (for example, land on the moon)
2. *Where* did the main event take place?
3. *When* did the main event take place?
4. *How* did the person accomplish his or her goal?

Step 2: Revise questions.

1. Look up sources of information on the Internet, in the library, and in newspapers. You may also look for information in the readings of this unit and other units in your book.
2. Ask new questions as you look up information. Revise your questions and write them down.
3. Use headings and tables of contents to help you locate and organize information. Also use graphic features to locate and organize information. Some graphic features are maps, graphs, time lines, and charts.
4. Ask your teacher to help you interpret the information in the graphic features. What do the graphic features tell you?
5. Review what you learned. Use the information from your research and your own prior knowledge to ask more questions you need answers to.

Step 3: Record information.

1. When you find something useful for your report, summarize it *in your own words*. Then make a note card of the source where you found it. Refer to the Research Process section of the Student Handbook.
2. If you find something that you want to quote in your report (that is, use someone else's exact words), you *must* copy the words exactly and put them in quotation marks (". . . "). Make a careful note of the source. In your report, you *must* use the quotation marks and show who originally said or wrote the words.
3. Evaluate your research. Review your notes. Make sure your information is useful.

Step 4: Organize your ideas.

1. Choose the parts of the person's story that you want to tell. Organize them in chronological order. Use the headings, tables of contents, and graphic features from your research to help you.
2. For each part of the story, list the facts, examples, and evidence that support it. You will use the outline in the next step to organize this information.

MULTI-LEVEL OPTIONS *Writer's Workshop*

Newcomer Have students draw pictures of people who were the first to do things. Help students add titles and captions to their drawings.

Beginning Have students work with partners to gather information for their reports. Remind them to try to use multiple sources for their research.

Intermediate Have students write drafts of their body paragraphs. Tell them to begin by writing topic sentences. Remind students that a topic sentence tells the main idea of a paragraph. Have them complete their paragraphs with sentences that contain supporting details.

Advanced Have students assume their subjects' identities and write their reports in autobiographical form. Remind students to use first-person writing. Tell them that they should imagine what their subjects thought, felt, and experienced.

Step 5: Write a draft by hand or on a computer.

1. Write a TITLE for your report.
2. Write an INTRODUCTION.
   a. In one sentence, state what you are going to talk about. (This is your **thesis statement.**)
   b. Explain why this is an important topic to understand.
3. Write the BODY (two or three supporting paragraphs).
   a. In each paragraph, state one of your ideas.
   b. After stating your idea, give supporting details or examples.
   c. Write about your ideas in chronological order.
4. Write a CONCLUSION. Briefly restate your thesis.
5. Write a bibliography, a list of your SOURCES (the places where you got your information).
6. Make grammar work for you.
   a. Use the past perfect tense to talk about past actions that happened before other past actions: *He had already tried to climb the mountain.*
   b. Use *yet* to show contrast: *He was cold and tired. Yet he continued on.*
   c. Use appositives to identify other people in the report: *Diana Chen, his teammate, was a big help.*

Step 6: Revise and edit your report.

1. Proofread your report to find errors in paragraph indentation, spelling, capitalization, and punctuation.
2. If you use a computer, use software such as an online dictionary or thesaurus. Check definitions and spellings.
3. Collaborate with a partner to proofread your report and give you feedback. Also proofread your partner's work and give feedback.
4. Revise your draft. Blend paragraphs together. Use transition words. Combine sentences using conjunctions.

Step 7: Publish.

1. Prepare a final draft. Create a Table of Contents to organize your information.
2. Create a class collection of these reports. Review them for their strengths and weaknesses.
3. Set your goals as a writer based on your writing and the writing of your classmates.

The Heinle Newbury House Dictionary

Student Handbook

UNIT 6
Apply and Expand

Step 5: Write a draft.

Review the suggested order: introduction, body, and conclusion. Remind students to use the various grammar tenses and forms when appropriate.

Step 6: Revise and edit your report.

Review editing and proofreading points. Give clarification and explanation as needed. Then, in pairs, have students share their reports and give each other feedback on their drafts.

Step 7: Publish.

Encourage students to make their reports interesting. Display final reports on a bulletin board or your school Web site. Allow time for students to read one another's reports.

Have students write a sentence explaining the most interesting fact they learned about the person they researched.

Portfolio

Students may choose to include their writings in their portfolios.

Content Connection *Science*

Provide students with a list of everyday items, such as a zipper, flat-bottomed paper bags, a ball-point pen, or an aspirin. Have students use the Internet or other sources to find out who invented the item. Ask them to gather information about the person, when the item was discovered or invented, and how it changed or contributed to everyday life.

Learning Styles *Visual*

Have students create visual aids to enhance their reports. Have students include one or more of the following:

— maps, charts, or graphs

— pictures of their subjects

— timelines, flowcharts, or other graphic organizers

— other illustrations, drawings, or pictures

Tell students to create their visual aids by hand or on a computer.

UNIT 6
Apply and Expand

Projects

Project 1: Make a Book About a New Place

1. **Represent your ideas** Help students arrange their pictures, maps, and information effectively using color, graphics, and text.
2. **Write a news report** Have students work in pairs to research current news in their new places. Instruct them to collaborate to compose and organize a news report of one current event. Have them practice their reports with another pair. Then instruct them to revise their news reports based on feedback. Have them give their news reports to the class.

Project 2: Write a Letter to the President

Teacher Resource Book: *Business Letter, p. 57*

1. **Explain an idea** Brainstorm a list of possible issues. Have students choose something that affects them personally.
2. **Collaborate with other writers** Have students work in pairs to compose their letters. Then instruct them to organize their letters so they follow format in steps 4–6. Ask pairs to share their letters with other pairs. Based on the feedback, have pairs collaborate to revise their letters.

Portfolio 

Students may choose to include their projects in their portfolios.

Projects

These projects will help you expand what you know about frontiers. Work alone, with a partner, or with a group.

Project 1: Make a Book About a New Place

Everyone goes to new places at some time. Find information and pictures about a new place and make a book about it.

1. Look through magazines and find pictures of several places where you have never been. Cut out these pictures, if you can.
2. Glue each of your pictures onto a piece of paper. On the paper, write the name of the place shown.
3. On a note card, write down some questions you have about these places. Research answers to your questions at your school library or on the Internet. Write the facts you learned at the bottom of the pieces of paper.
4. Use maps that show where this place is located. Use and interpret the maps to answer some of your questions. What do the maps tell you? Write this information next to your pictures.
5. Bind your pages together to make a book. Add to the book as you learn about new places that you might go.

Project 2: Write a Letter to the Presiden

If you could write a letter to the president of the United States, what would you say? Collaborate with a partner to write your letter.

1. Think about something important to you, to your family, or to your community.
2. How can the president help? Make a list of your ideas on a piece of paper or make a draft on the computer.
3. Use correct letter format. Refer to your Student Handbook.
4. In the opening paragraph, state your reason for writing.
5. In the next paragraph, give facts and examples to support your position.
6. In conclusion, tell again what you would like to happen and how the president can help.
7. Revise and edit your letter. Be sure to use the Editing Checklist in your Student Handbook and all the steps you learned in the Writer's Workshops.
8. Sign your letter in your best cursive handwriting when you have finished

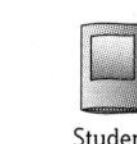
Student Handbook

MULTI-LEVEL OPTIONS *Projects*

Newcomer Have students draw pictures of themselves asking the President for help. Ask students to explain their drawings. Then help students add captions or speech balloons.

Beginning Have students draw pictures of themselves asking the President for help. Ask them to add captions or speech balloons that help explain what is happening in their pictures.

Intermediate Have students compile their letters. Help them submit their compiled letters to a newspaper, magazine, or other publication. If the letters are published, have students discuss how they feel about seeing their letters in print. ***Ask:*** *How might people react to these letters?*

Advanced Have students use the Internet, library, or other source to find the e-mail address for the President. Have students send their final drafts to the President. Ask students to share any responses with the class.

Further Reading

The books listed here explore the theme of frontiers. Read one or more of them. Write your thoughts and feelings about what you read. In your Reading Log, take notes on your answers to these questions:

1. In the books you have read, what common characteristics do the characters share?
2. How do the characters deal with the challenges presented by frontiers?
3. How are the experiences you read about similar to your own life experiences?

A Wrinkle in Time
by Madeleine L'Engle, Bantam Doubleday Dell Books for Young Readers, 1973. Meg and Charles, along with their friend Calvin, journey through time and space to find their father, who disappeared while working on a top-secret government project.

Lewis and Clark
by George E. Sullivan, Scholastic, Inc., 2000. Lewis and Clark kept journals of their 1804–1806 expedition to the Pacific Ocean. In this book, read about their journey in their own words.

They Had a Dream: The Civil Rights Struggle from Fredrick Douglass to Marcus Garvey to Martin Luther King Jr. and Malcom X
by Jules Archer, Penguin Putnam Books for Young Readers, 1996. This book chronicles the lives of important African-Americans in United States history.

Taking Charge: The Johnson White House
by Michael R. Beschloss, Simon & Schuster Children's, 2001. President Johnson tape-recorded all phone conversations and Oval Office meetings while he was in the White House. This book allows readers to read his thoughts and conversations about the Civil Rights Act and his meetings with Martin Luther King Jr.

Sarah, Plain and Tall
by Patricia MacLachlan, HarperCollins Children's Books, 1987. This book tells about life on the American prairie. Sarah, a new bride, comes to live with a family on the frontier and must adjust to her new life.

Dragon's Gate
by Laurence Yep, HarperCollins, 1994. This book gives an account of the lives of the Chinese immigrants who built the Transcontinental Railroad in the Sierra Mountains.

Across the Wide and Lonesome Prairie: The Oregon Trail Diary of Hattie Campbell
by Kristina Gregory, Scholastic, Inc., 1997. In her diary, 13-year-old Hattie tells the story of her trip from Missouri to Oregon. She writes about the joys and hardships her family faces as they make the long journey through the frontier.

Reading Log

Heinle Reading Library

UNIT 6
Apply and Expand

Further Reading

Teacher Resource Book: *Reading Log, p. 64*

Respond to Literature Have students select a book about the theme and prepare a written book report. Tell them to describe qualities and characteristics of the main characters. Ask them to include details of how the characters faced and dealt with problems and challenges in the story. Instruct students to give their own personal responses by pointing out similarities between their own lives and the lives of the characters.

Assessment Program: *Unit 6 Test pp. 97–102; End-of-Book Exam, pp. 103–108*

Skills Index

Grammar, Usage, and Mechanics

Adjectives, 130, 131, 201, 250, 404
comparative, 130, 250
superlative, 200

Adverbs, 38, 262, 263, 314

Affixes, 12, 100, 130, 144, 188, 262, 300, 314, 326, 340, 378

Appositives, 360, 409

Capitalization, 39, 149, 176, 177, 219, 281, 327, 345, 409

Clauses, 53, 276
dependent, 52, 53, 276, 281, 390
independent, 53
relative, 236, 281

Comma, 52, 276, 360

Complex Sentences, 52

Compound Sentences, 52, 75, 236

Compound Words, 26, 214

Conjunctions
and, 38, 188, 189
but, 188, 189
yet, 404, 409

Contractions, 70, 116, 117, 164

Infinitives, 250

Nouns, 130

Paragraph, 39

Parts of Speech, 164

Penmanship, 149, 345, 410

Possessives, 116, 117

Prefixes, 262, 300, 378

Prepositional Phrases, 164, 165, 189

Pronouns, 189, 214, 249, 405
first-person, 42, 53, 101, 131, 189, 204
referents, 214

Proper nouns, 176, 177

Punctuation, 101, 117, 281, 345
apostrophe, 281
contractions, 116, 117, 164
possessives, 116, 117
of clauses, 52, 53, 276, 390
commas, 52, 276, 360

Quotation Marks, 254, 299, 301, 377, 408

Resources
dictionary, 130, 262, 317, 325, 326, 340, 390, 393, 404
synonym finder, 303, 360
thesaurus, 360

Sentences
complex, 52
compound, 52, 75, 236
punctuation, 52, 53, 75, 101, 149, 219, 276, 281, 345, 360, 390, 409

Spelling, 301
-ed verb forms, 250
influence of languages and cultures, 52, 90
prefixes, 300, 378
root words, 52, 70, 276, 326, 378
suffixes, 12, 100, 130, 144, 188, 314, 340
use of resources to correct, 75, 149, 219, 281, 345, 409

Subject-Verb Agreement, 91, 326, 344

Suffixes, 12, 100, 130, 144, 188, 314, 340

Tenses
future, 100
future conditional, 116, 117
past, 12, 26, 70, 250, 251, 379
past continuous, 314, 315
past perfect, 378, 379, 405, 409
perfect
present perfect, 300, 344
present, 326
present conditional, 340, 344
present continuous tense, 144, 344
present perfect, 300, 344
simple present, 90, 91, 344
progressive (continuous), 144, 314, 315, 344

Verbs
be, 26, 27, 100, 250, 314
-ed forms, 250
modals, 12, 26, 70, 90–91, 100, 116–117, 144, 176, 250–251, 314, 326, 378
two-word verbs, 176

Listening and Speaking

Appreciation
aesthetic language, 4, 11, 141
oral interpretations, 406
oral reading
classic works, 180
contemporary works, 114, 128–129, 142–143, 199, 377

Audiences, 389
adapt spoken language for
diction, 359
usage, 359
word choice, 359
audience and setting
effective pitch, 73, 217, 261, 278, 279, 377
effective rate, 73, 217, 278, 299, 343, 377
effective tone, 73, 129, 187, 217, 261, 278, 279, 299, 389
effective volume, 73, 217, 261, 278, 299, 377
clarification and support, 278
with elaborations, 73, 99, 147, 343
with evidence, 72, 389, 406
with examples, 406
content area vocabulary
arts, 3, 263, 327, 329, 341
language arts, 101, 155, 237
math, 145, 177, 351
science, 13, 15, 27, 71, 82, 91, 165, 177, 265, 277, 303, 315, 325, 379
social studies, 29, 39, 41, 55, 81, 93, 103, 117, 119, 131, 133, 167, 179, 189, 191, 201, 203, 215, 225, 239, 251, 253, 287, 301, 317, 361, 363, 381, 391, 393, 405
dramatic interpretations
experiences, 163
plays, 117, 313
poems, 13, 145, 165
stories, 25, 377
evaluate
others' presentations, 73, 147, 149, 217, 278, 343, 389, 406, 407
own presentations, 73, 217, 278, 343
interviewing, 89, 129, 146, 175, 278, 403
providing information, 72
reaction, 192
reporting, 72, 146–147, 278–279
requesting, 11, 73, 76, 89, 146

Content Areas
arts, 3, 263, 327, 329, 341
language arts, 101, 155, 237
math, 145, 177, 351
science, 13, 15, 27, 71, 82, 89, 91, 165, 177, 265, 277, 303, 315, 325, 379
social studies, 29, 39, 41, 55, 81, 93, 103, 117, 119, 131, 133,

167, 179, 189, 191, 201, 203, 215, 225, 239, 251, 253, 287, 301, 317, 361, 363, 381, 391, 393, 405

Critical Listening
evaluate spoken message
content, 73, 99, 147, 217, 278, 343, 407
credibility, 149, 342, 407
delivery, 73, 217, 278, 299, 343, 389, 407
monitor understanding, 99, 147, 217, 278, 343, 407
perception of message, 73
persuasive techniques, 382, 391, 406–407
seek clarification, 73, 99, 147, 278, 343
speaker, 192
nonverbal message, 217
opinion, 69, 149, 394
perspective, 76, 407
purpose, 278
repetition, 382
verbal message, 73, 147, 156, 217, 278, 343, 407
verifiable fact, 69, 394, 406, 407

Culture, 53
connect
experiences, 42
ideas, 11, 40, 51, 69, 143, 146, 163, 166, 178, 190, 199, 213, 235, 249, 252, 264, 350, 359, 380, 394
information, 41, 50, 143, 239
insights, 42, 50
language use, 51, 143, 286, 345
oral traditions, 143, 155

Paired Interactions
compare and contrast, 1
debate, 69
description, 11, 249
dialogue, 187, 299, 313
identify
colloquial speech, 51
sequence of events, 37, 99
interview, 89, 129, 175, 278, 403
personal experience
describe, 11, 99, 249
discuss, 163, 275
personal opinion, expressing, 36, 68
personal opinion, supporting, 402
proofreading, 409
retell, 37
role-play, 25, 89, 175, 299
shared reading, 325
story, 143

Presentations
biography, 216–217, 278–279
debate, 69
descriptions, 99, 163
dialogue, 187, 299, 313, 377
discussion, 199
dramatic read-aloud, 117, 145, 165, 261, 377
evaluate, 69
others' presentations, 73, 343, 389, 406, 407
own presentations, 73, 217, 278, 343
interview, 89, 129, 146, 175, 278, 403
letter to the editor, 149
narrative, 143, 216–217, 278–279, 377
news report, 72–73
oral summary, 146–147, 342–343
oral traditions, 143
play
lines from a play, 313
scene from a play, 115
poem, 13, 145, 165
report, 278–279
role-play, 25, 89, 175, 299
shared reading, 325
speech, 72–73, 99, 192, 199, 201, 220, 389, 406–407
story, 143, 377

Purpose
determine purpose, 146, 199, 235, 254, 278, 342, 405, 408
distinguish intonation patterns, 115, 129, 377
distinguish sounds, 11, 316, 389
eliminate barriers, 175, 199, 316
organize, 235
produce intonation patterns, 115, 129, 377
produce sounds, 389
summarize, 235
take notes, 235
understand major idea, 217, 278, 407
understand supporting evidence, 407

Speaking Preparation
charts, 69, 115, 199, 275, 286
graphic organizers, 72
Internet resources, 72, 220
interview form, 175
note cards, 72, 278, 279
questions to answer, 72, 89, 146, 175, 216, 220, 278, 342
rehearse, 342, 377, 406
technology, 72, 216
visuals, 69, 72, 99, 220

Speaking Style
speech, 192, 199, 382

Reading

Comprehension
analyze characters, 10, 24, 36, 50, 51, 68, 69, 98, 114, 142, 198, 254, 339, 359
author purpose, 49, 161, 173, 197, 247, 259, 297, 308, 311, 387, 388, 397
author strategy, 24, 56, 231, 297, 308
build background, 3, 15, 29, 41, 55, 81, 93, 103, 119, 133, 155, 167, 179, 191, 203, 225, 239, 253, 265, 287, 303, 317, 329, 351, 363, 381, 393
cause and effect, 16, 18–23, 24, 36, 82, 88, 174, 186, 212, 248, 260, 324, 338, 358, 402
chronology, 98, 114, 175, 180, 182–185, 275, 352, 354–357, 394
compare and contrast, 11, 50, 76, 88, 128, 212, 226, 228–232, 234, 304, 402
connect, 3, 10, 15, 29, 41, 42, 44–49, 50, 55, 81, 93, 98, 103, 114, 119, 128, 133, 142, 143, 155, 167, 174, 179, 186, 191, 198, 203, 212, 225, 234, 239, 253, 265, 274, 286, 287, 303, 312, 317, 324, 329, 351, 363, 381, 393
details, 56, 58–67, 136, 137, 170–173, 266, 268–273, 376, 388, 394
dialogue, 56, 254, 256–259, 261, 288
draw conclusions, 50, 68, 98, 114, 120, 122–127, 128, 142, 204, 206–211, 274, 298, 312, 376, 382, 384–387, 388, 402
draw inferences, 4–9, 10, 68, 82, 84–87, 88, 114, 128, 174, 186, 198, 212, 234, 260, 298, 312, 330, 332–337, 338, 359, 388, 401
evaluate, 142, 162, 234, 260,

274, 312, 405
experience for comprehension, use of, 2, 54, 80, 92, 102, 118, 132, 154, 166, 202, 224, 238, 252, 316, 328
fact and opinion, 192, 388, 394, 396–401, 402
graphic organizers, 2, 40, 51, 201, 215, 240, 279, 304
identify, 24, 36, 51, 61, 98, 99, 114, 131, 186, 248, 253, 312, 358, 393
illustrations
analyzing, 162
"how-to" book, 330
images, 88
interpret, 88, 186, 198, 246, 260, 298, 313, 324, 410
judgments, making, 162, 198, 260
knowledge for comprehension, use of, 2, 14, 28, 40, 54, 80, 92, 102, 118, 132, 154, 166, 178, 190, 202, 224, 238, 252, 264, 286, 302, 316, 328, 350, 362, 380, 392
main idea and details, 10, 36, 56, 58–67, 68, 136, 137, 168, 170–173, 266, 268–273, 274, 338, 358, 376, 388, 402
make modifications
asking questions, 324, 358
rereading aloud, 11
searching for clues, 15, 179, 287, 363, 393
using reference aids, 13, 191
memoir, 204
mental images, 4, 98, 156, 158–161, 364, 366–375
monitor comprehension, 16, 156, 199, 266, 318, 364
narration, 56
outline, 318, 320–323
paraphrase, 24, 212, 376, 388, 402
predict, 24, 30, 31–35, 50, 120, 122–127, 128, 212, 288, 290–297
prior knowledge, 2, 14, 28, 40, 54, 80, 92, 102, 118, 132, 154, 166, 178, 190, 202, 224, 238, 252, 264, 286, 302, 316, 328, 350, 362, 380, 392
purposes for reading, 49, 173, 197, 247
adjust purpose, 11, 25, 37, 51, 69, 89, 99, 163, 175, 188, 213, 300, 310, 314, 347, 352, 377
to enjoy, 347, 377
establish purpose, 77, 151, 221, 304, 314, 347, 352, 377
to find out, 56, 58–67
to interpret, 352, 377
to solve problems, 352, 377
to understand, 10, 50
questions
different levels, 10, 24, 36, 50, 68, 88, 98, 114, 128, 142, 162, 174, 186, 198, 212, 234, 248, 260, 274, 298, 312, 324, 338, 358, 376, 388, 402
different types, 2, 28, 72, 76, 89, 92, 118, 149, 150, 224, 240, 249, 251, 263, 301, 328, 350
test-like questions, 14, 279, 302
recall facts, 10, 24, 36, 50, 68, 88, 98, 114, 128, 142, 162, 174, 180, 182–185, 186, 198, 212, 234, 248, 260, 274, 298, 302, 312, 324, 338, 352, 354–357, 358, 376, 388, 402
reflect, 198
sequence of events, 37, 99, 104, 105–113, 134, 136–139, 174, 175, 212, 274, 324, 376
setting, analyzing, 50, 98
similarities and differences across texts, 4, 101, 304
speculate, 174, 198, 298, 324, 338, 376
steps in process, 88, 274
study strategies, 234, 265, 324, 352, 382, 403
summarize, 68, 94, 96–97, 142, 245, 324
support inferences, 6, 7, 9, 65, 66, 82, 162, 337, 376, 401
text features
biography, 168, 304, 394
diary, 94, 180
drama, 304
fable, 4
fiction, 16, 94, 120, 134, 226, 364
first-person narrative, 42
folktale, 254
historical fiction, 94, 134
historical narrative, 30, 94
"how-to" book, 330
informational text, 82, 352, 361
journal, 134
memoir, 204
narrative, 30, 42, 288
nonfiction narrative, 30, 240
play, 104
poem, 4, 156
realistic adventure fiction, 16
realistic fiction, 16, 120
science fiction, 364
scientific informational text, 82
short story, 56, 71
speech, 192, 382
textbook, 318
text's structure/progression, 4
captions, 330
fable, 4
fiction, 226
first-person narrative, 53, 249
headings, 318, 361, 408
inductive organization, 266
locate information, 180, 182–185, 318, 352, 354–357
narrative, 53, 249, 288
recall information, 10, 24, 36, 50, 68, 98, 114, 128, 142, 162, 174, 180, 182–185, 186, 198, 212, 234, 248, 260, 274, 298, 302, 312, 324, 338, 352, 354–357, 376, 388, 402
subheadings, 318
textbook, 318
timeline, 134, 168, 246
visuals, 36, 59, 88, 162, 317, 330, 343, 354, 376
Content Areas
arts, 3, 263, 327, 329, 341
language arts, 101, 155, 237
math, 145, 177, 351
science, 13, 15, 27, 71, 82, 91, 165, 177, 265, 277, 303, 315, 325, 379
social studies, 29, 39, 41, 55, 81, 93, 103, 117, 119, 131, 133, 167, 179, 189, 191, 201, 203, 215, 225, 239, 251, 253, 287, 301, 317, 361, 363, 381, 391, 393, 405
Culture, 53
common characteristics, 42, 50
compare
others' experiences, 42, 50, 143
own experiences, 42, 50, 143, 248

connections, 41, 42, 50, 133, 143, 239, 286
distinctive characteristics, 143, 239, 248
themes, 54

Fluency
adjust reading rate, 50, 114, 198, 265, 312, 388
choral reading, 128, 402
echo reading, 162, 376
independent-level materials, 77, 221, 283, 413
instructional-level materials, 2, 14, 28, 40, 54, 80, 92, 102, 118, 132, 154, 166, 178, 190, 202, 224, 238, 252, 264, 286, 302, 316, 328, 350, 362, 380, 392
rapid word recognition, 36, 98, 212
read aloud, 10, 24, 128, 162, 198, 213, 261, 402
read chunks, 24, 68, 186, 234
read silently, 68, 186, 198, 234, 274, 298, 358
read to memorize, 142
read to scan, 248, 324, 325
repeated reading, 88, 174, 260, 298, 338

Genres, 16, 101
biography, 168, 304, 394
diary, 94, 101, 180
drama, 304
fable, 4
fiction, 16, 94, 120, 134, 226, 364
folktale, 254
historical fiction, 94, 134
"how-to" book, 330
informational text, 82, 318, 352, 361
journal, 101, 134
memoir, 101, 204
narrative, 113, 288
first-person, 42, 101, 129, 131, 189, 249
historical, 30
nonfiction, 30, 240
short story, 56
play, 104
poem, 4, 11, 141, 156
realistic fiction, 16, 120
science fiction, 363, 364
speech, 192, 382
story, 56

Inquiry and Research
charts, 13, 54, 80, 102, 120, 132, 133, 144, 154, 164, 166, 190, 224, 261, 299, 362, 380, 392
draw conclusions, 50, 68, 98, 114, 120, 122–127, 128, 142, 204, 206–211, 274, 298, 312, 376, 382, 384–387, 388, 402
electronic texts, 217
experts, 76, 177, 220, 277, 410
form and revise questions, 76, 218, 220, 403, 408, 410
graphic features, 72, 145, 408, 410
graphs, 216, 302, 410
maps, 28, 29, 41, 81, 93, 103, 119, 133, 167, 170, 179, 191, 203, 215, 239, 269, 279, 287, 290, 301, 351, 354, 410
timelines, 99, 134, 246
Venn Diagram, 304
informational sources, 224
library, 224, 225, 237
Internet, 76, 148, 150, 191, 216, 220, 279, 282, 346, 408, 410
make charts, 13, 54, 69, 74, 76, 80, 102, 115, 120, 131, 132, 133, 148, 154, 164, 166, 190, 199, 224, 261, 275, 282, 286, 341, 362, 380, 392
media, 73, 76, 147, 150, 217, 220, 279, 282, 343, 346, 407, 410
outline ideas, 235, 318, 320–323, 408–409
print resources, 73, 147, 192, 217, 242–246, 303, 317, 325, 393, 407
report, 408
research project, 76, 148, 150, 408, 410
speech, 72–73, 192, 220, 407
statements, 409
summarize and organize information, 224, 225
take notes, 408
technology presentation, 216, 217
text organizers
graphic features, 51, 165, 201, 215, 240, 242–246, 279, 304, 391
headings, 318, 361, 408
table of contents, 409
visuals, 216, 279

Literary Concepts
author's perspective, 97, 139, 141
cause and effect, 16, 18–23, 24, 36, 82, 88, 186, 212, 248, 260, 324, 338, 358, 402
chronological order, 114, 175, 180, 182–185, 275, 352, 354–357, 361, 394
compare and contrast, 50, 76, 88, 128, 212, 226, 228–232, 304, 306–311, 402
compare communication, 345
deductive organization, 266
inductive organization, 266
purpose of text, 49, 173, 197, 247, 259
entertain, 156, 288, 304
express, 42, 156, 180
influence/persuade, 74, 148–149, 344, 389
inform, 30, 82, 318
persuade, 389

Literary Response
compare and contrast ideas, themes, issues, 11, 50, 76, 88, 128, 162, 402
connect ideas, themes, issues, 77, 234, 312, 411
interpret, 88, 186, 198, 246, 260
through discussion, 69, 199, 213
through enactment, 25, 175, 313, 359
through journal writing, 77, 221, 382, 377
through media, 279, 324, 407, 410
make connections, 10, 42, 44–49, 98, 114, 128, 142, 155, 174, 186, 198, 212, 234, 274, 312, 324
offer observations, 338
raise questions, 89, 175, 218, 397
react, 68, 69, 221, 260
reading log, 51, 77, 99, 115, 163, 168, 175, 180, 199, 213, 226, 235, 261, 275, 299, 304, 325, 330, 352, 359, 377, 382, 389, 403
reflect, 198
speculate, 174, 198, 298, 324, 338, 376
support responses
own experiences, 142
relevant aspects of text, 6, 7, 9, 65, 66, 162, 204, 206–211, 256, 337, 376

Literary Terms
act, 304
analogy, 200, 234
character, 4, 16, 56, 94, 104, 120, 134, 226, 254, 304, 364
characterization, 339

changes, 10, 24, 50, 68, 261, 312
conflict, 68, 298, 312, 359
direct, 51
indirect, 51
motivation, 69
point of view, 42, 129, 249, 299, 304, 394
relationship, 10, 298, 312, 359
traits, 261
colloquial speech, 51
descriptive language, 325
dialogue, 56, 104, 134, 254, 261, 288
diary, 94, 101, 180
direct address, 180, 192, 382
excerpt, 14, 16, 28, 40, 42, 80, 92, 118, 132, 166, 178, 202, 224, 286, 302, 316, 350, 362, 380, 392
fiction, 16, 226
historical, 94, 134
realistic, 16, 120
scientific, 364
figurative language, 25, 200, 234, 390
simile, 25
first-person point of view, 42, 101, 129, 131, 189, 249
flashback, 99, 275, 277
folktale, 254
foreshadowing, 213
free verse, 140
graphics, 318
journal, 101, 134
lesson of a story, 254
memoir, 101, 204
metaphor, 143
mood, 199, 377
moral of a story, 4
narration, 56
narrator, 104
nonfiction, 240
novel, 16
personification, 37, 39
playwright, 115, 304
plot, 36, 104, 120, 226
point of view, 42, 97, 129, 217, 249, 299, 304, 394
problem resolution, 42
rhyme, 4, 11, 156, 163, 165
scene, 104, 115, 304
setting, 16, 94, 115, 120, 204, 352, 364
stage directions, 304, 312, 313
stanza, 4, 156
style, 129, 192, 199, 235, 339, 382
symbolism, 388
tale, 254
theater, 115, 304, 313
third-person point of view, 299, 301, 304, 394, 405
tone, 187, 189, 199, 201, 248
transitions, 175

Purposes
adjust purpose, 77, 151, 221, 304, 347, 411
appreciate writer's craft, 235, 259, 299, 347
complete forms, 73, 147, 217
entertain, 156, 161, 180, 308, 389
establish purpose, 17, 151, 221, 304, 347, 411
inform, 30, 173, 197, 247, 325, 327, 364, 389
make recommendation, 77, 352
models for writing, 27, 71, 177, 251, 405
take action, 151, 395
write a response, 347, 413

Reading Strategies, 4
cause and effect, 16, 18–23, 24, 36, 88, 174, 186, 212, 248, 269, 324, 338, 358, 402
chronology, 114, 175, 180, 182–185, 275, 352, 354–357, 394
compare and contrast, 1, 50, 128, 212, 226, 228–232, 304, 306–311, 402
compare with own experience, 10, 42, 44–49, 98, 114, 128, 142, 174, 186, 198, 234, 274, 312, 358
conclusions, 50, 68, 98, 114, 120, 122–127, 128, 142, 204, 206–211, 274, 298, 312, 376, 382, 384–387, 388, 402
dialogue to understand character, 254, 256–259, 261, 288
fact from opinion, 192, 388, 394, 396–401, 402
graphic sources, 240, 242–246
inferences, 4–9, 10, 68, 82, 84–87, 88, 114, 128, 174, 186, 198, 212, 234, 260, 312, 330, 332–337, 338, 359, 388, 401
main idea and details, 10, 36, 56, 58–67, 68, 136, 137, 168, 170–173, 266, 268–273, 274, 338, 358, 376, 388, 402
mental images, 4, 98, 156, 158–161, 364, 366–375
predict, 24, 30, 31–35, 50, 120, 122–127, 128, 212, 288, 290–297
represent text information in outline, 318, 320–323
sequence of events, 37, 99, 104, 105–113, 134, 136–139, 168, 174, 175, 212, 274, 324, 376
summarize, 68, 94, 96–97, 142, 245, 324
text evidence, 142, 330, 332–337, 382, 384–387

References, 277
dictionary, 3, 130, 133, 155, 163, 203, 236, 253, 262, 300, 317, 325, 326, 340, 390, 393, 404, 409
encyclopedia, 13, 191, 279
experts, 76, 177, 220, 277, 410
glossary/glosses, 90, 191, 265, 317
Internet, 76, 148, 150, 191, 216, 220, 279, 282, 346, 408, 410
magazines, 191
newspaper, 191
software, 281, 220
synonym finder, 167, 303, 360
thesaurus, 167, 360, 409

Text Sources
anthology, 75, 219
classic work, 182, 221
contemporary work, 18, 32, 44, 194, 290, 366, 384, 398, 413
electronic text, 73, 217
informational text, 82, 352, 361
Internet, 76, 148, 150, 191, 216, 220, 279, 282, 346, 408, 410
library, 224, 225, 237
manual, 220
novel, 77, 151, 221, 283, 347, 411
play, 105, 305
poetry, 4, 11, 156
textbook, 317, 318

Vocabulary Development
affixes, 12, 188, 300, 314, 326, 340, 378
analogies, 200, 234
compound words, 26, 214
connotative meaning, 55, 381, 390
content area words
arts, 3, 263, 327, 329, 341
language arts, 101, 155, 237
math, 145, 177, 351

science, 13, 15, 27, 71, 82, 91, 165, 177, 265, 277, 303, 315, 325, 379
social studies, 29, 39, 41, 55, 81, 93, 103, 117, 119, 131, 133, 167, 179, 189, 191, 201, 203, 215, 225, 239, 251, 253, 287, 301, 317, 361, 363, 381, 391, 393, 405
context clues, 15, 179, 287, 363, 393
denotative meaning, 52, 381, 390
derivatives, 52, 81, 236
draw on experiences, 265, 329, 351, 363
figurative language, 25, 200, 234, 390
homonyms, 41
key phrases, 10
key words, 239, 393
listening to selections, 114, 128, 142, 199, 377
multiple-meaning words, 41
personal dictionary, 13, 52, 55, 70, 81, 103, 130, 133, 144, 155, 167, 176, 188, 203, 225, 236, 262, 276, 300, 303, 314, 317, 326, 329, 340, 360, 363, 376, 393
reference aids, 3, 130, 133, 155, 163, 167, 191, 203, 265, 326, 340, 390, 393, 404
related words, 27, 29, 39, 71, 81, 88, 119, 131, 236, 239, 253
repetition, 225
root words, 52, 70, 90, 133, 236, 253, 276, 326, 378
strategies
LINK strategy, 103
word wheel, 81, 351
synonym finder, 3, 13, 167, 303, 360
synonyms, 3, 13, 93, 167, 303, 360
thesaurus, 167, 360
word origins, 52, 81, 90, 236, 262, 276, 326

Word Identification
context, 15, 179, 287, 363
contractions, 164
derivations, 52, 81, 236
dictionary, 53, 55, 81, 90, 130, 155, 203, 236, 253, 340, 390, 393, 404
glossary/glosses, 90, 191, 265, 317
language structure, 12, 38, 70, 164, 176, 188, 214, 308
letter-sound correspondences, 90
meanings, 52, 53, 133, 203, 214, 225, 253, 300, 325, 378, 381, 390, 404, 409
prefixes, 262, 300, 378
pronunciation, 90, 163
root words, 70, 133, 276, 378
Greek, 90, 276, 326
Latin, 52, 236, 276
suffixes, 12, 100, 130, 144, 188, 314, 340

Writing

Connections
authors
challenges, 72, 161, 211, 233, 273, 297
strategies used, 231, 297, 308
collaboration with other writers, 13, 146–147, 175, 213
correspondence
e-mail, 280–281
letter, 148–149
mail, 149, 280

Culture
compare and contrast, 150
others' experiences, 76

Forms
bibliography, 409
biography, 177, 277, 405
book, 410
dialogue, 117, 301
diary, 101, 189
editorial, 344
e-mail, 280–281
folktale, 263
"how-to" article, 341
informational text, 91, 361
instructions, 341
interview
form, 175
questions, 146, 175, 403
journal, 101, 134
letter, 148–149, 410
list, 74, 213, 392, 406
magazine article, 76, 150
memoir, 215
narrative, 74, 301, 379
first-person, 53, 101, 131, 189, 251
historical, 39
persuasive speech, 391, 406–407
play, 117
scene from a play, 315
poem, 11, 13, 145, 165
poster, 76, 150, 282
report, 72–73, 408–409
review, 75
science fiction, 379
speech, 201, 220, 391, 406–407
story, 237
realistic adventure story, 27
realistic story, 131
short story, 71
Web article/page, 76, 220

Inquiry and Research, 218, 282
concept map, 72, 165, 391
evaluation, 405, 408
guest speakers, 76, 148, 150, 220, 277
learning log, 150, 282, 411
on-line searches, 76, 148, 150, 177, 341
organize facts, 148, 216, 282, 408
organize ideas, 235, 344, 391, 408
outline, 235, 408–409
periodicals, 76, 150
presentations, 76, 216, 220
prior knowledge, 148
questions, 89, 146, 218, 220, 282, 397, 403, 408, 410
sources, citation of, 218, 408, 409
summarize facts, 282, 408
summarize ideas, 235
take notes, 235, 408
technology presentations, 72
timelines, 216

Literary Devices
characterization, 51, 53
chronological order, 361, 394, 408, 409
dialogue, 263
figurative language, 25, 391
flashback, 99, 277
incomplete sentences, 129, 131
metaphors, 143
personification, 37, 39
repetition, 391, 403
rhyming words, 11, 163, 165
table of contents, 409
thesis statement, 409
timeline, 39
tone, 187, 189, 199, 201
word choice, varying, 93

Purpose
appropriate form, 361, 412
appropriate literary devices, 11
audience and purpose, 389, 391
appropriate style, 235, 237, 339, 341, 391

appropriate tone, 187, 189, 199, 201
appropriate voice, 53, 101, 131, 189, 251, 301, 405
ideas, 27, 53, 71, 216, 251, 344, 366, 393, 410
literary response, 218
purposes
to develop, 27, 346
to discover, 76, 90, 155, 262, 288, 318, 392, 413
to entertain, 27, 74, 131, 301, 315, 379, 389
to express, 13, 53, 71, 145, 165, 215, 237, 251
to influence/persuade, 74, 148–149, 344, 389, 391, 410
to inform, 12, 39, 73, 91, 117, 145, 177, 201, 251, 263, 277, 280, 327, 361, 389
to instruct, 327, 341
to problem solve, 53
to record, 39, 101, 189, 215, 277, 405
to reflect on ideas, 117
transitions, 175

Writing Process
analyze writing, 27
develop drafts, 74, 148, 218, 280–281, 344, 409, 410
edit drafts, 75, 91, 149, 219, 281, 345, 361, 409, 410
evaluate writing
criteria, 75, 149, 216, 219, 281, 345
others' writing, 406
own writing, 75, 76, 91, 101, 145, 149, 201, 219, 220, 281, 345, 361, 409, 410
grammar, usage, and mechanics
adjectives, 131, 201
adverbs, 262, 263
capitalization, 39, 176, 177, 327
clauses, 53, 236, 237
conjunctions, 38, 188, 189, 404, 409
contractions, 117
paragraph, 39
possessives, 117
prepositional phrases, 165, 189
pronouns, 53, 249, 405
proper nouns, 177
punctuation, 53, 75, 101, 117, 149, 219, 281, 345, 409
prewriting strategies, 148
brainstorming, 145, 165, 280, 282, 344
charts, 74, 76, 131, 148, 282, 341
graphic organizers, 72, 165, 391
lists, 74, 76, 145
logs, 74, 101, 131, 218, 344, 379
notes, 72
story chart, 27
proofread, 75, 149, 219, 361, 409
publish, 75, 149, 219, 345, 409
reference materials, use of, 76, 148, 277, 341, 408
resource materials, use of, 76, 148, 277, 341, 408
review collection of written works, 75
revise drafts, 75, 91, 149, 219, 281, 345, 361, 409, 410
supporting ideas, 408, 409, 410
technology, use of, 72, 76, 148, 149
text structure/progression, 39, 53, 71
sequence of events, 91, 134, 175, 280

Viewing and Representing

Analysis
interpret and evaluate meaning, 1, 79, 88, 147, 153, 162, 223, 241–246, 279, 285, 324, 349, 404, 406
nonverbal messages, 343
media
compare and contrast, 73, 147, 217, 345, 407
effect, 147
electronic media, 73, 147, 217
film, 147
graphic organizers, 279
to influence, 343
to inform, 343
print media, 73, 147, 217, 242–246, 407
purpose, 147, 217, 343, 407
technology presentations, 217
video, 73, 147, 217, 279, 343, 407
visual media, 73, 147, 162, 217, 330, 343, 354, 376, 407
rank order, 145
visuals, 59, 88, 217, 317, 330, 343, 354, 376, 406

Content Areas
math, 145
social studies, 301

Interpretation
choice of style, elements, media, 88, 147
important events and ideas, 147, 246, 279, 324
media to compare ideas, 73, 147, 217, 402, 406

Production
assess message, 343, 407
media, 76, 150, 220, 282, 346, 410
technology, 72, 76, 216, 220
video, 313
visuals, 13, 72, 76, 131, 216, 220, 263, 282, 341, 345, 346, 410

Credits

Text

Unit 1

Pp. 6–7, THE RACE. Text copyright © 2001 by JENNIFER TRUJILLO. From the book *Love to Mamá: A Tribute to Mothers.* Permission arranged with Lee & Low Books Inc., New York, NY 10016.

Pp. 8–9, THE CAMEL DANCES. TEXT AND ILLUSTRATION COPYRIGHT © 1980 BY ARNOLD LOBEL. Used by permission of HarperCollins Publishers.

Pp. 17–23, THE HATCHET. Reprinted with the permission of Simon & Schuster Books for Young Readers, an imprint of Simon & Schuster Children's Publishing Division from HATCHET by Gary Paulsen. Copyright © 1987 Gary Paulsen. Audio rights: From *Hatchet* by Gary Paulsen. Copyright © 1987 by Gary Paulsen. Used by permission of Flannery Literary.

Pp. 31–35, ANTARCTIC ADVENTURE. From ANTARCTIC ADVENTURE: EXPLORING THE FROZEN SOUTH by Meredith Hooper. Published in the United States by DK Publishing, Inc. Text copyright © 2000 by Meredith Hooper. Reproduced by permission of Dorling Kindersley Ltd.

Pp. 43–49, YANG THE YOUNGEST. From YANG THE YOUNGEST AND HIS TERRIBLE EAR, copyright © 1992 by Lensey Namioka. Used by permission of Lensey Namioka. All rights are reserved by the Author.

Pp. 57–67, THE SCHOLARSHIP JACKET, by Marta Salinas. From *Nosotras: Latina Literature Today* edited by María del Carmen Boza, Beverly Silva, and Carmen Valle. Copyright © 1986 by Bilingual Press/Editorial Bilingüe (Arizona State University, Tempe, AZ). Reprinted by permission.

Unit 2

Pp. 83–87, WHY DO LEAVES CHANGE COLOR IN THE FALL?, by World Wide Web. From "Why Do Leaves Change Color in the Fall?" Published on-line at http://www.sciencemadesimple.com/leaves.html. Copyright © 1997 by Science Made Simple, Inc., PO Box 503, Voorhees, NJ 08043.

Pp. 95–97, ELIZABETH'S DIARY. From OUR STRANGE NEW LAND: ELIZABETH'S DIARY by Patricia Hermes. Copyright © 2000 by Patricia Hermes. Reprinted by permission of Scholastic Inc.

Pp. 105–113, AND NOW MIGUEL. COPYRIGHT © 1953 BY JOSEPH KRUMGOLD. Used by permission of HarperCollins Publishers. Adaptation from *U.S. Express* magazine, Jan. 1991. Reprinted by permission of Scholastic Inc. Audio rights: From adaptation of *...And Now Miguel* by Joseph Krumgold. Adaptation from *U.S. Express* magazine, Jan. 1991. Published by Scholastic Inc. Copyright © 1953 by Joseph Krumgold. Used by permission of Adam Krumgold.

Pp. 121–127, TUCK TRIUMPHANT. From TUCK TRIUMPHANT by Theodore Taylor, copyright © 1991 by Theodore Taylor. Used by permission of Doubleday, a division of Random House, Inc. Audio rights: From *Tuck Triumphant* by Theodore Taylor. Copyright © 1991 by Theodore Taylor. Used by permission of Watkins/Loomis, Inc.

Pp. 136–139, THE JOURNAL OF JESSE SMOKE. From THE JOURNAL OF JESSE SMOKE: A CHEROKEE BOY by Joseph Bruchac. Copyright © 2001 by Joseph Bruchac. Reprinted by permission of Scholastic Inc.

P. 140, ANCIENT WAYS. © 1999 Elvania Toledo. Originally appeared in *When the Rain Sings: Poems by Young Native Americans* (1999, Simon & Schuster/National Museum of the American Indian, Smithsonian Institution).

Unit 3

Pp. 157–161, LIFE DOESN'T FRIGHTEN ME. "Life Doesn't Frighten Me," copyright © 1978 by Maya Angelou, from AND STILL I RISE by Maya Angelou. Used by permission of Random House, Inc.

Pp. 169–173, MATTHEW A. HENSON. From FIVE BRAVE EXPLORERS by Wade Hudson. Copyright © 1995 by Just Us Books, Inc. Reprinted by permission of Scholastic Inc.

Pp. 181–185, ANNE FRANK: THE DIARY OF A YOUNG GIRL. From ANNE FRANK: THE DIARY OF A YOUNG GIRL by Anne Frank, translated by B.M. Mooyaart-Doubleday, copyright © 1952 by Otto H. Frank. Used by permission of Doubleday, a division of Random House, Inc.

Pp. 193–197, LANCE ARMSTRONG: CHAMPION CYCLIST, by President George W. Bush. From "Remarks by the President in Ceremony Honoring Lance Armstrong," on-line at http://www.whitehouse.gov/news/releases/2001/08/20010803-7.html.

Pp. 205–211, EARTHQUAKE. From *Water Buffalo Days* by Huynh Quang Nhuong. COPYRIGHT © 1997 BY HUYNH QUANG NHUONG. Used by permission of HarperCollins Publishers.

Unit 4

Pp. 228–231, THE LIBRARY CARD. From THE LIBRARY CARD by Jerry Spinelli. Copyright © 1997 by Jerry Spinelli. Reprinted by permission of Scholastic Inc.

P. 232, AT THE LIBRARY. Copyright © by Nikki Grimes. Published in IT'S RAINING LAUGHTER by Nikki Grimes, originally published by Dial Books for Young Readers, now published by Boyds Mills Press. Reprinted by permission of Curtis Brown, Ltd. All rights reserved.

Pp. 241–247, DISCOVERING THE INCA ICE MAIDEN. From *Discovering the Inca Ice Maiden: My Adventures on Ampato* by Johan Reinhard. Copyright © 1998 by Johan Reinhard. Reprinted by permission of National Geographic Society.

Pp. 255–259, THE ART OF SWORDSMANSHIP. From *One Hand Clapping: Zen Stories for All Ages,* Introduction by Rafe Martin, Illustrations by Junko Morimoto. Published by Rizzoli International Publications, Inc., New York.

Pp. 267–273, MAE JEMISON: SPACE SCIENTIST. From *Mae Jemison: Space Scientist* by Gail Sakurai. Copyright © 1995 by Children's Press® . Reprinted by permission. All rights reserved.

Unit 5

Pp. 289–297, HOW TIA LOLA CAME TO STAY. Copyright © 2001 by Julia Alvarez. Adapted from HOW TIA LOLA CAME TO ~~VISIT~~ STAY published by Alfred A. Knopf, a division of Random House, Inc. Reprinted by permission of Susan Bergholz Literary Services, New York. All rights reserved.

Pp. 306–308, HELEN KELLER. From IN THEIR OWN WORDS: HELEN KELLER by George Sullivan. Copyright © 2000 by George Sullivan. Reprinted by permission of Scholastic Inc.

Pp. 309–311, THE MIRACLE WORKER. Reprinted with the permission of Scribner, an imprint of Simon & Schuster Adult Publishing Group from THE MIRACLE WORKER by William Gibson. Copyright © 1956, 1957 William Gibson. Copyright © 1959, 1960 Tamarack Productions, Ltd., and George S. Klein & Leo Garel as trustees under three separate deeds of trust. Audio rights: From *The Miracle Worker* by William Gibson. Copyright © 1956, 1957 William Gibson. Copyright © 1959, 1960 Tamarack Productions, Ltd., and George S. Klein & Leo Garel as trustees under three separate deeds of trust. Used by permission of The Lantz Office.

Pp. 319–323, HEARING: THE EAR. Excerpt pp. 34–37 from DISCOVER THE WONDER: ELECTRICITY. Copyright © 1993 by Scott, Foresman and Company. Reprinted by permission of Pearson Education, Inc.

Pp. 331–337, THE ART OF MAKING COMIC BOOKS. From *The Art of Making Comic Books* by Michael Morgan Pellowski. Text copyright 1995 by Michael Morgan Pellowski. Illustration copyright 1995 by Howard Bender. Used by permission of the publisher, Lerner Publications Company, a division of Lerner Publishing Group. All rights reserved.

Unit 6

Pp. 353–357, THE LEWIS AND CLARK EXPEDITION. Excerpt pp. 374–375 from SCOTT FORESMAN SOCIAL STUDIES: THE UNITED STATES. Copyright

© 2003 by Pearson Education, Inc. Reprinted by permission.

Pp. 365–375, A WRINKLE IN TIME. Excerpt from "The Tesseract" from A WRINKLE IN TIME by Madeleine L'Engle. Copyright © 1962, renewed 1990 by Madeleine L'Engle Franklin. Reprinted by permission of Farrar, Straus and Giroux, LLC. Audio rights: From *A Wrinkle in Time* by Madeleine L'Engle. Published by Farrar, Straus & Giroux. Copyright © 1962 by Madeleine L'Engle Franklin. © renewed 1990. This usage granted by permission of Lescher & Lescher, Ltd. All rights reserved.

Pp. 383–387, I HAVE A DREAM. Reprinted by arrangement with the Estate of Martin Luther King Jr., c/o Writers House as agent for the proprietor New York, NY. *Copyright 1963 Dr. Martin Luther King Jr., copyright renewed 1991 Coretta Scott King.*

Pp. 396–397, LYNDON BAINES JOHNSON: OUR THIRTY-SIXTH PRESIDENT. From *Lyndon Baines Johnson: Our Thirty-Sixth President* by Melissa Maupin. Copyright © 2002 by The Child's World®, Inc. Reprinted by permission.

Pp. 398–401, SPEECH TO THE NATION: JULY 2, 1964. From *Public Papers of the Presidents of the United States: Lyndon B. Johnson, 1963–64.* Volume II, entry 446, pp. 842-844. Washington, D.C.: Government Printing Office, 1965.

Illustrators

Matthew Archambault: pp. 365–366, 368, 370–374 (© Matthew Archambault/Scott Hull Associates); **Anthony Carnabuci:** pp. 58–66 (© Anthony Carnabuci/HK Portfolio); **Margaret Chodos-Irvine:** pp. 255–258 (© Margaret Chodos-Irvine/Kolea Baker); **Viviana Diaz:** pp. 106–112 (© Viviana Diaz/Irmeli Holmberg); **James Edwards:** pp. 18–22 (© James Edwards/The Beranbaum Group); **Bill Ersland:** pp. 291–296 (© Bill Ersland/Irmeli Holmberg); **Tom Foty:** pp. 121–126 (© Tom Foty/Munro Campagna); **Gershom Griffith:** pp. 44–48 (© Gershom Griffith/Craven Design Studios); **Clint Hansen:** pp. 353, 356–357 (© Clint Hansen/Scott Hull Associates); **Laurie Harden:** p. 232 (© Laurie Harden/Christina A. Tugeau); **Rosanne Kaloustian:** pp. 241–245 (© Rosanne Kaloustian/Irmeli Holmberg); **John Kastner:** p. 140 (© John Kastner/The Beranbaum Group); **Mike Kasun:** pp. 331, 335 (© Mike Kasun/Munro Campagna); **Ron Mahoney:** pp. 136–138 (© Ron Mahoney/Wilkinson Studios, LLC); **Mapping Specialists, Ltd.:** pp. 28, 29, 41, 81, 93, 103, 119, 133, 167, 170, 179, 191, 203, 215, 239, 269, 287, 290, 301, 351, 354 (© Mapping Specialists, Ltd.); **Hilber Nelson:** pp. 228–230 (© Hilber Nelson/Kolea Baker); **Cheryl Kirk Noll:** pp. 95–96 (© Cheryl Kirk Noll/Christina A. Tugeau); **Precision Graphics:** pp. 3, 29, 84, 86, 91, 165, 317, 322, 379 (© Precision Graphics); **Carlotta Tormey:** p. 6 (© Carlotta Tormey/Wilkinson Studios, LLC); **Raoul Vitale:** pp. 155, 157–160 (© Raoul Vitale/Scott Hull Associates); **Suling Wang:** pp. 205–210 (© Suling Wang/Kolea Baker).

Author Photos

p. 7 (Jennifer Trujillo); p. 23 (Gary Paulsen); p. 27 (Theodore Taylor, © John Graves); p. 35 (Meredith Hooper, © Jennifer Tabor); p. 49 (Lensey Namioka); p. 97 (Patricia Hermes); p. 139 (Joseph Bruchac, © Michael Greenlar); p. 141 (Elvania Toledo); p. 161 (Maya Angelou, © Mitchell Gerber/CORBIS); p. 173 (Wade and Cheryl Hudson); p. 185 (Anne Frank, © Topham/The Image Works); p. 197 (George Bush, © Rick Friedman/Index Stock Imagery); p. 231 (Jerry Spinelli, © M. Elaine Adams); p. 247 (Johan Reinhard); p. 259 (Rafe Martin); p. 297 (Julia Alvarez, © Bill Eichner. Reprinted by permission of Susan Bergholz Literary Services, New York. All rights reserved.); p. 308 (George Sullivan); p. 311 (William Gibson, © William Inge Theatre Festival. Photo by: RJ Osborn); p. 337 (Michael Morgan Pellowski); p. 375 (Madeleine L'Engle, © 1992, Sigrid Estrada); p. 387 (Martin Luther King, Jr., © Flip Schulke/CORBIS); p. 397 (Melissa Maupin); p. 401 (Former President Lyndon B. Johnson, © CORBIS).

Photos

Alamy Images: (All © Alamy Images) p. 32 (© Frank Hurley/Royal Geographic Society/Alamy Images), p. 33 (© Frank Hurley/Royal Geographic Society/Alamy Images).

Art Resource: (All © Art Resource) p. 5 (*Jockeys,* Edgar Degas oil on paper, © Visual Arts Library/Art Resource, NY), pp. 78–79 (*Day and Night,* M.C. Escher, woodcut, 1938 © Cordon Art B.V./Art Resource), p. 135 (*Shoshone Women Watering Horse, ca. 1850's,* oil on canvas by Alfred Jacob Miller © The Newark Museum/Art Resource, NY).

The Bridgeman Art Library: (All © The Bridgeman Art Library) pp. 152–153 (*The Glacier de Tacconay,* from 'Scenes from the the Snowfields', engraved by Vincent Brooks and color litho by Edward Thomas Coleman © The Bridgeman Art Library), pp. 222–223 (*Louis Pasteur experimenting for the cure of hydrophobia in his laboratory, c.1885, pub. C. 1895 (print),* print by Adrien Emmanuel Marie, © The Bridgeman Art Library), pp. 348–349 (*The Rocky Mountains: Emigrants Crossing the Plains, 1866,* lithograph by Currier, N. and Ives, J.M. © The Bridgeman Art Library).

CORBIS: (All © Corbis) pp. I–1 (*Runners,* Robert Delaunay painting, © Archivo Iconografico, S.A./CORBIS), p. 15 (© Raymond Gehman/CORBIS), p. 17 (© Ric Ergenbright/CORBIS), p. 43 (© Roger Ressmeyer/CORBIS), p. 83 (© Julie Habel/CORBIS), p. 105 (*The Shepherd,* painting by Hubert Robert © Alexander Burkatowski/CORBIS), p. 117 (© Joseph Sohm; ChromoSohm, Inc./CORBIS), p. 169 © Bettmann/CORBIS), p. 171 (© Chris Rainier/CORBIS), p. 172 (© Bettmann/CORBIS), p. 193 (© Reuters NewMedia, Inc./CORBIS), p. 194 (© Reuters NewMedia, Inc./CORBIS), p. 263 (rug© Gian Berto Vanni/CORBIS, chair© Araldo de Luca/CORBIS, Panamanian © Danny Lehman/CORBIS, vase © Araldo de Luca/CORBIS), p. 265 (© CORBIS SYGMA), p. 267 (© NASA/Roger Ressmeyer/CORBIS), p. 270 (© CORBIS), p. 271 (© NASA/Roger Ressmeyer/CORBIS), p. 272 (© CORBIS), pp. 284–285 (© Danny Lehman/CORBIS), p. 289 (© Julie Habel/CORBIS), p. 305 (© Bettmann/CORBIS), p. 306 (© Bettmann/CORBIS), p. 307 (© Bettmann/CORBIS), p. 309 (© Bettmann/CORBIS), p. 310 (© Bettmann/CORBIS), p. 355 (© Bettmann/CORBIS), p. 383 (© Bettmann/CORBIS), p. 384 (© Bettmann/CORBIS), p. 385 (© Flip Schulke/CORBIS), p. 395 (© Hulton-Deutsch Collection/CORBIS), p. 396 (© Bettmann/CORBIS), p. 397 (© Bettmann/CORBIS), p. 398 (© Ted Streshinsky/CORBIS), p. 399 (© Flip Schulke/CORBIS), p. 400 (© Bettmann/CORBIS).

Cordon Art B.V.-Baarn-Holland: pp. 78–79 M. C. Escher's "Day and Night" © 2002 Cordon Art B.V. – Baarn – Holland. All rights reserved.

Getty Images: (All © Getty Images) p. 34 (© Getty Images), p. 57 (© David Young-Wolff/Getty Images), p. 87 (© Don Farrall/Getty Images), p. 87 (© David Bishop/FoodPix/Getty Images), p. 181 (© Anne Frank Fonds – Basel/Anne Frank House – Amsterdam/Getty Images), p. 184 (© Anne Frank Fonds – Basel/Anne Frank House – Amsterdam/Getty Images), p. 195 (© Ezra Shaw/Getty Images), p. 196 (© Ezra Shaw/Getty Images), p. 253 (© Lawrence M. Sawyer/Getty Images), p. 268 (© Andy Caulfield/Getty Images), pp. 289–297 (© Adam Crowley/Getty Images), p. 317 (© Getty Images), p. 323 (© Michael Dunning/Getty Images).

Imagebank: p. 31 (© Frans Lemmons/Imagebank).

The Image Works: (All © The Image Works) p. 182 (© Topham/The Image Works), p. 184 (© Topham/The Image Works).

Index Stock Imagery: p. 386 (© Henryk Kaiser/Index Stock Imagery).

Photo Edit: (All © Photo Edit) p. 227 (© Tom McCarthy/Photo Edit), p. 319 (© Tony Freeman/Photo Edit), p. 320 (© Mary Kate Denny/Photo Edit), p. 321 (© Robert Brenner/Photo Edit).

Photo Researchers: p. 323 (© G. Brederg/Photo Researchers).

Index

Author and Reading Selection Index

Alvarez, Julia, 289–297
"Ancient Ways," 140
"And Now Miguel," 105–113
Angelou, Maya, 157–161
"Anne Frank: The Diary of a Young Girl," 181–185
"The Art of Making Comic Books," 331–337
"The Art of Swordsmanship," 255–259
"At the Library," 232
"A Wrinkle In Time," 365–375
Bruchac, Joseph, 135–139
Bush, George W., 193–197
"The Camel Dances," 8–9
"Discovering the Inca Ice Maiden," 241–247
"Earthquake," 205–211
"Elizabeth's Diary," 95–97
Frank, Anne, 181–185
Gibson, William, 309–311
Grimes, Nikki, 232–233
"Hatchet," 17–23
"Hearing: The Ear," 319–323
"Helen Keller," 305–308
Hermes, Patricia, 95–97
Hooper, Meredith, 31–35
"How Tía Lola came to ~~Visit~~ Stay," 289–297
Hudson, Wade, 169–173
"I Have a Dream," 383–387
Johnson, Lyndon Baines, 398–401
"The Journal of Jesse Smoke," 135–139
King Jr., Martin Luther, 383–387
Krumgold, Joseph, 105–113
"Lance Armstrong: Champion Cyclist," 193–197
L'Engle, Madeleine, 365–375
"The Lewis and Clark Expedition," 353–357
"The Library Card," 227–231
"Life Doesn't Frighten Me," 157–161
Lobel, Arnold, 8–9
"Lyndon Baines Johnson: Our Thirty-Sixth President," 395–397
"Mae Jemison, Space Scientist," 267–273
"Matthew A. Henson," 169–173
Maupin, Melissa, 395–397
"The Miracle Worker," 309–311
Namioka, Lensey, 43–49
Nhuong, Huynh Quang, 205–211
Paulsen, Gary, 17–23
Pellowski, Michael Morgan, 331–337
"The Race," 5–7
Reinhard, Johan, 241–247
Sakurai, Gail, 267–273
Salinas, Marta, 57–67
"The Scholarship Jacket," 57–67
"Science Made Simple," 82–87
"Speech to the Nation: July 2, 1964," 398–401
Spinelli, Jerry, 227–231
Sullivan, George, 305–308
Taylor, Theodore, 121–127
Toledo, Elvania, 140–141
Trujillo, Jennifer, 5–7
"Tuck Triumphant," 121–127
"Yang the Youngest," 43

Skills Index

Grammar, Usage, and Mechanics

Adjectives, 130, 131, 201, 250, 404
capitalization, TE/243
comparative, 130, 250
superlative, 200
Adverbs, 38, 262, 263, 314; TE/123
Affixes, 12, 100, 130, 144, 188, 262, 300, 314, 326, 340, 378; TE/123
Appositives, 360, 409
Capitalization, 39, 149, 176, 177, 219, 281, 327, 345, 409
abbreviations of names and places, TE/173
acronyms, TE/271
adjectives, TE/243
exclamations, TE/337
headings, TE/321
names
countries and languages, TE/47
days of week, TE/35
months of year, TE/35
personal names, TE/7
place names, TE/113
proper names, TE/401
opening and closing of letter or diary, TE/185
proper nouns, TE/269
quotes, TE/229
titles
for people, TE/371
of works, TE/159, 321
Clauses, 53, 276
dependent, 52, 53, 276, 281, 390
independent, 53
relative, 236, 281
Cognates (*See* root words)
Comma, 52, 276, 360
multi-level options, TE/234
Complete Sentences, TE/129
Complex Sentences, 52
Compound Sentences, 52, 75, 236
Compound Words, 26, 214
Conjunctions
and, 38, 188, 189
but, 188, 189
yet, 404, 409
Contractions, 70, 116, 117, 164; TE/45
Infinitives, 250
Nouns, 130, 176, 177; TE/9, 269
Paragraph, 39
multi-level options, TE/234
Parts of Speech, 164; TE/176
Penmanship, 149, 345, 410
Possessives, 116, 117; TE/125, 387
Prefixes, 262, 300, 378
Prepositional Phrases, 164, 165, 189
Pronouns, 189, 214, 249, 405
first-person, 42, 53, 101, 131, 189, 204
multi-level options, TE/248, 298
referents, 214
Proper nouns, 176, 177; TE/269
Punctuation, 101, 117, 281, 345
apostrophe, 281
contractions, 116, 117, 164; TE/45
possessives, 116, 117; TE/125, 387
of clauses, 52, 53, 276, 390
colons, TE/197, 311
commas, 52, 276, 360; TE/59, 171, 247, 257, 293, 355, 399
dashes, TE/197
ellipsis, TE/61
hyphen, TE/97, 307, 333, 334
parentheses, TE/273
periods, TE/21
question marks, TE/111
quotation marks, TE/23, 291
quotes, TE/257
semicolons, TE/183
Quotation Marks, 254, 299, 301, 377, 408; TE/23, 291
Resources
dictionary, 130, 262, 317, 325, 326, 340, 390, 393, 404
synonym finder, 303, 360
thesaurus, 360
Sentences
complete, TE/129
complex, 52
compound, 52, 75, 236
multi-level options, TE/128
punctuation, 52, 53, 75, 101, 149, 219, 276, 281, 345, 360, 390, 409

Spelling, 301
abbreviations, TE/33
adverbs with *-ly* suffix, 38, 314; TE/123
alternative, TE/291
/au/ sound, TE/49
/aw/ sound, TE/141
c for */s/* sound, TE/87
ch for *k* word endings, TE/85
double consonants, words formed with, TE/245
-ed verb forms, 250; TE/209
f using *f, ph, gh,* TE/367
homophones, TE/195, 295
ie and *ei,* TE/137
influence of languages and cultures, 52, 90
ing endings, TE/323
it's and *its,* TE/161
long vowel sounds, TE/63, 231
-l or *-ll* word endings, TE/67
-ly suffix for adverbs, TE/123
ordinal numbers, TE/369
past tense words with *-y* ending, TE/211
plurals, TE/207
irregular, TE/385
nouns, TE/9
prefixes, 300, 378; TE/127
qu for *kw,* TE/397
r- controlled vowels, TE/19
root words, 52, 70, 276, 326, 378; TE/236, 276
silent letters
b, TE/107
gh, TE/109
h, TE/373
k, TE/259
l, TE/139
w, TE/335
suffixes, 12, 100, 130, 144, 188, 314, 340; TE/123
th and *t; thr* and *tr,* TE/357
use of resources to correct, 75, 149, 219, 281, 345, 409
Subject-Verb Agreement, 91, 326, 344
Suffixes, 12, 100, 130, 144, 188, 314, 340; TE/123
Tenses
future, 100
future conditional, 116, 117
past, 12, 26, 70, 250, 251, 379
past continuous, 314, 315
past perfect, 378, 379, 405, 409
perfect
present perfect, 300, 344
present, 326
present conditional, 340, 344
present continuous tense, 144, 344
present perfect, 300, 344
simple present, 90, 91, 344
progressive (continuous), 144, 314, 315, 344
Verbs
be, 26, 27, 100, 250, 314
-ed forms, 250
modals, 12, 26, 70, 90–91, 100, 116–117, 144, 176, 250–251, 314, 326, 378
multi-level options, TE/324
two-word verbs, 176

Listening and Speaking

Appreciation
aesthetic language, 4, 11, 141
oral interpretations, 406
oral reading
classic works, 180
contemporary works, 114, 128–129, 142–143, 199, 377
Audiences, 389
adapt spoken language for
diction, 359
usage, 359
word choice, 359
audience and setting
effective pitch, 73, 217, 261, 278, 279, 377
effective rate, 73, 217, 278, 299, 343, 377
effective tone, 73, 129, 187, 217, 261, 278, 279, 299, 389; TE/384
effective volume, 73, 217, 261, 278, 299, 377
clarification and support, 278
with elaborations, 73, 99, 147, 343
with evidence, 72, 389, 406
with examples, 406
content area vocabulary
arts, 3, 263, 327, 329, 341; TE/11, 41, 51, 93, 103, 121, 129, 163, 169, 213, 235, 275, 325, 331, 353
language arts, 101, 155, 237
math, 145, 177, 351; TE/181, 239, 267, 279, 299, 343, 393, 407
science, 13, 15, 27, 71, 82, 91, 165, 177, 265, 277, 303, 315, 325, 379; TE/95, 179, 203, 225, 265, 305, 363, 377, 409
social studies, 29, 39, 41, 55, 81, 93, 103, 117, 119, 131, 133, 167, 179, 189, 191, 201, 203, 215, 225, 239, 251, 253, 287, 301, 317, 361, 363, 381, 391, 393, 405; TE/15, 73, 135, 157, 193, 249, 319, 351, 389
technology, TE/31, 69, 155, 199, 255, 303, 317, 365
dramatic interpretations
experiences, 163
plays, 117, 313
poems, 13, 145, 165
stories, 25, 377
evaluate
others' presentations, 73, 147, 149, 217, 278, 343, 389, 406, 407
own presentations, 73, 217, 278, 343
interviewing, 89, 129, 146, 175, 278, 403
multi-level options, TE/388
providing information, 72
reaction, 192
reporting, 72, 146–147, 278–279
requesting, 11, 73, 76, 89, 146
Content Areas
arts, 3, 263, 327, 329, 341; TE/11, 41, 51, 93, 103, 121, 129, 163, 169, 213, 235, 275, 325, 331, 353
language arts, 101, 155, 237
math, 145, 177, 351; TE/181, 239, 267, 279, 299, 343, 393, 407
science, 13, 15, 27, 71, 82, 89, 91, 165, 177, 265, 277, 303, 315, 325, 379; TE/95, 179, 203, 225, 265, 305, 363, 377, 409
social studies, 29, 39, 41, 55, 81, 93, 103, 117, 119, 131, 133, 167, 179, 189, 191, 201, 203, 215, 225, 239, 251, 253, 287, 301, 317, 361, 363, 381, 391, 393, 405; TE/15, 73, 135, 157, 193, 249, 319, 351, 389
technology, TE/31, 69, 155, 199, 255, 303, 317, 365
Critical Listening
evaluate spoken message
content, 73, 99, 147, 217, 278, 343, 407
credibility, 149, 342, 407
delivery, 73, 217, 278, 299, 343, 389, 407
monitor understanding, 99, 147, 217, 278, 343, 407; TE/60
perception of message, 73
persuasive techniques, 382, 391, 406–407
seek clarification, 73, 99, 147, 278, 343
speaker, 192
nonverbal message, 217
opinion, 69, 149, 394
perspective, 76, 407
purpose, 278
repetition, 382
verbal message, 73, 147, 156, 217, 278, 343, 407
verifiable fact, 69, 394, 406, 407
Culture, 53
connect, TE/17, 57, 83, 105, 119, 133, 175, 241, 261, 289, 339, 381
experiences, 42; TE/43, 44, 45, 48, 57, 341
ideas, 11, 40, 51, 69, 143, 146, 163, 166, 178, 190, 199, 213, 235, 249, 252, 264, 350, 359, 380, 394
information, 41, 50, 143, 239
insights, 42, 50
language use, 51, 143, 286, 345
oral traditions, 143, 155
Paired Interactions
compare and contrast, 1
debate, 69
description, 11, 249
dialogue, 187, 299, 313; TE/49
identify
colloquial speech, 51

sequence of events, 9, 37; TE/7, 33, 183
interview, 89, 129, 175, 278, 403
personal experience
describe, 11, 99, 249
discuss, 163, 275
personal opinion, expressing, 36, 68
personal opinion, supporting, 402
proofreading, 409
retell, 37; TE/33
role-play, 25, 89, 175, 299; TE/47, 48, 61, 63, 65, 67, 112, 258
shared reading, 325; TE/19, 20, 21, 22, 23, 32, 33, 35, 49, 60, 61, 69, 84, 85, 97, 99, 124, 143, 163, 171, 172, 196, 210, 211, 229, 230, 242, 247, 291, 292, 293, 294, 295, 296, 297, 307, 310, 311, 313, 321, 332, 333, 334, 335, 336, 339, 355, 356, 357, 359, 367, 369, 371, 375, 380, 385, 386, 392, 399
story, 143

Presentations
biography, 216–217, 278–279
community connection, TE/81, 219
debate, 69
descriptions, 99, 163
dialogue, 187, 299, 313, 377
discussion, 199
dramatic read-aloud, 117, 145, 165, 261, 377
evaluate, 69
others' presentations, 73, 343, 389, 406, 407
own presentations, 73, 217, 278, 343
guest speakers, TE/25, 43, 282, 395
home connection, TE/37, 99, 115, 143, 147, 217, 281, 403
interview, 89, 129, 146, 175, 278, 403
letter to the editor, 149
multi-level options, TE/72–73, 146–147, 216–217, 220, 278–279, 282, 342–343, 346, 406–407
narrative, 143, 216–217, 278–279, 377
news report, 72–73
oral summary, 146–147, 342–343
oral traditions, 143
play
lines from a play, 313
scene from a play, 115
poem, 13, 145, 165
report, 278–279
role-play, 25, 89, 175, 299
shared reading, 325
speech, 72–73, 99, 192, 199, 201, 220, 389, 406–407
story, 143, 377

Purpose
determine purpose, 146, 199, 235, 254, 278, 342, 405, 408
distinguish intonation patterns, 115, 129, 377
distinguish sounds, 11, 316, 389
eliminate barriers, 175, 199, 316
multi-level options, TE/388
organize, 235; TE/175
produce intonation patterns, 115, 129, 377
produce sounds, 389
summarize, 235; TE/129, 170, 172, 229, 231, 233, 243, 246, 273, 291, 293, 295, 307, 310, 323, 357, 370, 374, 384, 399, 400
take notes, 235
understand major idea, 217, 278, 407
understand supporting evidence, 407

Speaking Preparation
charts, 69, 115, 199, 275, 286; TE/169
graphic organizers, 72; TE/118, 154, 352
Internet resources, 72, 220
interview form, 175
note cards, 72, 278, 279
questions to answer, 72, 89, 146, 175, 216, 220, 278, 342
rehearse, 342, 377, 406
technology, 72, 216
visuals, 69, 72, 99, 220; TE/171

Speaking Style
speech, 192, 199, 382

Reading

Comprehension, TE/7, 9, 18, 19, 20–23, 32–35, 44–49, 58–67, 84–87, 96–97, 106–113, 122–127, 136–141, 158–161, 170–173, 182–185, 194–197, 206–211, 228–233, 240–247, 256–259, 268–273, 290–297, 306–311, 320–323, 332–337, 354–357, 366–375, 384–387, 396–401
analyze characters, 10, 24, 36, 50, 51, 68, 69, 98, 114, 142, 198, 254, 339, 359; TE/20, 106, 111, 115, 123, 126, 137, 175, 184, 230, 242, 256, 257, 269, 271, 290, 306, 369, 371
analyze facts, TE/167, 372
author purpose, 49, 161, 173, 197, 247, 259, 297, 308, 311, 387, 388, 397; TE/308, 397
author strategy, 24, 56, 231, 297, 308
build background, 3, 15, 29, 41, 55, 81, 93, 103, 119, 133, 155, 167, 179, 191, 203, 225, 239, 253, 265, 287, 303, 317, 329, 351, 363, 381, 393; TE/367, 369, 374
cause and effect, 16, 18–23, 24, 36, 82, 88, 174, 186, 212, 248, 260, 324, 338, 358, 402; TE/85, 171
chronology, 98, 114, 175, 180, 182–185, 275, 352, 354–357, 394
compare and contrast, 11, 50, 76, 88, 128, 212, 226, 228–232, 234, 304, 402; TE/23, 35, 49, 113, 127, 140, 173, 185, 197, 211, 247, 259, 273, 297, 305, 311, 337, 357, 375, 387, 401
connect, 3, 10, 15, 29, 41, 42, 44–49, 50, 55, 81, 93, 98, 103, 114, 119, 128, 133, 142, 143, 155, 167, 174, 179, 186, 191, 198, 203, 212, 225, 234, 239, 253, 265, 274, 286, 287, 303, 312, 317, 324, 329, 351, 363, 381, 393; TE/101, 323, 387
community connection, TE/5, 25, 43, 205, 227, 383, 395
home connection, TE/55, 89
details, 56, 58–67, 136, 137, 170–173, 266, 268–273, 376, 388, 394
dialogue, 56, 254, 256–259, 261, 288; TE/291
draw conclusions, 50, 68, 98, 114, 120, 122–127, 128, 142, 204, 206–211, 274, 298, 312, 376, 382, 384–387, 388, 402; TE/115, 367, 373, 385, 401
draw inferences, 4–9, 10, 68, 82, 84–87, 88, 114, 128, 174, 186, 198, 212, 234, 260, 298, 312, 330, 332–337, 338, 359, 388, 401; TE/375
evaluate, 142, 162, 234, 260, 274, 312, 405; TE/135
experience for comprehension, use of, 2, 54, 80, 92, 102, 118, 132, 154, 166, 202, 224, 238, 252, 316, 328; TE/28, 43, 44, 45, 48, 57, 69
fact and opinion, 192, 388, 394, 396–401, 402
graphic organizers, 2, 40, 51, 201, 215, 240, 279, 304; TE/31, 56, 89, 102, 352, 364, 393
identify, 24, 36, 51, 61, 98, 99, 114, 131, 186, 248, 253, 312, 358, 393; TE/8, 46, 56, 66, 85, 107, 111, 122, 152, 171, 175, 183, 232, 385, 386, 387
illustrations
analyzing, 36, 59, 88, 162, 317, 330, 343, 354, 376; 162; TE/1, 5, 19, 21, 43, 57, 58, 79, 83, 84, 85, 121, 123, 153, 157, 169, 171, 181, 193, 195, 205, 206, 223, 229, 241, 244, 245, 255, 267, 268, 285, 289, 291, 294, 305, 307, 319, 331, 332, 333, 334, 335, 336, 349, 353, 355, 356, 365, 366, 368, 369, 370, 371, 372, 373, 374, 383, 395, 399
"how-to" book, 330
images, 88
interpret, 88, 186, 198, 246, 260, 298, 313, 324, 410; TE/22, 107, 115, 185
judgments, making, 162, 198, 260
knowledge for comprehension, use of, 2, 14, 28, 40, 54, 80, 92, 102, 118, 132, 154, 166, 178, 190, 202, 224, 238, 252, 264, 286, 302, 316, 328, 350, 362, 380, 392
main idea and details, 10, 36, 56, 58–67, 68, 136, 137, 168, 170–173, 266, 268–273, 274, 338, 358, 376, 388, 402; TE/400

make modifications, TE/307
asking questions, 324, 358
guided reading, TE/45, 46, 47, 123, 195, 209, 271, 398, 400
reading aloud, TE/65, 138, 183, 245, 246, 257, 270, 272, 273, 321, 332, 333, 370, 373, 374, 401
reciprocal reading, TE/59, 62, 64, 66, 137, 194, 207, 269, 272, 396, 397
rereading, TE/19, 20, 25, 33, 69, 86, 89, 99, 115, 143, 163, 183, 196, 199, 210, 229, 230, 242, 247, 258, 291, 294, 297, 299, 310, 313, 333, 335, 336, 339, 355, 356, 357, 359, 369, 371, 372, 375, 377, 385, 386, 389, 397
rereading aloud, 11; TE/45, 46, 47, 261
searching for clues, 15, 179, 287, 363, 393; TE/225, 332
shared reading, TE/9, 19, 20, 21, 22, 23, 32, 33, 35, 60, 61, 63, 67, 69, 85, 97, 106, 111, 124, 125, 126, 127, 138, 139, 143, 163, 171, 172, 182, 185, 197, 208, 210, 211, 229, 230, 231, 242, 244, 245, 246, 247, 256, 259, 291, 292, 293, 294, 295, 296, 297, 308, 309, 310, 311, 313, 321, 322, 323, 332, 333, 334, 335, 336, 337, 339, 355, 356, 357, 359, 367, 368, 369, 370, 371, 372, 373, 374, 375, 380, 385, 386, 392, 399, 401
using reference aids, 13, 191
memoir, 204
mental images, 4, 98, 156, 158–161, 364, 366–375; TE/209
monitor comprehension, 16, 156, 199, 266, 318, 364; TE/60
multi-level options, TE/6, 8, 18, 22, 32, 34, 44, 46, 48, 58, 60, 62, 64, 66, 84, 86, 96, 106, 110, 122, 124, 126, 136, 138, 140, 158, 160, 170, 172, 180, 182, 184, 194, 196, 206, 208, 210, 228, 230, 232, 240, 242, 244, 246, 256, 258, 268, 270, 272, 290, 292, 294, 296, 306, 308, 310, 320, 322, 332, 334, 336, 354, 356, 366, 368, 370, 372, 374, 384, 386, 396, 398, 400
narration, 56
outline, 318, 320–323
paraphrase, 24, 212, 376, 388, 402
predict, 24, 30, 31–35, 50, 120, 122–127, 128, 212, 288, 290–297; TE/78, 127, 139, 161, 182, 209, 246, 256, 257, 289, 310, 334, 335, 368
prior knowledge, 2, 14, 28, 40, 54, 80, 92, 102, 118, 132, 154, 166, 178, 190, 202, 224, 238, 252, 264, 286, 302, 316, 328, 350, 362, 380, 392; TE/5, 17, 31, 43, 57, 78, 83, 95, 105, 121, 135, 152, 157, 169, 181, 193, 205, 222, 223, 225, 227, 241, 255, 267, 284, 285, 289, 305, 309, 319, 331, 349, 351, 352, 353, 363, 365, 383, 391, 393, 395, 403
prologue, TE/18, 32, 194, 228, 290, 306, 366, 396, 398
purposes for reading, 49, 173, 197, 247
adjust purpose, 11, 25, 37, 51, 69, 89, 99, 163, 175, 188, 213, 300, 310, 314, 347, 352, 377
to enjoy, 347, 377
establish purpose, 77, 151, 221, 304, 314, 347, 352, 377
to find out, 56, 58–67
to interpret, 352, 377; TE/22, 107, 115, 185
to solve problems, 352, 377; TE/62
to understand, 10, 50
questions
different levels, 10, 24, 36, 50, 68, 88, 98, 114, 128, 142, 162, 174, 186, 198, 212, 234, 248, 260, 274, 298, 312, 324, 338, 358, 376, 388, 402
different types, 2, 28, 72, 76, 89, 92, 118, 149, 150, 224, 240, 249, 251, 263, 301, 328, 350; TE/60
test-like questions, 14, 279, 302
recall facts, 10, 24, 36, 50, 68, 88, 98, 114, 128, 142, 162, 174, 180, 182–185, 186, 198, 212, 234, 248, 260, 274, 298, 302, 312, 324, 338, 352, 354–357, 358, 376, 388, 402
reflect, 198
sequence of events, 37, 99, 104, 105–113, 134, 136–139, 174, 175, 212, 274, 324, 376; TE/7, 33, 107, 183
setting, analyzing, 50, 98
similarities and differences across texts, 4, 101, 304; TE/9, 23, 35, 49, 67, 87, 97, 113, 127, 141, 161, 173, 185, 197, 211, 233, 247, 259, 273, 297, 311, 323, 337, 357, 375, 387, 401
speculate, 174, 198, 298, 324, 338, 376
steps in process, 88, 274
study strategies, 234, 265, 324, 352, 382, 403
summarize, 68, 94, 96–97, 142, 245, 324; TE/129, 170, 172, 229, 231, 233, 243, 246, 273, 291, 293, 295, 307, 310, 323, 357, 370, 374, 384, 399, 400
support inferences, 6, 7, 9, 65, 66, 82, 162, 337, 376, 401
text features
analyze, TE/161, 384
biography, 168, 266, 304, 394; TE/268, 306, 307, 396
diary, 94, 180; TE/96, 182
drama, 304
fable, 4
fiction, 16, 94, 120, 134, 226, 364; TE/96, 140, 228, 232, 366, 375
first-person narrative, 42
folktale, 254; TE/256
historical fiction, 94, 134; TE/96, 140
historical narrative, 30, 94
"how-to" book, 330
informational text, 82, 352, 361; TE/320, 354, 357
italics, TE/233, 242, 268, 296, 297, 309, 375
journal, 134; TE/140
memoir, 204; TE/210
narrative, 30, 42, 288; TE/290, 296
nonfiction narrative, 30, 240; TE/242
play, 104; TE/106, 309
poem, 4, 156; TE/6, 158, 159
prologue, TE/18, 32, 194, 228, 290, 306, 366, 396, 398
realistic adventure fiction, 16
realistic fiction, 16, 120
science fiction, 364; TE/366, 375
scientific informational text, 82
short story, 56, 71
speech, 192, 382; TE/194, 384, 398, 400
textbook, 318; TE/320
text's structure/progression, 4; TE/197, 337, 364
captions, 330
fable, 4; TE/9
fiction, 226
first-person narrative, 53, 249; TE/46
headings, 318, 361, 408; TE/32, 320, 334, 335
inductive organization, 266
locate information, 180, 182–185, 318, 352, 354–357; TE/xvi
multi-level options, TE/42, 156, 168, 352, 364, 382, 394
narrative, 53, 249, 288; TE/46, 290
recall information, 10, 24, 36, 50, 68, 98, 114, 128, 142, 162, 174, 180, 182–185, 186, 198, 212, 234, 248, 260, 274, 298, 302, 312, 324, 338, 352, 354–357, 376, 388, 402
subheadings, 318
textbook, 318
timeline, 134, 168, 246; TE/357
visuals, 36, 59, 88, 162, 317, 330, 343, 354, 376; TE/1, 5, 19, 21, 43, 57, 58, 79, 83, 84, 85, 121, 123, 153, 157, 169, 171, 181, 193, 195, 205, 206, 223, 229, 241, 244, 245, 255, 267, 268, 285, 289, 291, 294, 305, 307, 319, 331, 332, 333, 334, 335, 336, 349, 353, 355, 356, 365, 366, 368, 369, 370, 371, 372, 373, 374, 383, 395, 399

Content Areas

arts, 3, 263, 327, 329, 341; TE/11, 41, 51, 93, 103, 121, 129, 163, 169, 213, 235, 275, 325, 331, 353
language arts, 101, 155, 237
math, 145, 177, 351; TE/181, 239, 267, 279, 299, 343, 393, 407
science, 13, 15, 27, 71, 82, 91, 165, 177, 265, 277, 303, 315, 325, 379;

TE/95, 179, 203, 225, 265, 305, 363, 377, 409
social studies, 29, 39, 41, 55, 81, 93, 103, 117, 119, 131, 133, 167, 179, 189, 191, 201, 203, 215, 225, 239, 251, 253, 287, 301, 317, 361, 363, 381, 391, 393, 405; TE/15, 73, 135, 157, 193, 249, 319, 351, 389
technology, TE/31, 69, 155, 199, 255, 303, 317, 365

Culture, 53
common characteristics, 42, 50
compare
others' experiences, 42, 50, 143
own experiences, 42, 50, 143, 248; TE/44, 45, 48, 57
connections, 41, 42, 50, 133, 143, 239, 286; TE/17, 43, 57, 83, 105, 119, 133, 175, 241, 261, 289, 339, 341, 381
distinctive characteristics, 143, 239, 248
themes, 54

Fluency
adjust reading rate, 50, 114, 198, 265, 312, 388
choral reading, 128, 402; TE/6, 7, 44, 109, 140, 141, 158, 159, 160, 161, 232, 233, 387
echo reading, 162, 376
independent-level materials, 77, 151, 221, 283, 347, 411
instructional-level materials, 2, 14, 28, 40, 54, 80, 92, 102, 118, 132, 154, 166, 178, 190, 202, 224, 238, 252, 264, 286, 302, 316, 328, 350, 362, 380, 392
rapid word recognition, 36, 212, 98
read aloud, 10, 24, 128, 162, 198, 213, 261, 402
read chunks, 24, 68, 186, 234
read silently, 68, 186, 198, 234, 274, 298, 358
read to memorize, 142
read to scan, 248, 324, 325
repeated reading, 88, 174, 260, 298, 338

Genres, 16, 101; TE/xvi, 78, 152
biography, 168, 266, 304, 394; TE/268, 396
diary, 94, 101, 180; TE/96, 182
drama, 304
fable, 4
fiction, 16, 94, 120, 134, 226, 364; TE/96, 140, 228, 232, 366, 375
folktale, 254; TE/256
historical fiction, 94, 134; TE/96, 140
"how-to" book, 330
informational text, 82, 318, 352, 361; TE/320, 354, 357
journal, 101, 134; TE/140
memoir, 101, 204; TE/210
narrative, 113, 288; TE/290, 296
first-person, 42, 101, 129, 131, 189, 249
historical, 30
nonfiction, 30, 240; TE/242
short story, 56
play, 104; TE/106, 309
poem, 4, 11, 141, 156; TE/6, 58, 159
realistic fiction, 16, 120
science fiction, 363, 364; TE/366, 375
speech, 192, 382; TE/194, 384, 398, 400
story, 56

Inquiry and Research
charts, 13, 54, 80, 102, 120, 132, 133, 144, 154, 164, 166, 190, 224, 261, 299, 362, 380, 392; TE/169, 205, 267, 319, 395
community connection, TE/149
draw conclusions, 50, 68, 98, 114, 120, 122–127, 128, 142, 204, 206–211, 274, 298, 312, 376, 382, 384–387, 388, 402; TE/115, 367, 373, 385, 401
electronic texts, 217
experts, 76, 177, 220, 277, 410
form and revise questions, 76, 218, 220, 403, 408, 410
graphic features, 72, 145, 408, 410; TE/136
diagram, 304; TE/9, 29, 67, 87, 233, 322
graphs, 216, 302, 410
maps, 28, 29, 41, 81, 93, 103, 119, 133, 167, 170, 179, 191, 203, 215, 239, 269, 279, 287, 290, 301, 351, 354, 410; TE/240, 385
timelines, 99, 134, 246; TE/357
Venn Diagram, 304; TE/9, 67, 87, 226, 233, 305
informational sources, 224
library, 224, 225, 237; TE/150
Internet, 76, 148, 150, 191, 216, 220, 279, 282, 346, 408, 410; TE/240, 327
make charts, 13, 54, 69, 74, 76, 80, 102, 115, 120, 131, 132, 133, 148, 154, 164, 166, 190, 199, 224, 261, 275, 282, 286, 341, 362, 380, 392; TE/169, 205, 267, 319
media, 73, 76, 147, 150, 217, 220, 279, 282, 343, 346, 407, 410
outline ideas, 235, 318, 320–323, 408–409
print resources, 73, 147, 192, 217, 242–246, 303, 317, 325, 393, 407; TE/150, 346
report, 408
research project, 76, 148, 150, 408, 410
speech, 72–73, 192, 220, 407
statements, 409
summarize and organize information, 224, 225; TE/357
take notes, 235, 408
technology presentation, 216, 217; TE/240
text organizers
graphic features, 51, 165, 201, 215, 240, 242–246, 279, 304, 391; TE/9, 29, 67, 87, 136, 233
headings, 318, 361, 408; TE/320, 334, 335
table of contents, 409; TE/xvi, 78, 101
visuals, 216, 279

Literary Concepts
author's perspective, 97, 139, 141; TE/185
cause and effect, 16, 18–23, 24, 36, 82, 88, 186, 212, 248, 260, 324, 338, 358, 402; TE/85, 171
chronological order, 114, 175, 180, 182–185, 275, 352, 354–357, 361, 394
compare and contrast, 50, 76, 88, 128, 212, 226, 228–232, 304, 306–311, 402; TE/23, 35, 49, 113, 127, 140, 173, 185, 197, 211, 247, 259, 273, 297, 305, 311, 337, 357, 375, 387, 401
compare communication, 345
deductive organization, 266
inductive organization, 266
multi-level options, TE/88, 174, 274
purpose of text, 49, 173, 197, 247, 259
entertain, 156, 288, 304
express, 42, 156, 180
influence/persuade, 74, 148–149, 344, 389
inform, 30, 82, 318
persuade, 389

Literary Response
compare and contrast ideas, themes, issues, 11, 50, 76, 88, 128, 162, 380, 402; TE/23, 35, 49, 113, 127, 140, 173, 185, 197, 211, 247, 259, 273, 297, 305, 311, 337, 357, 375, 387, 401
connect ideas, themes, issues, 77, 234, 312, 411; TE/1, 79, 153, 223, 285, 349, 383, 387
interpret, 88, 186, 198, 246, 260
through discussion, 69, 199, 213; TE/97, 107, 185, 195, 199, 332
through enactment, 25, 175, 313, 359; TE/22, 115, 315
through journal writing, 77, 221, 382, 377
through media, 279, 324, 407, 410
make connections, 10, 42, 44–49, 98, 114, 128, 142, 155, 174, 186, 198, 212, 234, 274, 312, 324; TE/202, 215, 323, 387
offer observations, 338
raise questions, 89, 175, 218, 397
react, 68, 69, 221, 260; TE/195
reading log, 51, 77, 99, 115, 163, 168, 175, 180, 199, 213, 226, 235, 261, 275, 299, 304, 325, 330, 352, 359, 377, 382, 389, 403
reflect, 198
speculate, 174, 198, 298, 324, 338, 376
support responses
own experiences, 142; TE/213
relevant aspects of text, 6, 7, 9, 65,

66, 162, 204, 206–211, 256, 337, 376
Literary Terms
act, 304
analogy, 200, 234, 326
character, 4, 16, 56, 94, 104, 120, 134, 226, 254, 304, 364; TE/8, 66, 111, 115, 122, 175
characterization, 339
changes, 10, 24, 50, 68, 261, 312
conflict, 68, 298, 312, 359
direct, 51
indirect, 51
motivation, 69
point of view, 42, 129, 249, 299, 304, 394
relationship, 10, 298, 312, 359
traits, 261; TE/175
colloquial speech, 51
descriptive language, 325
dialogue, 56, 104, 134, 254, 261, 288; TE/291
diary, 94, 101, 180; TE/96, 182
direct address, 180, 192, 382
excerpt, 14, 16, 28, 40, 42, 80, 92, 118, 132, 166, 178, 202, 224, 286, 302, 316, 350, 362, 380, 392
fiction, 16, 226; TE/96, 140, 228, 232, 375
historical, 94, 134; TE/96, 140
realistic, 16, 120
scientific, 364; TE/375
figurative language, 25, 200, 234, 390; TE/232, 386
simile, 25
first-person point of view, 42, 101, 129, 131, 189, 249
flashback, 99, 275, 277
folktale, 254; TE/256
foreshadowing, 213
free verse, 140
graphics, 318
journal, 101, 134; TE/140
lesson of a story, 254
memoir, 101, 204; TE/210
metaphor, 143
mood, 199, 377; TE/211, 384
moral of a story, 4
multi-level options, TE/10, 24, 36, 50, 68, 98, 114, 142, 162, 174, 186, 198, 212, 248, 260, 298, 312, 338, 359, 376, 402
narration, 56
narrator, 104; TE/109
nonfiction, 240; TE/242
novel, 16
personification, 37, 39
playwright, 115, 304
plot, 36, 104, 120, 226; TE/122
point of view, 42, 97, 129, 217, 249, 299, 304, 394; TE/49, 141, 401
problem resolution, 42
prologue, TE/18, 32, 194, 228, 290, 306, 366, 396, 398
rhyme, 4, 11, 156, 163, 165
scene, 104, 115, 304; TE/108
setting, 16, 94, 115, 120, 204, 352, 364; TE/122
stage directions, 304, 312, 313; TE/309
stanza, 4, 156; TE/6, 7, 140, 160
style, 129, 192, 199, 235, 339, 382
symbolism, 388
tale, 254
theater, 115, 304, 313
third-person point of view, 299, 301, 304, 394, 405
tone, 187, 189, 199, 201, 248; TE/211, 384
transitions, 175
Purposes
adjust purpose, 77, 151, 221, 304, 347, 411
appreciate writer's craft, 235, 259, 299, 347
complete forms, 73, 147, 217
entertain, 156, 161, 180, 308, 389
establish purpose, 17, 151, 221, 304, 347, 411
inform, 30, 173, 197, 247, 325, 327, 364, 389
make recommendation, 77, 352
models for writing, 27, 71, 177, 251, 405; TE/188, 327
take action, 151, 395
write a response, 347, 413
Reading Strategies, 4
cause and effect, 16, 18–23, 24, 36, 88, 174, 186, 212, 248, 269, 324, 338, 358, 402; TE/85, 171
chronology, 114, 175, 180, 182–185, 275, 352, 354–357, 394
compare and contrast, 1, 50, 128, 212, 226, 228–232, 304, 306–311, 402; TE/23, 35, 49, 113, 127, 140, 173, 185, 197, 211, 247, 259, 273, 297, 305, 311, 337, 357, 375, 387, 401
compare with own experience, 10, 42, 44–49, 98, 114, 128, 142, 174, 186, 198, 234, 274, 312, 358; TE/44, 45, 48, 57, 305
conclusions, 50, 68, 98, 114, 120, 122–127, 128, 142, 204, 206–211, 274, 298, 312, 376, 382, 384–387, 388, 402; TE/115, 367, 373, 385, 401
dialogue to understand character, 254, 256–259, 261, 288; TE/8, 111, 175
evaluate, TE/9, 23, 35, 49, 67, 87, 97, 113, 127, 141, 161, 173, 185, 197, 211, 233, 247, 259, 273, 297, 311, 323, 337, 357, 375, 387, 401
fact from opinion, 192, 388, 394, 396–401, 402
graphic sources, 240, 242–246
inferences, 4–9, 10, 68, 82, 84–87, 88, 114, 128, 174, 186, 198, 212, 234, 260, 312, 330, 332–337, 338, 359, 388, 401; TE/375
main idea and details, 10, 36, 56, 58–67, 68, 136, 137, 168, 170–173, 266, 268–273, 274, 338, 358, 376, 388, 402; TE/400
mental images, 4, 98, 156, 158–161, 364, 366–375; TE/209
multi-level options, TE/4, 16, 30, 38, 56, 82, 94, 104, 120, 134, 192, 204, 226, 254, 266, 288, 304, 318, 330
predict, 24, 30, 31–35, 50, 120, 122–127, 128, 212, 288, 290–297; TE/78, 127, 139, 161, 182, 209, 246, 256, 257, 289, 310, 334, 335, 368
represent text information in outline, 318, 320–323
selection preview, TE/5, 17, 31, 43, 57, 83, 95, 105, 121, 135, 157, 169, 181, 193, 205, 227, 241, 255, 267, 289, 305, 319, 331, 353, 365, 383, 395
sequence of events, 37, 99, 104, 105–113, 134, 136–139, 168, 174, 175, 212, 274, 324, 376; TE/7, 33, 107, 183
summarize, 68, 94, 96–97, 142, 245, 324; TE/129, 170, 172, 229, 231, 233, 243, 246, 273, 291, 293, 295, 307, 310, 323, 357, 370, 374, 384, 399, 400
text evidence, 142, 330, 332–337, 382, 384–387; TE/385
unit preview, TE/xvi, 78, 152, 222, 284, 348
unit theme, TE/xvi, 78, 152, 222, 284, 348
References, 277; TE/399
dictionary, 3, 130, 133, 155, 163, 203, 236, 253, 262, 300, 317, 325, 326, 340, 390, 393, 404, 409
encyclopedia, 13, 191, 279
experts, 76, 177, 220, 277, 410
glossary/glosses, 90, 191, 265, 317
Internet, 76, 148, 150, 191, 216, 220, 279, 282, 346, 408, 410; TE/240, 327
magazines, 191; TE/405
newspaper, 191; TE/405
software, 281, 220
synonym finder, 167, 303, 360
thesaurus, 167, 360, 409
Text Sources
anthology, 75, 219
classic work, 182, 221
contemporary work, 18, 32, 44, 194, 290, 366, 384, 398, 413
electronic text, 73, 217
informational text, 82, 352, 361
Internet, 76, 148, 150, 191, 216, 220, 279, 282, 346, 408, 410; TE/240, 327
library, 224, 225, 237; TE/150
manual, 220
novel, 77, 151, 221, 283, 347, 411
play, 105, 305
poetry, 4, 11, 156
textbook, 317, 318

Vocabulary Development
affixes, 12, 188, 300, 314, 326, 340, 378
analogies, 200, 234, 326; TE/335
compound words, 26, 214
connotative meaning, 55, 381, 390
content area words
arts, 3, 263, 327, 329, 341; TE/11, 41, 51, 93, 103, 121, 129, 163, 169, 213, 235, 275, 325, 331, 353
language arts, 101, 155, 237
math, 145, 177, 351; TE/181, 239, 267, 279, 299, 343, 393, 407
science, 13, 15, 27, 71, 82, 91, 165, 177, 265, 277, 303, 315, 325, 379; TE/95, 179, 203, 225, 265, 305, 363, 377, 409
social studies, 29, 39, 41, 55, 81, 93, 103, 117, 119, 131, 133, 167, 179, 189, 191, 201, 203, 215, 225, 239, 251, 253, 287, 301, 317, 361, 363, 381, 391, 393, 405; TE/15, 73, 135, 157, 193, 249, 319, 351, 389
technology, TE/31, 69, 155, 199, 255, 303, 317, 365
context clues, 15, 179, 287, 363, 393; TE/225, 332
denotative meaning, 52, 381, 390; TE/6, 7, 18, 19, 21, 32, 33, 45, 59, 85, 97, 107, 122, 123, 137, 140, 159, 171, 194, 195, 207, 232, 242, 256, 291, 296, 307, 309, 320, 321, 332, 334, 357, 366, 367, 369, 373, 375, 384, 396, 398
derivatives, 52, 81, 236
draw on experiences, 265, 329, 351, 363; TE/29, 103, 265
figurative language, 25, 200, 234, 390; TE/232, 386
home connection, TE/3, 167, 191, 253, 287, 329
homonyms, 41
key phrases, 10
key words, 239, 393; TE/29
listening to selections, 114, 128, 142, 199, 377
multi-level options, TE/2, 14, 28, 40, 54, 80, 92, 102, 118, 132, 154, 166, 178, 190, 202, 224, 238, 252, 264, 286, 302, 316, 328, 350, 362, 380, 392
multiple-meaning words, 41
personal dictionary, 13, 52, 55, 70, 81, 103, 130, 133, 144, 155, 167, 176, 188, 203, 225, 236, 262, 276, 300, 303, 314, 317, 326, 329, 340, 360, 363, 376, 393
reference aids, 3, 130, 133, 155, 163, 167, 191, 203, 265, 326, 340, 390, 393, 404
related words, 27, 29, 39, 71, 81, 88, 119, 131, 236, 239, 253; TE/183
repetition, 225
root words, 52, 70, 90, 133, 236, 253, 276, 326, 378; TE/236, 276
strategies
LINK strategy, 103
word wheel, 81, 351; TE/360, 390
synonym finder, 3, 13, 167, 303, 360
synonyms, 3, 13, 93, 167, 303, 360
thesaurus, 167, 360
word origins, 52, 81, 90, 236, 262, 276, 326

Word Identification
cognates (*See* root words); TE/T434–436
context, 15, 179, 287, 363; TE/225
contractions, 164
derivations, 52, 81, 236
dictionary, 53, 55, 81, 90, 130, 155, 203, 236, 253, 340, 390, 393, 404
glossary/glosses, 90, 191, 265, 317
language structure, 12, 38, 70, 164, 176, 188, 214, 308
letter-sound correspondences, 90
meanings, 52, 53, 133, 203, 214, 225, 253, 300, 325, 378, 381, 390, 404, 409; TE/6, 7, 18, 19, 21, 32, 33, 45, 59, 85, 97, 107, 122, 123, 137, 140, 159, 171, 194, 195, 207, 232, 242, 256, 291, 296, 307, 309, 320, 321, 332, 334, 357, 366, 367, 369, 373, 375, 384, 396, 398
prefixes, 262, 300, 378
pronunciation, 90, 163
root words, 70, 133, 276, 378; TE/236
Greek, 90, 276, 326; TE/276
Latin, 52, 236, 276; TE/276
suffixes, 12, 100, 130, 144, 188, 314, 340

Writing

Connections
authors
challenges, 72, 161, 211, 233, 273, 297
strategies used, 231, 297, 308
collaboration with other writers, 13, 146–147, 175, 213
community, TE/187, 313, 345
correspondence
e-mail, 280–281
letter, 148–149
mail, 149, 280
home, TE/75, 217, 281, 359
personal experiences, TE/131

Culture
compare and contrast, 150
others' experiences, 76

Forms
bibliography, 409
biography, 177, 277, 405
book, 410
dialogue, 117, 301
diary, 101, 189
editorial, 344
e-mail, 280–281
folktale, 263
"how-to" article, 341
informational text, 91, 361
instructions, 341
interview
form, 175
questions, 146, 175, 403
journal, 101, 134
letter, 148–149, 410
list, 74, 213, 392, 406
magazine article, 76, 150
memoir, 215
narrative, 74, 301, 379
first-person, 53, 101, 131, 189, 251
historical, 39
persuasive speech, 391, 406–407
play, 117
scene from a play, 315
poem, 11, 13, 145, 165
poster, 76, 150, 282
report, 72–73, 408–409
review, 75
science fiction, 379
speech, 201, 220, 391, 406–407
story, 237
realistic adventure story, 27
realistic story, 131
short story, 71
Web article/page, 76, 220

Inquiry and Research, 218, 282
concept map, 72, 165, 391
evaluation, 405, 408
guest speakers, 76, 148, 150, 220, 277
learning log, 150, 282, 411
on-line searches, 76, 148, 150, 177, 341
organize facts, 148, 216, 282, 408; TE/117, 379, 410
organize ideas, 235, 344, 391, 408; TE/117
outline, 235, 408–409; TE/277
periodicals, 76, 150
presentations, 76, 216, 220
prior knowledge, 148
questions, 89, 146, 218, 220, 282, 397, 403, 408, 410
sources, citation of, 218, 408, 409
summarize facts, 282, 408
summarize ideas, 235
take notes, 235, 408
technology presentations, 72
timelines, 216; TE/357, 361

Literary Devices
characterization, 51, 53
chronological order, 361, 394, 408, 409
dialogue, 263; TE/291
figurative language, 25, 391; TE/232
flashback, 99, 277
incomplete sentences, 129, 131
metaphors, 143
personification, 37, 39
repetition, 391, 403; TE/385, 387
rhyming words, 11, 163, 165
table of contents, 409; TE/xvi, 78
thesis statement, 409
timeline, 39; TE/357, 361
tone, 187, 189, 199, 201
word choice, varying, 93

Purpose
appropriate form, 361, 412
appropriate literary devices, 11
audience and purpose, 389, 391
appropriate style, 235, 237, 339, 341, 391
appropriate tone, 187, 189, 199, 201
appropriate voice, 53, 101, 131, 189, 251, 301, 405
ideas, 27, 53, 71, 216, 251, 344, 366, 393, 410
literary response, 218
purposes
to develop, 27, 346
to discover, 76, 90, 155, 262, 288, 318, 392, 413
to entertain, 27, 74, 131, 301, 315, 379, 389
to express, 13, 53, 71, 145, 165, 215, 237, 251
to influence/persuade, 74, 148–149, 344, 389, 391, 410
to inform, 12, 39, 73, 91, 117, 145, 177, 201, 251, 263, 277, 280, 327, 361, 389
to instruct, 327, 341
to problem solve, 53
to record, 39, 101, 189, 215, 277, 405
to reflect on ideas, 117
transitions, 175

Writing Process
analyze writing, 27
develop drafts, 74, 148, 218, 280–281, 344, 379, 409, 410; TE/361
edit drafts, 75, 91, 149, 219, 281, 345, 361, 409, 410
evaluate writing
criteria, 75, 149, 216, 219, 281, 345
others' writing, 75, 149, 219, 281, 345, 409
own writing, 75, 76, 91, 101, 145, 149, 201, 219, 220, 281, 345, 361, 409, 410; TE/261
grammar, usage, and mechanics
adjectives, 131, 201
adverbs, 262, 263
capitalization, 39, 176, 177, 327
clauses, 53, 236, 237
conjunctions, 38, 188, 189, 404, 409
contractions, 117
paragraph, 39
possessives, 117
prepositional phrases, 165, 189
pronouns, 53, 249, 405
proper nouns, 177
punctuation, 53, 75, 101, 117, 149, 219, 281, 345, 409
materials, use of, 76, 148, 277, 341, 408; TE/346
multi-level options, TE/12, 26, 52, 70, 74–75, 76, 90, 100, 112, 116, 130, 144, 148–149, 150, 164, 176, 188, 200, 214, 218–219, 236, 250, 262, 276, 280–281, 282, 300, 314, 326, 340, 344–345, 360, 378, 390, 404, 408–409, 410
prewriting strategies, 148
brainstorming, 145, 165, 280, 282, 344; TE/13, 201, 341, 391, 408
charts, 74, 76, 131, 148, 282, 341
graphic organizers, 72, 165, 391; TE/117, 189, 263, 361, 379, 405
lists, 74, 76, 145
logs, 74, 101, 131, 218, 344, 379
notes, 72
story chart, 27
proofread, 75, 149, 219, 361, 409
publish, 75, 149, 219, 345, 409
reference materials, use of, 76, 148, 277, 341, 408
resource materials, use of, 76, 148, 277, 341, 408; TE/346, 391
review collection of written works, 75
revise drafts, 75, 91, 149, 219, 281, 345, 361, 409, 410
supporting ideas, 408, 409, 410
technology, use of, 72, 76, 148, 149
text structure/progression, 39, 53, 71
sequence of events, 91, 134, 175, 280

Viewing and Representing

Analysis
interpret and evaluate meaning, 1, 79, 88, 147, 153, 162, 223, 241–246, 279, 285, 324, 349, 404, 406; TE/1, 5, 17, 43, 57, 58, 79, 83, 85, 95, 105, 121, 123, 153, 157, 169, 181, 193, 195, 205, 206, 223, 227, 229, 241, 244, 245, 255, 267, 268, 289, 291, 294, 305, 307, 319, 331, 332, 333, 334, 335, 336, 349, 353, 355, 356, 365, 366, 368, 369, 370, 371, 372, 373, 374, 383, 395, 399
nonverbal messages, 343
media
to clarify understanding, TE/367
compare and contrast, 73, 147, 217, 345, 407
effect, 147; TE/343
electronic media, 73, 147, 217
film, 147
graphic organizers, 279; TE/105, 217, 240, 288, 343, 353
to influence, 343
to inform, 343
print media, 73, 147, 217, 242–246, 407
purpose, 147, 217, 343, 407
technology presentations, 217; TE/240
video, 73, 147, 217, 279, 343, 407
visual media, 73, 147, 162, 217, 330, 343, 354, 376, 407; TE/1, 5, 19, 21, 43, 57, 58, 79, 83, 84, 85, 121, 123, 153, 157, 169, 171, 181, 193, 195, 205, 206, 223, 229, 241, 244, 245, 255, 267, 268, 285, 289, 291, 294, 305, 307, 319, 331, 332, 333, 334, 335, 336, 349, 353, 355, 356, 365, 366, 368, 369, 370, 371, 372, 373, 374, 383, 395, 399
rank order, 145
visuals, 59, 88, 217, 317, 330, 343, 354, 376, 406; TE/1, 5, 19, 21, 43, 57, 58, 79, 83, 84, 85, 121, 123, 153, 157, 169, 171, 181, 193, 195, 205, 206, 223, 229, 241, 244, 245, 255, 267, 268, 285, 289, 291, 294, 305, 307, 319, 331, 332, 333, 334, 335, 336, 349, 353, 355, 356, 365, 366, 368, 369, 370, 371, 372, 373, 374, 383, 395, 399

Content Areas
math, 145
social studies, 301

Interpretation
choice of style, elements, media, 88, 147; TE/1, 223, 349
important events and ideas, 147, 246, 279, 324
media to compare ideas, 73, 147, 217, 402, 406

Production
assess message, 343, 407
media, 76, 150, 220, 282, 346, 410
multi-level options, TE/76, 150, 220, 282, 346, 410
technology, 72, 76, 216, 220
video, 313
visuals, 13, 72, 76, 131, 216, 220, 263, 282, 341, 345, 346, 410; TE/177

Assessment

Assess, TE/1, 3, 4, 11, 12, 13, 15, 16, 26, 27, 29, 30, 37, 38, 39, 41, 42, 51, 52, 53, 55, 56, 69, 70, 73, 75, 79, 81, 82, 89, 90, 91, 93, 94, 99, 100, 101, 103, 104, 115, 116, 117, 119, 120, 129, 130, 131, 133, 134, 143, 144, 145, 147, 149, 153, 155, 156, 163, 164, 165, 167, 168, 175, 176, 177, 179, 180, 187, 188, 189, 191, 192, 199, 200, 201, 203, 204, 213, 214, 215, 217, 219, 223, 225, 226, 235, 236, 237, 239, 240, 249, 250, 251, 253, 254, 261, 262, 263, 265, 266, 275, 276, 277, 279, 281, 285, 287, 288, 299, 300, 301, 303, 304, 313, 314, 315, 317, 318, 325, 326, 327, 329, 330, 339, 340, 341, 343, 345, 349, 351, 352, 359, 360, 361, 363, 364, 377, 378, 379, 381, 382, 389, 390, 391, 393, 394, 403, 404, 405, 407, 409
Reteach and Reassess, TE/13, 27, 39, 53, 70, 91, 101, 117, 131, 145, 165, 177, 189, 201, 215, 237, 251, 263, 277, 301, 315, 327, 341, 361, 379, 391, 405

Learning Styles

Interpersonal, TE/69, 129, 147, 155, 219, 289, 383

Intrapersonal, TE/5, 105, 157, 179, 191, 193, 227, 241, 267, 299, 331, 365, 381

Kinesthetic, TE/3, 29, 51, 95, 163, 217, 249, 253, 305, 351

Linguistic, TE/31, 57, 121, 143, 149, 199, 313, 329, 377, 395

Mathematical, TE/25, 41, 83, 119, 133, 167, 265, 275, 317, 407

Musical, TE/43, 55, 75, 99, 175, 187, 281, 303, 343, 359, 403

Natural, TE/15, 89, 103, 135, 169, 203, 235, 279, 287, 339, 353

Verbal, TE/181, 205, 239, 255

Visual, TE/11, 17, 37, 73, 81, 93, 115, 213, 225, 261, 319, 325, 345, 363, 389, 393, 409

Activity Book Contents

Unit 1: Challenges

Chapter 1: The Race *and* The Camel Dances

Build Vocabulary: Define and Alphabetize Words
Writing: Punctuate Dialogue
Elements of Literature: Identify Words That Rhyme
Word Study: Analyze the Suffix *-er*
Grammar Focus: Study Past Tense Verbs *and* Use Past Tense Negatives, Questions, and Contractions
From Reading to Writing: Edit a Poem
Across Content Areas: Use Reference Sources

Chapter 2: Hatchet

Build Vocabulary: Identify New Words *and* Alphabetize Words
Writing: Capitalize Proper Nouns *and* Punctuate Sentence Endings
Elements of Literature: Identify Similes
Word Study: Understand Compound Words
Grammar Focus: Use the Past Tense of *Be and* Use the Past Tense of *Be* in Questions, Negatives, and Contractions
From Reading to Writing: Edit a Realistic Adventure Story
Across Content Areas: Use a Chart

Chapter 3: And Now Miguel

Build Vocabulary: Use Dictionary Guide Words and Context
Writing: Spell Words with the Suffix *-ly*
Elements of Literature: Identify Personification
Word Study: Use Adverbs
Grammar Focus: Use *And* to Join Two Words *and* Use *And* to Join Groups of Words
From Reading to Writing: Edit a Nonfiction Historical Narrative
Across Content Areas: Take Notes

Chapter 4: Yang the Youngest

Build Vocabulary: Use a Dictionary Entry
Writing: Use Capitalization and Commas with Dialogue
Elements of Literature: Analyze Characters
Word Study: Define Words with Latin Roots
Grammar Focus: Study Complex Sentences and Dependent Clauses *and* Study Dependent Clauses with Time Words
From Reading to Writing: Edit a First-Person Narrative
Across Content Areas: Use a Political Map

Chapter 5: The Scholarship Jacket

Build Vocabulary: Use Words About School *and* Identify Dictionary Definitions
Writing: Use *There, Their,* and *They're* Correctly
Elements of Literature: Analyze Character Motivation
Word Study: Identify Root Words
Grammar Focus: Use *Could* and *Could Not* for Past Ability *and* Use *Could* and *Could Not* with Questions and Contractions
From Reading to Writing: Edit a Short Story
Across Content Areas: Compare and Contrast

Unit 2: Changes

Chapter 1: Why Do Leaves Change Color in the Fall?

Build Vocabulary: Study Word Meaning
Writing: Use Commas After Introductory Time Phrases
Elements of Literature: Use Graphic Organizers to Describe Processes
Word Study: Use Pronunciation in Context
Grammar Focus: Study Simple Present Tense Verbs, Negatives, and Contractions *and* Form Simple Present Tense Questions
From Reading to Writing: Edit a Scientific Informational Text
Across Content Areas: Use Audio-Visual Resources

Chapter 2: Elizabeth's Diary

Build Vocabulary: Define Words Using Context Clues
Writing: Use Exclamation Points
Elements of Literature: Recognize and Interpret Flashbacks
Word Study: Understand the Suffix *-ty*
Grammar Focus: Use the Future Tense *and* Use *Will* with Future Tense Questions, Negatives, and Contractions
From Reading to Writing: Write an E-Mail Message
Across Content Areas: Use a Graphic Organizer for Taking Notes

Chapter 3: And Now Miguel

Build Vocabulary: Define Words Using Context
Writing: Use Periods and Question Marks
Elements of Literature: Identify Setting
Word Study: Contrast *Its* and *It's*
Grammar Focus: Study Future Conditional Sentences
From Reading to Writing: Write Dialogue
Across Content Areas: Use Graphic Organizers for Taking Notes

Chapter 4: Tuck Triumphant

Build Vocabulary: Study Word Meanings
Writing: Punctuate Dialogue
Elements of Literature: Analyze Characters in a First-Person Narrative
Word Study: Use the Suffix *-less*
Grammar Focus: Use Adjectives Before Nouns
From Reading to Writing: Edit a Realistic Story
Across Content Areas: Use Graphic Organizers to Compare Information

Chapter 5: The Journal of Jesse Smoke *and* Ancient Ways

Build Vocabulary: Understand Multiple Meaning Words
Writing: Capitalize Proper Nouns
Elements of Literature: Understand Metaphors
Word Study: Use the Suffix *-ness*
Grammar Focus: Use the Present Progressive Tense
From Reading to Writing: Edit a Poem
Across Content Areas: Use a Chart to Present Information

Unit 3: Courage

Chapter 1: Life Doesn't Frighten Me

Build Vocabulary: Define and Categorize Words
Writing: Change Spelling of Words Ending in *y*
Elements of Literature: Words that Rhyme
Word Study: Learn the Meaning of Contractions
Grammar Focus: Study Prepositional Phrases *and* Write and Edit Prepositional Phrases of Place
From Reading to Writing: Edit a Poem
Across Content Areas: Use Cluster Maps

Chapter 2: Matthew A. Henson

Build Vocabulary: Define Words Using Synonyms
Writing: Use Commas with Quotation Marks
Elements of Literature: Recognize Chronological Order and Transitions
Word Study: Recognize Proper Nouns
Grammar Focus: Identify Two-Word Verbs
From Reading to Writing: Edit a Biography
Across Content Areas: Use Audio-Visual Resources

Chapter 3: Anne Frank: The Diary of a Young Girl

Build Vocabulary: Connect to Images and Related Words
Writing: Spell Irregular Past Tense Verbs
Elements of Literature: Identify Tone in Diary Entries
Word Study: Learn About Suffixes
Grammar Focus: Compound Sentences with *But* and Use the Conjunction *But* to Introduce a Sentence
From Reading to Writing: Write a Diary Entry
Across Content Areas: Compare and Contrast Holiday Traditions

Chapter 4: Lance Armstrong: Champion Cyclist

Build Vocabulary: Identify Multiple Meaning Words
Writing: Capitalize Proper Nouns Related to Government and Sports
Elements of Literature: Understand the Style of a Speech

Word Study: Interpret Figurative Language
Grammar Focus: Analyze Comparative Adjectives *and* Analyze Comparative and Superlative Adjectives
From Reading to Writing: Edit a Speech
Across Content Areas: Use an Index

Chapter 5: Earthquake

Build Vocabulary: Identify Analogies
Writing: Use Semicolons
Elements of Literature: Recognize Foreshadowing
Word Study: Identify and Use Compound Words
Grammar Focus: Study Objective Case Pronouns *and* Use Subject, Object, and Possessive Pronoun Forms
From Reading to Writing: Learn Techniques for Writing Introductions
Across Content Areas: Use a Venn Diagram

Unit 4: Discoveries

Chapter 1: The Library Card *and* At the Library

Build Vocabulary: Define Words
Writing: Capitalize First Words in Dialogue
Elements of Literature: Compare and Contrast
Word Study: Understand Historical Influences on English Words
Grammar Focus: Relative Clauses with *That* as a Subject *and* Relative Clauses in Complete Sentences
From Reading to Writing: Edit a Story
Across Content Areas: Use the Library

Chapter 2: Discovering the Inca Ice Maiden

Build Vocabulary: Identify and Group Words
Writing: Punctuate Questions and Answers
Elements of Literature: Understand First-Person Point of View
Word Study: Spell *-ed* Forms of Verbs
Grammar Focus: Use *Be* + Adjective + Infinitive
From Reading to Writing: Edit a First-Person Nonfiction Narrative
Across Content Areas: Use an Informational Text

Chapter 3: The Art of Swordsmanship

Build Vocabulary: Define Words
Writing: Double Consonants Before Adding *-ed* or *-ing*
Elements of Literature: Examine Character Traits
Word Study: Find Word Origins and Prefixes
Grammar Focus: Use Adverbs to Show Time
From Reading to Writing: Edit a Tale
Across Content Areas: Find Art in Everyday Life

Chapter 4: Mae Jemison, Space Scientist

Build Vocabulary: Define Words
Writing: Distinguish Between *ie* and *ei*
Elements of Literature: Recognize Flashbacks
Word Study: Identify Greek and Latin Roots
Grammar Focus: Use and Punctuate Dependent Clauses with *Although*
From Reading to Writing: Edit a Biography
Across Content Areas: Compare a Table and an Article

Unit 5: Communication

Chapter 1: How Tía Lola Came to ~~Visit~~ Stay

Build Vocabulary: Use Context Clues
Writing: Capitalize Proper Nouns and Titles
Elements of Literature: Recognize Point of View
Word Study: Use the Prefixes *un-* and *im-*
Grammar Focus: Recognize the Present Perfect Tense *and* Use the Present Perfect Tense in Questions, Negatives, and Contractions
From Reading to Writing: Write a Narrative with Dialogue
Across Content Areas: Read a Weather Map

Chapter 2: Helen Keller *and* The Miracle Worker

Build Vocabulary: Use New Words in Context
Writing: Use a Colon
Elements of Literature: Write Stage Directions
Word Study: Use the Suffix *-ly*
Grammar Focus: Recognize and Use the Past Progressive Tense *and* Use the Past Progressive Tense with Questions, Negatives, and Contractions
From Reading to Writing: Edit a Scene from a Play
Across Content Areas: Use Audio-Visual Resources

Chapter 3: Hearing: The Ear

Build Vocabulary: Identify and Use Scientific Vocabulary
Writing: Use Dashes
Elements of Literature: Use Descriptive Language
Word Study: Identify Words with Greek Roots
Grammar Focus: Make Subjects and Verbs Agree in the Present Tense
From Reading to Writing: Edit Writing That Informs
Across Content Areas: Compare Texts

Chapter 4: The Art of Making Comic Books

Build Vocabulary: Group Words about Comic Books
Writing: Punctuate Exclamations
Elements of Literature: Recognize Writing Style
Word Study: Understand the Suffix *-ian*
Grammar Focus: Understand and Use the Present Conditional
From Reading to Writing: Write an Illustrated "How-to" Article
Across Content Areas: Match and Research Job Skills

Unit 6: Frontiers

Chapter 1: The Lewis and Clark Expedition

Build Vocabulary: Define Words Using Context Clues
Writing: Use Sentence Punctuation
Elements of Literature: Analyze Characters
Word Study: Use a Synonym Finder
Grammar Focus: Use Appositives
From Reading to Writing: Edit an Informational Text
Across Content Areas: Use Headings as You Read

Chapter 2: A Wrinkle in Time

Build Vocabulary: Define Words
Writing: Use Semicolons
Elements of Literature: Understand Mood
Word Study: Understand the Prefixes *un-*, *in-*, and *im-*
Grammar Focus: Identify the Past Perfect Tense *and* Use the Past Perfect Tense in Questions, Negatives, and Contractions
From Reading to Writing: Edit a Science Fiction Narrative
Across Content Areas: Use Graphic Organizers to Take Notes

Chapter 3: I Have a Dream

Build Vocabulary: Define Words
Writing: Review Capitalization Rules
Elements of Literature: Identify Audience and Purpose
Word Study: Recognize Figurative Language
Grammar Focus: Use Dependent Clauses with *That and* Identify and Use Complete Sentences
From Reading to Writing: Edit a Persuasive Speech
Across Content Areas: Use Graphs and Timelines

Chapter 4: Lyndon Baines Johnson *and* Speech to the Nation

Build Vocabulary: Use Synonyms
Writing: Spell Irregular Verbs
Elements of Literature: Recognize Repetition in a Speech
Word Study: Identify Adjectives
Grammar Focus: Use Conjunctions to Show Contrast
From Reading to Writing: Edit a Biography
Across Content Areas: Use Reference Maps

Student CD-ROM Contents

Unit 1: Challenges

Chapter 1: The Race *and* The Camel Dances

Build Vocabulary: Find Synonyms Using a Reference Aid
Capitalization: Names of People
Text Structure: Poem and Fable
Reading Strategy: Make Inferences
Elements of Literature: Distinguish Sounds of Rhyming Words
Word Study: Analyze the Suffix *-er*
Grammar Focus: Learning Past Tense Verbs

Chapter 2: Hatchet

Build Vocabulary: Use Context
Spelling: *r*-Controlled Vowels
Text Structure: Realistic Adventure Fiction
Reading Strategy: Identify Cause and Effect
Elements of Literature: Use Figurative Language
Word Study: Understand Compound Words
Grammar Focus: Use the Past Tense of the Verb *Be*

Chapter 3: Antarctic Adventure

Build Vocabulary: Identify Words about Ships
Spelling: Abbreviations for Weights, Measures, and Times
Text Structure: Historical Narrative
Reading Strategy: Predict
Elements of Literature: Identify Personification
Word Study: Use Adverbs
Grammar Focus: Use *and* to Join Words

Chapter 4: Yang the Youngest

Build Vocabulary: Identify Homonyms
Punctuation: Apostrophes in Contractions
Text Structure: First-Person Narrative
Reading Strategy: Compare a Reading with Your Experiences
Elements of Literature: Analyze Characters
Word Study: Define Words with a Latin Root
Grammar Focus: Study Complex Sentences with Dependent Clauses

Chapter 5: The Scholarship Jacket

Build Vocabulary: Learn Words about Emotions
Spelling: */k/* Sound Words
Text Structure: Short Stories
Reading Strategy: Find the Main Idea and Details
Elements of Literature: Analyze Character Motivation
Word Study: Identify Root Words
Grammar Focus: Use *Could* and *Couldn't* for Past Ability

Unit 2: Changes

Chapter 1: Why Do Leaves Change Color in the Fall?

Build Vocabulary: Use a Word Wheel
Spelling: Use *c* for /s/ Sound
Text Structure: Scientific Informational Text
Reading Strategy: Make Inferences
Elements of Literature: Identify Processes
Word Study: Use Pronunciation in Context: *ph*
Grammar Focus: Identify and Use the Simple Present Tense

Chapter 2: Elizabeth's Diary

Build Vocabulary: Use Varied Word Choices
Punctuation: Hyphens for Spelled-Out Numbers
Text Structure: Historical Fiction Diary
Reading Strategy: Summarize
Elements of Literature: Identify Flashbacks
Word Study: Understand the Suffix: *-ty*
Grammar Focus: Use the Future Tense with *will*

Chapter 3: And Now Miguel

Build Vocabulary: Use the LINK Strategy
Capitalization: Cities, States, Provinces
Text Structure: Play
Reading Strategy: Determine the Sequence of Events
Elements of Literature: Understand Scenes in a Play
Word Study: Contrast *Its* and *It's*
Grammar Focus: Identify and Use the Future Conditional

Chapter 4: Tuck Triumphant

Build Vocabulary: Identify Related Words
Punctuation: Apostrophes for Possession
Text Structure: Realistic Fiction
Reading Strategy: Draw Conclusions
Elements of Literature: Recognize Style in a First-Person Narrative
Word Study: Use the Suffix *-less*
Grammar Focus: Use Adjectives before Nouns

Chapter 5: The Journal of Jesse Smoke *and* Ancient Ways

Build Vocabulary: Find Root Words
Spelling: *i* before *e* Except after *c*
Text Structure: Historical Fiction Journal
Reading Strategy: Understand the Sequence of Events
Elements of Literature: Understand Metaphors
Word Study: Use the Suffix *-ness*
Grammar Focus: Use the Present Continuous Tense

Unit 3: Courage

Chapter 1: Life Doesn't Frighten Me

Build Vocabulary: Preview New Vocabulary
Capitalization: Titles
Text Structure: Poem
Reading Strategy: Use Images to Understand and Enjoy Poetry
Elements of Literature: Identify Rhyming Words
Word Study: Identify Contractions
Grammar Focus: Use Prepositional Phrases

Chapter 2: Matthew A. Henson

Build Vocabulary: Learn Synonyms with Reference Aids
Punctuation: Commas in a Series
Text Structure: Biography
Reading Strategy: Find the Main Idea and Supporting Details
Elements of Literature: Recognize Chronological Order and Transitions
Word Study: Recognize Proper Nouns
Grammar Focus: Identify Two-Word Verbs

Chapter 3: Anne Frank: The Diary of a Young Girl

Build Vocabulary: Use Context
Punctuation: Semicolons
Text Structure: Diary
Reading Strategy: Use Chronology to Locate and Recall Information
Elements of Literature: Understand Tone
Word Study: Use the Suffix *-ion*
Grammar Focus: Use Conjunctions to Form Complex Sentences

Chapter 4: Lance Armstrong: Champion Cyclist

Build Vocabulary: Use Multiple Reference Aids
Punctuation: Colons and Dashes
Text Structure: Speech
Reading Strategy: Distinguish Fact from Opinion
Elements of Literature: Identify Style, Tone, and Mood in a Speech
Word Study: Interpret Figurative Language
Grammar Focus: Use Superlative Adjectives

Chapter 5: Earthquake

Build Vocabulary: Use Reference Aids to Find Definitions
Spelling: Plurals and Past Tense
Text Structure: Memoir
Reading Strategy: Draw Conclusions and Give Support
Elements of Literature: Recognize Foreshadowing
Word Study: Form Compound Words
Grammar Focus: Identify Pronoun Referents

Unit 4: Discoveries

Chapter 1: The Library Card *and* At the Library

Build Vocabulary: Use Repetition to Find Meaning
Capitalization: Quotations
Text Structure: Fiction
Reading Strategy: Compare and Contrast
Elements of Literature: Recognize a Writing Style
Word Study: Understand Historical Influences on English Words
Grammar Focus: Identify Sentences with Relative Clauses

Chapter 2: Discovering the Inca Ice Maiden

Build Vocabulary: Understand Key Words and Related Words
Spelling: Double Consonants
Text Structure: Nonfiction Narrative
Reading Strategy: Use Graphic Sources of Information
Elements of Literature: Understand First-Person Point of View
Word Study: Spell *-ed* Forms of Verbs
Grammar Focus: Identify *Be* + Adjective + Infinitive

Chapter 3: The Art of Swordsmanship

Build Vocabulary: Identify Related Words
Punctuation: Commas within Quotations
Text Structure: Folktale
Reading Strategy: Use Dialogue to Understand Character
Elements of Literature: Examine Character Traits and Changes
Word Study: Find Word Origins and Prefixes
Grammar Focus: Use Adverbs to Show Time

Chapter 4: Mae Jemison, Space Scientist

Build Vocabulary: Adjust Reading Rate
Punctuation: Parentheses for Information
Text Structure: Inductive Organization
Reading Strategy: Find the Main Ideas and Supporting Details
Elements of Literature: Recognize Flashbacks
Word Study: Identify Greek and Latin Word Origins
Grammar Focus: Use and Punctuate Dependent Clauses with *Although* and *When*

Unit 5: Communication

Chapter 1: How Tía Lola Came to ~~Visit~~ Stay

Build Vocabulary: Use Context Clues
Spelling: *There, Their,* and *They're*
Text Structure: Narrative
Reading Strategy: Predict
Elements of Literature: Recognize Point of View
Word Study: Use the Prefixes *un-* and *im-*
Grammar Focus: Recognize the Present Perfect Tense

Chapter 2: Helen Keller *and* The Miracle Worker

Build Vocabulary: Find Synonyms for Action Verbs
Punctuation: Stage Directions
Text Structure: Biography and Drama
Reading Strategy: Compare and Contrast
Elements of Literature: Analyze Stage Directions
Word Study: Use the Suffix *-ly*
Grammar Focus: Recognize and Use Past Continuous Verbs

Chapter 3: Hearing: The Ear

Build Vocabulary: Identify Science Vocabulary
Spelling: Words Ending in *-ing*
Text Structure: Textbook
Reading Strategy: Represent Text Information in an Outline
Elements of Literature: Recognize Descriptive Language
Word Study: Identify Words with Greek Origins
Grammar Focus: Recognize Subject and Verb Agreement in the Present Tense

Chapter 4: The Art of Making Comic Books

Build Vocabulary: Learn Words about Art
Punctuation: Exclamations and Hyphens
Text Structure: Illustrated "How-To" Book
Reading Strategy: Make Inferences Using Text Evidence
Elements of Literature: Recognize Writing Style
Word Study: The Suffix *-ian*
Grammar Focus: Understand the Present Conditional

Unit 6: Frontiers

Chapter 1: The Lewis and Clark Expedition

Build Vocabulary: Use a Word Wheel
Spelling: *t, th, tr,* and *thr*
Text Structure: Informational Text
Reading Strategy: Use Chronology to Locate and Recall Information
Elements of Literature: Analyze Characters
Word Study: Use a Thesaurus and Synonym Finder to Find Synonyms
Grammar Focus: Use Appositives

Chapter 2: A Wrinkle in Time

Build Vocabulary: Use Context Clues
Capitalization: Titles
Text Structure: Science Fiction
Reading Strategy: Describe Mental Images
Elements of Literature: Understand Mood
Word Study: Understand the Suffixes *un-, in-,* and *im-*
Grammar Focus: Identify the Past Perfect Tense

Chapter 3: I Have a Dream

Build Vocabulary: Distinguish Denotative and Connotative Meanings
Punctuation: Possessives
Text Structure: Speech
Reading Strategy: Draw Conclusions with Text Evidence
Elements of Literature: Identify Audience and Purpose
Word Study: Recognize Figurative Language
Grammar Focus: Use Dependent Clauses with *That*

Chapter 4: Lyndon Baines Johnson: Our Thirty-Sixth President *and* Speech to the Nation: July 2, 1964

Build Vocabulary: Identify Key Words about Government
Capitalization: Proper Names
Text Structure: Biography
Reading Strategy: Distinguish Fact from Opinion
Elements of Literature: Recognize Repetition in a Speech
Word Study: Identify Adjectives
Grammar Focus: Use the Conjunction *Yet* to Show Contrast

English-Spanish Cognates

From the Reading Selections

Unit 1: Challenges

Unit 1, Chapter 1

The Race, *page 5*

enter	entrar
line	línea
mountain	montaña
rest	resto
rose	rosa
surprise	sorpresa

The Camel Dances, *page 8*

announced	anunció
applause	aplauso
basic	básico
camel	camello
desert	desierto
desire	deseo
fatigue	fatiga
frankly	francamente
invited	invitó
movement	movimiento
practiced	practicó
repeated	repitió
satisfaction	satisfacción
simply	simplemente
splendid	espléndido

Unit 1, Chapter 2

Hatchet, *page 17*

air	aire
baseball	béisbol
character	carácter
class	clase
clearly	claramente
combination	combinación
exasperation	exasperación
fine	fino
material	material
millions	millones
oxygen	oxígeno
person	persona
pilot	piloto
rock	roca
science	ciencia
visit	visitar

Unit 1, Chapter 3

Antarctic Adventure, *page 31*

abandon	abandonar
camp	campamento
coast	costa
continent	continente
cross	cruzar
decided	decidió
expedition	expedición
explorer	explorador
island	isla
miles	millas
move	mover
ocean	océano
October	octubre
penguins	pengüínos
saved	salvado
solid	sólido
terrible	terrible

Unit 1, Chapter 4

Yang the Youngest, *page 43*

attention	atención
bus	bus
company	compañía
confused	confundido
curious	curioso
family	familia
invaded	invadir
music	música
parents	parientes
parts	partes
panda	panda
patient	paciente
popular	popular
problems	problemas
respect	respeto
secretary	secretaria
students	estudiantes

Unit 1, Chapter 5

The Scholarship Jacket, *page 57*

adrenaline	adrenalina
appreciate	apreciar
athletic	atlético
attention	atención
case	caso
class	clase
colors	colores
coincidence	coincidencia
compare	comparar
complete	completo
continue	continuar
conversation	conversación
cost	costo
cruel	cruel
curve	curva
decided	decidió
delicate	delicado
dignity	dignidad
escaped	escapó
exception	excepción
favor	favor
front	frente
graduation	graduación
gym	gimnasio
history	historia
innocent	inocente
letters	letras
mile	milla
participate	participar
plants	plantas
represented	representado
tradition	tradición
uniform	uniforme

Unit 2: Changes

Unit 2, Chapter 1

Why Do Leaves Change Color in the Fall?, *page 83*

air	aire
article	artículo
carbon	carbón
chlorophyll	clorofila
colors	colores
combination	combinación
common	común
dioxide	dióxido
energy	energía
excess	exceso
different	diferente
during	durante
eventually	eventualmente
form	formar
gas	gas
material	material
occur	ocurrir
oxygen	oxígeno
pigments	pigmentos
prepare	preparar
product	producto
production	producción
science	ciencia
scientist	científico
separation	separación
simple	simple
violets	violetas
visible	visible

Unit 2, Chapter 2

Elizabeth's Diary, *page 95*

baby	bebé
Captain	capitán
diary	diario
expedition	expedición
hurricane	huracán
melon	melón
mosquitos	mosquitos
ocean	océano
rats	ratas

Unit 2, Chapter 3

And Now Miguel, *page 105*

basketball	básquetbol
direction	dirección
dozen	dozena
family	familia
idea	idea
impatiently	impacientemente
important	importante
ocean	océano
pasture	pastura
pilot	piloto
policeman	policía
practice	practicar
separated	separado
soldier	soldado
surprise	sorpresa
terrible	terrible

Unit 2, Chapter 4

Tuck Triumphant, *page 121*

adoption	adopción
family	familia
finally	finalmente
identification	identificación
immigration	imigración
introducing	introduciendo
Korean	coreano
lemon	limón
license	licencia
Martians	marcianos
minute	minuto
move	mover
novel	novela
possessions	posesiones

Unit 2, Chapter 5

The Journal of Jesse Smoke, *page 135*

companion	compañero
existence	existencia
secretary	secretaria
journal	jornal
mechanics	mecánicos
mile	milla
negotiate	negociar
observed	observé
pass	pasar
plantation	plantación
practical	práctico
soldiers	soldados

Ancient Ways, *page 140*

exercise	ejercicio
Indian	indio
present	presente
traditional	tradicional
vehicles	vehículos

Unit 3: Courage

Unit 3, Chapter 1

Life Doesn't Frighten Me, *page 157*

dragon	dragón
lion	león
magic	mágica
ocean	océano
panther	pantera

Unit 3, Chapter 2

Matthew A. Henson, *page 169*

adventure	aventura
area	área
authorized	autorizó
boots	botas

community	comunidad
different	diferente
disaster	desastre
explorer	explorador
famous	famoso
group	grupo
guide	guía
honor	honor
interested	interesado
medal	medalla
member	miembro
military	militar
minutes	minutos
move	mover
North Pole	Polo Norte
observation	observación
part	parte
planned	planeado
point	punto
polar	polar
presented	presentó
temperature	temperatura
victory	victoria

Unit 3, Chapter 3

Anne Frank: The Diary of a Young Girl, *page 181*

concentration camp	campo de concentración
diary	diario
escape	escape
idea	idea
immediately	inmediatemente
impression	impresión
memories	memorias
necessary	necesario
pair	par
pass	pasar
silence	silencio
visiting	visitando

Unit 3, Chapter 4

Lance Armstrong: Champion Cyclist, *page 193*

applause	aplauso
cancer	cáncer
champion	campeón
character	carácter
comment	comentar
competitor	competitor
Congress	Congreso
cyclist	ciclista
delegation	delegación
determination	determinación
event	evento
extraordinary	extraordinario
honored	honrado
inspired	inspirado
introduce	introducir
invited	invitado
observer	observador
present	presentar
president	presidente
privilege	privilegio
program	programa
Senate	Senado
serious	serio
similar	similar
triumph	triunfar
victory	victoria

Unit 3, Chapter 5

Earthquake, *page 205*

animals	animales
area	área
atmosphere	atmósfera
buffalo	búfalo
circumstances	circunstancias
disasters	desastres
domestic	domésticos
enemies	enemigos
enormous	enorme
escape	escapar
fruit	fruta
instincts	instinctos
jungle	jungla
limited	limitado
minutes	minutos
natural	natural
possible	posible
presence	presencia
preserve	preservar
regularity	regularidad
space	espacio
tigers	tigres

Unit 4: Discoveries

Unit 4, Chapter 1

The Library Card, *page 228*

air	aire
baby	bebé
basketball	básquetbol
common	común
collecting	colectando
different	diferente
electric	eléctrico
enemies	enemigos
enter	entrar
idea	idea
imagine	imaginar
insect	insecto
minute	minuto
move	mover
mysterious	misterioso
page	página
pass	pasar
rare	raro
vomiting	vomitar

At the Library, *page 232*

crystal	cristal
paradise	paradiso
pirates	piratas
prefer	preferir

Unit 4, Chapter 2

Discovering the Inca Ice Maiden, *page 241*

active	activo
assistant	asistente
camp	campo
cause	causar
circumstance	circunstancia
condition	condición
continue	continuar
decide	decidir
descend	descender
difficult	difícil
dozen	dozena
finally	finalmente
fragments	fragmentos
impossible	imposible
literally	literalmente
mile	milla
moment	momento
normal	normal
part	parte
plastic	plástico
possible	posible
preserved	preservado
probably	probablemente
rest	resto
rock	roca
route	ruta
sandals	sandalias
September	septiembre
simple	simple
specialists	especialistas
statues	estatuas
structure	estructura
surprise	sorpresa
textile	textil
victim	víctima
volcano	volcán

Unit 4, Chapter 3

The Art of Swordsmanship, *page 255*

attack	ataque
constant	constante
descend	descender
determination	determinación
entire	entero
extraordinary	extraordinario
finally	finalmente
gradually	gradualmente
impatience	impaciencia
patient	paciente
servant	serviente
student	estudiante

Unit 4, Chapter 4

Mae Jemison, Space Scientist, *page 267*

adult	adulto
African -American	afroamericana
art	arte
astronaut	astronauta
astronomer	astrónomo
Atlantic Ocean	Océano Atlántico
basic	básico
center	centro
class	clase
company	compañía
conditions	condiciones
control	controlar
experiments	experimentos
explorer	explorador
function	función
future	futuro
history	historia
imagination	imaginación
imagine	imaginar
information	información
interests	intereses
investigate	investigar
limited	limitado
medical	medical
medicine	medicina
minute	minuto
mission	misión
nausea	náusea
normally	normalmente
orbit	órbita
participation	participación
preparation	preparación
project	proyecto
public	público
responsibilities	responsabilidades
results	resultados
science	ciencia
September	septiembre
technology	technología
temperature	temperatura

Unit 5: Communication

How Tía Lola Came to ~~Visit~~ Stay, *page 289*

car	carro
chocolate	chocolate
circle	círculo
closet	closet
colorful	colorido
divorce	divorcio
favorite	favorito
idea	idea
impossible	imposible
license	licencia
memory	memoria
Mexican	mexicano
microphone	micrófono
moment	momento
move	mover
nervous	nervioso
office	oficina
palm tree	palma
problem	problema
public	público
resist	resistir

technical	técnico
terminal	terminal
tremendous	tremendo
visit	visita

Unit 5, Chapter 2

Helen Keller, *page 306*

alphabet	alfabeto
attention	atención
biography	biografía
continue	continuar
creature	creatura
decided	decidió
difficult	difícil
event	evento
form	formar
institution	institución
letters	letras
minute	minuto
mystery	misterio
particularly	particularmente
palm	palma

The Miracle Worker, *page 309*

automatically	automaticamente
distance	distancia
impatiently	impacientemente
muscle	músculo
palm	palma
possess	poseer
porch	porche
servant	serviente

Unit 5, Chapter 3

Hearing: The Ear, *page 320*

air	aire
balance	balancear
cars	carros
compact disks	discos compactos
connect	conectar
different	diferente
electric	eléctrico
energy	energía
example	ejemplo
guitar	guitarra
important	importante
interpret	interpretar
liquids	líquidos
microphone	micrófono
move	mover
muscles	músculos
music	música
nerves	nervios
parts	partes
pass	pasar
position	posición
radio	radio
siren	sirena
solids	sólidos
television	televisión
vibrate	vibrar

Unit 5, Chapter 4

The Art of Making Comic Books, *page 331*

absurd	absurdo
accent	acento
artist	artista
character	caracter
characteristics	características
combination	combinación
concept	concepto
correct	correcto
creative	creativo
crime	crimen
define	definir
detective	detective
dimension	dimensión
distinctive	distinto
experiment	experimentar
hero	heroe
history	historia
horror	horror
human	humano
imagination	imaginación
imperfect	imperfecto
industry	industria
interesting	interesante
introduce	introducir
magician	mágico
millionaire	millonario
monster	monstruo
pirate	pirata
politics	política
process	proceso
produce	producir
realistic	realístico
reality	realidad
science	ciencia
situation	situación
soldier	soldado
solid	sólido
technology	tecnología
universe	universo

Unit 6: Frontiers

Unit 6, Chapter 1

The Lewis and Clark Expedition, *page 353*

animals	animales
attention	atención
captain	capitán
climate	clima
contributions	contribuciones
establish	establecer
expedition	expedición
guide	guía
interpreters	intérpretes
map	mapa
members	miembros
minerals	minerales
Pacific Ocean	Océano Pacífico
plants	plantas
relationships	relaciones
route	ruta
territory	territorio

Unit 6, Chapter 2

A Wrinkle in Time, *page 365*

accept	aceptar
atmosphere	atmósfera
civilization	civilización
complete	completo
concept	concepto
confident	confidente
completely	completamente
different	diferente
difficult	difícil
dimension	dimensión
distance	distancia
enormous	enorme
evaporate	evaporar
expression	expresión
geometry	geometría
idea	idea
imagine	imagina
intolerable	intolerable
line	línea
moment	momento
movement	movimiento
mysterious	misterioso
planet	planeta
points	puntos
portion	porción
possible	posible
presence	presencia
rest	resto
science fiction	ciencia ficción
scientist	cientista
secret	secreto
silence	silencio
space	espacio
veins	venas
visible	visible
visit	visita

Unit 6, Chapter 3

I Have a Dream, *page 383*

character	carácter
color	color
create	crear
difficulties	dificultades
injustice	injusticia
liberty	libertad
nation	nación
oppression	opresión
spiritual	spiritual
symphony	sinfonía
transform	transformar

Unit 6, Chapter 4

Lyndon Baines Johnson: Our Thirty-sixth President, *page 396*

assassinated	asesinado
biography	biografía
continue	continuar
differences	diferencias
hotel	hotel
hours	horas
illegal	ilegal
minority	minoridad
nation	nación
president	presidente
problems	problemas
programs	programas
public	público
reserved	reservado
restaurant	restaurante
segregation	segregación
television	televisión
vice president	vice presidente
violence	violencia

Speech to the Nation: July 2, 1964, *page 398*

ability	abilidad
continent	continente
difficult	difícil
eliminate	eliminar
fortunes	fortunas
future	futuro
history	historia
honor	honor
hotels	hoteles
independence	independencia
justice	justicia
liberty	libertad
limit	limitar
nation	nación
occasion	ocasión
patriots	patriotas
personal	personal
political	política
public	público
respect	respetar
restaurant	restaurante
service	servicio
simple	simple
special	especial
valiant	valiente